EU Dumping Determinations and WTO Law

Global Trade Law Series

VOLUME 18

Kluwer Law International

EU Dumping Determinations and WTO Law

By

Henrik Andersen

Wolters Kluwer
Law & Business

AUSTIN BOSTON CHICAGO NEW YORK THE NETHERLANDS

Published by:
Kluwer Law International
PO Box 316
2400 AH Alphen aan den Rijn
The Netherlands
Website: www.kluwerlaw.com

Sold and distributed in North, Central and South America by:
Aspen Publishers, Inc.
7201 McKinney Circle
Frederick, MD 21704
United States of America
Email: customer.care@aspenpubl.com

Sold and distributed in all other countries by:
Turpin Distribution Services Ltd.
Stratton Business Park
Pegasus Drive, Biggleswade
Bedfordshire SG18 8TQ
United Kingdom
Email: kluwerlaw@turpin-distribution.com

Printed on acid-free paper.

ISBN 978-90-411-2827-0

Printed in Great Britain.

Lao Tzu, *Tao Te Ching XLIII*

The most submissive thing in the world can ride roughshod over the most unyielding in the world – that which is without substance entering that which has no gaps.

That is why I know the benefit of taking no action.
The teaching that uses no words, the benefit of taking no action, these are beyond the understanding of all but a very few in the world.

[Translated by D. C. Lau]

Table of Contents

Preface

This book concerns one of the major challenges in the field of globalization: *Anti-dumping*. More specifically, the book looks into whether EU dumping determinations of products from Asian countries are in conformity with WTO law. The reason for looking into this question is my major interest in globalization and its challenges in the field of international trade and public international law. Different cultures with different legal backgrounds and understandings of law have to interact with one another. On one hand, globalization is the opening of markets between states to the better good of the world consumer and world producers, but on the other hand, the opening of markets might also oust national producers because of cheaper products in the global market, or it might be a reason for strong political powers to exploit weaker states.

Anti-dumping is just one set of several rules dealing with the impacts of globalization. On the international level, WTO anti-dumping law ensures a mechanism for importing countries to impose duties on foreign products with dumped prices, i.e., the export price is lower than the domestic price of the like product in the exporting country. Such a mechanism should *ceteris paribus* lead to a reduction in the import of the dumped products, and the anti-dumping rules may then be seen as an obstacle to trade between states. However, such rules may be justified in the light of undesired outcomes by predatory pricing, where the exporter lowers the export prices in order to eliminate the competitors in the importing country and thereafter raises the prices.

The application of the anti-dumping instrument by WTO Members is often controversial because of the protectionist character of anti-dumping, in which inefficient industries are protected from foreign competition. The legal framework within the WTO has some loopholes that leave wide discretion to the investigating authorities to determine that a product is dumped, thereby emphasising the protectionist nature of anti-dumping. The use of anti-dumping becomes even more controversial when WTO Members use the anti-dumping tool beyond the legal scope of WTO law. The questions raised in this book concern the EU dumping determinations and their conformity with WTO law. The EU has a magnificent impact on global politics and the global trade, and the EU should take a leading position in turning the global wheels by ensuring the conformity with the legal standards under public international law. In so doing, the EU can secure that EU importers and foreign exporters can rely on the international set of anti-dumping law and the legal certainty of law. Furthermore, anti-dumping deserves much more attention in legal research than it has so far been given. This book is just a modest contribution to the research in the anti-dumping field.

This book is a revised version of my PhD thesis. The book would not have been possible without the inspiration, support, comments, etc. from several people and organizations to whom I owe my deepest regards.

I want to thank Copenhagen Business School for offering me the opportunity to undertake a PhD project, and City University of Hong Kong for supporting my research stay in Hong Kong in 2006. Furthermore, I want to thank Otto Mønsteds Fond and Konsul Axel Nielsens Mindelegat for financial support.

I want to thank in particular my supervisors for inspiration and interesting discussions. From Copenhagen Business School, I would like to thank Professor, dr.jur. Jens Fejø, Associate Professor, PhD, Lynn Roseberry and Professor, PhD, Verner Worm; and from City University of Hong Kong, Professor Gu Minkang. I also want to thank the members of the PhD Assessment Committee for providing me with some very useful and interesting comments about my work upon which I may continue my journey into the universe of research; Professor, PhD, Ulla Neergaard from Copenhagen Business School, Professor, PhD, Pär Halström from Umeå University, and Associate Professor, PhD, Pernille Wegener Jessen from Aarhus School of Business, Aarhus University. I also owe my deepest thanks to my colleagues at Copenhagen Business School, in particular Associate Professor, PhD, Kim Østergaard for convincing me to do a PhD, and Associate Professor, PhD, Christina Tvarnø and Head of Department, Professor, PhD, Steen Treumer for interesting discussions. Furthermore, I want to thank Lecturer Sharma Charu from City University of Hong Kong.

Also, I want to thank Administrative Officer Marie Pade Andersen and Translation Service Manager Susanne Askham for linguistic and grammatical editing.

I want to thank my family and friends for their support and understanding through the often challenging times: My parents, Søren and Annie Andersen; my sister Dorte Andersen; and the rest of my family: Bent Rohde Nielsen, Pia Bergstrøm Frederiksen, Oskar Rohde Bergstrøm, Anton Rohde Bergstrøm, Helene Hilligsøe, Anne Hilligsøe, Mads Hilligsøe, Morten Hilligsøe and Jørgen Rasmussen. To my Danish friends: Rene Thastum Jespersen, Peter Lille Frøen Rasmussen, Anne-Mette Hansen, Jesper Eier Engberg, Peter G. Uru and Pia Johannessen, Christian and Lone Lund Jørgensen, Martin Beo and Janni Dam Wied, Peder Bissen and Marie Lindeløv, Mette and Jerome Venet, Charlotte and Allan Gravsen, Anne-Sofie Aggerbeck-Lauritzen, Helene and Anders Fertin, and Andreas Petersen. To my Hong Kong friends: Leony Quion, Lesley Chui Suk Yin, Annie Chan, Donnie Dong, and Kelvin Wangchao. Also,

I want to thank the staff at Harbour Plaza Resort City in Hong Kong. Furthermore, I want to thank people in the TaijiQuan, YiQuan and Cheng Hsin field, in particular Master Torben Bremann, Master Wee Kee Jin, Grand Master Sam Tam, Grand Master Peter Ralston, Peter Hass, Jeppe Turck, Jesper Andersen Møller and Klaus Kornø Rasmussen. Also, I want to thank everybody at the Wudang Taoist Kung Fu Academy in Wudang, China. Furthermore, I want to thank my high school teacher, Jim Skov Jensen, from Greve Gymnasium, for being the first one to introduce me to GATT back in a history class in 1991.

I certainly want to thank Kluwer Law International for supporting the idea of publishing the PhD as a book. In particular, I want to thank the editors: Lou Rolla and Professor Ross Buckley for their suggestions on how to improve my work.

The present book would have not been completed without inspiration from many different writers on WTO and EU anti-dumping law. The writings and discussions by Edwin Vermulst in *The 10 Major Problems With the Anti-dumping Instrument in the European Community*, by Harold Wenig in *The European Community's Anti-dumping System: Salient Features*, by Pierre Didier in *The WTO Anti-dumping Code and EC Practice* and by Yuhan Liu in *Anti-dumping Measures and China* have all been great inspirations to me in writing this book. The first three articles are printed in *Journal of World Trade*, and the last-mentioned article is printed in *Journal of Financial Crime*.

The first book I ever read about WTO/GATT was *The GATT/WTO Dispute Settlement System – International Law, International Organizations and Dispute Settlement* from 1997 by Ernst-Ulrich Petersmann – an excellent work. It inspired me to look into the field of WTO. Most books about general WTO law include a chapter or section about anti-dumping law. I highly recommend looking into *The Law and Policy of the World Trade Organization*, by Peter Van den Bossche, from 2005. The book distinguishes itself by its wide coverage of complicated WTO law. Another interesting book is *Modern GATT Law – A Treatise on the General Agreement on Tariffs and Trade*, from 2005, by Raj Bhala. The author builds his writing on WTO law around the provisions in GATT 1994. Another great contribution to the discussion is *WTO Law – from a European perspective*, from 2006, edited by Birgitte Egelund Sørensen, Michael Steinicke, and Karsten Engsig Sørensen, which compares similarities and differences between the WTO and the EU systems. The chapter on anti-dumping, written by Pernille Wegener Jessen, includes a section on EU law on anti-dumping circumvention. Guiguo Wang has written about WTO – with China as the central subject – in *The Law of the WTO – China and the Future of Free Trade*, from 2005. The second edition of *The World Trade Organization – Law, Practice, and Policy*, from 2006, by Mitsuo Matsushita, Thomas J. Schoenbaum and Petros C. Mavroidis, is also excellent. The authors provide a very interesting discussion regarding the sources of WTO law. Furthermore, throughout the book, the authors make a number of suggestions to improve WTO law.

For those interested in the background of WTO law, the extensive three-volume work by Terence P. Stewart (ed.); *The GATT Uruguay Round – A Negotiating History*, from 1993, is recommended. The section on anti-dumping is written by Terence P. Stewart, Susan G. Markel, and Michael T. Kerwin. I also encourage those interested to look into *The World Trading System*, from 1989, by John H. Jackson, who writes about the policy background of GATT law – and the tension between a rule-oriented system and national discretion.

With respect to writings about WTO anti-dumping law, I would suggest looking into *The WTO Anti-dumping Agreement*, from 2005, by Edwin Vermulst. The author makes critical remarks on the application of anti-dumping law by both WTO Members and the DSB. Edwin Vermulst has also – together with Folkert Graafsma – written *WTO Anti-dumping, Subsidies and Safeguards*, from 2005, where an overview of anti-dumping disputes before panels and Appellate Body is provided. For a more detailed book on WTO anti-dumping law, *A Handbook Anti-dumping Investigations*, from 2003, by Judith Czako, Johan Human and Jorge Miranda, can be suggested.

For those interested in EU anti-dumping law, Ivo Van Bael and Jean-Francois Bellis have written *Anti-dumping and Other Trade Protection Laws of the EC*, of which the fourth edition is from 2004. The book gives an excellent overview of – and critical approach to – anti-dumping law in EU. Furthermore, the authors provide an overview of the anti-dumping cases in EU from initiation of investigation to termination – and further development – of cases from 1995 to 2004.

For a comparative study of the evolution of WTO/GATT and EU anti-dumping law, Wenxi Li's doctoral thesis *Anti-dumping Law of WTO/GATT and EC – Gradual Evolution of Anti-dumping Law in Global Economic Integration*, from 2001 is a must-read. The author makes suggestions on how to improve the existing anti-dumping laws towards more credibility.

About the trade relation between EU and China, I highly recommend *EC Trade Law Following China's Accession to the WTO*, by Jan Hoogmartens, from 2004, which includes some interesting discussions about the non-market economy approach in anti-dumping matters.

If the reader of this book wants to contact me for clarifications about my work or with suggestions for improvement, he or she should not hesitate to do so at: henriklaw@yahoo.com.

Henrik Andersen

Chapter 1
Introduction

1.1 DUMPING AND ITS ELEMENTS

The World Trade Organization (WTO) was established in 1995 as the successor of the General Agreements on Tariffs and Trade (GATT). One aim of the WTO is to increase production and trade between WTO Members, and the intended means to achieve this is breaking down trade barriers and reducing tariffs between WTO Members.[1] Exceptions are made when a WTO Member is involved in unfair trade practice.[2] Unfair trade practice can be either a situation where the WTO Member subsidizes export products or a situation where the producers are dumping the prices of exported products.[3] The present book focuses on dumping.

Within the WTO framework, dumping is defined in Article VI.1 of GATT 1994 as occurring when 'products of one country are introduced into the commerce of another country at less than the normal value'. The term 'normal value' usually refers to the domestic price of the product in the exporting country. An example of dumping is if the domestic price in, for example, India of bed linen manufactured by Indian producers is 5 Rupees (INR) per sheet and the export price from Indian producers to importers in the European Union (EU) is only INR 3 per sheet. By subtracting the export price from the normal value, the 'dumping margin' of INR 2 per sheet is found.

Dumping is condemned under WTO law. If a WTO Member finds that imported products are dumped and the dumped prices cause injury to the industry

---

1. See preamble of the Agreement Establishing the World Trade Organization.
2. R. Bhala, *Modern GATT Law – A Treatise on the General Agreement on Tariffs and Trade* (London: Sweet & Maxwell, 2005), 683.
3. See for instance R. Bhala, Ibid., 683-684 and E. Vermulst, *The WTO Anti-dumping Agreement* (Oxford: Oxford University Press, 2005b), 11.

in the importing WTO Member State, then WTO law permits the importing member to impose an anti-dumping duty on the dumped products.

The EU, a member of the WTO and subject to WTO law,[4] has adopted rules on protection against dumping in the *Basic Regulation*,[5] which is adopted with regard to Article 133 of the Treaty Establishing the European Community (the EC Treaty). The EU Commission (the Commission) carries out the anti-dumping investigation. The Commission has the power to impose provisional anti-dumping duties during the investigation. After concluding the investigation, the Commission makes a proposal to the EU Council (the Council) about imposing a definitive anti-dumping duty on the injuriously dumped products. The Council may endorse the proposal in a definitive Regulation. The Regulations by the Commission and the Council are under review of the EC courts, i.e., the Court of First Instance and the EC Court.

To identify dumping, the Commission and the Council go through four steps:

(1) the allegedly dumped product is defined;
(2) the normal value is determined;
(3) the export price is determined; and
(4) a comparison between the normal value and export price is made.

The aim of this book is to examine whether the EU legislation on dumping, the practice adopted by the Commission and the Council, as well as the EC courts reviews of dumping determinations of products from Asian countries in particular, are in conformity with WTO law.

The approach taken here is mainly based on a WTO perspective, although other perspectives are used when necessary for clarification of certain matters.

In the following section, the aim is further elaborated, and the reason why this question is of interest and how this book may contribute in the field of international trade will be discussed.

1.2 THE CHALLENGES AND DISCUSSIONS CONCERNING DUMPING DETERMINATIONS

It may justifiably be asked why it is interesting to look into the world of dumping determinations. After all, it appears just to be a matter of comparing a normal value with an export price of a product. If the export price is below the normal value, the

4. See more in Ch. 2 below.
5. Council Regulation (EC) No. 384/96 of 22 Dec. 1995 on protection against dumped imports from countries not members of the European Community, OJ L 56, 6 Mar. 1996, pp. 1-20, amended in Council Regulation (EC) No. 2331/96 of 2 Dec. 1996, OJ L 317, 6 Dec. 1996, pp. 1-2; Council Regulation (EC) No. 905/98 of 27 Apr. 1998, OJ L 128, 30 Apr. 1998, pp. 18-19; Council Regulation (EC) No. 2238/2000 of 9 Oct. 2000, OJ L 257, 11 Oct. 2000, pp. 2-3; Council Regulation (EC) No. 1972/2002 of 5 Nov. 2002, OJ L 305, 7 Nov. 2002, pp. 1-3; Council Regulation (EC) No. 461/2004 of 8 Mar. 2004, OJ L 77, 13 Mar. 2004, pp. 12-20; and Council Regulation (EC) No. 2117/2005 of 21 Dec. 2005, OJ L 340, 23 Dec. 2005, p. 17.

product is dumped. However, different methods of defining a product, different methods of determining the normal value and the export price and different methods of comparing the normal value and the export price may lead to several different dumping margins. In the following section, some of the complexities in determining dumping are described. The issues raised in this section are examined throughout the book.

In section 1.2.2, it is elaborated why it is interesting to look into whether EU dumping determinations are in conformity with WTO law.

1.2.1 Dumping Determinations

The problematic nature of the four elements i.e., product, normal value, export price, and comparison, is briefly discussed in this part.

1.2.1.1 Product

In order to impose an anti-dumping duty, the investigating authorities must define the particular product that is allegedly being dumped. If bed linen from India is being dumped, then the anti-dumping duty should only address bed linen and not, e.g., T-shirts produced in India, as there is a clear difference between bed linen and T-shirts in terms of their functions and probably also their substitutionality. However, merely defining the allegedly dumped product will not suffice. The investigating authorities must also define a domestically sold product that is identical to the product under consideration in the exporting country, in order to find a price that can be compared with the export price. If bed linen were the allegedly dumped product, it would not be reasonable to compare the export price of bed linen with the price of domestic sales of bananas. Chapter 3 deals with the question of whether the EU product determinations are in conformity with WTO law.

1.2.1.2 Normal Value

In the above example of dumping, it was assumed that the normal value would be 5 Indian rupees (INR), as the domestic price of the product was INR 5. If the example is modified slightly, and it is assumed instead that the domestic price is INR 3 and the export price is also INR 3, and furthermore that the product sold on the domestic market is like the product sold for export, then the dumping margin will be 0, and therefore the product is not dumped and should not be imposed with an anti-dumping duty.

However, the domestic price may be disregarded. There may be reasons to regard the actual domestic price between the Indian producer and the domestic buyer as unreliable. For example, if the domestic sale is made between the Indian producer and an associated domestic buyer, the price of INR 3 may not be a reflection of a normal market transaction price; therefore the domestic price for this transaction cannot serve as a normal value. It is necessary to examine what the criteria for a domestic price to qualify as normal value are and to examine the conditions for disregarding a domestic price in the normal value determination.

The question then is how the normal value is found when the domestic price is disregarded. If the producer has made more than this particular transaction with other buyers who are not associated with the producer, the prices from those transactions can serve as basis for comparison with the export price. For example, if the producer has made 100 domestic sales, where one of those is made to an associated buyer and must be disregarded, but the other 99 transactions are reliable, then a normal value can be based on those 99 other transactions. The situation becomes much more complicated if it is assumed that the producer has only made the one transaction the price of which is disregarded – or if the producer has made 100 transactions, but all with an associated buyer, and all disregarded. This will result in there being an export price of INR 3, but no domestic price with which to compare the export price. Both the WTO and EU legislation provide mechanisms to determine normal value by other means than the actual domestic price, for example by constructing a normal value based on cost of production, sales, general and administrative costs (SAG) and a reasonable profit. However, the constructed normal value may end up being higher than the domestic price that has been disregarded; for example, if the domestic price of 3 is disregarded and the constructed normal value is, e.g., 5, then dumping occurs. The situation has then gone from non-dumping (3 minus 3 is 0) to dumping (5 minus 3 is 2; therefore the price is dumped).

As indicated by this example, the normal value rules have mechanisms to amend the actual domestic price. The actual domestic price cannot be taken for granted, as the domestic price may be disregarded, and the normal value may be based by other means than the actual domestic price. See more about the general rules on normal value, and the alternatively based normal value determinations, in chapter 4.

Normal value may be an even more complicated phenomenon concerning dumped products from non-market or transition economies. A non-market economy is an economy where prices and supply are determined through government planning rather than by market forces. A transition economy is here understood as an economy transitioning from a non-market towards a market economy.[6] Normal value may not be based on the actual domestic prices for countries with a non-market or transition economy, as those prices are not seen as reliable due to state interference in price, cost and output determination. Instead, the normal value may be based on prices from a producer in an 'analogue country', which is a country with a market economy and which is considered as appropriate. Under WTO and EU law, China is regarded as a transition economy.[7] The normal value may therefore be based on prices from an analogue country, unless the Chinese producer can demonstrate that the actual domestic price in China is based on market forces. Often, the Chinese producer cannot bear the burden of proof. In that

---

6. Changho Sohn, 'Treatment of Non-market Economy Countries under the World Trade Organization Anti-dumping Regime', *Journal of World Trade* 39 (4) (2005): 764.
7. See more in Ch. 7 below.

case, the result may be that the normal value will end up being much higher than the Chinese producer expected. For example, if the Chinese producer has a domestic price of 3 Yuan Renmibi (CNY) and the export price is CNY 3, then the price of the product appears not to be dumped. However, if the Chinese producer has bought raw materials from a Chinese producer that is suspected of being under state interference with respect to price setting, then the Chinese producer's claim of market economy treatment will be rejected. Therefore, the domestic price of CNY 3 is not reliable. Instead, the domestic price may be based on the price by a producer in an analogue country, for example the US. If it is assumed that the US domestic price is the same as CNY 5, then the normal value for the Chinese producer will be CNY 5, and the product from the Chinese producer is then dumped (5 minus 3 is 2). See more about the dumping determinations of products originating from China in Chapter 7.

As seen here, the normal value is not easily defined by just referring to the actual domestic price. Naturally, the mechanism to disregard domestic prices and the mechanism to determine 'new' domestic prices cannot lead to objective results, because it is not possible to find the correct domestic price. Instead, those mechanisms will lead to a normal value that contains some artificial elements and to protests from producers and importers if the normal value ends up being higher than the actual domestic price.

1.2.1.3 Export Price

It is not only the domestic price that may be disregarded and based on other factors. The export price between the producer in the exporting country and the importer also may be disregarded. If, for example, the importer is associated with the producer in the exporting country, the price may not be reliable. In line with the normal value situation, the export price may have to be based on other means.

Therefore, the export price may not always be what it appears to be. The actual export price may be disregarded and found by other means. See more about matters of export price in Chapter 5.

1.2.1.4 Comparison

The normal value must be compared with the export price in order to determine the dumping margin. The comparison includes three types of questions:

The first question deals with the comparability of the two prices. The factors behind the normal value and export price may be different, and the domestic price and export price may be a reflection of such differences. For example, assume that the Indian producer has made a domestic sale to an Indian wholesaler at a domestic sales price of INR 3 per sheet, the Indian wholesaler has made a sale to an Indian retailer at a price of INR 4, and the Indian producer has made the export sale to an EU importer at an export price of INR 3 per sheet. Clearly, if the normal value is based on the price between the Indian wholesaler and the Indian retailer (i.e., the normal value is INR 4), but the export price is based on the price between the

Indian producer and the EU importer (price is INR 3), this will lead to a dumping margin of 1 (4-3 = 1). However, if the normal value is based on the domestic price between the Indian producer and the Indian wholesaler, then it is not a case of dumping. Due to such differences, the normal value and export price may have to be adjusted in situations where the prices come from transactions of different levels of trade.

Another example could be that the sales conditions between the Indian producer and the Indian wholesaler differ from the sales conditions between the Indian producer and the EU importer. If, for example, the Indian producer has to pay transportation costs and insurance of the domestic sale, and those costs are INR 1 per sheet, the producer may add those costs to the price; this means that the overall domestic price will be INR 4 per sheet. If the EU importer pays the same transportation costs and insurance of the export sale to the EU, and the export price is thus INR 3 per sheet, then dumping occurs (4-3 = 1), unless the normal value is adjusted for the transportation costs and the price of insurance.

The second question deals with the actual calculation of the dumping margin, when the export price is compared with the normal value. If the situation is that the Indian producer has only made one domestic sale and only one export sale, then it will present no problems to subtract the single export price from the single domestic price. The challenge occurs if the producer has made 100 domestic sales and, for example, 30 export sales. The question here is how to determine one dumping margin out of a great numbers of both domestic and export transactions.

The second question also leads to problems about *zeroing*. Zeroing occurs when the calculation of the dumping margin is made. Consider the following example: The Indian producer has 3 domestic sales and 3 export sales. The domestic sales and export sales take place at the same time, comprise the same number of bed linen, and have the same sales conditions. We assume that all the prices of the domestic sales are INR 4 per sheet. The export prices are different. In this example, the comparison is made by a *transaction-to-transaction* method, in which the price from each export transaction is compared with the price from each domestic transaction. The transaction-to-transaction method operates under the underlying assumption that both export and domestic transactions are comparable and in equal numbers. The export price of the first sale is 5, the export price of the second sale is 4 and the export price of the third sale is 3. If each domestic transaction price is compared with each export sales price, the result is as follows:

	Domestic price	*Export price*	*Calculation for each transaction*
Sale 1	INR 4	INR 5	− 1
Sale 2	INR 4	INR 4	0
Sale 3	INR 4	INR 3	+ 1

This will result in the following intermediary calculations: −1, 0, and 1. If those calculations are summed into one overall dumping margin, it will be 0 (−1 + 0 + 1 = 0). This means that the price of the bed linen has not been dumped. However, if the −1 calculation from the first transaction is 'zeroed', i.e., −1 is changed to 0, the aggregation will result in a positive overall dumping margin of 1 (0 + 0 + 1 = 1). The new aggregation method, where the negative numbers are zeroed, has now resulted in dumping of INR 1 per sheet.

Another zeroing method is to be found under the *weighted-average-to-transaction* method. If, for example, the domestic transactions and the export transactions are unequal in number, the authorities may have to calculate a weighted average of the domestic transactions. If only a weighted average price for the domestic price has been calculated and the price from specific export transaction is compared to the weighted average, this is called weighted-average-to-transaction calculation. Under this method, zeroing takes place if prices from export transactions higher than the weighted average domestic price are disregarded. Consider this example: There are 5 domestic transactions; all are comparable to the export transactions, but there are only three export transactions. The prices from the domestic transactions differ. The price of the first domestic transaction is INR 2 per sheet, the price of the second domestic transaction is INR 3 per sheet, the third domestic transaction is INR 4 per sheet, the fourth domestic transaction is INR 5 per sheet and, finally, the fifth domestic transaction is INR 6 per sheet. The weighted average normal value is 4, as (2+3+4+5+6)/(number of transactions = 5) = 4. For the three export transactions, the following prices are used: INR 2 per sheet, INR 4 per sheet, and INR 6 per sheet. The calculations will then be:

	Domestic price as a weighted average	*Export price*	*Calculation for each transaction*
Sale 1	INR 4	INR 2	+ 2
Sale 2	INR 4	INR 4	0
Sale 3	INR 4	INR 6	– 2

By including all the export transactions, the sum is 0, i.e., the product has not been dumped, as 2 + 0 + −2 is 0. If the export transaction with an export price higher than the weighted average domestic price is disregarded, the result will be a positive dumping margin, as 2 + 0 = 2. The zeroing here occurs because of the exclusion of some export prices.

Zeroing becomes much more complicated if the dumping margin was based on a *weighted-average-to-weighted-average* method. Under this calculation method, both the normal value and the export price are found through a weighted average calculation and then compared. If we use the numbers from the above example, the weighted-average export price will be 4, as (2+4+6)/(number of export transactions = 3) = 4. As the weighted average domestic price is also 4, the dumping margin will be 0, and the conclusion will be that dumping is not taking place. In Chapter 6, it will be demonstrated how the EU authorities found a way to zero under the weighted-average-to-weighted-average method.

Finally, the third question deals with whether the dumping margin will be individually or generally determined for the producers under investigation. An individual dumping margin is based on the domestic and export prices by the single producer, whereas a general margin is based on the prices from a group of producers.

The few examples presented above show that the comparison between the export price and the normal value is not merely a simple subtraction. There are several adjustable factors included at the comparison level, and these may lead to different dumping margins – depending on how those factors are applied. See more about such matters in Chapter 6. Concerning the individual and general margins, special EU rules apply for China; these are described in chapter 7.

1.2.2 EU Dumping Determinations and WTO Law

The product, normal value, export price and comparison are all regulated under both WTO and EU law. As each of the 4 elements may be determined by different methods, dumping may be artificially created by a WTO Member in order to keep out foreign competition. This section gives a brief introduction to some of the questions that have led this author to examine whether EU dumping determinations towards Asian countries are in conformity with WTO law.

The starting point is the overall aim of the WTO. As mentioned above, one aim of the WTO is to enhance production, raise living standards, etc., by reducing tariffs and barriers to trade, as well as to eliminate discriminatory behaviour. In that light, the rules on anti-dumping may be seen as an exception. Anti-dumping duties raise the prices of imported products and may thus serve as a trade-restricting, rather than trade-advancing, instrument between WTO Members.[8]

One rationale for allowing anti-dumping duties in a WTO context is to afford WTO Members a tool with which to meet unfair trade from other producers in other countries and to counter predation. Predation is the situation where the exporter intentionally lowers the price on the importing market in order to oust competitors in the importing market and gain monopoly power.[9] Predation may result in loss in welfare economy, as the predator, after having ousted the

8. G. Marceau, *Anti-dumping and Anti-Trust Issues in Free Trade Areas* (Oxford: Oxford University Press, 1994), 26.
9. See, for different definitions of 'predation', C. Ahlborn & B. Allen, 'The Napp Case: A Study of Predation ?', *World Competition* 26 (2) (2003): 233 et seq.

competitors, will raise the prices to the disadvantage of consumers.[10] Prior to the establishment of GATT in 1948, dumping of prices was a matter of national concern to several countries. The dumped products would cause injury to national industries – and in some instances, the exporting country would even set up import barriers, which would keep the injured industries from re-dumping. Anti-dumping duties were a possibility to offset dumping.[11]

Even though the application of the anti-dumping instrument may have justifiable impacts by protecting competition in the importing country from unfair trade practices, there is another side to the coin: National authorities often abuse the anti-dumping instrument to protect national interests.[12] Industries in the importing country may try to persuade their national authorities to impose anti-dumping duties on imported products as a strategy to retain market power.[13] If the WTO Member wants to protect an inefficient domestic industry from outside competition, the imposition of anti-dumping duties may reduce competition. Article VI of GATT 1947 was introduced as a rule to permit the use of anti-dumping duties on one hand, but on the other hand also to limit possible abuse of anti-dumping duties by national authorities.[14] If the EU uses the anti-dumping instrument beyond the limits of WTO law, the aim of the WTO may be more difficult to achieve and may result in reduced economic welfare.[15]

The fact is that the EU is a frequent user of anti-dumping duties on imported products. From 1 January 1995 to 31 December 2006, the EU reported 231 anti-dumping measures towards other WTO countries to the WTO Committee on Anti-dumping Practices. In that period, the EU was the third largest user of anti-dumping measures, only surpassed by India with 331 anti-dumping measures and the US with 239 anti-dumping measures.[16] Low-cost products from Asian countries have been subject to EU anti-dumping duties in particular because of the fear that EU industries would be run over by cheaper Asian products,[17] the main target being China.[18]

---

10. M. Matsushita, T. H. Schoenbaum & P. C. Mavroidis, *The World Trade Organization – Law, Practice, and Policy*, 2nd edn (Oxford: Oxford University Press, 2006), 398.
11. See more in Ch. 2 below.
12. M. Matsushita, T. H. Schoenbaum & P. C. Mavroidis, *The World Trade Organization – Law, Practice, and Policy*, 2nd edn (Oxford: Oxford University Press, 2006), 401.
13. Commission Decision 2003/7/EC of 13 Dec. 2000 relating to a proceeding under Art. 82 of the EC Treaty (COMP/33.133-D: Soda-ash – ICI) (notified under document number C(2000) 3796) (Text with EEA relevance), OJ L 010, 15 Jan. 2003, pp. 33-50, recital 53.
14. G. Marceau, *Anti-dumping and Anti-Trust Issues in Free Trade Areas* (Oxford: Oxford University Press, 1994), 134.
15. E. U. Petersmann, *The GATT Dispute Settlement System – International Law, International Organizations and Dispute Settlement* (The Hague: Kluwer Law International, 1997), 67.
16. See statistics at: <www.wto.org/english/tratop_e/adp_e/adp_e.htm>.
17. See S. S. Das, 'Evolution and Political Economy of Trade Protectionism: Anti-dumping and Safeguard Measures', *IIMB Management Review* 17 (4) (2005): 56.
18. See the Semi-Annual report under Art. 16.4 of the ADA for the EU by the WTO Committee on anti-dumping practices, G/ADP/N/139/EEC, 6 Apr. 2006 in particular Annex II and V. See also E. Vermulst, 'The 10 Major Problems With the Anti-dumping Instrument in the European Community', *Journal of World Trade* 39 (1) (2005a), 106. Furthermore, T. J. Prusa has

In spite of the frequent use of anti-dumping duties, the EU is rarely challenged in the WTO system, where the Dispute Settlement Body (DSB) settles disputes between WTO Members. Initially, disputes are settled through negotiations; if such negotiations fail, a panel is set up to prepare a recommendation on the pertinent legal and factual matters. The panel's recommendation can be appealed to the Appellate Body.[19] So far, the EU has been a respondent in only three cases.[20] The limited number of WTO cases with the EU as a respondent has led Wenig to claim that the EU system in itself provides a system that ensures conformity between its anti-dumping measures and WTO law.[21] Other commentators, who argue that EU dumping determinations are in conflict with WTO law, challenge Wenig's proposition. Vermulst claims that the Council's decision-making process lacks transparency, thus inviting 'leak and abuse'.[22] Vermulst states that the lack of transparency goes all the way through to the dumping determination; particularly, the normal value and export price end up being constructed rather than based on the actual prices, and at the comparison level, the EU resorts to a zeroing method. Vermulst finds that all those matters can be challenged in the WTO system.[23] In addition, Didier writes that the EU violates WTO law in dumping determinations.[24] Furthermore, EU's non-market approach towards China is criticized. Yuhan Liu, in opposition to Wenig, writes:

> Most of these investigations against China resulted in artificially high anti-dumping duties or minimum undertakings, which severely undermined the competitive capability of many Chinese industries involved, and virtually excluded them from the European market (. . .). The principal reason for this unfair and reprehensible outcome is the imposition of non-market status on China by the EU anti-dumping regime.[25]

Vermulst is in line with Yuhan Liu and finds that the EU system lacks predictability for the exporting Chinese producers to find out whether market economy

demonstrated that on a world wide basis, East Asian countries account for the highest growth in anti-dumping cases against them. See T. J. Prusa, 'East Asia's Anti-dumping Problem', *World Economy* 29 (6) (2006): 743 et seq.

19. See more in Ch. 2 below about Panels and Appellate Body.
20. *EC – Bed linen*, WT/DS/141, *EC – Tube or Pipe Fittings*, WT/DS/219 and *EC – Salmon (Norway)*, WT/DS/337 (case is pending).
21. H. Wenig, 'The European Community's Anti-dumping System: Salient Features', *Journal of World Trade* 39 (4) (2005): 790.
22. E. Vermulst, 'The 10 Major Problems with the Anti-dumping Instrument in the European Community', *Journal of World Trade* 39 (1) (2005a): 106.
23. Ibid., 106-110.
24. P. Didier, 'The WTO Anti-dumping Code and EC Practice – Issues for Review in Trade Negotiations', *Journal of World Trade* 35 (1) (2001): 33 et seq.
25. Yuhan Liu, 'Anti-dumping Measures and China', *Journal of Financial Crime* 12 (3) (2005): 273 et seq. See also Xiang Liu & H. Vandenbussche, *EU Anti-dumping Cases against China: An Overview and Future Prospects with Respect to China's WTO Membership* (LICOS Discussion Paper, LICOS Centre for Transition Economies, Katholieke Universiteit Leuven, 2002), 3.

treatment can be granted.[26] Wenig disagrees and elaborates on some of the challenges faced by the Commission during the investigation of dumped products from transition economies, for example, the lack of cooperation from exporters from transition economies. Wenig concludes: 'The EC has developed a reasonable and predictable set of criteria and methods to deal with these problems.'[27]

The different perceptions represented here make it interesting to conduct an in-depth examination of the EU's dumping determinations and their compliance with WTO law. The present book contributes to that discussion. Furthermore, if the EU wants to maintain its record with a low number of challenges in the WTO dispute settlement system in relation to the huge number of anti-dumping measures released by the EU institutions, it is necessary to point out areas where the EU may not be acting in conformity with WTO law. This study is therefore a tool for the EU institutions to consider whether EU legislation or EU practices need changes in order to reach consistent WTO compliance. This book contributes in the legal political area *de lege ferenda* and *de sententia ferenda*. Furthermore, the book will contribute to applicants of laws on dumping by describing, structuring and analyzing the content of WTO law on dumping and the EU's compliance with WTO law.

The focus in this book is mostly on the substantial part of dumping determinations, which is only one of several conditions that must be fulfilled in order to impose an anti-dumping duty. For example, within both the WTO and the EU frameworks, it is also a requirement that the dumped products injure the industry in the importing country, i.e., the EU industry. The injury requirement implies both an injury test and a causation test before an anti-dumping duty can be imposed. In addition, both frameworks require several procedural aspects by the investigating authorities. The injury requirements and the procedural requirements are not discussed here, unless these are of relevance for the dumping determination. Furthermore, EU anti-dumping legislation requires that the imposition of an anti-dumping duty is in the Community interest. In Chapter 2, those conditions will be touched upon in brief, as further reference to those conditions will be made in the analysis of the dumping determinations in Chapters 3-7. Therefore, in order to get a hold on the different concepts in the anti-dumping area – concepts used in this book – those conditions will be described. The reason for taking up the narrow focus of only dumping is that the dumping determination in itself has several complex tests to determine the product, normal value, export price and comparison.

The EU measures, which are examined here, are mainly measures towards *Asian countries*. The main reason for delimiting the EU measures to those applying to Asian countries, and not including EU measures addressing products from North and South American Countries, Africa, etc., is the vast number of anti-dumping regulations that, because of the EU's focus on Asia, particularly concern the

26. E. Vermulst, 'The 10 Major Problems With the Anti-dumping Instrument in the European Community', *Journal of World Trade* 39 (1) (2005a): 110 et seq.
27. H. Wenig, 'The European Community's Anti-dumping System: Salient Features', *Journal of World Trade* 39 (4) (2005): 793 et seq.

increasing imports from Asian countries. However, measures towards non-Asian countries are included when it is necessary for the description or explanation of certain matters, where the measures towards Asian countries seem insufficient. In particular, the reviews by the EC courts used here include a broader group of countries than Asian. The reason for including such cases is their binding effect on the Commission and the Council. It is assumed that the Commission and the Council will act in conformity with the rulings by the EC courts and consider those rulings in their anti-dumping practice towards Asian countries.[28]

1.2.3 The Legal Approach

The approach to the subject is here a legal one combined with a few related legal political aspects. It must be noted that anti-dumping is also subject to analyses in other disciplines. Economists are certainly discussing dumping and anti-dumping law and whether the anti-dumping legislation and application of it by national authorities will result in loss of global economic welfare.[29] Although it is generally agreed that predation may lead to monopoly power and subsequent higher prices for consumers,[30] some economists question whether predation is likely to happen because, historically, predatory pricing has never been successful.[31] Furthermore, in economic theories the rationale behind predatory pricing is debated.[32] Other economists argue that even if predation may happen, the anti-dumping instrument is not likely to detect predation.[33] Although discussions regarding the economic

28. See more in Section 1.3.3 below.
29. R. D. Willig, 'Economic Effects of Anti-dumping Policy', in *The WTO and Anti-dumping*, eds. D. R. Nelson & H. Vandenbussche (Cheltenham Glos: Edward Elgar Publishing Ltd, 2005), 291-292; J. E. Stieglitz, 'Dumping on Free Trade: The U.S. Import Trade Laws', *Southern Economic Journal* 64 (2) (1997): 409; M. Krauss, *How Nations Grow Rich* (Oxford: Oxford University Press, 1997), 24-25; M. N. Rothbard; *Protectionism and the Destruction of Prosperity* (monograph: Ludwig Von Mises Institute, 1986), 4; B. M. Hoekman & P. C. Mavroidis, 'Dumping, Anti-dumping and Antitrust', *Journal of World Trade* 30 (1) (2006): 29 et seq.; J. D. Reitzes, 'Anti-dumping Policy', in *The WTO and Anti-dumping*, eds. D. R. Nelson & H. Vandenbussche (Cheltenham Glos: Edward Elgar Publishing Ltd, 2005), 408-409; S. P. Anderson, N. Schmidt & J. Thisse, 'Who Benefits from Anti-dumping Legislation?', in *The WTO and Anti-dumping*, eds. R. Nelson & H. Vandenbussche (Cheltenham Glos: Edward Elgar Publishing Ltd, 2005), 424-425.
30. See B. Hindley & P. A. Messerlin, *Anti-dumping Industrial Policy – Legalized Protectionism in the WTO and What To Do About It* (Washington, DC: The AEI Press, 1996), 6.
31. M. N. Rothbard; *Protectionism and the Destruction of Prosperity* (monograph: Ludwig Von Mises Institute, 1986), 4 and J. Viner, *Dumping – A Problem in International Trade*, Reprint of Economic Classics (New York: Augstus M. Kelley Publishers, 1966), 133.
32. J. E. Stieglitz, 'Dumping on Free Trade: The U.S. Import Trade Laws', *Southern Economic Journal* 64 (2) (1997): 404 et seq.
33. See R. D. Willig, 'Economic Effects of Anti-dumping Policy', in *The WTO and Anti-dumping*, eds. D. R. Nelson & H. Vandenbussche (Cheltenham Glos: Edward Elgar Publishing Ltd, 2005), 303 et seq.

impacts of the dumping determinations are interesting, they lie outside the scope of this book.

While on the subject of predation, it should be noted that the issue of predation is not only found under anti-dumping law. National and EU competition laws deal with predation as well. For example, under EU law, Article 82 of the EC Treaty prohibits abuse of a dominant position. In *AKZO*, the EC Court found that predatory behaviour by a dominant company is abuse of a dominant position.[34] A second example is Indian law. Pursuant to Article 4.1 and Article 4.2(a)(ii) of the Competition Act,[35] a dominant company is prohibited from abusing its dominant position by imposing unfair and discriminatory prices, including predation.[36] A third example is the newly promulgated anti-monopoly law of the People's Republic of China, which entered into force in August 2008; the law's Article 17.2 prohibits a dominant company from selling products below costs without justifiable causes.[37]

This double set of laws – competition law and anti-dumping law – to catch predatory behaviour has led commentators to discuss whether an international competition law should replace WTO anti-dumping law.[38] So far, WTO Members have established a Working Group on the Interaction between Trade and Competition Policy, but an international agreement on competition policies has not been concluded.[39] Whether an international competition law should replace the anti-dumping rules is not further discussed in this book.

The legal approach is not without reservations. There are several political and diplomatic elements in the WTO system. Such elements may have an impact in the determination of law and may then make law a hazier concept. WTO law must therefore be understood in that context. Jackson writes:

> [I]t now seems clear that WTO represents a further enhancement (compared to the GATT whose evolution was in this direction anyway) in the direction of rule orientation.[40]

---

34. *AKZO*, Case C-62/86, judgment of the EC Court on 3 Jul. 1991, ECR 1991, p. I-3359, Para. 70.
35. The Competition Act, 2002, No. 12 of 2003.
36. See more about Indian competition law in S. Chakravarthy, 'India', in *Competition Policy and Development in Asia*, eds. D. H. Brooks and S. J. Evenett (Hampshire: Palgrave Macmillan, 2005), 107-160.
37. The Anti-monopoly Law of the People's Republic of China, adopted at the 29th meeting of the Standing Committee of the Tenth National People's Republic of China on 30 Aug. 2007. See unofficial English translation at <www.chinalawinfo.com>.
38. See for instance Wenxi Li, *Anti-dumping Law of WTO/GATT and EC – Gradual Evolution of Anti-Dumping Law in Global Economic Integration* (Lund: Lund University, 2001), 385-387; G. Marceau, *Anti-Dumping and Anti-Trust Issues in Free Trade Areas* (Oxford: Oxford University Press, 1994); J. E. Stieglitz, 'Dumping on Free Trade: The U.S. Import Trade Laws', *Southern Economic Journal* 64 (2) (1997): 420; M. Matsushita, T. H. Schoenbaum & P. C. Mavroidis, *The World Trade Organization – Law, Practice, and Policy*, 2nd edn (Oxford: Oxford University Press, 2006), 433-436.
39. M. Matsushita, T. H. Schoenbaum & P. C. Mavroidis, *The World Trade Organization – Law, Practice, and Policy*, 2nd edn (Oxford: Oxford University Press, 2006), Ch. 22.
40. J. H. Jackson, 'Global Economics and International Economic Law', *Journal of International Economic Law* 1 (1) (1998): 17.

Jackson finds that WTO law is heading in the direction of *rule orientation*, which, according to Jackson, can be described the following way:

> The 'rule orientated approach' focuses the disputing parties' attention on the rule, and on predicting what an impartial tribunal is likely to conclude about the application of a rule. This in turn, will lead to greater certainty and predictability which is essential in international affairs, particularly economic affairs driven by market orientated principles of decentralized decision making, with participation by millions of entrepreneurs. (. . .)
>
> The phrase 'rule orientation' is used here to contrast with phrases such as 'rule of law', and 'rule-based system'. Rule orientation implies a less rigid adherence to 'rule' and connotes some fluidity in rule approach (especially since it accommodates some bargaining or negotiation).[41]

A rule-oriented system is characterized by its predictable legal outcome. It is not the same as a rule of law system, because some bargaining power may interfere with the rule application. Therefore, it cannot be expected that a dispute between WTO Members will go through traditional judicial stages, as is the case in national systems.[42] At the same time, the rule-oriented system must also be seen as a contrast to a power-oriented system such as the GATT system. Petersmann, who supports the idea of rule orientation, writes about power orientation:

> A power-oriented technique suggests discussions, negotiations or dispute settlement in which one party asserts or uses the relative power at its disposal in order to influence the conduct of the other party.[43]

The difference between power orientation and rule orientation lies not only in the degree of predictability in the application of norms, but also in the matter of which norms a country should apply in its ordinary conduct towards other WTO Members – and which norms a Member can expect other countries will follow in the relation between the countries.

The findings in this book about the EU conformity with WTO law in the anti-dumping area have reservations due to the rule-oriented nature of WTO law. A statement in this book that the EU is violating a WTO provision may be perceived as a negotiation tool whereby disputes are resolved through diplomacy and may not easily be carried through the judicial systems. In such a case, the negotiation power between the parties has an impact on the determination of law.

41. Ibid., 6.
42. However, it may in several national systems be questioned whether politics in fact may have an impact on judicial decisions.
43. E. U. Petersmann, *The GATT Dispute Settlement System – International Law, International Organizations and Dispute Settlement* (The Hague: Kluwer Law International, 1997), 66.

In Chapter 2, WTO law as a rule-oriented system concerning anti-dumping matters will be discussed by looking into three factors:

(1) The evolution of anti-dumping legislation under the GATT/WTO system. Here it is claimed that the legislation has limited the discretionary power of the WTO Members.
(2) The system of dispute settlement and sanctions concerning anti-dumping matters. Here it is claimed that the WTO system has a court-like system, but still with several negotiation possibilities.
(3) The EU approach to WTO law in anti-dumping matters.

The findings in Chapters 3-7 must be seen in the light of the findings in chapter 2. Therefore, a claim in this book of WTO-inconsistent behaviour by the EU authorities may have another outcome if the case is resolved through negotiations.

1.3 SOURCES OF WTO ANTI-DUMPING LAW AND THE EU MEASURES

The establishment of WTO law in the anti-dumping field is not easily done by glancing at the texts of the different WTO agreements. The agreements regulating the anti-dumping field are not very transparent and contain several unclear elements in terms of their text as well as structure. Furthermore, the anti-dumping area is regulated by two agreements, and there may be some inconsistencies between them. In addition, the Panels and the Appellate Body cannot overrule the national authorities' interpretations of the WTO anti-dumping provisions if those interpretations are 'permissible'.

In this section, the different sources of WTO law in the anti-dumping field are discussed. Furthermore, a few words are said about the interpretation of the WTO provisions governing anti-dumping.

Besides the challenges to establish WTO law, the EU anti-dumping measures are also special by nature. This section ends up with a brief discussion of the different EU sources used here and their interrelationship with one another.

1.3.1 WTO Sources

The WTO agreements do not provide for a catalogue of sources of WTO law, and there is no official guidance concerning the exact sources to look into when matters of WTO law arise. In literature, the definition of sources of WTO law varies from narrow approaches, where WTO agreements are the only sources of WTO law, to wider approaches that include non-binding sources.[44] In this book, the concept of

44. See for discussion about sources of WTO law: M. Matsushita, T. H. Schoenbaum & P. C. Mavroidis, *The World Trade Organization – Law, Practice, and Policy*, 2nd edn (Oxford: Oxford University Press, 2006), Ch. 2; B. T. Daniel, 'Interpretation, Sources of Law and

'sources of WTO law' is in line with that provided by Van den Bossche, who writes:

> Not all sources of WTO law (. . .) are of the same nature or are on the same legal footing. Some sources provide for specific legal rights and obligations for WTO Members that theses Members can enforce through WTO dispute settlement. Many other sources (. . .) do not in and by themselves provide for specific, enforceable rights and obligations. They are nevertheless sources of WTO law as they 'clarify' or 'define' the law that applies between WTO Members on WTO matters.[45]

1.3.1.1 The WTO Agreements and Decisions from the Ministerial Conference

The principal source of WTO law is the Marrakesh Agreement Establishing the WTO (WTO Agreement).[46] All other WTO agreements are annexed to it. The annexed agreements form an integral part of the WTO Agreement and are binding on the WTO Members; see Article II.2 of the WTO Agreement.

The most important annexed agreements treated for this volume are those about anti-dumping. There are two agreements: First of all, GATT 1994, Article VI concerns anti-dumping. The wordings of Article VI of GATT 1994 are only found by consulting GATT 1947. The other agreement is the Agreement on Implementation of Article VI of the General Agreement on Tariffs and Trade (Anti-dumping Agreement (ADA)). Article VI of GATT 1994 is elaborated on in the ADA, where in particular Article 2 concerns dumping determination.

In case of conflict between the WTO Agreement on one side and GATT 1994 and ADA on the other, the WTO Agreement prevails, due to the *principle of lex superior* in Article XVI.3 of the WTO Agreement. The relationship between Article VI of GATT 1994 and provisions of the ADA is provided in Article 1 of ADA:

> An anti-dumping measure shall be applied only under the circumstances provided for in Article VI of GATT 1994 and pursuant to investigations initiated[47] and conducted in accordance with the provisions of this Agreement.

Precedents', in *WTO Law – From an European perspective*, eds. B. Egelund Olsen, M. Steinicke & K. Engsig Sørensen (København: Forlaget Thomson, 2006), 76-80; G. Marceau, 'Conflicts of Norms and Conflicts of Jurisdiction – The Relationship between the WTO Agreement and MEAs and Other Treaties', *Journal of World Trade* 35 (6) (2001): 1081 et seq.; J. Pauwelin, *Conflict of Norms in Public International Law* (Cambridge: Cambridge University Press, 2003); P. Van den Bossche, *The Law and Policy of the World Trade Organization* (Cambridge: Cambridge University Press, 2005), 44-64.

45. P. Van den Bossche, *The Law and Policy of the World Trade Organization* (Cambridge: Cambridge University Press, 2005), 44.
46. See *US – Gasoline*, W/DS2/AB/R, report of the Appellate Body on 29 Apr. 1996. See also P. Van den Bossche, *The Law and Policy of the World Trade Organization* (Cambridge: Cambridge University Press, 2005), 44.
47. The footnote in Art. 1 states: 'The term "initiated" as used in this Agreement means the procedural action by which a Member formally commences an investigation as provided in Art. 5.'

> The following provisions govern the application of Article VI of GATT 1994 in so far as action is taken under anti-dumping legislation or regulations.

It is furthermore provided in Article 18.1 of the ADA:

> No specific action against dumping of exports from another Member can be taken except in accordance with the provisions of GATT 1994, as interpreted by this Agreement.[48]

In *US – 1916 Act*, the Appellate Body stated that Article VI of GATT 1994 must be read in conjunction with the ADA because Article VI of GATT 1994 and the ADA are both part of the WTO Agreement.[49] The Appellate Body furthermore referred to the Panel finding and stated that the applicability of Article VI of GATT 1994 implies the applicability of the ADA.[50] Therefore, Article VI of GATT 1994 and ADA are bound together, where ADA is elaborating the provision of Article VI of GATT 1994.

Decisions from the Ministerial Conference in relation to WTO rounds are also sources of WTO law. The Ministerial Conference consists of all the WTO Members and holds meetings every two years.[51] Through such decisions, the Ministerial Conference can add new rights and obligations or amend existing rules.[52] Furthermore, new WTO Members can only be accepted through a decision made by the Ministerial Conference.[53] In this book, the decision on Accession of China into the WTO is very important.[54] The Accession Agreement for China specifies the special rules for China, where also the non-market treatment in the anti-dumping field is regulated. Therefore, the Accession Agreement and its protocols will be used. The legal status of the Accession Agreement and its protocols and the relationship between the Accession Agreement and the other relevant WTO agreements, i.e., the WTO Agreement, GATT 1994 and the ADA, will be discussed in Chapter 7.

1.3.1.2 Panel and Appellate Body Reports

In this book, there is a wide reference to reports of Panels and Appellate Body in the determination of WTO law. When a Panel or Appellate Body releases a report, it must be adopted in the WTO system by the WTO Members; see more in Section 2.3. In the following part, a few comments are made on the legal status of unadopted

48. In a footnote in Art. 18.1, it is provided: 'This is not intended to preclude action under other relevant provisions of GATT 1994, as appropriate.'
49. *US – 1916 Act*, WT/DS136/AB/R and WT/DS162/AB/R, report of the Appellate Body on 28 Aug. 2000, para. 114.
50. Para. 133, with reference to the Panel report in *US – 1916 Act (EC)*, WT/DS136/R, report of the Panel on 31 Mar. 2000, para. 6.165. See also the Panel in *Thailand – H-Beams*, WT/DS122/R, report of the Panel on 28 Sep. 2000, para. 7.120.
51. Art. IV.1 of the WTO Agreement.
52. Art. IX and X of the WTO agreement.
53. Art. XII of the WTO Agreement.
54. WT/L/432, 23 Nov. 2001, Decision by the Ministerial Conference on 10 Nov. 2001.

and adopted reports from the GATT system and the adopted reports from the WTO system.

So far, it has never happened in the WTO that a report from the Panel or Appellate Body has not been adopted.

According to Article IX.2 of the WTO Agreement, the Ministerial Conference and the General Council have the *exclusive authority* to adopt interpretations of the WTO Agreement and the annexed agreements. The General Council is represented by all WTO Members, and meetings are held when so required to carry out the functions of the WTO. The General Council is authorized to act on behalf of the Ministerial Conference.[55] The Panels and Appellate Body have no such exclusive authority as the Ministerial Conference and the General Council do. Therefore, the question is whether reports of the Panels and the Appellate Body have a binding power in future cases. It should be noted that it seems the Ministerial Conference and General Council have only rarely exercised their right to adopt an authoritative interpretation of the WTO agreements.[56] An example is the interpretation of the WTO Agreement on Trade-Related Aspects of Intellectual Property Rights (TRIPS) which according to the Ministerial Conference can and should be interpreted and implemented in a manner supportive of WTO Members' right to protect public health and, in particular, to promote access to medicines for all.[57]

The Appellate Body itself has defined the legal status of Panel and Appellate Body reports. In *Japan – Alcoholic Beverages II*,[58] the Panel regarded both adopted GATT Panel reports and WTO Panel reports as subsequent practice in line with Article 31.3(b) of the Vienna Convention on the Law of Treaties and held that such reports were an integral part of the WTO Agreement.[59] The Appellate Body, however, rejected the Panel's standpoint and stated that Panel reports were only binding on the parties in a specific dispute and that reports had to be adopted by the WTO Members. In doing so, the Appellate Body referred to Article IX.2 of the WTO Agreement. However, the Appellate Body stressed the importance of adopted Panel reports because they are an important part of the GATT acquis, because subsequent Panels refer to them and because they create *legitimate expectations* among the WTO Members. The Appellate Body agreed with the Panel's standpoint that unadopted Panel reports have no legal value.[60]

In *US Shrimps (Article 21.5 – Malaysia)*,[61] the Appellate Body stated that its findings about the status of Panel reports in *Japan – Alcoholic Beverages II* also

55. Art. IV.2 of the WTO Agreement.
56. See P. Van den Bossche, *The Law and Policy of the World Trade Organization* (Cambridge: Cambridge University Press, 2005), 145.
57. WT/Min(01)/Dec/02; Declaration of the TRIPS Agreement and Public Health by the Ministerial Conference, 20 November 2001, para. 4.
58. *Japan – Alcoholic Beverages II*, WT/DS8/AB/R, WT/DS10/AB/R and WT/DS11/AB/R, report of the Appellate Body on 4 Oct. 1996.
59. See para. 6.10 in the Panel report in *Japan – Alcoholic Beverages II*, WT/DS8/AB/R, WT/DS10/AB/R and WT/DS11/AB/R, report of the Panel 11 Jul. 1996.
60. Para. 14 of the Appellate Body report.
61. *US – Shrimp (Art. 21.5 – Malaysia)*, WT/DS58/AB/RW, report of the Appellate Body on 22 Oct. 2001.

cover Appellate Body reports; this meant that they should be taken into account by Panels and Appellate Body because they establish *legitimate expectations*.[62] It is a consistent practice by Panels and Appellate Body to refer to former reports,[63] as expressed by a Panel in *US – Shrimp (Ecuador)*:[64]

> We have, as is our duty, carefully taken into consideration the Appellate Body's reasoning in US – Softwood Lumber V and taken into consideration the consistent line of the Appellate Body reports.[65]

Panel and Appellate Body reports are therefore of legal value to future cases. The consistency in practice is also in accordance with Article 3.2 of the *Understanding on Rules and Procedures Governing the Settlement of Disputes* (DSU), which provides that 'dispute settlement system of the WTO is a central element in providing security and predictability to the multilateral trading system'.

In this book, adopted GATT and WTO reports of Panels and Appellate Body are regarded as sources of law.[66]

1.3.1.3 Customary International Law

Customary international law refers to a practice between states. This practice must have some sort of duration, it must be consistent and it must be general.[67]

Customary international law is part of the source complex of WTO law. It is provided in Article 3.2 of the Dispute Settlement Understanding (DSU) that the WTO agreements must be clarified in accordance with customary rules on interpretation of international law. The most important aspect of customary international law for this book is the reference to the Vienna Convention on the Law of Treaties, which the Panels and Appellate Body regard as having attained status as customary in public international law; see more in paragraph 1.3.2 below.

62. Para. 109.
63. See about GATT Panel reports para. 82-85 in *US – Corrosion-Resistant Steel Sunset Review*, WT/DS244/AB/R, report of the Appellate Body on 15 Dec. 2003. In that case, which regarded whether a nonmandatory measure can be challenged, it is interesting to note that the Appellate Body, by elaborating its findings in *US – 1916 Act*, initially mentions GATT practice and *thereafter* refers to provisions in the ADA. In regard to WTO Panel and Appellate Body report, see for instance *EC – Bed linen*, WT/DS141/AB/R, report of the Appellate Body on 1 Mar. 2001, para. 83 and *US – Softwood Lumber V*, WT/DS264/AB/R, report of the Appellate Body on 11 Aug. 2004, para. 162.
64. *US – Shrimp (Ecuador)*,WT/DS335/R, report of the Panel on 30 Jan. 2007.
65. Para. 7.41.
66. See, for discussion in literature about Panel and Appellate Body reports, M. Matsushita, T. H. Schoenbaum & P. C. Mavroidis, *The World Trade Organization – Law, Practice, and Policy*, 2nd edn. (Oxford: Oxford University Press, 2006), 58-64; R. Bhala, *Modern GATT Law – A Treatise on the General Agreement on Tariffs and Trade* (London: Sweet & Maxwell, 2005), xvii-xviii; P. Van den Bossche, *The Law and Policy of the World Trade Organization* (Cambridge: Cambridge University Press, 2005), 56; and D. Palmeter & P. Mavroidis, 'The WTO Legal System: Sources of Law', *American Journal of International Law* 92 (1998): 401.
67. I. Brownlie, *Principles of Public International Law*, 5th edn (Oxford: Oxford University Press, 1998), 5-11.

1.3.1.4 Principles of Law

In this book, reference is also made to principles of law.[68] The Appellate Body and Panels frequently refer to principles of law, which serve to fill gaps in the WTO system.[69] Two principles in particular will be referred to: the non-discrimination principle and the fairness principle.

The 'non-discrimination principle' is a cornerstone in WTO law.[70] Several provisions in GATT 1994 require non-discriminatory treatment. Under Article I of GATT 1994, there is the most-favoured-nation requirement, according to which WTO Members must not favour one WTO Member over another. Article III of GATT 1994 provides *national treatment* of imported products, which implies that a WTO Member cannot treat domestic products more favourably than imported products. Whereas Articles I and III deal with nation-based discrimination, Article X.3(a) of GATT 1994 provides a more general prohibition against discrimination.[71] Pursuant to Article X.3(a), WTO Members are required to 'administer in a uniform, impartial and reasonable manner all its laws, regulations, decisions and rulings' pertaining to valuation of products for customs purposes, rates of duty, taxes and other charges, import and export requirements, restrictions or prohibitions, and other import affecting conditions. A Panel stated in *Argentina – Hides and Leather* that Article X.3 applies to discrimination against *traders* and is not limited to discrimination between nations.[72] Furthermore, the wording of Article X.3(a) implies that it is the *administration* of laws, regulations, decisions and rulings – and not the laws, regulations, decisions and rulings themselves – which must not be discriminatory. In the same case, the Panel stated that administrative regulations can also be subject to Article X.3(a).[73] The Panel statement supports the claim that Article X.3(a) is an expression of the general principle of non-discrimination.[74] In this book, reference is made to the non-discrimination principle. However, it is not examined whether the EU is discriminating between different countries in anti-dumping investigations. Instead, the principle is applied to situations where there may be discriminating treatment of producers from the same country.

The 'fairness principle' appears in practice as guiding the ADA, in particular Article 2.4, although neither Panels nor Appellate Body have explicitly used the term 'fairness principle' – with one dissenting Panellist as an exception.[75] The fairness principle can be derived from two situations in practice.

---

68. See V. D. Degan, *Sources of International Law* (The Hague: Kluwer Law International, 1997), 136-141 and I. Brownlie, ibid., 15-19.
69. P. Van den Bossche, *The Law and Policy of the World Trade Organization* (Cambridge: Cambridge University Press, 2005), 58.
70. Ibid., 39-41 and 308.
71. Ibid., 309.
72. *Argentina – Hides and Leather*, WT/DS155/R, report of the Panel on 19 Dec. 2000, para. 11.68.
73. Para. 11.71.
74. P. Van den Bossche, *The Law and Policy of the World Trade Organization* (Cambridge: Cambridge University Press, 2005), 309.
75. *US – Zeroing (EC)*, WT/DS294/R, report of the Panel on 31 Oct. 2005, para. 9.14.

First, with reference to Article 2.4 of the ADA, the Appellate Body stated in *EC – Bed linen* that the requirement of fair comparison in Article 2.4 is not limited to the actual comparison between normal value and export price; rather it is a *general obligation* that informs all of Article 2 of the ADA.[76] This requirement was even further elaborated in *US – Zeroing (EC)*, where the Appellate Body stated:

> We recall that the Panel found, first, that the 'fair comparison' language in the first sentence of Article 2.4 creates an *independent obligation*, and, *secondly, that the scope of this obligation is not exhausted by the general subject matter expressly addressed by paragraph 4 (that is to say, the price comparability).* (. . .) On the substantive meaning of the term 'fair comparison', we also agree with the Panel that the legal rule set out in the first sentence of Article 2.4 is expressed in terms of a general and abstract standard. One implication of this is that this requirement is also applicable to proceedings governed by Article 9.3.[77] (Emphasis added)

The Appellate Body repeated its viewpoints in *US – Softwood Lumber V (Article 21.5 – Canada)*.[78] A Panel stated in *US – Zeroing (Japan)* that the *indeterminate standard of fairness* underlies Article 2.4 of the ADA, but it cannot render more specific provisions in the ADA inoperative.[79] However, in *Egypt – Steel Rebar*, a Panel found that the fairness provided in Article 2.4 would not be a general obligation in the ADA.[80] Based on the legal reasoning by the Appellate Body in the above-mentioned cases, it must be assumed that the Panel finding is not correct.

Second, in *US – Hot-Rolled Steel*, the Appellate Body, without specific reference to the provisions regarding normal value determination, found that investigating authorities are obligated to be fair in the calculation of normal value because additional costs will distort the comparison.[81] This indicates that the investigating authorities must not be biased in the calculation of normal value, because the normal value will be compared with the export price. In the same case, the Appellate Body stated about Article 2.1 and the term 'ordinary course of trade'[82] of the ADA:

> Although we believe that the Anti-dumping Agreement affords WTO Members discretion to determine how to ensure that normal value is not distorted through the inclusion of sales that are not 'in the ordinary course of trade', that discretion is not without limits. In particular, the discretion must be exercised

76. *EC – Bed linen*, WT/DS141/AB/R, report of the Appellate Body on 1 Mar. 2001, para. 59.
77. *US – Zeroing (EC)*, WT/DS294/AB/R, report of the Appellate Body on 18 Apr. 2006, para. 146.
78. *US – Softwood Lumber V (Art. 21.5 – Canada)*, WT/DS264/AB/WR, report of the Appellate Body on 15 Aug. 2006, para. 133.
79. *US – Zeroing (Japan)*, WT/DS322/R, report of the Panel on 20 Sep. 2006, para. 7.158.
80. *Egypt – Steel Rebar*, WT/DS211/R, report of the Panel on 8 Aug. 2002, paras 7.333-7.335.
81. *US – Hot-Rolled Steel*, WT/DS184/AB/R, report of the Appellate Body on 24 Jul. 2001, paras 167-168.
82. See Ch. 4 below.

in an even-handed way that is fair to all parties affected by an anti-dumping investigation.[83]

The general statement by the Appellate Body in *US – Hot-Rolled Steel*, together with the argumentations in the other cases, indicates that a fairness principle runs through the entire ADA.[84] In this book, reference will be made to the fairness principle in situations where the ADA is not sufficiently clear concerning dumping determinations.

1.3.1.5 Other Sources

Occasionally, the Appellate Body will refer to dictionaries in order to get an ordinary meaning of a word. Even though the Appellate Body does not elaborate on the use of dictionaries, it must be assumed that the use of dictionaries only applies in situations where it has not been possible to find an ordinary meaning of a specific word in the context of the ADA. See for example *EC – Bed linen*,[85] and *US – Softwood Lumber V (Article 21.5 – Canada)*.[86] In this book, Black's Law Dictionary will be used to define words when no guidance can be found elsewhere in the sources of law. Furthermore, writings by some experts in the WTO and anti-dumping field will also be used here, both for discussion and inspiration, and for supporting the points of view presented in the book.

Some commentators refer to the reports by the Group of Experts as contributing to the development of anti-dumping law.[87] The Group of Experts was appointed in 1958 to discuss anti-dumping duties and GATT anti-dumping law[88] and released two reports.[89] In *US – Softwood Lumber (Article 21.5 – Canada)*, the Appellate Body made it clear that these reports are of limited legal value because they date back to 1959 and 1960.[90] However, a Panel referred to the Group of Experts as supporting its conclusion in *US – Zeroing (Japan)*.[91] It must in this regard be stressed that in that particular case, the Panel had made

83. Para. 150.
84. E. Vermulst, *The WTO Anti-dumping Agreement* (Oxford: Oxford University Press, 2005b), 25, n. 37.
85. *EC – Bed linen*, WT/DS141/AB/R, report of the Appellate Body on 1 Mar. 2001, para. 57, where the n. 24 refers to *The Concise Oxford Dictionary of Current English* (Oxford: Clarendon Press, 1995), 269, in order to find the ordinary meaning of the word 'comparable'.
86. *US – Softwood Lumber V (Art. 21.5 – Canada)*, WT/DS264/AB/RW, report of Appellate Body of 15 Aug. 2006, para. 138, n. 231.
87. See for instance Wenxi Li, *Anti-dumping Law of GATT/WTO and EC – Gradual Evolution of Anti-dumping Law in Global Economic Integration* (Lund: Lund University, 2001), 36-37.
88. Ibid.
89. First report on 24 Apr. 1959, L/978, second report on 29 Jan. 1960, L1141. See more in Ch. 2 below.
90. *US – Softwood Lumber V (Art. 21.5 – Canada)*, WT/DS264/AB/RW, report of the Appellate Body of 15 Aug. 2006, para. 121.
91. *US – Zeroing (Japan)*, WT/DS322/R, report of the Panel on 20 Sep. 2006.

its conclusion before the Appellate Body had released its findings in *US – Softwood Lumber (Article 21.5 – Canada)*,[92] and thus it cannot be concluded that the Panel also would have referred to the Group of Experts if the findings by the Appellate Body had been released before the Panel report. In spite of their limited legal value, according to the Appellate Body, the reports issued by the Group of Experts are still of significant value in understanding the development of anti-dumping law in the GATT and WTO framework. In this book, the reports will be used as supporting argumentation and to underpin the description of the evolution of GATT/WTO anti-dumping law into a rule-oriented system.[93]

In accordance with Article 16.1 of the ADA, a Committee on Anti-dumping Practices has been established. The Committee consists of all the WTO Members. It serves as a consultant in anti-dumping matters upon request by WTO Members. Furthermore, the Committee conducts annual reviews of the implementation and operation of the ADA.[94] The Committee has established subsidiary bodies such as the Ad Hoc Group on Implementation and the Informal Group on Anti-Circumvention.[95] The Committee can issue recommendations, which are not legally binding. However, for this book such recommendations can serve as an interpretative tool.[96]

1.3.2 Interpretation of WTO Agreements

The interpretation method used here of Article VI of GATT 1994 and of provisions in the ADA is inspired by the interpretation methods applied by Panels and, in particular, by the Appellate Body. This section contains a brief discussion of the interpretative methods by Panels and Appellate Body of the WTO Agreements, including ADA and GATT 1994.

1.3.2.1 General Interpretative Approach

The WTO agreements must be interpreted in accordance with the customary rules of public international law; see Article 3.2. of the DSU. Article 17.6(ii) of ADA also contains an explicit reference to the interpreting rules of customary international law. In this regard, it is settled practice by Panels and Appellate

92. See the Panel report, n. 741, where the Panel refers to the Panel report of *US – Softwood Lumber (Art. 21.5 – Canada)*, and also mentions the pending appeal. As will later be discussed regarding zeroing in transaction-to-transaction situations, it would have been in place for the Panel to postpone its findings in the *US – Zeroing (Japan)* until after the findings of the Appellate Body in *US – Softwood Lumber (Art. 21.5 – Canada)*.
93. See Ch. 2 below.
94. See Art. 18.6 of the ADA.
95. E. Vermulst, *The WTO Anti-dumping Agreement* (Oxford: Oxford University Press, 2005b), 217.
96. Ibid., 218 and I. Van Bael & J. F. Bellis, *Anti-dumping and Other Trade Protection Laws of the EC*, 4th edn (The Hague: Kluwer Law International, 2004), 514.

Body to refer to Articles 31 and 32 of the Vienna Convention on the Law of Treaties (Vienna Convention). According to the Appellate Body, the Vienna Convention 'has attained status of a rule of customary or general international law'.[97] This statement finds support from practice by, for example, the International Court of Justice (ICJ) and in literature.[98]

Articles 31 and 32 of the Vienna Convention provide:

Article 31 General rule of interpretation

1. A treaty shall be interpreted in good faith in accordance with the ordinary meaning to be given to the terms of the treaty in their context and in the light of its object and purpose.
2. The context for the purpose of the interpretation of a treaty shall comprise, in addition to the text, including its preamble and annexes:
   (a) any agreement relating to the treaty which was made between all the parties in connexion with the conclusion of the treaty;
   (b) any instrument which was made by one or more parties in connexion with the conclusion of the treaty and accepted by the other parties as an instrument related to the treaty.
3. There shall be taken into account, together with the context:
   (a) any subsequent agreement between the parties regarding the interpretation of the treaty or the application of its provisions;
   (b) any subsequent practice in the application of the treaty which establishes the agreement of the parties regarding its interpretation;
   (c) any relevant rules of international law applicable in the relations between the parties.
4. A special meaning shall be given to a term if it is established that the parties so intended.

Article 32 Supplementary means of interpretation

Recourse may be had to supplementary means of interpretation, including the preparatory work of the treaty and the circumstances of its conclusion, in order to confirm the meaning resulting from the application of Article 31, or to determine the meaning when the interpretation according to Article 31:

(a) leaves the meaning ambiguous or obscure; or
(b) leads to a result which is manifestly absurd or unreasonable.

---

97. *US – Gasoline*, WT/DS2/AB/R, report of the Appellate Body on 29 Apr. 1996, p. 17.
98. See for instance *Oil Platforms, Islamic Republic of Iran v. USA*, General List no. 90, judgment by the ICJ of 12 Dec. 1996. para. 23. See also O. Spiermann, *Moderne Folkeret*, 3rd revised edn (København: Jurist- og Økonomforbundets Forlag, 2006), 125-126 and A. H. Qureshi, *Interpreting WTO Agreements – Problems and Perspectives* (Cambridge: Cambridge University Press, 2006), 4.

The guiding principle is the principle of good faith,[99] which also informs the entire ADA.[100] According to Querishi, the principle of good faith includes two propositions:

1) The principle of effective treaty interpretations, where a treaty is to be given meaning to all terms.[101] In this line of thought, the Appellate Body also refuses readings of a text that will reduce or nullify paragraphs or whole clauses of the text; see for example *US – Gasoline*.[102]
2) The interpretation should not lead to absurd or unreasonable results.[103]

According to the Appellate Body, the starting point is the text of the treaty. The Appellate Body usually has a narrow approach to the text. In this line of thought, the Appellate Body has stated that the principles of interpretation in Article 31 of the Vienna Convention 'neither require nor condone the imputation into a treaty of words that are not there or the importation into a treaty of concepts that were not intended'.[104] If the parties' intention does not explicitly refer to a particular obligation, then the Panels and the Appellate Body usually refuse to read it into the text.[105] With respect to the object and purpose of ADA, there is no preamble in the ADA. A few Panels, however, have noted that one of the fundamental goals of the ADA is to ensure that objective determinations are made based to the extent possible on facts.[106]

Furthermore, the Appellate Body finds guidance in the context. If a specific obligation under one provision is not expressed in the provision under interpretation, the Appellate Body usually rejects reading such a condition into the text.[107]

Support may be found in the preparatory works to the ADA, where it may be demonstrated that during the negotiations, the negotiators may have discussed whether to include specific obligations or rights in the provisions.[108] During the

---

98. See more about the principle of good faith in Cheng Bin, *General Principles of Law as Applied by International Courts and Tribunals* (Reprint, Cambridge: Cambridge Grotius Publications Ltd, 1987), 107; and A. H. Qureshi, *Interpreting WTO Agreements – Problems and Perspectives* (Cambridge: Cambridge University Press, 2006), 13.
99. *US – Hot Rolled Steel*; WT/DS184/AB/R, report of the Appellate Body on 24 Jul. 2001, para. 101.
101. A. H. Qureshi, *Interpreting WTO Agreements – Problems and Perspectives* (Cambridge: Cambridge University Press, 2006), 13.
102. *US – Gasoline*, WT/DS2/AB/R, report of the Appellate Body on 29 Apr. 1996, p. 23.
103. A. H. Qureshi, *Interpreting WTO Agreements – Problems and Perspectives* (Cambridge: Cambridge University Press, 2006), 13.
104. *EC – Bed linen*,WT/DS141/AB/R, report of the Appellate Body on 1 Mar. 2001, para. 83; *India – Patents (US)*, WT/DS50/AB/R, report of the Appellate Body on 19 Dec. 1997, para. 45.
105. *US – Hot-Rolled Steel*, WT/DS184/AB/R, report of the Appellate Body on 24 Jul. 2001, para. 166-167; *EC – Tube or Pipe Fittings*, WT/DS219/AB/R, report of the Appellate Body on 22 Jul. 2003, para. 101 and 110-111; *Thailand – H – Beams*, WT/DS122/R, report of the Panel on 28 Sep. 2000, para. 7.89; *Argentina – Poultry Anti-dumping Duties*, WT/DS241/R, report of the Panel on 22 Jul. 2003, para. 7.153.
106. See Panel in *US – Steel Plate*, WT/DS206/R, report of the Panel on 28 Jun. 2002, para. 7.60, and *US – Hot Rolled Steel*, WT/DS184/R, report of the Panel on 28 Feb. 2001, para. 7.55.
107. *EC – Bed linen*, WT/DS141/AB/R, report of the Appellate Body on 31 Mar. 2001, paras 79-84.
108. *US – Stainless Steel*, WT/DS179/R, report the Panel of 22 Dec. 2000, para. 6.111, n. 53.

Uruguay Round, different drafts were discussed before the final Uruguay ADA was made. In particular, the Carlisle I draft, the Carlisle II draft, the New Zealand I draft, the New Zealand II draft, the New Zealand III draft and the Dunkel draft are significant. However, some of the drafts are unpublished working papers with no document numbers. Extracts from those drafts can be found in *Understanding the WTO Anti-dumping Agreement, Negotiation History and Subsequent Interpretation* by James P. Durling and Matthew R. Nicely from 2002, and in *The GATT Uruguay Round – A Negotiating History (1986-1992), Volume II*: *Commentary* by Terence B. Stewart from 1993. Those drafts – or preparatory works – will support some of the standpoints made here about obligations/rights that should not be read into the ADA.

1.3.2.2 National Interpretation: Article 17.6(ii) of the ADA

In the 'last minute' of the Uruguay Round, the US insisted that the Panels and Appellate Body cannot overrule 'permissible' interpretations of the ADA by national authorities.[109] The result was Article 17.6(ii) of the ADA, which provides:

> [T]he panel shall interpret the relevant provisions of the Agreement in accordance with customary rules of interpretation of public international law. Where the panel finds that a relevant provision of the Agreement admits of more than one permissible interpretation, the panel shall find the authorities' measure to be in conformity with the Agreement if it rests upon one of those permissible interpretations.

The question is, though, whether it is possible to end up with more than one 'permissible' interpretation of the text in an ADA provision.

In that respect, the different approaches to law from different legal cultures must be noted. See Craig, who writes that the EC Court will produce one interpretation of the particular provision: it may find that the Commission has some wide discretion due to economic considerations, but there will still be one interpretation of the provision under which the discretion can be carried out. In the US, the Supreme Court may be open to several interpretations in some cases. In *Chevron v. Natural Res. Def. Council*, the US Supreme Court stated that a permissible interpretation by an agency might be accepted even though a court may adopt another interpretation of the particular provision.[110] The difference between the EC Court and the US Supreme Court is that the former will find only one correct interpretation, while the US Supreme Court may allow different 'permissible' interpretations.[111]

The point of departure is the actual text of Article 17.6(ii) of ADA, where ambiguous wordings of a provision in the ADA may end up with more than one

109. G. N. Horlick & E. C. Shea, 'The World Trade Organization Anti-dumping Agreement', *Journal of World Trade* 29 (1995): 30.

110. *Chevron v. Natural Res. Def. Council*, 467 U.S. 837 (1984), 467 U.S. 837, 842-844.

111. See D. Craig, *EU Administrative Law* (Oxford: Oxford University Press, 2006), 436.

permissible interpretation. In addition, in case the interpretation of a provision should lead to a conclusion that allows the investigating authorities some discretion, Panels and Appellate Body must accept the investigating authorities' decisions under such discretion. Furthermore, the good faith requirement in Article 31 of the Vienna Convention implies that Article 17.6(ii) of ADA cannot be nullified; therefore, under some circumstances, there may be more than one permissible interpretation of the provisions in ADA.

The Appellate Body has concluded that a permissible interpretation after Article 17.6(ii), second sentence, 'is one which is found to be appropriate after application of the pertinent rules of the Vienna Convention'.[112] Rightly, the method to determine the interpretation(s) must be based on the Vienna Convention. Several commentators have argued that the Vienna Convention is constructed to lead to only *one* permissible interpretation of the provisions.[113] However, as stated above, an interpretation may lead to a conclusion where discretion is left to the investigating authorities.

It is interesting to note that Panels have been more open to interpretations from national authorities, contrary to the Appellate Body, which often refuses interpretations other than its own and therefore does not allow as much discretion as Panels.[114] The reluctance to allow national interpretations by the Appellate Body has led to criticism in literature.[115] Nevertheless, it seems that the Appellate Body finds an interpretation by WTO Members permissible if both parties to a dispute agree on the interpretation.[116]

In this book, the interpretations by national authorities will only be given little weight, in line with the approach by the Appellate Body. Article VI of GATT 1994 together with provisions of the ADA is here being interpreted narrowly.

1.3.3 EU Dumping Measures and Judicial Reviews

In this section it is discussed which EU measures are used to induce general assertions about EU dumping determinations and their relation to the EC courts.

112. *US – Hot Rolled Steel*, WT/DS184/AB/R, report of the Appellate Body on 24 Jul. 2001, para. 60. See also *Mexico – Corn Syrup (Art. 21.5 – US)*, WT/DS132/AB/RW, report of the Appellate Body on 22 Oct. 2001, para. 130.
113. See J. P. Durling & M. R. Nicely, *Understanding the WTO Anti-dumping Agreement, Negotiation History and Subsequent Interpretation* (London: Cameron May, 2002), 585; E. Vermulst, *The WTO Anti-dumping Agreement* (Oxford: Oxford University Press, 2005b), 229; G. N. Horlick & E. C. Shea, 'The World Trade Organization Anti-dumping Agreement', *Journal of World Trade* 29 (1) (1995): 30; and O. Spiermann, *Moderne Folkeret*, 3rd revised edn (København: Jurist- og Økonomforbundets Forlag, 2006), 123.
114. See in general throughout the book.
115. See for instance J. Greenwald, 'WTO Dispute Settlement: An Exercise in Trade Law Legislation?', *Journal of International Trade Law* 6 (1) (2003): 117 et seq.
116. *US – Hot Rolled Steel*, WT/DS184/AB/R, report of the Appellate Body on 24 Jul. 2001, para. 172.

The legal fundament to make dumping determinations under EU law is Article 133 of the EC Treaty about external relations, according to which the Council upon proposal by the Commission is to implement common commercial policies in regard to third countries. With regard to Article 133, the basic Regulation was adopted by the Council. The basic Regulation contains substantial and procedural rules in anti-dumping investigations, and, for this study, the text of the provisions is the starting point to be examined under WTO law. The Commission may impose provisional anti-dumping duties by Regulation.[117] Upon proposal by the Commission, the Council may impose definitive anti-dumping duties by Regulation.[118] The provisional and definitive Regulations serve as administrative practice.[119]

The Regulations are under review by the EC Court and the Court of First Instance.[120] Therefore, if a certain practice by the Commission or Council is found by the EC Court or Court of First Instance to be in violation of EU law, then such practice is disregarded in this book.

Until 1994, the judicial control of anti-dumping regulations was only controlled by the EC Court. The Court of First Instance had no jurisdiction in anti-dumping matters.[121] This may indicate that the Council had an interest in keeping the judicial control as limited as possible – and keeping wide political power in anti-dumping matters. The scope of judicial reviews of Council Regulations has also been tried before the EC Court in *Eurocoton v. Council*,[122] where the Council claimed that in anti-dumping cases, the Council acts as a legislator, not as an administrative body like the Commission does in competition cases. Therefore, according to the Council, the procedures in the anti-dumping investigation would not be subject to judicial reviews.[123] The EC Court, however, rejected this standpoint and stated that 'anti-dumping proceedings are similar in several respects to an administrative procedure'.[124] The EC Court continued and defined the Council's role in the anti-dumping procedures and the nature of the specific anti-dumping regulations:

> In such matters, the Council acts under rules – the basic regulation – which set well-defined limits to the powers of the institutions and offer procedural safeguards to the economic operators concerned and to their professional associations.

---

117. Arts 7 and 14.1 of the basic Regulation.
118. Arts 9.4 and 14.1 of the basic Regulation.
119. See right below in the minimized text.
120. Art. 230 of the EC Treaty.
121. Council Decision 94/149/ECSC EC of 7 Mar. 1994 amending Decision 93/350/Euratom, ECSC, EEC amending Decision 88/591/ECSC, EEC, Euratom establishing a Court of First Instance of the European Communities, Art. 1.
122. *Eurocoton v. Council*, Case C-76/01 P, judgment of the Court of 30 Sep. 2003. ECR 2003 P I-10091.
123. Para. 40
124. Para. 69.

> In so doing, the Council acts within a regulatory framework which it has imposed on itself, specifying the conditions in which an anti-dumping regulation may be adopted as well as the Council's room for manoeuvre as to whether or not to adopt such measures.[125]

Reviews by the EC courts on the practice by the Commission and the Council are examined here. Although the Commission and the Council Regulations are under judicial review, the Commission and the Council have a high degree of discretion in determining dumping and injury. First, the basic Regulation offers several provisions that give the Commission and the Council discretionary powers, for example Article 2.1, second sentence, where the domestic price *may* be based on other sellers' prices if the actual exporter does not produce or sell domestically.[126] Second, the EC courts have limited the judicial review due to the complexity in the economic, political and legal situations of the trade protective area.[127] The judicial review is therefore limited to verifying whether the relevant procedural rules have been complied with, whether the facts on which the disputed choice is based have been accurately stated, and whether there has been a manifest error of appraisal or a misuse of powers.[128]

Some Commission decisions are regarded as anti-dumping measures. Until 2002, the Commission was the only imposer of duties concerning products under the Treaty establishing the European Coal and Steel Community (ECSC). This has resulted in a few anti-dumping cases concerning imported steel. In accordance with Article 14.1 of Commission Decision 2277/96/ECSC of 28 November 1996 on protection against dumped imports from countries not members of the ECSC, the Commission could make decisions that imposed both provisional and definitive duties. The 2277/96 decision was homogenous with the basic Regulation in regard to dumping determination.[129] In 2002, the ECSC expired and the products covered

---

125. Para. 70-73.
126. See D. Craig, *EU Administrative Law* (Oxford: Oxford University Press, 2006), 433-434.
127. See for instance *Tokyo Bearings and others v. Council*, Case 240/84, judgment of the EC Court of 7 May 1987, ECR 1987, p. 1809, para. 19; *Sinochem v. Council*, Case T-97/95, judgment of the Court of First Instance on 29 Jan. 1998. ECR 1998, p. 85, para. 51; *Thai Bicycle Industry v. Council*, Case T-118/96, judgment of the Court of First instance of 17 Jul. 1998, ECR 1998, p. II-2991, para. 32; *Arne Mathisen v. Council*; Case T-340/99, judgment of the Court of First Instance of 4 Jul. 2002, ECR 2002, p. II-2905; *Shanghai Teraoka Electronic v. Council*, Case T-35/01, judgment of the Court of First Instance on 28 Oct. 2004, ECR 2004, p. II-3663, para. 48 and *Shandong v. Council*, Case T-413/03, judgment of the Court of First Instance on 13 Jul. 2006, ECR II-not yet reported, para. 61.
128. See for instance *Tokyo Bearings and others v. Council*, Case 240/84, judgment of the EC Court of 7 May 1987, ECR 1987, p. 1809, para. 19; *Nölle v. Council*, Case C-16/90, judgment of the EC Court on 22 Oct. 1991, ECR 1991, p. I-5163, para. 12; *Ferchimex v. Council*, Case T-164/94, judgment of the Court of First Instance on 28 Sep. 1995, ECR 1995, p. II-2681, para. 67; *Thai Bicycle Industry v. Council*, Case T-118/96, judgment of the Court of First instance of 17 Jul. 1998, ECR 1998, p. II-2991, para. 54.
129. Recital 6 in the 2277/96 Decision.

by the 2277/96 Decision were transferred to the basic Regulation.[130] Some Commission Decisions are used in this study.

The use of Regulations and Decisions has some limitations, as the Commission and the Council are not always very informative and do not always state clear reasons for their findings. Therefore, it may not always be possible to state the argumentation behind a finding in a specific Regulation or Decision.

An example can be found about the calculation methodology of the dumping margin, where the lack of information in the Regulations makes it difficult to establish the factors on which the Commission and the Council base their conclusions. In Chapter 6, matters about the practice of 'zeroing' are discussed. 'Zeroing' is a very questionable method by which to calculate the dumping margin. For now, it is worth mentioning that the Council, which used to rely on such a method, did not mention its calculation methodology in its Regulations. This has now resulted in a case before the EC Court regarding the annulment of such a Regulation due to lack of information.[131]

---

130. Council Regulation (EC) No. 963/2002 of 3 Jun. 2002 laying down transitional provisions concerning anti-dumping and anti-subsidy measures adopted pursuant to Commission Decisions No. 2277/96/ECSC and No. 1889/98/ECSC, as well as pending anti-dumping and anti-subsidy investigations, complaints and applications pursuant to those Decisions, OJ L 149, 7 Jun. 2002, p. 3-7, and Council Regulation (EC) No. 1310/2002 of 19 Jul. 2002 amending Regulation (EC) No. 963/2002 laying down transitional provisions concerning anti-dumping and anti-subsidy measures adopted pursuant to Commission Decisions No. 2277/96/ECSC and No. 1889/98/ECSC, as well as pending anti-dumping and anti-subsidy investigations, complaints and applications pursuant to those Decisions, OJ L 192, 20 Jul. 2002, pp. 9-10.
131. See *Metro*, C-245/05, OJ, C 205. 20 Aug. 2005, p. 10.

Chapter 2

WTO Law as a Rule-Oriented System

When EU dumping determinations are evaluated under WTO law, the elements characterizing WTO law must be kept in mind. A finding in this book of WTO inconsistent behaviour by the EU can be criticized for several reasons. For example, a violation by the EU of its WTO obligations may not imply that it will be reflected in the EU system in future dumping determinations, and an alleged violation of a specific provision in the ADA may not imply that it is easily brought before the DSB.

Thus, this chapter is about how WTO law is understood in this book and the reservations applying to the findings throughout the book. As already mentioned in Chapter 1, WTO law may be seen as a rule-oriented system. The meaning of rule orientation is substantiated in this chapter.

This chapter also serves another purpose in providing an overview of the anti-dumping rules. In the following chapters, reference will be made to other aspects of the anti-dumping rules than just the specific rules on dumping.

The starting point in Section 2.1 is the evolution of anti-dumping legislation under the GATT and WTO system. In Section 2.2, a brief overview of the anti-dumping rules of today is provided. It will be claimed that the WTO rules today leave less discretion to the investigating authorities than was the case under GATT law. The nature of the WTO anti-dumping legislation is less power-oriented than in the early GATT days.

Section 2.3 is about the enforcement of WTO law in the WTO system. It is here claimed that the DSB has become more judicialized than it was under the GATT time, although the starting point for settling disputes is based on political solutions.

Finally, in Section 2.4 the EU approach to WTO law on dumping is examined. It is claimed here that to some extent the EU applies the WTO rules in the EU system.

2.1 EVOLUTION OF ANTI-DUMPING LAW IN GATT/WTO

The practice of anti-dumping of products can be traced back to ancient times.[1] The first major measure towards dumping was reported in the late 1700s, when US industries suffered from allegedly dumped products from England. In 1816, the US enacted a Tariff Act, the aim of which was to protect the US industry from allegedly predatory English export prices. During the late 1800s, the protected US industries would engage in dumping of export prices of products to Canada and Australia, and English industries claimed to be suffering from dumped products by German and French exporters. The Governments in the US and Germany would furthermore facilitate dumping by establishing systems of export bounties to the exporting producers.[2]

In 1904, William S. Fielding, the Finance Minister of Canada, claimed that the proper method to meet dumping was 'to impose special duties upon dumped goods'.[3] Canada introduced specific anti-dumping measures in its Customs Act of 1904. Dumping was no longer under the general customs tariffs.[4] In making this move, Canada served as an example for other countries that introduced anti-dumping legislation in the following years: New Zealand in 1905, Australia in 1906 and South Africa in 1914.[5]

The purpose of anti-dumping measures was to avoid unfair trading practices by exporting companies and countries, and in particular to protect domestic industries from aggressive export prices from German industries. The domestic German market was protected by high tariffs on imported goods, and the German industries would create cartels, which facilitated the possibilities of dumping behaviour.[6]

During World War I, the decline in trade between nations led several countries to establish industries of products that usually had been imported. In the inter-war period, those new industries became vulnerable to the import of low priced products. As a result, other countries like the US and Japan introduced specific anti-dumping legislation.[7]

Dumping matters were discussed not only on the national level. On the *international level*, the focus on dumping was increasing,[8] and in 1926, the economist Jacob Viner delivered *A Memorendum on Dumping* at the League of Nation

1. J. Viner, *Dumping – A Problem in International Trade* (Reprint of Economic Classics, New York: Augstus M. Kelley Publishers, 1966), 374.
2. Ibid., 36-50.
3. Ibid., 193.
4. Ibid., 192-193.
5. T. P. Stewart, *The GATT Uruguay Round: A Negotiating History – Vol. II* (Deventer: Kluwer Law and Taxation Publishers, 1993), 1391.
6. J. Viner, *Dumping – A Problem in International Trade* (Reprint of Economic Classics, New York: Augstus M. Kelley Publishers, 1966), 51-66.
7. T. P. Stewart, *The GATT Uruguay Round: A Negotiating History – Vol. II* (Deventer: Kluwer Law and Taxation Publishers, 1993), 1395.
8. Ibid., 1404-1405.

in Geneva.[9] After World War II, the US and the United Kingdom made proposals to regulate international trade and establish the International Trade Organization (ITO).[10] It was suggested in the proposal that the application of anti-dumping measures should be dealt with by the ITO.[11]

At that time, the UN[12] established the United Nations Economic and Social Council (ECOSOC), the purpose of which was to draft an ITO Charter. At an ECOSOC meeting in London in 1946, a resolution was adopted to promote international trade, and a Preparatory Committee was established to elaborate on the ITO Charter draft.[13] The US prepared a draft charter including provisions about commercial policy. The US Draft Charter was the basis for the discussions made by the Preparatory Committee at its First Session in London. It included suggestions to an international anti-dumping legislation.[14] The ITO charter, also called the Havana Charter,[15] included the provisions of GATT 1947. GATT 1947 was signed on 30 October 1947 and entered into force on 1 January, 1948. The idea was to let GATT 1947 work temporarily until the ITO Charter could be brought into force.[16] However, the ITO Charter was never put into life, because the interest gap between the industrialized and developing countries was too wide.[17]

2.1.1 Anti-dumping in GATT: from Beginning to the Kennedy Round

Article VI of GATT 1947 gave the GATT contracting parties an overall framework to impose anti-dumping duties on injuring dumped goods. The provision was

9. J. Viner, *Dumping – A Problem in International Trade* (Reprint of Economic Classics, New York: Augstus M. Kelley Publishers, 1966), 347.
10. See Report from Second Session of the Preparatory Committee of the United Nations Conference on Trade and Employment, Seventh Meeting held on Thursday, 30 Oct. 1947, E/PC/T/PV.2/7, p. 5. See also World Trade Organization, *Guide to GATT Law and Practice – Volume I* (Geneva: World Trade Organization, 1995), 2 and T. P. Stewart, *The GATT Uruguay Round: A Negotiating History – Vol. II* (Deventer: Kluwer Law and Taxation Publishers, 1993), 1405.
11. T. P. Stewart, *The GATT Uruguay Round: A Negotiating History – Vol. II* (Deventer: Kluwer Law and Taxation Publishers, 1993), 1405.
12. The UN Charter was signed on 26 Jun. 1945 by 51 signatories. See J. O'Brien, *International Law* (London: Cavendish Publishing Ltd, 2001), 697-699.
13. The Prepatory Committee consisted of members from Australia, Belgium-Luxembourg Economic Union, Brazil, Canada, Chile, China, Cuba, Czechoslovakia, France, India, Lebanon, Netherlands, New Zealand, Norway, South Africa, the Soviet Union, the UK and the US. See WTO (1995), at p. 4, n. 1.
14. F. Snyder, 'The Origins of the "Nonmarket Economy": Ideas, Pluralism and Power in EC Anti-dumping Law about China', *European Law Journal* 7 (4) (2001): 379.
15. The final act for the establishment of ITO was drafted in Havana at conference from 21 Nov. 1947 to 24 Mar. 1948, cf. p. 5 in the Final Act of the United Nations Conference on Trade and Employment.
16. E. U. Petersmann, *The GATT Dispute Settlement System – International Law, International Organizations and Dispute Settlement* (The Hague: Kluwer Law International, 1997), 70.
17. Wang Gui Guo, *The Law of The WTO – China and the Future of Free Trade* (Hong Kong: Sweet & Maxwell Asia, 2005), 6.

restricted to price dumping and did not concern other kinds of dumping, such as service, exchange and social, which had been discussed during the negotiations.[18]

Dumping was not forbidden in GATT 1947, but condemned. Article VI also provided that the anti-dumping duty should not be greater than the dumping margin. Dumping was defined as export prices 'less than its normal value, if the price of the product exported from one country to another (a) is less than the comparable price, in the ordinary course of trade, for the like product when destined for consumption in the exporting country, or (b) in the absence of such domestic price, is less than either (i) the highest comparable price for the like product for export to any third country in the ordinary course of trade, or (ii) the cost of production of the product in the country of origin plus a reasonable addition for selling cost and profit'.

Article VI, on the one hand, is an exception to the general aim of market access, as anti-dumping duties may be seen as a trade barrier.[19] Furthermore, Article VI is an exception to the most-favoured-nation requirement in GATT 1947, Article I. According to which GATT contracting parties are not allowed to discriminate in the imposition of customs duties and charges of any kind to import of the like product from other GATT contracting parties, as the anti-dumping duties are targeted products from specific GATT contracting parties.[20] On the other hand, Article VI was also meant to ensure that anti-dumping duties could not serve as a protectionist means by national authorities.[21] Therefore, Article VI required that the calculation of dumping margins should be based on comparable prices, and non-paid indirect taxes could not be added.[22]

Article VI provides that both dumping and injury are necessary conditions to impose an anti-dumping duty, but it offers no procedural guidelines. Furthermore, the definition of dumping lacks guidelines regarding 'comparable price', 'ordinary course of trade', 'like product' and 'destined for consumption in the exporting country'. In addition, no guidelines are provided on the calculation methods between the normal value and export price, although, '[d]ue allowance shall be made in each case for differences in conditions and terms of sale, for differences in taxation, and for other differences affecting price comparability'. The original Article VI.1 contained a footnote clarifying that 'hidden dumping', where the resale price from an importer associated with the exporter is lower than the invoiced price by the exporter and below the normal value, was also price dumping. In hidden dumping situations, the export price can then be based on the resale

18. T. P. Stewart, *The GATT Uruguay Round: A Negotiating History* (Deventer: Kluwer Law and Taxation Publishers, 1993), 1406.
19. B. M. Hoekman & M. M. Kostecki, *The Political Economy of the World Trading System – From GATT to the WTO* (Oxford: Oxford University Press, 1995), 32.
20. GATT Contracting Parties, twelfth session, Anti-dumping & Countervailing Duties – GATT Secretariat Analysis of Legislation, L/712, 23 Oct. 1957, 5.
21. G. Marceau, *Anti-dumping and Anti-Trust Issues in Free Trade Areas* (Oxford: Oxford University Press, 1994), 134.
22. GATT Contracting Parties, twelfth session, Anti-dumping & Countervailing Duties – GATT Secretariat Analysis of Legislation, L/712, 23 Oct. 1957, 6.

price by the importer – and not the actual export price from the sale between the associated exporter and importer. Article VI did not offer more clarification. The lack of guidelines left the GATT contracting parties with wide discretionary power as to the application of anti-dumping rules and imposition of anti-dumping duties on imported products.[23] Different approaches by different GATT contracting parties led to allegations by some GATT contracting parties that other GATT contracting parties abused their national anti-dumping law as a trade barrier to foreign products. This was in conflict with the purpose of GATT to reduce trade barriers.[24] GATT anti-dumping law lacked predictability.

2.1.1.1 Non-market Economies

One of the first steps towards clearer rules addressed products from non-market economy countries. The end of World War II saw two major political blocs – East and West. The Western bloc based its values on capitalism, with the market as allocating resources and as a price regulating mechanism, whereas the Eastern bloc was founded on the socialistic economy, in which prices of consumer and factor goods and resource allocation were determined by the State, and the State was the owner of the resources.[25] Regarding anti-dumping matters, the problem in determining prices and costs could be the reliance on the domestic prices from the nations in the Eastern bloc. The price would not be the result of the market forces, but the result of the State's determination. In addition, the State in a Communist country would be able to allocate resources to companies with a lower anti-dumping margin.[26]

In 1955, the issue of finding the normal value for goods originating from non-market economies was raised by Czechoslovakia to a GATT Working Party. It was considered whether Article VI.1(b) should be amended in order to deal with products from non-market economy countries. The result was an interpretative note to Article VI.1 (b),[27] which reads:

> 'It is recognized that, in the case of imports from a *country which has a complete or substantially complete monopoly of its trade and where all domestic prices are fixed by the State, special difficulties may exist in determining price comparability* for the purposes of paragraph 1, and in such cases importing contracting parties may find it necessary to take into account the possibility that *a strict comparison with domestic prices in such a country may not always be appropriate*'. (Emphasis added)

23. T. P. Stewart, *The GATT Uruguay Round: A Negotiating History* (Deventer: Kluwer Law and Taxation Publishers, 1993), 1409-1410.
24. J. H. Jackson, *The World Trading System* (London: The MIT Press, 1989), 226.
25. F. Snyder, 'The Origins of the "Nonmarket Economy": Ideas, Pluralism and Power in EC Anti-dumping Law about China', *European Law Journal* 7 (4) (2001): 378 et seq.
26. Ibid.
27. L/334; Report of the Working Party on Barriers to Trade other than Restrictions or Tariffs, report of 1 Mar. 1955, para. 6.

The interpretative note as suggested by the Working Party was adopted by the GATT contracting parties on 3 March 1955. The note states that domestic prices from GATT contracting parties, where prices are fixed by the State and the State controls the resources, may not be useful as references for the determination of the normal value. However, it is not elaborated on in the interpretative note what sort of methodologies should be used in cases involving dumping from such countries. For example, there are no alternative suggestions as to how to determine a normal value for a non-market economy country. However, the note opens up the opportunity to base the normal value for a non-market economy country on other prices and costs than those found in the particular country. In subsequent US anti-dumping practice, normal value for non-market countries would be based on prices from a producer in a country with a market economy.[28] That practice has later been imported to EU practice.[29]

2.1.1.2 The Group of Experts

In 1958, Norway and Sweden suggested that a group of anti-dumping experts from the contracting parties should be set up to discuss the technical requirements to national anti-dumping legislation in regard to normal value, export price, like product, injury, administrative requirements, etc.[30] Based on the suggestion, a Group of Experts was established. The Group of Experts delivered two reports, the first of which was released in 1959.[31] In that report, it commented: on the export price, which should be the ex-factory price; normal value should be adjusted for the quantities sold compared to the export; how to calculate several domestic prices into one normal value; the alternatives to domestic prices in Article VI (b)(i)-(ii) were not hierarchic, but were only to be used when a normal value could not be based on the general rule in Article VI (a); indirect dumping, where exports go through a transit country, would also fall under the anti-dumping duty; and like product should be delimited to products of same physical characteristics. The Group of Experts furthermore provided clarification regarding injury, domestic industry, justification of provisional anti-dumping duties, and the importance of hearings and the duration of the validity of the anti-dumping duties.[32]

In 1960, the second report from the Group of Experts was published.[33] In its second report, the Group of Experts emphasized that anti-dumping duties are only to be imposed if actual dumping occurs and if the dumped prices cause or threaten

---

28. F. Snyder, 'The Origins of the "Nonmarket Economy": Ideas, Pluralism and Power in EC Anti-dumping Law about China', *European Law Journal* 7 (4) (2001): 384 et seq.
29. See Ch. 7 below.
30. *Anti-dumping and Countervailing Duties*, proposals by the Norwegian and Swedish delegations for further action by the GATT contracting parties, L/908, 11 Nov. 1958.
31. First Report of the Group of Experts on Anti-dumping and Countervailing Duties, L/978, delivered on 24 Apr. 1959.
32. Para. 6-23.
33. Second Report of the Group of Experts on Anti-dumping and Countervailing Duties, L/1141, delivered on 29 Jan. 1960.

to cause injury to the domestic industry in the importing country. The dumping determinations should be made firm-specific, if possible. The Group of Experts furthermore commented on production costs and SAG and their content. In addition, 'sales dumping', where an importer sells below the export price, may be regarded as dumping if the importer is compensated by the exporter. Finally, requirements to the investigating authorities were suggested about initiation of investigation, hearings, etc.[34]

2.1.2 The Kennedy Round (1963-1967)

Through negotiation rounds, the GATT contracting parties would make amendments to GATT and the tariff levels and provide agreements to elaborate on specific provisions of GATT 1947. However, those agreements were not necessarily signed by *all* the GATT contracting parties, and this left the agreements with some uncertainty regarding their application to the GATT contracting parties that did not accept the agreements.[35]

The first five of those negotiation rounds were in Geneva in 1947, Annecy in 1949, Torquay in 1951, Geneva in 1956 and Dillon in 1960-1961. They did not concern the anti-dumping field.[36] The first important step to clarify Article VI of GATT 1947 would come in the Kennedy Round from 1963 to 1967 by the Kennedy ADA, where the suggestions from the Group of Experts would be influential on the negotiations and future development of the clarification of Article VI.[37]

The Kennedy ADA would govern the application of Article VI and brought a number of clearer guidelines into the use of Article VI. The preamble was based on the statement from the Group of Experts that imposition of anti-dumping duties 'should not constitute an unjustifiable impediment to international trade and that anti-dumping duties may be applied against dumping only if such dumping causes or threatens material injury to an established industry or materially retards the establishment of an industry'.

Article 2 of the Kennedy ADA dealt with the dumping determination, and it provided as follows:

- *Like product* would now be defined as a product alike in all respects to the product under consideration, or in absence of such product, another product with close resemblance to the product under consideration.[38]
- In *transit-export sales* through an intermediary country, the export price should normally be based on the export price from the intermediary country

---

34. Paras 5-29.
35. J. H. Jackson, *The World Trading System* (London: The MIT Press, 1989), 89.
36. P. Van den Bossche, *The Law and Policy of the World Trade Organization* (Cambridge: Cambridge University Press, 2005), 82.
37. T. P. Stewart, *The GATT Uruguay Round: A Negotiating History* (Deventer: Kluwer Law and Taxation Publishers, 1993), 1417.
38. Art. 2(b).

to the importing country, unless the products would be transhipped through the intermediary country, where the price from the country of origin should be used.[39]

- The *alternatives to the actual domestic price* in Article VI.1 (b) were clarified. When there was no sale of the like product in the ordinary course of trade, or when due to the particular market situation such sales do not permit a proper comparison, the dumping margin would be based on the alternatives (third-country price or construction based on costs, SAG and profit). The 'particular market situation' was supposed to deal with non-market economy countries.[40] It was further clarified that profit should not exceed the profit normally realised on sales of products of the same general category of products in the domestic market of the country of origin.[41]
- *Alternatives to export price* was also provided in the Kennedy ADA. In case of no export price or unreliable export price due to association or compensatory arrangements between the exporter and importer, the export price may be based on the first resale price to an independent customer, or in case of no resale in the same condition as imported, on such reasonable basis as the national authorities determine.[42]
- Rules regarding *comparison between the normal value and export price* were also elaborated. The comparison should be fair and based on the same level of trade, normally the ex-factory level for sales made nearly the same time as possible. Also, due allowance should be made to differences in conditions and terms of sale, taxation and other differences that affect price comparability.[43]

The Kennedy ADA also provided elaboration of injury, definition of the term 'industry' and several rules addressing the investigation and evidence.[44]

Furthermore, the Kennedy ADA also provided the 'lesser duty rule', stating that it was desirable that the duty be less than the dumping margin, 'if such lesser duty would be adequate to remove the injury to the domestic country'.[45] The introduction of the lesser duty rule in GATT law indicates that the use of the anti-dumping instrument by GATT contracting parties should be limited, as a GATT contracting party should only impose the minimum possible anti-dumping duty.[46] However, it would still be at the discretion of the national authorities to decide whether a duty less than the dumping margin should apply in specific cases.

39. Art. 2(c).
40. F. Snyder, 'The Origins of the "Nonmarket Economy": Ideas, Pluralism and Power in EC Anti-dumping Law about China', *European Law Journal* 7 (4) (2001): 387 et seq.
41. Art. 2(d).
42. Art. 2(e).
43. Art. 2(f).
44. See in general the Kennedy ADA.
45. Art. 8(a).
46. G. Marceau, *Anti-dumping and Anti-Trust Issues in Free Trade Areas* (Oxford: Oxford University Press, 1994), 134-135.

Furthermore, a 'de minimis rule' was introduced, as cases would be terminated if the dumping margin, or the volume of dumped import, or the injury, was negligible.[47]

The parties to the Kennedy ADA would have to inform the GATT contracting parties about changes in the national anti-dumping laws, respectively, and report annually on the administration of their national anti-dumping laws and provide summaries of the cases.[48]

Furthermore, Article 17 provided that a Committee on Anti-dumping Practices should be established, composed of parties to the ADA. The Committee should afford the parties an opportunity to consult it on matters concerning the administration of anti-dumping matters.

The Kennedy ADA brought some guidelines to the investigating authorities. The wide discretion under Article VI of GATT 1947 now seemed to be limited under the elaborating provisions in the ADA.

2.1.3 The Tokyo Round (1973-1979)

In the following GATT Round, the Tokyo Round from 1973-1979, the GATT contracting parties would not make any amendments concerning provisions concerning dumping determinations. Article 2 from the Kennedy ADA was reproduced in Article 2 of the Tokyo Round, although the use of paragraph letters was changed to paragraph numbers.[49] However, several issues were raised during the Tokyo Round. There was a call for clarification of the ADA concerning sales below costs and allowances about price comparability,[50] but those issues would not be reflected in Article 2 of the Tokyo ADA. Instead, those suggestions would find their way into the ADA at the following round: the Uruguay Round.

The Tokyo Round instead brought some changes regarding injury, stating that dumping would no longer be required as the principal cause of the injury.[51] In other areas the Tokyo ADA would clarify the rules on procedural aspects, rules about undertakings, and rules about the dispute settlement.[52]

Article 14 provided that GATT Members would have to report to the Committee on Anti-dumping Practices all preliminary and final anti-dumping actions taken. Furthermore, all the GATT Members would have to submit a report on anti-dumping actions taken every six months. The Committee was now a central

47. Art. 5(c).
48. Arts 15 and 16.
49. For instance, Art. 2(f) of the Kennedy ADA became Art. 2.6 in the Tokyo ADA.
50. See T. P. Stewart, *The GATT Uruguay Round: A Negotiating History* (Deventer: Kluwer Law and Taxation Publishers, 1993), 1439-1455.
51. See differences in Art. 3 of the Kennedy ADA and Art. 3 of the Tokyo ADA. See also T. P. Stewart, Ibid., 1456.
52. T. P. Stewart, *The GATT Uruguay Round: A Negotiating History* (Deventer: Kluwer Law and Taxation Publishers, 1993), 1461.

body concerning the anti-dumping investigations and imposition of anti-dumping duties by the parties to the agreement.

2.1.4 The Uruguay Round (1986-1994)

The next GATT Round was the Uruguay Round from 1986 to 1994, where several amendments and clarifications were brought into the ADA. Furthermore, the WTO was established, and the ADA became a binding agreement on *all* WTO Members.

Concerning dumping determination, the Uruguay Round elaborated on the following points:

- Low volume sales could now be disregarded as not comparable with the export price.[53]
- Sales below costs were now being regulated.[54] Before the Uruguay Round, several GATT Members had introduced a practice to disregard sales below costs in the normal value determination.[55] The Uruguay Round finally brought some elaboration into the ADA about the circumstances required before such sales may be disregarded.
- Rules about how to calculate cost and cost allocation were introduced.[56]
- Rules on calculating SAG and profits were introduced.[57]
- The adjustment mechanism for differences affecting price comparability became more detailed, and it was now required that a fair comparison be made between normal value and export price.[58]
- There was an elaboration on currency conversion concerning the comparison between normal value and export prices.[59]
- The calculation of the dumping margin was elaborated. Before the Uruguay Round, in calculating of dumping margins some GATT Members, in particular the EU[60] and the US, would use zeroing by comparing a weighted-average normal value with specifically selected export transactions in order to address targeted dumping.[61] In Chapter 1, this was called the *weighted-average-to-transaction* method. The practice of the

53. Art. 2.2 together with Art. 2.1 of ADA.
54. Art. 2.2.1 of ADA.
55. T. P. Stewart, *The GATT Uruguay Round: A Negotiating History* (Deventer: Kluwer Law and Taxation Publishers, 1993), 1543.
56. Art. 2.2.1.1 of ADA.
57. Art. 2.2.2 of ADA.
58. Art. 2.4 of ADA. See also J. P. Durling & M. R. Nicely, *Understanding the WTO Anti-dumping Agreement, Negotiation History and Subsequent Interpretation* (London: Cameron May, 2002), 86.
59. Art. 2.4.1 of ADA.
60. See for instance the EC Court in *Tokyo Bearings and others v. Council*, Case 240/84, Judgment of the EC Court of 7 May 1987. ECR 1987, p. 1809, paras 11-24.
61. T. P. Stewart, *The GATT Uruguay Round: A Negotiating History* (Deventer: Kluwer Law and Taxation Publishers, 1993), 1537-1540.

> weighted-average-to-transaction method had been tested before a GATT Panel in *EC – Cotton Yarn*,[62] where the Panel found that the zeroing method was not part of the adjustment of normal value and export price for price comparability, as zeroing was the next step in the calculation of the dumping margin. The zeroing was therefore not inconsistent with GATT law.[63] Several other GATT Members had concerns over this methodology, and the conclusion of the Uruguay Round was that the weighted-average-to-transaction methodology could only be used under exceptional circumstances.[64] The principal methods would be a comparison between either a weighted-average normal value and a weighted-average export price, or a transaction-to-transaction comparison between normal value and export price.[65]

The Uruguay Round also brought a few amendments to the injury rules and to the procedural rules. Furthermore, the de minimis rule was elaborated, as negligible percentages were put on dumping margins and volume of dumped imports.

In the following section, the result from the Uruguay ADA is described. This provides the reader an overview of the WTO anti-dumping rules, as Chapters 3-7 contain references to provisions in the ADA other than those specifically dealing with dumping.

2.2 THE WTO ANTI-DUMPING RULES: AN OVERVIEW

This section is divided into two subsections about the substantial rules and procedural rules, respectively.

2.2.1 Substantial Rules

The substantial rules can be divided into two areas. The first is the topic of this book: dumping. The other area is injury. Before anti-dumping measures can be imposed on a product from another country, both dumping and injury must be established by the investigating authorities.[66]

---

62. *EC – Cotton Yarn*, ADP 137, report by Panel of 4 Jul. 1995. See for more examples from GATT Panel practice in E. Vermulst, *The WTO Anti-dumping Agreement* (Oxford: Oxford University Press, 2005b), 54-56.
63. Paras 500-501.
64. T. P. Stewart, *The GATT Uruguay Round: A Negotiating History* (Deventer: Kluwer Law and Taxation Publishers, 1993), 1538-1540.
65. Art. 2.4.2 of the ADA.
66. Art. VI of GATT 1994.

2.2.1.1 Dumping

It was stated above that the Uruguay Round brought a series of important changes to the rules about dumping determinations.[67] Those amendments were carried out in Article 2 of the ADA. The specific rules are analyzed in Chapters 3-7. An overview of the rules is provided here:

- Article 2.1 defines dumping and the requirements to normal value; see Chapter 4.
- Article 2.2 regards the alternatives to the domestic price; see Chapter 4 and also Chapter 7.
- Article 2.3 concerns the export price; see Chapter 5.
- Article 2.4 is about the comparison between the normal value and export price; see Chapter 6.
- Article 2.5 regards export sales through intermediary countries; see Chapter 4.
- Article 2.6 defines the term 'like product'; see Chapter 3.

2.2.1.2 Injury

The dumped goods must cause injury or threat of injury to the producers of the like product in the importing country.[68] Producers in the importing country of the like product, i.e., products like the imported dumped products, must be injured by the dumped product. Thus, the injury test also serves as a means to define the scope of imported products that fall under the anti-dumping duty. If a dumped product is not like the injured products in the importing country, the anti-dumping duty cannot be imposed. The injury test consists of several elements:

- *Domestic industry*: Definition of the injured industry in the importing country. The reference for this definition is the like product as the one dumped.[69]
- *Material injury*: The investigating authorities must examine both the volume of the dumped import and its effect on the prices in the importing market, as well as the consequent impact of these imports on the producers in the importing country, in order to determine material injury.[70] The examinations must be based on positive evidence and must be objective.[71]

---

67. See 2.1.4.
68. Art. VI.1 of GATT 1994 and Art. 3 of ADA.
69. Art. 4 of ADA.
70. Art. 3.1 of ADA. The term 'material injury' follows from Art. VI (1) of GATT 1994 and fn. 9 in ADA.
71. Art. 3.1 of ADA. See Appellate Body in both *US – Hot-rolled Steel*, WT/DS184/AB/R, report of the Appellate Body on 24 Jul. 2001, paras 192-193 and 204-206, and *Thailand – H-Beams*, WT/DS122/AB/R, report of the Appellate Body on 12 Mar. 2001, para. 107-111 both reports regard 'positive evidence'.

- *Causality*: It must be demonstrated by the investigating authorities that the dumped goods are causing the injury. First, the investigating authorities must demonstrate the injury by an examination of *all* relevant evidence before them. Second, it must be examined whether any known factors are causing injury to the domestic industry in the importing country, like volume and prices of imports not sold at dumped prices, contraction in demand or changes in the patterns of consumption, trade-restrictive practices of and competition between the foreign and domestic producers, developments in technology and the export performance, and productivity of the domestic industry.[72]
- *Threat of material injury:* Even if there is no actual injury, a threat of injury by dumped products may lead to imposition of an anti-dumping duty. Such determination must be based on facts and not merely on allegation, conjecture or remote possibility. The central question in this regard is whether the dumped product can create a change in circumstances that leads to an injury.[73] The investigating authorities should regard four non-exhaustive factors: the significant rate of increase of the dumped imports, the capacity of the exporter, price effect on domestic prices and inventories of the product being investigated.[74] Anti-dumping measures in regard to threat must be decided with special care.[75]

2.2.2 Procedural Rules

The procedural rules relate to the requirements for initiating an investigation, the administrative rules during the investigation, the measures possible, and the rules about reviews.

2.2.2.1 Initiation of the Investigation

An anti-dumping investigation is initiated by the investigating authorities upon a written application by or on behalf of the domestic producers in the importing country.[76] The investigating authorities may only under special circumstances initiate the investigation without any written application from the domestic industry.[77] The application must include evidence of dumping and injury as well as information about the applicant, a complete description of the allegedly dumped product, domestic prices in the exporting country, and the injury factors of the evolution of volume of the allegedly dumped product and the effect on the

72. Art. 3.5 of the ADA.
73. See Panel in *Egypt – Steel Rebar*, WT/DS211/R, report of the Panel on 8 Aug. 2002, para. 7.91.
74. Art. 3.7 of the ADA.
75. Art. 3.8 of the ADA.
76. Art. 5.1 of the ADA.
77. Art. 5.6 of the ADA.

domestic industry.[78] The application is not supposed to include any analysis of the information; rather the application must contain information in the sense of evidence in support of the allegations.[79]

The investigating authorities must examine the accuracy and adequacy of the evidences provided in the application to determine whether there is sufficient evidence to justify the initiation of an investigation.[80] However, an initiation of investigation can only be made if the investigating authority finds that the application has been made by or on behalf of the domestic industry.[81] Furthermore, the application must not be published by the authorities unless it is decided to initiate an investigation. Yet, before the initiation of investigation, the authorities must notify the government in the exporting country about the application.[82] The notification should be made as soon as possible after the receipt by the investigating authorities of a properly documented application and as early as possible before the decision is taken regarding initiation of an investigation.[83] The notification can be either oral or written.[84]

Article 5.8 of the ADA is a de minimis and negligible provision. The margin of dumping is to be considered de minimis if the margin is less than 2% of the export price. Furthermore, if the volume of the dumped import from one country is less than 3% of imports of the like product in the importing country, the volume is regarded as negligible. In case of de minimis margin or negligible volume, the application of initiating the anti-dumping investigation shall be rejected, and the investigation shall be terminated. Exceptions are made in cases where individual countries that count for less than 3% of the import collectively account for more than 7% of the import of the like product in the importing country. The provision of Article 5.8 applies both to pre-initiation and post-initiation situations.[85]

2.2.2.2 Investigation

According to Article 12 of the ADA, a public notice must be given when investigations are initiated, when preliminary and final determinations are made, including provisional measures, and on conclusion or suspension of definitive duties.

---

78. Art. 5.2 of the ADA.
79. See Panel in *Mexico – Corn Syrup*, WT/DS132/R, report of the Panel on 28 Jan. 2000, para. 7.76 and Panel in *Thailand – H-Beams*, report of Panel on 28 Sep. 2000, which refers to the *Mexico – Corn Syrup* case, cf. paras 7.75-7.76.
80. Art. 5.3 of the ADA.
81. Art. 5.4 of the ADA.
82. Art. 5.5 of the ADA.
83. Recommendation Concerning the Timing of the Notification under Art. 5.5 of the Committee on Anti-dumping Practices, G/ADP/5 of 3 Nov. 1998. See also Panel in *Guatemala – Cement II*, WT/DS156/R, report of the Panel on 24 Oct. 2000, paras 8.76-8.83.
84. *Thailand – H-Beams*, WT/DS122/R, report of the Panel on 28 Sep. 2000, para. 7.89. See in the same case the discussion about the content of notification, para. 7.91.
85. See Panel in *Guatemala – Cement II*, WT/DS156/R, report of the Panel on 24 Oct. 2000, para. 8.72.

There is a time limit for the duration of the investigation. After Article 5.10 of the ADA, the investigation must, except in special circumstances, be concluded within one year from the date of initiation. Exceptions can be made in special circumstances, but the time limit may in no case be longer than 18 months. The data to take into account is based on prices, costs, etc. from the investigating period, which is the period of data collection. The Committee on Anti-dumping Practices has recommended the investigating period normally be one year and in any case no less than six months, ending as close to the date of initiation of the investigation as is practicable.[86]

Article 6 of the ADA concerns evidence and due process in the investigation.[87] Article 6.1 provides that all interested parties must be given notice of the information that is required by the authorities and ample opportunity to present evidence. 'Interested parties' are defined in Article 6.11 in a non-exhaustive list.

In Article 6.1.1, a minimum period of 30 days to reply to questionnaires must be given to exporters or foreign producers. Furthermore, interested parties participating in the investigation must be given access to written evidence provided by other parties, unless such information is confidential.[88] All other parties must be given access to information that is relevant to their case, non-confidential and used by the investigating authorities in the investigation. Those interested parties must also be given opportunity to prepare presentations based on this information.[89] In addition, the known exporters and the authorities in the exporting country must be provided with the full text of the application of initiation of an anti-dumping investigation, apart from confidential information.[90] Other interested parties must also be given access to the application on request. Rules regarding confidentiality are provided in Article 6.5. Article 6.2 provides *all* interested parties the right to a hearing. However, there is no obligation for interested parties to participate in such hearings. Before a definitive decision is made, the authorities must inform all interested parties of the facts upon which the decision is made. It must take place in sufficient time for the parties to defend their interests.[91]

Pursuant to Article 6.10, it is a general rule to determine *individual dumping margins* for each known producer or exporter. Exceptions can be made in situations

---

86. *Recommendation Concerning the Period of Data Collection for Anti-dumping Investigations* of the Committee on Anti-dumping Practices, G/ADP/6, on 16 May 2000. See also E. Vermulst, *The WTO Anti-dumping Agreement* (Oxford: Oxford University Press, 2005b), 9.
87. See in regard to due process Appellate Body in *US – Oil Country Tubular Goods Sunset Reviews*, WT/DS268/AB/R, report of the Appellate Body on 29 Nov. 2004, para. 241 and Panel in *US – Oil Country Tubular Goods Sunset Reviews (Art. 21.5 – Argentina)*, WT/DS268/RW, report of the Panel on 30 Nov. 2006, para. 7.120; Panel in *Guatemala – Cement II*, WT/DS156/R, report of the Panel on 24 Oct. 2000, apparently distinguishing between fundamental rights in Art. 6.1 and Art. 6.2, cf. paras 8.178 and 8.179.
88. Art. 6.1.2. See also Panel in *Argentina – Poultry Anti-dumping Duties*, WT/DS241/R, report of the Panel on 22 Apr. 2003, para. 7.153.
89. Art. 6.4.
90. Art. 6.1.3.
91. Art. 6.9.

where the number of exporters, producers, importers or types of products is so large that individual determinations will be impracticable. Under those circumstances, the authorities may use *sampling techniques*. The selection of producers in the sample should preferably be made after consulting and with the consent of the producers, exporters or importers concerned.[92] However, individual margin must be determined for those producers or exporters that are not part of the sample if they submit the necessary information within the time limit. Only if the number of producers or exporters is so large that individual examinations 'would be unduly burdensome *and* prevent the timely completion of the investigation' may the examination be based on the samples.[93]

2.2.2.3 Measures and Anti-dumping Duties

According to Article 7.1 of the ADA, the investigating authorities may apply provisional measures towards the imported products if the conditions in Article 5 are met, provided there is a preliminary affirmative determination of dumping and injury, and such a measure is necessary to prevent injury. Such measures can take the form of a provisional anti-dumping duty – or preferably as security by cash deposit or bond.[94] Provisional measures cannot be applied sooner than 60 days from the date of initiation.[95] A provisional measure has a time limit and can apply for a maximum of 6 months, but must be limited to the shortest time as possible.[96]

The producer may offer a price undertaking to the investigating authorities. If such an undertaking is accepted, the anti-dumping proceedings are suspended or terminated. Price undertakings cannot, however, be sought or accepted unless the investigating authorities have made a preliminary affirmative determination of injurious dumping.[97]

If a price undertaking is not sought or accepted, the investigating authorities can impose a definitive anti-dumping duty on the imported products if all the substantial and procedural conditions are fulfilled.[98] The anti-dumping duty must be collected on a non-discriminatory basis, where the investigating authorities must, unless it is impracticable, fulfil several administrative conditions about naming all suppliers of the products.[99]

The anti-dumping duty must not exceed the dumping margin; cf. Article 7.5, together with Article 9.3. This, however, is desirable if the anti-dumping duty is

92. Art. 6.10.1 of the ADA.
93. Art. 6.10.2 of the ADA.
94. Art. 7.2 of the ADA.
95. Art. 7.3 of the ADA.
96. Art. 7.4 of the ADA.
97. Art. 8.1 and Art. 8.2 of the ADA.
98. Art. 9.1 of the ADA.
99. Art. 9.2 of the ADA.

less than the dumping margin if a lesser duty is sufficient to remove the injury to the industry in the importing country; see Article 9.1. This is the *lesser duty rule*.[100]

If the investigating authorities use a sampling technique in accordance with Article 6.10, the anti-dumping margin for those producers that have not been selected for the sample must not exceed the weighted-average margin of dumping established with respect to the selected producers.[101]

The anti-dumping duty must remain in force to the extent necessary to counteract injurious dumping. However, any definitive anti-dumping duty must be terminated no later than five years after the imposition, unless it is determined in a review that removal of the duty will lead to continuation or recurrence of injurious dumping.[102]

The investigating authorities must make reviews of the need for the continued imposition of dumping. The reviews may be carried out on the initiative of the investigating authorities; when a reasonable time has elapsed,[103] where the 5-year rule, mentioned above, is the maximum time;[104] or upon request by any interested parties, who submit positive information substantiating the need for a review.[105]

Article 13 of the ADA requires the WTO Members to maintain judicial, arbitral or administrative tribunals to review administrative actions to final anti-dumping determinations and to determinations taken on the reviews just mentioned. Those tribunals and their procedures shall be independent of the authorities who are responsible for the measures under review.

2.2.3 Final Words

From the point of departure in Article VI of GATT 1947 with an overall set of rules to cope with dumping matters, through elaborations in the Kennedy ADA and Tokyo ADA, the anti-dumping legislation of the WTO has evolved into a complex body of detailed rules.

The wordings of Article VI of GATT 1947 left a wide discretion to the GATT contracting parties in their approach to dumping, but at the same time there was a call for more unification in national dumping approaches, as the anti-dumping instrument was allegedly being abused to keep competition away from the importing markets.

The more detailed rules in the present ADA may on one hand serve as a limitation on national discretion by unification in national anti-dumping law.

100. See for instance E. Vermulst, *The WTO Anti-dumping Agreement* (Oxford: Oxford University Press, 2005b), 171; J. Czako, J. Human & J. Miranda, *A Handbook on Anti-dumping Investigations* (Cambridge: Cambridge University Press, 2003), 75-76.
101. Art. 9.4 of the ADA.
102. Art. 11.1 together with Art. 11.3.
103. Art. 11.2.
104. Art. 11.3.
105. Art. 11.2.

Such unification could be seen as a step in the direction of more clarity and predictability in the anti-dumping system. However, the complex body of rules may have another side to it. The rules may be so complicated and structured in such a way that an immediate reading of them leads to confusion, thus leading to the conclusion that the rules themselves conflict with one another. It has not been examined in this part whether this could be the case, but it at least appears to be so for the dumping determinations in Chapters 3-7.

If the aim of the WTO is to be achieved, the laws on dumping must be clear and transparent. The national authorities should have clear guidance about the scope of discretion left to them. If the EU violates WTO law, it may not be a result of intentional behaviour by the EU authorities, but it may be a result of unclear WTO law. Under the present Doha Round, the EU has, in a submission to the negotiating group on WTO rules, asked for clearer legislation in light of the Panel and Appellate Body reports.[106] Furthermore, commentators are divided into two groups, disagreeing on the needs for changes in law. The first group claims that WTO law has a vague and unclear definition of dumping that is easily abused by national authorities.[107] The other group claims that WTO anti-dumping law provides discretion that is limited by activist application by Appellate Body beyond its powers under the DSU and the WTO Agreement.[108] Nevertheless, the evolution in the GATT/WTO shows a trend in reducing the national discretionary power and some more clarity in law. However, several areas could be improved concerning transparency in law. Some of those will be mentioned throughout the book.

---

106. See; Submission from the European Communities Concerning the Agreement on Implementation of Art. VI of GATT 1994 (Anti-dumping Agreement) to the Negotiating Group on Rules in regard to WTO Doha Development Agenda Negotiations of Jul. 2002.
107. See for instance B. M. Hoekman & P. C. Mavroidis, 'Dumping, Anti-dumping and Antitrust', *Journal of World Trade* 30 (1) (2006): 29 et seq.; P. Didier, 'The WTO Anti-dumping Code and EC Practice – Issues for Review in Trade Negotiations', *Journal of World Trade* 35 (1) (2005): 33 et seq.; Wenxi Li, *Anti-dumping Law of WTO/GATT and EC – Gradual Evolution of Anti-dumping Law in Global Economic Integration* (Lund: Lund University, 2001), 387; D. Bekker, 'The Strategic Use of Anti-dumping in International Trade' *South African Journal of Economics* 74 (3) (2006): 505; M. Finger (ed), *Anti-dumping – How It Works and Who Gets Hurt* (Michigan: The University of Michigan Press, 2003), preface pp. vii-viii; G. N. Horlick, 'How the GATT became protectionist – An Analysis of the Uruguay Round Draft Final Anti-dumping Code', *Journal of World Trade* 27 (5) (2003): 7 et seq.; R. Bhala, *Modern GATT Law – A Treatise on the General Agreement on Tariffs and Trade* (London: Sweet & Maxwell, 2005), 685.
108. See J. Greenwald, 'WTO Dispute Settlement: An Exercise in Trade Law Legislation?', *Journal of International Trade Law* 6 (1) (2003): 117 et seq., and D. K. Tarullo, 'Paved with good intentions: the dynamic effects of WTO review of anti-dumping action', *World Trade Review* 2 (3) (2003): 379. Apparently also M. Matsushita, T. H. Schoenbaum & P. C. Mavroidis, *The World Trade Organization – Law, Practice, and Policy*, 2nd edn (Oxford: Oxford University Press, 2006), 908-910.

2.3 THE ENFORCEMENT OF WTO ANTI-DUMPING LAW IN THE WTO SYSTEM

In this part, the evolution of the dispute settlement system is described. It is claimed that the system has changed from a power-oriented system to a rule-oriented system.

Above, it was found that GATT was originally meant to be a temporary body until the much more complex ITO would take over. ITO legislation provided rules on dispute settlement. The starting point would be diplomatic solutions between the parties. If no such solutions were found, the disputing parties could be referred to the *Executive Board*,[109] which would consist of 18 members from ITO states.[110] Those 18 members would be appointed by the *Conference*, which consisted of *all* members of the ITO.[111] The Executive Board would come up with a decision, which could be reviewed by the Conference.[112] However, Conference decisions could be brought before the ICJ, the decisions of which would be binding to the Conference.[113]

2.3.1 Dispute Settlement under GATT 1947

GATT 1947 contained two provisions dealing with disputes. Article XXII sets out a right for GATT contracting parties to seek consultation on GATT matters. Article XXIII points out the requirements for asking the GATT contracting parties to recommend solutions to the dispute.

Pursuant to Article XXIII.1 of GATT 1947, a GATT contracting party that considers that any benefit accruing to it directly or indirectly under GATT 1947 is being nullified or impaired by another party may approach the other GATT contracting party in order to reach a satisfactory adjustment on the matter. Article XXIII.1 provides three causes that can form the basis of a claim:

(1) the GATT contracting party is not able to carry out its obligation – this is called a violation complaint;
(2) the application of a measure, whether or not it conflicts with GATT 1947 – this is called a non-violation complaint; or
(3) the existence of any other situation – these are called a situation complaint.[114]

Thus, the GATT dispute settlement system was only applicable to GATT contracting parties, not to citizens in the GATT contracting states.

---

109. Art. 94 of the ITO Charter.
110. Art. 78.1 of ITO Charter.
111. Art. 74.1 of ITO Charter.
112. Art. 95.1 of ITO Charter.
113. Art. 96 of ITO Charter.
114. E. U. Petersmann, *The GATT Dispute Settlement System – International Law, International Organizations and Dispute Settlement* (The Hague: Kluwer Law International, 1997), 73.

If no satisfactory solution is found, the parties may refer the matter to the contracting parties.[115] In the early GATT days, working parties, consisting of *all* the GATT Members, would propose a solution. Working parties would therefore also consist of the parties to the dispute. According to Petersmann, such solutions were based on considerations that were more political than legal, as the working parties consisted of governmental representatives instead of lawyers.[116]

Eventually, the working parties were replaced by Panels, which were composed of 3-5 experts from other GATT contracting parties. Consequently, the parties to the dispute would no longer have any direct influence on the content of a recommendation but would still have influence on the composition of Panels. By replacing working Parties with Panels, GATT took a step in a more rule-oriented direction.[117]

In 1955, Article XXIII.2 was amended in order to provide the GATT contracting parties with a retaliation tool. If the circumstances are serious enough, a GATT contracting party could suspend the application to any other contracting party or parties of such concessions or other obligations under GATT 1947 as they determined appropriate in the circumstances.[118] The GATT contracting parties could authorize retaliation by a majority of votes. However, during the GATT time the retaliation was only applied once.[119]

During the Tokyo Round, a DSU was concluded. In Article 7 of the Tokyo DSU, it was provided that customary practice in the field of dispute settlement should be continued in future. Prior to the Tokyo Round, a customary practice had been developed in which a GATT contracting member was *compensated* if an immediate withdrawal of a GATT inconsistent measure was impracticable. This customary GATT practice was written into the annex to the Tokyo DSU.[120]

Although there are indications of rule orientation in the use of Panels instead of working parties, and in the introduction of sanction tools of compensation or retaliation for not bringing GATT inconsistent measures into conformity with GATT law, the GATT system was still power-oriented in regard to adoption of Panel recommendations. The recommendations from Panels needed to be adopted in unison by *all* GATT Member States, including the parties to the dispute.[121] The blocking option of GATT Panel reports was reflected in cases regarding anti-dumping. During the time from 1947 to the establishment of the WTO, only 5 out of 9 Panel reports regarding anti-dumping were adopted:

---

115. Art. XXIII.2 of GATT 1947.
116. E. U. Petersmann, *The GATT Dispute Settlement System – International Law, International Organizations and Dispute Settlement* (The Hague: Kluwer Law International, 1997), 84.
117. J. H. Jackson, *The World Trading System* (London: The MIT Press, 1989), 93.
118. T. P. Stewart, *The GATT Uruguay Round: A Negotiating History* (Deventer: Kluwer Law and Taxation Publishers, 1993), 2675.
119. J. H. Jackson, *The World Trading System* (London: The MIT Press, 1989), 96.
120. Para. 5 in the Annex.
121. P. Van den Bossche, *The Law and Policy of the World Trade Organization* (Cambridge: Cambridge University Press, 2005): 176-177.

- *Swedish – Anti-dumping Duties*[122] was adopted on 26 February 1955;
- *New Zealand – Imports of electrical transformers from Finland*[123] was adopted on 18 July 1985;
- *US – Anti-dumping Duties against Imports of Fresh and Chilled Atlantic Salmon*[124] was adopted on 27 April 1994;
- *Korea – Anti-dumping Duties on Imports of Polyacetal Resins from the United States*[125] was adopted on 27 April 1993; and
- *EC – Anti-dumping Duties on Imports of Cotton Yarn from Brazil*[126] was adopted on 30 October 1995.

Four other Panel anti-dumping reports were blocked.[127] Another GATT Panel report can be added to the list of adopted anti-dumping cases, as *EEC – Regulation on Imports of Parts and Components*[128] concerned EU rules regarding circumvention of anti-dumping duties. The issue was not regarded under Article VI of GATT 1947 but was instead dealt with under the discrimination provision in Article III.2 of GATT 1947.[129]

In this regard, it must be noted that in other areas than the anti-dumping area, the frequency of adopted GATT Panel reports was apparently higher.[130]

2.3.2 WTO Dispute Settlement

In 1985, the GATT contracting parties established a preparatory Committee to determine the subjects to be discussed during the Uruguay Round. One of the

---

122. *Swedish – Anti-dumping Duties*, L/328 – 3S/81, report of the Panel on 23 Feb. 1955.
123. *New Zealand – Imports of electrical transformers from Finland*, L/5814 – BISD 32S/55, report of the Panel on 19 Jun. 1985.
124. *US – Anti-dumping Duties against Imports of Fresh and Chilled Atlantic Salmon*, ADP/87, report of the Panel on 30 Nov. 1992.
125. *Korea – Anti-dumping Duties on Imports of Polyacetal Resins from the United States*, ADP/92 – BISD 40S/205, report of the Panel on 2 Apr. 1993.
126. *EC – Anti-dumping Duties on Imports of Cotton Yarn from Brazil*, ADP/137, report of the Panel on 4 Jul. 1995.
127. See an overview of cases in E. U. Petersmann, *The GATT Dispute Settlement System – International Law, International Organizations and Dispute Settlement* (The Hague: Kluwer Law International, 1997), Annex A. From this index the following anti-dumping Panel reports were not adopted; *US – Imposition of Anti-dumping Duties on Imports of Seamless Stainless Steel Hollow Products from Sweden*, ADP/47, report by Panel on 20 Aug. 1990, *US – Anti-dumping Duties in the US on Gray Portland Cement Clinker Imported from Mexico*, ADP/82, report by Panel on 7 Sep. 1992; *US – Anti-dumping Duties on Imports of Stainless Steel Plate from Sweden*, ADP/117, report by Panel on 24 Feb. 1994; and *EC – Anti-Dumping Duties on Audio Tapes in Cassettes Originating in Japan*, ADP/136, report by Panel on 28 Apr. 1995.
128. *EEC – Regulation on Imports of Parts and Components*, L/6657 – BISD 37S/132, report of the Panel of 22 Mar. 1990.
129. Para. 5.9 and 5.11 of the Panel report.
130. J. H. Jackson, *The World Trading System* (London: The MIT Press, 1989), 99.

subjects the Committee pointed at was the DSB. The Committee particularly stressed the adoption of and the compliance with Panel reports by the GATT contracting parties.[131] During the Uruguay Round, a new DSU was enacted.

The new DSU still has the diplomatic solution as a starting point, as WTO Members affirm their adherence to the principles in Article XXII and Article XXIII of GATT 1947.[132] Before a Panel is established, the parties to the dispute must seek consultation. If the consultation fails to settle the dispute within 60 days after a request for consultation is received, it may be requested to establish a Panel.[133] In addition, the system is only applicable to WTO Members, not citizens.

The new DSU also directed the DSB into a more judicialized system than the GATT system.[134] First, the Appellate Body was introduced. Panel reports can now be appealed to the Appellate Body,[135] which is a standing body consisting of 7 permanent members in which the disputing parties have no appointing rights to the composition of Appellate Body in the particular cases.[136] The Appellate Body may uphold, modify, or reverse the legal findings and conclusions by Panels,[137] although the Appellate Body has a limited power to deal only with matters regarding law covered in the Panel report, and legal interpretations developed by the Panel can be appealed.[138] Factual matters are entirely left to Panels.

Second, the vetoing right for a GATT Member to block a recommendation by Panels was amended. Now, both un-appealed Panel and Appellate Body recommendations have to be adopted unless *all* WTO Members reject the adoption, i.e., with consensus.[139] Nevertheless, the WTO Members still have the right to seek an authoritative interpretation outside the DSB at the Ministerial Conference, as mentioned in the previous chapter.[140] A final interpretation is left to the Ministerial Conference and the General Council, which is represented by all WTO Members.

Third, when a Panel or Appellate Body finds that national measures are inconsistent with WTO law, the WTO Member shall put the measure into conformity with WTO law.[141] The implementation by the WTO Member of the recommendation is under surveillance by the DSB.[142] The compliance must be carried out immediately,[143] unless immediate compliance is impracticable. In such cases, the

131. T. P. Stewart, *The GATT Uruguay Round: A Negotiating History* (Deventer: Kluwer Law and Taxation Publishers, 1993), 2722.
132. Art. 3.1 of the DSU.
133. Art. 4.7 of the DSU.
134. E. U. Petersmann, The GATT Dispute Settlement System – International Law, International Organizations and Dispute Settlement (The Hague: Kluwer Law International, 1997), Ch. 5.
135. DSU Art. 16.4.
136. DSU Art. 17.
137. DSU Art. 17.13.
138. DSU Art. 17.6.
139. DSU Art. 16.4 and Art. 17.14.
140. DSU Art. 3.9.
141. DSU Art. 19.1 together with Art. 21.
142. DSU Art. 21.3.
143. DSU Art. 21.1.

WTO Member is given a reasonable time to implement the recommendation.[144] If the Panel or Appellate Body recommendation is not implemented by the WTO Member within the reasonable period, the WTO Member must upon enter into negotiations about compensating the other party to the dispute. If no satisfactory compensation can be agreed upon within 20 days after the reasonable time period, the DSB may authorize the other party to suspend its application of concessions or other WTO obligations towards the WTO Member.[145] Compensation or retaliation is not preferred over full implementation.[146] This condition seems not to be fully carried out by some WTO Members, including the EU, which seems to regard the compensatory sanction as an alternative to full implementation.[147] Finally, pursuant to Article 21.5 of the DSU, in the event of disagreements between the disputing parties whether the WTO Member who has violated WTO law has brought the measure into WTO conformity in accordance with the recommendations from the Panel or Appellate Body, a Panel is established to deal with such matters. This is a so-called 'compliance case'.[148]

Apparently, a violation of Article VI of GATT 1994 or the ADA will not in itself release the sanctions. Compensation – and if that is not working, retaliation – is a result of non-implementation of the recommendation by Panels and the Appellate Body. However, Panels and the Appellate Body may suggest ways in which the WTO Member could implement the recommendation.[149] Such *suggestions* may give Panels and Appellate Body the possibility to suggest revocation of the WTO violating measure and refund of the collected duty.[150] A Panel has dealt with that issue. In *Guatemala – Cement II*,[151] Mexico requested that Guatemala – in addition to revoking the illegal anti-dumping duty – should refund the anti-dumping duty already paid over three and a half years.[152] The Panel ruled that Guatemala should revoke the anti-dumping measure but declined to rule that Guatemala had to refund the anti-dumping duties collected over the three and a half years.[153]

Anti-dumping disputes are also regulated in Article 17 of the ADA. It appears that the rules in ADA and in DSU are complementary, and not in conflict with each other; see Appellate Body in *Guatemala Cement I*.[154] The starting point of a dispute is the same as under DSU, where a mutually satisfactory resolution

144. DSU Art. 21.3.
145. DSU Art. 22.2.
146. DSU Art. 22.1.
147. See the EC Court in *Portugal v. Council*, case C-149/96, judgment of the EC Court on 23 Nov. 1999, ECR 1999, p. I-8395, paras 36-40.
148. See P. Van den Bossche, *The Law and Policy of the World Trade Organization* (Cambridge: Cambridge University Press, 2005), 280-282.
149. DSU Art. 19.1.
150. See E. Vermulst, *The WTO Anti-dumping Agreement* (Oxford: Oxford University Press, 2005b), 260-261.
151. *Guatemala – Cement II;* WT/DS156/R, report of the Panel on 24 Oct. 2001.
152. Para. 9.4.
153. Paras 9.6-9.7.
154. *Guatemala – Cement I*, WT/DS60/AB/R, report of the Appellate Body on 2 Nov. 1998, para. 65-67.

must be sought.[155] However, a Panel is only established if no solution is found *and* if the investigating authority has taken final action to impose a definitive anti-dumping duty on the products or a price undertaking has been accepted. A provisional measure may also be brought before a Panel if the provisional duty has a significant impact on the complaining WTO Member.[156] In Chapter 1, the special rules about national interpretation of the ADA were discussed.

2.3.3 Final Comments

The starting point of the GATT anti-dumping legislation was Article VI of GATT 1947, which in itself was only vaguely worded and left the investigating authorities several interpretative alternatives. Over the years, the GATT anti-dumping legislation became more complex by a set of detailed rules intended to unify the national application of anti-dumping measures. The major problem during the GATT years was to settle disputes by the dispute settlement system, as recommendations from GATT Panels were often blocked by a party to the dispute. GATT law was then to be seen in the light of the political considerations that GATT Members could exercise in disputes.

The establishment of WTO brought several changes in the rule-oriented direction. Article VI of GATT 1994 was further elaborated by an even more complicated set of rules than before. There were now guidelines about different calculation methods, and the rules on adjustment of normal value and export price were enhanced. However, Article 17.6(ii) of the ADA provided guidelines for accepting permissible interpretations by national authorities, although, in WTO practice, they seem not to have had much impact.[157] The DSB was judicialized by introducing the Appellate Body and by amending the adoption rules to the effect that recommendations from Panels or Appellate Body are adopted unless there is consensus among *all* WTO Members that the adoption of the recommendation should be blocked. However, there is still a diplomatic basis in the disputes, both at the initial stage of the cases and in compliance cases. Furthermore, a violation of the anti-dumping rules is not sanctioned unless recommendations from Panels or Appellate Body are not followed. In addition, the WTO system does not ensure a mechanism for citizens to bring a case before a Panel or Appellate Body. It is left to the WTO Members to ensure such a mechanism. Therefore, a finding of a violation of WTO anti-dumping law in this book does not mean that such a violation can be tried by a foreign producer or an EU importer in the DSB, unless a WTO Member brings the case before the DSB.

155. Art. 17.3 of the ADA.
156. Art. 17.4 of the ADA.
157. See Section 1.3.2.2.

2.4 EU IN GATT/WTO

In this section, the connection between the WTO system and the EU system is described. First, a few words about the EU as a WTO Member. Next, a description of the EU anti-dumping legislation is provided in light of GATT/WTO law. Finally, the application of WTO law in the EU system is described. As illustrated above, citizens cannot themselves use the WTO system to bring a case before the DSB, and the question is whether WTO law is applicable in the EU system by the EC courts.

2.4.1 THE EU AS A WTO MEMBER

The EU had not been one of the GATT contracting parties, albeit all EU Members individually were GATT contracting parties. The EU, however, was to be found at the negotiation tables during the GATT Rounds, and the EU had become a party to the concluded agreements.[158]

With Decision 94/800, the Council approved the WTO Agreement and the annexes attached to it, including the ADA.[159] The EU signed the *Final Act embodying the results of the Uruguay Round of Multilateral Trade Negotiations* and thereby became a full member of WTO.[160]

The EU has committed itself to the WTO Agreement, where it is provided in Article XVI(4) of the WTO Agreement that Members 'shall ensure the conformity of its laws, regulations and administrative procedures with its obligations as provided in the annexed Agreements'. Furthermore, the EU shall follow the recommendations from Panels and Appellate Body.[161]

It is further provided in Article 18.1 of the ADA that '[n]o specific action against dumping of exports from another Member can be taken except in accordance with the provisions of GATT 1994, as interpreted by this Agreement'. Furthermore, according to Article 18.4, each Member must 'take all necessary steps, of a general or particular character, to ensure, not later than the date of entry into force of the WTO Agreement for it, the conformity of its laws, regulations and administrative procedures with the provisions of this Agreement as they apply for the Member in question'.

---

158. K. Lenaerts & P. Van Nuffel, *Constitutional Law of the European Union* (London: Thomson/ Sweet & Maxwell, 2005), 840.
159. Council Decision 94/800/EC of 22 Dec. 1994 concerning the conclusion on behalf of the European Community, as regards matters within its competence, of the agreements reached in the Uruguay Round multilateral negotiations (1986-1994) OJ L 336, 23 Dec. 1994, p. 1-2, Art. 1.
160. K. Lenaerts & P. Van Nuffel, *Constitutional Law of the European Union* (London: Thomson/ Sweet & Maxwell, 2005), 841.
161. Art. II.2 of the WTO Agreement together with Art. 19.1 and Art. 21 of the DSU.

The EU has therefore accepted to act in conformity with the WTO anti-dumping legislation in Article VI of GATT 1994 and ADA, and furthermore agreed to follow adopted Panel and Appellate Body reports directed at the EU.

The EU is special by nature by consisting of 27 WTO Member States. At WTO negotiation meetings, the EU has a number of votes equal to the number of EU Member States that are Members of WTO.[162] In the inter-relationship between the 27 EU Member States, anti-dumping duties are prohibited. Initially, under Article 91 of the European Economic Community (EEC) Treaty of 1957,[163] the EU Member states could invoke anti-dumping duties on products from other EU Member States by authorization from the Commission. This provision expired in 1968, when the transitional period for establishing the common market ended.[164] The end of the transitional period was also the start of the common commercial policy under Article 113 of the EEC Treaty.[165] The EU was now given full power in anti-dumping matters, and the first basic Regulation was enacted.[166] Under the present basic Regulation, the Council has the power to impose definitive anti-dumping duties and to collect provisional anti-dumping duties upon proposal by the Commission.[167] The Commission is empowered to impose the provisional anti-dumping duty on foreign goods, but it cannot collect such duties.[168]

Although the EU has the full power to impose anti-dumping duties on the imported products, the EU Member States are represented in the Advisory Committee.[169] The Advisory Committee must be consulted by both the Commission and the Council during the anti-dumping investigation; for example, the anti-dumping duty cannot be imposed on the imported goods without prior consultation of the Advisory Committee.[170] Furthermore, the customs agencies in the EU Member States ensure the practical collection of anti-dumping duties.[171] Any measures taken by the Commission and Council are under review of the EC courts; see Article 230 of the EC treaty;[172] and the EU is thus fulfilling Article 13 of the ADA.

---

162. WTO Agreement, Art. IX.
163. Art. 91 has been deleted from the EC Treaty.
164. Art. 8 of the EEC Treaty.
165. Now Art. 133 of the EC Treaty.
166. Regulation (EEC) No. 459/68 of the Council of 5 Apr. 1968 on protection against dumping or the granting of bounties or subsidies by countries which are not members of the European Economic Community, OJ L 93, 17 Apr. 1968, p. 1-12. See also P. Wegener Jessen, 'Anti-dumping', in *WTO Law – from an European Perspective*, eds. B. Egelund Olsen, M. Steinicke and K. Engsig Sørensen (København: Forlaget Thomson, 2006), 414-415.
167. Art. 9.4 of the basic Regulation.
168. Art. 7.4 of the basic Regulation.
169. I. Van Bael and J. F. Bellis, *Anti-dumping and Other Trade Protection Laws of the EC*, 4th edn (The Hague: Kluwer Law International, 2004), 21.
170. Art. 9.4 of the Basic Regulation.
171. I. Van Bael & J. F. Bellis, *Anti-dumping and Other Trade Protection Laws of the EC*, 4th edn (The Hague: Kluwer Law International, 2004), 21.
172. See Ch. 1 above.

2.4.2 Evolution of EU Anti-dumping Legislation in Light of GATT/WTO Law

The evolution of EU anti-dumping legislation since the first basic Regulation in 1968 has been a reflection of the development in the GATT legislation. The Kennedy ADA found its way into EU legislation, but the Tokyo ADA – and also the ADA from the Uruguay Round – would also to some extent reflect the development taking place in the EU anti-dumping practice by the Commission and Council.

The 1968 basic Regulation[173] provides in its preamble that the basic Regulation 'must be drawn up with due regard for the rules laid down in Article VI of the GATT and in the Agreement on Implementation of that Article'. The reference to GATT/WTO has been consistent in the subsequent basic Regulations. The text of the substantial part of the 1968 basic Regulation regarding dumping and injury bears a close resemblance to the Kennedy ADA.[174] One of the major *differences* between the GATT rules and the EU rules is the requirement under EU law that the imposition of the anti-dumping duty be in the interest of the Community.[175] Furthermore, the 1968 basic Regulation specifies the different roles between the Commission, the Council and the Member states.[176]

The 1968 basic Regulation was superseded by the 1979 basic Regulation.[177] The 1979 basic Regulation was concluded by the Council in order to make the necessary amendments to the EU anti-dumping legislation due to the amendments in GATT law following the Tokyo Round.[178] The 1979 basic Regulation would reflect the Tokyo ADA. Yet, the 1979 basic Regulation made further specifications that are not contained in the Tokyo ADA. Dumping determinations concerning non-market economies were specified.[179] Due to an increase in the anti-dumping measures in the EU in the early 1980s, several procedural amendments were made,

173. Regulation (EEC) No. 459/68 of the Council of 5 Apr. 1968 on protection against dumping or the granting of bounties or subsidies by countries which are not members of the European Economic Community, OJ L 93, 17 Apr. 1968, p. 1-12. Amended by Council Regulation (EEC) No. 1411/77 of 27 Jun. 1977 amending Regulation (EEC) No. 459/68 on protection against dumping or the granting of bounties or subsidies by countries which are not members of the European Economic Community, OJ L 160, 30 Jun. 1977, p. 4, and by Council Regulation (EEC) No. 1681/79 of 1 Aug. 1979 amending Regulation (EEC) No. 459/68 on protection against dumping or the granting of bounties or subsidies by countries which are not members of the European Economic Community, OJ L 196, 2 Aug. 1979, pp. 1-6.
174. Ibid., p. 54.
175. Art. 15.1 (a) and Art. 17 of the 1968 Basic Regulation.
176. See for instance Art. 16 and Art. 21 of the 1968 basic Regulation.
177. Council Regulation (EEC) No. 3017/79 of 20 Dec. 1979 on protection against dumped or subsidized imports from countries not members of the European Economic Community, OJ L 339, 31 Dec. 1979, p. 1-14. Amended by Council Regulation (EEC) No. 1580/82 of 14 Jun. 1982 amending Regulation (EEC) No. 3017/79 on protection against dumped or subsidized imports from countries not members of the European Economic Community, OJ L 178, 22 Jun. 1982, p. 9.
178. See preamble to the 1979 Basic Regulation.
179. Art. 2.5 of the 1979 Basic Regulation.

and in 1984 a new basic Regulation came into force.[180] Just 4 years later, the 1984 basic Regulation was replaced by the 1988 basic Regulation.[181] The 1988 basic Regulation amended the dumping and injury provisions and introduced a circumvention provision, according to which a definitive duty could be imposed on goods assembled in the EU if there was an association between the EU assembler and a foreign producer who was subject to an anti-dumping duty. The rule was found to be inconsistent with GATT law by a GATT Panel in *EEC – Regulation on Imports of Parts and Components*,[182] as the circumvention rule violated Article III.2, first sentence, of GATT 1947.[183] The Panel did not examine the rule under Article VI of GATT 1947.[184] Subsequently, the specific circumvention rule in the 1988 basic Regulation was suspended by the Commission,[185] and later the circumvention rule was amended.[186] In 1994 a new basic Regulation was enacted;[187] this was intended to take the ADA from the Uruguay Round into account. However, the 1994 basic

180. See Wenxi Li, Anti-dumping Law of WTO/GATT and EC – Gradual Evolution of Anti-dumping Law in Global Economic Integration (Lund: Lund University, 2001), 56. Council Regulation (EEC) No. 2176/84 of 23 Jul. 1984 on protection against dumped or subsidized imports from countries not members of the European Economic Community, OJ L 201, 30 Jul. 1984, pp. 1-16, amended in Council Regulation (EEC) No. 1761/87 of 22 Jun. 1987 amending Regulation (EEC) No. 2176/84 on protection against dumped or subsidized imports from countries not members of the European Economic Community, OJ L 167, 26 Jun. 1987, pp. 9-10.
181. Council Regulation (EEC) No. 2423/88 of 11 Jul. 1988 on protection against dumped or subsidized imports from countries not members of the European Economic Community, OJ L 209, 2 Aug. 1988, p. 1-17, amended by Council Regulation (EC) No. 521/94 of 7 Mar. 1994 on the introduction of time limits for investigation procedures carried out against dumped or subsidized imports from countries not members of the European Community and amending Regulation (EEC) No. 2423/88, OJ L 66, 10 Mar. 1994, pp. 7-9, and by Council Regulation (EC) No. 522/94 of 7 Mar. 1994 on the streamlining of decision-making procedures for certain Community instruments of commercial defence and amending Regulations (EEC) No. 2641/84 and No. 2423/88, OJ L 66, 10 Mar. 1994, pp. 10-11.
182. *EEC – Regulation on Imports of Parts and Components*, BISD 37S/132, Report by Panel of 22 Mar. 1990.
183. Para. 5.9. Art. III.2, first sentence, of GATT 1947 (now GATT 1994) provides: '[T]he products of the territory of any contracting party imported into the territory of any other contracting party shall not be subject, directly or indirectly, to internal taxes or other internal charges of any kind in excess of those applied, directly or indirectly, to like domestic products.'
184. Para. 5.11.
185. I. Van Bael & J. F. Bellis, *Anti-dumping and Other Trade Protection Laws of the EC*, 4th edn (The Hague: Kluwer Law International, 2004), 343-345.
186. See s. 2.4.2.3.
187. Council Regulation (EC) No. 3283/94 of 22 Dec. 1994 on protection against dumped imports from countries not members of the European Community, OJ L 349, 31 Dec. 1994, amended by Council Regulation (EC) No. 355/95 of 20 Feb. 1995 amending Regulation (EC) No. 3283/94 on protection against dumped imports from countries not members of the European Community, OJ L 41, 23 Feb. 1995, p. 2, and by Council Regulation (EC) No. 1251/95 of 29 May 1995 amending Regulation (EC) No. 3283/94 on protection against dumped imports from countries not members of the European Community, OJ L 122, 2 Jun. 1995, p. 1-1.

Regulation was only short-lived and was replaced by the present basic Regulation in 1996 due to material linguistic errors.[188]

On an overall level, the present basic Regulation has a similar structure to that of the ADA, although the basic Regulation is more elaborate than the ADA, particularly in procedural matters. In the following sections, a few of the major differences between the basic Regulation and the ADA will be pointed out.

2.4.2.1 Community Interest

Under EU law, it is required that the imposition of an anti-dumping duty is in the interest of the Community; see Article 7.1 of the basic Regulation regarding provisional duties and Article 9.4 regarding definitive duties. In Article 21.1, it is provided that Community interest determination must be based on an appreciation of all the various interests taken as a whole, including the interests of the domestic industry, users and consumers.

In the WTO framework, Article 9.1 of ADA, it is provided that even though the two foregoing conditions, dumping and injury, are met, the investigating authorities can nevertheless decide not to impose an anti-dumping duty on the importing dumped goods. Therefore, including a rule about Community interest does not present a violation of WTO law.

2.4.2.2 Guaranties of Rights in Anti-dumping Cases

The basic Regulation provides rules about rights of the producers, exporters, etc. in anti-dumping matters. Besides the administrative rules under the basic Regulation, it follows from case law that where the Community institutions have a wide power of appraisal, respect for the rights guaranteed by the Community legal order in administrative procedures is even more fundamentally important.[189] For example, this implies that the investigating authorities in their use of information about exporters and importers are required to comply with the rights of a defence. The investigating authorities must take into account all the relevant circumstances in the case and appraise the facts of the matter with all due care before a decision is made.[190]

Under EU law, the basic rights under administrative law appear to be more extensive than what is required under WTO law. Basically, WTO law appears merely to provide a general framework of due process during the investigation.[191]

---

188. Wenxi Li, *Anti-dumping Law of WTO/GATT and EC – Gradual Evolution of Anti-dumping Law in Global Economic Integration* (Lund: Lund University, 2001), 57.
189. *Shandong v. Council*, Case T-413/03, judgment of the Court of First Instance on 13 Jul. 2006, ECR 2006, p. II-2243, para. 63. See also K. Lenaerts & P. Van Nuffel, *Constitutional Law of the European Union* (London: Thomson/Sweet & Maxwell, 2005), 716-717.
190. *Nölle*, Case C-16/90, judgment of the EC Court on 22 Oct. 1991, ECR p. I-5163, para. 13, and in particular *Shandong v. Council*, Case T-413/03, judgment of the Court of First Instance on 13 Jul. 2006, ECR II-not yet reported, paras 64-66 and 96.
191. Art. 6 of the ADA.

2.4.2.3 Circumvention

Article 13 of the basic Regulation regards circumvention.[192] Circumvention refers to situations where exporters who have been imposed with anti-dumping duties may export their goods to the EU through a country that is not included in the original anti-dumping regulation. In such situations, the Commission will examine any changes in the trade pattern from the suspected countries and the country included in the anti-dumping measure to the EU.[193] Circumvention will also include situations where the exporters modify the product that is subject to an anti-dumping duty in order to let the product fall outside the product definition in the anti-dumping regulation. In this line, assembly processes in EU or third countries can also be regarded as circumvention.[194] If changes in the trade pattern

---

192. Circumvention is defined in Art. 13.1 as 'a change in the pattern of trade between third countries and the Community or between individual companies in the country subject to measures and the Community, which stems from a practice, process or work for which there is insufficient due cause or economic justification other than the imposition of the duty, and where there is evidence of injury or that the remedial effects of the duty are being undermined in terms of the prices and/or quantities of the like product, and where there is evidence of dumping in relation to the normal values previously established for the like product, if necessary in accordance with the provisions of Art. 2.'
193. See for instance *Polyethylene Terephthalate Film*, Council Regulation (EC) No. 1975/2004 of 15 Nov. 2004, extending the definitive anti-dumping duty imposed by Regulation (EC) No. 1676/2001 on imports of polyethylene terephthalate (PET) film originating, inter alia, in India to imports of PET film consigned from Brazil and from Israel, whether declared as originating in Brazil or Israel or not, OJ L 342, 18 Nov. 2004, p. 1-7, recitals 20-31; *Coumarin*, Council Regulation (EC) No. 2272/2004 of 22 Dec. 2004 extending the definitive anti-dumping duty imposed by Regulation (EC) No. 769/2002 on imports of coumarin originating in the People's Republic of China to imports of coumarin consigned from India or Thailand, whether declared as originating in India or Thailand or not, OJ L 396, 31/12/2004, pp.18-27, recitals 18-34; *Steel Ropes and Cables*, Council Regulation (EC) No. 1886/2004 of 25 Oct. 2004 extending the definitive anti-dumping duty imposed by Council Regulation (EC) No. 1796/1999 on imports of steel ropes and cables originating, inter alia, in the People's Republic of China to imports of steel ropes and cables consigned from Morocco, whether declared as originating in Morocco or not, and terminating the investigation in respect of imports from one Moroccan exporter, OJ L 328, 30 Oct. 2004, pp. 1-6, recitals 15-24; and *Certain Ringbinder Mechanisms II*, Council Regulation (EC) No. 1208/2004 of 28 Jun. 2004 extending the definitive anti-dumping measures imposed by Regulation (EC) No. 119/97 on imports of certain ring-binder mechanisms originating in the People's Republic of China to imports of the same product consigned from the Socialist Republic of Vietnam, OJ L 232, 1 Jul. 2004, pp. 1-8, recitals 19-40.
194. *Gas-fuelled, non-refillable Pocket Flint Lighters*, Council Regulation (EC) No. 192/1999 of 25 Jan. 1999 extending the definitive anti-dumping duty, imposed by Regulation (EEC) No. 3433/91 on imports of gas-fuelled, non-refillable pocket flint lighters originating in the People's Republic of China to imports of certain disposable refillable pocket flint lighters originating in the People's Republic of China or consigned from or originating in Taiwan and to imports of non-refillable lighters consigned from or originating in Taiwan, and terminating the proceeding in respect of imports of non-refillable lighters consigned from Hong Kong and Macao, OJ L 22, 29 Jan. 1999, p. 1-9, recital 9. In the particular case, refills were added to lighters in order to fall under a different CN-code not subject to the anti-dumping duty. In practice the lighters were sold as non-refillable; *Integrated Electronic Compact Fluorescent Lamps (CFL-i)*,

or modification of products cannot be justified or due cause or economic reasons, the existing anti-dumping regulation can be extended to cover the other third countries.

The extension of the anti-dumping duty to include other countries will imply that the prices are dumped and the EU producers are injured. The dumping determination is based on the normal value from the original investigation.[195]

It has so far not been possible to reach an agreement between WTO Members regarding rules on circumvention. It is not clear whether circumvention can fall under the existing ADA.[196]

2.4.2.4 Regulations Inconsistent with EU Law

On rare occasions, the anti-dumping duty imposed by the Commission or the Council may be found to be inconsistent with the basic Regulation by the EC courts. A violation of EU law may result in duty drawback and damages.

It follows from Article 233 of the EC Treaty that 'the institution or institutions whose act has been declared void or whose failure to act has been declared contrary to this Treaty shall be required to take the necessary measures to comply with the judgment of the Court of Justice'. The necessary measures may be amending the duties retroactively, where excess duty paid has been reimbursed to the exporter,[197] or if the entire duty is illegally imposed, a reimbursement of the entire duty paid.[198]

Under Article 288.2 of the EC Treaty, the EU institutions are liable in non-contractual matters where damage has been caused by the EU institutions. In *Commission v. Fresh Marine*, the EC Court stated that three conditions must be met in order to incur liability for damages in non-contractual relations:

(1) the infringed-upon rule of law must be intended to confer rights on individuals;
(2) the breach must be sufficiently serious; and

Council Regulation (EC) No. 866/2005 of 6 Jun. 2005 extending the definitive anti-dumping measures imposed by Regulation (EC) No. 1470/2001 on imports of integrated electronic compact fluorescent lamps (CFL-i) originating in the People's Republic of China to imports of the same product consigned from the Socialist Republic of Vietnam, the Islamic Republic of Pakistan and the Republic of the Philippines, OJ L 145, 9 Jun. 2005, pp. 1-15, recitals 22 and 42. In the particular case, both transhipment and assembly operations took place.

195. Art. 13.1 of the Basic Regulation. See also I. Van Bael & J. F. Bellis, *Anti-dumping and Other Trade Protection Laws of the EC*, 4th edn (The Hague: Kluwer Law International, 2004), 490.

196. Committee on Anti-dumping Practices, G/L/123, 29 Oct. 1996, para. 21. See also Informal Group on anti-Circumvention, paper from New Zealand, G/ADP/IG/W/52, 8 Mar. 2007.

197. *Stainless Steel Fasteners and Parts thereof I*, Council Regulation (EC) No. 695/2003 of 14 Apr. 2003 amending Regulation (EC) No. 393/98 imposing a definitive anti-dumping duty on imports of stainless steel fasteners and parts thereof originating in the People's Republic of China, India, the Republic of Korea, Malaysia, Taiwan and Thailand, OJ L 99, 17 Apr. 2003, pp. 22-23, recital 4.

198. Notice concerning anti-dumping measures on imports of para-cresol originating in the People's Republic of China, OJ C 296, 6 Dec. 2006, p. 30.

(3) there must be a direct causal link between the breach of the obligation resting on the author of the act and the damage sustained by the injured parties.[199]

A violation of EU anti-dumping law by the Commission and/or the Council may then result in both duty payback and liability for damages.

WTO law does not require that illegally imposed duties must also be paid back, nor are their any requirements of paying damages in situations where Article VI of GATT 1994 or provisions in the ADA have been violated.

2.4.3 Application of WTO Law in the EU System

A State can have different approaches to how an international treaty, like the WTO Agreement and its annexed agreements, will apply in the national system. In literature, two concepts have been developed: *monism* and *dualism*.[200] In the monistic theory, public international law is an integral part of the municipal system. From an EU perspective – if the EU is understood as a single legal personality – a monistic approach will mean that treaties with third countries and other sources of public international law can be invoked by EU citizens before the EC Court and Court of First Instance and may overrule EU law if EU law is not in accordance with public international law.

In the dualistic theory, public international law is not an integral part of national law. International treaties, etc., can only be invoked before the courts if they have been implemented in national law. National law and public international law are two distinct legal systems. From an EU perspective, this would mean that EU citizens should not be able to invoke international treaties, etc., before the EC Court and Court of First Instance, unless the treaties had been implemented into the EU system.

Article 300 of the EC treaty provides that international agreements that the EU has entered into are binding on the EU institutions. It is not provided whether international treaties are applicable before the EC Court. The EC Court has dealt with those matters and has a generally monistic approach to international treaties, i.e., international agreements are applicable in the Community, which means that international treaties can be invoked and enforced by the EC Court. For an example of this, see *Hageman*,[201] where the EC Court stated its competence to interpret an international treaty with Greece[202] because the treaty was entered into

---

199. *Commission v. Fresh Marine*, Case C-472/00, judgment of the EC Court on 10 Jul. 2003, ECR 2003, p. I-7541, para. 25.

200. See more about monism and dualism in H. Kelsen, *General Theory of Law and State* (translated by Anders Wedberg)(Harvard: Harvard University Press, 1945), 363-364; A. Ross, *Folkeret* (6th revised version by O. S. Andersen, T. Lehmann and P. Magid, Copenhagen, Nyt Nordisk Forlag Arnold Busck, 1984), pp. 67-71; R. Nielsen and C. D. Tvarnøe, *Retskilder og retsteorier* (Copenhagen: Jurist- og Økonomforbundets Forlag, 2005), 142-143.

201. *Hageman*, Case 181/73, judgment of the EC Court on 30 Apr. 1974, ECR 1974, p. 449.

202. In 1974, Greece was not a member of the EU. Greece became a member in 1981.

by the Council according to Article 300 and 310.[203] Furthermore, in *Kupferberg*, the EC Court has stated that an international treaty may be directly applicable even though the international treaty has no direct applicability in the judicial system of the contracting party to the international treaty.[204]

2.4.3.1 The Effect of GATT/WTO Provisions in EU

Contrary to what is stated above, the application of GATT provisions in the Community or before the EC courts has been an exception to the rule.

In *International Fruit Company*, the EC Court was dealing with the question of applicability of GATT provisions on Community measures in the national court systems for the first time. The EC Court stated that it was first to be investigated whether the Community was bound by the international agreement. Next, the national courts only have jurisdiction over the validity of the Community measures at stake if the international agreement confers rights of citizens in the Community, which they can invoke before the national courts.[205] The EC Court found that GATT provisions do bind the Community, but that the GATT provisions have no direct effect, i.e., they cannot be invoked by citizens before national or EC courts. The EC Court stressed the flexibility of GATT and the fact that conflicts between the parties to a dispute should be resolved through negotiations. Furthermore, the EC Court noted the possibility to withdraw from GATT obligations in situations with serious threat of damage.[206]

GATT, then, does bind the EU, which is expected in light of the *pacta sunt servanda* principle of public international law. This means that the EU must fulfil its obligation towards other GATT Member states but that GATT law is not applicable before the EC Court.

However, the EC Court has modified – or elaborated – the approach to GATT/WTO law. First, with the Fediol doctrine from *Fediol v. Commission*, the EC Court stated that in situations where the EU intends to implement a particular obligation assumed in the context of the WTO, the EC Court can make a review of EU measures in light of the WTO provisions.[207]

In *Nakajima v. Council*, the EC Court found that the ADA is applicable in the EU system because of the express reference in the basic Regulation to Article VI of GATT 1994.[208] This has become known as the Nakajima doctrine.[209]

---

203. Paras 3-5.
204. *Kupferberg*, Case 104/81, judgment of the EC Court on 26 Oct. 1982, ECR 1982, p. 3641, para. 18.
205. *International Fruit Company*, Joined cases 21-24/72, judgment of the EC Court of 12 Dec. 1972. ECR 1972, p. 1219, paras 7 and 8.
206. Paras 20-27.
207. *Fediol v. Commission*, Case 70/87, judgment of the EC court on 22 Jun. 1989, ECR 1989, p. 1781, paras 19-22.
208. *Nakajima v. Council*, Case C-69/89, judgment of the EC Court on 7 May 1991, ECR 1991, p. I-2069, paras 30-32.
209. See Court of First Instance in *Chiquita v. Commission*, Case T-19/01, judgment of the Court of First Instance on 3 Feb. 2005, ECR 2005, p. II-315.

Those two doctrines now constitute settled practice.[210] However, the scope of applicability of the ADA in the EU system needs further clarification and elaboration by the EC Court. For example, in *Petrotub and Republica v. Council*, the Court of First Instance refused to apply the ADA but was overruled by the EC Court. In the actual case, the requirement to state reasons for applying a weighted-average-to-transaction method under Article 2.4.2 of the ADA was not written into Article 2.11 of the basic Regulation, and in a specific case, the Council had not provided a very detailed reason for its application of the method. The Council stated that Article 2.4.2 of the ADA is not applicable before the EC Court.[211] On appeal, the EC Court stated that the provisions in the Article VI of GATT 1994 and ADA must be taken into account because the basic Regulation explicitly refers to the ADA in its preamble, and thus it is intended to implement the rules in Article VI of GATT 1994 and the ADA into EU law.[212] Therefore, the EC Court must review the EU measures in light of Article VI of GATT 1994 and the ADA and must interpret those provisions in a manner consistent with international law.[213] In the particular case, the EC Court stated that the requirement to state reasons was met in Article 253 of the EC Treaty. As the Council had not stated reasons in the contested regulation, the Council regulation was annulled. It still needs to be clarified whether a violation of Article VI or the ADA, as found by the EC courts, is sufficient to annul a Commission or Council Regulation, or whether such annulment is only possible if the violation of WTO law is also a violation of EU law.

It is not only before the EC courts that the WTO anti-dumping legislation can be tried. It is also seen that the Commission and the Council refer to and interpret WTO anti-dumping legislation.[214]

2.4.3.2 Panel and Appellate Body Anti-dumping Reports in EU

It is still not clear whether Panel or Appellate Body reports are binding on the EU institutions. The Council has enacted Regulation 1515/2001,[215] the purpose of which is to permit the Council to bring EU anti-dumping measures into conformity

210. See for instance *Biret v. Council*, Case C-93/02 P, judgment of the EC court on 30 Sep. 2003, ECR 2003, p. I-497, para. 61, and *Fruchthandelsgesellschaft*, C-307/99, Order of the Court of 2 May 2001, ECR 2001, p. I-3159, para. 27.
211. *Petrotub and Republica v. Council*, Case T-34/98, judgment of the Court of First Instance on 15 Dec. 1999, ECR p. II-3837, para. 48.
212. *Petrotub and Republica v. Council*, Case C-76/00, judgment of the EC Court on 9 Jan. 2003, ECR p. I-79, paras 52-55.
213. Para. 56-57.
214. See as example *Certain Footwear with Uppers of Leather*, Council Regulation (EC) No. 1472/2006 of 5 Oct. 2006 imposing a definitive anti-dumping duty and collecting definitely the provisional duty imposed on imports of certain footwear with uppers of leather originating in the People's Republic of China and Vietnam, OJ L 275, 6 Oct. 2006, p. 1-41, recitals 74-75.
215. Council Regulation (EC) No. 1515/2001 of 23 Jul. 2001 on the measures that may be taken by the Community following a report adopted by the WTO Dispute Settlement Body concerning anti-dumping and anti-subsidy matters, OJ L 201, 26 Jul. 2001, pp. 10-11.

with Panel and Appellate Body reports.[216] Council regulation 1515/2001 was adopted in order to provide guidelines in situations where EU measures are inconsistent with WTO law.[217] Prior to this regulation, both Panels and the Appellate Body had found the zeroing methodology used by the Commission and the Council to be inconsistent with WTO law.[218]

In situations where a Panel or Appellate Body finds EU measures inconsistent with WTO law, the Council can by simple majority, upon a proposal submitted by the Commission after consultation of the Advisory Committee, repeal or amend the inconsistent regulation or adopt any other special measures that are deemed to be appropriate in the circumstances; cf. Article 1.1. The 1515/2001 regulation also makes it possible to conduct a review before repealing, amending or adopting other measures.[219] Furthermore, the Council can suspend the disputed or amended measure.[220]

The Council has referred to the *EC – Bed linen*[221] Appellate Body report and *EC – Tube or Pipe Fittings*[222] Panel report in the amendment regulations to the original ones.[223] In both cases, the Panel and Appellate Body had found some Commission and Council anti-dumping regulations inconsistent with WTO law. The reference to those reports indicates a willingness by the Council to follow the WTO recommendations directed towards EU.

Article 2 of the 1515/2001 regulation deals with the situation where EU measures have not been tried by a Panel or Appellate Body, but their interpretations of

---

216. Recital 4.
217. See also Notice regarding the anti-dumping measures in force following a ruling of the Dispute Settlement Body of the World Trade Organization adopted on 12 Mar. 2001, OJ C 111, 8 May 2002 P. 0004-0005.
218. See more about *EC – Bed linen*, WT/DS141/AB/R, report of the Appellate Body on 1 Mar. 2001 and WT/DS141/R, report of the Panel on 30 Oct. 2000 and *EC – Tube or Pipe Fittings*, WT/DS219/R, report of the Panel on 7 Mar. 2003 in Section 6.2.2.3.1 below.
219. Art. 1.3.
220. Art. 1.4.
221. *EC – Bed linen*, WT/DS141/R, report of the Panel on 30 Oct. 2000, and WT/DS/141/AB/R, report of the Appellate Body on 1 Mar. 2001.
222. *EC – Tube or Pipe Fittings*, WT/DS219/AB/R, report by Appellate Body on 22 Jul. 2003.
223. See regarding *EC – Bed linen*; Cotton-*type Bed linen*; Council Regulation (EC) No. 1644/2001 of 7 Aug. 2001 amending Regulation (EC) No. 2398/97 imposing a definitive anti-dumping duty on imports of cotton-type bed linen originating in Egypt, India and Pakistan and suspending its application with regard to imports originating in India, OJ L 219, 14 Aug. 2001, p. 1-11, where the Council referred to the Appellate Body report in recital 2 and then amended and suspended the original regulation in regard to India, cf. Art. 1 and 2, whereas Egypt and Pakistan were not included in the amendment and suspension, cf. recital 15. Instead, the dumping determinations for Egypt and Pakistan were amended in another Council regulation.

    See regarding *EC – Tube or Pipe Fittings; Malleable Cast Iron Tube or Pipe Fittings*, Council Regulation (EC) No. 436/2004 of 8 Mar. 2004 amending Regulation (EC) No. 1784/2000 imposing a definitive anti-dumping duty and collecting definitively the provisional duty imposed on imports of certain malleable cast iron tube or pipe fittings originating in Brazil, the Czech Republic, Japan, the People's Republic of China, the Republic of Korea and Thailand, OJ L 72, 11 Mar. 2004, p. 15-22. The Council referred to the findings in the Appellate Body report in recitals 2-4 and then based the amended regulation on those findings, cf. recital 9.

Article VI or the ADA in other cases indicate that the EU measures may be inconsistent with WTO law. In such situations, the Council can take any of the measures mentioned in Article 1.1. In *Cotton-type Bed linen I*, the Council took such measures with reference to Article 2. The Council took the interpretation of the Appellate Body in the *EC – Bed linen* case into account.[224] The result was that the EU regulation regarding Egypt was suspended and the EU regulation regarding Pakistan was terminated.[225]

Measures taken under Council regulation 1515/2001 have effect *ex nunc* and therefore only apply to future anti-dumping duties. Duties that have been collected by the EU authorities prior to such measures will not be reimbursed, unless this is provided elsewhere.[226] It must therefore be assumed that according to this regulation, a violation of WTO law does not imply that the anti-dumping duty collected will be paid back. This is in accordance with WTO law as stated above.

However, it must be stressed that the Council Regulation leaves it to the discretion of the Council to determine whether it will comply with Panel and Appellate Body reports. The Council Regulation may then be in conflict with a Court Opinion by the EC Court. In Court Opinion 1/91,[227] the EC Court stated that when an international agreement provides its own court system, the EU institutions, including the EC Court, are bound by decisions made by that court.[228] However, the question is whether the DSB is regarded as a court system, due to the wide negotiating options in disputes; see more about this Opinion below.

In practice by the Court of First Instance, reference has been made to reports from Panel and Appellate Body, for example in *Shanghai Teraoka Electronic v. Council*.[229] Shanghai Teraoka Electronic was a Chinese producer of electronic weighing scales and exported them mainly to the EU market. In 2000, the Council imposed a definitive anti-dumping duty on imports of electronic weighing scales originating from China, South Korea and Taiwan.[230] The Court of First Instance initially rejected the argument by the Chinese company of market economic treatment. Later, the Court of First Instance had to consider the complaint that the

224. *Cotton-type Bed linen I*, Council Regulation (EC) No. 160/2002 of 28 Jan. 2002 amending Council Regulation (EC) No. 2398/97 imposing a definitive anti-dumping duty on imports of cotton-type bed linen originating in Egypt, India and Pakistan, and terminating the proceeding with regard to imports originating in Pakistan, OJ L 26, 30 Jan. 2002, p. 1-4, recital 5.
225. Arts 1 and 2 of the *Cotton-type Bed linen I Regulation*.
226. Art. 3.
227. Opinion of the EC Court delivered pursuant to the second subparagraph of Art. 228 (1) of the Treaty. Draft agreement between the Community, on the one hand, and the countries of the European Free Trade Association, on the other, relating to the creation of the European Economic Area, Opinion 1/91, 14 Dec. 1991, ECR p. I-6079.
228. See para. 3 in the summary.
229. *Shanghai Teraoka Electronic v. Council*, Case T-35/01, judgment of the Court of First Instance on 28 Oct. 2004, ECR 2004, p. II-3663.
230. *Certain electronic weighing scales (REWS)*, Council Regulation (EC) No. 2605/2000 of 27 Nov. 2000 imposing definitive anti-dumping duties on imports of certain electronic weighing scales (REWS) originating in the People's Republic of China, the Republic of Korea and Taiwan, OJ L 301, 30 Nov. 2000, pp. 42-60.

Council had failed to analyze all the relevant economic factors when determining injury. The Chinese company claimed that the Council infringed Article 3.5 of the basic Regulation. It then referred to the *EC – Bed linen* Panel report,[231] where the Panel assessed Article 3.4 of the ADA, which is almost identical in its wording and context to Article 3.5 in the basic Regulation. The Council asserted that the Panel report had no direct effect in the legal system in the Community.

Firstly, the Court of First Instance referred to the consistency of Community legislation with WTO law when provisions are intended specially to give effect to international agreements. The Court of First Instance went on to assess the consistency of Article 3.5 of the basic regulation with Article 3.4 of the ADA. It stated:

> Consequently, Article 3(5) of the basic regulation is, in itself, consistent with the 1994 Anti-dumping Code. *However, according to the applicant, the Community institutions acted in breach of their obligation to evaluate all the relevant factors, which follows from the interpretation given to Article 3(4) of that code in the bedlinen report, in that they failed to take account of two of the factors listed in Article 3(5) of the basic regulation (. . .). It must therefore be examined whether or not the Community institutions evaluated those two factors.*[232] (Emphasis added)

The Court of First Instance concluded that the Council had considered the two factors. Apparently, the Court of First Instance followed the interpretation made by the Panel.

In *Ritek and Prodisc v. Council*, the Court of First Instance made a more detailed analysis of the Appellate Body report, *EC – Bed linen*,[233] and applied the report in its determination of EU law. However, the Court of First Instance did not rule upon whether the reports from the DSB were binding for the judiciary bodies in EU.[234] In this regard, it must be noted that the case before the Court of First Instance did not involve both the parties, i.e., EU and India, from the WTO dispute in *EC – Bed linen*.[235] In WTO law, the reports only bind the parties in the specific case, but they create expectations in future cases and must therefore be taken into consideration in the determination of WTO law; see more about this in Chapter 1.

Although there is reference to Panel and Appellate Body reports by the Court of First Instance, a violation of WTO law does not in itself imply that the EC courts may follow the line immediately. In *Portugal v. Council*, the EC Court stated that although a Panel or Appellate Body may find that the EU has acted inconsistently with WTO law, the DSU ensures a mechanism for negotiations if the

231. *EC – Bed linen*, WT/DS141/R, report of the Panel on 30 Oct. 2000.
232. Paras 140 and 141.
233. *EC – Bed linen*, WT/DS141/AB/R, report of Appellate Body on 1 Mar. 2001.
234. *Ritek and Prodisc v. Council*, Case T-274/02, judgment of the Court of First Instance of 24 Oct. 2006. ECR 2006, p. II-4305, paras 97-107.
235. See more about the *EC – Bed linen* case throughout this book.

recommendations are not implemented within a reasonable period of time.[236] The case dealt with WTO provisions that were not under the Nakajima or Fediol doctrines and thus not applicable in the EU system.[237] It cannot be concluded that the EC Court would reach same conclusions about interpretations of the ADA that are applicable before the EC courts.

A case is pending before the EC Court in *Ikea*,[238] where the EC Court has to decide whether a recommendation by the Appellate Body that a provision of the ADA has been violated by EU also constitutes a violation of provisions in the basic Regulation. In his opinion, the Advocate General has referred to the Court Opinion 1/91. The Advocate General finds that the DSB does not have the characteristics of a judicial body because of the negotiation element in disputes and the possibility to disregard a prompt compliance with a Panel or Appellate Body recommendation. The Advocate General has therefore concluded that the EC Court is not bound by the recommendation from the Appellate Body.[239]

All in all, the application of the reports of Panels and Appellate Body in the EU system is still not clear. There may be doubts on whether the EC courts feel obligated to apply such reports when the EU legislation is being interpreted. However, it is seen that in some instances, the Court of First Instance has referred to such reports.

2.5 FINAL WORDS

WTO law is here seen as a rule-oriented system. The special rules about dumping have evolved into a more rule-complex body than they were in the initial GATT period, and they leave less discretion to the national authorities. However, WTO law must still be seen as a system with several political opportunities for parties in the disputes to have an impact on the interpretation of Article VI of GATT 1994. Furthermore, the WTO rules only apply to states in the WTO system, not to citizens. Producers under anti-dumping investigation who feel that their rights under WTO law are being infringed must therefore rely on either a request for consultation from their own country, or the importing country having a court system where WTO law is applicable.

A violation of WTO law does not in itself cause sanctions towards the violating WTO Member. Only in situations where a recommendation by a Panel or Appellate Body is not implemented by a WTO Member, compensation – and if that is not possible, retaliation – is the sanction tool. The question is whether the lack of sanctions *ex tunc* is an invitation to WTO Members not to comply with WTO law,

236. *Portugal v. Council*, Case C-149/96, judgment of the EC Court on 23 Nov. 1999, ECR 1999, p. I-8395, paras 36-40.
237. Para. 51.
238. *Ikea*, Case 351/04, *Ikea v. Commissioners of Customs & Excise*, OJ C 262, 23 Oct. 2004, p. 18.
239. *Ikea*, Case C-351/04, opinion of Advocate General Leger, delivered on 6 Apr. 2006, points 89-98.

unless a Panel or Appellate Body has recommended that WTO law is being violated.

Under the EU system, Article VI of GATT 1994 and ADA are to some extent applicable before the Court of First Instance and the EC Court. WTO law may then be applicable to citizens who regard a measure by the Commission or the Council as inconsistent with WTO legislation. Apparently, the reports by Panels and Appellate Body are also taken into account in the EU system, both in the 1515/2001 regulation and at the Court of First Instance. The legal value of those reports in the EU system still needs further clarification. However, a report by a Panel or Appellate Body appears not to lead to an immediate compliance by the EC courts, as the EC Court has emphasized the diplomatic means in the DSB as a right to apply if a recommendation by a Panel or Appellate Body is against an EU measure.

If the EC courts find that an anti-dumping measure by the Commission or the Council is inconsistent with EU law, such a measure will be annulled and lead to reimbursement of the paid duty. It is still not clear whether a WTO provision can stand alone in the EU system.

In Chapter 1, it was stated that the approach used here consists of narrow interpretations of specific WTO provisions on dumping. However, the interpretations and findings made throughout the book fall under the reservations made here, as there are political elements in the WTO system reducing the predictability of WTO law.

Chapter 3
Product under Consideration and Like Product

A product is dumped if the price of the exported product is lower than the price of the like product when sold in the exporting country. The dumping determination depends on prices of an exported product and prices of a domestically sold product. There are two main issues about the product under investigation and the like product:

First, the product definition demarcates the goods that may be imposed with an anti-dumping duty. If, for example, the Commission and the Council investigate bed linen from India, it seems unreasonable if Indian export of shoes were to be included in the investigation. Shoes are different from bed linen. Although it seems unreasonable to include shoes under the product definition of bed linen, the situation would be different if the question regarded two sorts of bed linen of different qualities due to different production techniques. If the allegedly dumped product is high-quality bed linen, the question could then be whether low-quality bed linen should be included in the examination. There is also another point to be made concerning the definition of the product under consideration: If a producer does not sell the like product domestically, the normal value for that producer may be based on alternative means and, under certain circumstances, on data provided by the other producers under the investigation.[1] Naturally, the broader the product scope, the wider a spectrum of data from different types of products under the general product definition that may serve as basis for the determination of a normal value for the particular producer. In this chapter, it is examined whether there are any guidelines about how to make the product definition, which types of products should be included under the definition and whether the EU product definition is in conformity with WTO law.

1. See more in Ch. 4 below about Art. 2.2.2 (i)-(iii) of the ADA and Art. 2.1, second sentence and Art. 2.6(a)-(c) of the basic Regulation.

Next, the 'like product' in the exporting country must be defined. To use the same example as that above, the export sales price of bed linen cannot be compared with the domestic sales prices of shoes. The question is how the 'like product' is determined.

A 'like product' definition is not only made in regard to the dumping determination. 'Like product' is also determined for the injury test, where the exported product must cause injury to the like product in the importing country.[2] Furthermore, 'like product' is used in regard to the special rules that apply on Chinese products.[3] In this chapter, the like product refers only to the product in the exporting country for dumping determination purposes.

The starting point in this chapter is a description of WTO legislation and practice for the product under consideration, i.e., the allegedly dumped product that is subject to investigation, and for the like product. Next, EU legislation and practice regarding the product under consideration and the like product is examined under WTO law.

3.1 WTO LEGISLATION

There are no guidelines in Article VI of GATT 1994 or in the ADA to define the product under consideration. In accordance with Article VI of GATT 1994 and Article 2.1 of the ADA, a product is dumped if it is sold at the export market at a price less than the domestic price. Therefore, the scope of product in the dumping determination must be defined as the allegedly dumped product.

In Section 2.2.2, it was mentioned that in order to initiate an anti-dumping investigation, a few conditions must be met. The domestic industry must submit the information and necessary evidence that the defined product is being dumped injuriously.[4] The investigating authorities may also, under special circumstances, initiate an investigation without an application from the domestic industry if there is sufficient evidence to indicate injurious dumping.[5] The product being investigated shall be defined in accordance with the facts about injurious dumping. Nevertheless, there is no guidance about how to determine the *types* of products falling under the defined product. For example, as mentioned above, is low-quality bed linen to be included in the investigation if the product defined is bed linen?

Apparently, the lack of clear guidelines under WTO legislation leaves wide discretion to the investigating authorities to determine the product scope, although it remains subject to the requirement of sufficient evidence of injurious dumping.

---

2. See Art. 3.2 of the ADA. See also Panel in *Korea – Certain Paper*, WT/DS312/R, report of the Panel on 28 Oct. 2005, para. 7.219. See Art. 3.2 of the Basic Regulation.
3. See Art. 15(a)(i)-(ii) of the Protocol on the Accession of the People's Republic of China, WT/L/432 of 23 Nov. 2001 and Art. 2.7(a) of the basic Regulation.
4. Arts 5.1 and 5.2 of the ADA.
5. Art. 5.6 of the ADA.

The like product is defined in Article 2.6 of the ADA, which reads:

> Throughout this Agreement the term 'like product' ('produit similaire') shall be interpreted to mean a product which is identical, i.e., alike in all respects to the product under consideration, or in the absence of such a product, another product which, although not alike in all respects, has characteristics closely resembling those of the product under consideration.

Based on this text, the starting point of defining the domestic products must be to identify those products identical to the product under consideration. 'Identical' means *alike in all respects* to the allegedly dumped product. The identical requirement is exempted in situations where there is no identical domestically sold product. Under those circumstances, the 'like product' must have characteristics of close resemblance to the product under consideration. It is not further provided how a test of close resemblance must be made.

It should be noted that under Article 2.4, which is described in details in Chapter 6, a mechanism is provided to assure that differences affecting the price comparability between normal value and export price must be adjusted. For example, this provision takes into account physical differences, and this indicates that some differences may exist between the domestic sold product and the exported product.

3.2 PRACTICE BY PANELS AND APPELLATE BODY

In the following part, the practice of Panels and Appellate Body concerning a product under consideration and like product is examined. This part starts with the product under consideration. Next, the like product will be discussed.

3.2.1 Product under Consideration

The product under consideration is not defined under WTO legislation. In the following, it will be examined whether some guidelines about product definition can be found in practice.

3.2.1.1 No Criteria to Determine Product under Consideration

It appears from practice that the definition of the product under consideration is entirely left to the discretion of the investigating authorities.

In *US – Zeroing (Japan)*, the Appellate Body stated that a product may be defined by the investigating authorities,[6] and that the definition is usually made in the light of an application from the domestic industry to initiate an investigation under Article 5.2 of the ADA or, in special circumstances, Article 5.6 of the ADA.[7]

---

6. *US – Zeroing (Japan)*, WT/DS322/AB/R, report of the Appellate Body on 9 Jan. 2007, para. 115.
7. Footnote 302 re para. 115.

In *US – Softwood Lumber V*, a Panel noted about the product under consideration and Article 2.6 of the ADA:

> As the definition of 'like product' implies a comparison with another product, it seems clear to us that the starting point can only be the 'other product', being the allegedly dumped product. Therefore, once the product under consideration is defined, the 'like product' to the product under consideration has to be determined on the basis of Article 2.6. However, in our analysis of the AD Agreement, we could not find any guidance on the way in which the 'product under consideration' should be determined.[8]

The line in this case was also used in *Korea – Certain Paper*.[9] There are no guidelines in the ADA or in Article VI of GATT 1994 concerning determining the product. The investigating authorities are, however, bound by the conditions in Article 5.2 or Article 5.6 of the ADA when defining the product.

In that line, the Appellate Body has on several occasions accepted that the product definition may be broad and that several types of products may be included under the general product definition.[10]

The inclusion of several types of products under the general product definition has led to questions about whether the investigating authorities must define the *characteristics* from one single product under investigation, those shared by *all* the types that are being investigated. This question was raised in *US – Softwood Lumber V* concerning a discussion about 'like product' and 'product under consideration'. The US Department of Commerce (USDOC) had imposed an anti-dumping duty on softwood lumber from Canada. The USDOC had considered a broad category of softwood lumber with several different types of softwood lumber. Canada claimed that the definition of 'like products' by the USDOC did not match some of the products under consideration, and that therefore, those products should have been dealt with in a different investigation. Canada referred to Article. 2.6 of the ADA and claimed that Article 2.6 suggested a three-step approach, which the USDOC had disregarded: 'First, the investigating authority must identify the characteristics of the product under consideration. Second, it must identify the characteristics of each product proposed for inclusion in the like product. Third, it must determine whether the characteristics of each are identical or, if not, then closely resembling those of the product under consideration.' Canada argued that the USDOC had not defined the product under consideration and had not compared the characteristics

8. *US – Softwood Lumber V*, WT/DS264/R, Report of the Panel on 13 Apr. 2004, para. 7.153.
9. *Korea – Certain Paper*, WT/DS312/R, report of the Panel on 28 Oct. 2005, apparently para. 7.216 and also para. 7.221.
10. See for instance both Panel and Appellate Body in *EC Bed linen*, WT/DS141/AB/R, report of the Appellate Body on 1 Mar. 2001, para. 53, and WT/DS141/R, report of the Panel on 30 Oct. 2000, para. 6.117, and indirectly *US – Softwood Lumber V (Art. 21.5 – Canada)*, WT/DS264/AB/RW, report of the Appellate Body on 15 Aug. 2006, para. 104.

of the different types of products with the product under consideration as a whole.[11] The Panel stated:

> Canada considers that, rather than comparing the overall scope of the product under consideration with the overall scope of the like product, Article 2.6 requires that each individual item within the 'like product' must be 'like' each individual item within the 'product under consideration'. This in effect means that there must be 'likeness' within both the product under consideration and within the like product. As Canada itself has stated, '[t]he terms 'product under consideration' and 'like product' must be limited to a single group of products sharing characteristics'. Once again, however, we see no basis to imply such a condition into the *AD Agreement.* While there might be room for discussion as to whether such an approach might be an appropriate one from a policy perspective, whether to require such an approach is a matter for the Members to address through negotiations. It is not our role as a panel to create obligations which cannot clearly be found in the *AD Agreement* itself.[12]

According to the Panel, there is no mention in the ADA that the different types of products that fall under the product definition must be alike. Apparently, in the Panel's reasoning, the different types of products under the overall product definition need not be alike in the terms of likeness provided in Article 2.6. Thus, the product definition may cover a broad scope of different types that may not be alike.

The finding by the Panel in *US – Softwood Lumber V* was supported by another Panel in *Korea – Certain Paper*, where the Korean Trade Commission (KTC) had determined the product under consideration to be plain copier paper and wood-free printing paper originating from Indonesia. The KTC had made an individual dumping calculation for plain copier paper and wood-free printing paper respectively and had made one final, single margin covering both types of paper.[13] Indonesia claimed that the two types of products – plain copier paper and wood-free printing paper – were not like products, 'because they have differences with respect to physical characteristics, end-uses, substitutability, market sectors in which they compete, HS nomenclatures and manufacturing processes'.[14] That argument was rejected by the Panel:

> We note that these two, together, constituted 'the product under consideration' in the investigation at issue. We see no basis in Article 2.6 for the proposition that the like product definition also applies to the definition of 'the product under consideration'. We are aware of no provision in Article 2.6, or any other article in the Agreement, that contains a definition of 'the product under consideration' itself.[15]

11. *US – Softwood Lumber V*, WT/DS264/R, report of the Panel on 13 Apr. 2004, paras 7.140-7.142.
12. Paras 7.172-7.173.
13. *Korea – Certain Paper*, WT/DS312/R, report of the Panel on 28 Oct. 2005, para. 7.223.
14. Para. 7.216. HS nomenclature is an international harmonized system nomenclature governed by the Convention on the Harmonized Commodity Description and Coding System.
15. Para. 7.221. In n. 242, the Panel referred to the Panel finding in *US – Softwood Lumber V*.

The rejection by the Panel has two important aspects:

- The different types or sub-groups of products, which fall under the 'product under consideration' definition, do not have to be alike in the sense provided in Article 2.6.
- There are no criteria regarding physical characteristics, end-uses, substitutability, markets where they compete etc. to define the product.

Overall, the investigating authorities have absolute discretion to determine the product under consideration, as long as the evidential requirements under Article 5.2 or, in some situations, Article 5.6 of the ADA are met. The product under consideration can then be determined to include different types of products, which may not be alike. The requirements of likeness in Article 2.6 do not apply to the different types under the general product under consideration. Furthermore, there are no requirements that the product under consideration must be demarcated by criteria of, for example, interchangeability between the different types of products, competition between products, qualitative differences etc.

3.2.1.2 The Binding Definition

By being allowed extensive discretion in defining a product, it could be assumed that some WTO Members would define the product broadly and include some types of products which, seen separately, are not dumped. However, the Appellate Body has provided some limitations to the methods used by investigating authorities when they work with broad definitions of the product under consideration.

In *EC – Bed linen*, the Commission and the Council had defined the product under investigation to be cotton type bed linen, which included several different types of bed linen. During the investigation, the EU authorities would then, when appropriate, leave some types of products out of the dumping calculation but include those same types when imposing the anti-dumping duty. This puzzle of calculations by including and excluding types of products, but imposing all of them with an anti-dumping duty, led to higher dumping margins. The Appellate Body made a clear limitation on arbitrary use – and non-use – of some types of products under the general definition during the investigation. The Appellate Body stated:

> Thus, of its own accord, the European Communities clearly identified cotton-type bed linen as the product under investigation in this case. This is undisputed in this appeal. *Having defined the product as it did, the European Communities was bound to treat that product consistently thereafter in accordance with that definition.*[16] (Emphasis added)

The product definition by the investigating authorities is binding throughout the investigation. The statement by the Appellate Body is in line with the fairness principle, which states that the treatment of a product – or the types falling under

16. *EC – Bed linen*, WT/DS141/AB/R, report of the Appellate Body on 1 Mar. 2001, para. 53.

the definition – must be even-handed throughout the investigation. Investigating authorities are not allowed to define a product that includes several types falling under the product definition and then leave some types out during the investigation that are later imposed with a dumping duty. If the investigating authorities want to leave some types out of the product investigation, the product definition must also reflect the narrower scope.

In *Mexico – Steel Pipes and Tubes*, Guatemala claimed that the Mexican anti-dumping authority, Economía, had excluded pipes and tubes in the preliminary investigation and then included pipes and tubes in the final dumping determination without a proper examination of the information submitted by the exporter pertaining to the added products.[17] According to Guatemala, Mexico had violated several provisions in ADA, including Article 2;[18] Article 2.1 had been violated, as dumping margins had not been calculated for the added products; Article 2.4 had been violated, as there was no fair comparison since not all pricing information for the added products was used; Article 2.6 had been violated, as the product definition had been changed during the investigation without positive evidence and without an impartial and objective examination of the facts, although Article 2.6 does not prohibit that the product and like product definitions may be changed during the investigation.[19] Mexico claimed that the ADA did not contain a definition of the product concerned and that Economía had correctly considered the physical characteristics and technical and commercial interchangeability of the products at issue.[20]

The Panel found that during the investigation, Economía had changed the product definition twice without gathering or analyzing information pertaining to the added products.[21] The Panel found that Mexico had violated Article 6.8 of the ADA by rejecting data submitted from the exporter and relying on available facts, as there was no evidence that the exporter had acted in a deliberately misleading manner in terms of the data it provided in its questionnaire response, at verification, or at any other point, to justify such a rejection.[22] Furthermore, Mexico had violated procedural rules in Article 6.8 by not informing the producer from Guatemala that its information had been rejected.[23] The Panel then exercised its right to judicial economy and did not make any findings about whether Mexico had violated Article 2 of the ADA by changing the product scope. Instead, the Panel referred to its finding about Article 6.8 and stated:

> We recall that these findings are related in part to the expansions of the scope of the investigated product during the course of the investigation. Furthermore, and in any case, as a result of these findings, Economía's final determination of dumping as a whole – in respect of the entire expanded product

17. *Mexico – Steel Pipes and Tubes*, WT/DS331/R, Report of the Panel on 8 Jun. 2007, para. 7.62.
18. Para. 3.1.
19. Para. 7.202.
20. Para. 3.2.
21. Para. 7.105.
22. Para. 7.183.
23. Para. 7.190.

> scope – was inconsistent with the Anti-dumping Agreement. On this basis we do not consider it necessary to, and thus do not, make findings on these remaining claims pertaining to Economía's final determination of dumping.[24]

The Panel has not ruled whether the change of product definition is a violation of the above-mentioned provisions in Article 2. In this case, the fact that Article 6.8 regarding evidence was violated was sufficient to rule that the dumping determination with the broadened product scope made by Economía was in violation of the ADA. Interestingly, the Panel refers in this conclusion to the ADA – and not to specific provisions in the ADA. The Panel's finding supports the finding by the Appellate body in *EC – Bed linen*, as the product definition is binding on the investigating authorities. It is a violation of the ADA to impose an anti-dumping duty on a type of product if that type of product has not been included in the product definition.

3.2.2 Like Product

This section concerns the practice about 'like product' and how 'like product' is defined. The dumping determination is based on a comparison between the price of the allegedly dumped product and the price of the 'like product' from domestic sales. The term 'like product' is defined in Article 2.6 of the ADA.

'Like product' is also found in other WTO agreements, but the scope of like product varies according to the particular agreement.[25] Therefore, practice about 'like product' from other agreements will not show a clear picture about the ADA, and therefore only practice about the ADA is used here.

It must be noted that a Panel has questioned the obligatory character of Article 2.6. In *US – Softwood Lumber V*,[26] the Panel first of all stated that Article 2.6 of the ADA 'is a definitional article, and as such it is not clear to us that it contains *in itself* obligations on Members, or in any event that it could be the basis for an *independent* violation'.[27]

Thereby, the Panel states that Article 2.6 does not in itself impose obligations on the WTO Members. Article 2.6 must then be used in combination with other provisions. As already mentioned, the term 'like product' is mentioned in several provisions of the ADA.

In the same case, the Panel clarified how the 'like product' is to be determined:

> In our view, this means that the 'like product', for purposes of the dumping determination, is the product which is destined for consumption in the exporting country. *The 'like product' is therefore to be compared with the allegedly*

24. Para. 7.205.
25. See Appellate Body in *Japan – Alcoholic Beverages II*, WT/DS8, WT/DS10 and WT/DS11/AB/R, report of the Appellate Body on 4 Oct. 1996, p. 21.
26. *US – Softwood Lumber V*, WT/DS264/R, Report of the Panel on 13 Apr. 2004.
27. Para. 7.146.

dumped product, which is generally referred to in the AD Agreement as the 'product under consideration'.(. . .) [T]he starting point can only be the product allegedly being dumped and that the product to be compared to it for purposes of the dumping determination, and the product the producers of which are allegedly being injured by the dumped product, is the 'like product' for purposes of the dumping and injury determinations, respectively.

Article 2.6 therefore defines the basis on which the product to be compared to the 'product under consideration' is to be determined, that is, a product which is either identical to the product under consideration, or in the absence of such a product, another product which has characteristics closely resembling those of the product under consideration. *As the definition of 'like product' implies a comparison with another product, it seems clear to us that the starting point can only be the 'other product', being the allegedly dumped product. Therefore, once the product under consideration is defined, the 'like product' to the product under consideration has to be determined on the basis of Article 2.6. However, in our analysis of the AD Agreement, we could not find any guidance on the way in which the 'product under consideration' should be determined.*[28] (Emphasis added)

The basis for determining the like product is the product being dumped – i.e., the product under consideration. The general rule is that the like product is identical to the product under consideration. In the absence of an identical product, the like product must therefore be based on the characteristics from the product under consideration. The connection between the product under consideration and the like product seems to be based on product characteristics – not the competition between the products. This finding may be slightly modified by another Panel in *Korea – Certain Paper*, where the Panel stated:

We note that Article 2.6 takes 'the product under consideration' as the starting point of the definition of 'like product'. It then stipulates that the like product is *the product that is identical* to the product under consideration, or one *that has physical characteristics that closely resemble those of the product under consideration.* The phrase 'Throughout this Agreement' indicates that this definition applies to the definition of like product for both dumping and injury determinations in an anti-dumping investigation. Therefore, once the product under consideration is defined, the IA has to make sure that the product it is using in its injury determination is like the product under consideration. As long as that determination is made consistently with the parameters set out in Article 2.6, the IA' s like product definition will be WTO-consistent.[29] (Emphasis added)

The Panel repeats the findings from *US –Softwood Lumber V*, as the product under consideration is the base for the like product determination. However, one change is that this Panel seems not to rank the identical products over those closely

28. Para. 7.152-153.
29. *Korea – Certain Paper*, WT/DS312/R, report of the Panel on 28 Oct. 2005, para. 7.219.

resembling the product under consideration. The Panel does not stress that products closely resembling the product under consideration are to be used in the absence of an identical product. The Panel states that the like product must be identical to the product under consideration *or* have *physical characteristics* that closely resemble those of the product under consideration. The fact that the need for physical characteristics closely resembling the product under consideration is stressed indicates that a like product definition based solely on substitutionality between the product under consideration and like product is not sufficient.

3.3 EU LEGISLATION

In line with WTO legislation, there is no provision that defines the product under consideration or the types to be included. However, in the notice of initiation, the Commission must indicate the product concerned; see Article 5.10 of the basic Regulation.

The term 'like product' is defined in Article 1.4:

> [T]he term 'like product' shall be interpreted to mean a product which is identical, that is to say, alike in all respects, to the product under consideration, or in the absence of such a product, another product which although not alike in all respects, has characteristics closely resembling those of the product under consideration.

The wording of Article 1.4 is a reproduction of Article 2.6 of the ADA. The like product is one identical to the product under consideration. In the absence of a product identical to the product under consideration, the like product is one with characteristics closely resembling those of the product under consideration.

In addition, EU law has an adjustment mechanism for differences affecting price comparability between normal value and export price. That mechanism includes adjustments for physical differences between the product under investigation and the like product. See more in chapter 6 about Article 2.10 of the basic Regulation.

Concerning the dumping determination, 'like product' refers to the domestically sold product under different situations. For the normal value determination, the domestic price must be for the like product; see Article 1.2. The domestic sale of the like product must be representative; see Article 2.2. Rules for construction of the normal value for the like product are stated in Article 2.3. The calculation of SAG and profits will generally be based on the producer's domestic sales of the like product. In the normal value determination for China, the price from producers in analogue countries must be based on the like product; see Article 2.7(a).

3.4 EU PRACTICE

Concerning the product under consideration and like product, the Commission and the Council make a two-step determination. First, the product under consideration –

and the types falling under the definition – is defined. Next, the like product for both dumping and injury is defined.[30] By having the product under consideration as the starting point for the like product definition, the EU authorities are acting in conformity with the guidelines prescribed by Panels and Appellate Body under WTO law.

As Appellate Body has also stated, the investigating authorities are bound by the definition of the product under consideration throughout the investigation. In this chapter it is not further discussed whether this rule is followed by the EU authorities, but matters in that regard will be brought up in subsequent chapters.

3.4.1 Product under Investigation

The initial step taken by the Commission is to prepare a Notice of initiation of anti-dumping proceedings in the Official Journal (OJ).[31] The Commission must define the product concerned in overall terms; see Article 5.10 of the basic Regulation. It will also be mentioned which exporting country is subject to the investigation.

The following part deals with the factors used by the Commission and the Council when determining whether a type of product falls inside the product definition.

3.4.1.1 Physical, Chemical, and Technical Characteristics

The main guideline to determine whether a product falls inside or outside the product concerned is the physical, technical, and chemical characteristics resembling the product description.[32] If a product does not share the same physical,

30. *Certain Iron or Steel Ropes and Cables*, Council Regulation (EC) No. 1601/2001 of 2 Aug. 2001 imposing a definitive anti-dumping duty and definitively collecting the provisional anti-dumping duty imposed on imports of certain iron or steel ropes and cables originating in the Czech Republic, Russia, Thailand and Turkey, OJ L 211, 4 Aug. 2001, pp. 1-19, recital 16.
31. Several conditions must be met before the Commission publishes the Notice in the OJ. The complainants, which are usually producers in the EU, must provide the commission with sufficient evidence regarding dumping and injury before the proceeding is initiated; cf. Arts 5.9 and 5.7 of the basic Regulation.
32. See for instance *Certain Magnesia Bricks*, Council Regulation (EC) No. 1659/2005 of 6 Oct. 2005 imposing a definitive anti-dumping duty and collecting definitively the provisional duty imposed on imports of certain magnesia bricks originating in the People's Republic of China, OJ L 267, 12 Oct. 2005, pp. 1-14, recital 8; *Certain Graphite Electrode Systems*, Commission Regulation (EC) No. 1009/2004 of 19 May 2004 imposing a provisional anti-dumping duty on imports of certain graphite electrode systems originating in India, OJ L 183, 20 May 2004, pp. 61-82, recital 14, endorsed in Council Regulation (EC) No. 1629/2004 of 13 Sep. 2004 imposing a definitive anti-dumping duty and collecting definitively the provisional duty imposed on imports of certain graphite electrode systems originating in India, OJ L 295, 18 Sep. 2004, pp. 10-14, recital 6; *Certain Plastic Sacks and Bags*, Council Regulation (EC)

technical, or chemical characteristics, it will not be investigated – and thus falls outside the anti-dumping measures.[33] In consequence, the EU institutions have to disregard products that do not have the same physical characteristics or the same use. See for example *Polyethylene Terephthalate Film*, where the Council stated:

> Finally, the investigation showed that metallised PET film has to be distinguished from film, which is reinforced, laminated, supported or similarly combined with other materials. These processes modify the basic physical, chemical and technical characteristics of PET film to such an extent that the resulting product cannot be considered to be the product concerned.[34]

It is seen that the Council has stressed consumer perception concerning the physical characteristics between two products. In *Cotton-type Bed linen I*, the Council was met with the argument that handloom products, which are fabric woven on looms operated purely by hand or foot, should be excluded from the investigation of bed linen. The Council stated in this regard:

> As regards the request to exclude handloom products, while the use of different production methods is not in itself a reason relevant to the definition of the like product, *it was found that handloom items had physical characteristics different from those of other bed linen*, notably through a less regular and looser weave. *This difference led to a different consumer perception of handloom products* which was reinforced by the fact that handloom products are often sold through particular sales channels such as charity shops which are not available to Community producers.[35] (Emphasis added)

It is not clear from the statement whether the Council suggests that the physical criteria are met only in situations where the consumers perceive the items as physically different. However, it must be assumed that consumer perception in

---

No. 1425/2006 of 25 Sep. 2006 imposing a definitive anti-dumping duty on imports of certain plastic sacks and bags originating in the People's Republic of China and Thailand, and terminating the proceeding on imports of certain plastic sacks and bags originating in Malaysia, OJ L 270, 29 Sep. 2006, pp. 4-41, recital 37. See also I. Van Bael & J.F. Bellis, *Anti-dumping and Other Trade Protection Laws of the EC*, 4th edn (The Hague: Kluwer Law International, 2004), 159.

33. See for instance about physical differences; mini-disc and CD-Rs in *Recordable Compact Disks*, Council Regulation (EC) No. 1050/2002 of 13 Jun. 2002 imposing a definitive anti-dumping duty and collecting definitively the provisional duty imposed on imports of recordable compact disks originating in Taiwan, OJ L 160, 18 Jun. 2002, pp. 2-13, recital 12.
34. *Polyethylene Terephthalate Film*, Council Regulation (EC) No. 1676/2001 of 13 Aug. 2001 imposing a definitive anti-dumping duty and collecting definitively the provisional duty imposed on imports of PET film originating in India and the Republic of Korea, OJ L 227, 23 Aug. 2001, pp. 1-14, recital 11.
35. *Cotton-type Bed linen I*, Commission Regulation (EC) No. 1069/97 of 12 Jun. 1997 imposing a provisional anti-dumping duty on imports of cotton-type bed linen originating in Egypt, India and Pakistan, OJ L 156, 13 Jun. 1997, pp. 11-33, endorsed in Council Regulation (EC) No. 2398/97 of 28 Nov. 1997 imposing a definitive anti-dumping duty on imports of cotton-type bed linen originating in Egypt, India and Pakistan, OJ L 332, 4 Dec. 1997, pp. 1-18, recital 7 in the Council regulation.

this case just supports the argumentation. It will be demonstrated below that in other situations, consumer perception is disregarded.

The term 'same physical characteristics' is broadly interpreted, which will also be revealed in the following sections. In this line, the Council stated in *Certain Plastic Sacks and Bags*, where the exporters of different types of plastic bags argued that the scope of product was too broad by including all sorts of plastic bags, which had different applications:

> In this respect it should be noticed that the basic Regulation does not require that investigations cover products that are identical in all aspects, e.g., in terms of production process, pricing, sales channels, uses or consumer perception. Rather, it has been the Commission's consistent practice to require that for product types to be considered as a single product it is enough that they share the same basic physical, technical and/or chemical characteristics.[36]

As WTO law provides wide discretion to the investigating authorities regarding the product definition, and there are no requirements about shared characteristics between the different types included in the investigation, the line by the Commission and the Council with emphasis on the shared physical, technical or chemical characteristics seems to be in conformity with WTO law.

In the following sections, some of the other factors taken into account by the Commission and the Council in product determination are described.

3.4.1.2 The CN Codes

One way of delimiting the product scope is using the product's *Combined Nomenclature Code* (CN code), which is a coding system for classifying products for customs and statistics.[37] In several cases, the Commission and the Council have found support in the CN codes to frame the product under investigation.[38]

---

36. *Certain Plastic Sacks and Bags*, Council Regulation (EC) No. 1425/2006 of 25 Sep. 2006 imposing a definitive anti-dumping duty on imports of certain plastic sacks and bags originating in the People's Republic of China and Thailand and terminating the proceeding on imports of certain plastic sacks and bags originating in Malaysia, OJ L 270, 29 Sep. 2006, pp. 4-41, recital 38.
37. Council Regulation (EEC) No. 2658/87 of 23 Jul. 1987 on the tariff and statistical nomenclature and on the Common Customs Tariff, OJ L 256, 7 Sep. 1987, pp. 1-675, with several amendments, Art. 1.
38. See for instance *Tungsten Carbide and Fused Tungsten Carbide*, Commission Regulation (EEC) No. 763/90 of 26 Mar. 1990 imposing a provisional anti-dumping duty on imports of tungsten carbide and fused tungsten carbide originating in the people's Republic of China and terminating the anti-dumping proceeding concerning imports of those products from the Republic of Korea, OJ L 83, 30 Mar. 1990, pp. 36-44, recital 10, endorsed in Council Regulation (EEC) No. 2737/90 of 24 Sep. 1990 imposing a definitive anti-dumping duty on imports of tungsten carbide and fused tungsten carbide originating in the People's Republic of China and definitively collecting the provisional duty, OJ L 264, 27 Sep. 1990, pp. 7-11, recital 9, reviewed in Council Regulation (EC) No. 2268/2004 of 22 Dec. 2004 imposing a definitive anti-dumping duty on imports of tungsten carbide and fused tungsten carbide originating in the People's

Although the CN codes might support the delimitation of the product, it is also seen in Council and Commission practice that some products that fall under a different CN code than the one identified for the investigation can still be considered as product under investigation. In *Sacks and Bags Made of Polyethylene or Polypropylene*,[39] the Commission had imposed a provisional duty on woven sacks and bags of a kind used for the packaging of goods, not knitted or crocheted, obtained from a polyethylene or polypropylene strip or the like of woven fabrics, weighing 120gr/m^2 or less and originating in India, Indonesia and Thailand.[40] The product fell under the CN codes 6305 32 81 and 6305 33 91.[41] One importer of 'big bags' weighing 120 g/m^2 claimed before the Council that big bags belonged under a different CN code and thus should not be covered by the proceeding.[42] The Council, however, stated:

> The Provisional Duty Regulation mentioned, in recital 6 thereof, that the product concerned falls within CN codes 6305 32 81 and 6305 33 91. *However, the Commission became aware that the sacks and bags concerned in the present investigation can be classified under CN codes 3923 21 00, 9323 29 10 and 3923 29 90 while still meeting the description of the product concerned if made from a fabric which is either woven from a strip wider than 5 mm or laminated on both sides to an extent visible to the naked eye*. Therefore, sacks and bags falling under the description of the product concerned and classified under CN codes other than those provisionally disclosed should also be covered by the present investigation. *Therefore, the conclusions set out in the Provisional Duty Regulation concerning the definition of the product concerned and the like product are confirmed.*[43] (Emphasis added)

The Council emphasizes the description of the product over the CN Code classification. This means that the EU authorities can include products that are outside

Republic of China, OJ L 395, 31 Dec. 2004, pp. 56-67, recital 15; *Certain Footwear with Textile Uppers*, Commission Regulation (EC) No. 165/97 of 28 Jan. 1997 imposing a provisional anti-dumping duty on imports of certain footwear with textile uppers originating in the People's Republic of China and Indonesia, OJ L 029, 31 Jan. 1997, pp. 3-18, recitals 13-15, endorsed in Council Regulation (EC) No. 2155/97 of 29 Oct. 1997 imposing a definitive anti-dumping duty on imports of certain footwear with textile uppers originating in the People's Republic of China and Indonesia and collecting definitively the provisional duty imposed, OJ L 298, 1 Nov. 1997, pp. 1-18, recital 7.

39. *Sacks and Bags Made of Polyethylene or Polypropylene*, Commission Regulation (EC) No. 45/97 of 10 Jan. 1997 imposing a provisional anti-dumping duty on imports of sacks and bags made of polyethylene or polypropylene originating in India, Indonesia and Thailand, OJ L 12, 15 Jan. 1997, pp. 8-20 endorsed in Council Regulation (EC) No. 1950/97 of 6 Oct. 1997 imposing a definitive anti-dumping duty on imports of sacks and bags made of polyethylene or polypropylene originating in India, Indonesia and Thailand and collecting definitively the provisional duty imposed, OJ L 276, 9 Oct. 1997, pp. 1-8.
40. Art. 1 of the Commission Regulation.
41. Ibid.
42. Recital 9 of the Council Regulation.
43. Recital 11 of the Council Regulation.

the CN Codes mentioned in the initial notice or the provisional regulation in the investigation. The Council has elaborated its application of CN codes in *Certain Magnesia Bricks*,[44] where the notice of initiation of the anti-dumping procedure listed two CN codes, but the actual investigation included products under other CN codes. The Council stated:

> However, CN codes which are mentioned in the notice of initiation are given for information only and are not binding, as it is the product description, in particular the physical and chemical characteristics, which is relevant for the scope of the investigation. Consequently, all types of magnesia bricks sharing the same basic physical and chemical characteristics and having basically the same use, should be covered by the investigation, regardless of their customs classification. The scope of the investigation has thus not been extended. The investigation has clarified that the product concerned should legally be imported under CN codes ex68159100, ex68159910 and ex68159990. If, however, it was found that the product concerned was mistakenly declared under a different CN code, the investigation also covered that product.[45]

Based on this finding, the application of CN codes is not binding, but merely informative. The description of the product is binding, and in particular, the physical and chemical characteristics are relevant in framing the investigation.

In this line, the Commission and the Council have refused to delimit the scope of product definition even though the product definition would cover a large number of CN codes. In *Certain Footwear with Uppers of Leather,*[46] the product definition covered 33 different CN codes. One of the parties argued that the Commission should make individual dumping investigations for the different types of shoes. The Commission stated as follows – and this was later endorsed by the Council:

> The number of different CN codes covered by the product definition is, as such, also irrelevant for the question as to whether a product definition is broad or narrow. The relevant criteria applied in order to determine whether or not the product, subject of an investigation, can be considered a single product,

---

44. *Certain Magnesia Bricks*, Council Regulation (EC) No. 1659/2005 of 6 Oct. 2005 imposing a definitive anti-dumping duty and collecting definitively the provisional duty imposed on imports of certain magnesia bricks originating in the People's Republic of China, OJ L 267, 12 Oct. 2005, pp. 1-14.
45. Recital 8.
46. *Certain Footwear with Uppers of Leather*, Commission Regulation (EC) No. 553/2006 of 23 Mar. 2006 imposing a provisional anti-dumping duty on imports of certain footwear with uppers of leather originating in the People's Republic of China and Vietnam, OJ L 098, 6 Apr. 2006, pp. 3-54 endorsed in Council Regulation (EC) No. 1472/2006 of 5 Oct. 2006 imposing a definitive anti-dumping duty and collecting definitely the provisional duty imposed on imports of certain footwear with uppers of leather originating in the People's Republic of China and Vietnam, OJ L 275, 6 Oct. 2006, pp. 1-41.

i.e., its basic physical and technical characteristics, are set out in detail above.[47]

However, the Commission and Council have been reluctant to include other CN Codes in the product definition if they covered misclassified products. In *Malleable Cast Iron Tube or Pipe Fitting*, one interested party argued that the product under consideration – which was under CN code 7307 19 10 – was also imported into the EU under other CN codes. Therefore, the interested party argued that those CN codes should also be included in the investigation. The Council refused the claim, because if malleable fittings were imported under other CN codes, then they were misclassified.[48]

As already stated, WTO law offers wide discretion to the investigating authorities in defining the product under investigation. The application of physical, technical, and chemical characteristics seems to be in conformity with WTO law, as mentioned above. However, the EU authorities must make sure that the application of CN codes does not appear to be a part of the product definition, but only a guideline. If it appears from the initial product description or from the Commission and Council Regulations that the CN codes delimit the product scope, it may be a violation of WTO law to include products from other CN codes. As the Appellate Body has stated in *EC – Bed linen*, the definition of the product under investigation binds the investigating authorities.

3.4.1.3 Interchangeability

The Commission and the Council have paid attention to competition between the types of products or their interchangeability. If there is no interchangeability or no competition between some types, the products may be excluded from the investigation. In *Malleable Cast Iron Tube or Pipe Fittings*, the Council refused the claim of an interested party to include unthreaded fittings under the product definition of pipe fittings. The Council found that unthreaded fittings 'as such are not in competition with the product under consideration and are not interchangeable with it'.[49]

In *Certain Footwear with Textile Uppers*, the Council found that slippers were not suitable for outdoor use and were not interchangeable with outdoor shoes. This appeared – according to the Council – also to be the consumers' perception. Slippers and outdoor shoes could not be regarded as one single product.[50]

---

47. Recital 33 in the Commission Regulation – endorsed in recital 39 of the Council Regulation.
48. *Malleable Cast Iron Tube or Pipe Fittings*, Council Regulation (EC) No. 1784/2000 of 11 Aug. 2000 imposing a definitive anti-dumping duty and collecting definitively the provisional duty imposed on imports of certain malleable cast iron tube or pipe fittings originating in Brazil, the Czech Republic, Japan, the People's Republic of China, the Republic of Korea and Thailand, OJ L 208, 18 Aug. 2000, pp. 8-23, recitals 10-11.
49. *Malleable Cast Iron Tube or Pipe Fittings*, ibid., recital 12.
50. *Certain Footwear with Textile Uppers*, Council Regulation (EC) No. 2155/97 of 29 Oct. 1997 imposing a definitive anti-dumping duty on imports of certain footwear with textile uppers

However, in another shoe case, *Certain Footwear with Uppers of Leather,*[51] the basic physical, chemical, or technical differences were stressed – but the interchangeability and consumer perception were rejected. In its provisional regulation, the Commission had left special technology athletic footwear (STAF) out of the investigation of footwear other than sportswear because of differences in the basic physical and technical characteristics, sales channels, end-use and consumer perception.[52] In the same case, the Commission rejected the argument put forward by the EU industry that STAF should be included in the product definition because there was a fashion trend by consumers to use such shoes for other than sport, which puts STAF in competition with casual footwear. The Commission stated:

> In this respect, even if fashion trends may have had an impact on the consumer's choice and preferences, they certainly do not affect the essential basic physical and technical characteristics of a product, and therefore do not alter the above conclusions.[53]

The statement by the Commission supports the above claim that the main determinants in the product definition are the physical, technical, and chemical characteristics between the range of types or sub-groups of products that fall under the product definition – not the interchangeability or competitiveness between them. The Council upheld the Commission's findings,[54] where the Council – due to the EU producers' contesting of the Commission findings – stated that the EU producers did not contest that STAF has different physical and technical characteristics.[55] Since the EU producers could not contradict the Commission's findings on the differences between the basic physical and technical characteristics, STAF and the footwear under investigation could not be regarded as one single product.

In situations where types of products cannot easily be distinguished but their end uses are different, those different types will be regarded as a single product if they are in competition and share the same basic physical, technical, or chemical characteristics. See *Polyester Staple Fibres I,*[56] in which the Commission stated:

---

originating in the People's Republic of China and Indonesia and collecting definitively the provisional duty imposed, OJ L 298, 1 Nov. 1997, pp. 1-18, recital 8.

51. *Certain Footwear with Uppers of Leather*, Commission Regulation (EC) No. 553/2006 of 23 Mar. 2006 imposing a provisional anti-dumping duty on imports of certain footwear with uppers of leather originating in the People's Republic of China and Vietnam, OJ L 098, 6 Apr. 2006, pp. 3-54 endorsed in Council Regulation (EC) No. 1472/2006 of 5 Oct. 2006 imposing a definitive anti-dumping duty and collecting definitely the provisional duty imposed on imports of certain footwear with uppers of leather originating in the People's Republic of China and Vietnam, OJ L 275, 6 Oct. 2006, pp. 1-41.
52. See the Commission Regulation, recitals 12-19.
53. Recital 21.
54. Recitals 19 and 39 in the Council Regulation.
55. Recital 14 in the Council Regulation.
56. *Polyester Staple Fibres I*, Commission Regulation (EC) No. 1472/2000 of 6 Jul. 2000 imposing a provisional anti-dumping duty on imports of polyester staple fibres originating in India and the Republic of Korea, OJ L 166, 6 Jul. 2000, pp. 1-13, endorsed in Council Regulation (EC)

> The different types are considered as one product for the purpose of the investigation in the sense that the basic physical characteristics of the different types do not entail any significant differences, even though the uses and the quality of PSF sold might differ. There exist no clear dividing lines between the various types as there is overlapping and consequently competition between adjacent types.[57]

The basic physical characteristics are nearly the same – but their uses are different. There are several types with competition between *adjacent* types, but not competition between all types under the general product definition. As there is no clear dividing line between the different types, they are regarded as one product. The Council affirmed the Commission Regulation:

> Regarding the use of the product concerned, significant overlapping, substitution and competition between different types of PSF was found. The investigation has shown that there is no clear dividing line between the various types which would establish a unique link between physical product characteristics and the use of the product and that, consequently, the available evidence does not allow a product differentiation on this basis. In that respect, it is also underlined that the results of independent laboratory analysis cannot possibly determine definitely the ultimate use of the product. Consequently, the various types of PSF involved should be considered as forming one single product for the purposes of this proceeding.[58]

This line has been followed in other cases. In *Steel Ropes and Cables*, it was claimed by some exporters that a distinction should be made between steel wire ropes (SWR) for general use and those for industry specific use. The Council refused such a distinction because all SWR shared the same physical and technical characteristics. The Council further added to its argumentation:

> The various types of SWR can be classified into a number of product groups reflecting their physical and technical characteristics. *While SWR in groups in the top end and in the bottom end of the range are clearly not interchangeable, SWR in adjoining groups have been found to be interchangeable*. It was concluded that a certain degree of overlapping and competition existed between SWR in different groups. Given this overlap between the groups, no clear dividing line could be established at any point in the range of SWR.(. . .). In conclusion, given that all SWR were found to have the same basic physical and technical characteristics and use, *even if differences existed between SWR in the top end and bottom end of a range, since competition exists between SWR in adjacent groups, it was concluded that all products in the range*

No. 2852/2000 of 22 Dec. 2000 imposing a definitive anti-dumping duty and definitively collecting the provisional duty imposed on imports of polyester staple fibres originating in India and the Republic of Korea, OJ L 332, 28 Dec. 2000, pp. 17-31.

57. Recital 18, endorsed by Council, recital 10.
58. Recital 9.

> *formed one single product and therefore all SWR were considered to be one product.*[59] (Emphasis added)

See also *Certain Ring Binder Mechanisms II*. The Council stated:

> Several hundred different models of RBMs were sold during the IP in the Community. The models varied by size, shape and number of rings, the size of the base plate and the system to open the rings (pull open or opening trigger). In the absence of a clear dividing line in the range of RBMs and given that all of them have the same basic physical and technical characteristics, and that the models of RBMs can, *within certain ranges*, replace each other, the Commission established that all RBMs constitute one single product for the purpose of the present proceeding.[60] (Emphasis added)

The Commission and the Council have continued this practice in cases where there is no clear dividing line between the different ranges of products.[61] It is obvious that the Council is willing to extend the scope of the product definition to all types of products that are or can be interchangeable. However, the different types may not be in competition with one another, but may be in competition with adjacent types.

Under WTO law, it is not required that different types be in competition with one another to be under a general product definition.

3.4.1.4 Qualitative Differences

On several occasions, the EU authorities have rejected exporters' claim about exclusion of their products with a different qualities than the products concerned. In *Ferro-Silico-Manganese*, the Council made this general statement:

> In this respect, it is noted again that although certain slight differences exist within the range of qualities which go to make up the like product, all qualities

59. *Steel Ropes and Cables*, Council Regulation (EC) No. 1796/1999 of 12 Aug. 1999 imposing a definitive anti-dumping duty, and collecting definitively the provisional duty imposed, on imports of steel ropes and cables originating in the People's Republic of China, Hungary, India, Mexico, Poland, South Africa and Ukraine and terminating the anti-dumping proceeding in respect of imports originating in the Republic of Korea, OJ L 217, 17 Aug. 1999, pp. 1-13, recitals 6-8.
60. *Certain Ring Binder Mechanisms II*, Council Regulation (EC) No. 976/2002 of 4 Jun. 2002 imposing a definitive anti-dumping duty on imports of certain ring binder mechanisms (RBM) originating in Indonesia and terminating the anti-dumping proceeding in respect of imports of certain RBM originating in India, OJ L 150, 8 Jun. 2002, pp. 1-16, recital 17.
61. See also *Synthetic Fibres of Polyester II*, Council Regulation (EC) No. 1728/1999 of 29 Jul. 1999 imposing a definitive anti-dumping duty on imports of synthetic fibres of polyesters originating in Taiwan and terminating the proceeding in respect of imports of synthetic fibres of polyesters originating in the Republic of Korea, OJ L 204, 4 Aug. 1999, pp. 3-12, recital 13; *Certain Ring Binder Mechanisms II*, Council Regulation (EC) No. 976/2002 of 4 Jun. 2002 imposing a definitive anti-dumping duty on imports of certain ring binder mechanisms (RBM) originating in Indonesia and terminating the anti-dumping proceeding in respect of imports of certain RBM originating in India, OJ L 150, 8 Jun. 2002, pp. 1-16, recital 17.

> can be considered to be a single product since their main physical and technical characteristics and uses are the same.[62]

It is seen in subsequent practice that the authorities disregard the differences in qualities when the scope of product is being established.[63] See for example recent practice in *Certain Graphite Electrode Systems* and *Lever Arch Mechanisms.*

In *Certain Graphite Electrode Systems*, the Commission investigated graphite electrodes and/or nipples used for such electrodes in order to examine whether the imported goods from India were being sold at dumped prices. One of the raw materials used in the production of the product concerned was a petroleum coke – a by-product of the oil industry. One Indian producer claimed that his products did not fall within the definition of the product concerned, because he did not use a premium needle coke, which is a top quality petroleum coke. The Commission stated:

> Indeed, different qualities of petroleum coke can be used for producing graphite electrode systems. *However, it is the basic physical and technical characteristics of the end product and its end uses, irrespective of the raw materials used, which determine the product definition.* If graphite electrodes and nipples used for such electrodes originating in India and imported into the Community meet the basic physical and technical characteristics as described in the product definition, they are considered product concerned. Therefore, the claim was rejected.[64] (Emphasis added)

The Council did not add any comment to the product definition in its Regulation imposing the definitive duty and collecting the provisional duty.[65]

---

62. *Ferro-Silico-Manganese*, Council Regulation (EC) No. 495/98 of 23 Feb. 1998 imposing a definitive anti-dumping duty on imports of ferro-silico-manganese originating in the People's Republic of China, amending Regulation (EC) No. 2413/95 in respect of anti-dumping measures concerning imports of ferro-silico-manganese originating in Ukraine and terminating the proceeding in respect of imports of ferro-silico-manganese originating in Brazil, South Africa and Russia, OJ L 062, 3 Mar. 1998, pp. 1-18, recital 17.
63. See for instance *Granular Polytetrafluoroethylene (PTFE)*; Council Regulation (EC) No. 1987/2005 of 2 Dec. 2005 imposing a definitive anti-dumping duty and collecting definitively the provisional duty imposed on imports of granular polytetrafluoroethylene (PTFE) originating in Russia and the People's Republic of China, OJ L 320, 8 Dec. 2005, pp. 1-19, recitals 9-10; *Sulphanilic Acid*; Commission Regulation (EC) No. 575/2002 of 3 Mar. 2002 imposing a provisional anti-dumping duty on imports of sulphanilic acid originating in the People's Republic of China and in India, OJ L 87, 4 Apr. 2002, pp. 28-44 endorsed in Council Regulation (EC) No. 1339/2002 of 22 Jul. 2002 imposing a definitive anti-dumping duty and collecting definitively the provisional duty imposed on imports of sulphanilic acid originating in the People's Republic of China and India, OJ L 196, 25 Jul. 2002, pp. 11-18, recitals 7-9.
64. *Certain Graphite Electrode Systems*, Commission Regulation (EC) No. 1009/2004 of 19 May 2004 imposing a provisional anti-dumping duty on imports of certain graphite electrode systems originating in India, OJ L 183, 20 May 2004, pp. 61-82, recital 14.
65. *Certain Graphite Electrode Systems*, Council Regulation (EC) No. 1629/2004 of 13 Sep. 2004 imposing a definitive anti-dumping duty and collecting definitively the provisional duty

Similarly, in *Lever Arch Mechanisms*, where some factors, such as the quality and thickness of the steel, the size of the mechanisms, and the surface treatment, were different, the Commission stressed that the products had the same basic physical and technical characteristics and were used for the same purposes. Consequently, the Commission regarded the different types of products as one single product.[66] The Council endorsed the Commission's finding.[67]

The wide discretion under WTO law may imply that the rejection by the EU authorities of considering the qualitative differences when the product defined is in conformity with WTO law. Yet, if the low quality and high quality products are not in competition, and the EU industry is only producing high quality products, the low quality products should not be under the investigation if there is no injurious impact on the EU industry. That would follow from Article 5.2 and Article 5.6 of the ADA, where there must be evidence of a causal link between the product defined and the injury on the domestic industry in order to initiate an investigation. If such link is not demonstrated, the investigation shall be terminated. Apparently, if the product definition covers a wider scope of types of products, where some types due to qualitative differences are not causing injury on the EU industry, then such products should be left out from the investigation.

3.4.1.5 Different Functionality and Patented Products

The Commission and the Council have rejected arguments about leaving products with some differences in functionality compared to the overall defined product under consideration out of the investigation.[68] In a similar vein, the Commission and the Council may reject arguments of patented products with an improved functionality. This was seen in *Certain Plastic Sacks and Bags*, where a Malaysian exporter of bags with a patented dispensing mechanism, which was not produced by EU producers, claimed that the patented product with its special functionality should be left out of the investigation. The Council stated:

> However this patented feature, while intended to bring a functional advantage over other carrier bags, does not represent a sufficient difference in physical

---

imposed on imports of certain graphite electrode systems originating in India, OJ L 295, 18 Sep. 2004, pp. 10-14, recital 6.

66. *Lever Arch Mechanisms*, Commission Regulation (EC) No. 134/2006 of 26 Jan. 2006 imposing a provisional anti-dumping duty on imports of lever arch mechanisms originating in the People's Republic of China, OJ L 023, 27 Jan. 2006, pp. 13-33, recital 13.
67. *Lever Arch Mechanisms*, Council Regulation (EC) No. 1136/2006 of 24 Jul. 2006 imposing a definitive anti-dumping duty and collecting definitively the provisional duty imposed on imports of lever arch mechanisms originating in the People's Republic of China, OJ L 205, 27 Jul. 2006, pp. 1-12, recitals 8-9.
68. See *Certain Electronic Weighing Scales (REWS)*, Council Regulation (EC) No. 2605/2000 of 27 Nov. 2000 imposing definitive anti-dumping duties on imports of certain electronic weighing scales (REWS) originating in the People's Republic of China, the Republic of Korea and Taiwan, OJ L 301, 30 Nov. 2000, pp. 42-60, recital 11.

> characteristics for the bags in question to be considered a separate product. Indeed, they remain basically interchangeable with other carrier bags, with or without similar patented systems.[69]

In line with this practice, patented products will not be excluded from the product definition, either because they are covered by an intellectual property right protection or because there is an exclusive sales contract between the producer and the EU importer. See for example the Council statement in *Lever Arch Mechanism:*

> It is considered that a patented design or an exclusive contract between an exporting producer and a European user for a certain type of product does not, as such, justify the exclusion of this type from the definition of the product concerned or the like product. A [lever arch mechanism] with all its characteristics remains the product concerned irrespective of whether it is patented or purchased via an exclusive contract.[70]

Under WTO law, it is the product from a specific country that is targeted under an anti-dumping investigation, not the product from specific producers. The text of the ADA contains no exception for producers with certain intellectual or certain contractual rights. Therefore, producers with certain rights, like a patent, may not be excluded from the investigation by the Commission and the Council if the patented product falls under the product definition. The practice by the Commission and the Council therefore seems to be in conformity with WTO law

3.4.1.6 Different Production Techniques

The EU institutions seem to rely on a test based only on the physical, technical, or chemical characteristics, when examining whether a specific type of product is included in the investigation. Yet, in *Polyethylene Terephthalate Film*, the Council made an opening to exclude products that had been produced through different production processes than the product defined. The producers under investigation had claimed that metallized polyethylene terephthalate (PET) film should be excluded from the product under consideration – base PET film – because the metallized PET film needed further processing. The producers also claimed that metallized PET film was categorized under another CN Code than the products

---

69. *Certain Plastic Sacks and Bags*, Council Regulation (EC) No. 1425/2006 of 25 Sep. 2006 imposing a definitive anti-dumping duty on imports of certain plastic sacks and bags originating in the People's Republic of China and Thailand, and terminating the proceeding on imports of certain plastic sacks and bags originating in Malaysia, OJ L 270, 29 Sep. 2006, pp. 4-41, recital 37.
70. *Lever arch mechanisms*, Council Regulation (EC) No. 1136/2006 of 24 Jul. 2006 imposing a definitive anti-dumping duty and collecting definitively the provisional duty imposed on imports of lever arch mechanisms originating in the People's Republic of China, OJ L 205, 27 Jul. 2006, pp. 1-12, recital 8.

concerned. In its regulation imposing a provisional anti-dumping duty, the Commission has stated that the products, metallized film and base film, had the same physical characteristics and were interchangeable. The differences in application were, in the Commission's point of view, only minor, and the two types were to be regarded as the same product.[71] The Council endorsed the Commission's standpoint,[72] and added:

> It should be noted that the fact that an additional production step is required for the production of metallised PET film, with resulting higher cost of production and sales price, is not an element which could justify *per se* the exclusion of a certain type of PET film from the product scope of the proceeding.[73] (Emphasis added)

The Council further stated that only in situations where the metallized film was reinforced, laminated, supported, or combined with other materials, their basic physical, chemical, and technical characteristics would be different to an extent that would exempt them from being regarded as the product concerned. Only in such instances would they be classified under another CN code. For that reason, the exporting product – metallized film – fell under the product definition.[74]

In its definition of the scope of product, the Commission only regarded the elements of physical characteristics and interchangeability, whereas the Council also regarded the additional production steps and thus the higher costs and sales price. Even though, in this particular case, the Council does not endorse the argument by the exporting producers to exclude metallized PET film, it seems that the Council will not deny the possibility that different production methods, which result in different costs and sales prices for the producers, can be taken into consideration. This follows from the emphasized wordings, where the Council says it cannot exclude products with different production processes per se. The main factors to determine whether a product falls under the product definition still seem to be the physical, technical, or chemical characteristics.

However, in *Malleable Cast Iron Tube or Pipe Fittings*, the Council found there was no competition between the product concerned – pipe fittings – and unthreaded fittings. The Council also paid attention to the further steps in the production of threaded fittings compared with the unthreaded. One interested

71. *Polyethylene Terephthalate Film*, Commission Regulation (EC) No. 367/2001 of 23 Feb. 2001 imposing a provisional anti-dumping duty on imports of PET film originating in India and the Republic of Korea, OJ L 055, 24 Feb. 2001, pp. 16-39, recital 19.
72. *Polyethylene Terephthalate Film*, Council Regulation (EC) No. 1676/2001 of 13 Aug. 2001 imposing a definitive anti-dumping duty and collecting definitively the provisional duty imposed on imports of PET film originating in India and the Republic of Korea, OJ L 227, 23 Aug. 2001, pp. 1-14, recital 9.
73. Recital 10.
74. Recital 11.

party asserted that the product under investigation should be extended to include unthreaded fittings.[75] The Council refused the claim and stated:

> [U]nthreaded fittings do not fall within the definition of the product under consideration. In fact, they are an intermediate product necessitating further manufacturing steps which give the product under consideration one of its essential characteristics, i.e., its joining mechanism. *As a consequence, unthreaded fittings as such are not in competition with the product under consideration and are not interchangeable with it*. Moreover, *the investigation showed that the threading represents a significant step in the manufacturing process in terms of value added to the malleable fitting, in particular in consideration of the high level of labour involved in that step*. Therefore, they cannot be considered to form one single product together with threaded malleable fittings, i.e., the product under consideration.[76] (Emphasis added)

It is questionable why the Council does not refer to the main criteria: physical, technical, or chemical characteristics in its argumentation. It appears that the different production processes and lack of competition are the main determinants.

In other situations, the Commission and the Council have justified the inclusion of products with different production techniques by referring to the adjustment in Article 2.10. In *Sulphanilic Acid*, interested parties claimed that the definition of the product was incorrect because there were two grades of sulphanilic acid that and the EU institutions should distinguish between those two sorts and thus make two different investigations. The interested parties claimed that the purified grade could be used in all applications, whereas non-purified grades were not useful in the production of optical brighteners and food dyes. Consequently, according to the interested parties, there was no interchangeability between the two grades.[77] The Council stated:

> The fact that interchangeability may only be in one direction in certain applications because of concerns about impurities is therefore not considered to be sufficient justification that purified and technical grades constitute different products which should be treated separately in two different investigations. Whilst accepting that *the purification process adds certain additional costs to the production process*, it is recalled that these *were taken into account when making a fair comparison* between the different grades produced by the

75. *Malleable Cast Iron Tube or Pipe Fittings*, Council Regulation (EC) No. 1784/2000 of 11 Aug. 2000 imposing a definitive anti-dumping duty and collecting definitively the provisional duty imposed on imports of certain malleable cast iron tube or pipe fittings originating in Brazil, the Czech Republic, Japan, the People's Republic of China, the Republic of Korea and Thailand, OJ L 208, 18 Aug. 2000, pp. 8-23, recital 10.
76. Recital 12.
77. *Sulphanilic Acid*, Council Regulation (EC) No. 1339/2002 of 22 Jul. 2002 imposing a definitive anti-dumping duty and collecting definitively the provisional duty imposed on imports of sulphanilic acid originating in the People's Republic of China and India, OJ L 196, 25 Jul. 2002, pp. 11-18, recital 7.

Community industry and those imported from the countries concerned for the purposes of calculating the level of price undercutting and the injury elimination level.[78] (Emphasis added)

The Council seems to make cost adjustment at the comparison level in this particular case, which could justify the inclusion of products with different production techniques. However, there is no clear line compared to the *Polyethylene Terephthalate Film* case mentioned above.

In *Cotton-type Bed linen I*, the EU authorities have rejected the argument that different production techniques lead to an exclusion of a product from the investigation.[79] See citation mentioned above in 3.4.1.1.

Based on the wide discretion left to the investigating authorities, the unclear Commission and Council practice seems not to be a violation of WTO law. Only if it can be proved that the Commission and the Council discriminate between different countries or between different producers will this be in conflict with the non-discrimination principle. However, such conclusions cannot be reached based on the data used here.

3.4.2 Like Product

The price of the allegedly dumped product must be compared with the price of the like product sold on the domestic market in the exporting country.

The EU authorities always define the like product right after having defined the product under consideration. The 'like product' determination between the exported product and the domestically sold product is usually not disputed. This may be caused by the fact that the dumping determination will usually be based on a comparison of the domestic and export price between specific types of products – and not for the overall category of the product under investigation.[80] Furthermore, differences affecting price comparability, for example qualitative differences between the product under consideration and the like product, are adjusted for in accordance with Article 2.10, see more on the adjustments in Section 6.1.

78. Recital 8.
79. *Cotton-type Bed linen I*, Commission Regulation (EC) No. 1069/97 of 12 Jun. 1997 imposing a provisional anti-dumping duty on imports of cotton-type bed linen originating in Egypt, India and Pakistan, OJ L 156, 13 Jun. 1997, pp. 11-33, endorsed in Council Regulation (EC) No. 2398/97 of 28 Nov. 1997 imposing a definitive anti-dumping duty on imports of cotton-type bed linen originating in Egypt, India and Pakistan, OJ L 332, 4 Dec. 1997, pp. 1-18, recital 7. See also *Tartaric Acid*, Council Regulation (EC) No. 130/2006 of 23 Jan. 2006 imposing a definitive anti-dumping duty and collecting definitively the provisional duty imposed on imports of tartaric acid originating in the People's Republic of China, OJ L 23, 27 Jan. 2006, pp. 1-7, recital 10.
80. See for instance *Polyester Staples Fibres I*, Council Regulation (EC) No. 2852/2000 of 22 Dec. 2000 imposing a definitive anti-dumping duty and definitively collecting the provisional duty imposed on imports of polyester staple fibres originating in India and the Republic of Korea, OJ L 332, 28 Dec. 2000, pp. 17-31, recitals 24 and 41.

In practice, most disagreements between the Commission/Council and the producers concern the likeness between the exported product and the production by EU industries for the injury determination,[81] in particular concerning situations where the like product may not even be produced by EU producers, but the EU producers have the facilities to do so.[82] The injury practice is not further elaborated in this book.

The practice of the Commission and the Council to determine the like product for the dumping determination reveals a close resemblance to the one established under the definition of the product under consideration. The main factors in determining whether a domestically sold product is like the product under investigation are the basic physical, technical, or chemical resemblances between them. If they share the same basic physical, technical, or chemical characteristics, they are alike. This is established practice.[83]

---

81. See for instance *Malleable Cast Iron Tube or Pipe Fittings*, Council Regulation (EC) No. 1784/2000 of 11 Aug. 2000 imposing a definitive anti-dumping duty and collecting definitively the provisional duty imposed on imports of certain malleable cast iron tube or pipe fittings originating in Brazil, the Czech Republic, Japan, the People's Republic of China, the Republic of Korea and Thailand, OJ L 208, 18 Aug. 2000, pp. 8-23, recital 17. See also *Canon II*, Case C-171/87, judgment of the EC Court on 10 Mar. 1992, ECR 1992, p. I-1237, paras 46-49.
82. See for instance *Stainless Steel Fasteners and Parts thereof II*, Council Regulation (EC) No. 1890/2005 of 14 Nov. 2005 imposing a definitive anti-dumping duty and collecting definitively the provisional duty imposed on imports of certain stainless steel fasteners and parts thereof originating in the People's Republic of China, Indonesia, Taiwan, Thailand and Vietnam and terminating the proceeding on imports of certain stainless steel fasteners and parts thereof originating in Malaysia and the Philippines, OJ L 302, 19 Nov. 2005, pp. 1-13, recital 15. See apparently *Cotton-type Bed Linen I*, Commission Regulation (EC) No. 1069/97 of 12 Jun. 1997 imposing a provisional anti-dumping duty on imports of cotton-type bed linen originating in Egypt, India and Pakistan, OJ L 156, 13 Jun. 1997, P. 0011-0033 endorsed in Council Regulation (EC) No. 2398/97 of 28 Nov. 1997 imposing a definitive anti-dumping duty on imports of cotton-type bed linen originating in Egypt, India and Pakistan, OJ L 332, 4 Dec. 1997, pp. 1-18, recital 5.
83. *Synthetic Fibre Ropes*, Commission Regulation (EC) No. 18/98 of 7 Jan. 1998 imposing a provisional anti-dumping duty on imports of synthetic fibre ropes originating in India, OJ L 4, 8 Jan. 1998, pp. 28-38, recital 9, endorsed in Council Regulation (EC) No. 1312/98 of 24 Jun. 1998 imposing a definitive anti-dumping duty on imports of synthetic fibre ropes originating in India and collecting definitively the provisional duty imposed, OJ L 183, 26 Jun. 1998, pp. 1-8, recital 8; *Polyester Staple Fibres I*, Commission Regulation (EC) No. 1472/2000 of 6 Jul. 2000 imposing a provisional anti-dumping duty on imports of polyester staple fibres originating in India and the Republic of Korea, OJ L 166, 6 Jul. 2000, pp. 1-13, recital 19, endorsed in Council Regulation (EC) No. 2852/2000 of 22 Dec. 2000 imposing a definitive anti-dumping duty and definitively collecting the provisional duty imposed on imports of polyester staple fibres originating in India and the Republic of Korea, OJ L 332, 28 Dec. 2000, pp. 17-31, apparently recital 9, and Council Regulation (EC) No. 428/2005 of 10 Mar. 2005 imposing a definitive anti-dumping duty on imports of polyester staple fibres originating in the People's Republic of China and Saudi Arabia, amending Regulation (EC) No. 2852/2000 imposing a definitive anti-dumping duty on imports of polyester staple fibres originating in the Republic of Korea and terminating the anti-dumping proceeding in respect of such imports originating in Taiwan, OJ L 071, 17 Mar. 2005, pp. 1-33, recital 27; *Lever Arch Mechanisms*, Commission Regulation (EC) No. 134/2006 of 26 Jan. 2006 imposing a provisional anti-dumping duty on imports of lever

Even though the 'like product' may be based on physical characteristics – in line with the Panel suggestion – the term 'physical' may be broadly defined to include a broad range of different types. In *Shanghai Bicycles Corporation v. Council*, the Court of First Instance stressed that when types – in this case, bicycles – cannot be clearly divided into sub-groups, and competition exists between those sub-groups, it is not sufficient to establish different functions or different needs. The Court of First Instance concluded that 'like product' covers all bicycles, all categories merged together.[84] With this statement, the 'like product' may cover those types which are competing – at least in those situations where there is no clear dividing line between the different types. However, this also indicates that the term 'physical' is not a narrow concept. In this regard, it seems closely related to the 'physical' concept used for the determination of product under consideration.

In a more recent case, *Cotton-type bed linen II*, the Council refused to regard consumer bed linen 'like' grey cloth used as an intermediary product for industrial use.[85] The broad concept of 'physical characteristics' has its limits.

The question is though, whether a broad definition of 'like product' is in line with WTO law. Under WTO legislation, a textual reading of Article 2.6 of the ADA – and in this line Article 1.4 of the basic Regulation – suggests that the like product must be identical to the product under consideration. In the absence of such a product, the like product must be one that, although not alike in all respects, has characteristics closely resembling those of the product under consideration. It is not apparent from the information provided in the regulations whether the Commission and the Council in fact first look for 'identical' products and then look for products with characteristics closely resembling the product under investigation. However, in *Korea – Certain Paper*, a Panel seems to have stated that the likeness condition in Article 2.6 is fulfilled if the products are either identical or have physical characteristics closely resembling each other. Based on the Panel statement, it cannot be concluded that the EU practice is in violation of WTO law. Furthermore, Article 2.4 of the ADA requires that differences between the product under investigation and the like product shall be adjusted for if the price comparability is affected by such differences. Therefore, it can be assumed that under

arch mechanisms originating in the People's Republic of China, OJ L 23, 27 Jan. 2006, pp. 13-33, recital 14, endorsed in Council Regulation (EC) No. 1136/2006 of 24 Jul. 2006 imposing a definitive anti-dumping duty and collecting definitively the provisional duty imposed on imports of lever arch mechanisms originating in the People's Republic of China, OJ L 205, 27 Jul. 2006, pp. 1-12, recital 10; *Tartaric Acid*; Commission Regulation (EC) No. 1259/2005 of 27 Jul. 2005 imposing a provisional anti-dumping duty on imports of tartaric acid originating in the People's Republic of China, OJ L 200, 30 Jul. 2005, pp. 73-90, recitals 12, endorsed in Council Regulation (EC) No. 130/2006 of 23 Jan. 2006 imposing a definitive anti-dumping duty and collecting definitively the provisional duty imposed on imports of tartaric acid originating in the People's Republic of China, OJ L 023, 27 Jan. 2006, pp. 1-7, recital 11.

84. *Shanghai Bicycle Corporation v. Council*, Case T-170/94, judgment of the Court of First Instance of 25 Sep. 1997. ECR 1997, p. II-1383, para. 67-71.

85. *Cotton-type Bed linen II*, Council Regulation (EC) No. 695/2006 of 5 May 2006 amending Regulation (EC) No. 397/2004 imposing a definitive anti-dumping duty on imports of cotton-type bedlinen originating in Pakistan, OJ L 121, 6 May 2006, pp. 14-26, recital 34.

WTO law there is some room for differences between the product under investigation and the like product as long as such differences are being adjusted. See more in Section 6.1 below.

3.5 FINAL COMMENTS

There are no clear guidelines in the WTO legislation or in WTO practice regarding the determination of the product under consideration. The investigating authorities have wide discretion to define the product being investigated, as long as the requirements in Article 5.2 and Article 5.6 of the ADA are met. However, the Appellate Body has stated that once the product has been defined and it includes different types or sub-groups of the product under investigation, the investigating authorities must treat all the different types and the different sub-groups in line with the definition. The investigating authorities cannot on one hand leave out one of the types under the product definition if this would lead to higher dumping margin – and on the other hand impose an anti-dumping duty on that type of product. This statement implies that the product definition frames the entire investigation. Yet, there is no guidance on how to determine the types to be included in the product scope.

EU legislation does not define the product under consideration or give guidance on the types to be included under the product definition. However, in Commission and Council practice, some guidelines may be found, as types that share the same physical, technical, or chemical characteristics as the product defined are included. The Commission and the Council may also look into other factors, but the main determinants are the physical, technical, or chemical characteristics. This practice used by the Commission and the Council seems to be in conformity with the WTO obligations, due to the wide discretion.

Under WTO law, the like product determination is regulated in Article 2.6 of the ADA, according to which the like product must be identical to the product under consideration or, in the absence of such product, to a product with characteristics closely resembling the product under consideration. This apparent hierarchical order seems not to be fully reflected in practice. Furthermore, a Panel has stressed that 'characteristics closely resembling' means *physical characteristics.*

The 'physical' criteria can be criticized. Article 2.6 of the ADA does not provide that 'characteristics closely resemblance' must be physical. The requirement of putting a 'physical' condition into the ADA has also been on the negotiation table a few times. Already in the 1950's, the Group of Experts dealt with some issues concerning the 'like product',[86] before the Kennedy Round. The Group agreed that the likeliness between products should be based on the physical character of the products. In addition, different types of the like product should be adjusted at the comparison level.[87] The Group of Experts also commented on the

86. First Report of the Group of Experts on Anti-dumping and Countervailing Duties, L/978, 24 Apr. 1959.
87. Para. 12.

interpretation of 'like product'. The term 'should not be interpreted either too broadly so as to cover products of a different kind with higher prices on the internal market, nor too stringently so as to elude the application of paragraph 1(a) of Article VI'.[88] During the negotiations of the Uruguay Round, attempts were made to provide some criteria for the determination of the like product. In the initial Carlisle I and II text, it was provided:

> Throughout this Code the term 'like product' ('produit similaire') shall be interpreted to mean a product which is identical, i.e., alike in all respects to the product under consideration, or in the absence of such a product, another product which, although not alike in all respects, has *both physical, technical and/or chemical characteristics and applications or uses* closely resembling those of the product under consideration. *Minor variations among these products, such as those resulting from the changes in fashion, and quality differences shall not preclude a finding that products are like within the meaning of this paragraph. Slightly altered or developed versions of a product may be like that product if the above-mentioned criteria are met.* (Emphasis added) ('Code' is another term for the ADA)

Yet, the criteria of physical, technical, or chemical characteristics did not find its way into the ADA, and therefore the finding by the Panel in *Korea – Certain Paper* may be taking a step too far by reading a physical criterion into Article 2.6. It must further be noted that Article 2.4 of the ADA provides that when the prices are compared, '[d]ue allowance shall be made in each case, on its merits, for differences which affect price comparability, including differences in conditions and terms of sale, taxation, levels of trade, quantities, physical characteristics, and any other differences which are also demonstrated to affect price comparability'. Article 2.4 opens up for some physical differences between the product under consideration and the like product.

The Commission and the Council use similar approaches in determining the like product as used in the product definition. The Commission and the Council stress the physical resemblance between the product under consideration and the like product. It is not clear from the information in the Regulations whether the Commission and the Council examine whether the products are identical before evaluating the physical similarities between the product under consideration and the like product. From the text of Article 2.6 of the ADA, the Commission and the Council are supposed to make such an exercise before they look for products resembling the product under consideration, but it seems not to be fully reflected in Panel practice. It cannot clearly be concluded then that the EU practice is in violation of WTO law

88. Para. 13.

Chapter 4
Normal Value

In this chapter, it is examined whether determination of normal value within the EU system is in conformity with the WTO law. The normal value is used for comparison with the export price in order to determine dumping, and it is based on domestic prices in the exporting country.

The chapter is divided into two sections. In Section 4.1, focus is on the general rule that normal value is based on the actual domestic prices from transactions between the producer in the exporting country and domestic buyers. Here it is examined what the conditions are for the actual domestic prices to qualify as normal value, and the circumstances for disregarding actual domestic prices.

Section 4.2 deals with the alternative means to establish the normal value if the normal value cannot be based on the actual domestic prices.

The rules on normal value for Chinese producers are different and are therefore explored separately in Chapter 7. Only when the special rules on normal value for Chinese producers are derogated from will the Chinese producers be treated under the general rules as described in this chapter.

4.1 GENERAL RULE: ACTUAL DOMESTIC PRICE

In this section, the general rule on normal value is explored, and the rules for disregarding the actual domestic prices are examined. In practice, a producer only rarely claims that the actual domestic prices are to be disregarded;[1] this may indicate that producers prefer to have normal value based on the actual

1. See *Cotton-type Bedlinen II*, Council Regulation (EC) No. 695/2006 of 5 May 2006 amending Regulation (EC) No. 397/2004 imposing a definitive anti-dumping duty on imports of cotton-type bed linen originating in Pakistan, OJ L 121, 6 May 2006, pp. 14-26, recital 28, and *EC – Cotton Yarn*, ADP/137, report of the Panel on 4 Jul. 1995, paras 467-469.

domestic prices from transactions to the domestic buyers instead of having the normal value constructed.

The first step in this section is to provide a framework of WTO law on normal value. The point of departure is the WTO legislation in Article VI.1(a)(i) of GATT 1994 and Article 2.1 of the ADA. In order to clarify some of the concepts in those provisions, support is found elsewhere in the ADA. Subsequently, the application of those rules by Panels and Appellate Body is examined. In Section 4.1.3, the EU legislation on normal value is examined under WTO law. Subsequently, the EU practice of the Commission, the Council and the EC courts is examined under WTO law.

4.1.1 WTO Legislation

Normal value is not directly defined under Article VI of GATT 1994 or in the ADA. Instead, recourse may be taken to the general definition of dumping in Article VI.1(a)(i) of GATT 1994 and Article 2.1 of the ADA, which reads:

> For the purpose of this Article, a product is to be considered as being introduced into the commerce of an importing country at less than its normal value, if the price of the product exported from one country to another is less than the *comparable price, in the ordinary course of trade, for the like product when destined for consumption in the exporting country*. (Emphasis added)

The general rule under WTO legislation is that normal value is based on prices that meet four conditions:

- the price must be *comparable* with the export price;
- the price originates from a transaction in the *ordinary course of trade*;
- the price is that of a *like product* to the exported product; and
- the price is based on a transaction *destined for consumption in the exporting country*.

According to this reading, if one of the four conditions on normal value is not met, the actual price cannot serve as a basis for a comparison with the export price and must therefore be left out of the normal value determination. The four conditions will be elaborated on in the following section.

4.1.1.1 Comparable Prices

The sales between the allegedly dumped products and the domestic sales must be comparable. Article VI of GATT 1994 and Article 2.1 do not further define what a comparable price is. The context may shed some light on the term 'comparable'. Article 2.2 of the ADA, which concerns the alternatives to actual domestic prices,[2]

2. See more in Section 4.2 below, about the alternatives to the actual domestic price in the normal value determination.

provides the grounds for using those alternatives. Two of those grounds in Article 2.2 are related to prices that 'do not permit a proper comparison':

- the particular market situation; and
- the low volume of sales.

A '*particular market situation*' is not further defined. This has its roots in the situation in non-market economy states,[3] and the wordings of a particular market situation found its way into the Kennedy ADA as a consequence of the non-market performance by some Communist GATT Member states; see chapter 2. However, it is not clear whether other market types will fall under the 'particular market' category in Article 2.2. It must be assumed that the investigating authorities have wide discretion to determine whether there is a particular market situation due to lack of clear guidelines in the WTO text.

'L*ow-volume sales*' is defined in note 2 to Article 2.2. It is provided:

> Sales of the like product destined for consumption in the domestic market of the exporting country shall normally be considered a sufficient quantity for the determination of the normal value if such sales constitute 5 per cent or more of the sales of the product under consideration to the importing Member, provided that a lower ratio should be acceptable where the evidence demonstrates that domestic sales at such lower ratio are nonetheless of sufficient magnitude to provide for a proper comparison.

Therefore, the investigating authorities may disregard domestic sales when they are below the 5% threshold, as such prices do not permit a proper comparison with the export price.

Attention must also be paid to Article 2.4 of the ADA, which concerns the adjustment for differences affecting price comparability between normal value and export price. Prices that for some reason may not seem comparable at the point of departure can be adjusted. However, it is not clear whether the investigating authorities are required to include prices that are not comparable due to one of the reasons provided in Article 2.4, but which may be comparable after adjustment, or whether the investigating authorities have the discretion to disregard such prices.

4.1.1.2 Ordinary Course of Trade

A domestic sale that is not in the ordinary course of trade will fall outside the indirect normal value definition in Article 2.1. The concept of 'ordinary course of trade' is not defined in Article VI of GATT 1994 or in the ADA, and this suggests a wide discretion to the investigating authorities.

An example of prices which may not derive from the ordinary course of trade is provided in Article 2.2.1, which states that the investigating authorities *may*

3. F. Snyder, 'The Origins of the "Nonmarket Economy": Ideas, Pluralism and Power in EC Anti-dumping Law about China', *European Law Journal* 7 (4) (2001): 387 et seq.

disregard domestic prices if they are below per unit (fixed and variable) costs plus sales, administrative and general costs (SAG), as these are not being in the ordinary course of trade. Pursuant to Article 2.2.1, such prices

> may be disregarded in determining normal value only if the authorities[4] determine that such sales are made within an extended period of time in substantial quantities and are at prices which do not provide for the recovery of all costs within a reasonable period of time. If prices which are below per unit costs at the time of sale are above weighted average per unit costs for the period of investigation, such prices shall be considered to provide for recovery of costs within a reasonable period of time.

The conditions must be considered cumulatively, note the word 'and'. Thus, three criteria must be met in order for the investigating authorities to leave out sales below costs.

First, sales must take place within an extended period of time, which according to an added note 'should normally be one year but shall in no case be less than six months'. The investigating authorities cannot disregard single transactions being below costs, but must examine the pattern of prices and costs from the investigating period which is normally one year.[5] It is not clear under what circumstances the investigating authorities can depart from the one-year rule, but the minimum period in which sales below costs cannot be disregarded as being outside the ordinary course of trade is six months.[6]

Next, the sales must be made in substantial quantities. In a note added to the provision, it is elaborated that the term 'substantial quantity' describes when the weighted-average selling price is below the weighted average per unit costs, which includes all transactions under consideration for establishing the normal value; or when not less than 20% of the *volume* of domestic sales are made below per unit costs.

Van Bael and Bellis are sceptical about the 20% rule and write: 'This methodology (...) accordingly tends to increase the artificial character of dumping findings.'[7]

Finally, if the costs will be recovered by the prices within a reasonable time, the sales cannot be disregarded. 'A reasonable period of time' is as a minimum the period of investigation.

---

4. A note is annexed to the provision: 'When in this Agreement the term "authorities" is used, it shall be interpreted as meaning authorities at an appropriate senior level.'
5. See Section 2.2.2.2 above.
6. See also Wenxi Li, *Anti-dumping Law of WTO/GATT and EC – Gradual Evolution of Anti-dumping Law in Global Economic Integration* (Lund: Lund University, 2001), 77.
7. I. Van Bael & J.F. Bellis, *Anti-dumping and Other Trade Protection Laws of the EC*, 4th edn (The Hague: Kluwer Law International, 2004), 57.

The three conditions make it possible for the producer to place a new product on the market if it is assumed that the costs – including sunk costs – may result in below per unit cost in the introductory stage of the product.

Vermulst, who is highly critical of the below cost rule, demonstrates that dumping may occur when there is no price discrimination.[8] There are four transactions of equal weight and the production cost per unit is 90:

- transaction 1 on 1 June: domestic price is 50 and export price is 50;
- transaction 2 on 10 June; domestic price is 100 and export price is 100;
- transaction 3 on 15 June; domestic price is 150 and export price is 150;
- transaction 4 on 20 June; domestic price is 200 and export price is 200.

In this particular case, there is no price discrimination at all. Nevertheless, the first transaction has a lower domestic price than the production cost, and that transaction is 25% of the total volume. Thereby, that particular transaction can be disregarded. The result is that the weighted average of the remaining domestic price will be 150 ((100 + 150 + 200)/3) compared with the weighted-average export price, which is 125 ((50 + 100 + 150 + 200)/4). This will result in dumping of 25 per export transaction.

The wording of Article 2.2.1 leave much discretion to the national authorities to determine whether low costs sales should be excluded; note the term 'may'. The discretion may have a huge impact in the dumping determination.

Consider this situation: The producer has just introduced a new product type into the market. The producer decides that the unit price must be the same as for the two older types, which is EUR 100 per unit. For the new product, there have been quite high sunk costs, and the average unit cost for the first year is 150. The other two types of product both have average unit costs of EUR 50. All three types of product are sold in equal volume, i.e., the new product exceeds the 20% rule.

If the sales below costs test can be made for each type, *all* the domestic transactions of the new product can be disregarded. If the export price is the same, i.e., 100, and the domestic price for the new product is instead constructed – based on costs, SAG and profits – then dumping occurs. However, if no distinction between the three types can be made, costs can be spread over the three types. Then unit cost will be 83.33 ((50 + 50 + 150)/3) – less than 100 – and the domestic prices for the new product cannot be disregarded.

Didier finds it problematic that it is not provided that the burden of proof should be on the investigating parties; therefore, some investigating authorities put the burden of proof on the producers.[9]

8. See E. Vermulst, *The WTO Anti-dumping Agreement* (Oxford: Oxford University Press, 2005b), 22-23.
9. See P. Didier, 'The WTO Anti-dumping Code and EC Practice – Issues for Review in Trade Negotiations', *Journal of World Trade*, 35 (1) (2001): 35.

4.1.1.3 Like Product

Normal value is based on a price of a product 'like' the allegedly dumped product under investigation.

A domestic sale of chicken, for example, cannot be used as a standard of reference to the export of bananas. 'Like product' was discussed in the preceding chapter, where it was concluded that under WTO law it is defined in Article 2.6 of the ADA, and that according to practice the like product must have physical resemblance to the product exported.

4.1.1.4 Destined for Consumption in the Exporting Country

Pursuant to Article 2.1 and Article VI of GATT 1994, the prices must originate from the like product destined for consumption in the exporting country. The meaning of 'destined for consumption in the exporting country' is not elaborated on in the text.

The notion 'exporting country' needs further clarification in situations where the actual exports do not come from the country of the production of the product under investigation. Such sales occur when the product is not imported directly from the country of origin, i.e., where the product originates from. The imports come, rather, from an intermediary country. For example, if Indian producers export bed linen to buyers in Thailand, and those buyers re-export the bed linen to importers in the EU, the question will be whether the normal value is to be based on either:

- the domestic prices from transactions in the country of origin, i.e., prices from transactions between the Indian producer and Indian buyers; or
- the domestic prices from transaction in the country of transhipment, i.e., prices between the Thai importer and its domestic buyers.

Article 2.5 of the ADA regards those issues, and it reads:

> In the case where products are not imported directly from the country of origin but are exported to the importing Member from an intermediate country, the price at which the products are sold from the country of export to the importing Member shall normally be compared with the comparable price in the country of export. However, comparison may be made with the price in the country of origin, if, for example, the products are merely transshipped through the country of export, or such products are not produced in the country of export, or there is no comparable price for them in the country of export.

In cases where the export takes place from a country other than the one where the product is actually produced, the normal value will normally be based on the prices from the *exporting country*. Referring to the above example, normal value is based on prices from domestic transactions in Thailand. This rule may be exempted from, and the price be based on, domestic transactions in the country of origin, i.e., the domestic prices in sales between the Indian producer and the Indian buyers if, *for example*, the export country serves as a transhipment destination, the products are not produced in the exporting country or the prices are not comparable in the exporting country.

It is not clear whether the term 'for example' suggests that the list for exempting from the general rule is or is not exhaustive.

4.1.2 Practice by Panels and Appellate Body

In the following section, the practice by Panels and Appellate Body on the general rules on normal value will be examined in order to provide a clearer frame of WTO law on normal value. It is settled practice that normal value is based on the actual domestic prices from transactions in the exporting country; only when criteria in Article 2.2 are met may normal value be based on alternatives.[10] In this section, the practice of disregarding domestic transactions is discussed, where Article 2.1 is the point of departure.

First, a number of general statements regarding Article VI.1 of GATT 1994 and Article 2.1 by the Appellate Body are presented. Next, practices relating to the general rules on normal value and to the exclusions of the actual domestic transactions are examined. Practice relating to 'like product' is not part of the discussion – see more in Chapter 3.

4.1.2.1 General Statements about Article VI of GATT 1994, Article 2.1 of the ADA and Normal Value

The question in this section is whether there is a general outline for circumstances where domestic transactions shall be included in the normal value determination and circumstances for disregarding domestic prices from the normal value.

The starting point is Article VI of GATT 1994 and Article 2.1 of the ADA, which do not directly define normal value. In *US – Hot-Rolled Steel*, the Appellate Body stated:

> The text of Article 2.1 expressly imposes four conditions on sales transactions in order that they may be used to calculate normal value: first, the sale must be 'in the ordinary course of trade'; second, it must be of the 'like product'; third, the product must be 'destined for consumption in the exporting country'; and, fourth, the price must be 'comparable'.[11]

The Appellate Body further stated that the four conditions are exhaustive and that sales cannot be disregarded for other than the four conditions.[12] If all four conditions are met by the transaction, the prices from the transaction shall be used to

10. See Panel and Appellate Body practice in Section 4.2.2.1 below.
11. *US – Hot-Rolled Steel*, WT/DS184/AB/R, report of the Appellate Body on 24 Jul. 2001, para. 165.
12. Para. 166.

determine normal value.[13] The Appellate Body furthermore states regarding the 'ordinary course of trade' condition that if a sale does not take place in the ordinary course of trade, it must be disregarded.[14] It must be supposed that sales that are not 'of the like product', 'destined for consumption in the exporting country' or 'comparable' must also be disregarded. The reading of Article 2.1 by the Appellate Body therefore implies that the investigating authorities are required to determine the normal value on prices that are based on comparable prices of the like product made in the ordinary course of trade when destined for consumption in the ordinary course of trade. Investigating authorities must not delimit or add further conditions to the normal value determination.

However, a Panel stated in *Argentina – Poultry Anti-dumping Duties* that Article 2.1 of the ADA is silent about whether *all* domestic transactions shall be included in the normal value determination. The Panel then looked into Article 2.2.1 and found that under Article 2.1, together with Article 2.2.1, domestic prices may only be disregarded from the normal value determination under special circumstances provided in the text.[15] It is not clear whether the Panel refers to the circumstances provided in Article 2.1. The case dealt with issues over zeroing and is further described in Section 6.2.2.3.1.

The scope of application of Article 2.1 is not straightforward. In *US – Zeroing (Japan)*, the Appellate Body stated:

> Article 2.1 of the Anti-dumping Agreement and Article VI:1 of the GATT 1994 are definitional provisions. They set out a definition of 'dumping' for the purposes of the Anti-dumping Agreement and the GATT 1994. The definitions in Article 2.1 and Article VI:1 are no doubt central to the interpretation of other provisions of the Anti-dumping Agreement, such as the obligations relating to, inter alia, the calculation of margins of dumping, volume of dumped imports, and levy of anti-dumping duties to counteract injurious dumping. But, Article 2.1 and Article VI:1, read in isolation, do not impose independent obligations.[16]

According to this statement, Article VI.1 of GATT 1994 and Article 2.1 of the ADA do not impose obligations on the WTO Members. The statement is made by the Appellate Body about whether 'zeroing' is inconsistent with Article VI.1 of GATT 1994 and Article 2.1 of the ADA. Zeroing will be dealt with in Section 6.2. The statement is not made about the conditions for normal value. However, the statement seems to be very generally made about the (non-)obligatory character of those two provisions – and therefore it may imply that the four conditions cannot

---

13. See also Panel in *US – Oil Country Tubular Goods Sunset Reviews (Art. 21.5 – Argentina)*, WT/DS268/RW, report of the Panel on 30 Nov. 2006, para. 7.76.
14. Para. 139.
15. *Argentina – Poultry Anti-dumping Duties*, WT/DS241/R, report of the Panel on 22 Apr. 2003, para. 7.272.
16. *US – Zeroing (Japan)*, WT/DS322/AB/R, report of the Appellate Body on 9 Jan. 2007, para. 140.

independently serve as a basis for a claim of violation of the normal value determination. In other words: the conditions regarding normal value may be based on other provisions in the ADA, where Article 2.1 of ADA and Article VI.1 of GATT 1994 will only serve as an interpretation tool.

In other cases, Article 2.1 has indirectly served as a basis for determining the conditions of normal value. See for example Appellate Body in *EC – Tube or Pipe Fittings:*

> Article 2.1 of the Anti-dumping Agreement identifies a product as 'dumped' where the product is introduced into the commerce of another country at 'less than its normal value'. 'Normal value' is understood by virtue of that provision to be the 'price, in the ordinary course of trade, for the like product when destined for consumption in the exporting country'.[17]

In *US – Oil Country Tubular Goods Sunset Reviews (Article 21.5 – Argentina),* a Panel stated:

> As Article 2.1 makes clear, the starting point for normal value is 'the comparable price, in the ordinary course of trade' for the like product when destined for consumption in the exporting country.[18]

According to this Panel, the four conditions in Article 2.1 are the starting point in the determination of normal value. It is not apparent whether the Panel would also allow further conditions to determine normal value.

The problem here is the unclear scope of discretion left to the national authorities to determine whether domestic transactions should be disregarded or not. It cannot be solely concluded that the four conditions in Article VI.1 of GATT 1994 and Article 2.1 are exhaustive if the provision does not in itself impose obligations on the national authorities, and it is then not clear what the exact criteria are. However, the practice in each of the four conditions is described in the following sections.

4.1.2.2 Comparable Prices

The first condition in Article VI.1(a) and Article 2.1 of the ADA is for normal value to be based on prices comparable with the export price. As stated above, Article 2.2 offers some guidance, as prices from sales in a particular market or insufficient sales may not be regarded as comparable. Furthermore, Article 2.4 of ADA is an adjustment mechanism, which ensures that prices that may contain some differences affecting price comparability are made comparable.[19]

---

17. *EC – Tube or Pipe Fittings*; WT/DS219/AB/R, report of Appellate Body 22 Jul. 2003, para. 93.
18. *US – Oil Country Tubular Goods Sunset Reviews (Art. 21.5 – Argentina)*, WT/DS268/RW, report of the Panel on 30 Nov. 2006, para. 7.76.
19. *US – Hot-Rolled Steel*, WT/DS184/AB/R, report of the Appellate Body on 24 Jul. 2001, para. 167.

Even though Article 2.2 mentions a particular market situation, as well as low-volume sales as situations where prices will not be comparable, it may not exhaust the term 'comparable' in Article 2.1. As stated by the Appellate Body in *US – Hot-Rolled Steel*, Article 2.2 deals with the construction of normal value when there are no sales of the like product in the ordinary course of trade, or when the domestic price is not comparable due to a particular market situation or low-volume sales. The test by the Appellate Body is to evaluate domestic transactions under Article 2.1 and disregard sales that are not comparable with the export price. If such non-comparable sales can be categorized under one of the two groups in Article 2.2, the price must be based on one of the methods provided in Article 2.2[20]

The question is, however, whether the investigating authorities are required to consult Article 2.4 before concluding that prices are not comparable. This question needs to be clarified in practice.

A particular market situation has not been tested by a WTO body. However, it was tested by a GATT Panel in *EC – Cotton Yarn*. Brazil claimed that the normal value determination by the EU authorities should not be based on prices from domestic transactions, due to a particular market situation in Brazil. Due to high inflation in Brazil, the Brazil Cruzeiro (Cr) dollar had been frozen to the US dollar. As export sales were paid in USD and inflation continued, the prices from domestic transactions should then be disregarded due to the particular market situation in Brazil.[21] EU rejected the Brazilian argument and claimed that only if the freezing of the exchange rate had an impact on the domestic prices could such prices be disregarded.[22]

The Panel noted that the particular market situation itself was not a basis for disregarding domestic prices. Rather, it was only if the particular market situation had an impact on the domestic prices and if there were '*something intrinsic to the nature of the sales themselves that dictates they cannot permit a proper comparison*'[23] that the sales were to be disregarded.

As Brazil had not been able to demonstrate that the special market situation had an impact on the domestic prices, the Brazilian claim was dismissed by the Panel.[24]

The statement by the Panel suggests that the actual domestic prices must be preferred, even though a particular market exists, if the domestic prices from transactions on such a particular market are comparable with the export price. Only if the particular market has an impact on the domestic prices, such that such prices cannot be compared to the export price, must such prices be disregarded.

Low-volume sales has not been clarified in WTO practice. However, in *US – Softwood Lumber V (Article 21.5 – Canada)*, the Appellate Body stated that 'there

20. Ibid., para. 163.
21. *EC – Cotton Yarn*, ADP/137, report of the Panel on 4 Jul. 1995, paras 467-469.
22. Para. 472.
23. Para. 478.
24. Paras 479 and 483.

is nothing in the text of Article 2.2 that prohibits an investigating authority from dividing the product under investigation into product types or models'.[25]

The challenge with the statement comes when taking footnote 2 to Article 2.2 into account. It is provided that the 5% test is made for the 'product under consideration'. This opens up the question of whether the 5% test can be done for particular types, or whether the 5% low-volume test must be made for the overall product under consideration. There are obvious differences between a 5% test of the product as such and of the type-to-type differentiated products.

For example, the producer makes three types of products:

- type A, with a domestic sale of 6 units and export of 100 units;
- type B, also with a domestic sale of 6 units and export of 100 units; and
- type C, with a domestic sale of 4 units and export of 100 units.

From the type-to-type based calculation, both type A and B will be 6% of the export sales, and therefore they must be sold in sufficient quantities on the domestic market to be comparable with the export prices. Type C will only be 4% of the export sales and must be disregarded. If the 5% test is only applicable to the 'product under consideration' as such, the picture will be different. For all types A, B and C, there will be a domestic sale of 16 units. The export sales will be 300 units. The domestic sales will then be 5.333% of the export sales, and therefore all the domestic sales must be included in the normal value.

From a textual approach, the 5% test should be done for the overall product under consideration – not the different types. This reading is supported by Vermulst.[26]

This reading of the footnote regarding Article 2.2 may be in conflict with the statement by the Appellate Body if the statement is meant as a general expression of Article 2.2 in relation to differentiation of the product under consideration into different types. Therefore, the Appellate Body should make further clarification in this regard.

It must be emphasized that the statement by the Appellate Body in *US – Softwood Lumber V (Article 21.5 – Canada)* is made about an interpretation of Article 2.4.2, where Article 2.2 serves as the context – therefore the statement by the Appellate Body must be seen in this light. It is not further elaborated whether the statement implies that product differentiation can take place at all steps in the dumping determination – therefore the statement raises a number of questions. The fact that products can be divided into different types during the investigation is in line with the findings in Chapter 3 and with Article 2.4.2 practice, where investigating authorities may make multiple margins for different types under the weighted-average-to-weighted-average method.[27]

---

25. *US – Softwood LumberV. (Art. 21.5 – Canada)*, WT/DS264/AB/RW, report of the Appellate Body on 15 Aug. 2006, para. 104.
26. See E. Vermulst, *The WTO Anti-dumping Agreement* (Oxford: Oxford University Press, 2005b), 30-32.
27. See *US – Softwood Lumber V*, WT/DS264/AB/R, report of the Appellate Body on 11 Aug. 2004, para. 80. See more in Ch. 6 below.

Under the EU section, it will be further discussed whether the 5% test can be type-to-type-based. For now, it is sufficient to conclude that practice regarding the comparability of the normal value with the export price is very limited.

4.1.2.3 Ordinary Course of Trade

The second normal value condition under Article VI.1 of GATT 1994 and Article 2.1 of ADA is the requirement that normal value be based on sales made in the ordinary course of trade. The concept of 'ordinary course of trade' is not clearly defined in GATT 1994 or in the ADA. The Appellate Body has shed some light on the term 'ordinary course of trade'. In *US – Hot-Rolled Steel*, the Appellate Body found:

> Investigating authorities *must* exclude, from the calculation of normal value, all sales which are not made 'in the ordinary course of trade'.[28] (Emphasis added)

On a general level, the Appellate Body states that domestic sales not made in the ordinary course of trade must be disregarded in the normal value determination. The condition mentioned in Article 2.1 is not an option for the investigating authorities to include or exclude sales not made in the ordinary course of trade.

The question is, then, what constitutes a sale made inside/outside the ordinary course of trade? Above, some guidance was found in Article 2.2.1 of the ADA, where sales below costs and SAG may be regarded as not having taken place in the ordinary course of trade. The Appellate Body stated in *US – Hot-Rolled Steel* that the methods mentioned in Article 2.2.1 do not constitute an exhaustive list of the range of those available to determine whether a transaction between two parties is made in the ordinary course of trade or not.[29] 'Ordinary course of trade' is therefore a wider concept than just sales below costs situations in Article 2.2.1.

In the following sections, a number of criteria from the *US – Hot-Rolled Steel* case about the determination of 'ordinary course of trade' will be examined. So far, *US – Hot-Rolled Steel* is the only case that has dealt with matters about ordinary course of trade.

4.1.2.3.1 A Definition of Ordinary Course of Trade

In *US – Hot-Rolled Steel*, the Appellate Body accepted a definition of 'ordinary course of trade' provided by the USDOC. The Appellate Body stated:

> The Anti-dumping Agreement does not define the term 'in the ordinary course of trade'. Before the Panel, Japan referred with approval to the definition of this term given by USDOC in its questionnaire and, *for the purposes of this*

28. *US – Hot-Rolled Steel*, WT/DS184/AB/R, report of Appellate Body on 24 Jul. 2001, para. 145.
29. Para. 147.

> *appeal, we are content to work with this definition.* That USDOC definition states:
>
> Generally, sales are in the ordinary course of trade if made under conditions and practices that, for a reasonable period of time prior to the date of sale of the subject merchandise, have been normal for sales of the foreign like product.
>
> *In terms of the above definition*, Article 2.1 requires investigating authorities to exclude sales not made 'in the ordinary course of trade', from the calculation of normal value, *precisely to ensure that normal value is, indeed, the 'normal' price of the like product, in the home market of the exporter. Where a sales transaction is concluded on terms and conditions that are incompatible with 'normal' commercial practice for sales of the like product, in the market in question, at the relevant time, the transaction is not an appropriate basis for calculating 'normal' value.*[30] (Emphasis added)

The Appellate Body refers to the definition provided by the USDOC and will 'work' with this definition. The definition is then used in combination with Article 2.1 of the ADA, according to which transactions that fall outside the definition provided by the USDOC must be excluded from the investigation. Those are transactions which are considered outside of 'normal' commercial practice. The Appellate Body later states that the ADA affords the WTO Members discretionary powers to determine whether sales take place in the ordinary course of sale or whether they fall outside the scope of ordinary course of sale.[31]

The definition by the USDOC is made up of four criteria:

- The conditions for the sale must be normal in the light of other sales of the like product in the market.
- The practice in the sale between the parties must be normal in light of the practice in other sales.
- The conditions and practice must have been normal for a reasonable period of time prior to the date of sale of the product under investigation. The normality must be seen in light of the practice in the market in some time.
- The sale is of the like product.

These four criteria are very generally formulated. They include the two 'normality' criteria, which are in line with the statement by the Appellate Body that ordinary course of trade price must be 'normal'. The USDOC definition further includes that normality must be based on practice over a reasonable period of time. The like product criterion is already found in one of the four conditions in Article 2.1 of the ADA.

The wide discretion allowing the investigating authorities to define ordinary course of trade is not without limits. The Appellate Body stated that the ordinary

30. Paras 139-140.
31. Para. 148.

course of trade criterion is intended to ensure that the normal value is 'indeed, the "normal" price of the like product'. The criteria to define ordinary course of trade must assure that prices from 'normal' transactions between the producer and the domestic buyer are reflected in the normal value, whereas prices from abnormal transactions must be excluded. The Appellate Body provided some examples of sales that may not be in the ordinary course of trade:[32]

- Sales between companies with 'common ownership'. They may be legally distinct persons.
- Sales between parties with common control.
- Sales where prices are below or higher than the market prices. However, the 'ordinary course of trade' evaluation cannot be based solely on a comparison between market prices and prices from transactions, which are examined under the ordinary course of trade test; see more on this below.
- Sales between totally independent parties may be outside the ordinary course of trade, for example, a liquidation sale.

The Appellate Body further stated:

> Clearly, the lower the degree of common ownership, implying common control, between the parties to a sales transaction, the less likely it is that the transaction will not be 'in the ordinary course of trade'.[33]

According to the Appellate Body, sales between associated partners may be disregarded because they are not made in the ordinary course of trade. The closer the legal or financial bond between the producer and the domestic buyer, the greater the likelihood that sales between them are not in the ordinary course of trade. After Article 2.1, such sales should be disregarded. However, the examples provided by the Appellate Body are not a negative demarcation of 'ordinary course of trade'. Sales between parties with, for example, common control, may still be ordinary. It is not sufficient to make a per se exclusion of some sales without looking into the character of the sale; see more in the next paragraph about testing the sale. The Appellate Body just gives some guidance about the likelihood for sales being outside the ordinary course of trade.

It is also apparent that the Appellate Body will not label any sales as not being in the ordinary course of trade per se. Furthermore, it can be argued – as in the next paragraph – that, at a minimum, associates must have the opportunity to demonstrate that sales between them are in fact made in the ordinary course of trade.

Although it is not clear whether this definition will work in other cases, the requirement for normality in the transactions is the yardstick by which ordinary course of trade is determined. The next paragraph deals with the test used to determine whether the ordinary course of trade condition is met.

32. Paras 141-143.
33. Para. 143.

4.1.2.3.2 Tests to Determine Ordinary Course of Trade

In *US – Hot-Rolled Steel*, the USDOC used an 'arms-length' test to determine whether sales between associated parties took place in the ordinary course of trade. The USDOC would find the weighted average sales prices from the producer to an associate. If this amount was 99.5% or less of the weighted-average sales price from the producer to all un-associated parties – the so-called 'ordinary course of trade price' – all the sales between the producer and the associate would be disregarded as being not in the ordinary course of trade.

According to the US, the 99.5% threshold would indicate that the affiliation between the producer and the associated party had affected the price between them. However, the arms-length test would only indicate whether the sales price between the associates would be lower than the reference sales – not higher, as only sales with prices lower than the ordinary course of trade price were included.[34] The Appellate Body stated:

> We note that determining whether a sales price is higher or lower than the 'ordinary course' price is not simply a question of comparing prices. Price is merely one of the terms and conditions of a transaction. *To determine whether the price is high or low, the price must be assessed in light of the other terms and conditions of the transaction.* Thus, the volume of the sales transaction will affect whether a price is high or low. Or, the seller may undertake additional liability or responsibilities in some transactions, for example for transport or insurance. These, and a number of other factors, may be expected to affect an assessment of the price.[35] (Emphasis added)

The investigating authorities may find an 'ordinary course of trade price' as a basis for testing the 'normality' of a sales transaction. Differences between such a test price and the sales prices between the producer and domestic buyer can be explained by several reasons, and the investigating authorities must these take into account. A simple comparison between the 'ordinary course' price and the actual price is not a sufficient test to determine whether sales are inside or outside the ordinary course of trade.[36] Therefore, a test must include an examination of reasons behind any lower prices than the ordinary course of trade price; this may – in spite of the affiliation – be explained by normal market conditions.

There can be many reasons why the price would be lower than sales between unrelated parties. For example, if the exporter and the associated party are able to economize their transaction costs between them due to a close relationship, the sales price between them will then become lower. A lower price between two associates that is based on cost efficiency may still be a result of the market forces.

---

34. See paras 131-132.
35. Para. 142.
36. See also J. P. Durling & M. R. Nicely, *Understanding the WTO Anti-dumping Agreement, Negotiation History and Subsequent Interpretation* (London: Cameron May, 2002), 29.

The Appellate Body further noted that the practice by the USDOC 'does not involve any right for an exporter to demonstrate that sales to affiliates were, in the light of all of the circumstances, actually in the ordinary course of trade, even though they fell below the 0.5% downward range'.[37] A test to determine 'ordinary course of trade' cannot automatically exclude some sorts of sales without giving the producer and domestic buyer the opportunity to demonstrate that the transactions between them are made in the ordinary course of trade. The statement by the Appellate Body further supports the above claim that some types of sales cannot per se be disregarded as not taking place in the ordinary course of trade.

The next step for the Appellate Body was to focus on the different approaches by the USDOC to low-price sales and high-price sales between associates. The low-price sales would be tried according to the arms-length test, whereas high-price sales – prices higher than the ordinary course of trade price – would only be disregarded if the producer demonstrated that such prices were 'aberrationally' or 'artificially' high.[38] The inclusion of high prices and exclusion of low prices in the normal value determination will raise the normal value – and thereby the likelihood of dumping.

The Appellate Body commented on the burden on the producers to demonstrate that prices were artificially high and noted that, under Article 2.1. it is the investigating authorities – not the producers – that must ensure that the normal value is based on sales made in the ordinary course of trade. Therefore, it is doubtful to place the burden on the producers.[39]

Finally, the Appellate Body compared the two methods for low and high prices and stated:

> In our view, there is a lack of even-handedness in the two tests applied by the United States, in this case, to establish whether sales made to affiliates were 'in the ordinary course of trade'. The combined application of these two rules operated systematically to raise normal value, through the automatic exclusion of marginally low-priced sales, coupled with the automatic inclusion of all high-priced sales, except those proved, upon request, to be aberrationally high priced. The application of the two tests, thereby, disadvantaged exporters.[40]

The Appellate Body refers to the fairness principle in the normal value determination. Investigating authorities cannot on one hand refuse low-price sales from the normal value and on the other hand include high price sales. The test must be even-handed for both low- and high-price sales. The Appellate Body states in a footnote that the fairness principle does not require that the tests to verify low- and high-price must be identical.[41] This may be seen in the light of the above statements about the different reasons behind low or high prices.

---

37. Para. 149.
38. Para. 151.
39. Para. 153.
40. Para. 154.
41. See n. 113.

In sum, the findings in *US – Hot-Rolled Steel* indicate that 'ordinary course of trade' is defined as transactions taking place in normal trade. To test whether such a transaction is normal, the national authorities cannot rely only on a simple comparison of prices from some types of transactions with prices from other types of transactions, for example between associates. The test requires some flexibility where normality may be proved present, although the prices are higher or lower than the ordinary course of trade price. The test also implies the fairness principle. National authorities cannot treat some information in one way and then disregard the same information in another, just to be able to disregard the transaction as not ordinary.

4.1.2.4 Destined for Consumption in the Exporting Country

The fourth and final condition in Article VI.1 (a) and Article 2.1 of the ADA is the requirement that:

- the product must be destined for consumption, and
- it is in the exporting country.

In transhipment situations, where the product is not imported from the country of origin, but comes from an intermediary country, Article 2.5 offers guidelines stating as a rule that normal value shall be based on prices from the actual exporting country.

There is no practice to clarify the terms 'consumption' and 'exporting country'. The only statement about Article 2.5 is found by a Panel in *US – Hot-Rolled Steel*, where the Panel in a footnote found that '[a]rticle 2.5 deals with the situation where the products are not imported from the country of origin directly'.[42] This statement does not shed any light on the term 'exporting country'.

4.1.2.5 Replacing Price in Downstream Sales between Associates

The text in the ADA and Article VI of GATT 1994 does not clearly rule on how domestic transactions between a producer and an associated buyer must be dealt with. Above, it was seen that the Appellate Body found that such transactions could fall outside the ordinary course of trade requirement. The Appellate Body, however, has had a different approach to sales between associated parties if the sales could be categorized as 'downstream sales'. The product is *resold* by the associated domestic buyer to an independent customer in the exporting market. Downstream sales are not to be confused with situations where the associated buyer uses the product as an intermediary part in his own production.

In *US – Hot-Rolled Steel*, a downstream situation was tried before the Appellate Body. In the particular case, the investigating authority replaced the prices from the domestic sales between the producer and the associated partner with the

42. *US – Hot-Rolled Steel*, WT/DS184/R, report of the Panel on 28 Feb. 2001, n. 88 re para. 7.116.

prices from the sale between the associated buyer and first independent buyer. Japan argued that such a replacement was not permissible under Article 2.1, and that the actual price between the producer and the associate was the proper domestic price. A Panel supported the Japanese argument.[43]

The Appellate Body reversed the Panel's findings. The Appellate Body referred to Article 2.1 and mentioned the four conditions. It then stated:

> In our view, provided that all of the explicit conditions in Article 2.1 of the Anti-dumping Agreement are satisfied, the identity of the seller of the 'like product' is not a ground for precluding the use of a downstream sales transaction when calculating normal value. In short, we see no reason to read into Article 2.1 an additional condition that is not expressed.[44]

Normal value may then be based on the price paid by the first independent buyer. The Appellate Body makes a narrow interpretation of Article 2.1, and cannot find a legal basis for including the 'seller' as a condition.

The interpretation by the Appellate Body could seem like an open door inviting national authorities to use downstream prices in situations where such prices are higher than the actual domestic price asked by the producer. The Appellate Body, however, set up a limitation to such practice by referring to Article 2.4 of the ADA:

> We do not mean to suggest that the identity of the seller is irrelevant in calculating normal value under Article 2.1 of the Anti-dumping Agreement. *However, to ensure that prices are 'comparable', the Anti-dumping Agreement provides a mechanism, in Article 2.4, which allows investigating authorities to take full account of the fact, as appropriate, that a relevant sale was not made by the exporter or producer itself, but was made by another party. Article 2.4 requires that a 'fair comparison' be made between export price and normal value*. This comparison 'shall be made at the same level of trade, normally at the ex-factory level'. In making a 'fair comparison', Article 2.4 mandates that due account be taken of 'differences which affect price comparability', such as differences in the 'levels of trade' at which normal value and export price are calculated.[45] (Emphasis added)

Pursuant to Article 2.4 of the ADA, allowances shall be made when prices from downstream sales replace the prices from sales between the producer and the associated buyer. For example, the resale price may be higher than the price between the producer and the associated buyer due to extra costs from having the associated buyer as an intermediary party, whereas the export price may be based on the actual price between the producer and the importer without such extra costs.

43. Ibid., paras 7.113-7.114.
44. *US – Hot-Rolled Steel*, WT/DS184/AB/R, report of Appellate Body on 24 Jul. 2001, para. 166.
45. Para. 167.

In the Panel report, the Panel referred to Article 6.10 about the general rule that dumping margins are made for each individual producer, in support of rejecting the method applied by the USDOC.[46] The Appellate Body also refused the reference to Article 6.10. The rejection was based on the fact that even though the downstream prices are used, it is still possible to make an individual margin for the exporter or producer concerned.[47]

Japan – and the Panel – referred to Article 2.3 as a context to support the rejection of using replacement prices as normal value. Article 2.3 of the ADA provides that downstream sales prices can be used in the export price determination. This is also provided in the 'Hidden Dumping' note added to Article VI.1 of GATT 1994. There is no express reference to replacement prices to the normal value in Article 2.1 – or in the alternatives in Article 2.2 – and therefore the drafters of the ADA have not intended to disregard prices in downstream sales between the producer and the associated buyer.[48] Without any further elaboration, this interpretation of Article 2.1 and 2.3 was rejected by the Appellate Body, which was satisfied with the terms under Article 2.1.[49]

Under WTO law, the actual domestic prices between a producer and an associated buyer may be replaced by the price paid to the first independent customer, when normal value is determined.

The following sections deal with EU legislation and practice concerning general conditions for domestic prices in the normal value determination, in order to determine whether EU legislation and practice is in conformity with WTO law.

4.1.3 EU Legislation

The EU legislation on normal value is to some extent a reproduction of the WTO legislation, although the structure in EU legislation is quite different. Article 1.2 of the basic Regulation contains the general definition of dumping. It provides:

> A product is to be considered as being dumped if its export price to the Community is less than a comparable price for the like product, in the ordinary course of trade, as established for the exporting country.

The definition of dumping provides a comparison between the export price and

(1) a comparable price;
(2) of the like product;
(3) in the ordinary course of trade;
(4) in the exporting country.

---

46. Para. 7.114 of the Panel report.
47. Para. 170 of the Appellate Body report.
48. Para. 7.117 of the Panel report.
49. Para. 171 of the Appellate Body report.

The conditions for normal value are nearly the same as under WTO law. The difference is that under WTO law, the definition of dumping – and the indirect definition of normal value – implies the condition of 'destined for consumption', which is not found under the EU dumping definition. That condition is, however, found elsewhere in the basic Regulation.

Under EU law, the requirements for normal value are explicitly provided in Article 2.1, first sentence:

> The normal value shall normally be based on the prices paid or payable, in the ordinary course of trade, by independent customers in the exporting country.

This goes one step further than the WTO legislation, where it is not explicitly written into the legislation that normal value is based on the prices from transactions in the ordinary course of trade to independent customers. Article 2.1 further reads:

> However, where the exporter in the exporting country does not produce or does not sell the like product, the normal value may be established on the basis of prices of other sellers or producers.
>
> Prices between parties which appear to be associated or to have a compensatory arrangement with each other may not be considered to be in the ordinary course of trade and may not be used to establish normal value unless it is determined that they are unaffected by the relationship.
>
> In order to determine whether two parties are associated account may be taken of the definition of related parties set out in Article 143 of Commission Regulation (EEC) 2454/93 of 2 July 1993 laying down provisions for the implementation of Council Regulation (EEC) No. 2913/92 establishing the Community Customs Code(6).

The conditions of normal value as found under Article 1.2 and Article 2.1 of the Basic Regulation will be described in the following section.

4.1.3.1 The Price Is Based on Sales to Independent Customers

As a rule, normal value must be based on prices to independent customers, cf. Article 2.1. This condition is not found in the WTO legislation. It must be noted that Article 2.1 in this regard opens up to some discretion, as the normal value must 'normally' be based on such prices. Concerning WTO law – in particular the findings by Appellate Body in *US – Hot-Rolled Steel* – it would not be in conformity with WTO law to disregard prices between associated parties without a proper examination of whether such sales are in fact in the ordinary course of trade. It must be assumed from the term 'normally' that the rule in Article 2.1 of the basic Regulation can be waived.

4.1.3.2 Comparability between Normal Value and Export Price

Pursuant to Article 1.2 of the basic Regulation, the normal value must be comparable with the export price. Dumped prices that are not comparable with the export price will be disregarded in the normal value determination. There is no definition of what constitutes 'comparable sales' under Article 1.2.

Article 2.3 offers some guidance, as it provides that when there is a *particular market situation*, prices from sales of the like product do not permit proper comparison with the export price. This is in line with the WTO text in Article 2.2 of the ADA.

The particular market situation is further clarified in the second sentence of Article 2.3 of the basic Regulation. A particular market situation 'may be deemed to exist, inter alia, when prices are artificially low, when there is significant barter trade, or when there are non-commercial processing arrangements'. In recital 3 to Regulation 1972/2002 amending the basic Regulation, it is provided that the examples given in the sentence do not exclude the possibility that other types of 'particular market situations' may exist. Recital 3 also provides guidelines about when a market is 'a particular market':

> This would be situations, where demand and supply are not well reflected in the market signals, and thereby can have an impact on the determination of prices and costs.

According to GATT practice, prices from such a particular market are only to be excluded in the normal value determination if the prices affect the comparability with the export price. Therefore, the examples of particular markets in the EU text, which are also only 'deemed to exist', cannot be used as justification for disregarding prices per se unless the comparability is affected.

4.1.3.3 Ordinary Course of Trade

The prices must come from sales in the ordinary course of trade between the producer and the domestic buyer. The term 'ordinary course of trade' is not defined, but some examples of sales not in the ordinary course of trade are found elsewhere in Article 2.1, third sentence. Sales between associated parties, or sales between parties with a compensatory agreement, may not be considered as having taken place in the ordinary course of trade. In Article 2.4, sales below costs may be excluded as sales not made in the ordinary course of trade. The sales in connection with association and sales below costs are elaborated on in the following.

4.1.3.3.1 Sales between Associated Parties

Domestic sales between associated parties will be left out of the investigation as not made in the ordinary course of trade unless it is demonstrated by the associated parties, or by the parties having a compensatory agreement, that the price between them is unaffected by their relationship. When the term 'associated' is determined, account may be taken of the definition of 'related parties' set out in Article 143 of Commission Regulation (EEC) 2454/93 of 2 July 1993, laying down provisions for the implementation of Council Regulation (EEC) No. 2913/92 establishing the

Community Customs Code; see Article 2.1, fourth sentence.[50] Article 143 provides:

1. Persons shall be deemed to be related only if:

   (a) they are officers or directors of one another's businesses; (b) they are legally recognized partners in business; (c) they are employer and employee; (d) any person directly or indirectly owns, controls or holds 5 % or more of the outstanding voting stock or shares of both of them; (e) one of them directly or indirectly controls the other; (f) both of them are directly or indirectly controlled by a third person; (g) together they directly or indirectly control a third person; or (h) they are members of the same family. Persons shall be deemed to be members of the same family only if they stand in any of the following relationships to one another: – husband and wife, – parent and child, – brother and sister (whether by whole or half blood), – grandparent and grandchild, – uncle or aunt and nephew or niece, – parent-in-law and son-in-law or daughter-in-law, – brother-in-law and sister-in-law.

2. For the purposes of this title, persons who are associated in business with one another in that one is the sole agent, sole distributor or sole concessionaire, however described, of the other shall be deemed to be related only if they fall within the criteria of paragraph 1.

There is wide discretion under WTO law for determining ordinary course of trade, which may be situations with association. However, it must be observed that the association cannot by itself serve as a basis for excluding sales as not being in the ordinary course of trade. If the associates are able to demonstrate that the relatedness is not affecting the price, the sales will be regarded as ordinary.

It is not clear from the EU legislation how the first and third sentences of Article 2.1 are related. In the first sentence, it is provided that the normal value is based on prices made in the ordinary course of trade to independent of customers. That could exclude transactions made between a producer and a dependent customer per se. In the third sentence, it is provided that sale from a producer to an associated buyer is not regarded as being part of the ordinary course of trade, unless the associated parties can demonstrate that the interrelationship has no effect on the price. Does the difference in terminology 'independent customer' and 'associated parties' imply that the producer and *dependent customer* are not offered the opportunity to demonstrate that the price is not affected by the dependence between them? In my view, the dependence between the producer and a domestic customer will fall under the definition of associated parties. It would therefore be appropriate

50. Art. 1.1 of the Council Regulation 1972/2002 amending the basic Regulation adds to Art. 2.1 of the basic Regulation that in the determination of 'associated parties' the definition of related parties set out in Art. 143 of Commission Regulation (EEC) 2454/93 of 2 Jul. 1993 laying down provisions for the implementation of Council Regulation (EEC) No. 2913/92 establishing the Community Customs Code(6).

if EU legislators would correct this legislative detail, which might otherwise lead to confusion.

4.1.3.3.2 Sales below Costs and SAG

Article 2.4 of the basic Regulation regulates the circumstances under which sales below costs may be disregarded as not being in the ordinary course of trade. Article 2.4 reads:

> Sales of the like product in the domestic market of the exporting country, or export sales to a third country, at prices below unit production costs (fixed and variable) plus selling, general and administrative costs may be treated as not being in the ordinary course of trade by reason of price, and may be disregarded in determining normal value, only if it is determined that such sales are made within an extended period in substantial quantities, and are at prices which do not provide for the recovery of all costs within a reasonable period of time.
>
> If prices which are below costs at the time of sale are above weighted average costs for the period of investigation, such prices shall be considered to provide for recovery of costs within a reasonable period of time.
>
> The extended period of time shall normally be one year but shall in no case be less than six months, and sales below unit cost shall be considered to be made in substantial quantities within such a period when it is established that the weighted average selling price is below the weighted average unit cost, or that the volume of sales below unit cost is not less than 20 % of sales being used to determine normal value.

The wording of Article 2.4 of the basic Regulation is nearly identical to that of Article 2.2.1 of the ADA. The footnote to Article 2.2.1 of the ADA, about the extended period and the substantial quantities, has been written into Article 2.4, third sentence, of the basic Regulation.

Rather, the WTO codified a longstanding EU practice, where there was a 20% threshold about substantial quantity.[51]

Sales below costs are only regarded as not being in the ordinary course of trade in the following situations:

- The sales below costs are made within an extended period. This extended period of time will normally be one year. The period can be less than one year, but shall in no case be less than six months. Thus, the Commission and the Council cannot disregard sales below costs if they are not made in this extended period of time.
- The sales must be in substantial quantities within the extended period. The sales are made in substantial quantities when (1) the weighted average

51. See I. Van Bael & J. F. Bellis, *Anti-dumping and Other Trade Protection Laws of the EC*, 4th edn (The Hague: Kluwer Law International, 2004), 57.

selling price is below the weighted average unit costs, or (2) the volume of sales below costs is 20% or more of the sales used to determine the normal value.

– The prices below costs must not provide for recovery of all costs within a reasonable period of time. Such prices will make a recovery within a reasonable time if they are above the weighted average costs for the period of investigation.

The wordings are in line with the wordings provided by WTO law, Article 2.2.1, including footnotes, of the ADA.

4.1.3.4 Normal Value Shall Be Based on the Price in the Exporting Country

Pursuant to Article 1.2 and Article 2.1 of the basic Regulation, normal value is based on the price in the exporting country. In situations where the exports come from an intermediary country, like transhipment, Article 1.3 of the basic Regulation provides:

> The exporting country shall normally be the country of origin. However, it may be an intermediate country, except where, for example, the products are merely transhipped through that country, or the products concerned are not produced in that country, or there is no comparable price for them in that country.

Article 1.3, first sentence, lays down the general rule that the exporting country is the *country of origin*, and the normal value is based on the price from the country of origin. In situations involving direct export from a producer of the allegedly dumped product to EU importers, this provision does not cause doubts as to the conformity with WTO law.

The uncertainty of conformity of Article 1.3 in the basic Regulation with WTO law may instead arise in situations where the producer of the product exports to a third country, and from this country the product is re-exported to EU. For example, if an Indian producer of bed linen exports to Thailand and the Thai importers sell to EU importers, the EU wordings may indicate that the normal value is based on the prices in India instead of in Thailand. Such an interpretation of the EU legislation may be in conflict with WTO law, where the general rule is that the intermediary country is regarded as the *exporting country*.

Article 1.3, second sentence, of the basic Regulation provides an exception to the general rule, as the intermediary country may be regarded as the *exporting country* unless the products are merely transhipped through that country, the products are not produced in the intermediary country, or there are no comparable prices in the intermediary country. The EU institutions may then grant exemptions from the general rule and base the normal value on prices from the intermediary country – in line with WTO law.

4.1.3.5 The Sale Must Be of the Like Product

The 'like product' is defined in Article 1.4 of the basic Regulation. In Chapter 3, it was demonstrated that 'like product' must share the same physical, chemical or technical characteristics as the product under investigation.

4.1.3.6 Low-Volume Sales

Article 2.2 of the basic Regulation concerns the requirement of domestic sales being representative in order to serve as a basis for normal value. Article 2.2 provides:

> Sales of the like product intended for domestic consumption shall normally be used to determine normal value if such sales volume constitutes 5 % or more of the sales volume of the product under consideration to the Community. However, a lower volume of sales may be used when, for example, the prices charged are considered representative for the market concerned.

Pursuant to Article 2.2 of the basic Regulation, sales below 5% of the export sales are generally regarded as insufficient to base normal value upon. Such sales may be disregarded.

The exclusion of sales below 5% of the export sales is in accordance with footnote 2 to Article 2.2 of the ADA. The only difference between EU and WTO law is that under WTO law, low-volume sales are regarded as not comparable with the export price. Under EU law, low-volume sales are not categorized as sales 'not permitting a proper comparison'. Instead, low-volume sales have their own category.

4.1.3.7 Destined for Consumption

Article 2.2 of the basic Regulation states that '[s]ales of the like product intended for domestic consumption shall normally be used to determine normal value'. An *a contrario* interpretation of this text could indicate that domestic sales not destined for consumption may be excluded. Such an interpretation of Article 2.2 finds support in Article 5.1, which requires that, in their application for initiation of an investigation, the EU producers must provide the Commission with information regarding the domestic prices 'at which the product in question is sold when destined for consumption in the domestic markets of the country or countries of origin or export'.

The 'destined for consumption' requirement under WTO law is apparently fulfilled by Article 2.2 and Article 5.1 of the basic Regulation.

4.1.4 EU Practice

In this section, the practice by the Commission, the Council and the EC courts on the general rules on normal value is examined. In practice, the general rule is to base normal value on the actual domestic prices between the producer and the domestic buyers if the sales are representative in the ordinary course of trade for the like product in the exporting country.[52] The EC courts have established that the alternative methods to determine normal value, which are described in Section 4.2, are only subsidiary to a normal value based on the actual domestic price.[53] The statement by the EC courts is in line with WTO law.[54]

In the following sections, the situations where domestic prices are disregarded from the normal value determination by the EU authorities are examined.

4.1.4.1 Comparable Prices

It is only on rare occasions that the Commission and the Council disregard the actual domestic prices for not being comparable with the export price. Mostly, the differences between normal value and export price are adjusted under Article 2.10 of the basic Regulation in order to make the prices comparable. See more about the adjustment of prices in Chapter 6.

The term 'comparable price' is not elaborated upon in EU legislation, but in Article 2.3 prices from 'particular market situations' are not regarded as comparable with the export price.

One example where the Commission and the Council referred to 'a particular market' in order to disregard domestic prices is *Polyester Stable Fibres I*. The producer sold polyester stable fibre as intermediary products to final product producers on the domestic market in the exporting country. The final product was then exported. The producers of polyester stable fibres did, however, get some export

52. *Synthetic Fibres of Polyesters I*, Council Regulation (EC) No. 907/97 of 20 May 1997 amending Regulation (EEC) No. 54/93 imposing a definitive anti-dumping duty on imports of synthetic fibres of polyesters originating in India and the Republic of Korea, OJ L 131, 23 May 1997, pp. 1-3; *Polyester Staple Fibres I*, Commission Regulation (EC) No. 1472/2000 of 6 Jul. 2000 imposing a provisional anti-dumping duty on imports of polyester staple fibres originating in India and the Republic of Korea, OJ L 166, 6 Jul. 2000, pp. 1-13, recitals 27-33, apparently endorsed in Council Regulation (EC) No. 2852/2000 of 22 Dec. 2000 imposing a definitive anti-dumping duty and definitively collecting the provisional duty imposed on imports of polyester staple fibres originating in India and the Republic of Korea, OJ L 332, 28 Dec. 2000, pp. 17-31; *Polyethylene Terephthalate Film*, Commission Regulation (EC) No. 367/2001 of 23 Feb. 2001 imposing a provisional anti-dumping duty on imports of PET film originating in India and the Republic of Korea, OJ L 55, 24 Feb. 2001, pp. 16-39, recitals 28-31, endorsed in Council Regulation (EC) No. 1676/2001 of 13 Aug. 2001 imposing a definitive anti-dumping duty and collecting definitively the provisional duty imposed on imports of PET film originating in India and the Republic of Korea, OJ L 227, 23 Aug. 2001, pp. 1-14, recital 14.
53. See *Canon I*, Joined cases 277/85 and 300/85, judgment of the EC Court of 5 Oct. 1988, ECR 1988, p. 5731, para. 11; *Matsushita I*, Case C-175/87, judgment of the EC Court of 10 Mar. 1992, ECR 1992, p. I-1409, para. 17; *Thai Bicycle Industry v. Council*, Case T-118/96, judgment of the Court of First Instance on 17 Jul. 1998, ECR 1998, p. II-2991, para. 46; *Matsushita II*, Case C-104/90, judgment of the EC Court of 13 Oct. 1993, ECR 1993, p. I-4981, paras 9-15; and *Ajinomoto and NutraSweet v. Council and Commission*, Joined cases C-76/98 P and C-77/98 P, judgment of the EC Court of 3 May 2001, ECR 2001, p. II-3223, para. 37.
54. See Section 4.2.2.1 below.

advantages, although their sales addressed the domestic market. The Council and the Commission argued that a 'particular market situation' existed because the transaction (local export sale) between the producer under investigation and the final producer was not subject to domestic sales tax, was normally invoiced in USD and paid for by letters of credit, and was subject to duty drawback arrangements. According to the Council and the Commission, this is evidence of a particular market situation. The actual domestic prices between the producer and the domestic buyers were then disregarded.[55]

Under WTO law, it follows from Article 2.1 that sales that are not comparable must be disregarded. Such a situation may be sales on 'a particular market', as 'such sales do not permit a proper comparison'. However, it is not sufficient that a particular market exists to disregard the transactions taking place on that particular market. The particular market situation must have an impact on the domestic prices, and there must be something intrinsic to the sales themselves that dictates they cannot serve as a proper comparison with the export price.[56] There seems to be no further conditions for disregarding prices as not being comparable, and it might leave wide discretionary powers to the investigating authorities to determine the comparability between the normal value and export price.

The question is, then, whether sales with state subsidies or tax allowances are not comparable with export prices. The Council Regulation does not elaborate on why the prices from the sales do not permit a proper comparison with the export price. It cannot be concluded on that basis that the practice in *Polyester Stable Fibres I* is in conformity with or in violation of WTO law. However, if the Council solely bases its conclusion on the elements characterizing the particular market situation and does not find a link between that situation and the domestic prices, it may violate WTO law.

4.1.4.2 Ordinary Course of Trade

The term 'ordinary course of trade' is not defined under EU law. Pursuant to EU legislation, sales between associated parties, or sales between parties with a compensatory arrangement, may be regarded as not taking place in the ordinary course of trade.[57] In practice, cases involving compensatory agreements are a rare phenomenon,[58] whereas associations are more common. Furthermore, sales

---

55. *Polyester Staple Fibres I*, Commission Regulation (EC) No. 1472/2000 of 6 Jul. 2000 imposing a provisional anti-dumping duty on imports of polyester staple fibres originating in India and the Republic of Korea, OJ L 166, 6 Jul. 2000, pp. 1-13 endorsed in Council Regulation (EC) No. 2852/2000 of 22 Dec. 2000 imposing a definitive anti-dumping duty and definitively collecting the provisional duty imposed on imports of polyester staple fibres originating in India and the Republic of Korea, OJ L 332, 28 Dec. 2000, pp. 17-31. See recital 29 of the Council Regulation.
56. *EC – Cotton Yarn*, ADP/137, report of Panel on 4 Jul. 1995, paras 467-469.
57. See Art. 2.1 of the basic Regulation.
58. See I. Van Bael & J.F. Bellis, *Anti-dumping and Other Trade Protection Laws of the EC*, 4th edn (The Hague: Kluwer Law International, 2004), 59. See as an example *Certain Polyester Yarn*, Council Regulation (EEC) No. 407/83 of 21 Feb. 1983 amending Regulation (EEC)

below costs may be disregarded as not being made in the ordinary course of trade.[59]

In *Goldstar v. Council*, the EC Court commented on the concept of ordinary course of trade:

> The ordinary course of trade is a concept which relates to the nature of sales themselves. It is designed to exclude, for the determination of the normal value, situations in which sales on the domestic market are not made under conditions corresponding to the ordinary course of trade, in particular where a product is sold at a price below production costs or where transactions take place between parties which are associated or have a compensatory arrangement with each other.[60]

The term 'ordinary course of trade' is related to the actual domestic sales transactions. If sales are not made in the ordinary course of trade, they must be disregarded in the normal value determination in line with WTO law.

In the following section, situations involving sales between associated parties are examined. Subsequently, practice relating to sales below costs is examined. Finally, situations with local export sales are discussed.

4.1.4.2.1 Sales between Associated Parties

According to Article 2.1, third sentence, in the basic Regulation, the EU authorities *may* disregard prices between associated parties as not having been made in the ordinary course of trade, unless the associated parties can demonstrate that the association or compensatory arrangements do not affect the price.[61] However, Article 2.1, first sentence, provided that normal value shall *normally* be based on prices to independent customers. The question in that regard is whether the Commission and the Council disregard sales between associated parties per se, which would be a violation of WTO law. However, Article 2.1, first sentence, uses the term 'normally', which suggests that the authorities can derogate from the rule.

In *Stainless Steel Fasteners and Parts thereof I*, the Council made an analysis of the prices between two associated parties to determine whether prices between the parties were at arm's length compared to prices to unrelated customers.[62]

No. 3439/80 imposing a definitive anti-dumping duty on imports of certain polyester yarn originating in the United States of America, OJ L 050, 23 Feb. 1983, p. 1, where the domestic buyer brought the raw material himself to the company in question and was only charged for texturing. Such arrangement was not considered as a sale in the ordinary course of trade.

59. Art. 2.4 of the basic Regulation.
60. *Goldstar v. Council*, Case C-105/90, judgment of the EC Court of 13 Feb. 1992, ECR 1992, p. I-677, para. 13. See also *Ajinomoto and NutraSweet v. Council and Commission*, Joined cases C-76/98 P and C-77/98 P, judgment of the Court of 3 May 2001, ECR 2001, p. II-3223, para. 38.
61. See also Court of First Instance in *Petrotub and Republica v. Council*, Joined cases T-33/98 and T-34/98, judgment of the Court of First Instance of 15 Dec. 1999, ECR 1999, p. II-3837, paras 73-74.
62. *Stainless Steel Fasteners and Parts thereof I*, Council Regulation (EC) No. 393/98 of 16 Feb. 1998 imposing a definitive anti-dumping duty on imports of stainless steel fasteners and parts

It is not apparent from the Regulation whether the analysis is a direct comparison of the prices between the associated parties and sales to non-associated parties, or whether the analysis goes beyond the price setting by including the different factors that influence the price, like quantity, quality, transport, etc.

In *Polyester Staple Fibres (PSF) II*, it appears that the Commission did not carry out a further test as to whether the sales between the related parties could in fact have been made in the ordinary course of trade. The Commission stated:

> One of the two investigated Indonesian exporting producers made some sales of the product concerned to a related user on the domestic market. Pursuant to Article 2(1) of the basic Regulation, these sales were not considered to be in the ordinary course of trade and were not used to establish normal value.[63]

The recital does not reveal whether the Commission considered making an ordinary course of trade test of the sales between the associated parties; rather, it appears that the Commission disregarded the sales per se due to the association.

Under WTO law, there is wide discretion to determine whether sales are made in the ordinary course of trade. The closer the relationship between the parties, the greater the likelihood that sales are not made in the ordinary course of trade. However, the investigating authorities must test whether sales are ordinary, i.e., 'normal'. Therefore, prices cannot per se be disregarded without being tested. The test must take into account several factors that may have an impact on the price between the associated parties. It is not sufficient to disregard the actual domestic price by merely comparing it with a price from a transaction between unrelated parties. Furthermore, the associated parties shall be given an opportunity to demonstrate that the sales between them are made in the ordinary course of trade.

The information from these Regulations is limited. It cannot be concluded whether the Commission and the Council carry out such tests as required under WTO law. It would have been preferable if the Commission and the Council would elaborate their findings in these cases in order to make the legal basis for their findings transparent.

4.1.4.2.2 Prices below Costs and SAG

Pursuant to Article 2.4, sales below costs and SAG may be disregarded if such sales are made within an extended period in substantial quantities and the loss is not recovered within a reasonable period of time.

---

thereof originating in the People's Republic of China, India, the Republic of Korea, Malaysia, Taiwan and Thailand, OJ L 50, 20 Feb. 1998, pp. 1-14, recital 21.

63. *Polyester Staple Fibres (PSF) II*, Commission Regulation (EC) No. 124/2000 of 20 Jan., 2000 imposing a provisional anti-dumping duty on imports of polyester staple fibres (PSF) originating in Australia, Indonesia and Thailand, OJ L 16, 21 Jan. 2000, pp. 30-49, recital 44, apparently endorsed in Council Regulation (EC) No. 1522/2000 of 10 Jul. 2000 imposing a definitive anti-dumping duty on imports of synthetic staple fibres of polyester originating in Australia, Indonesia and Thailand and collecting definitively the provisional duty imposed, OJ L 175, 14 Jul. 2000, pp. 10-28.

In practice, the first and third conditions about 'extended period' and 'loss is not recovered within a reasonable period of time' are followed by the Commission and the Council. Apparently, the WTO requirements are also met; see 4.1.3.3.2, although the information in the Regulations is limited. It is therefore not possible to read the actual methods used in determining the 'extended period' and 'loss is not recovered within a reasonable period of time'.[64] What is more interesting is the EU practice concerning the second condition that sales must be in substantial quantities.

Pursuant to Article 2.4, third sentence, sales below costs are sold in substantial quantities when the weighted-average selling price is below the weighted average unit costs, or when the volume of sales below costs is not less than 20% of the sales used to determine normal value. It is established practice that only one of those two criteria has to be fulfilled in order to regard sales below costs made in substantial quantities;[65] this also has been confirmed by the Court of First Instance in *Petrotub and Republica v. Council*.[66] This part was not appealed to the EC Court.

This practice is in line with WTO law. It follows from footnote 5 to Article 2.2.1 of the ADA that the substantial quantity condition is met when the weighted average selling price is below weighted average per unit costs, *or* the volume of sales below costs represents no less than 20% of the total volume.

---

64. See as examples: *Stainless Steel Fasteners and Parts thereof I*, Commission Regulation (EC) No. 1732/97 of 4 Sep. 1997 imposing a provisional anti-dumping duty on imports of stainless steel fasteners and parts originating in the People's Republic of China, India, Malaysia, the Republic of Korea, Taiwan and Thailand, OJ L 243, 5 Sep. 1997, pp. 17-36, recitals 14, 17 and 20, endorsed in Council Regulation (EC) No. 393/98 of 16 Feb. 1998 imposing a definitive anti-dumping duty on imports of stainless steel fasteners and parts thereof originating in the People's Republic of China, India, the Republic of Korea, Malaysia, Taiwan and Thailand, OJ L 50, 20 Feb. 1998, pp. 1-14, recital 28; and *Certain Graphite Electrode Systems*, Commission Regulation (EC) No. 1009/2004 of 19 May 2004 imposing a provisional anti-dumping duty on imports of certain graphite electrode systems originating in India, OJ L 183, 20 May 2004, pp. 61-82, recitals 18-19, apparently endorsed in Council Regulation (EC) No. 1629/2004 of 13 Sep. 2004 imposing a definitive anti-dumping duty and collecting definitively the provisional duty imposed on imports of certain graphite electrode systems originating in India, OJ L 295, 18 Sep. 2004, pp. 10-14.
65. See examples: *Cotton-type Bed linen I*, Commission Regulation (EC) No. 1069/97 of 12 Jun. 1997 imposing a provisional anti-dumping duty on imports of cotton-type bed linen originating in Egypt, India and Pakistan, OJ L 156, 13 Jun. 1997, pp. 11-33, recital 25; *Sacks and Bags Made of Polyethylene or Polypropylene*, Commission Regulation (EC) No. 45/97 of 10 Jan. 1997 imposing a provisional anti-dumping duty on imports of sacks and bags made of polyethylene or polypropylene originating in India, Indonesia and Thailand, OJ L 12, 15 Jan. 1997, pp. 8-20, recital 14, endorsed in Council Regulation (EC) No. 1950/97 of 6 Oct. 1997 imposing a definitive anti-dumping duty on imports of sacks and bags made of polyethylene or polypropylene originating in India, Indonesia and Thailand and collecting definitively the provisional duty imposed, OJ L 276, 9 Oct. 1997, pp. 1-8, recitals 13 and 16; and *Synthetic Fibres of Polyesters I*, Council Regulation (EC) No. 907/97 of 20 May 1997 amending Regulation (EEC) No. 54/93 imposing a definitive anti-dumping duty on imports of synthetic fibres of polyesters originating in India and the Republic of Korea, OJ L 131, 23 May 1997, pp. 1-3, recital 10.
66. *Petrotub and Republica v. Council*, Joined cases T-33/98 and T-34/98, judgment of the Court of First Instance of 15 Dec. 1999, ECR 1999, p. II-3837, para. 85.

However, in EU practice, a 10% rule has been developed, which does not appear in EU legislation. If the volume of profitable sales exceeds 10% of the entire domestic sales volume – but is less than 20% of the entire domestic sales volume – the EU authorities will disregard the below costs sales but will include the remaining profitable sales in the normal value. If the volume of profitable sales is *10% or less* of the volume of domestic sales, *all* the domestic sales will be disregarded as not having taken place in the ordinary course of trade.

Apparently, the 10% rule took form in 1997. In *Synthetic Fibres of Polyesters I* and *Sacks and Bags Made of Polyethylene or Polypropylene*, both from 1997, the rule had not yet been applied.[67] However, the rule has been used consistently since then.[68] The Court of First Instance has apparently endorsed the rule.[69]

---

67. *Synthetic Fibres of Polyesters I*; Council Regulation (EC) No. 907/97 of 20 May 1997 amending Regulation (EEC) No. 54/93 imposing a definitive anti-dumping duty on imports of synthetic fibres of polyesters originating in India and the Republic of Korea, OJ L 131, 23 May 1997, pp. 1-3, recital 10; and *Sacks and Bags Made of Polyethylene or Polypropylene*; Commission Regulation (EC) No. 45/97 of 10 Jan. 1997 imposing a provisional anti-dumping duty on imports of sacks and bags made of polyethylene or polypropylene originating in India, Indonesia and Thailand, OJ L 12, 15 Jan. 1997, pp. 8-20, recital 14, endorsed in Council Regulation (EC) No. 1950/97 of 6 Oct. 1997 imposing a definitive anti-dumping duty on imports of sacks and bags made of polyethylene or polypropylene originating in India, Indonesia and Thailand and collecting definitively the provisional duty imposed, OJ L 276, 9 Oct. 1997, pp. 1-8, recital 16.
68. *Cotton-type Bed linen I*, Commission Regulation (EC) No. 1069/97 of 12 Jun. 1997 imposing a provisional anti-dumping duty on imports of cotton-type bed linen originating in Egypt, India and Pakistan, OJ L 156, 13 Jun. 1997, pp. 11-33, recital 26, endorsed in Council Regulation (EC) No. 2398/97 of 28 Nov. 1997 imposing a definitive anti-dumping duty on imports of cotton-type bed linen originating in Egypt, India and Pakistan, OJ L 332, 4 Dec. 1997, pp. 1-18, recital 19; *Potassium Permanganat*, Commission Regulation (EC) No. 178/98 of 23 Jan. 1998 imposing a provisional anti-dumping duty on imports of potassium permanganate originating in India and the Ukraine, OJ L 019, 24 Jan. 1998, pp. 23-34, recital 11, endorsed in Council Regulation (EC) No. 1507/98 of 13 Jul. 1998 imposing a definitive anti-dumping duty on imports of potassium permanganate originating in India and the Ukraine and collecting definitively the provisional duty imposed OJ L 200, 16 Jul. 1998, pp. 4-8, recital 8; *Synthentic Fibre Ropes*, Commission Regulation (EC) No. 18/98 of 7 Jan. 1998 imposing a provisional anti-dumping duty on imports of synthetic fibre ropes originating in India, OJ L 004, 8 Jan. 1998, pp. 28-38, recital 12, endorsed in Council Regulation (EC) No. 1312/98 of 24 Jun. 1998 imposing a definitive anti-dumping duty on imports of synthetic fibre ropes originating in India and collecting definitively the provisional duty imposed ,OJ L 183, 26 Jun. 1998, pp. 1-8, recital 10; *Certain Unbleached Cotton Fabrics*, Commission Regulation (EC) No. 773/98 of 7 Apr. 1998 imposing a provisional anti-dumping duty on imports of certain unbleached cotton fabrics originating in the People's Republic of China, Egypt, India, Indonesia, Pakistan and Turkey, OJ L 111, 9 Apr. 1998, pp. 19-64, recital 51; *Stainless Steel Bars*, Commission Regulation (EC) No. 1084/98 of 28 May 1998 imposing a provisional anti-dumping duty on imports of stainless steel bars originating in India, OJ L 155, 29 May 1998, pp. 3-13, recital 14; *Polyethylene Terephthalate Film*, Commission Regulation (EC) No. 367/2001 of 23 Feb. 2001 imposing a provisional anti-dumping duty on imports of PET film originating in India and the Republic of Korea, OJ L 055, 24 Feb. 2001, pp. 16-39, recital 31, endorsed in Council Regulation (EC) No. 1676/2001 of 13 Aug. 2001 imposing a definitive anti-dumping duty and collecting definitively the provisional duty imposed on imports of PET film originating in India and the Republic of Korea, OJ L 227, 23 Aug. 2001, pp. 1-14, recital 14.
69. *Thai Bicycles Industry v. Council*, Case T-118/96, judgment of the Court of First Instance on 17 Jul. 1998, ECR 1998, p. II-2991, paras 47-48.

From a WTO perspective, the 10% rule applied by the Commission and the Council may be questionable, although it has not been tried before a Panel or Appellate Body. Based on the text of Article 2.2.1 in the ADA, only the sales below costs can be disregarded. 'Sales' refers to the below cost sales. It does not seem that investigating authorities may disregard sales above costs and SAG when a certain percentage of the overall sales below costs and SAG are reached.

Furthermore, by looking into the context of Article 2.2.1 of the ADA, it is provided in Article 2.2 that *all* sales may be disregarded in situations where they are not comparable due to low-volume sales being below 5%. Such a rule is not found concerning sales below costs in Article 2.2.1. Nowhere in the ADA is it possible to find any basis for disregarding *all* domestic sales, when only a percentage of the total sales are below costs. If the drafters of the ADA had wished that when some sales are below cost then *all* sales can be disregarded in the normal value determination, they would have written it into the ADA. The 10% rule applied by the Commission and the Council may then present a violation of WTO law.

The practice used by the Commission and the Council also reveals that the below cost-based examination is made per product type and not for the overall product under consideration.[70] The question is whether the type-to-type based examination is in conformity with WTO law.

It follows both from the text of Article 2.2.1 and footnote 5 that sales are below costs if the prices on the domestic market are below *per unit* costs of production. The domestic prices are then compared with the unit costs and not with the weighted-average costs of the like product. Therefore, a practice where the below cost determination is type-to-type based instead of based on the overall product may be in conformity with WTO law. Furthermore, it provided in note 5 re Article 2.2.1 of the ADA that the sales will be in 'substantial quantities when the authorities establish that the weighted-average selling price *of the transactions under consideration* for the determination of normal value is below the weighted average per unit costs, or that the volume of sales below per unit costs represents not less than 20% *of the volume sold in the transactions under consideration* for the determination of normal value'. The determination goes for *transactions under consideration*, not for the like product. From a textual approach, this indicates that in situations where the investigating authorities divide the product under consideration into different types in order to carry out an examination of each type, the cost determination can be made for each type. If the drafters of the ADA wished to make the below cost determination for the overall like product, they could have written it into the Article 2.2.1 and its notes. This is what the drafters did, for example, in note 2 re Article 2.2 about the

70. See as example *Polyethylene Terephthalate Film*, Council Regulation (EC) No. 366/2006 of 27 Feb. 2006 amending Regulation (EC) No. 1676/2001 imposing a definitive anti-dumping duty on imports of PET film originating, inter alia , in India, OJ L 068, 8 Mar. 2006, pp. 6-14, recital 20.

5% rule on representative sales volumes in Article 2.2, where it is made 'of the sales of the product under consideration'.

Therefore, a below cost determination based on the different types of the product seems not to be in violation of WTO law.

4.1.4.2.3 Local Export Sales

On a few occasions, the Commission and the Council have stated that 'local export' sales in Korea are disregarded from the normal value determination as not being in the ordinary course of trade.[71] A 'local export' sale is a domestic transaction of the product from the producer to a domestic buyer, who uses the product as intermediary elements in a final product destined for export. The producer may get some export advantages, for example, exemption from domestic taxes.

Under WTO law, sales on the market must be tested for their 'normality'. It may be questioned whether the Commission and the Council, by disregarding local export sales as not being in the ordinary course of trade, are using the right label. Indeed, the Commission and the Council seem to test the *market conditions* and not the *actual sales conditions*. If all producers in Korea get the same advantages by selling an intermediary product to an exporting producer of the final product, it seems that the market conditions for those producers are the same. In this regard, it must be noted that the EC Court stated in *Goldstar v. Council* that 'ordinary course of trade is a concept which relates to the nature of sales themselves'.[72] This statement supports the claim that ordinary course of trade refers to the actual sales, not the market conditions. If the market conditions are of such a special nature that sales on such markets are to be disregarded, such sales are not under WTO law comparable with the export price due to the *particular market situation*. The Commission and the Council also applied that rule on local export sales in *Polyester Stable Fibres I*;[73] see 4.1.4.1 *above*.

---

71. *Polyester Staple Fibres I*, Commission Regulation (EC) No. 1472/2000 of 6 Jul. 2000 imposing a provisional anti-dumping duty on imports of polyester staple fibres originating in India and the Republic of Korea, OJ L 166, 6 Jul. 2000, pp. 1-13, endorsed in Council Regulation (EC) No. 2852/2000 of 22 Dec. 2000 imposing a definitive anti-dumping duty and definitively collecting the provisional duty imposed on imports of polyester staple fibres originating in India and the Republic of Korea, OJ L 332, 28 Dec. 2000, pp. 17-31, recital 29; *Polyethylene Terephthalate Film*, Commission Regulation (EC) No. 367/2001 of 23 Feb. 2001 imposing a provisional anti-dumping duty on imports of PET film originating in India and the Republic of Korea, OJ L 55, 24 Feb. 2001, pp. 16-39, recital 57, endorsed in Council Regulation (EC) No. 1676/2001 of 13 Aug. 2001 imposing a definitive anti-dumping duty and collecting definitively the provisional duty imposed on imports of PET film originating in India and the Republic of Korea, OJ L 227, 23 Aug. 2001, pp. 1-14, recitals 28-29.
72. *Goldstar v. Council*, Case C-105/90, judgment of the EC Court of 13 Feb. 1992, ECR 1992, p. I-677, para. 13.
73. *Polyester Stable Fibres I*, Commission Regulation (EC) No. 1472/2000 of 6 Jul. 2000 imposing a provisional anti-dumping duty on imports of polyester staple fibres originating in India and the Republic of Korea, OJ L 166, 6 Jul. 2000, pp. 1-13 endorsed in Council Regulation (EC) No.

4.1.4.3 Low-Volume Sales

Pursuant to Article 2.2 of the basic Regulation, domestic sales volume below 5% of the export sales volume to the EU may be disregarded. Such sales are not regarded as representative in finding a proper normal value.

4.1.4.3.1 The Two 5% Tests

In Commission and Council practice, there is a two-step approach when determining whether domestic sales are representative. The EU authorities will first test *all* domestic sales of the like product against *all* exported sales. This examination is not based on types. It is an examination of the overall scope of the product under consideration. If domestic sales volume is below 5% of export sales volume, the domestic sales are not considered representative and are therefore disregarded.[74]

If domestic sales volume of the like product is or exceeds 5% of the export sales volume, the second 5% test is carried out. The second 5% test is based on the different *types of products* that all fall under the generally defined product category.

The EU institutions can, according to their own practice, disregard domestic prices if the second test is not passed by the producer. An example is *Synthetic Fibres of Polyesters I*, where the Council stated:

> Although the company's total domestic sales of the like product constituted more than 5 % of the volume of export sales to the Community, it was found that for the product type sold to the Community the domestic sales volume for the corresponding type was below this threshold and the prices could not be considered representative for the market concerned[75]

The application of the two tests is a consistent practice by the EU authorities.[76] By using two tests in determining whether the domestic sales volume is sufficient

---

2852/2000 of 22 Dec. 2000 imposing a definitive anti-dumping duty and definitively collecting the provisional duty imposed on imports of polyester staple fibres originating in India and the Republic of Korea, OJ L 332, 28 Dec. 2000, pp. 17-31.

74. See *Polyester Stable Fibres I*, Council Regulation (EC) No. 428/2005 of 10 Mar. 2005 imposing a definitive anti-dumping duty on imports of polyester staple fibres originating in the People's Republic of China and Saudi Arabia, amending Regulation (EC) No. 2852/2000 imposing a definitive anti-dumping duty on imports of polyester staple fibres originating in the Republic of Korea and terminating the anti-dumping proceeding in respect of such imports originating in Taiwan, OJ L 071, 17 Mar. 2005, pp. 1-33, recital 29.
75. *Synthetic Fibres of Polyesters I*, Council Regulation (EC) No. 1489/96 of 23 Jul. 1996 amending Regulation (EEC) No. 54/93 imposing a definitive anti-dumping duty on imports of synthetic fibres of polyesters originating in India and the Republic of Korea. OJ L 189, 30 Jul. 1996, pp. 10-12, recital 9.
76. See as examples *Sacks and Bags Made of Polyethylene or Polypropylen*, Commission Regulation (EC) No. 45/97 of 10 Jan., 1997 imposing a provisional anti-dumping duty on imports of sacks and bags made of polyethylene or polypropylene originating in India, Indonesia and Thailand, OJ L 12, 15 Jan. 1997, pp. 8-20, recitals 14 and 19, endorsed in Council Regulation

to be representative, the EU authorities will end up disregarding more domestic sales by the exporters than would be the case in situations with only the first overall test.

An example will show the differences in the test. Consider the situation in which an exporter of allegedly dumped Polyethylene terephthalate (PET) film sells two types of PET film – metalized and base film. Both types of film are exported and sold on the domestic market. Assume that the producer exports to the EU 1000 t of metalized film and 1000 t of base film. Thus, the overall export of the like PET film are 2000 t. Domestically, the sales are 100 t of metalized film and 40 t of base film. In all, there is a sale of 140 t of the like product on the domestic market.

When the first test is done, based on the overall product scope, there is a domestic sale of 7% of the export volume, and the sales are representative. When the second test is done – the type-to-type based test – the result will be as follows: The domestic sale of metalized PET film turns out to be 10% of the export of metalized PET film. The domestic sale of base film will only be 4% of the export of base film. Therefore, the domestic sales of base film will be disregarded.

It must also be noted that even though the conditions are met for one type and not for another, none of them will be regarded as representative if the overall sales are not sufficient. Consider the previous example with the PET film, where the export of metalized film is 1000 t and the export of base film is 1000 t – in all, 2000 t. Assume that metalized film are sold by 55 t domestically, and base film are sold at only 40 t. For the general product, there will only be a domestic sale of

(EC) No. 1950/97 of 6 Oct. 1997 imposing a definitive anti-dumping duty on imports of sacks and bags made of polyethylene or polypropylene originating in India, Indonesia and Thailand and collecting definitively the provisional duty imposed, OJ L 276, 9 Oct. 1997, pp. 1-8, recital 16; *Certain Polyethylene Terephthalate I*, Commission Regulation (EC) No. 1742/2000 of 4 Aug. 2000 imposing a provisional anti-dumping duty on imports of certain PET originating in India, Indonesia, Malaysia, the Republic of Korea, Taiwan and Thailand, OJ L 199, 5 Aug. 2000, pp. 48-77, recitals 14-16, and Council Regulation (EC) No. 366/2006 of 27 Feb. 2006 amending Regulation (EC) No. 1676/2001 imposing a definitive anti-dumping duty on imports of PET film originating, inter alia, in India, OJ L 068, 8 Mar. 2006, pp. 6-14, recitals 17-18; *Certain Iron or Steel Ropes and Cables*, Commission Regulation (EC) No. 230/2001 of 2 Feb. 2001 imposing a provisional anti-dumping duty on certain iron or steel ropes and cables originating in the Czech Republic, Russia, Thailand and Turkey and accepting undertakings offered by certain exporters in the Czech Republic and Turkey, OJ L 034, 3 Feb. 2001, pp. 4-27, recital 19, endorsed in Council Regulation (EC) No. 1601/2001 of 2 Aug. 2001 imposing a definitive anti-dumping duty and definitively collecting the provisional anti-dumping duty imposed on imports of certain iron or steel ropes and cables originating in the Czech Republic, Russia, Thailand and Turkey, OJ L 211, 4 Aug. 2001, pp. 1-19, recital 24; *Sulphanic Acid*, Commission Regulation (EC) No. 575/2002 of 3 Mar. 2002 imposing a provisional anti-dumping duty on imports of sulphanilic acid originating in the People's Republic of China and in India, OJ L 087, 4 Apr. 2002, pp. 28-44, recitals 13-15; *Certain Graphite Electrode Systems*, Commission Regulation (EC) No. 1009/2004 of 19 May 2004 imposing a provisional anti-dumping duty on imports of certain graphite electrode systems originating in India, OJ L 183, 20 May 2004, pp. 61-82, recitals 16-18.

4.75% of the export sale. Thus *all* the sales will be disregarded, even though the domestic sale of metalized film on a type-to-type calculation will be 5.5% of the export sale.

Compared to WTO law, it is provided in footnote 2 to Article 2.2 that the quantity of sales of the like product is sufficient to determine normal value 'if such sales constitute 5% or more of the sales of the *product under consideration*'. The question is, then, whether the two-step approach by the EU is in conformity with the requirement in Article 2.2 and footnote 2.

From a textual approach, domestic sales of the like product take place in a sufficient quantity if they constitute 5% or more of the sales of the *product under consideration to the importing Member*. The yardstick is sales of the product under consideration, and based on this the percentage of the like product is determined. In Chapter 3 it was found that under WTO law, the product under consideration is the product defined by the investigating authorities as that allegedly dumped, and the investigating authorities are bound by that definition; see the Appellate Body statement in *EC – Bed linen*.[77] Upon defining a product as the 'product under investigation', that definition must also be reflected when applying the 5% rule.

As it is not provided in the footnote that the 5% calculation may be made for specific types under the general category of the product under consideration, a type-based test may violate WTO law. This suggests that EU is violating WTO law by making the type-to-type-based test.

However, as the Appellate Body pointed out in *US – Softwood Lumber V (Article 21.5 – Canada)*, there is nothing in Article 2.2 that prohibits the investigating authorities from dividing the product under investigation into different types.[78] Nevertheless, this statement may not imply that under the 5% test the type-to-type-based test may be done. Note 2 re Article 2.2 does not in itself prohibit the possibility of making a product division for other steps under the anti-dumping investigation. For example, the comparison between normal value and export price may be made more easily by dividing the product into types. Article 2.2 does not, on the other hand, allow WTO Members to depart from the wordings in the note. Even though several steps in the anti-dumping investigation may be made through a type-to-type comparison, this does not imply that the 5% test may be used on specific types. Therefore, the use of the type-to-type-based test by the EU authorities may be in violation of WTO law. This reading of the ADA is also supported by Vermulst.[79]

4.1.4.3.2 Disregard of Some Products from the 5% Calculation

The EU authorities may disregard some domestically sold products when calculating the percentage of domestic sales. The exclusion of such domestically sold

77. *EC – Bed linen*, WT/DS141/AB/R, report of the Appellate Body on 1 Mar. 2001, para. 53.
78. *US – Softwood Lumber V(Art. 21.5 – Canada)*, WT/DS264/AB/RW, report of the Appellate Body on 15 Aug. 2006, para. 104.
79. See E. Vermulst, *The WTO Anti-dumping Agreement* (Oxford: Oxford University Press, 2005b), 30-32.

products will lead to a lower percentage of domestic sales compared to the export and will thus increase the likelihood of disregarding domestic sales.

In *Polyethylene Terephthalate Film*, the Council disregarded second grade film, which some exporters sold on the domestic market from the low-volume determination. The film sold for export to the EU was first grade film. The Council found that second grade film was not 'directly comparable' with first grade film. Those domestic sales were therefore excluded from the calculation of the normal value. Another exporter sold three different grades on the domestic market. Often, the first grade film and second grade film were sold en masse with third grade film – and at the price of third grade film because it was a stock-clearance. The export sales were all first grade film. The Council found that the domestic sales were not comparable with the export sales.[80]

In this particular case, the third grade films were excluded from the investigation because they were not exported to the EU. This leaves an open question. If the third grade film had been sold to the EU, would the Council then – after having made its type-to-type based differentiation – also have made another differentiation based on the grades of the different types of film?

It could be argued that since the Council disregarded the third grade film in this particular case because it is not 'directly comparable', a more specific differentiation would also be used in the situation with export of the third grade film.

Such exclusion of products from the 5% test can only be justified from a WTO perspective when the products being excluded are either not 'like' in the sense of Article 2.6 of the ADA or not destined for consumption. According to note 2 re Article 2.2, the provision addresses low-volume 'sales of the like product destined for consumption in the domestic market in the exporting country.' The Council bases its argument on direct comparability and different grades of quality. It is not incorrect that such sales may be disregarded from the 5% test, but the argumentation may have to go hand in hand with the argumentation used by the Commission and the Council in their 'like product' determination. It is not contained in the WTO text that some products may be excluded from the low-volume test due to non-comparability.

Furthermore, the overall product definition is important in this regard as a reference for the 'like product' determination. If the Commission and the Council in fact use a broad product definition that may include those low grade products, then had they been exported to the EU, the low grade products would also be 'like' in the sense given in Article 2.6 of the ADA and would therefore be included. The broader the definition, the greater the likelihood of including a broad range of domestically sold products in the low-volume determination. As stated by the Appellate Body in *EC – Bed linen*, the product scope frames the investigation.[81]

---

80. *Polyethylene Terephthalate Film*, Council Regulation (EC) No. 366/2006 of 27 Feb. 2006 amending Regulation (EC) No. 1676/2001 imposing a definitive anti-dumping duty on imports of PET film originating, inter alia, in India, OJ L 068, 8 Mar. 2006, pp. 6-14, recital 18.
81. See Section 3.2.1.2 below.

4.1.4.3.3 *Acceptance of Domestic Sales Below 5%*

It follows from the wording of Article 2.2 of the basic Regulation that even a domestic sales volume below 5% of the export sales volume may still be used if the prices at the domestic market are representative.

In *Malleable Cast Iron Tube or Pipe Fittings*, the only exporting producer that had a domestic sale below the 5% limit argued that the exemption should be applied. The Council stated:

> *It is the consistent practice of the Community institutions* not to use prices of products or product types that are not sold in representative quantities in order to determine the normal value. *Only when sales volumes are equal to or exceed the 5 % threshold will the Commission consider that the sales are sufficiently representative to form a basis for normal value.* No factors were found which would justify a deviation from the normal practice by using a volume of sales lower than the 5 % threshold.[82]

By stating that only sales volumes equal to or above 5% can be regarded as representative, the Council seemed to make a per se exclusion of domestic sales below 5% of export sales. It is not clear which factors would justify the use of sales below 5%.

However, in recent practice the rejection of all sales below 5% may have changed. In the amendment to *Cotton-Type Bed linen II*, the Council carried out an examination of the characteristics of the market and the sales organization for three exporters whose domestic sales were only 2.2%, 0.5% and 0.2% of the sales to the EU; following the examination, those sales were rejected.[83] This indicates a willingness by the Commission and the Council to undertake concrete examinations of sales below 5%.

According to Van Bael and Bellis, the Council Regulations rarely use the exception to the 5% rule.[84] The authors refer to one case in *Farmed Atlantic Norway* where the Council accepted two exporters' volume below 5%, but above 4%, because Norwegian statistics showed that the total domestic volume for *all* domestic sales was 5.2% of the total export sales.[85]

---

82. *Malleable Cast Iron Tube or Pipe Fittings*, Council Regulation (EC) No. 1784/2000 of 11 Aug. 2000 imposing a definitive anti-dumping duty and definitively collecting the provisional duty imposed on imports of certain malleable cast iron tube or pipe fittings originating in Brazil, the Czech Republic, Japan, the People's Republic of China, the Republic of Korea and Thailand, OJ L 208, 18 Aug. 2000, pp. 8-23, recital 25.
83. *Cotton-Type Bedlinen II*, Council Regulation (EC) No. 695/2006 of 5 May 2006 amending Regulation (EC) No. 397/2004 imposing a definitive anti-dumping duty on imports of cotton-type bedlinen originating in Pakistan, OJ L 121, 6 May 2006, pp. 14-26, recital 25.
84. I. Van Bael & J.F. Bellis, *Anti-dumping and Other Trade Protection Laws of the EC*, 4th edn (The Hague: Kluwer Law International, 2004), 54-55.
85. *Farmed Atlantic Norway*, Council Regulation (EC) No. 1890/97 of 26 Sep. 1997 imposing a definitive anti-dumping duty on imports of farmed Atlantic salmon originating in Norway – Council Declaration, OJ L 267, 30 Sep. 1997, pp. 1-18, recital 15.

Concerning WTO law, it is provided in note 2 to Article 2.2 of the ADA that there cannot be a per se rejection of sales volume below 5%, because a lower ratio shall be accepted where the evidence demonstrates that the domestic sales provide for a proper comparison. The question is, though, under what exceptional circumstances can sales below 5% be included in the normal value determination? It appears, however, that there is wide discretion left to the investigating authorities to make that determination. The Council has demonstrated a willingness to examine concrete matters in order to determine whether the general 5% rule will be exempted. Thus, the recent EU practice seems to be in conformity with the WTO requirements.

4.1.4.4 Exporting Country

In EU legislation, the normal value is based on prices from the exporting country.[86] In practice, the Commission and the Council base the normal value on transactions taking place in the exporting country; this is not questionable. The problem arises in situations where two countries are involved in export:

- the country of origin; and
- the exporting country is an intermediary country between the country of origin and the EU.

The question is then on which criteria normal value is to be based.

In Article 1.3 of the basic Regulation, first sentence, the general rule is that the exporting country is the country of origin. This may be exempted from in situations that involve intermediary countries. There are only a few cases of the situation in which a product is transhipped through another country, and all of those cases are prior to the 1996 basic Regulation. Under the former basic Regulation, the wordings about such sales were different – which means that there is some hesitation about making analogue conclusions from the application of that Regulation to the present basic Regulation. According to Van Bael and Bellis, the EU institutions 'almost systematically rejected requests by exporters to base normal value on prices in an intermediary country from which the products were exported to the Community'.[87]

Under the present WTO regime, such rejections would infringe upon WTO law, as the general rule is to base the normal value on the domestic prices in the *exporting country*, unless the products are transhipped through the exporting

---

86. Arts 1.2 and 2.1 of the basic Regulation.
87. I. Van Bael & J.F. Bellis, *Anti-dumping and Other Trade Protection Laws of the EC*, 4th edn (The Hague: Kluwer Law International, 2004), 45-47. See from practice *Colour Television Receivers*, Commission Regulation (EC) No. 2376/94 of 27 Sep. 1994 imposing a provisional anti-dumping duty on imports of colour television receivers originating in Malaysia, the people's Republic of China, the Republic of Korea, Singapore, and Thailand, OJ L 255, 1 Oct. 1994, pp. 50-69, recitals 55-56, endorsed in Council Regulation (EC) No. 710/95 of 27 Mar. 1995 imposing a definitive anti-dumping duty on imports of colour television receivers originating in Malaysia, the People's Republic of China, the Republic of Korea, Singapore, and Thailand and collecting definitively the provisional duty imposed, OJ L 73, 1 Apr. 1995, pp. 3-12, recital 15.

country, or the products are produced in the exporting country or there is no comparable price for them in the exporting country.

It should be noted that in cases where the imposition of an anti-dumping duty is circumvented by selling through an intermediary country, such sales fall under the EU circumvention rules described in Section 2.4.2.3. The difference between the circumvention situations and the situation described here is that circumvention takes place *after* the imposition of an anti-dumping duty, whereas the situation with intermediary countries described in this section takes place *before* the imposition of the anti-dumping duty.

4.1.4.5 Destined for Consumption in the Exporting Country

In line with WTO law, EU legislation includes that the like product must be destined for consumption in the exporting country. Based on the Regulations used in this study, it seems that the 'destined for consumption' requirement has not been challenged. However, in one particular case it can be questioned whether that requirement was tried under different labels.

This case is *Polyester Stable Fibres I*, which was mentioned in Section 4.1.4.1 *above*. A number of Korean producers had *domestic sales* of polyester stable fibres to final producers. Polyester stable fibre was the product under investigation. In the domestic sales in Korea, polyester stable fibres were sold as intermediary products to final producers who exported the final product. The sales from the producer of polyester stable fibres to final producers were not subject to domestic taxes. In the Commission Regulation, it was stated:

> [T]hese sales were subject to administrative arrangements specific to export sales as they were not subject to domestic sales tax, they were normally invoiced in US dollars and paid for by letters of credit, they were subject to duty drawback arrangements and they were normally classified as local export sales in the companies' accounting records. *In these circumstances, these sales were excluded from the domestic sales listings.*[88] (Emphasis added)

The rejection by the Commission of including those sales in the normal value determination is not based on any of the mentioned criteria in the dumping provisions. The Commission takes a more liberal role and bases the rejection of the prices from the specific transactions on 'these circumstances'.

In the Council Regulation, the producers claimed that there was no legal basis to disregard those sales. In search of a legal basis in EU law, the Council referred to a 'particular market situation' and 'ordinary course of trade'.

---

88. *Polyester Stable Fibres I*, Commission Regulation (EC) No. 1472/2000 of 6 Jul. 2000 imposing a provisional anti-dumping duty on imports of polyester staple fibres originating in India and the Republic of Korea, OJ L 166, 6 Jul. 2000, pp. 1-13, endorsed in Council Regulation (EC) No. 2852/2000 of 22 Dec. 2000 imposing a definitive anti-dumping duty and definitively collecting the provisional duty imposed on imports of polyester staple fibres originating in India and the Republic of Korea, OJ L 332, 28 Dec. 2000, pp. 17-31, recital 53.

However, in the Regulation amending the PSF Regulation, the Council based its reason for disregarding the domestic prices on another factor. The transactions were disregarded in the normal value determination because '*the product was ultimately destined for export*'.[89] It was no longer a matter under the ordinary course of trade condition or the particular market situation. The polyester stable fibres were sold for export, not domestic sale, and thus the prices must be disregarded.

If the only reason for disregarding those sales is the fact that – after being incorporated into another product – they are exported, it may be questioned under WTO law whether EU violates the condition that sales destined for consumption in the exporting country shall be included in the normal value determination.

In the present case, a domestic buyer incorporates the intermediary product into a final product. The transaction between the producer and the domestic buyer of the intermediary product takes place in the exporting country. Furthermore, the product is used by the domestic buyer as an intermediary element in a final product that is produced in the exporting country. It therefore appears that the domestic buyer is the *consumer* of the product. In this line, Vermulst argues that sales where the product is intermediary to another product should be regarded as consumed.[90]

The question is, however, whether the export of a final product – which includes the like product as an intermediary product – is sufficient to regard the like product as *exported*. Looking at the text of Article 2.1 of the ADA, it appears the normal value includes the prices from sales in the exporting country of the like product. Such an interpretation implies that the transaction between the producer and the domestic buyer, before the product is being consumed, must be taken into account, and that such transactions cannot be disregarded as being export sales. The reason for disregarding the domestic prices in the specific case may then be a violation of WTO law.

4.1.4.6 Downstream Sales between Associates

In situations with downstream sales between associates, where an associated buyer resells the product, it follows from Article 2.1 of the basic Regulation, first sentence, that normal value is based on the price in the ordinary course of trade to the first independent customer.

In practice, the Commission and the Council use the resale price as a basis for normal value. Already before Article 2.1 was established, the Commission and the

89. *Polyester Stable Fibres I*, Council Regulation (EC) No. 428/2005 of 10 Mar. 2005 imposing a definitive anti-dumping duty on imports of polyester staple fibres originating in the People's Republic of China and Saudi Arabia, amending Regulation (EC) No. 2852/2000 imposing a definitive anti-dumping duty on imports of polyester staple fibres originating in the Republic of Korea and terminating the anti-dumping proceeding in respect of such imports originating in Taiwan, OJ L 71, 17 Mar. 2005, pp. 1-33, recital 115.
90. Vermulst gives an example with Polyester Staple Fibres, though without referring to the EU cases mentioned above. See E. Vermulst, *The WTO Anti-dumping Agreement* (Oxford: Oxford University Press, 2005b), 19-20.

Council had developed a practice of disregarding the actual prices from sales transactions between associated parties when the product was meant for resale.[91] This practice was also tried – and endorsed – by the EC Court.[92] In addition, after the 1996 basic Regulation was introduced, the practice of disregarding the price between the producer and associated buyer and instead using the first resale price has continued.[93]

A few points must be made, as there seems to be confusion in some cases as regards the reason for disregarding – or rather replacing – the sales price between the producer and the associated buyer. In *Stainless Steel Fasteners and Parts thereof I*, the Commission stated about Taiwanese exporters:

> These two related exporting producers sold the product concerned on the domestic market both through a related reselling company and directly to unrelated customers. Where the product types were sold to the related reselling company, it was considered, pursuant to the third paragraph of Article 2 (1) of the Basic Regulation, that *those sales were not made in the ordinary course of trade. In these cases, normal value was established on the basis of the prices at which the product was first resold to an independent customer.*[94]

---

91. *Electronic Typewriters*, Commission Regulation (EEC) No. 3643/84 of 20 Dec. 1984 imposing a provisional anti-dumping duty on imports of electronic typewriters originating in Japan and terminating the anti-dumping proceeding with regard to Nakajima All Co. Ltd, OJ L 335, 22 Dec. 1984, pp. 43-48, endorsed in Council Regulation (EEC) No. 1698/85 of 19 Jun. 1985 imposing a definitive anti-dumping duty on imports of electronic typewriters originating in Japan, OJ L 163, 22 Jun. 1985, pp. 1-11.
92. See *Canon I*, Joined cases 277/85 and 300/85, judgment of the Court (Fifth Chamber) of 5 Oct. 1988, ECR 1988, p. 5731; paras 11-12; *Matsushita I*, Case C-175/87, judgment of the EC Court of 10 Mar. 1992, ECR 1992, p. I-1409, paras 11-17; *Matsushita II*, Case C-104/90, judgment of the EC Court of 13 Oct. 1993, ECR 1993, p. I-4981, paras 9-15.
93. *Certain Tube or Pipe Fittings of Iron and Steel I*, Commission Regulation (EC) No. 2318/95 of 27 Sep. 1995 imposing a provisional anti-dumping duty on imports of certain tube or pipe fittings, of iron or steel, originating in the People' s Republic of China, Croatia and Thailand and terminating the anti-dumping proceeding in respect of imports of these fittings, originating in the Slovak Republic and Taiwan, OJ L 234, 3 Oct. 1995, pp. 4-15, recital 25, endorsed in Council Regulation (EC) No. 584/96 of 11 Mar. 1996 imposing a definitive anti-dumping duty on imports of certain tube or pipe fittings, of iron or steel, originating in the People's Republic of China, Croatia and Thailand, and collecting definitively the provisional duty imposed, OJ L 84, 3 Apr. 1996, 1-7, recital 14; *Stainless Steel Fasteners and Parts thereof I*, Commission Regulation (EC) No. 1732/97 of 4 Sep. 1997 imposing a provisional anti-dumping duty on imports of stainless steel fasteners and parts originating in the People's Republic of China, India, Malaysia, the Republic of Korea, Taiwan and Thailand, OJ L 243, 5 Sep. 1997, pp. 17-36, recital 22, endorsed in Council Regulation (EC) No. 393/98 of 16 Feb. 1998 imposing a definitive anti-dumping duty on imports of stainless steel fasteners and parts thereof originating in the People's Republic of China, India, the Republic of Korea, Malaysia, Taiwan and Thailand, OJ L 50, 20 Feb. 1998, pp. 1-14, recital 21. See also I. Van Bael & J.F. Bellis, *Anti-dumping and Other Trade Protection Laws of the EC*, 4th edn (The Hague: Kluwer Law International, 2004), 51.
94. *Stainless Steel Fasteners and Parts thereof I*, Commission Regulation (EC) No. 1732/97 of 4 Sep. 1997 imposing a provisional anti-dumping duty on imports of stainless steel fasteners and parts originating in the People's Republic of China, India, Malaysia, the Republic of Korea,

The Commission states that the transactions between the related companies are 'not in the ordinary course of trade'. Such sales therefore should be disregarded. However, if sales are not made in the ordinary course of trade, there seems to be no legal basis for applying the first resale price. As we will see in next section, under WTO law there are only two alternatives when prices are disregarded for not being in the ordinary course of trade. Those alternatives are:

(1) third-country prices; or
(2) normal value based on costs, SAG and a reasonable profit.

Instead, the statement by the EC Court in *Canon I* seems more appropriate, as it was found that the resale price to the first independent buyer 'of the product may be properly regarded as the prices actually paid for the product in the exporting country or country of origin in the ordinary course of trade'.[95] The EC Court thereby uses the transaction between the associated buyer and the independent buyer as the starting point for the normal value determination: it does use not the transaction between the producer and the associated buyer, which in that case is merely regarded as one unit due to the interdependency.

Furthermore, it is not elaborated in EU practice under what circumstances a relation between the producer and associate buyer is so close that they are no longer considered independent. It is not clear whether Article 143 of Commission Regulation (EEC) 2454/93 of 2 July 1993, which lays down provisions for the implementation of Council Regulation (EEC) No. 2913/92, which establishes the Community Customs Code, which is suggested in Article 2.1, fourth sentence, to determine 'associated', also applies in the situation of resale. If that is the case, and if, for example, the owner of one of the associated companies has a minimum of 5% or more of the outstanding voting stock or shares, then the producer and the associate will be regarded as associated in the sense of Article 2.1.[96]

Compared to WTO law, the EU approach to downstream sales through associated parties is not in itself a violation of WTO law. The Appellate Body has accepted first resale price in such situations, although the argumentation behind this differs from the one presented by the EU institutions. In EU practice, a problem occurs if sales that are not in the ordinary course of trade are linked to resale prices.

Taiwan and Thailand, OJ L 243, 5 Sep. 1997, pp. 17-36, recital 22. Apparently endorsed by the Council, though the Council does not mention the term 'ordinary course of trade', cf. recital 21 in the Council Regulation (EC) No. 393/98 of 16 Feb. 1998 imposing a definitive anti-dumping duty on imports of stainless steel fasteners and parts thereof originating in the People's Republic of China, India, the Republic of Korea, Malaysia, Taiwan and Thailand, OJ L 50, 20 Feb. 1998, pp. 1-14.

95. *Canon I*, Joined cases 277/85 and 300/85, judgment of the Court (Fifth Chamber) of 5 Oct. 1988. ECR 1988, p. 5731, para. 67.
96. See Art. 143(d) of Commission Regulation (EEC) No. 2454/93 of 2 Jul. 1993 laying down provisions for the implementation of Council Regulation (EEC) No. 2913/92 establishing the Community Customs Code.

4.2 ALTERNATIVES TO THE ACTUAL DOMESTIC PRICES

The general rule to base normal value on the actual domestic price between the producer and the domestic buyer may be exempted from, and normal value based instead on alternative methods. As seen in the preceding section, the prices from transactions between a producer of the allegedly dumped product and a domestic buyer may be disregarded. The result could be that *all* such prices are disregarded, and therefore the normal value cannot be based on any domestic transactions between the producer and the buyer. Another situation might be that a producer of the product under investigation does not have any domestic sales at all, but only produces for the export markets. In that situation, the normal value cannot be based on domestic prices.

It must here be recalled that the anti-dumping investigation is addressed imported products from a specific country and not products from a specific producer. Some exporting producers may therefore be in a situation with no domestic sales while still being subject to the anti-dumping investigation.[97]

In this section, it is examined whether EU legislation and practice are in conformity with WTO law on the alternatives to actual domestic prices.

Two questions will be considered:

(1) What are the circumstances in which alternative means to determine normal value should be applied?
(2) What alternatives may be used?

The establishment of normal value based on alternative means has resulted in much debate over the methods to determine normal value. It is argued that the alternative methods used may result in arbitrary and higher dumping margins than would be the case if the actual domestic prices had been used.[98] In the anti-dumping cases, producers will generally argue that the actual domestic prices should be used as a reference to the export price for the dumping determination. Still, there are situations where exporters will argue that the actual prices should be disregarded and the normal value should be constructed; see for example *Cotton-type Bed linen II*,[99] although this is a rare exception.

---

97. See Section 2.2.2 below. See, for instance, the requirements in the application for an initiation of an anti-dumping investigation in Art. 5.2 (ii) of the ADA and the requirement of informing all interested parties, which includes exporters and foreign producers of the product under investigation, cf. Art. 6.1 and Art. 6.11 of the ADA.
98. See for instance E. Vermulst, *The WTO Anti-dumping Agreement* (Oxford: Oxford University Press, 2005b), 35-37; and Wenxi Li, *Anti-dumping Law of WTO/GATT and EC – Gradual Evolution of Anti-dumping Law in Global Economic Integration* (Lund: Lund University, 2001), 62.
99. *Cotton-type Bed linen II*; Council Regulation (EC) No. 695/2006 of 5 May 2006 amending Regulation (EC) No. 397/2004 imposing a definitive anti-dumping duty on imports of cotton-type bed linen originating in Pakistan, OJ L 121, 6 May 2006, pp. 14-26, recital 28. See also *EC – Cotton Yarn*, ADP/137, report of the Panel on 4 Jul. 1995, paras 467-469.

The starting point in this section is WTO legislation and practice by Panels and Appellate Body on alternatives to the actual domestic price. Subsequently, EU legislation and practice by the Commission, the Council and the EC courts will be discussed under the WTO obligations.

4.2.1 WTO Legislation

Article VI.1(b) of GATT 1994 and Article 2.2 of the ADA provide two alternatives to the actual domestic price. Article VI.1(b) provides that a product is dumped if the export price

- is less than the comparable price, in the ordinary course of trade, for the like product when destined for consumption in the exporting country;
- 'or in the absence of such domestic price, is less than either (i) the highest comparable price for the like product for export to any third country in the ordinary course of trade, or (ii) the cost of production of the product in the country of origin plus a reasonable addition for selling cost and profit'.

Article 2.2 of the ADA provides:

> When there are no sales of the like product in the ordinary course of trade in the domestic market of the exporting country or when, because of the particular market situation or the low volume of the sales in the domestic market of the exporting country, such sales do not permit a proper comparison, *the margin of dumping shall be determined by comparison with a comparable price of the like product when exported to an appropriate third country, provided that this price is representative, or with the cost of production in the country of origin plus a reasonable amount for administrative, selling and general costs and for profits.* (Emphasis added)

The alternatives provided in Article VI.1(b) of GATT 1994 and Article 2.2 of the ADA are the same. It is either:

- the highest comparable price for the like product for export to any third country in the ordinary course of trade (the third-country price); or
- the cost of production of the product in the country of origin plus a reasonable addition for administrative, SAG and profit.

The reasons for applying the alternatives seem a bit more comprehensive under Article VI.1(b) of GATT 1994 than under Article 2.2 of the ADA. Under Article VI.1(b), there must be recourse to the alternative methods when there is no comparable price, in the ordinary course of trade, for the like product when destined for consumption in the exporting country. Under Article 2.2 of the ADA, the alternatives apply when there is no sale in the ordinary course of trade for the like product, or when the price is not comparable due to low-volume sales or a particular market situation. Under Article 2.2 of the ADA, it appears that the alternatives do not apply in situations where domestic prices have been disregarded for not being destined for consumption in the exporting country.

In the following sections, the WTO legislation on the two alternatives: third-country price and constructed value will be elaborated.

4.2.1.1 Third-Country Price

The third-country price alternative is differently phrased in Article VI.1(b)(i) and Article 2.2 of the ADA. Article VI.1(b)(i) contains no condition that the third-country prices must be *representative*.

Another difference is with the term '*highest comparable price'* in Article VI.1(b)(i), which is not found in Article 2.2 in the ADA. Article 2.2 provides instead that the third-country price must be *comparable* with the export price. Clearly, the higher third-country price used as normal value, the greater likelihood of finding dumping. Based on the preparatory work in Carlisle I, where 'highest' price was suggested but did not find its way into the final text, it must be assumed with the change in Article 2.2 that the investigating authorities will have to base the third-country price on *all* comparable prices and not on the highest comparable third-country price. This has not yet been disputed.

Article 2.2 also brought into the text that the selected country must be *appropriate*, whereas Article VI.1(b)(i) provides '*any third country*'. The different terms 'appropriate' and 'any' suggest that, under Article 2.2, the investigating authorities have discretionary powers to choose a third country, but the discretion must include an examination of different countries in order to find an 'appropriate' third country. The 'appropriateness' has not yet been tried by Panels or Appellate Body.

Article 2.2.1 of the ADA provides that sales to third countries at prices below per unit (fixed and variable) plus SAG may be disregarded in determining the normal value. The authorities then have the discretion to leave out such transactions from the normal value determination, or they may have to establish the normal value by using the second alternative, i.e., construction of normal value on costs, SAG and profits.

4.2.1.2 Normal Value Based on Costs, SAG and Profits

The other alternative to the actual domestic price is construction of the price based on costs, reasonable SAG and profits. The wordings in Article VI(b)(ii) and Article 2.2 of ADA do not present any apparent differences. Both texts provide that the calculation of SAG and profits must be 'reasonable'. The purpose of constructing a normal value is to find a price that would have been derived if the transaction had been ordinary or the market had been under normal market conditions.[100]

100. See T. P. Stewart, *The GATT Uruguay Round: A Negotiating History – Vol. II* (Deventer: Kluwer Law and Taxation Publishers, 1993), 1554.

The ADA provides further guidelines on how to determine costs and SAG and profit. Article 2.2.1.1 deals with cost calculation. SAG and profits are regulated in Article 2.2.2.

4.2.1.2.1 Calculation of Costs, Article 2.2.1.1 of the ADA

Article 2.2.1.1 of the ADA on cost determination provides:

> For the purpose of paragraph 2, costs shall normally be calculated on the basis of records kept by the exporter or producer under investigation, provided that such records are in accordance with the generally accepted accounting principles of the exporting country and reasonably reflect the costs associated with the production and sale of the product under consideration. Authorities shall consider all available evidence on the proper allocation of costs, including that which is made available by the exporter or producer in the course of the investigation provided that such allocations have been historically utilized by the exporter or producer, in particular in relation to establishing appropriate amortization and depreciation periods and allowances for capital expenditures and other development costs. Unless already reflected in the cost allocations under this sub-paragraph, costs shall be adjusted appropriately for those non-recurring items of cost which benefit future and/or current production, or for circumstances in which costs during the period of investigation are affected by start-up operations.

In the first sentence of Article 2.2.1.1, it is stated that as a rule, the investigating authorities must base the cost calculation on data provided by the exporter or producer under investigation. Such data can be disregarded for two reasons:

(1) if they are not in conformity with 'generally accepted accounting principles of the exporting country'; or
(2) they do not 'reflect the costs associated with the production and sale of the product under consideration'.

The second sentence deals with cost allocation, where all available evidence must be considered by the investigating authorities when the cost data is analyzed. This includes evidence on allocation during the course of investigation if they have been used historically.

The third and final sentence deals with cost adjustment. It is stated that 'costs shall be adjusted appropriately for those non-recurring items of cost which benefit future and/or current production, or for circumstances in which costs during the period of investigation are affected by start-up operations'. It is added in a note:

> The adjustment made for start-up operations shall reflect the costs at the end of the start-up period or, if that period extends beyond the period of investigation, the most recent costs which can reasonably be taken into account by the authorities during the investigation.

The note provides that start-up costs must be adjusted to reflect costs at the end of the start-up period.

The investigating authorities must take into account that some sunk costs might benefit future production, and therefore such costs must be adjusted to a level suitable for the relevant price, as it would have been had there been a domestic price in the ordinary course of trade. For example, companies may make preparatory investigations before entering a market or before setting up production. In an anti-dumping investigation, the investigating authorities must take into consideration that such investments or sunk costs may not be expected to yield a profit in the short run, and therefore the costs must be adjusted to a lower level. The same goes for start-up costs, which at the initial stage of production can be relatively high per unit production but eventually will be lowered due to economies of scale.

4.2.1.2.2 Calculation of SAG and Profits

Calculation of SAG and profits is regulated in Article 2.2.2 in the ADA. The amounts of SAG and profits must be based 'on actual data pertaining to production and *sales in the ordinary course of trade of the like product* by the exporter or producer'. This means that the investigating authorities must use data from the ordinary course of trade submitted from the producer.

It is further provided in Article 2.2.2:

> When such amounts cannot be determined on this basis, the amounts may be determined on the basis of:
>
> (i) the actual amounts incurred and realized by the exporter or producer in question in respect of production and sales in the domestic market of the country of origin of the same general category of products;
> (ii) the weighted average of the actual amounts incurred and realized by other exporters or producers subject to investigation in respect of production and sales of the like product in the domestic market of the country of origin;
> (iii) any other reasonable method, provided that the amount for profit so established shall not exceed the profit normally realized by other exporters or producers on sales of products of the same general category in the domestic market of the country of origin.

It follows from the wording that the method in Article 2.2.2 is the principal method, and that the three other methods in Article 2.2.2(i) – (iii) only apply 'when such amounts cannot be determined on this basis'.

The first alternative in Article 2.2.2(i) provides that SAG and profits be based on amounts incurred and realized by the producer of products in *the same general category*. Thus, the product scope used to determine SAG and profits may be wider than the like product. The question is then how the scope of products in the same general category should be determined compared to 'like product'.

The second alternative in Article 2.2.2(ii) provides a method through which the investigating authorities look into the data from the *other producers under investigation*. In such cases, SAG and profits must be calculated as a weighted average of the amounts incurred and realized by those other producers.

The third alternative in Article 2.2.2 (iii) provides wide discretion to the investigating authorities in offering the possibility of using '*any other reasonable method*' to determine SAG and profit. However, the third alternative is limited, as the 'profit' – but not SAG – must not exceed the weighted average profit normally realized by other producers of the same general category of the product.

4.2.2 Practice by Panels and Appellate Body

In this part, the practice by Panels and Appellate Body concerning the alternatives to the actual domestic prices is described. First, some general statements about Article VI.1 of GATT 1994 and Article 2.2 of the ADA are examined. Thereafter, practice regarding costs, SAG and profits is described.

4.2.2.1 General Statements about Article 2.2 and Article VI

The wordings in Article VI.1 and Article 2.2 of the ADA contained some differences regarding reasons for applying the alternatives. Article VI.1 of GATT 1994 seemed to include a broader scope of reasons than Article 2.2 of the ADA. However, in Section 1.3.1.1 it was found that Article VI of GATT 1994 and provisions in the ADA are not in conflict, but that the ADA is elaborating on Article VI of GATT 1994. In the relationship between Article VI.1.b and Article 2.2 of the ADA, a Panel stated in *Thailand – H-Beams* that by resolving a claim under Article 2.2 of the ADA, the same claim under Article VI.1.b of GATT 1994 is also resolved.[101] This suggests that a reading of Article 2.2 can only lead to the same result as a reading of Article VI of GATT 1994. In *US – Hot-Rolled Steel*, the Appellate Body stated that *Article 2.2 regulates the construction of normal value when domestic sales are disregarded for the reasons mentioned in Article 2.2.*[102] In *EC – Tube or Pipe Fittings*, the Appellate Body stated:

> Article 2.2 makes clear that an alternative basis for deriving 'normal value' must be relied upon by an investigating authority where one of three conditions exists:
>
> (a) there are no sales in the exporting country of the like product in the ordinary course of trade; or
> (b) sales in the exporting country's market do not 'permit a proper comparison' because of 'the particular market situation'; or
> (c) sales in the exporting country's market do not 'permit a proper comparison' because of their low volume.[103]

101. *Thailand – H-Beams*, WT/DS122/R, report of the Panel on 28 Sep. 2000, para. 7.120.
102. *US – Hot-Rolled Steel*, WT/DS184/AB/R, report of the Appellate Body on 24 Jul. 2001, para. 163.
103. *EC – Tube or Pipe Fittings*, WT/DS219/AB/R, report of the Appellate Body on 22 Jul. 2003, para. 94.

In *US – Oil Country Tubular Goods Sunset Reviews (Article 21.5 – Argentina)*, the Panel stated that '[o]nly in the circumstances set forth in Article 2.2 may an investigating authority look to alternative bases to home market prices, such as costs, when determining normal value'.[104]

The practice is that normal value based on alternatives only applies when:

(1) there are *no* sales in the ordinary course of trade of the like product;
(2) a particular market exists; or
(3) the sales are of low volume.

This may indicate that Article VI.1 of GATT 1994 must be read narrowly and that the alternatives to the actual domestic price only apply when one of those three conditions is met. It can be added that if the negotiators of the ADA had meant to include a broader scope of reasons for applying the alternatives, they would have written them into Article 2.2.

Once one of the three conditions is met, Article VI.1 (b) of GATT 1994 and Article 2.2 of the ADA suggest two alternatives to the actual domestic price to determine the normal value:

(1) third-country prices; or
(2) normal value based on costs, SAG and profits.

Concerning the relationship between third-country price and constructed price, a textual reading of both Article 2.2 of ADA and Article VI.1 (b)(i)-(ii) suggests that the alternatives must be equal. Therefore, the national authorities have discretion to choose either producer's export sales price to another third country, or construct the normal value based on costs, reasonable amount of SAG and profits.

This reading finds support in GATT practice about Article VI of GATT 1947. In the GATT Panel report in *Swedish Anti-dumping Duties*, the Panel stated:

> The Panel was of the opinion that if the Swedish authorities considered that it was not possible to find 'a comparable price in the ordinary course of trade for the like product when determined for consumption in the exporting country', no provisions in the General Agreement would prevent them from using one of the other two criteria laid down in Article VI.[105]

According to the GATT Panel, the investigating authorities have absolute discretion in choosing between the two alternatives.

This reading of Article VI is supported by the preparatory work to the present ADA. In the New Zealand I and II text, it was suggested that when the actual price was disregarded, the normal value should be based on '(a) a comparable price of the like product when exported to an appropriate third country or countries (. . .) or (b) *when this is not possible* the constructed value of the like product' (emphasis

104. *US – Oil Country Tubular Goods Sunset Reviews (Art. 21.5 – Argentina)*, WT/DS268/RW, report of the Panel on 30 Nov. 2006, para. 7.76.
105. *Swedish – Anti-dumping Duties*, L/328 – 3S/81, report of the Panel on 23 Feb. 1955, para. 28.

added). This indicates that the negotiators discussed the possibility of creating a hierarchy between the two methods. The hierarchy was, however, left out again in the final text of Article 2.2, which supports the suggestion that there is discretion to the investigating authorities to choose between the alternatives in Article 2.2, when the domestic price has been disregarded, or when there is no domestic price, for the reasons mentioned in Article 2.2.

Finally, it must be noted that the normal value determination for a producer may include both prices from actual domestic sales and 'prices' based on the alternative means. Such a normal value mix may occur in situations with multiple averaging, where the normal value is determined by including intermediary calculations of different types of the product under investigation. For example, an intermediary normal value for one type of the like product is based on actual domestic prices, whereas the intermediary normal value for another type of the like product is based on an alternative calculation. In *US – Softwood Lumber V (Article 21.5 – Canada)*, the Appellate Body stated that '*there is nothing in the text of Article 2.2 that prohibits an investigating authority from dividing the product under investigation into product types or models.*'[106] Furthermore, the Appellate Body found that the investigating authorities are not limited '*when the conditions are met, to use constructed normal value for one particular model or type, but not for others.*'[107]

In practice, the use of third-country prices has not resulted in any disputes. The questions raised above about *appropriate* country can therefore not be solved by looking into practice. The construction of normal value based on costs, SAG and profits has resulted in some cases concerning both cost calculation in Article 2.2.1.1 and the determination of SAG and profits in Article 2.2.2. Those cases are analyzed in the following.

4.2.2.2 Calculation of Costs

Article 2.2.1.1 of the ADA concerns cost calculation. In the first sentence, the general rule is that the national authorities must use cost data from the particular producer if the data is in accordance with generally accepted accounting principles and they reflect the costs associated with production and sale of the product under investigation. In *Egypt – Steel Rebar*, Turkey claimed that the Egyptian Investigating Authority (IA) should have allowed short-term interest earnings in the cost calculation for Turkish steel rebar producers.[108] This claim was rejected by Egypt.[109] The Panel interpreted Article 2.2.1.1, first sentence, and stated:

> [W]e believe that the provision itself makes clear that the calculation of costs in any given investigation must be determined based on the merits, in the light

---

106. *US – Softwood Lumber V (Art. 21.5 – Canada)*, WT/DS264/AB/RW, report of the Appellate Body on 15 Aug. 2006, para. 104.
107. Para. 104.
108. *Egypt – Steel Rebar*, WT/DS211/R, report of the Panel on 8 Aug. 2002, para. 7.389.
109. Para. 7.390.

> of the particular facts of that investigation. This determination in turn hinges on whether a particular cost element does or does not pertain, in that investigation, to the production and sale of the product in question in that case. Thus, in particular, *we must consider the details of the evidence of record in order to reach a conclusion as to whether, in the rebar investigation, there was evidence in the record that the short-term interest income was 'reasonably' related to the cost of producing and selling rebar, and that the IA thus should have included it in the cost of production calculation.*[110] (Emphasis added)

The term 'cost' depends on its link to the actual production of the product under consideration. If there is no reasonable link between expenses and the production or sale of the product, the expenses do not qualify as cost in the sense of Article 2.2.1.1. In order to assess whether there is such a connection between the alleged cost element and the cost of production and sales cost, the cost determination must be based on the facts of a particular case. In the particular case, the Panel could not find such a link between the short-term interests and the costs of production or sales costs. Therefore, the claim by Turkey was rejected by the Panel.[111]

The second sentence in Article 2.2.1.1 regards the cost allocation where all available evidence must be taken into account, including that evidence provided under the course of investigation if has historically been utilized. In *US – Softwood Lumber V*, the Appellate Body clarified the term 'consider all available evidence on the proper allocation of costs'. In its cost calculation, the investigating authorities in the US, the USDOC, had adopted a methodology in which a percentage of the total financial expenses for the company was allocated to the production of the like product on the basis of comparison of total cost of products sold for the entire production with the total cost of the like product. One producer claimed that the production of the like product required fewer assets than the total production of all products, and therefore the producer allocated the financial expenses on the different business segments based on the total assets for each product as a percentage of the total assets needed for all products.[112] With those two different methodologies to determine the allocation of costs, the question before the Panel was whether the USDOC had to compare the different methodologies before determining the allocation of costs. In the Panel report, it was concluded:

> In our view, Article 2.2.1.1, when stating that '[a]uthorities shall consider all available evidence on the proper allocation of costs', *does not require that investigating authorities compare various allocation methodologies to assess their advantages and disadvantages* but to 'consider' all available evidence on

110. Para. 7.393.
111. Para. 7.426. See also E. Vermulst, *The WTO Anti-dumping Agreement* (Oxford: Oxford University Press, 2005b), 34-36.
112. *US – Softwood Lumber V*, WT/DS264/AB/R, report by Appellate Body of 11 Aug. 2004, paras 119-120.

> the proper allocation of costs. We find that DOC met the requirement set forth in Article 2.2.1.1.[113] (Emphasis added)

The Panel therefore refused that investigating authorities should evaluate different methodologies when all evidence had been considered. The Appellate Body reversed the Panel finding. The Appellate Body looked into the ordinary meaning of the term 'consider' and concluded with reference to a dictionary that it meant to 'reflect on' or 'weigh the merits of'. Therefore, investigating authorities were required to reflect on and to weigh the merits of all available evidence on the proper allocation of costs.[114] However, it could not be read into the term 'consider' that the investigating authority was required to 'compare' advantages and disadvantages between different allocation methodologies. Instead, the requirement under 'consider all available evidence' would vary from case to case, and in some cases a comparison could therefore not be required.[115] The Appellate Body then stated:

> However, in other instances – such as where there is *compelling evidence* available to the investigating authority that more than one allocation methodology potentially may be appropriate to ensure that there is a proper allocation of costs-the investigating authority may be required to 'reflect on' and 'weigh the merits of' evidence that relates to such alternative allocation methodologies, in order to satisfy the requirement to 'consider all available evidence'. Thus, although the second sentence of Article 2.2.1.1 does not, as a general rule, require investigating authorities to compare allocation methodologies to assess their respective advantages and disadvantages in each and every case, *there may be particular instances in which the investigating authority may be required to compare them in order to satisfy the explicit requirement of the second sentence of Article 2.2.1.1 to 'consider all available evidence on the proper allocation of costs'*.[116] (Emphasis added)

The Appellate Body limits the discretion of investigating authorities. If a producer can demonstrate by compelling evidence that other allocation methodologies are more appropriate than the one suggested by the investigating authority, this must be considered by the investigating authority. Therefore, the investigating authorities cannot exclude convincing allocation methodologies in the allocation of cost determination. However, the Appellate Body does not provide further guidelines about the scope of 'compelling evidence' needed to ensure that investigating authorities consider other allocation methodologies. The Appellate Body also

113. *US – Softwood Lumber V*, WT/DS264/R, report of the Panel on 13 Apr. 2004, para. 7.238.
114. *US – Softwood Lumber V*, WT/DS264/AB/R, report by Appellate Body of 11 Aug. 2004, para. 133.
115. Paras 137-138.
116. Para. 138.

exercised judicial economy and did not interpret the term 'historically utilized' in Article 2.2.1.1, second sentence.[117]

The third sentence in Article 2.2.1.1, about sunk costs, has apparently not been tried by a Panel or Appellate Body.

4.2.2.3 Calculation of SAG and Profits

Besides cost determination, the alternative normal value includes reasonable SAG and profits. Pursuant to Article 2.2.2 of the ADA, a reasonable amount of SAG and profits must be based on the producer's data from the sales in the ordinary course of trade of the like product. When it cannot be determined on this basis, SAG and profits are based on:

- The amount from sales of 'the same general category of products' by the producer.
- Weighted average of domestic sales of the like product by other producers.
- Any other reasonable method. The amount of profit must not exceed the profit normally realized by other exporters' sale of products in the same general category.

The SAG and profits concluded must therefore be 'reasonable'. In *Thailand – H-Beams*, the Panel stated that all the methods in Article 2.2.2 will, when applied correctly, end up with a reasonable amount of SAG and profit.[118]

In the following sections, Panel and Appellate Body practice concerning Article 2.2.2 and its subparagraphs is described.

4.2.2.3.1 Principal Method in Article 2.2.2

The wording of Article 2.2.2 indicate a hierarchy between the method described in Article 2.2.2 and the methods in the subparagraphs of Article 2.2.2, where SAG and profits under the principal method rely on actual data from the producer. In practice, the Appellate body has stressed this hierarchy and made statements about what data must be excluded from SAG and profits determination under the principal method.

In *EC – Tube or Pipe Fittings*, the Appellate Body had to determine whether data from sales that had been excluded due to low volume of domestic sale had to be included in the SAG and profits determination. EU had disregarded the domestic price of some Brazilian producers in accordance with Article 2.1 and then constructed the normal value based on SAG and profits in accordance with Article 2.2. The data used to determine SAG and profits were based on those sales that were disregarded as non-representative in the first place. Brazil contested the

117. Para. 142.
118. *Thailand – H-Beams*, WT/DS122/R, report of the Panel on 28 Sep. 2000, paras 7.119-7.125.

use of data from those sales as consistent with Article 2.2.2 of the ADA.[119] The Appellate Body stated:

> Examining the text of the chapeau of Article 2.2.2, we observe that this provision imposes a general obligation ('shall') on an investigating authority to use 'actual data pertaining to production and sales in the ordinary course of trade' when determining amounts for SG&A and profits. Only '[w]hen such amounts cannot be determined on this basis' may an investigating authority proceed to employ one of the other three methods provided in sub-paragraphs (i)-(iii). *In our view, the language of the chapeau indicates that an investigating authority, when determining SG&A and profits under Article 2.2.2, must first attempt to make such a determination using the 'actual data pertaining to production and sales in the ordinary course of trade'. If actual SG&A and profit data for sales in the ordinary course of trade do exist for the exporter and the like product under investigation, an investigating authority is obliged to use that data for purposes of constructing normal value; it may not calculate constructed normal value using SG&A and profit data by reference to different data or by using an alternative method.*
>
> As the Panel correctly observed, it is meaningful for the interpretation of Article 2.2.2 that Article 2.2 specifically identifies low-volume sales in addition to sales outside the ordinary course of trade.
>
> In contrast to Article 2.2, the chapeau of Article 2.2.2 explicitly excludes only sales outside the ordinary course of trade. The absence of any qualifying language related to low volumes in Article 2.2.2 implies that an exception for low-volume sales should not be read into Article 2.2.2. (. . .). Accordingly, we conclude that a requirement that low-volume sales be excluded from the calculation of SG&A and profits cannot be read into the text of Article 2.2.2.[120] (Emphasis added)

First, the Appellate Body makes it clear that the method in Article 2.2.2 is the principal method in determining SAG and profits.

Next, concerning the data used in the SAG and profits determination using the principal method, data from sales made outside the ordinary course of trade have to be excluded from the SAG and profits determination. Data from low-volume sales must be included in the SAG and profits determination, because low-volume sales are *not* regarded as sales outside the ordinary course of trade; see Section 4.1.1.1, where such sales are grouped in the 'comparable' category.

The Appellate Body has made a similar statement in *EC – Bed linen*. The Appellate Body stated that data from sales not made in the ordinary course of trade must be disregarded under the principal method in Article 2.2.2. The Appellate Body stressed the text of Article 2.2.2: '*actual data pertaining to production and*

119. *EC – Tube or Pipe Fittings*, WT/DS219/AB/R, report of the Appellate Body on 22 Jul. 2003, paras 86-87.
120. Paras 97-98.

sales in the ordinary course of trade'.[121] If sales are not in the ordinary course of trade and therefore must be disregarded, then SAG and profits must be based on one of the three alternative methods in Article 2.2.2(i)-(iii).

From the interpretation by the Appellate Body, it must be assumed that the investigating authorities cannot depart from the principal method in Article 2.2.2 even though sales are of low volume. Article 2.2.2 is not an alternative to the other methods in Article 2.2.2(i)-(iii). Therefore, if sales are made in the ordinary course of trade, regardless of their low volume, data from such sales must be included in the SAG and profits determination.

4.2.2.3.2 Relationship between the Subparagraphs in Article 2.2.2(i), (ii) and (iii)

If the actual data from the exporter cannot be used to determine constructed value due to sales not made in the ordinary course of trade of the like product, the alternative methods in Article 2.2.2 (i)-(iii) will be applied. It has been questioned whether there is a hierarchy among the three alternatives.

In *Thailand – H-Beams*, a Panel stated that there is no hierarchy between the three subparagraphs in Article 2.2.2(i)-(iii).[122] It was further elaborated by a Panel in *EC – Bed linen*:

> Looking first at the text of Article 2.2.2, *we see nothing that would indicate that there is a hierarchy among the methodological options listed in subparagraphs (i) to (iii).* Of course, they are listed in a sequence, but this is an inherent characteristic of any list, and does not in and of itself entail any preference of one option over others. Moreover, we note that where the drafters intended an order of preference, the text clearly specifies it. Thus, Article 2.2.2 provides 'When such amounts cannot be determined on this basis . . . 'an investigating authority may turn to subparagraphs (i) to (iii). There is no similar language regarding the subparts themselves. *Had the drafters wished to indicate a hierarchy among the three options, surely they would have done so in a manner that made that hierarchy explicit.* Certainly, we would have expected something more than simply a numbered listing. Thus, in context, it seems clear to us that the mere order in which the options appear in Article 2.2.2 has no preferential significance.[123] (Emphasis added)

The Panel rule is, then, that there is no hierarchy between the three alternatives. It is left to the investigating authorities to decide which of the three methods is preferred. In this regard, it should be added that during the Uruguay Round negotiations, a model was suggested containing a hierarchy between the different alternatives, but this was changed during the several drafts that followed.[124]

---

121. *EC – Bed linen*, WT/DS141/AB/R, report of the Appellate Body on 1 Mar. 2001, para. 82.
122. *Thailand – H-Beams*, WT/DS122/R, report of the Panel on 28 Sep. 2000, para. 7.123.
123. *EC – Bed linen*, WT/DS141/R, report of the Panel on 20 Oct. 2000, para. 6.59.
124. See Arts 2.2.4, 2.2.4.1 and 2.2.4.2 of the Carlisle II Text.

Therefore, the national authorities have absolute discretion to determine which of the methods under Article 2.2.2(i)-(iii) may be used when the principal method in Article 2.2.2 cannot be used to determine SAG and profits.

4.2.2.3.3 Data from Sales Not Made in the Ordinary Course of Trade

As found above, the Appellate Body stated in *EC – Tube or Pipe Fittings*[125] that data from sales not in the ordinary course of trade have to be excluded from the SAG and profits determination under the principal method in Article 2.2.2. The question is then whether this exclusion of data from sales outside the ordinary course of trade also goes for the alternative methods under Article 2.2.2(i)-(iii).

The Appellate Body has dealt with the issue concerning Article 2.2.2(ii) in *EC – Bed linen*.[126] The Panel had concluded in its report that data from sales outside the ordinary course of trade must be excluded from the determination under the alternative methods. The Panel based its finding on a general principle of excluding sales not in the ordinary course of trade from the calculation of normal value. This principle would apply in Article 2.2 and Article 2.2.2 with subparagraphs. The Panel therefore concluded that it is a permissible interpretation of Article 2.2.2(ii) to exclude data from sales not in the ordinary course of trade.[127]

The Appellate Body reversed the Panel's finding. The Appellate Body stressed the text of Article 2.2.2(ii), according to which data must be based on '*amounts actually incurred and realized*'. Referring to a dictionary, the Appellate Body found that 'realized' includes both profits and losses. Therefore, data from sales not made in the ordinary course of trade must be included in the SAG and profits determination under Article 2.2.2(ii). The Appellate Body found additional support for its textual finding in the context, where the principal method in Article 2.2.2 explicitly excludes data from sales not made in the ordinary course of trade. Since there is no explicit exclusion of data from sales not made in the ordinary course of trade under Article 2.2.2(ii), this type of data must be included in the method in Article 2.2.2(ii).[128]

It must be assumed that the finding by the Appellate Body also covers the interpretation of the term '*actual amounts incurred and realized*' in Article 2.2.2(i), as an interpretation of Article 2.2.2(i) in the context of Article 2.2.2 would give the same result.

Concerning Article 2.2.2(iii), the method to determine SAG and profits may be freer. However, the limit is 'profit realized' by other exporters of the same category of products, and the method must be reasonable. It must be assumed that data from sales made outside the ordinary course of trade must be included in the profit determination, if this is reasonable.

---

125. *EC – Tube or Pipe Fittings*, WT/DS219/AB/R, report of the Appellate Body on 22 Jul. 2003.
126. *EC – Bed linen*, WT/DS141/AB/R, report of the Appellate Body of 31 Mar. 2001.
127. *EC – Bed linen*, WT/DS141/R, report of the Panel on 30 Oct. 2000, paras 6.84-6.87.
128. Paras 79-84.

4.2.2.3.4 The Same General Category of Products, Article 2.2.2(i)

Under Article 2.2.2(i), SAG and profits are based on data from the producer in question in respect to products that are in the same '*general category*' as the product under investigation. It is not further elaborated on in the text how the 'same general category of product' should be defined, but as indicated above, the same general category of products is an extension of the product definition. This means that it will include a broader category of products than the like product.

In *Thailand – H-Beams*, the Panel was presented with a dispute about the narrowness of the same general category of products. Thailand had imposed an anti-dumping duty on angles, shapes and sections of iron or non-alloy steel and H-Beams from Poland. Thailand had accepted a claim from Poland that JIS and DIN H-beams were not like products due to physical and production process differences, and JIS was excluded from the investigation. However, the domestic sales of the like product were disregarded due to insufficient sales, and the normal value was constructed based on costs, SAG and profits in accordance with Article 2.2.2(i). The Thai authorities based the same general category of products on both H-Beams, and JIS. Poland claimed that the category was too narrow and that the Thai authorities should have included a broader category of products in its SAG and profits determination in order to get a more representative result. The Panel stated that Article 2.2.2(i) did not provide any guidance on how to define 'the same general category of products' and the narrowness or width of the scope of it.[129] The Panel then looked at the chapeau and overall structure of Article 2.2.2 and Article 2.2 and found some guidance. The Panel noted that Article 2.2.2 and Article 2.2 '*concern the establishment of an appropriate proxy for the price "of the like product in the ordinary course of trade in the domestic market of the exporting country" when that price cannot be used*'.[130] When the actual data cannot be used, the alternatives in Article 2.2.2(i) and Article 2.2.2(ii) extend the sources of data to be used either from a wider product scope in Article 2.2.2(i), or by including data from other producers in Article 2.2.2(ii). This confirmed that the intention is to establish a price as close as possible to the price of the like product.[131] Referring to this context, the Panel concluded:

> [T]he use under subparagraph (i) of a narrower rather than a broader 'same general category of products' certainly is permitted. Indeed, the narrower the category, the fewer products other than the like product will be included in the category, and this would seem to be fully consistent with the goal of obtaining results that approximate as closely as possible the price of the like product in the ordinary course of trade in the domestic market of the exporting country.[132]

---

129. *Thailand – H-Beams*, WT/DS122/R, report of the Panel on 28 Sep. 2000, para. 7.111.
130. Para. 7.112.
131. Para. 7.112.
132. Para. 7.113.

The Panel does not provide any criteria to determine the 'same general category of products', but some guidance is found. 'The same general category of products' must be as close as possible to the like product. That is the intention of Article 2.2 and 2.2.2.

It must be assumed that the same argument will be used to put a limit on too broadly defined general categories of products. This finds support in another statement by the Panel regarding whether a narrow scope is representative. The Panel stated:

> The broader the category, the more products other than the like product will be included, and thus in our view the more potential there will be for the constructed normal value to be unrepresentative of the price of the like product. We therefore disagree with Poland that Article 2.2.2(i) requires the use of broader rather than narrower categories, and believe to the contrary that the use even of the narrowest general category that includes the like product is permitted.[133]

Investigating authorities are not free to make too broad a scope of general categories of similar products. The broader the scope, the further away from the intentions behind Article 2.2 and Article 2.2.2 it goes – and thus the further away from the possible price of the like product. However, there are no guidelines provided by the Panel on how to determine the scope. It must be assumed that the narrowest scope is the 'like product', which has to share the same physical characteristics as the product under consideration.[134]

4.2.2.3.5 Weighted Average, Article 2.2.2(ii)

Under Article 2.2.2(ii), SAG and profits are based on the weighted average of the amounts incurred by other producers under investigation.

In *EC – Bed linen*, it was disputed whether the weighted average amounts of SAG and profits could be based on data from a *single* other producer of the like product or data needed to derive from more than one other producer. The Panel found that it as a permissible interpretation to use data from only one single other exporter.[135]

The Appellate Body did not agree with the Panel. The Appellate Body stressed that 'weighted average' implies data from more than one other producer. It is impossible to make a weighted average from data of only one other producer.[136] The Appellate Body ended its argumentation by stating:

> In our view, then, the use of the phrase 'weighted average', combined with the use of the words 'amounts' and 'exporters or producers' in the plural in the text of Article 2.2.2(ii), clearly anticipates the use of data from more than one exporter or producer. We conclude that the method for calculating amounts for

133. Para. 7.115.
134. See Section 3.2.2 above.
135. *EC – Bed linen*, WT/DS141/R, report of the Panel on 30 Oct. 2000, paras 6.70-6.71.
136. *EC – Bed linen*, WT/DS141/AB/R, report of the Appellate Body on 31 Mar. 2001, paras 72-75.

> SG&A and profits set out in this provision can only be used if data relating to more than one other exporter or producer is available.[137]

The Appellate Body makes a clear limitation in the use of Article 2.2.2(ii), which only applies to situations where the amount of SAG and profits can be based on data from more than one other producer. If there is a market with only one other exporter, the investigating authorities will have to base their SAG and profits determination on one of the other alternatives offered in Article 2.2.2(i) or Article 2.2.2(iii). Furthermore, in situations with more than one other producer on the market, the investigating authorities cannot select data from only one of those other producers. The investigating authorities are then prevented from going solely after the data from the exporter with the highest profit.

4.2.2.3.6 Any Other Reasonable Method, Article 2.2.2(iii)

The third alternative method to determine SAG and profits seems more flexible, as the investigating authorities may use '*any other reasonable method*'. This method is limited, as the profit found must not 'exceed the profit normally realized by other exporters or producers' of 'products of the same general category in the domestic market in the country of origin'.

The third alternative still needs to be tested in practice. There are therefore no further guidelines about 'any other reasonable method'.

Based on the above findings about Article 2.2.2(i) and Article 2.2.2(ii), it must be assumed that the data used to determine 'profit' must include data from more than one exporter; note the plural forms 'exporters' and 'producers'. Such an interpretation will be in line with the findings made by the Appellate Body in *EC – Bed linen*. Furthermore, the term 'products of the same general category' may also be determined under the conditions stated by the Panel in *Thailand – H-Beams*, where the same general category under Article 2.2.2(i) must be as close to the 'like product' as possible.

In the following sections, EU legislation and EU practice on the alternative means to determine normal value – and the reasons for applying the alternatives – are examined under the findings of WTO law.

4.2.3 EU Legislation

Under EU law, the alternatives to the actual domestic price are provided in the basic Regulation in Article 2.1, second sentence, and Article 2.3. Article 2.1, second sentence, reads:

> [W]here the exporter in the exporting country does not produce or does not sell the like product, the normal value may be established on the basis of prices of other sellers or producers.

137. Para. 76.

Article 2.3 of the basic Regulation provides:

> When there are no or insufficient sales of the like product in the ordinary course of trade, or where because of the particular market situation such sales do not permit a proper comparison, the normal value of the like product shall be calculated on the basis of the cost of production in the country of origin plus a reasonable amount for selling, general and administrative costs and for profits, or on the basis of the export prices, in the ordinary course of trade, to an appropriate third country, provided that those prices are representative.

Pursuant to Article 2.1, the alternative to the actual domestic price is prices from *other sellers or producers if the producer does not produce or sell the product*. This alternative is not provided under WTO law, and it may therefore be a violation of WTO law. Under WTO law, the only alternatives to the actual domestic price are:

- third-country prices; or
- construction on costs, SAG and profits.

Article 2.3 offers the WTO alternatives:

- third-country prices; or
- normal value constructed on costs, SAG and profits.

EU legislation does not elaborate any further on third-country prices, though it elaborates in the basic Regulation on cost calculation in Article 2.5 and on SAG and profits in Article 2.6.

The reasons for applying the alternatives in Article 2.3 are the same as under WTO law:

- no sales in the ordinary course of trade;
- low-volume sales; or
- the particular market situation.

The relationship between Article 2.1 and Article 2.3 of the basic Regulation is not clear from the wording. It seems that both provisions address no sale situations as a basis for applying their alternatives respectively. It is not clear which of the provisions prevail in no sale situations, or whether the Commission and the Council have absolute discretion in such situations to choose the alternative normal value.

4.2.3.1 Calculation of Costs

Article 2.5 of the basic Regulation deals with the determination of costs. Article 2.5, first sentence, is a reproduction of the wordings of the first sentence of Article 2.2.1.1 of the ADA. Costs must be based on data kept by the producer under investigation if normal accounting principles are followed. In the second sentence of Article 2.5 of the basic Regulation, it is added:

> If costs associated with the production and sale of the product under investigation are not reasonably reflected in the records of the party concerned, they

> shall be *adjusted or established* on the basis of the *costs of other producers or exporters in the same country* or, *where such information is not available or cannot be used*, on *any other reasonable basis, including information from other representative markets.*[138] (Emphasis added)

If the record kept by the producer does not reflect the cost in a reasonable manner, the cost must either be adjusted or based on data from other producers in the same country. If those data cannot be used either, the cost is determined in a reasonable manner.

The third and fourth sentence of Article 2.5 read:

> Consideration shall be given to evidence submitted on the proper allocation of costs, provided that it is shown that such allocations have been historically utilized. In the absence of a more appropriate method, preference shall be given to the allocation of costs on the basis of turnover. Unless already reflected in the cost allocations under this subparagraph, costs shall be adjusted appropriately for those non-recurring items of cost which benefit future and/or current production.

This means that the Commission must consider all evidence submitted to it on the allocation of costs that has been historically utilized by the producer in question. This provision differs from Article 2.2.1.1, second sentence of the ADA, as the WTO rule provides that *all available evidence* must be considered on a *proper* allocation of costs, including the allocation method historically used by the producer. Apparently, WTO law is not limited to historically used allocation methods by the producer as a principal method to determine the cost allocation.

The fifth sentence of Article 2.5 closely resembles the wordings of the third sentence of Article 2.2.1.1 of the ADA. The Commission must adjust costs appropriately for all sunk costs that will benefit future and/or current production. Yet, the fifth sentence does not include anything about start-up costs, as provided in the WTO text. Start-up costs are instead dealt with in the sixth sentence of Article 2.5 of the basic Regulation:

> Where the costs for part of the period for cost recovery are affected by the use of new production facilities requiring substantial additional investment and by low capacity utilization rates, which are the result of start-up operations which take place within or during part of the investigation period, the average costs for the start-up phase shall be those applicable, under the abovementioned allocation rules, at the end of such a phase, and shall be included at that level, for the period concerned, in the weighted average costs referred to in the second sub-paragraph of paragraph 4. [This is referring to the situation where the prices are lower than the productions costs, but higher than the weighted average costs.]

---

138. Art. 1.3 in Council Regulation (EC) No. 1972/2002 of 5 Nov. 2002 amending Regulation (EC) No. 384/96 on the protection against dumped imports from countries not members of the European Community, OJ L 305, 7 Nov. 2002, 1-3.

According to the wordings, the following two conditions must be fulfilled in order to get an adjustment for start-up costs:

- Costs are affected by the use of *new production facilities*, which are required to be *substantial additional investments*.
- Costs are affected by low capacity rates as a result of the start-up costs.

The EU rules on start-up costs seem like a limitation compared to Article 2.2.1.1 of the ADA, where start-up costs are not limited to only 'new production facilities'. In addition, the requirement of 'additional' costs, which furthermore have to be 'substantial', is a clear limitation. Thus, start-up costs, which are not a substantial part of the sunk costs, may not have to be adjusted by the Commission; this in the end can result in a higher constructed value.

If the conditions are met in Article 2.5, sixth sentence, the average cost for the start-up phase is adjusted to the end of the start-up period. This is in line with note 6 to Article 2.2.1.1 of the ADA, which provides that the adjustment must be made based on the costs at the end of the period.

Regarding the period of the start-up phase, Article 2.5, seventh and eighth sentence, reads:

> The length of a start-up phase shall be determined in relation to the circumstances of the producer or exporter concerned, but shall not exceed an appropriate initial portion of the period for cost recovery. For this adjustment to costs applicable during the investigation period, information relating to a start-up phase which extends beyond that period shall be taken into account where it is submitted prior to verification visits and within three months of the initiation of the investigation.

The first point to notice is that it must be a case-by-case determination by the Commission regarding the length of the start-up phase for the producer. The next point to notice is that if the start-up phase is longer than the investigation period, the producer must submit information in that regard to the Commission before verification visits and within three months of the investigation in order to get adjustments.

Under WTO law, footnote 6 re Article 2.2.1.1 of the ADA, the investigating authorities have wide discretion to determine which start-up costs will be taken into account when the start-up phase goes beyond the investigation period. It may be questioned, however, whether the EU text leaves sufficient discretion to the Commission and the Council to determine or adjust those cost factors that are not explicitly mentioned in the Article 2.5 of the basic Regulation.

4.2.3.2 Calculation of SAG and Profit

The second element in the construction of normal value is SAG and profits. In line with the WTO text in Article 2.2.2 of ADA, Article 2.6 of the basic Regulation provides that a reasonable SAG and profits must be based on actual data pertaining to production and sales, in the ordinary course of trade, of the like product by the exporter or producer under investigation. In addition, under EU law this principal method is to be departed from, '*when such amounts cannot be determined on this basis*'. The alternatives in Article 2.6(a)-(c) provide:

(a) the weighted average of the actual amounts determined for other exporters or producers subject to investigation in respect of production and sales of the like product in the domestic market of the country of origin;
(b) the actual amounts applicable to production and sales, in the ordinary course of trade, of the same general category of products for the exporter or producer in question in the domestic market of the country of origin;
(c) any other reasonable method, provided that the amount for profit so established shall not exceed the profit normally realized by other exporters or producers on sales of products of the same general category in the domestic market of the country of origin.

The text of Article 2.6(a)-(c) has some resemblance to Article 2.2.2(i)-(iii) in the ADA, but there are also some apparent differences. The first method in Article 2.2.2(i) of the ADA, where SAG and profits are based on the data on a broader category of products from the producer, comes second in the EU legislation under Article 2.6(b) of the basic Regulation. The second method in Article 2.2.2(ii) of the ADA, SAG and profits based on other producers' data of the like product, comes first in Article 2.6(a) of the basic Regulation. The difference in the construction between the alternatives in WTO and EU legislation is not a violation of WTO law, as there is no hierarchy between the alternatives in WTO law.

The first alternative in Article 2.6(a) shows a remarkable difference from Article 2.2.2(ii) of the ADA. Under the EU text, the weighted average is based on amounts 'determined' for other producers. Under WTO law, the weighted average is based on amounts 'incurred and realized' by other producers. Above, it was found that this requirement includes sales with both profits and losses. As pointed out by Van Bael and Bellis, the EU text offers an opportunity for the Commission and the Council to leave out sales not in the ordinary course of trade, like sales below costs. This may be in violation of WTO law, as data from sales not in the ordinary course of trade must be included under the method in Article 2.2.2(ii);[139] see above in 4.2.2.3.3.

The alternative in Article 2.6(b) also differs from the WTO text in Article 2.2.2(i) of the ADA. Under Article 2.6(b) of the basic Regulation, the actual amounts must be based on sales in the ordinary course of trade, and therefore sales below costs may be disregarded. Under Article 2.2.2(i) of the ADA, it is provided that the amounts are 'incurred and realized' by the producer. The conflict with WTO law may therefore be the same as mentioned above, concerning the difference between Article 2.6(a) of the basic Regulation and Article 2.2.2(ii) of

139. See I. Van Bael & J. F. Bellis, *Anti-dumping and Other Trade Protection Laws of the EC*, 4th edn (The Hague: Kluwer Law International, 2004), 74.

the ADA.[140] As stated by the Appellate Body in *EC – Bed linen*,[141] sales with both profits and losses must be included in the determination of SAG and profits in the Article 2.2.2(i) method.

Article 2.6(c) of the basic Regulation is a reproduction of Article 2.2.2(iii) of the ADA.

4.2.4 EU Practice

As stated by both the EC Court and the Court of First Instance, the alternative methods to determine normal value are *subsidiary* to the actual domestic price, and that principle can only be derogated from when there are no sales of the like product in the ordinary course of trade or when such sales do not permit a proper comparison.[142]

Under Article 2.1, second sentence, of the basic Regulation, the alternative suggested is other producers' domestic prices, when the producer does not produce or sell the like product, whereas the alternatives under Article 2.3 are third country prices or normal value based on costs, SAG and profits, when there are no or insufficient sales in the ordinary course of trade or where the particular market situation does not permit a proper comparison.

In this section, it is examined how the EU institutions apply the alternatives in Article 2.1 and Article 2.3; whether there is a hierarchy between the alternatives and what the necessary conditions of applying the alternatives are. The practice is regarded under WTO law on such matters.

4.2.4.1 Relationship between Article 2.1 and Article 2.3

The Commission and the Council practice reveal a hierarchy between the alternative in Article 2.1 and the alternatives in Article 2.3. In *Sacks and bags made of polyethylene or polypropylene*,[143] the Commission based the normal value

---

140. See also I. Van Bael & J.F. Bellis, ibid., 74.

141. *EC – Bed linen*, WT/DS141/AB/R, report of the Appellate Body of 31 Mar. 2001, paras 79-84.

142. See for instance *Canon I*, Joined cases 277/85 and 300/85, judgment of the Court of 5 Oct. 1988, ECR 1988, p. 5731, para. 11; *Matsushita I*, Case C-175/87, judgment of the EC Court of 10 Mar. 1992, ECR 1992, p. I-1409, para. 17; *Thai Bicycles Industry v. Council*, Case T-118/96, judgment of the Court of First Instance of 17 Jul. 1998, ECR 1998, p. II-2991, para. 46; *Matsushita II*, Case C-104/90, Judgment of the EC Court of 13 Oct. 1993, ECR 1993, p. I-04981, paras 9-15; and *Ajinomoto and NutraSweet v. Council*, Joined cases C-76/98 P and C-77/98 P, judgment of the EC Court of 3 May 2001, ECR 2001, p. II-3223, para. 37.

143. *Sacks and Bags Made of Polyethylene or Polypropylene*, Commission Regulation (EC) No. 45/97 of 10 Jan. 1997 imposing a provisional anti-dumping duty on imports of sacks and bags made of polyethylene or polypropylene originating in India, Indonesia, and Thailand, OJ L 12, 15 Jan. 1997, 8-20 endorsed in Council Regulation (EC) No. 1950/97 of 6 Oct. 1997 imposing a definitive anti-dumping duty on imports of sacks and bags made of polyethylene or polypropylene originating in India, Indonesia, and Thailand and collecting definitively the provisional duty imposed, OJ L 276, 9 Oct. 1997, pp. 1-8.

for one producer on the sales of other producers' domestic prices in accordance with Article 2.1, instead of on a constructed value under Article 2.3.[144] The producer argued that the normal value should be based on a constructed value in accordance with Article 2.3. In the Council Regulation, the Council made the following statement:

> In accordance with Article 2 (1) of the Basic Regulation, normal value is normally based on domestic prices. If a producer does not make sufficient domestic sales in the ordinary course of trade, normal value must be established on the basis of other producers' sales prices for the comparable product, because *it can be assumed that the use of other producers' prices produces a more accurate normal value than construction from the cost of production. Only in the absence of representative domestic sales by other producers, or if such sales prices are not suitable, will normal value be constructed in accordance with Article 2 (3)* of the Basic Regulation. However, the producer in question did not advance any argument as to why the use of other producers' prices should not have been suitable.[145] (Emphasis added)

According to the Council, there is a hierarchy between the alternative method in Article 2.1 and the alternative methods in Article 2.3. The Council finds that prices from other producers are preferred because those prices may be more accurate than a constructed price. The alternative methods in Article 2.3 only apply if the sale by the other producers is of low volume or the sales are not suitable.

The argument by the Council can be contradicted; the problem of using other producers' domestic price instead of the two other alternatives – constructed price or price to a third country – is that a more efficient producer, who sells at a lower domestic price than the competitors, will have a disadvantage. Consider this situation:

> An Indian producer sells bed linen in the domestic market to a price of INR 5. The domestic competitors cannot sell at this low price, and instead they sell the product at INR 6. The reason why the Indian producer can sell at only INR 5 is due to a more efficient production and higher knowledge. However, the Indian producer mainly exports his product to the EU, so his domestic sale only represents an insignificant part of his entire sales. The export price to the EU is also INR 5, which means that the producer is actually not dumping. Yet, when the producer's domestic sales are disregarded because of the insufficient sales in the ordinary course of trade, the new domestic price for the

144. *Sacks and Bags Made of Polyethylene or Polypropylene*, Commission Regulation (EC) No. 45/97 of 10 Jan. 1997 imposing a provisional anti-dumping duty on imports of sacks and bags made of polyethylene or polypropylene originating in India, Indonesia and Thailand, OJ L 12, 15 Jan. 1997, pp. 8-20, recital 15.
145. *Sacks and Bags Made of Polyethylene or Polypropylene*, Council Regulation (EC) No. 1950/97 of 6 Oct. 1997 imposing a definitive anti-dumping duty on imports of sacks and bags made of polyethylene or polypropylene originating in India, Indonesia, and Thailand and collecting definitively the provisional duty imposed, OJ L 276, 9 Oct. 1997, pp. 1-8, recital 14.

Indian producer will be based on the other producers' price, i.e., the domestic price will then be INR 6. This will then result in dumping, when the comparison between the normal value and export price is made because 6-5 equals 1.

From this example, it is demonstrated that the Council argument may not always be right. Another contradiction to the preferred method is that in the alternative methods – third sale price and constructed price based on SAG and profits – the price determination will to a large extent depend on amounts that the particular producer can control. In third-country prices, the producer determines those prices. In the construction of the normal value, the amounts are based on the producer's own data. If the costs are low due to cost efficiency, this will be reflected in the constructed normal value. The same goes for a producer with low SAG. Under the preferred method by the Commission and the Council, the data to determine normal value is out of the producer's control.

It is settled practice by the EU authorities to prefer other producers' domestic sales, in order to establish a reference to the export price of the producer that has no domestic sales – or whose domestic sales are not representative or whose prices are unreliable.[146]

One exception is found in a non-adopted Commission Regulation.[147] The Commission used the construction method of the normal value in accordance with Article 2.3 – not normal value based on other producers' domestic prices.[148] However, as stated, the particular Regulation was not endorsed by the Council but ended in a case before the Court of First Instance in *Eurocoton v. Council II*,[149]

146. See from the practice of the Commission and the Council: *Hematite Pigs Iron*, Commission Decision No. 962/98/ECSC of 7 May 1998 repealing Decisions No. 1751/94/ECSC and No. 55/96/ECSC with respect to the imposition of definitive anti-dumping duties on imports of hematite pig iron originating in Brazil, the Czech Republic, Poland, Russia and the Ukraine, OJ L 135, 8 May 1998, pp. 7-17, recital 16; *Polyethylene Terephthalate Film*, Commission Regulation (EC) No. 367/2001 of 23 Feb. 2001 imposing a provisional anti-dumping duty on imports of PET film originating in India and the Republic of Korea, OJ L 55, 24 Feb. 2001, pp. 16-39, recital 31, endorsed in Council Regulation (EC) No. 1676/2001 of 13 Aug. 2001 imposing a definitive anti-dumping duty and collecting definitively the provisional duty imposed on imports of PET film originating in India and the Republic of Korea, OJ L 227, 23 Aug. 2001, pp. 1-14, recital 14; *Certain Ringbinder Mechanisms I*, Council Regulation (EC) No. 976/2002 of 4 Jun. 2002 imposing a definitive anti-dumping duty on imports of certain ring binder mechanisms (RBM) originating in Indonesia and terminating the anti-dumping proceeding in respect of imports of certain RBM originating in India, OJ L 150, 8 Jun. 2002, pp. 1-16, recital 25; *Certain Footwear with Uppers of Leather*, Council Regulation (EC) No. 1472/2006 of 5 Oct. 2006 imposing a definitive anti-dumping duty and collecting definitely the provisional duty imposed on imports of certain footwear with uppers of leather originating in the People's Republic of China and Vietnam, OJ L 275, 6 Oct. 2006, pp. 1-41, recitals 99-100.

147. *Certain Unbleached Cotton Fabrics*, Commission Regulation (EC) No. 773/98 of 7 Apr. 1998 imposing a provisional anti-dumping duty on imports of certain unbleached cotton fabrics originating in the People's Republic of China, Egypt, India, Indonesia, Pakistan, and Turkey, OJ L 111, 9 Apr. 1998, pp. 19-64.

148. See recitals 53, 74, 124, 127 and 142.

149. *Eurocoton v. Council II*, Case T-192/98, judgment of the Court of First Instance of 17 Mar. 2005, ECR 2005, p. II-2.

where the Council's decision not to endorse the Regulation was set aside.[150] The Court of First Instance did not, however, make any findings in regard to the particular issue raised here. The legal value of the Commission Regulation must therefore be limited, and the exceptional finding by the Commission cannot overshadow the huge number of Regulations in which other producers' prices are the preferred method.

Wenxi Li is very critical about using other sellers' prices. He finds that the investigating authorities may *choose* data from other sellers that will lead to artificial dumping – and disregard data leading to a lower or negative dumping margin.[151]

The alternatives in Article 2.3 of the basic Regulation will only apply under exceptional circumstances, when:

- there is no other producer; or
- there is no or insufficient sales by the other producer;[152] or
- there is no likeness between the products.[153]

The application of other producers' prices as the preferred alternative to the actual domestic price may be a violation of WTO law. Article VI.1(b) of GATT 1994 and

150. See also Chs 1 and 2 below.

151. Wenxi Li, *Anti-dumping Law of WTO/GATT and EC – Gradual Evolution of Anti-dumping Law in Global Economic Integration* (Lund: Lund University, 2001), 159.

152. *Stainless Steel Fasteners and Parts thereof I*, Commission Regulation (EC) No. 1732/97 of 4 Sep. 1997 imposing a provisional anti-dumping duty on imports of stainless steel fasteners and parts originating in the People's Republic of China, India, Malaysia, the Republic of Korea, Taiwan, and Thailand, OJ L 243, 5 Sep. 1997, pp. 17-36, recital 15, endorsed in Council Regulation (EC) No. 393/98 of 16 Feb. 1998 imposing a definitive anti-dumping duty on imports of stainless steel fasteners and parts thereof originating in the People's Republic of China, India, the Republic of Korea, Malaysia, Taiwan and Thailand, OJ L 50, 20 Feb. 1998, pp. 1-14, recital 14; *Sacks and Bags Made of Polyethylene or Polypropylene*, Commission Regulation (EC) No. 45/97 of 10 Jan. 1997 imposing a provisional anti-dumping duty on imports of sacks and bags made of polyethylene or polypropylene originating in India, Indonesia and Thailand, OJ L 12, 15 Jan. 1997, pp. 8-20, recital 15, endorsed in Council Regulation (EC) No. 1950/97 of 6 Oct. 1997 imposing a definitive anti-dumping duty on imports of sacks and bags made of polyethylene or polypropylene originating in India, Indonesia and Thailand, and collecting definitively the provisional duty imposed, OJ L 276, 9 Oct. 1997, pp. 1-8, recital 16, Council Regulation (EC) No. 96/1999 of 12 Jan. 1999 amending Regulation (EC) No. 1950/97 imposing a definitive anti-dumping duty on imports of sacks and bags made of polyethylene or polypropylene originating in India, Indonesia, and Thailand and collecting definitively the provisional duty imposed, OJ L 11, 16 Jan. 1999, pp. 1-4, recital 10; and apparently *Certain Footwear with Uppers of Leather or Plastics*, Council Regulation (EC) No. 467/98 of 23 Feb. 1998 imposing a definitive anti-dumping duty on imports of certain footwear with uppers of leather or plastics originating in the People's Republic of China, Indonesia and Thailand, OJ L 60, 28 Feb. 1998, pp. 1-29, recitals 29, 30 and 62.

153. *Stainless Steel Fasteners and Parts thereof I*, Council Regulation (EC) No. 393/98 of 16 Feb. 1998 imposing a definitive anti-dumping duty on imports of stainless steel fasteners and parts thereof originating in the People's Republic of China, India, the Republic of Korea, Malaysia, Taiwan, and Thailand, OJ L 50, 20 Feb. 1998, pp. 1-14, recital 14.

Article 2.2 of the ADA identify only two alternative methods, one of which '*shall*' be used if there are no sales in the ordinary course of trade of the like product, or due to low-volume sales or sales on a particular market.

In *EC – Tube or Pipe Fittings*, the Appellate Body defined 'shall' in regard to Article 2.2.2 of the ADA. The Appellate Body stated in general terms that 'shall' means to impose an obligation on the investigating authority.[154] This general definition of 'shall' must be assumed to work for Article 2.2 of the ADA.

Therefore, under Article VI.1(b) of GATT 1994 and Article 2.2 of the ADA, the Commission and the Council are obligated to use one of the two alternative methods if there are no sales in the ordinary course of trade, if there are low-volume sales or if there are sales in a market with a particular situation. This interpretation finds support in the context. Under Article 2.2.2 and its subparagraphs, it is explicitly provided that under certain circumstances, data from *other producers* may be used in the SAG and profits determination. Article VI.1(b) of GATT 1994 and Article 2.2 of the ADA contain no explicit reference to the use of prices from other producers. Had the drafters preferred that prices from other sellers should be an alternative to the actual domestic price – apart from situations under Article 2.2.2 and its subparagraphs – they would have written it into the text of Article VI.1(b) or Article 2.2.

The text of Article 2.1, second sentence, of the basic Regulation and the practice applied by the Commission and the Council may therefore be in violation of WTO law.

4.2.4.2 Article 2.3: Rejection of Third-Country Prices

When the Commission and the Council have departed from the preferred alternative in Article 2.1 of the basic Regulation, the secondary alternatives are third-country prices or construction of normal value based on costs, SAG and profits.

In practice, the Commission and the Council rarely use third-country prices to determine normal value based on prices from the producer to another appropriate third country.[155] The Council stated in *Ferro-Silicon* that the reason for not applying the third country method is the risk that those sales may also be dumped.[156]

154. *EC – Tube or Pipe Fittings*, WT/DS219/AB/R, report of the Appellate Body on 22 Jul. 2003, para. 97.
155. See I. Van Bael & J. F. Bellis, *Anti-dumping and Other Trade Protection Laws of the EC*, 4th edn (The Hague: Kluwer Law International, 2004), 64 and Wenxi Li, *Anti-dumping Law of WTO/GATT and EC – Gradual Evolution of Anti-dumping Law in Global Economic Integration* (Lund: Lund University, 2001), 89.
156. *Ferro-Silicon*, Council Regulation (EEC) No. 341/90 of 5 Feb. 1990 accepting undertakings and imposing a definitive anti-dumping duty on imports of ferro-silicon originating in Iceland, Norway, Sweden, Venezuela or Yugoslavia, except those sold for export to the Community by companies whose undertakings have been accepted, OJ L 38, 10 Feb. 1990, pp. 1-8, recital 15.

Instead, the Commission and the Council base the normal value on the costs and reasonable SAG and profits.

The rejection of third-country prices is not in violation of WTO law. As stated above, there is no hierarchy between third-country prices and construction of prices based on costs, SAG and profits in Article 2.2 of ADA and Article VI.1 (b)(i)-(b)(ii) of GATT 1994. The Commission and the Council have therefore absolute discretion to choose between those two alternatives.

In the following sections, the practice of constructing normal value based on costs, SAG and profits is examined. First, the practice regarding costs and Article 2.5 of the basic Regulation is examined. Thereafter, the practice regarding SAG and profits and Article 2.6 and its subparagraphs is examined.

4.2.4.3 Construction of Costs

Article 2.5 of the basic Regulation does not define costs, but costs are based on records kept by the producer. It may be necessary to make adjustments in the cost determination and exclude/include certain types of costs. The Commission and the Council have adjusted costs in situations where the same costs have been reported both as cost and as SAG and the producer has demonstrated that there is such an overlap.[157] The Commission and the Council seem to be willing to make adjustments for costs if the producer demonstrates that there is a link between costs and production.[158] Under WTO law, costs must be adjusted, but wide discretion is left to the investigating authorities to make such determinations. However, if there is a link between costs and production or sales, such costs must be included in the costs determination.

157. See *Cotton-type Bed linen I*, Council Regulation (EC) No. 2398/97 of 28 Nov. 1997 imposing a definitive anti-dumping duty on imports of cotton-type bed linen originating in Egypt, India and Pakistan, OJ L 332, 4 Dec. 1997, pp. 1-18, recital 16.

158. *Barium Carbonate*, Commission Regulation (EC) No. 145/2005 of 28 Jan. 2005 imposing a provisional anti-dumping duty on imports of barium carbonate originating in the People's Republic of China, OJ L 027, 29 Jan. 2005, pp. 4-23, recitals 50-51, endorsed in Council Regulation (EC) No. 1175/2005 of 18 Jul. 2005 imposing a definitive anti-dumping duty and collecting definitively the provisional duty imposed on imports of barium carbonate originating in the People's Republic of China, OJ L 189, 21 Jul. 2005, pp. 15-23, recital 10; *Certain Polyethylene Terephthalate I*; Council Regulation (EC) No. 2604/2000 of 27 Nov. 2000 imposing a definitive anti-dumping duty and collecting definitively the provisional duty imposed on imports of certain PET originating in India, Indonesia, Malaysia, the Republic of Korea, Taiwan and Thailand, OJ L 301, 30 Nov. 2000, pp. 21-41, recital 29; *Certain Iron or Steel Ropes and Cables*, Commission Regulation (EC) No. 230/2001 of 2 Feb. 2001 imposing a provisional anti-dumping duty on certain iron or steel ropes and cables originating in the Czech Republic, Russia, Thailand and Turkey and accepting undertakings offered by certain exporters in the Czech Republic and Turkey, OJ L 34, 3 Feb. 2001, pp. 4-27, recital 45, endorsed in Council Regulation (EC) No. 1601/2001 of 2 Aug. 2001 imposing a definitive anti-dumping duty and definitively collecting the provisional anti-dumping duty imposed on imports of certain iron or steel ropes and cables originating in the Czech Republic, Russia, Thailand and Turkey, OJ L 211, 4 Aug. 2001, pp. 1-19, recital 42.

In EU practice, cost allocation depends on a historical utilization by the producer. If there is no historic use of the suggested allocation method, it may not be used.[159]

WTO law provides wide discretion to the investigating authorities to make such cost allocations, and it seems reasonable to use a historic record as a proper standard for cost allocation. However, according to WTO law, cost allocation must be based on a case-to-case specific determination. If the producer is able to demonstrate through compelling evidence that a specific allocation methodology should apply, the investigating authorities have to consider such a methodology, regardless of the historic use by the producer. Based on the EU practice, it cannot be concluded that the Commission and the Council would not be willing to exercise such discretion. Neither is it apparent from those cases that the Commission and the Council will depart from the use of historic records in cost allocation.

Adjustments of start-up costs are made if the conditions in Article 2.5 are met.[160] The Commission and the Council will not allow adjustments for start-up costs if the particular situation is not specified in Article 2.5; see for example *Polyethylene Terephthalate Film.*[161]

It may be a violation of WTO law, cf. Article 2.2.1.1 of the ADA, if the Commission and the Council bind themselves to the conditions in Article 2.5. In Article 2.2.1.1 of the ADA, it is provided that costs *shall* be adjusted appropriately for circumstances in which costs are affected by start-up costs. Therefore, the Commission and the Council may have to carry out an examination of the specific facts in particular cases in order to determine whether start-up costs must be adjusted. By locking themselves into a narrow interpretation of Article 2.5 of

---

159. See for instance *Bicycles II*, Council Regulation (EC) No. 397/1999 of 22 Feb. 1999 imposing a definitive anti-dumping duty on imports of bicycles originating in Taiwan and collecting definitively the provisional duty imposed, OJ L 049, 25 Feb. 1999, pp. 1-14, recital 13; *Cotton-type Bed linen I*; Commission Regulation (EC) No. 1069/97 of 12 Jun. 1997 imposing a provisional anti-dumping duty on imports of cotton-type bed linen originating in Egypt, India, and Pakistan, OJ L 156, 13 Jun. 1997, pp. 11-33, recital 36, endorsed in Council Regulation (EC) No. 2398/97 of 28 Nov. 1997 imposing a definitive anti-dumping duty on imports of cotton-type bed linen originating in Egypt, India and Pakistan, OJ L 332, 4 Dec. 1997, pp. 1-18, recital 15.

160. See for instance recital 21 in *Certain Flat-rolled Products of Iron or Non-alloy Steel, of a Width of 600 mm or more*; Commission Decision No. 1357/2001/ECSC of 4 Jul. 2001 amending Decision No. 283/2000/ECSC imposing a definitive anti-dumping duty on imports of certain flat-rolled products of iron or non-alloy steel, of a width of 600 mm or more, not clad, plated or coated, in coils, not further worked than hot-rolled, originating, inter alia, in India, OJ L 182, 5 Jul. 2001, pp. 27-33. See for other cases I. Van Bael & J.F. Bellis, *Anti-dumping and Other Trade Protection Laws of the EC*, 4th edn (The Hague: Kluwer Law International, 2004), 67, n. 95.

161. *Polyethylene Terephthalate Film*; Commission Regulation (EC) No. 367/2001 of 23 Feb. 2001 imposing a provisional anti-dumping duty on imports of PET film originating in India and the Republic of Korea, OJ L 55, 24 Feb. 2001, pp. 16-39, recital 41, endorsed in Council Regulation (EC) No. 1676/2001 of 13 Aug. 2001 imposing a definitive anti-dumping duty and collecting definitively the provisional duty imposed on imports of PET film originating in India and the Republic of Korea, OJ L 227, 23 Aug. 2001, pp. 1-14, recital 19.

the basic Regulation, the Commission and the Council may not exercise the appropriate discretion.

4.2.4.4 Calculation of SAG and Profits

Pursuant to Article 2.3 of the basic Regulation, a reasonable SAG and profits will be added to the costs in order to construct normal value. The EU authorities have shown in their practice that if the producer can demonstrate that some SAG is not related to the sales of the domestic product, they will be excluded from the SAG determination.[162] In the same line, SAG that are used by the producer for export sales – not domestic sales – will be excluded from the SAG and profits determination.[163] That practice seems to be in conformity with the fairness principle, as there appears not to be an uneven use of data.

The principal method to determine SAG and profits is provided in Article 2.6. In practice, SAG will be based on the amounts incurred by the producer with regard to domestic sales of the like product, whereas profit will be based on the weighted-average profit margin for products sold in sufficient quantities in the ordinary course of trade by the producer.[164]

The principal method can be exempted from by the three alternatives in 2.6(a) – (c). In practice, the EU authorities have disregarded the producer's own SAG and profits information for the following reasons: low-volume sales or sales below costs. Those two reasons for departing from the principal method in Article 2.6 are examined in the following. Subsequently, the application of the alternative methods in the subparagraphs to Article 2.6 will be examined.

4.2.4.4.1 Low-Volume Sales

The EU authorities have rejected the SAG and profits data from the producer when the domestic prices have been disregarded because of low-volume or no domestic sales.[165] As a result, the reason in Article 2.3 for disregarding the actual domestic prices of the producer – not representative domestic sales – will also apply in Article 2.6. In *Stainless Steel Fasteners and Parts thereof I*, it became apparent

162. See *Recordable Compact Disks*; Council Regulation (EC) No. 1050/2002 of 13 Jun. 2002 imposing a definitive anti-dumping duty and collecting definitively the provisional duty imposed on imports of recordable compact disks originating in Taiwan, OJ L 160, 18 Jun. 2002, pp. 2-13, recital 18.

163. See *Stainless Steel Fasteners and Parts thereof I*, Council Regulation (EC) No. 393/98 of 16 Feb. 1998 imposing a definitive anti-dumping duty on imports of stainless steel fasteners and parts thereof originating in the People's Republic of China, India, the Republic of Korea, Malaysia, Taiwan and Thailand, OJ L 50, 20 Feb. 1998, pp. 1-14, recital 22.

164. *Polyethylene Terephthalate Film*; Council Regulation (EC) No. 390/2005 of 7 Mar. 2005 terminating the partial interim review of the anti-dumping measures applicable to imports of PET film originating, inter alia, in India, OJ L 63, 10 Mar. 2005, pp. 1-3, recital 15.

165. See for instance *Sacks and Bags Made of Polyethylene or Polypropylene*; Commission Regulation (EC) No. 45/97 of 10 Jan. 1997 imposing a provisional anti-dumping duty on imports of sacks and bags made of polyethylene or polypropylene originating in India, Indonesia and

that data from low-volume domestic sales could instead serve as a basis for SAG and profits determination under Article 2.6(c).[166] However, in *Sulphanilic Acid*, the Commission stated:

> For the product type which was not sold in representative quantities on the domestic market, normal value had to be constructed. In order to determine the constructed normal value, the cooperating exporting producer's own sales, general and administrative (SG&A) costs incurred and weighted average profit realised on domestic sales of the like product, in the ordinary course of trade, during the IP, were added to the average cost of manufacturing during the IP, pursuant to Article 2(6) of the basic Regulation.[167]

The Council endorsed the argumentation by the Commission.[168] This statement seems to represent a change in practice, since low-volume sales are used to find SAG and profits under Article 2.6 – and thus it will not have to be based on an Article 2.6(c) determination. The investigating authorities seem to follow this

---

Thailand, OJ L 12, 15 Jan. 1997, pp. 8-20, recital 15, endorsed in Council Regulation (EC) No. 1950/97 of 6 Oct. 1997 imposing a definitive anti-dumping duty on imports of sacks and bags made of polyethylene or polypropylene originating in India, Indonesia and Thailand and collecting definitively the provisional duty imposed, OJ L 276, 9 Oct. 1997, pp. 1-8, recital 16; and Council Regulation (EC) No. 1763/2002 of 30 Sep. 2002 amending Regulation (EC) No. 1950/97 imposing definitive anti-dumping measures on imports of sacks and bags made of polyethylene or polypropylene originating, inter alia, in India, OJ L 267, 4 Oct. 2002, pp. 1-7, recital 32; *Certain Footwear with Uppers of Leather or Plastics*; Council Regulation (EC) No. 467/98 of 23 Feb. 1998 imposing a definitive anti-dumping duty on imports of certain footwear with uppers of leather or plastics originating in the People's Republic of China, Indonesia and Thailand, OJ L 60, 28 Feb. 1998, pp. 1-29, recitals 30 and 62; *Cotton-type Bedlinen II*; Council Regulation (EC) No. 695/2006 of 5 May 2006 amending Regulation (EC) No. 397/2004 imposing a definitive anti-dumping duty on imports of cotton-type bedlinen originating in Pakistan, OJ L 121, 6 May 2006, pp. 14-26, recital 32; *Certain Electronic Weighing Scales (REWS)*; Council Regulation (EC) No. 2605/2000 of 27 Nov. 2000 imposing definitive anti-dumping duties on imports of certain electronic weighing scales (REWS) originating in the People's Republic of China, the Republic of Korea and Taiwan, OJ L 301, 30 Nov. 2000, pp. 42-60, recital 20.

166. *Stainless Steel Fasteners and Parts thereof I*, Commission Regulation (EC) No. 1732/97 of 4 Sep. 1997 imposing a provisional anti-dumping duty on imports of stainless steel fasteners and parts originating in the People's Republic of China, India, Malaysia, the Republic of Korea, Taiwan and Thailand, OJ L 243, 5 Sep. 1997, pp. 17-36, recital 18, endorsed in Council Regulation (EC) No. 393/98 of 16 Feb. 1998 imposing a definitive anti-dumping duty on imports of stainless steel fasteners and parts thereof originating in the People's Republic of China, India, the Republic of Korea, Malaysia, Taiwan, and Thailand, OJ L 50, 20 Feb. 1998, pp. 1-14, recital 16.
167. *Sulphanilic Acid*, Commission Regulation (EC) No. 575/2002 of 3 Mar. 2002 imposing a provisional anti-dumping duty on imports of sulphanilic acid originating in the People's Republic of China and in India, OJ L 87, 4 Apr. 2002, pp. 28-44, recital 18.
168. *Sulphanilic Acid*, Council Regulation (EC) No. 1339/2002 of 22 Jul. 2002 imposing a definitive anti-dumping duty and collecting definitively the provisional duty imposed on imports of sulphanilic acid originating in the People's Republic of China and India, OJ L 196, 25 Jul. 2002, pp. 11-18, apparently recitals 12 and 17.

practice in some cases,[169] although the overall line of the Commission and the Council is not clear.

Under WTO law, it follows from Article 2.2.2 that SAG and profits '*shall* be based on the actual data pertaining to production and sales in the ordinary course of trade of the like product by the producer or producer under investigation'. Above, it was found that the term 'shall' means to impose an obligation on the investigating authorities. The Commission and the Council are therefore obligated to use data that derive from the ordinary course of trade. The principal method in Article 2.2.2 of the ADA can only be departed from when the sales do not take place in the ordinary course of trade, cf., Appellate Body in *EC – Tube or Pipe Fittings*.[170] The Appellate Body furthermore stated that '[t]he absence of any qualifying language related to low volumes in Article 2.2.2 implies that an exception for low-volume sales should not be read into Article 2.2.2'.[171]

Also, in other areas of the ADA, a national requirement of representative sales, which is not written into a specific provision of the ADA, is rejected. See for example regarding reviews in Article 9.5, where a national requirement of a certain volume of export was rejected by a Panel in *Mexico – Anti-dumping Measures on Rice*.[172] The Appellate Body upheld the Panel findings.[173]

As long as data are in the ordinary course of trade, as defined within the WTO framework, the data cannot be disregarded in the SAG and profits determination. Furthermore, had the drafters wished that the investigating authorities be permitted to disregard data from low-volume sales, they would have stated this in Article 2.2.2 of the ADA.

For the above reasons, the practice applied by the Commission and the Council, according to which data from low-volume sales are used to construct SAG and profit, is in accordance with WTO law, whereas the other practice, where data from low-volume sales are disregarded as not being in the ordinary course of trade, may be in violation of WTO law.

4.2.4.4.2 Sales below Costs

When calculating profits, the EU authorities disregard data from unprofitable sales if the conditions in their Article 2.4 practice are met. In Section 4.1.4.2.2 above,

---

169. See for example *Certain Ringbinder Mechanisms II*, Council Regulation (EC) No. 976/2002 of 4 Jun. 2002 imposing a definitive anti-dumping duty on imports of certain RBM originating in Indonesia and terminating the anti-dumping proceeding in respect of imports of certain RBM originating in India, OJ L 150, 8 Jun. 2002, pp. 1-16, recitals 27-29.
170. *EC – Tube or Pipe Fittings*, WT/DS219/AB/R. Report by Appellate Body 22 Jul. 2003, para. 94.
171. Para. 98.
172. *Mexico – Anti-dumping Measures on Rice*, WT/DS295/R, report of the Panel of 6 Jun. 2005, para. 7.266.
173. *Mexico – Anti-dumping Measures on Rice*, WT/DS295/AB/R, report of the Appellate Body of 29 Nov. 2005, para. 321.

sales below cost were disregarded if the sales volume constituted 20% or more of the domestic sales volume. The Commission and the Council also disregard such sales in the profit calculation.[174]

Under WTO law, Article 2.2.2 of the ADA and practice by the Appellate Body, sales not in the ordinary course of trade must be disregarded.[175] In Article 2.2.1, sales below cost are regarded as being outside the ordinary course of trade. The practice by the Commission and the Council is in line with WTO law.

In Section 4.1.4.2.2 *above*, it was also found that *all sales* were disregarded if the volume of profitable domestic sales was less than 10%. In this line, all sales are disregarded under the principal method in Article 2.6, and profit is based on one of the three exceptions in Article 2.6(a) – (c).[176] The Court of First Instance has endorsed this practice. In *Thai Bicycle Industry v. Council*, the Court of First Instance found:

> [I]n the absence of a specific legal provision, that threshold gives the economic operators concerned a measure of legal certainty with respect to the assessment by the institutions as to whether the profits realized by a producer on its profitable domestic sales of the like product are representative. In the light of that guarantee, the 10% threshold should be upheld and may be derogated from only in exceptional cases[177]

The practice of disregarding profit data from all sales when the 10% limit is exceeded may be a violation of WTO law. In Section 4.1.4.2.2, it was found to be a violation of Article 2.2.1 of the ADA to disregard all sales in the normal value determination. Such sales cannot be disregarded as not being in the ordinary course of trade. It must follow from Article 2.2.2 that such profitable sales – even though they constitute less than 10% of all the domestic sales – must be included in the SAG and profits determination. The statement by the Court of First Instance about representative profitable domestic sales is not convincing, as Article 2.2 of the ADA already contains a 5% limit of representative sales, and furthermore – as

174. See *Stainless Steel Fasteners and Parts thereof I*, Council Regulation (EC) No. 393/98 of 16 Feb. 1998 imposing a definitive anti-dumping duty on imports of stainless steel fasteners and parts thereof originating in the People's Republic of China, India, the Republic of Korea, Malaysia, Taiwan and Thailand, OJ L 50, 20 Feb. 1998, pp. 1-14, recitals 17 and 20.

175. See Section 4.2.2.3.1 above.

176. *Certain Electronic Weighing Scales (REWS)*, Council Regulation (EC) No. 2605/2000 of 27 Nov. 2000 imposing definitive anti-dumping duties on imports of certain REWS originating in the People's Republic of China, the Republic of Korea, and Taiwan, OJ L 301, 30 Nov. 2000, pp. 42-60, recital 20. Apparently also *Polyethylene Terephthalate Film*; Council Regulation (EC) No. 390/2005 of 7 Mar. 2005 terminating the partial interim review of the anti-dumping measures applicable to imports of PET film originating, inter alia, in India, OJ L 63, 10 Mar. 2005, pp. 1-3, recital 15, where only profit from sales in the ordinary course of trade would be included.

177. *Thai Bicycles Industry v. Council*, Case T-118/96, judgment of the Court of First Instance on 17 Jul. 1998, ECR 1998, p. II-2991, para. 71.

stated by the Appellate Body – even data from sales which are not representative must be included in the SAG and profits determination under Article 2.2.2.[178]

4.2.4.5 Weighted Average: Article 2.6(a)

When the principal method to determine SAG and profits in Article 2.6 in the basic Regulation is departed from, the Commission and the Council have established a hierarchy between the alternatives in Article 2.6(a), Article 2.6(b) and Article 2.6(c), in which Article 2.6(a) is the preferred method. Therefore, SAG and profits are based on the weighted average of the actual amounts determined for other producers in respect of production and sales of the like product.

If the method in Article 2.6(a) cannot be used, the method in Article 2.6(b) will be the next in the hierarchic order.[179] Article 2.6(a) is departed from when there is no other producer with a representative domestic sale.[180] It is not a violation of WTO law to prefer the method in Article 2.6(b) to Article 2.6(c) in such situations, as there is no hierarchy between the methods provided in Article 2.2.2(i), 2.2.2(ii) and Article 2.2.2(iii) of the ADA. The Commission and the Council may use whatever method they prefer, as long as the necessary conditions for applying it are fulfilled.

In situations with only *one* other producer, the Commission and the Council practice of departing from the method in Article 2.6(a) seems ambiguous. In *Certain Footwear with Uppers of Leather or Plastics*, the Council found it sufficient to use the amounts of SAG and profits for only one producer with a representative domestic sale. The Council stated:

> In this respect, it was considered, in accordance with Article 2(6)(a) of the Basic Regulation, that the amounts of SG&A and profit of the producer/exporter which did have sufficient domestic sales (. . .) should be used to

178. See Section 4.2.2.3.1 above and *EC – Tube or Pipe Fittings*, WT/DS219/AB/R, report of the Appellate Body on 22 Jul. 2003, paras 97-98.

179. *Cotton-type Bed linen II*, Council Regulation (EC) No. 695/2006 of 5 May 2006 amending Regulation (EC) No. 397/2004 imposing a definitive anti-dumping duty on imports of cotton-type bed linen originating in Pakistan, OJ L 121, 6 May 2006, pp. 14-26, recital 32; *Synthetic Fibre Ropes*, Commission Regulation (EC) No. 18/98 of 7 Jan. 1998 imposing a provisional anti-dumping duty on imports of synthetic fibre ropes originating in India, OJ L 4, 8 Jan. 1998, pp. 28-38, recital 12, endorsed in Council Regulation (EC) No. 1312/98 of 24 Jun. 1998 imposing a definitive anti-dumping duty on imports of synthetic fibre ropes originating in India and collecting definitively the provisional duty imposed, OJ L 183, 26 Jun. 1998, pp. 1-8, recital 10.

180. *Synthetic Fibre Ropes*; Commission Regulation (EC) No. 18/98 of 7 Jan. 1998 imposing a provisional anti-dumping duty on imports of synthetic fibre ropes originating in India, OJ L 4, 8 Feb. 1998, pp. 28-38, recital 12, endorsed in Council Regulation (EC) No. 1312/98 of 24 Jun. 1998 imposing a definitive anti-dumping duty on imports of synthetic fibre ropes originating in India and collecting definitively the provisional duty imposed, OJ L 183, 26 Jun. 1998, pp. 1-8, recital 10.

construct normal value for the six other Indonesian producers/exporters in the sample[181]

SAG and profits data from only one producer was also found sufficient in *Cotton-type Bed linen I*, where the normal value was based on samples.[182] The Council stated that only one producer from the sample had a representative domestic sale and that Article 2.6(a) is not excluded when there is only one producer.[183] A case is pending in *Ikea*,[184] where the EC Court has to rule on whether it is consistent with Article 2.6(a) to establish SAG and profits with data from only one producer. In his opinion, the Advocate General stated that it is not a violation of Article 2.6(a), in particular if there is only one other producer with representative domestic sales.[185]

In recent Commission and Council practice, the Commission and the Council have changed their approach to situations with only one other producer.[186] In *Cotton-type Bed linen II*, the Council made the following statement about the determination of SAG and profits for producers who did not have representative domestic sales:

> The SG&A expenses and profit could not be established on the basis of Article 2(6)(a) of the basic Regulation since only one company had representative domestic sales.[187]

Based on that statement, it is not sufficient to establish SAG and profits under the method in Article 2.6(a) if there is only *one* other producer. If the *Cotton-type Bed linen II* represents a new line in EU practice, that line is in accordance with WTO Law. As stated above, the Appellate Body has emphasized the plural forms in Article 2.2.2(ii) of the ADA, and therefore a weighted average cannot be based on only one other producer. A counterargument to the Advocate General in *Ikea* is

181. *Certain Footwear with Uppers of Leather or Plastics*; Council Regulation (EC) No. 467/98 of 23 Feb. 1998 imposing a definitive anti-dumping duty on imports of certain footwear with uppers of leather or plastics originating in the People's Republic of China, Indonesia and Thailand, OJ L 60, 28 Feb. 1998, pp. 1-29, recital 30.
182. *Cotton-type Bed linen I*; Commission Regulation (EC) No. 1069/97 of 12 Jun. 1997 imposing a provisional anti-dumping duty on imports of cotton-type bed linen originating in Egypt, India and Pakistan, OJ L 156, 13 Jun. 1997, pp. 11-33, endorsed in Council Regulation (EC) No. 2398/97 of 28 Nov. 1997 imposing a definitive anti-dumping duty on imports of cotton-type bed linen originating in Egypt, India and Pakistan, OJ L 332, 4 Dec. 1997, pp. 1-18.
183. Recital 18 in the Council Regulation.
184. *Ikea*; Case 351/04, *Ikea v. Commissioners of Customs & Excise*, OJ C 262, 23 Nov. 2004, p. 18.
185. *Ikea*, Case 351/04, opinion of Advocate General Leger, delivered on 6 Apr. 2006, point 132-134.
186. See for instance *Cotton-type Bed linen I*, Council Regulation (EC) No. 2239/2003 of 17 Dec. 2003 terminating the partial interim review and the expiry review concerning the anti-dumping measures imposed by Regulation (EC) No. 2398/97 on imports of cotton-type bed linen originating, inter alia, in India, OJ L 333, 20 Dec. 2003, pp. 3-8.
187. *Cotton-type Bed linen II*; Council Regulation (EC) No. 695/2006 of 5 May 2006 amending Regulation (EC) No. 397/2004 imposing a definitive anti-dumping duty on imports of cotton-type bed linen originating in Pakistan, OJ L 121, 6 May 2006, pp. 14-26, recital 32.

that the investigating authorities could apply one of the other methods in Article 2.6(b) or Article 2.6(c) if there is only one other producer.

The practice by the Commission and the Council does raise another question. Only data from producers with *representative sales* will be used in the SAG and profits calculation. As stated above, this requirement is not a violation of WTO law as long as the method in Article 2.6(a) is departed from. The situation is different, however, if the method in Article 2.6(a) is applied, but data from producers with sales below 5% are left out of the SAG and profits determination.

According to Article 2.2.2(ii) of ADA, the weighted average of the other producers is based on 'the actual amounts incurred and realized' by those producers. In *EC – Bed linen*, the Appellate Body found that 'realized' means that sales with profit and losses must be used in the weighted average.[188] The producers also realize data from low-volume sales. Furthermore, it can be argued that Article 2.2.2(ii) does not explicitly exclude low-volume sales, whereas in the context it is provided in Article 2.1 together with Article 2.2 that such sales are disregarded. This interpretation suggests that the EU practice of disregarding low-volume sales under the method in Article 2.6(a) is a violation of Article 2.2.2(ii) of the ADA.

4.2.4.6 The Same General Category of Products: Article 2.6(b)

Under the second method in Article 2.6(b), SAG and profits shall be based on the actual amounts applicable to production and sales, in the ordinary course of trade, *of the same general category of products* for the *producer or producer* in question in the domestic market of the country of origin. This means that the product definition will be of significance because the 'same general category of products' must be products with some similarities with the investigated product.

The Commission found in *Certain Footwear with Textile Uppers* that footwear with *plastic uppers*, which were not subject to the proceeding, was in the same general category as footwear with *textile uppers*.[189]

In *Certain Footwear with Uppers of Leather or Plastics*, the product under consideration was non-sports footwear.[190] The Council found that *sports shoes and*

188. *EC – Bed linen*, WT/DS141/AB/R, report of the Appellate Body on 31 Mar. 2001, paras 79-84.

189. *Certain Footwear with Textile Uppers*, Commission Regulation (EC) No. 165/97 of 28 Jan. 1997 imposing a provisional anti-dumping duty on imports of certain footwear with textile uppers originating in the People's Republic of China and Indonesia, OJ L 029, 31 Jan. 1997, pp. 3-18, recital 27, endorsed in Council Regulation (EC) No. 2155/97 of 29 Oct. 1997 imposing a definitive anti-dumping duty on imports of certain footwear with textile uppers originating in the People's Republic of China and Indonesia and collecting definitively the provisional duty imposed. OJ L 298, 1 Nov. 1997, pp. 1-18.

190. *Certain Footwear with Uppers of Leather or Plastics*, Council Regulation (EC) No. 467/98 of 23 Feb. 1998 imposing a definitive anti-dumping duty on imports of certain footwear with uppers of leather or plastics originating in the People's Republic of China, Indonesia and Thailand, OJ L 60, 28 Feb. 1998, pp. 1-29, recital 15.

sports wear was of the same general category as *non-sports shoes*. SAG and profits was then based on the sales of sports shoes and sports wear.[191]

As in WTO law, the Commission and the Council have wide discretion to determine the same general category of products. However, the discretion has certain limits, as the aim is to establish a price as close as possible to the like product. Therefore, the broader the category of products, the less likely it is that SAG and profits will reflect the actual SAG and profit. Under WTO law, it is a case-by-case examination, and it cannot be concluded here whether the EU adheres to WTO law or not.

The Commission and the Council have rejected the method in Article 2.6(b) in cases where the producer concerned did not have representative sales, in the ordinary course of trade, of the same general category of products.[192] Within the WTO framework, there is no hierarchy between the subparagraphs; see Section 4.2.2.3.2 above. The Commission and the Council may then choose another method than the one in Article 2.6(c). However, it may violate Article 2.2.2(i) of the ADA if the Commission and the Council apply the method in Article 2.6(b) but leave out data from non-representative sales and only use data from representative sales to determine SAG and profit; see Section 4.2.4.5 above.

4.2.4.7 Third Method: Any Other Reasonable Method – Article 2.6(c)

If the other two methods in Article 2.6(a) and Article 2.6(b) are not applicable, the third method in Article 2.6(c) will be applied by the Commission and the Council.[193] In such a situation, the determination of SAG and profits must be based on a method that is 'reasonable', where profit must not exceed weighted-average profit of other producers of the product in the same general category.

In *Certain Tungsten Electrodes*, the Commission used the profit by EU producers. In that regard, the Commission stated:

> In the absence of any other reasonable basis, it was decided to use the profit margin realized in the past by the Community industry, before the impact of Chinese imports was felt on the market.[194]

---

191. Recital 62.
192. *Cotton-type Bed linen II*, Council Regulation (EC) No. 695/2006 of 5 May 2006 amending Regulation (EC) No. 397/2004 imposing a definitive anti-dumping duty on imports of cotton-type bed linen originating in Pakistan, OJ L 121, 6 May 2006, pp. 14-26, recital 32.
193. See *Certain Footwear with Uppers of Leather*, Council Regulation (EC) No. 1472/2006 of 5 Oct. 2006 imposing a definitive anti-dumping duty and collecting definitely the provisional duty imposed on imports of certain footwear with uppers of leather originating in the People's Republic of China and Vietnam, OJ L 275, 6 Oct. 2006, pp. 1-41, recital 102.
194. *Certain Tungsten Electrodes*, Commission Regulation (EC) No. 1350/2006 of 13 Sep. 2006 imposing a provisional anti-dumping duty on imports of certain tungsten electrodes originating in the People's Republic of China, OJ L 250, 14 Sep. 2006, p. 10-33, recital 33.

This indicates that the use of the profit margins from EU producers only applies when no other reasonable methods of calculating the profit can be found.

There have also been cases where data from low-volume sales have found their way into the SAG and profits determination under Article 2.6(c). For example, in *Stainless Steel Fasteners and Parts thereof I*, the Commission disregarded the producer's own SAG and profits because domestic sales were below the 5% threshold defined in Article 2.3.[195] The Council stated:

> In this respect, it is considered that the fact that the domestic sales are not made in representative quantities is not in itself sufficient to disregard the data pertaining to these sales in the context of Article 2(6)(c) of the Basic Regulation.[196]

In this specific case, the data regarding SAG from the producer were used in the construction because the amount was in line with the weighted average of SAG of the other producers. Profit, however, differed significantly from the other producers and was therefore disregarded.[197]

In the *Cotton-type Bed linen II*, only one company had representative domestic sales. The SAG and profits were then based on the weighted average of its SAG and profits combined with the weighted-average SAG and profits for two companies with a non-representative sale of 2.2% and 0.2%.[198] The Council stated in that regard:

> In fact, it was considered that the domestic sales of these latter two companies, although not representative for the purpose of using domestic prices to calculate their own normal value, were sufficient to ensure that the related SG&A and profit could be considered as reliable for the purpose of applying Article 2(6)(c) of the basic Regulation.[199]

In the same case, the Council rejected a proposal by one producer to use the producer's own records of domestic sales to calculate the SAG and profits. However, the domestic sales were not of the like product and thus could not serve as a proper reference for the SAG and profits determination.[200]

---

195. *Stainless Steel Fasteners and Parts thereof I*, Commission Regulation (EC) No. 1732/97 of 4 Sep. 1997 imposing a provisional anti-dumping duty on imports of stainless steel fasteners and parts originating in the People's Republic of China, India, Malaysia, the Republic of Korea, Taiwan and Thailand, OJ L 243, 5 Sep. 1997, pp. 17-36, recital 18.
196. *Stainless Steel Fasteners and Parts thereof I*, Council Regulation (EC) No. 393/98 of 16 Feb. 1998 imposing a definitive anti-dumping duty on imports of stainless steel fasteners and parts thereof originating in the People's Republic of China, India, the Republic of Korea, Malaysia, Taiwan and Thailand, OJ L 50, 20 Feb. 1998, pp. 1-14, recital 16.
197. Recital 16 of the Council Regulation and recital 18 of the Commission Regulation.
198. *Cotton-type Bed linen II*, Council Regulation (EC) No. 695/2006 of 5 May 2006 amending Regulation (EC) No. 397/2004 imposing a definitive anti-dumping duty on imports of cotton-type bed linen originating in Pakistan, OJ L 121, 6 May 2006, pp. 14-26, recital 32.
199. Recital 33.
200. Recital 35.

In *Certain Footwear with Uppers of Leather or Plastics*, SAG and profits were based on the sales of other domestic producers' sale of products of the same general category. The Council found that sports shoes and sportswear were of the same general category as the product under investigation, non-sport footwear.[201] The EU authorities used a similar method in *Certain Footwear with Textile Uppers*.[202]

In *Certain Footwear with Uppers of Leather*, the Council based the SAG and profits determination on the amounts found for other producers *in other investigations* when those producers had domestic sales in the ordinary course of trade in accordance with Article 2.2.[203]

Under WTO law, there appears to be wide discretion in the application of the method in Article 2.2.2(iii). It is to a large extent left to the Commission and the Council to determine a reasonable method of finding SAG and profit. As long as the conditions for the profit determination are fulfilled, and the product scope is as close to the like product as possible, there seems to be no violation of WTO law in the abovementioned cases. It must be noted here that the method of using profit data from the EU producers seems to be the last resort.

4.3 FINAL COMMENTS

Chapter 4 was divided into two sections. Section 4.1 dealt with the general rules on normal value, whereas Section 4.2 concerned alternative ways of determining normal value.

In Section 4.1, it was found that under EU law, normal value is generally based on the actual price between the producer and the domestic buyer, which is also the rule under WTO law. WTO law has indirect conditions for normal value under Article VI.1 of GATT 1994 and Article 2.1 of the ADA, where the actual domestic prices are used if they are comparable with the export price and come from sales in the ordinary course of trade for the like product when destined for consumption in the exporting country.

---

201. *Certain Footwear with Uppers of Leather or Plastics*, Council Regulation (EC) No. 467/98 of 23 Feb. 1998 imposing a definitive anti-dumping duty on imports of certain footwear with uppers of leather or plastics originating in the People's Republic of China, Indonesia and Thailand, OJ L 60, 28 Feb. 1998, pp. 1-29, recital 62.
202. *Certain Footwear with Textile Uppers*, Commission Regulation (EC) No. 165/97 of 28 Jan. 1997 imposing a provisional anti-dumping duty on imports of certain footwear with textile uppers originating in the People's Republic of China and Indonesia, OJ L 029, 31 Jan. 1997, pp. 3-18, recital 28, endorsed in Council Regulation (EC) No. 2155/97 of 29 Oct. 1997 imposing a definitive anti-dumping duty on imports of certain footwear with textile uppers originating in the People's Republic of China and Indonesia and collecting definitively the provisional duty imposed, OJ L 298, 1 Nov. 1997, pp. 1-18, recital 35.
203. *Certain Footwear with Uppers of Leather*; Council Regulation (EC) No. 1472/2006 of 5 Oct. 2006 imposing a definitive anti-dumping duty and collecting definitely the provisional duty imposed on imports of certain footwear with uppers of leather originating in the People's Republic of China and Vietnam, OJ L 275, 6 Oct. 2006, pp. 1-41, recital 103.

However, a few points must be made about WTO law and the requirements for normal value. The Appellate Body has in one instance, in *US – Zeroing (Japan)*, stated that Article 2.1 of ADA does *not impose obligations* on the WTO Members; however in other cases, the Panels and the Appellate Body appear to have stressed the conditions in Article 2.1 as *requirements* to the WTO Members.[204] The statement in *US – Zeroing (Japan)* leads to some uncertainty as to what conditions must be met to use the actual domestic prices as normal value – and what the conditions are for disregarding the actual domestic prices. The statement by the Appellate Body in *US – Zeroing (Japan)* was also commented on by the Norwegian representative in the so-called 'minutes meeting' in the DSB.[205]

The scope of discretion left to the investigating authorities may then be wider than the standpoint represented here, where it has been argued that the conditions in Article 2.1 must be met. It could be suggested that WTO legislation could provide a clear definition of normal value with the exact requirements to the price used for comparison with the export price. Furthermore, a clear definition of normal value – and when to exclude some domestic transactions – will also prevent investigating authorities from finding ways of *zeroing* low-priced domestic transactions as the situation was in *Argentina – Poultry Anti-dumping Duties*,[206] described in Chapter 6, Section 6.2.2.3.1 below.

It appears that EU legislation and practice have similar conditions, although the categorization is different. The different categories are not in themselves a violation of WTO law. Furthermore, the EU legislation provides that sales must be made to independent customers, but at the same time it leaves room for discretion about sales in the ordinary course of trade between associated parties, where the last part seems to be in conformity with the requirement under WTO law.

In EU practice, a domestic price is rarely disregarded for not being comparable. In situations where local export sales are disregarded due to the particular market situation, the reason based on non-comparability seems to be the right WTO category if it is demonstrated that the market has a particular situation and that the particular market situation affects the price comparability.

EU practice on sales not made in the ordinary course of trade also includes local export sales, which may violate WTO law. Sales between associated parties may also be disregarded for not being in the ordinary course of trade, where EU practice appears to conform with WTO law, although the Regulations lacks information whether the EU disregards such sales per se without testing the sales for their 'normality'.

Sales below costs may be disregarded by the EU institutions as not being in the ordinary course of trade, where the EU institutions follow the 20% test as prescribed under WTO law. However, the EU also applies a 10% test, and this may violate WTO law.

---

204. *US – Zeroing (Japan)*, WT/DS322/AB/R, report of Appellate Body on 9 Jan. 2007, para. 140.
205. WT/DSB/M/225, on 8 Mar. 2007, paras 81-83.
206. *Argentina – Poultry Anti-dumping Duties*, WT/DS241/R, report of the Panel on 22 Apr. 2003.

In the low-volume sales determination, the Commission and the Council apply two tests. The general test is in conformity with WTO law, whereas the type-to-type-based test may be a violation of WTO law.

According to EU practice, local export sales have been disregarded because the product was ultimately destined for export. As stated above, prices from local export sales may be disregarded as not being comparable with the export price. The argumentation that such sales are destined for export may violate the 'destined for consumption in the exporting country' requirement under WTO law.

Downstream sales between associates are not explicitly regulated in WTO legislation. The Appellate Body has found that the application of the resale price to the first independent customer is not a violation of WTO law.

In *US – Hot-Rolled Steel*, the Appellate Body found that the normal value may be based on the first resale price to an independent customer in downstream sales situations between associated parties. The Panel had reached another conclusion. The focus by the Appellate body is on the seller of the product, and by referring to Article 2.1, the Appellate Body found that this provision does not provide any rule as to who the seller is. The Appellate Body could have substantiated its argumentation by referring to Article 2.2 and its subparagraphs, where the constructed normal value is based on records kept by the *producer or exporter*. Article 2.2 shows that 'seller' is not limited to just be a producer but can also be an exporter.

However, the finding by the Appellate Body is not that straightforward. The adjustment mechanism in Article 2.4 provides that *a fair comparison* between normal value and export price must be made *at the same general level of trade, normally at the ex-factory level*. In the spirit of Article 2.4, it would therefore be reasonable to suggest that in situations where normal value and export price originate from the same level of trade, the starting point for normal value would be that price, which could then be adjusted for the factors reflecting the association, affecting price comparability. By allowing the use of resale prices, it seems that the situations are being turned upside down; there are export and domestic sales from the producer at the same level of trade, but the price from the domestic sale is replaced by the resale price, which is then adjusted back to the ex-factory level.

Furthermore, as pointed out by the Panel, resale prices are explicitly written into the export price provision in Article 2.3; if there is no export or the export price is unreliable, the resale price to the first independent customer must be used. Resale prices are not provided as an alternative to the actual domestic price. However, the reference to Article 2.3 has some reservations; whereas the export price is limited to the price from the transaction between the exporting country and the importing country, there may nevertheless be several domestic prices of the like product due to several transactions in the domestic distribution chain.

However, by allowing the resale price in downstream sales situations, the investigating authorities now have the discretion to:

- Use the resale price from the first independent customer. It appears that the actual price between the associated parties under this method may be disregarded per se.

– Make an ordinary course of test, in order to determine whether the price between the associated parties is to be disregarded; then, if there are no sales in the ordinary course of trade, base the normal value on one of the two methods provided in Article 2.2.

By having those two alternatives, the method preferred by an investigating authority is not predictable. Under the first mentioned alternative, the investigating authorities are not required to test whether the sale between the producer and the associated buyer is made in the ordinary course of trade, whereas under the second alternative, the investigating authorities must make a test. In situations where two associated parties strictly use a market-based price between them, then under the first alternative such prices may be disregarded, and the normal value will instead be artificially made by adjusting the first resale price to the first independent buyer back to the same level of trade.

Furthermore, by using the argumentation of the Appellate Body, there seems to be no hindrance to using a resale price also in situations where the producer is *not* associated with the domestic buyer. Article 2.1 does not explicitly provide that the resale price from a buyer who is not associated with the producer cannot serve as a basis for normal value as long as it is adjusted back to the same general level of trade. There is no requirement that the normal value must be made to the first independent customer.

It seems there are several loopholes in the WTO system, which makes WTO law unpredictable in situations of downstream sales. It could be suggested that under the normal value definition, it would be clear on which seller the normal value will generally be based, and under such circumstances the price from other domestic sellers may be used as normal value.

The EU approach to downstream sales between associates is in accordance with the wide discretion offered under WTO law. The EU uses the first resale price to an independent customer. It appears that the EU also provides a test in order to determine whether the price between the associated parties is in the ordinary course of trade. Although the use of a test seems reasonable and allows prices between associates if the prices come from a normal market transaction, it may violate WTO law if the price is disregarded for not being in the ordinary course of trade and then replaced by the resale price. Under Article 2.2 of the ADA, it is clear that resale price is not an alternative to the prices that have been disregarded for not being in the ordinary course of trade.

Section 4.2 dealt with the alternatives to the actual domestic prices when they have been disregarded or when there are no domestic prices. EU law suggested three alternatives where the use of other sellers' prices may be a violation of WTO law, while WTO law only offers two alternatives: third-country prices and construction based on costs, SAG and profits.

In EU practice, the constructed normal value based on costs, SAG and profits is the preferred method if other sellers' prices cannot be used. It is in conformity with WTO law to prefer the constructed normal value to the third-country prices, as those alternatives are equal under WTO law.

WTO law provides a provision about cost determination and a provision about SAG and profit. It must be noted that in both *US – Softwood Lumber V* and *EC – Bed linen*, Panels have been overruled in the interpretation of those provisions; this may indicate that the text of those provisions is not that clear. Concerning the construction of normal value, the cost determination had some vagueness under WTO law. It was not clear when investigating authorities had to compare different allocation methods. The Commission and the Council make adjustments when there is a link between costs and production, and this is in line with WTO law. However, in EU law there may be some problems about the adjustment of start-up costs, where the conditions to make adjustment – also the line followed in practice – may be a violation of WTO law. Furthermore, it was not clear whether the Commission and the Council also are willing to compare alternative cost allocation methods.

SAG and profits must be established by using data from sales in the ordinary course of trade. This is the principal method under both WTO and EU law. WTO law requires that data from low-volume sales – which under WTO law is not the 'ordinary course of trade' category – must be used in the SAG and profits determination. EU has had a mixed practice in that regard and has occasionally disregarded such data in conflict with WTO law. Furthermore, the Commission and the Council also reject data from all sales in below costs situations when the 10% limit is reached; in Section 4.1 this was found to violate WTO law. In addition, concerning SAG and profits determination under the principal method, there is no legal basis under WTO law to reject such data.

When the principal method cannot be used, WTO law contains three equal alternatives. In EU practice these are put into a hierarchy, which is not in violation of WTO law. In the EU, the preferred method is the method where SAG and profits are based on a weighted average of amounts of other producers. The practice revealed, however, that on some occasions the Commission and the Council have based SAG and profits on data from only one other producer. Such an approach is in violation of WTO law; subsequently, the Commission and the Council have apparently changed the approach to conform to WTO law. Furthermore, the Commission and the Council may disregard data from unrepresentative sales, and this may also violate WTO law. The second method used in the EU system, SAG and profits based on data from the particular producer of the same general category of products, showed inconsistency with WTO law only when data from unrepresentative sales were disregarded. The third method applied by the Commission and the Council – SAG and profits calculated in any other reasonable manner – could not be questioned under WTO law.

Chapter 5
Export Price

In this chapter, it is examined whether the EU determination of the export price of the dumped product is in conformity with WTO law.

As is the case with normal value determination, the determination of the export price is a challenge in situations where sales take place between related parties. In those situations, the export price may not be regarded as reliable, because the export price may be lower or higher than the prices between unrelated parties in the ordinary course of trade. The questions discussed in this chapter are the same as in the previous chapter. The first question seeks to investigate under what circumstances the actual export price between a producer and an importer may be disregarded. The second question is then aimed at determining the alternatives if the export price is disregarded.

The export price determination is rarely challenged compared to the normal value determination, and the rules are less complicated than those applying to normal value.

The starting-point in this chapter is WTO law on export price. First, the legislation is described, and next the practice by the Panels and the Appellate Body is described. As the export price determination only rarely gives rise to disputes, the practice is limited to concern adjustment of export price. After providing the WTO legal framework on the export price, the EU legislation and practice is examined under WTO law.

5.1 WTO LEGISLATION

WTO legislation contains no definition of the export price. Indirect guidance can be found in the dumping definition in Article VI.1 of GATT 1994 and Article 2.1 of the ADA, where the export price is the price of the allegedly dumped product that is exported from one country to another.

It is not further elaborated in Article VI of GATT 1994 or Article 2.1 of the ADA whether the export price is the ex-factory price or the price when the product enters the importing country. In between the ex-factory and the entrance into the importing country, there may be transportation costs, insurance, freight, customs, etc. that may affect the price of the product. However, under Article 2.4, which is examined in the next chapter, the normal value and export price must be adjusted to be comparable.

WTO legislation regulates specific situations where the export price is to be disregarded. Note 1 re Article VI.1 provides:

> Hidden dumping by associated houses (that is, the sale by an importer at a price below that corresponding to the price invoiced by an exporter with whom the importer is associated, and also below the price in the exporting country) constitutes a form of price dumping with respect to which the margin of dumping may be calculated on the basis of the price at which the goods are resold by the importer.

Hidden dumping takes place in situations where the exporter and importer are associated, and the importer resells the product at prices below the purchase price. In that situation, the price between the related parties may be disregarded and the export price based on the resale price to the first independent customer. The note re Article VI has now been manifested in Article 2.3 of the ADA, which reads:

> In cases where there is no export price or where it appears to the authorities concerned that the export price is unreliable because of association or a compensatory arrangement between the exporter and the importer or a third party, the export price may be constructed on the basis of the price at which the imported products are first resold to an independent buyer, or if the products are not resold to an independent buyer, or not resold in the condition as imported, on such reasonable basis as the authorities may determine.

Article 2.3 provides alternatives to the export price if:

- there is no export price; or
- the export price is unreliable *because of association or compensatory agreements*.

According to the provision, it is left to the investigating authorities to determine when the export price is unreliable because of association or compensatory agreement, as the investigating authorities may use the constructed export price '*where it appears to the authorities*' that the actual export price is unreliable.

If one of those conditions is met, the investigating authorities may construct the export price on the resale price to the first independent customer. If the product is not resold to an independent customer or if the product is not resold in the same conditions, then the investigating authorities have discretionary powers to determine the export price on such reasonable basis as they determine.

There are also specific rules about adjustment of the constructed export price. Article 2.4 of the ADA provides that a fair comparison must be made between the normal value and the export price. Article 2.4, fourth sentence, refers explicitly to the constructed export prices in Article 2.3 and states that 'allowances for costs, including duties and taxes, incurred between importation and resale, and for profits accruing, should also be made'.

When the resale price or any other reasonable price is used as the export price, the investigating authorities should therefore make such allowances. For example, in the resale price situation, the investigating authorities should take into account that the resale price may include some costs, for example transportation costs, which would not be there if the actual export price had been used.

In the next section, a few statements by Appellate Body and Panels are described. Issues over export prices are a rare phenomenon in the WTO dispute settlement system, and there is no practice about the export price determination. The unproblematic nature of the export price determination may also be seen in the evolution of the text of Article 2.3, which is a reproduction of the text of the Kennedy ADA and the Tokyo ADA. It has not been necessary to make any amendments to the text.

5.2 PRACTICE BY PANELS AND APPELLATE BODY

In WTO practice, reference to Article 2.3 is rare, and it has not been directly stated when the actual export price between exporter and importer can be departed from. In *US – Hot-Rolled Steel,* the Appellate Body concluded that resale prices in downstream sales in *normal value* determinations are permitted, although resale prices are only explicitly provided in regard to export prices, 'when the export price is unreliable because of association'.[1] It must be assumed that the export price can only be made from a resale price if the requirement of either association or compensatory agreement is met, cf. Article 2.3.

Although some reservations must be made to draw such a conclusion from the particular case because it regarded normal value, it was more apparent in *US – Stainless Steel,* where a Panel made a number of statements about construction of the export price. The investigating authorities in the US, the USDOC, had determined the export price based on the price to the first independent customer because the Korean producer, Pohang Iron and Steel Company (POSCO), was associated with the US importer, Pohang Steel America Corporation (POSAM). The USDOC had adjusted the export price, i.e., the resale price for amounts originating from unpaid sales from an independent buyer who went bankrupt and had not paid POSAM for the product. USDOC had deducted the amount of unpaid sales from the price to other first independent buyers. The US claimed it was part of constructing the export price under Article 2.3 of the ADA. Korea claimed that the adjustment should be dealt with under Article 2.4 of the ADA, and that the specific adjustments were impermissible under that provision. The Panel made a distinction

1. *US – Hot-Rolled Steel*, WT/DS184/AB/R, report of Appellate Body on 24 Jul. 2001, para. 171.

between the different purchasers of the allegedly dumped product. In situations with sales to unrelated buyers, the adjustments were considered under Article 2.4, third sentence.[2] See more about adjustments in next chapter. In situations where the adjustments for the unpaid sales were made for sales to related buyers, it was regarded as part of constructing the export price.[3] It would then be a question regarding Article 2.3 and Article 2.4, fourth sentence, of the ADA.

In the relation between Article 2.3 and 2.4, fourth sentence, the Panel stated:

> In our view, both Article 2.3 and Article 2.4 play an important role in respect of the construction of export prices. When determining whether dumping exists, Article 2.1 usually requires a comparison of the export price with the comparable price, in the ordinary course of trade, for the like product when destined for consumption in the exporting country. *Article 2.3, however, authorizes a Member to construct the export price where, inter alia, the actual export price is unreliable because of association between the exporter and the importer.* As discussed in section VI.C.2.(b)(i), it was pursuant to this authorization that the DOC disregarded the export price charged by POSCO to its affiliated importer POSAM in these investigations and instead constructed the export price.
>
> *Further, Article 2.3 specifies that the export price may be constructed on the basis of the price at which the imported products are first resold to an independent buyer. It is clear from this language that, while the price charged to the first independent buyer is a starting-point for the construction of an export price, it is not itself the constructed export price. Nor does Article 2.3 itself contain any guidance regarding the methodology to be employed in order to construct the export price. Rather, the only rules governing the methodology for construction of an export price are set forth in Article 2.4 of the AD Agreement*, which provides that, '[i]n the cases referred to in paragraph 3, allowances for costs, including duties and taxes, incurred between importation and resale, and for profits accruing, should also be made'. Although the United States repeatedly refers to these allowances as 'Article 2.3 adjustments', the provision governing these allowances is found in Article 2.4 and it is therefore evident to us that a claim regarding the appropriateness of allowances made to construct an export price may be made pursuant to that Article.[4] (Emphasis added)

According to this statement, Article 2.3 of the ADA permits the investigating authorities to construct an export price when the actual export price is disregarded because it is unreliable due to association. Article 2.3, however, does not provide any guidance on how to construct the export price. Guidance to construct the export price is based on Article 2.4, fourth sentence.

---

2. *US – Stainless Steel*, WT/DS179/R, report of the Panel on 22 Dec. 2000, paras 6.71-6.80.
3. Paras 6.62-6.69.
4. Paras 6.90-6.91.

The US then claimed that even though Article 2.4 provides guidance on the construction of the export price, it is not mandatory to make such adjustments due to the text in Article 2.4, fourth sentence, where allowances for costs, etc. 'should' be made. The Panel stated that in the ordinary meaning, 'should' is generally a non-mandatory expression. It would work as non-mandatory in situations where the investigating authorities did not make allowances for factors that would result in a lower margin. The Panel then stated that allowances under Article 2.4, fourth sentence, are binding on the investigating authorities, and that investigating authorities are not permitted to make allowances in addition to those listed under Article 2.4, fourth sentence. In that respect, the Panel distinguished between the allowances made for *price comparability*, which is elaborated on in the next chapter, in Article 2.4, *third sentence*, and the allowances made for construction of the export price. The investigating authorities cannot make allowances for the constructed export price based on factors from Article 2.4, third sentence.[5]

The Panel was now ready to examine whether the deduction of an amount of unpaid sales from the price charged by the associated importer POSAM to the first independent customer was a permissible allowance for costs incurred between importation and resale under Article 2.4, fourth sentence, in the construction of the export price.

The Panel noted that the purpose of making such allowances is to '*construct a reliable export price to use in lieu of the actual export price*'.[6] The Panel stated:

> Read in light of this object and purpose, *we recognize that costs related to the resale transaction but not incurred in a temporal sense between the date of importation and resale could as a general matter be considered to be 'incurred between importation and resale' and thus deducted in order to construct an export price*. Nor do we preclude that an amount to cover the risk of non-payment might be considered to be such a cost. *We do not believe, however, that this interpretation of costs 'incurred between importation and resale' can be stretched to include costs that not only were not incurred in an accounting sense until after the date of resale but which were entirely unforeseen at that time*. In this regard, we observe that, while we agree with the United States that as a general principle a related importer may be expected to establish price based on costs plus profit, a price certainly cannot be expected to reflect an amount for costs that were entirely unforeseen at the time the price was set. *To deduct costs which not only were incurred after the date of resale but which were entirely unforeseen at that time would not result in a 'reliable' export price in the sense of the price that would have been paid by the related exporter had the sale been made on a commercial basis.*[7] (Emphasis added)

The cost allowances under Article 2.4, fourth sentence, are not only limited to those costs that are incurred in the time between import and resale by the related

5. Paras 6.92-6.95.
6. Para. 6.99.
7. Para. 6.100.

importer, as costs from the resale may be adjusted. However, if the costs are both unforeseen costs, like the bankruptcy of the independent customer and they incur after the time of resale, they cannot be regarded as costs incurred in the time between import and resale. Such costs cannot be adjusted under Article 2.4, fourth sentence. The Panel then rejected the argument by the US.[8]

The findings by the Panel in *US – Stainless Steel* are the only ones directly dealing with export prices in WTO practice. In the following sections, EU legislation and EU practice are regarded under WTO law.

5.3 EU LEGISLATION

In contrast to the WTO legislation, the concept of export price is explicitly defined under EU legislation. Article 2.8 of the basic Regulation reads:

> The export price shall be the price actually paid or payable for the product when sold for export from the exporting country to the Community.

The export price is the price when the product is sold for export *from* the exporting country, not the price when the product crosses the EU border.

Article 2.9 of the basic Regulation provides:

> In cases where there is no export price or where it appears that the export price is unreliable because of an association or a compensatory arrangement between the exporter and the importer or a third party, the export price may be constructed on the basis of the price at which the imported products are first resold to an independent buyer, or, if the products are not resold to an independent buyer, or are not resold in the condition in which they were imported, on any reasonable basis.
>
> In these cases, adjustment for all costs, including duties and taxes, incurred between importation and resale, and for profits accruing, shall be made so as to establish a reliable export price, at the Community frontier level.
>
> The items for which adjustment shall be made shall include those normally borne by an importer but paid by any party, either inside or outside the Community, which appears to be associated or to have a compensatory arrangement with the importer or exporter, including usual transport, insurance, handling, loading and ancillary costs; customs duties, any anti-dumping duties, and other taxes payable in the importing country by reason of the importation or sale of the goods; and a reasonable margin for selling, general and administrative costs and profit.

The first sentence of Article 2.9 is an importation of the WTO wordings from Article 2.3 of the ADA. The export price can be based on resale prices to the first

8. Para. 6.101.

independent buyer or, if that is not possible, on 'a reasonable basis' – which is left to the discretion of the Commission and the Council. The conditions for this are:

- there is no export price; or
- the export price is unreliable due to association or compensatory agreement.

The term 'associated' was defined in the last chapter in normal value situations under Article 2.1, fourth sentence, with reference to Article 143 of Commission Regulation (EEC) No. 2454/93 of 2 July 1993 laying down provisions for the implementation of Council Regulation (EEC) No. 2913/92 establishing the Community Customs Code. The question is whether this definition also covers the situations under Article 2.9, as there is no explicit reference to Article 143 of the mentioned Regulation. It is here worth noting that the definition of associated parties under Article 2.1, fourth sentence, came into the basic Regulation with Council Regulation 1972/2002 amending the basic Regulation.[9] It follows from the preamble of the 1972/2002 Regulation that it is expedient to give guidance as to when parties may be considered as related for the purpose of determining dumping, and then reference is made to the 2454/93 Regulation. Given the reference to dumping determinations and not just normal value determinations, it must be assumed that the definition also covers the Article 2.9 situations.

The second sentence of Article 2.9 closely resembles Article 2.4, fourth sentence, of the ADA. The Commission and the Council must make adjustments for the additional costs that are incurred between the import and the resale of the product, when the export price is based on a resale price.

The third sentence of Article 2.9 is a catalogue of costs that are adjusted for in the resale situations. Those costs are transport, insurance, handling, loading and ancillary. Under Article 2.4 of the ADA, fourth sentence, the term *costs* is not defined. This may indicate that there is wide discretion to the investigating authorities to define costs under national law.

Article 2.9 of the basic Regulation, third sentence, furthermore provides that adjustments are to be made for customs duties, anti-dumping duties and taxes related to the importation. The WTO text only provides that duties and taxes are to be adjusted, and the text is silent about anti-dumping duties. Given the lack of a definition of *duties* in the ADA, it must be assumed that there is wide discretion to define 'duties', and therefore that constructed export price may be adjusted for anti-dumping duties under WTO law.

Finally, Article 2.9, third sentence, provides that adjustments must be made for SAG and profits. Compared to WTO law, it may be questioned whether SAG must be adjusted. The text of Article 2.4 of the ADA, fourth sentence, only refers to 'profits', not to SAG. However, when looking into the context of Article 2.4 of the ADA, fourth sentence, it is worth noting that cost under Article 2.2 refers to cost of production, which is one element in the constructed normal value. SAG and profits

9. Council Regulation (EC) No. 1972/2002 of 5 Nov. 2002 amending Regulation (EC) No. 384/96 on the protection against dumped imports from countries not members of the European Community, OJ L 305, 7 Nov. 2002, pp. 1-3.

are the other elements in the constructed normal value. The term 'costs' under Article 2.4, fourth sentence, must be assumed to be a more comprehensive concept, as there is no explicit reference to 'cost of production'. Therefore, under a general concept of costs, SAG may fall under costs to be included under the general definition. Based on such a reading, the inclusion of SAG in the text of Article 2.9, third sentence, of the basic Regulation seems to be in conformity with WTO law.

In the following section, the practice regarding export price by the Commission and the Council towards Asian countries, as well as that at the EC courts, is examined under WTO law.

5.4 EU PRACTICE

In this section, it is first examined how the EU authorities deal with the general rule that export price is based on the price actually paid, and under what circumstances the actual export price is disregarded. Subsequently, the EU practice on the alternatives to the actual domestic price will be examined.

5.4.1 Actual Export Price

The general rule of the export price in Article 2.8 of the basic Regulation is to use the actual export prices paid or payable. In practice, the Commission and the Council also follow the principle of basing the export price on the actual export price paid by the importer.[10]

---

10. See for instance *Synthetic Fibre Ropes*, Commission Regulation (EC) No. 18/98 of 7 Jan. 1998 imposing a provisional anti-dumping duty on imports of synthetic fibre ropes originating in India, OJ L 4, 8 Jan. 1998, pp. 28-38, recital 13, endorsed in Council Regulation (EC) No. 1312/98 of 24 Jun. 1998 imposing a definitive anti-dumping duty on imports of synthetic fibre ropes originating in India and collecting definitively the provisional duty imposed, OJ L 183, 26 Jun. 1998, pp. 1-8, recital 11; *Polyester Staple Fibres I*, Commission Regulation (EC) No. 1472/2000 of 6 Jul. 2000 imposing a provisional anti-dumping duty on imports of polyester staple fibres originating in India and the Republic of Korea, OJ L 166, 6 Jul. 2000, pp. 1-13, recital 36, indirectly endorsed in Council Regulation (EC) No. 2852/2000 of 22 Dec. 2000 imposing a definitive anti-dumping duty and definitively collecting the provisional duty imposed on imports of polyester staple fibres originating in India and the Republic of Korea, OJ L 332, 28 Dec. 2000, pp. 17-31, recitals 14 and 36; *Sulphanilic Acid*, Commission Regulation (EC) No. 575/2002 of 3 Mar. 2002 imposing a provisional anti-dumping duty on imports of sulphanilic acid originating in the People's Republic of China and in India, OJ L 87, 4 Apr. 2002, pp. 28-44, recital 20, endorsed in Council Regulation (EC) No. 1339/2002 of 22 Jul. 2002 imposing a definitive anti-dumping duty and collecting definitively the provisional duty imposed on imports of sulphanilic acid originating in the People's Republic of China and India, OJ L 196, 25 Jul. 2002, pp. 11-18, recital 15; *Granular Polytetrafluoroethylene (PTFE)*, Commission Regulation (EC) No. 862/2005 of 7 Jun. 2005 imposing provisional anti-dumping duties on imports of granular polytetrafluoroethylene (PTFE) originating in Russia and the People's Republic of China, OJ L 144, 8 Jun. 2005, pp. 11-36, recital 59, endorsed in Council Regulation

5.4.1.1 Disregarding the Actual Export Price

In Article 2.9, first sentence, it is provided that when an export price is unreliable because of association or compensatory agreement, the export price may be determined on basis of first resale price to an independent customer or, if that is not possible, on any reasonable basis. In the following sections, the practice about disregarding the export price is examined.

5.4.1.1.1 Association and Compensatory Agreements

In practice, the Commission and the Council disregard the actual export prices between an exporter and an associated EU importer; they use the alternative method.[11]

Furthermore, sales between parties with a compensatory agreement are also disregarded and the export price then based on the resale price to the first independent customer. There have been a few cases before the Court of First Instance regarding the requirement that the Commission and the Council establish that a compensatory agreement has been reached between the exporter and the importer.

In *Miwon v. Council*,[12] a Korean company, Miwon, manufactured monosodium glutamate and sold it to importers in the EU. In the first anti-dumping investigation, an undertaking had been accepted.[13] In a review of the anti-dumping

(EC) No. 1987/2005 of 2 Dec. 2005 imposing a definitive anti-dumping duty and collecting definitively the provisional duty imposed on imports of granular PTFE originating in Russia and the People's Republic of China, OJ L 320, 8 Dec. 2005, pp. 1-19, recital 26; *Certain Polyethylene Terephthalate II*, Council Regulation (EC) No. 192/2007 of 22 Feb. 2007 imposing a definitive anti-dumping duty on imports of certain polyethylene terephthalate originating in India, Indonesia, Malaysia, the Republic of Korea, Thailand and Taiwan following an expiry review and a partial interim review pursuant to Art. 11(2) and 11(3) of Regulation (EC) No. 384/96, OJ L 59, 27 Feb. 2007, pp. 1-33, recital 28; *Certain Plastic Sacks and Bags,* Council Regulation (EC) No. 1425/2006 of 25 Sep. 2006 imposing a definitive anti-dumping duty on imports of certain plastic sacks and bags originating in the People's Republic of China and Thailand, and terminating the proceeding on imports of certain plastic sacks and bags originating in Malaysia, OJ L 270, 29 Sep. 2006, pp. 4-41, recital 52.

11. *Certain Side-by-side Refrigerators;* Commission Regulation (EC) No. 355/2006 of 28 Feb. 2006 imposing a provisional anti-dumping duty on imports of certain side-by-side refrigerators originating in the Republic of Korea, OJ L 59, 1 Mar. 2006, pp. 12-33, recital 23, endorsed in Council Regulation (EC) No. 1289/2006 of 25 Aug. 2006 imposing a definitive anti-dumping duty and collecting definitively the provisional duty imposed on imports of certain side-by-side refrigerators originating in the Republic of Korea, OJ L 236, 31 Aug. 2006, pp. 11-17, recital 19.
12. *Miwon v. Council*, Case T-51/96, judgment of the Court of First Instance of 30 Mar. 2000, ECR 2000, p. II-1841.
13. *MSG*, Council Regulation (EEC) No. 1798/90 of 27 June 1990 imposing a definitive anti-dumping duty on imports of MSG originating in Indonesia, the Republic of Korea, Taiwan, and Thailand and definitively collecting the provisional anti-dumping duty imposed on such imports, OJ L 167, 30 June 1990, p. 1, amended by Council Regulation (EEC) No. 2966/92 of 12 Oct. 1992, OJ L 299, 1992, p. 1, and by Council Regulation (EEC) No. 2455/93 of 2 Sep. 1993,

measures, the Commission found that the importers had resold monosodium glutamate at a loss during the entire period of investigation to purchasers in the EU. Furthermore, the undertaking had been violated. The Commission concluded that the export price was unreliable because the resale with losses and the violation of the undertaking indicated that there was a compensatory agreement between Miwon and the importers in the EU. Miwon challenged those findings and argued that the Commission and the Council had violated Article 2.8(b) of the 1988 basic Regulation, which has a close resemblance to Article 2.9 of the present basic Regulation, by constructing the export price instead of using the actual export price charged by Miwon.

The Court of First Instance emphasized that the Commission and the Council may determine that there is a compensatory agreement between an exporter and an importer without having actual evidence of its existence. It is sufficient that 'it appears' that a compensatory agreement exists.[14] The Court of First Instance noted that all the importers resold the product at a loss, i.e., at prices below the purchase price plus SAG and a reasonable profit.[15] The Court of First Instance then stated:

> Whilst, as the defendant rightly concedes, an importer may for one reason or another decide not to make a profit on a given transaction, it would none the less be extraordinary if none of the importers who cooperated had made any profit on the imports in question and yet they all, none the less, continued to import the product throughout the investigation period.[16]

The Court of First Instance continued and stated:

> [T]he importers' pricing behaviour must be regarded as a relevant factor for the purposes of establishing the unreliability of the export prices reported by the applicant and/or the existence of compensatory arrangements.[17]

Miwon was not able to make any satisfactory explanation for this pricing behaviour.[18] The Court of First Instance then rejected the claim by Miwon.[19]

From this ruling by the Court of First Instance, it can be concluded that a compensatory agreement can exist, even if there is no actual evidence of such an agreement. The pricing behaviour by the importers is a relevant factor to determine

---

OJ L 225, 1993, p. 1. MSG produced and exported by companies from which undertakings had been accepted by the Commission pursuant to Commission Decision 92/493/EEC of 12 Oct. 1992 accepting undertakings offered in connection with the review of anti-dumping measures applicable to certain imports of MSG originating in Indonesia and terminating the investigation, OJ L 299, 1992, p. 40, and Commission Decision 93/479/EEC of 30 Jul. 1993 accepting undertakings offered in connection with the review of anti-dumping measures applicable to certain imports of MSG originating in Indonesia, the Republic of Korea, Taiwan and Thailand, OJ L 225, 1993, p. 35.

14. Para. 40.
15. Paras 46-47.
16. Para. 50.
17. Para. 53.
18. Para. 64.
19. Para. 86.

the existence of such an agreement. A continuous resale at prices below the purchase price plus a sum of SAG and reasonable profit indicates that a compensatory agreement exists, and therefore the export price may be disregarded.

In *Kundan and Tata v. Council*, the Court of First Instance had to deal with a situation in which the Council said that a compensatory agreement existed *between the producer and the exporter, who were both in the same country*. The exporter resold the product to an importer in EU. The product, stainless steel fasteners, was manufactured by an Indian producer, Kundan, and sold to a domestic buyer, Tata, which resold the product to EU importers at prices approximately 10% lower than the prices Kundan charged Tata. The pricing policy was explained with reference to a system established by the Indian Government – the so-called Pass Book Scheme – where import duties on imported raw materials were reimbursed when products were exported. Tata obtained import duty credits for the products exported to the EU, which enabled it to absorb the difference between the prices Kundan charged for the products in question and the prices at which it resold those products on the Community market.[20] Kundan and Tata had an arrangement between them according to which an amount of 75% of the import credits obtained by Tata under the Pass Book Scheme would be transferred to Kundan by means of a corresponding increase in the price paid by Tata to Kundan.[21]

The Council found that an export price based on the price charged by Kundan to Tata was unreliable due to a compensatory agreement, and the export price was instead based on the resale price charged by Tata to the EU importers.

The question before the Court of First Instance was whether the Council had committed a manifest error of assessment in finding that the price between Kundan and Tata was unreliable on account of the special arrangement between them. The Court of First Instance found that the EU investigating authorities had not proved that Kundan and Tata had entered into an association or a compensatory arrangement with each other, but they inferred such an association or compensatory arrangement essentially from the finding that the resale prices charged by Tata to the EU importers were below the prices charged by Kundan.[22] The Court of First Instance then stated:

> That method is not contrary to either the letter or the spirit of Article 2(9) of the basic regulation. *It is apparent from that provision, and in particular from the use of the term 'where it appears', that the institutions have a certain latitude in deciding whether it is appropriate to apply that article and that recourse may be had to the constructed export price not only where the institutions obtain evidence of the existence of a compensatory arrangement but also where such an arrangement appears to exist.*[23] (Emphasis added)

---

20. *Kundan and Tata v. Council,* Case T-88/98, judgment by the Court of First Instance on 21 Nov. 2001, ECR 2002, p. II-4897, paras 17-18.
21. Para. 73.
22. Para. 60.
23. Para. 61.

In the same paragraph, the Court of First Instance made an analogue reference to the finding in *Miwon v. Council*. It was also concluded in that case that it is sufficient that 'it appears' that a compensatory agreement is made in order to disregard the actual prices and instead construct the export price.

Subsequently, the Court of First Instance analyzed whether the pricing policy enabled the Council to infer the existence of a compensatory arrangement between Kundan and Tata. The Court of First Instance found that the price between Kundan and Tata was influenced by the benefits accruing to Tata from the Pass Book Scheme because Kundan and Tata had arranged to share those benefits, which was reflected in the price between them.[24] The influence on the price was such as to render the prices charged between the Kundan and Tata unreliable for several reasons:

The Pass Book Scheme left Kundan and Tata possibilities for arrangements to share the benefits it generated. For example, the benefits to the holder of the Pass Book were determined on the basis of an estimate by the Indian authorities of the quantity of imported raw materials contained in the product exported, based on the standard norms.[25]

The Pass Book Scheme implied that the duties reimbursed were calculated on the basis of standard norms, and not on factual determination of actual import. This implied that when Tata placed an order at Kundan, Tata could calculate the duty reimbursed from the export in advance. By having the 25 per cent arrangement between them, Tata and Kundan could then arrange the price to make Tata obtain the same profit margin regardless of the price Tata charged the EU importers.[26]

The 25 per cent arrangement between Tata and Kundan, which implied that Kundan would get an transfer of 75 per cent of the reimbursed import duty by means of increasing the price between Kundan and Tata, enabled Kundan and Tata to show a higher export price.[27]

The Court of First Instance could then conclude that the Council had not made a manifest error in finding the price between Kundan and Tata unreliable because a compensatory arrangement existed between them.[28]

From these judgments, it can be concluded that it is not a requirement that the Commission and the Council be able to demonstrate that a factual compensatory arrangement exists. It is sufficient that such an arrangement can be inferred due to the wording in Article 2.9 'it appears'. Under such circumstances, the Commission and the Council will have discretionary powers to find criteria by which it is determined that prices may be unreliable due to such an arrangement. It is common to both *Miwon v. Council* and *Kundan and Tata v. Council* that the pricing policy

24. Paras 75-76.
25. Paras 79-80.
26. Para. 81.
27. Para. 82.
28. Para. 83.

between the producer and buyer was an important factor in determining whether a compensatory agreement existed. Furthermore, if a compensatory agreement between the parties is alleged, then the resale price being below the purchase price is a strong indication that such an agreement in fact exists.

Under WTO law, wide discretion is given to the investigating authorities to determine whether a compensatory agreement exists or not. This is not a factual determination; rather, the investigating authorities are to determine *where it appears* that such an agreement exists, cf. Article 2.3 of the ADA. Such an interpretation finds support in the context of Article 2.3 of the ADA. For example, under the dumping definition in Article 2.1 of the ADA, dumping is only to be determined 'if' the export price is below the comparable price, in the ordinary course of trade, for the like product when destined for consumption. The dumping determination is based on a factual finding of an export price below the normal value. If the negotiators had wanted to have clear evidence of the existence of a compensatory agreement, they would not have inferred the words 'where it appears'. The findings by the Commission, Council and Court of First Instance seem to be within the wide limits of WTO law.

5.4.1.1.2 Other Reasons for Disregarding the Actual Export Price

Apart from being disregarded due to association or a compensatory agreement, the question is whether an export price may be disregarded for other reasons. In *Cotton-type Bed linen II*, a number of Pakistani producers claimed that some exports should be excluded from the anti-dumping investigation, as they were not made in the ordinary course of trade and only represented less than 2% of all export sales. The EU industry opposed this claim and stated that those sales should be taken into account, as they were common in the sector. The Council refused the claim by the EU producers and excluded the particular export sales because those sales were not common in the sector and the sales were only of a small volume.[29]

It is worth noting that the Pakistani producers wanted the export prices to be disregarded. However, under WTO law, export prices can only be disregarded in the situations listed in Article 2.3 or under the weighted-average-to-transaction method provided in Article 2.4.2 of the ADA, which is elaborated on in the Section 6.2. Otherwise, disregarding some export transactions may lead to artificial high dumping margins if the disregarded export transactions are, for example, those with a high export price. In *Cotton-type Bed linen II*, it would then have been more appropriate to justify the exclusion of the particular sales if the particular type of product would not cause or threat to cause injury to the EU industry.

---

29. *Cotton-type Bed linen II*; Council Regulation (EC) No. 695/2006 of 5 May 2006 amending Regulation (EC) No. 397/2004 imposing a definitive anti-dumping duty on imports of cotton-type bedlinen originating in Pakistan, OJ L 121, 6 May 2006, pp. 14-26, recitals 47-48.

5.4.1.2 Sales through a Trading House

The question concerning sales through intermediary parties is what the export price is. If, for example, an Indian producer of bed linen makes a domestic sale to an unrelated domestic buyer who exports the product to an importer in EU, the question is whether the export price will be based on the actual price between the exporter and importer or on the price between the producer and the intermediary buyer.

In practice, the Commission and the Council will generally base the export price on the price between the producer and the exporter, i.e., the intermediary seller, if the exporter is unrelated, and if the producer is aware that the product will be resold for export.[30] Therefore, in situations where the export of the product is made through an intermediary part, like a trading house, the price which is to be regarded as dumped will not as a general rule be the actual price between the exporter and importer, but instead the price between the producer and the exporter.

Furthermore, if a producer (producer 1) is acting both as a producer of one type of the product under investigation which is being exported, and as an intermediary exporter of another type of the product under consideration which is produced by another producer (producer 2) under investigation, producer 1 is regarded as an agent of the second type of the product under consideration. The dumping margin for producer 1 will solely be based on the type of product the producer has in fact produced.[31]

This general rule is deviated from if the producer and the intermediary exporter are associated. See for example *Stainless Steel Fasteners and Parts thereof I*, which resulted in the *Kundan and Tata v. Council* case described above. In that case, the producer, Kundan, and the intermediary party, Tata, were located in the same country from which Tata exported the product. Due to the abovementioned

---

30. *Certain Ball Bearings and tapered Roller Bearings*, Council Regulation (EEC) No. 1739/85 of 24 Jun. 1985 imposing a definitive anti-dumping duty on imports of certain ball bearings and tapered roller bearings originating in Japan, OJ L 167, 27 Jun. 1985, pp. 3-9, recital 11; *Stainless Steel Fasteners and Parts thereof I,* Commission Regulation (EC) No. 1732/97 of 4 Sep. 1997 imposing a provisional anti-dumping duty on imports of stainless steel fasteners and parts originating in the People's Republic of China, India, Malaysia, the Republic of Korea, Taiwan and Thailand, OJ L 243, 5 Sep. 1997, pp. 17-036, recitals 29, 33 and 34, apparently endorsed in Council Regulation (EC) No. 393/98 of 16 Feb. 1998 imposing a definitive anti-dumping duty on imports of stainless steel fasteners and parts thereof originating in the People's Republic of China, India, the Republic of Korea, Malaysia, Taiwan and Thailand, OJ L 50, 20 Feb. 1998, pp. 1-14, recital 33.
31. *Certain Prepared or Preserved Sweetcorn*; Commission Regulation (EC) No. 1888/2006 of 19 Dec. 2006 imposing a provisional anti-dumping duty on imports of certain prepared or preserved sweetcorn in kernels originating in Thailand, OJ L 364, 20 Dec. 2006, pp. 68-91, recital 34, endorsed in Council Regulation (EC) No. 682/2007 of 18 Jun. 2007 imposing a definitive anti-dumping duty and collecting definitively the provisional duty imposed on imports of certain prepared or preserved sweetcorn in kernels originating in Thailand, OJ L 159, 20 Jun. 2007, pp. 14-25, recitals 15-19.

compensatory agreement, the export price was based on the price paid by the first independent buyer.[32]

Under WTO law, the situations with the intermediary parties are not directly regulated. The question is then whether an export price based on the price between the producer and an intermediary exporter may be used instead of the export price between the exporter and the importer. Pursuant to Article 2.1, the export price is of the product *exported from one country to another.* It is hardly convincing to argue that a sale of a product between a producer and an exporter, located in the same country, is export from one country to another. A textual interpretation therefore suggests that the export price must be based on the price between the exporter and the importer, not between the producer and the exporter. This reading is supported in the context. Article 2.3 of the ADA reads that when the export price is unreliable because of an association or compensatory agreement between *the exporter and the importer or a third party,* the export price may be constructed. Clearly, Article 2.3 is addressing situations where there is a close relationship between *the exporter* – not the producer – and the importer or a third party. The export price, which may be disregarded, is then a price from the actual export transaction. Furthermore, Article 2.2 and its sub-paragraphs provide that SAG and profits for normal value shall be based on records kept by *the exporter or producer.* Apparently, there may be a distinction between the producer and the exporter.

The exporter and producer may be the same, for example, when the producer exports directly to EU importers.

Under the general EU rule about the non-association situations, it was emphasized that the producer knew that the sale to the exporter was meant for export. It cannot be rejected that in situations, where the producer did not have such knowledge, the EU authorities may base the export price on the actual export sale. The possible violation of WTO law may then be limited to situations where the export price is based on the price between the producer and exporter, when the producer knows that the product is only transited through the exporters.

In the situations with association between the producer and the exporter, the EU institutions base the export price on the price paid by the first independent buyer if the importer is the first independent buyer. As there are strong arguments for basing the export price on the price between the exporter and importer, it seems convincing to determine the export price on such basis. Therefore, such practice is in conformity with WTO law.

---

32. *Stainless Steel Fasteners and Parts thereof I*, Council Regulation (EC) No. 393/98 of 16 Feb. 1998 imposing a definitive anti-dumping duty on imports of stainless steel fasteners and parts thereof originating in the People's Republic of China, India, the Republic of Korea, Malaysia, Taiwan and Thailand, OJ L 50, 20 Feb. 1998, pp. 1-14, recital 29.

5.4.2 Alternative Export Price

The general rule in EU legislation is to determine the export price based on the ex-factory price. If that price is unreliable due to association or compensatory agreement, the principal method is the *resale price to first independent customer*, see Article 2.9 of the basic Regulation. If the product is not resold to an independent buyer, or the product is not resold in the same condition, then the export price must be based on reasonable criteria.

It is the settled practice of the Commission and the Council to apply the principal method and use the first resale price in situations with associated parties.[33] The Commission and the Council will adjust the export price in accordance with Article 2.9. In situations where the export price is based on the resale price to the first independent buyer, the Commission and the Council will deduct a reasonable profit from the price paid by the independent buyer and adjust for costs incurred between importation and resale by the associated importer.[34]

33. *Stainless Steel Fasteners and Parts thereof I*, Commission Regulation (EC) No. 1732/97 of 4 Sep. 1997 imposing a provisional anti-dumping duty on imports of stainless steel fasteners and parts originating in the People's Republic of China, India, Malaysia, the Republic of Korea, Taiwan and Thailand, OJ L 243, 5 Sep. 1997, pp. 17-36, recital 39, apparently endorsed in Council Regulation (EC) No. 393/98 of 16 Feb. 1998 imposing a definitive anti-dumping duty on imports of stainless steel fasteners and parts thereof originating in the People's Republic of China, India, the Republic of Korea, Malaysia, Taiwan and Thailand, OJ L 50, 20 Feb. 1998, pp. 1-14; *Sulphanilic Acid*, Commission Regulation (EC) No. 575/2002 of 3 Mar. 2002 imposing a provisional anti-dumping duty on imports of sulphanilic acid originating in the People's Republic of China and in India, OJ L 87, 4 Apr. 2002, pp. 28-44, recital 21, endorsed in Council Regulation (EC) No. 1339/2002 of 22 Jul. 2002 imposing a definitive anti-dumping duty and collecting definitively the provisional duty imposed on imports of sulphanilic acid originating in the People's Republic of China and India, OJ L 196, 25 Jul. 2002, pp. 11-18, recital 15; *Polyethylene Terephthalate II*, Council Regulation (EC) No. 192/2007 of 22 Feb. 2007 imposing a definitive anti-dumping duty on imports of certain polyethylene terephthalate originating in India, Indonesia, Malaysia, the Republic of Korea, Thailand and Taiwan following an expiry review and a partial interim review pursuant to Art. 11(2) and Art. 11(3) of Regulation (EC) No. 384/96, OJ L 59, 27 Feb. 2007, pp. 1-33, recital 29.
34. *Polyester Staple Fibres I*, Commission Regulation (EC) No. 1472/2000 of 6 Jul. 2000 imposing a provisional anti-dumping duty on imports of polyester staple fibres originating in India and the Republic of Korea, OJ L 166, 6 Jul. 2000, pp. 1-13, recital 37, endorsed in Council Regulation (EC) No. 2852/2000 of 22 Dec. 2000 imposing a definitive anti-dumping duty and definitively collecting the provisional duty imposed on imports of polyester staple fibres originating in India and the Republic of Korea, OJ L 332, 28 Dec. 2000, pp. 17-31, recitals 35-36; *Sulphanilic Acid*, Commission Regulation (EC) No. 575/2002 of 3 Mar. 2002 imposing a provisional anti-dumping duty on imports of sulphanilic acid originating in the People's Republic of China and in India, OJ L 87, 4 Apr. 2002, pp. 28-44, recital 21, endorsed in Council Regulation (EC) No. 1339/2002 of 22 Jul. 2002 imposing a definitive anti-dumping duty and collecting definitively the provisional duty imposed on imports of sulphanilic acid originating in the People's Republic of China and India, OJ L 196, 25 Jul. 2002, pp. 11-18, recital 15; *Certain Polyethylene Terephthalate II*, Council Regulation (EC) No. 192/2007 of 22 Feb. 2007 imposing a definitive anti-dumping duty on imports of certain polyethylene terephthalate originating in India, Indonesia, Malaysia, the Republic of Korea, Thailand and Taiwan following an expiry review and a partial interim review pursuant to Art. 11(2) and Art. 11(3) of Regulation (EC) No. 384/96, OJ L 59, 27 Feb. 2007, pp. 1-33, recital 29.

The information in the Regulations is limited, but if the adjustments only include costs, duties, SAG and profits that have incurred in the time between import and resale, they are in accordance with the Panel finding in *US – Stainless Steel* mentioned above.

The Commission and the Council may depart from the resale price to the first independent customer if the product has been changed, i.e., it is not in the same condition as when it was imported. The export price may then be based on any other reasonable basis.[35]

The resale price to the first independent customer has also been departed from in other situations. In *Certain side-by-side Refrigerators*,[36] the Council faced a situation where the profit margin had been based on what appeared to be the price between the related importer and an independent buyer. However, after disclosure it was realized that the profit margin was based on the profit margin of the first independent customer. Since the Council could not determine a profit margin on any other prices from sales to first independent customer, the profit was established on another reasonable basis.[37]

When the export price is based on any other reasonable basis, the Commission and the Council may base the export price on other export transactions by the exporter if the exporter has sales to importers with no association or no compensatory agreement.[38] If it is not possible to construct an export price on data from other export sales to independent importers, the Commission and the Council may use the data from other producers.[39]

---

35. *Polyethylene Terephthalate Film*, Commission Regulation (EC) No. 367/2001 of 23 Feb. 2001 imposing a provisional anti-dumping duty on imports of PET film originating in India and the Republic of Korea, OJ L 55, 24 Feb. 2001, pp. 16-39, recital 58, endorsed in Council Regulation (EC) No. 1676/2001 of 13 Aug. 2001 imposing a definitive anti-dumping duty and collecting definitively the provisional duty imposed on imports of PET film originating in India and the Republic of Korea, OJ L 227, 23 Aug. 2001, pp. 1-14, recital 30.
36. *Certain side-by-side Refrigerators*, Commission Regulation (EC) No. 355/2006 of 28 Feb. 2006 imposing a provisional anti-dumping duty on imports of certain side-by-side refrigerators originating in the Republic of Korea, OJ L 59, 1 Mar. 2006, pp. 12-33, endorsed in Council Regulation (EC) No. 1289/2006 of 25 Aug. 2006 imposing a definitive anti-dumping duty and collecting definitively the provisional duty imposed on imports of certain side-by-side refrigerators originating in the Republic of Korea, OJ L 236, 31 Aug. 2006, pp. 11-17.
37. *Certain side-by-side Refrigerators*, Council Regulation (EC) No. 1289/2006 of 25 Aug. 2006 imposing a definitive anti-dumping duty and collecting definitively the provisional duty imposed on imports of certain side-by-side refrigerators originating in the Republic of Korea, OJ L 236, 31 Aug. 2006, pp. 11-17, recital 18.
38. *Polyethylene Terephthalate Film*, Commission Regulation (EC) No. 367/2001 of 23 Feb. 2001 imposing a provisional anti-dumping duty on imports of PET film originating in India and the Republic of Korea, OJ L 55, 24 Feb. 2001, pp. 16-39, recital 58, endorsed in Council Regulation (EC) No. 1676/2001 of 13 Aug. 2001 imposing a definitive anti-dumping duty and collecting definitively the provisional duty imposed on imports of PET film originating in India and the Republic of Korea, OJ L 227, 23 Aug. 2001, pp. 1-14, recital 30.
39. *Certain side-by-side Refrigerators*, Council Regulation (EC) No. 1289/2006 of 25 Aug. 2006 imposing a definitive anti-dumping duty and collecting definitively the provisional duty imposed on imports of certain side-by-side refrigerators originating in the Republic of Korea, OJ L 236, 31 Aug. 2006, pp. 11-17, recital 18.

Under WTO law, the reasons for departing from the resale price to the first independent customer are limited to situations when the product is not resold or not resold in the same condition. When the Commission and the Council have departed from the first resale price to the first independent customer because of changed product conditions, this is in conformity with Article 2.3 of the ADA.

The other situation, in *Certain side-by-side Refrigerators*,[40] in which the resale price to the first independent customer is departed from because the profit data came from the first independent buyer and not the intermediary part, is more questionable. Under WTO law, the only reasons for departing from the principal alternative method are when the product is not resold to an independent customer, or if the product conditions have changed. In the specific case, it seems as though the Council lacks sufficient information to determine the profit margin and therefore decides to base it on another reasonable method. However, it is the investigating authorities' own responsibility that the data submitted to them is adequately accurate to make a dumping determination; see Article 6.6 of the ADA. Even in situations where the producer, exporter, etc. refuses access to or otherwise does not provide the necessary information, the Commission and the Council have to base the resale price on the available facts; see Article 6.8 of the ADA. For its application, see Section 6.3.2.1. Therefore, it may be a violation of WTO law to determine the export price on any other reasonable basis in the circumstances described.

5.5 FINAL COMMENTS

In WTO practice, the determination of the export price does not lead to many issues – and practice is only very limited. The term 'export price' is not directly defined under WTO law, whereas under EU law, export price is defined as the price actually paid or payable for the product when sold for export from the exporting country to the EU.

The reasons for departing from the actual export price are the same under EU law as under WTO law. If the parties are associated, or if it appears that a compensatory agreements exists, the export price must be based on the price paid by the first independent customer. The reasons for departing from the actual export price are also reflected in EU practice. Due to wide discretion under WTO law, the practice by the EU institutions seems to be in conformity with WTO law.

In sales through trading houses located in the exporting country, in EU practice the price between the producer and the trading house serves as the export price. However, it appears to be limited to situations where the producer has

---

40. *Certain side-by-side Refrigerators*, Commission Regulation (EC) No. 355/2006 of 28 Feb. 2006 imposing a provisional anti-dumping duty on imports of certain side-by-side refrigerators originating in the Republic of Korea, OJ L 59, 1 Mar. 2006, pp. 12-33, endorsed in Council Regulation (EC) No. 1289/2006 of 25 Aug. 2006 imposing a definitive anti-dumping duty and collecting definitively the provisional duty imposed on imports of certain side-by-side refrigerators originating in the Republic of Korea, OJ L 236, 31 Aug. 2006, pp. 11-17.

knowledge of the resale. Under WTO law, the export price shall be based on the price between the exporter and the importer. Therefore, the EU may violate WTO law on that point.

The principal alternative to the actual export price is the price to the first independent customer. In EU practice, the principal alternative is departed from if there is a change in the product conditions; this is in conformity with WTO law. It is more questionable whether the EU practice of departing from the first resale price in situations where the profit data is insufficient is in conformity with WTO law.

When the alternatives to the actual export price are used, the EU legislation is clearer than WTO law in defining the costs and duties that may be adjusted. The clearer definitions in the EU legislation seem to be in conformity with WTO law because of the wide discretion left to national law.

Chapter 6
Comparison between Normal Value and Export Price

This chapter deals with the rules of comparison between normal value and export price in order to determine the dumping margin. It is examined whether EU comparison methodologies are in conformity with the methodologies prescribed under WTO law. The chapter is divided into three parts.

In part 6.1, the EU legislation and practice of adjustment of normal value and export price to make the prices comparable is examined under WTO law. As it cannot be expected that domestic transactions and export transactions take place at the same time, in the same quantities, etc., those differences may affect the normal value and export price. Therefore, in order to make a fair comparison between normal value and export prices, adjustment for such differences will be made. In Chapters 4 and 5, it was already mentioned that under WTO law an adjustment mechanism is provided in Article 2.4 of the ADA. Part 6.1 regards that mechanism, its application by Panels and Appellate Body, and EU conformity with WTO law.

Part 6.2 discusses the calculation of the dumping margin. It will be examined what calculation methods to determine the dumping margin are allowed under WTO law. In Chapter 1, some examples of *zeroing* were provided to demonstrate the problematic nature of calculating the dumping margin, and different results may come up depending on the chosen method.

In part 6.3, some general remarks are made about whether the dumping margin is made for individual producers or for a group of producers, i.e., general dumping margins. In Chapter 2 it was noted that the point of departure under WTO law is to calculate individual dumping margins. These however may have exceptions, for example in situations where the number of producers is so large that individual dumping determinations are impracticable, so that sampling techniques may be applied. There may be other situations where a general margin is calculated. Those other situations are briefly touched upon in part 6.3. As dumping margins for

Chinese producers receive special treatment under EU law, the rules on China are described in Chapter 7.

6.1 ADJUSTING NORMAL VALUE AND EXPORT PRICE

This part deals with the adjustment made for normal value and export price for differences affecting price comparability. The starting point is defining a framework of WTO law on such matters, first by looking into WTO legislation. Next is to find the outlines from practice by Panels and Appellate Body. Thereafter, EU legislation and EU practice is examined.

6.1.1 WTO Legislation

The adjustment mechanism of normal value and export price is provided in Article 2.4 of the ADA:

> A fair comparison shall be made between the export price and the normal value. This comparison shall be made at the same level of trade, normally at the ex-factory level, and in respect of sales made at as nearly as possible the same time. Due allowance shall be made in each case, on its merits, for differences which affect price comparability, including differences in conditions and terms of sale, taxation, levels of trade, quantities, physical characteristics, and any other differences which are also demonstrated to affect price comparability.[1] In the cases referred to in paragraph 3, allowances for costs, including duties and taxes, incurred between importation and resale, and for profits accruing, should also be made. If in these cases price comparability has been affected, the authorities shall establish the normal value at a level of trade equivalent to the level of trade of the constructed export price, or shall make due allowance as warranted under this paragraph. The authorities shall indicate to the parties in question what information is necessary to ensure a fair comparison and shall not impose an unreasonable burden of proof on those parties.

The first sentence provides the general principle that the comparison between export price and normal value must be *fair*. In Chapter 1, it was claimed that the fairness principle in the first sentence informs the entire ADA.

The second sentence provides guidelines for the level of comparison, which is '*normally*' the ex-factory level and provides that the comparison between export price and normal value must be made for sale made at 'as nearly as possible the same time'. The second sentence of Article 2.4 thus has two requirements: First, it

1. It is provided in a footnote: 'It is understood that some of the above factors may overlap, and authorities shall ensure that they do not duplicate adjustments that have been already made under this provision.'

is ensured that the export price and normal value are based on prices at the same level of trade. This requirement may cover the situations described in Chapter 4 with downstream sales prices, where the normal value may be based on the price paid by the first independent customer and may be on a different level in the distribution chain than the buyer in the importing country if the producer exports directly to the importer. Therefore, the normal value must be adjusted to reflect a price on the ex-factory level in line with the export price. Second, the second sentence of Article 2.4 has a time requirement, as the comparison of prices must be for export and domestic transactions made as nearly the same time as possible.

There can be several reasons why prices differ over time. For example, if the product under investigation is seasonal, like strawberries, it must be expected that the prices for strawberries out of season are higher than the prices for strawberries in season. Therefore, if the export transactions were made for strawberries in season, it would easily lead to a positive dumping margin if the export prices were compared to prices from domestic transactions out of season.

The third sentence of Article 2.4 regards the requirement to make adjustments for factors affecting price comparability. The provision lists a number of factors that may affect the prices, such as conditions and terms of sale, taxation, levels of trade, quantities, physical characteristics, and any other differences that are demonstrated to affect price comparability. The list of factors provided is not exhaustive, as 'any other differences which are also demonstrated to affect price comparability' shall be adjusted to ensure price comparability. In a footnote, it is furthermore provided that the investigating authorities must make sure that double adjusting does not take place. The third sentence of Article 2.4 leaves wide discretion to the investigating authorities about how the adjustments are made.

The fourth and fifth sentences of Article 2.4 concern the adjustment of the export price. In the previous chapter, it was found that Article 2.4, fourth sentence, addresses the construction of the export price. When the export price is based on first resale prices, allowances must be made for duties, taxes and profit that may be added to the export price due to the use of prices from the forward link in the distribution chain. Otherwise, as provided in the fifth sentence of Article 2.4, the normal value must be adjusted to the same level as the one on which the export price is based.

The sixth sentence of Article 2.4 provides requirements for the burden of proof, which must not be too heavy on the producers or exporters. In addition, the authorities must indicate the information needed to ensure a fair comparison of export price and normal value.

Although Article 2.4 provides requirements regarding adjusting the normal value and export price to make those prices comparable with each other, no guidelines are provided about *how* those adjustments can be made. It must therefore be assumed that the investigating authorities have the discretion to make the calculation of the adjustment.[2]

---

2. See J. Czako, J. Human & J. Miranda, *A Handbook on Anti-dumping Investigations* (Cambridge: Cambridge University Press, 2003), 119.

The requirement under Article 2.4 to ensure a fair comparison between normal value and export price can also include a conversion of currencies. For example, if the Indian exporting producer of bed linen exports at prices based on EUR, but domestic sales are made in INR, the comparison between normal value and export price must include a conversion between EUR and INR. Article 2.4.1 of the ADA provides requirements about such a conversion of currencies:

> When the comparison under paragraph 4 requires a conversion of currencies, such conversion should be made using the rate of exchange on the date of sale,[3] provided that when a sale of foreign currency on forward markets is directly linked to the export sale involved, the rate of exchange in the forward sale shall be used. Fluctuations in exchange rates shall be ignored and in an investigation the authorities shall allow exporters at least 60 days to have adjusted their export prices to reflect sustained movements in exchange rates during the period of investigation.

The general rule is to use the exchange rate for conversion of currencies on the date of the sale. In forward sales, the exchange rate must be based on the forward sale. Fluctuations in exchange rates must be ignored, and the exporters must have at least sixty days to adjust their export prices to reflect the movements in the exchange rates.

In the following section, the practice by Panels and Appellate Body regarding the adjustment of normal value and export price to ensure fair price comparability is described.

6.1.2 Practice by Panels and Appellate Body

Initially, a series of general statements by Panels and Appellate Body about Article 2.4 and adjustment is described. Thereafter, some of the specific rulings about adjustments are described.

Under the first sentence of Article 2.4, the purpose is to ensure that the comparison between normal value and export prices is fair. The term 'fair' was defined by the Appellate Body in *US – Softwood Lumber V (Article 21.5 – Canada)* 'to connote impartiality, even-handedness, or lack of bias'.[4] In *US – Hot-Rolled Steel*, the Appellate Body stated that it rests on the investigating authorities, not on the producers, to ensure a fair comparison,[5] Therefore, the use of data at the comparison level must be even-handed and impartial, and it is the investigating authorities

3. It is added in a footnote: 'Normally, the date of sale would be the date of contract, purchase order, order confirmation, or invoice, whichever establishes the material terms of sale.'
4. *US – Softwood Lumber V (Art. 21.5 – Canda)*, WT/DS264/AB/RW, report of the Appellate Body on 15 Aug. 2006, para. 138.
5. *US – Hot-Rolled Steel,* WT/DS184/AB/R, report of the Appellate Body on 24 Jul. 2001, para. 178, see also *US – Softwood Lumber V*, WT/DS264/R, report of the Panel on 13 Apr. 2004, para. 7.166.

that have to ensure the fair comparison. In *Argentina – Ceramic Tiles*, a Panel stated:

> Article 2.4 places the obligation on the investigating authority to make due allowance, in each case on its merits, for differences which affect price comparability.[6]

Under Article 2.4, the investigating authorities are then obligated to make the necessary adjustments for difference affecting price comparability.[7] Furthermore, in *US – Softwood Lumber V*, a Panel stated that the adjustments must be based on a case-by-case determination based on facts.[8] The Panel also commented on the relationship between the obligation to ensure the fair comparison and the burden of proof on the producers in the last sentence of Article 2.4:

> Based on our understanding of Article 2.4, we consider that the duty of an investigating authority to ensure a fair comparison cannot signify that an investigating authority must grant any claimed adjustment. On the other hand, we are of the view that an investigating authority in possession of the requisite evidence substantiating a claimed adjustment would not be justified in rejecting that claimed adjustment. Finally, bearing in mind the text of Article 2.4, we consider that this provision does not impose on investigating authorities any particular method for examining whether any given difference affects price comparability.[9]

The investigating authorities are not required to adjust for every factor suggested by the producers, but the investigating authorities are required to make the necessary adjustments provided the evidence is convincing. Furthermore, the Panel states that the investigating authority has wide discretion to determine what method will be applied to examine whether adjustments need to be made or not.

In the following part, a number of cases about adjustments are described. Panels and Appellate Body have made statements about differences affecting price comparability and conditions and terms, levels of trade, physical differences, conversion of currencies and other differences.

6.1.2.1 Differences Affecting Price Comparability and Conditions and Terms

Pursuant to Article 2.4, third sentence, the investigating authorities are required to make adjustments for differences that affect price comparability, including differences in conditions and terms in the contractual obligations in the export and domestic sales, respectively.

---

6. *Argentina – Ceramic Tiles,* WT/DS189/R, report of the Panel on 28 Sep. 2001, para. 6.113.
7. See also *Argentina – Poultry Anti-dumping Duties*, WT/DS241/R, report of the Panel on 22 Apr. 2003, para. 7.235.
8. *US – Softwood Lumber V*, WT/DS264/R, report of the Panel on 13 Apr. 2004, para. 7.170.
9. Para. 7.167.

In *US – Stainless Steel*, the Panel was faced with a situation where the US investigating authority, DOC, had adjusted the normal value by adding unpaid sales from a bankrupt purchaser to the normal value of all other domestic sales. Korea challenged this adjustment and claimed that it had not been demonstrated by the US that the unpaid sales had affected price comparability between the export price and normal value.[10] The US asserted that unpaid sales were direct selling expenses and were encompassed as expenses related to payment terms in a contract. Therefore, unpaid sales did affect the price comparability.[11]

The Panel examined Article 2.4 of the ADA and found that Article 2.4, third sentence 'identifies five specific categories of 'differences which affect price comparability': differences in conditions and terms of sale, taxation, levels of trade, quantities, and physical characteristics'.[12] The Panel then looked into the category 'differences in conditions and terms' to determine whether unpaid sales were encompassed by that category. After interpreting 'term' and 'condition', the Panel stated:

> [W]e consider that, read as a whole, the phrase 'conditions and terms of sale' refers to the bundle of rights and obligations created by the sales agreement, and 'differences in conditions and terms of sale' refers to differences in that bundle of contractual rights and obligations. Thus, to the extent that there are, for example, differences in payment terms in the two markets, a difference in the conditions and terms of sale exists. The failure of a customer to pay is not a condition or term of sale in this sense, however. Rather, non-payment involves a situation where the purchaser has violated the 'conditions and terms of sale' by breaching its obligation to pay for the merchandise in question.[13]

The Panel finds that 'conditions and terms' are related to the bundle of rights in a contract. An unpaid sale is not a condition or term but rather a violation of the bundle of rights and thus a violation of the conditions and terms in the contract. The Panel further stated:

> We recall that Article 2.4 identifies 'differences in conditions and terms of sale' as one of several 'differences which affect price comparability'. Thus, the notion of price comparability informs our interpretation of 'differences in conditions and terms of sale'. In our view, *the requirement to make due allowance for differences that affect price comparability is intended to neutralise differences in a transaction that an exporter could be expected to have reflected in his pricing*. A difference that could not reasonably have been anticipated and thus taken into account by the exporter when determining the price to be charged for the product in different markets or to different customers is not a difference that affects the comparability of prices within the

10. *US – Stainless Steel*, WT/DS179/R, report of the Panel on 22 Dec. 2000, para. 6.71.
11. Para. 6.74.
12. Para. 6.73.
13. Para. 6.75.

> meaning of Article 2.4. This reinforces our view that the phrase 'differences in conditions and terms of sale' cannot permissibly be interpreted to encompass an unanticipated failure of a customer to pay for certain sales.[14] (Emphasis added)

The purpose of making adjustments for differences that affect price comparability is to neutralize the differences that the producer *could expect to have reflected his pricing*. On a more general level, the adjustments are limited to those situations that are taken into account by a producer in the price setting. Differences which the producer could not have taken into account in connection with the price setting do not affect price comparability.

The Panel finally noted that the five categories in Article 2.4, third sentence, do not exhaust the possibilities of making adjustments for other differences affecting price comparability,[15] but in the particular case, the US had not argued that its practice was justified on such other basis. The adjustments for unpaid sales made by the DOC were then found not to be a permissible interpretation of Article 2.4, third sentence.[16]

6.1.2.2 Levels of Trade

According to Article 2.4, second sentence, price comparability must take place at the same level of trade, normally the ex-factory level. Article 2.4, third sentence, lists level of trade as a category to be adjusted for to ensure price comparability between export price and normal value.

In *Argentina – Poultry Anti-dumping Duties*, two Brazilian exporters of poultry, Sadia and Avipal, were imposed with Argentinean anti-dumping duties. In the comparison between normal value and export price, the Argentinean investigating authorities, DCD, had not made adjustments for domestic freight costs, which could affect the normal value. The export price, however, was based on ex-factory prices without freight costs. Brazil claimed that it was a violation of Article 2.4 not to make adjustments for such differences. The Panel stated generally:

> Argentina has not argued that it would not have been appropriate in principle to make the adjustment for freight costs. This is entirely reasonable, since it seems to us that under normal circumstances there is an obvious inconsistency with Article 2.4 if an investigating authority compares f.o.b. export prices with 'delivered' domestic prices, because such a comparison would not be made at the same level of trade.[17]

---

14. Para. 6.77.
15. See also *Korea – Certain Paper*, WT/DS312/R, report of the Panel on 28 Oct. 2005, para. 7.138.
16. *US – Stainless Steel*, WT/DS179/R, report of the Panel on 22 Dec. 2000, paras 6.79-6.80.
17. *Argentina – Poultry Anti-dumping Duties*, WT/DS241/R, report of the Panel on 22 Apr. 2003, para. 7.235.

Generally, differences in freight costs between the export sale and domestic sale are to be adjusted for under Article 2.4 to ensure that the prices compared reflect the same level of trade.

The DCD further claimed that the Brazilian exporters had not submitted satisfactory documentation for the freight costs. Sadia had only submitted freight costs on an annual basis – not for each transaction. This argument was rejected by the Panel because the questionnaire for the investigation did not exclude data based on an annual report.[18] However, the other exporter, Avipal, had not provided any documentation for the freight costs, and therefore the DCD were entitled to reject the claim from Avipal.[19]

In the same case, Brazil claimed that Argentina had violated Article 2.4 in having ignored the information provided by Brazil documenting that normal value differed from the export price in respect to tax, finance costs, sales commission and freight costs. Argentina claimed the information received by the DCD was in Portuguese, not Spanish, which is spoken in Argentina. Therefore, the DCD was within its right to ignore the information.[20] The Panel rejected the claim by Argentina because the DCD had used the same data in Portuguese to adjust the normal value upwards due to differences affecting price comparability.[21] This argument by the Panel is also supported by the fairness principle.

6.1.2.3 Physical Differences

When physical differences between the exported and domestically sold product affect price comparability, adjustments must be made for such differences.

In *Argentina – Ceramic Tiles*, the Argentinean investigating authorities, the DCD, had refused to make adjustments between the *different models* of ceramic tiles and failed to provide any alternative methods to deal with the physical differences between the domestic sold and exported products. The producers from EU sold many different models that varied in design, colour, etc. The DCD had instead made adjustments for the *differences in sizes* of the product under investigation. There were three sizes of the tiles, 20 × 20, 30 × 30 and 40 × 40 cm. The Panel stated:

> Article 2.4 places the obligation on the investigating authority to make due allowance, in each case on its merits, for differences which affect price comparability, including differences in physical characteristics. The last sentence of Article 2.4 provides that the authorities shall indicate to the parties in question what information is necessary to ensure a fair comparison. *We believe that the requirement to make due allowance for such differences, in each case on its merits, means at a minimum that the authority has to evaluate identified differences in physical characteristics to see whether an adjustment is*

18. Para. 7.236.
19. Para. 7.239.
20. Paras 7.241-7.242.
21. Para. 7.248.

> *required to maintain price comparability and to ensure a fair comparison between normal value and export price* under Article 2.4 of the AD Agreement, and to adjust where necessary.[22] (Emphasis added)

Argentina also claimed that the information provided by the EU producers had not been sufficient. The Panel stated that, if the information was unsatisfactory, the DCD 'could and should have', under Article 2.4, requested additional information. The Panel noted further that the DCD had made adjustments for other physical differences, but only the 'most important' ones. The Panel concluded that Argentina had violated Article 2.4 by failing to make adjustments for physical differences affecting price comparability.[23]

The Panel establishes a minimum standard concerning physical differences. If such differences are identified, the authorities are required to make adjustments to ensure a fair comparison. The investigating authorities cannot claim that information is insufficient if the investigating authorities have not indicated clearly what information is needed to make the particular adjustment.

In *Argentina – Poultry Anti-dumping Duties*, Argentina was again accused of violating Article 2.4 of the ADA. The DCD had raised *all* the Brazilian exporters' domestic prices by 9.09% due to physical differences between the domestically sold goods – poultry with feet and heads – and the exported goods – poultry without feet and heads. It was not disputed that adjustment should be made for those differences. The issue before the Panel was that the DCD made adjustment for *all* the exporters, including those exporters who both exported and sold domestically poultry *without* feet and heads. The DCD made this general adjustment due to conflicting evidence from the Brazilian domestic trade organization, JOX, and the questionnaires submitted by each Brazilian producer to the DCD.

The Panel found that Argentina had violated Article 2.4 of the ADA. The conflicting information from JOX did not serve as a sufficient basis to conclude that *all* exporters had a domestic sale of poultry with feet and heads, since it was only information from a single producer which had such inconsistencies. The DCD should instead have pursued the evidential differences further.[24]

In *US – Softwood Lumber V*, Canada claimed that the US investigating authority, the DOC, should have made adjustments for differences in dimension of lumber. The Panel held that the DOC had fulfilled the necessary requirements in examining whether such adjustments should be made and had tested whether the differences had an impact on manufacturing costs and sales costs.[25] The Panel stated:

> A discernible pattern of price differences is in our view necessary for a conclusion that a given difference affects price comparability. If, as here,

22. *Argentina – Ceramic Tiles*, WT/DS189/R, report of the Panel on 28 Sep. 2001, para. 6.113.
23. Paras 6.115-6.117.
24. *Argentina – Poultry Anti-dumping Duties*, WT/DS241/R, report of the Panel on 22 Apr. 2003, para. 7.259.
25. *US – Softwood Lumber V*, WT/DS264/R, report of the Panel on 13 Apr. 2004, para. 7.176.

> prices of types compared fluctuated against each other, criss-crossing themselves in many instances, without following any established pattern, we fail to see how an unbiased and objective investigating authority could be obligated to come to a conclusion that differences in dimension affect price comparability.[26]

According to the Panel, there must be a clear pattern in the domestic prices that is different from the pattern in the export prices in order to conclude that a difference in dimension has an effect on the prices. If there are no such differences in the pattern of prices, it cannot be concluded that there is an effect regarding the differences of the dimensions of lumber on the comparability between normal value and export price. The Panel furthermore found that Canada had not suggested any other methods about data examination to the DOC:

> In our view, exporters could have been more forthcoming in suggesting ways in which DOC should have marshalled the data before it. Had the respondents argued that DOC should have examined data in a particular way, in light of the specific facts of the case, and had DOC analysed that data in an unreasonable manner, thus determining that differences in dimension were not demonstrated to have affected price comparability, we might have found that the United States acted inconsistently with Article 2.4. This, however, we do not find to be the case.[27]

The producers should therefore also give suggestions for other methodologies to determine whether price differences have an effect on price comparability if the investigating authorities have not been able to discover such an effect on the price comparability.

6.1.2.4 Conversion of Currencies

Comparison of an export price in one currency with the normal value in another currency can cause some inaccuracies that will affect price comparability. Article 2.4.1 of the ADA provides some guidance in this regard. The provision was tested by a Panel in *US – Stainless Steel*, where the US investigating authority, the DOC, allegedly had converted the prices from the domestic sales in Korea from USD into Korean won (KRW) – and then re-converted the won prices back into USD in order to compare with the currency of the export prices which were in USD. The US had claimed that no double conversion took place because initially the domestic prices reported to DOC had been in KRW, but were later changed to US dollars.

The Panel stated in general terms:

> Article 2.4.1 sets forth rules with respect to the conversion of currencies to be applied '[w]hen the comparison under paragraph 4 requires a conversion of

26. Ibid.
27. Para. 7.183.

> currencies . . . ' While Article 2.4.1 does not spell out the precise circumstances under which currency conversions are to be avoided, *we consider that it does establish a general – and in our view, self-evident – principle that currency conversions are permitted only where they are required in order to effect a comparison between the export price and the normal value.* We note that a contrary interpretation would call into doubt the utility of the introductory clause of Article 2.4.1. If the drafters had not intended to establish a rule that currency conversions be performed only when required, they could easily have drafted Article 2.4.1 to provide that 'Currency conversions should be made using the rate of exchange on the date of sale. . . . '. Further, such an interpretation could result in the unusual situation where currency conversions that were required in order to perform a comparison under Article 2.4 would be subject to the rules set forth in Article 2.4.1, but unnecessary currency conversions could be performed without regard to the rules of Article 2.4.1.
>
> We need not here arrive at any general understanding as to when currency conversions are or are not required within the meaning of Article 2.4.1, nor do we express any view regarding Korea's 'reasonable alternative' test. *Rather, we consider it sufficient to conclude, for the purposes of this dispute, that currency conversion is not 'required', and would thus not be permissible under Article 2.4.1, in instances where the prices being compared are already in the same currency.*[28] (Emphasis added)

The Panel stated that in situations where the domestic sales in the exporting country take place in the same currency as the export price, investigating authorities cannot make a conversion of the currency to a currency of the place of the domestic sales and then re-convert it.

In the case at hand, the Panel then examined the facts before the DOC and found that the prices from one exporter were invoiced both in KRW and in USD, but actually paid in KRW. In addition, KRW prices were determined as of the date of invoice and remained fixed irrespective of any subsequent changes in the KRW/USD exchange rate between the date of invoice and the date of payment. The Panel stated that the DOC had made an unbiased and objective assessment of the evidence before it and could conclude that the domestic sales were made in KRW – not in USD.[29] Regarding the other Korean exporter, the Panel reached the opposite conclusion because the prices paid by the domestic purchasers – although in KRW – were different from the prices on the invoice. The prices actually paid followed the KRW/USD exchange rate. This would lead an unbiased and objective authority to conclude that the domestic prices were *not* made in KRW.[30]

28. *US – Stainless Steel*, WT/DS179/R, report by the Panel on 22 Dec. 2000, paras 6.11-6.12.
29. Para. 6.31.
30. Para. 6.39.

6.1.2.5 Other Differences

As already mentioned, the list of factors in Article 2.4, third sentence, that justify adjustments is not exhaustive. All differences that may affect price comparability should be examined by the investigating authorities in order to find whether the prices are in fact affected by differences and thus cannot be compared on a fair basis unless adjustments are made.

In *Korea – Certain Paper,* some Indonesian producers, Indah Kiat and Pindo Deli, made a domestic sale through a trading house, Cakrawala Mega Indah (CMI), but carried out the export sales to Korea themselves. Indonesia claimed that the Korean authorities, KTC, should have made adjustments for certain marketing activities, which were carried out and charged by the CMI on the domestic market. The KTC had based the normal value for the Indonesian producers on construction, including SAG and interests, but had not adjusted for the alleged expenses by using CMI on the domestic market. The Indonesian producers had dissimilar expenses in their export sales.[31] The Panel found:

> We note that Article 2.4 of the Agreement, which generally requires the IA to carry out a fair comparison between the normal value and the export price, specifically mentions levels of trade as one possible item for which an adjustment may be needed. In addition to providing a non-exhaustive list of items for which adjustments may be needed, Article 2.4 also generally stipulates that necessary adjustments have to be made with respect to any other factor which affects price comparability. Consequently, to make a prima facie case, *Indonesia has to demonstrate to the Panel that there was (1) a difference (2) that affected price comparability between the normal value and the export price* for which the KTC failed to make an adjustment.[32] (Emphasis added)

To claim that adjustments must be made for factors affecting price comparability, the complainant must demonstrate that there is a difference in factors related to normal value and export price and that those factors affect the price comparability between normal value and export price. The Panel found that Indonesia had not been able to demonstrate that differences existed to affect the price comparability:

> *[T]he fact that a trading company handles domestic or export sales of the subject product does not in and of itself mean that there is a difference that affects price comparability and that an adjustment has to be made under Article 2.4. The interested party claiming such an adjustment has to demonstrate that the involvement of the trading company gives rise to a difference that affects price comparability.* We note that, (...) Indonesia repeatedly referred to the costs incurred by CMI as the trading company handling domestic sales of Indah Kiat and Pindo Deli. This, in our view, is not enough

31. *Korea – Certain Paper*, WT/DS312/R, report by the Panel on 28 Oct. 2005, paras 7.135 and 7.139.
32. Para. 7.138.

> to demonstrate that CMI's involvement created a difference between the normal values and the export prices of Indah Kiat and Pindo Deli which affected price comparability. We are not convinced that there were sales-related services rendered by CMI with respect to domestic sales of Indah Kiat's and Pindo Deli's products in the Indonesian market which were not rendered in these two companies' export sales to Korea. Indonesia has failed to make a prima facie case in this regard. We therefore reject Indonesia's claim.[33] (Emphasis added)

When sales take place through a trading house, and the price charged by the trading house may be higher than the sales price between the producer and the trading house, it is not sufficient to claim for adjustments. Only if it is demonstrated that there are different factors affecting the price comparability between the export price and normal value will adjustments be made. In the particular case, Indonesia did not demonstrate that the marketing expenses that CMI incurred in the domestic sale were not incurred by the producers in their export sales. Therefore, the KTC was not obligated to make adjustments for such alleged differences.

In the following sections, the conformity of EU legislation and practice with WTO law is examined.

6.1.3 EU Legislation

The general rule for adjustment of factors affecting price comparability is provided in Article 2.10 of the basic Regulation:

> A fair comparison shall be made between the export price and the normal value. This comparison shall be made at the same level of trade and in respect of sales made at as nearly as possible the same time and with due account taken of other differences which affect price comparability. Where the normal value and the export price as established are not on such a comparable basis due allowance, in the form of adjustments, shall be made in each case, on its merits, for differences in factors which are claimed, and demonstrated, to affect prices and price comparability. Any duplication when making adjustments shall be avoided, in particular in relation to discounts, rebates, quantities and level of trade. When the specified conditions are met, the factors for which adjustment can be made are listed as follows:
>
> (a) Physical characteristics: An adjustment shall be made for differences in the physical characteristics of the product concerned. The amount of the adjustment shall correspond to a reasonable estimate of the market value of the difference.
>
> (b) Import charges and indirect taxes: An adjustment shall be made to normal value for an amount corresponding to any import charges or

33. Para. 7.147.

indirect taxes borne by the like product and by materials physically incorporated therein, when intended for consumption in the exporting country and not collected or refunded in respect of the product exported to the Community.

(c) Discounts, rebates and quantities: An adjustment shall be made for differences in discounts and rebates, including those given for differences in quantities, if these are properly quantified and are directly linked to the sales under consideration. An adjustment may also be made for deferred discounts and rebates if the claim is based on consistent practice in prior periods, including compliance with the conditions required to qualify for the discount or rebates.

(d) Level of trade: (i) An adjustment for differences in levels of trade, including any differences which may arise in OEM (Original Equipment Producer) sales, shall be made where, in relation to the distribution chain in both markets, it is shown that the export price, including a constructed export price, is at a different level of trade from the normal value and the difference has affected price comparability which is demonstrated by consistent and distinct differences in functions and prices of the seller for the different levels of trade in the domestic market of the exporting country. The amount of the adjustment shall be based on the market value of the difference. (ii) However, in circumstances not envisaged under (i), when an existing difference in level of trade cannot be quantified because of the absence of the relevant levels on the domestic market of the exporting countries, or where certain functions are shown clearly to relate to levels of trade other than the one which is to be used in the comparison, a special adjustment may be granted.

(e) Transport, insurance, handling, loading and ancillary costs: An adjustment shall be made for differences in the directly related costs incurred for conveying the product concerned from the premises of the exporter to an independent buyer, where such costs are included in the prices charged. Those costs shall include transport, insurance, handling, loading and ancillary costs.

(f) Packing: An adjustment shall be made for differences in the directly related packing costs for the product concerned.

(g) Credit: An adjustment shall be made for differences in the cost of any credit granted for the sales under consideration, provided that it is a factor taken into account in the determination of the prices charged.

(h) After-sales costs: An adjustment shall be made for differences in the direct costs of providing warranties, guarantees, technical assistance and services, as provided for by law and/or in the sales contract.

(i) Commissions: An adjustment shall be made for differences in commissions paid in respect of the sales under consideration. The term 'commissions' shall be understood to include the mark-up received by a trader of the product or the like product if the functions of such a trader are similar to those of an agent working on a commission basis.

(j) Currency conversions: When the price comparison requires a conversion of currencies, such conversion shall be made using the rate of exchange on the date of sale, except that when a sale of foreign currency on forward markets is directly linked to the export sale involved, the rate of exchange in the forward sale shall be used. Normally, the date of sale shall be the date of invoice but the date of contract, purchase order or order confirmation may be used if these more appropriately establish the material terms of sale. Fluctuations in exchange rates shall be ignored and exporters shall be granted 60 days to reflect a sustained movement in exchange rates during the investigation period.

(k) Other factors: An adjustment may also be made for differences in other factors not provided for under subparagraphs (a) to (j) if it is demonstrated that they affect price comparability as required under this paragraph, in particular that customers consistently pay different prices on the domestic market because of the difference in such factors.

The first sentence of Article 2.10 of the basic Regulation is a reproduction of Article 2.4, first sentence, of the ADA. The general headline is that the comparison must be fair. The second sentence of Article 2.10 of the basic Regulation differs from the second sentence of Article 2.4 of the ADA in one notable respect because, under the EU provision, that the same level of trade is normally the ex-factory level is not included. Furthermore, under Article 2.10(d) of the basic Regulation, level of trade is listed as a factor to be adjusted. The phrase 'normally the ex-factory level' is also absent under that provision. It may be a violation of WTO law if the comparison is in practice performed at other levels than that suggested, although the word 'normally' under Article 2.4 of the ADA, second sentence, prescribes some discretion to the investigating authorities.

The third sentence of Article 2.10 of the basic Regulation provides that if it is claimed and demonstrated that differences affect price comparability, adjustments must be made. The third sentence does not include a list of factors that may be adjusted. The third sentence therefore differs from Article 2.4 of the ADA, third sentence. However, the list of factors follows in Article 2.10(a)-(k) of the basic Regulation. The list of factors is wider under the EU provision than under the WTO provision. The EU list includes:

(a) physical characteristics;
(b) import charges and indirect taxes;
(c) discounts, rebates and quantities;
(d) level of trade;
(e) transport, insurance, handling, loading and ancillary costs;
(f) packing;
(g) credit;
(h) after-sales costs;
(i) commissions;
(j) currency conversions; and
(k) other factors.

However, the last factor, 'other factors', was not included in the original basic Regulation, but came with the amendment to that Regulation in 1996.[34] Consequently, the basic Regulation was brought into conformity with the non-exhaustive list of factors in Article 2.4, third sentence, of the ADA.

Under the fourth sentence of Article 2.10 of the basic Regulation, the footnote re Article 2.4 has been reproduced. The Commission and the Council must avoid making any double adjustments.

Article 2.10 of the basic Regulation lacks some important aspects of Article 2.4 of the ADA. Under the EU provision, it is not mentioned that the burden of proof on the producers, etc., must not be too unreasonable. It must therefore be evaluated on a case-by-case determination whether the EU authorities put a too unreasonable burden on the producers.

6.1.4 EU Practice

In the following, practice by the EU investigating authorities and by the EC courts is described. Under WTO law, wide discretion is given to the investigating authorities, and an evaluation under WTO law should be made on a case-by-case basis, with *all* the necessary information required to make such an examination. The information used here is solely based on information from Regulations and a few judgments from the EC courts, and not on the actual information submitted by the producers. Therefore, the examination of EU practice under WTO law is made with some reservations.

6.1.4.1 Differences in Physical Characteristics: Article 2.10(a)

Article 2.10(a) of the basic Regulation provides that adjustment must be made for physical differences that affect price comparability. In practice, the Commission and the Council make those adjustments for physical differences affecting the prices, including differences in quality.[35]

If a producer requests for adjustments, but cannot demonstrate a link between the physical differences and the prices, the Commission and the Council will refuse to adjust for physical differences.[36] Nor are adjustments made for physical

34. Council Regulation (EC) No. 2331/96 of 2 Dec. 1996 amending Regulation (EC) No. 384/96 on protection against dumped imports from countries not members of the European Community, OJ L 317, 6 Dec. 1996, pp. 1-2.
35. *Certain Polyethylene Terephthalate I*, Council Regulation (EC) No. 496/2002 of 18 Mar. 2002 amending Regulation (EC) No. 2604/2000 imposing a definitive anti-dumping duty on imports of certain polyethylene terephthalate originating, amongst other countries, in India, OJ L 78, 21 Mar. 2002, pp. 4-6, recital 17.
36. *Synthetic Fibre Ropes*, Commission Regulation (EC) No. 18/98 of 7 Jan. 1998 imposing a provisional anti-dumping duty on imports of synthetic fibre ropes originating in India, OJ L 4, 8 Jan. 1998, pp. 28-38, recital 15, endorsed in Council Regulation (EC) No. 1312/98 of 24 Jun. 1998 imposing a definitive anti-dumping duty on imports of synthetic fibre ropes

differences if the domestically sold product and the exported product share the same internal technical codes given by the company.[37]

Concerning the rules upheld by the Commission and the Council, it must be recalled that under WTO law, the burden of proof placed on the producer must not be unreasonable. However, if the Commission and the Council make a thorough examination and cannot establish a link between the physical differences and the prices, and the producers do not provide any other methodologies to support a claim for adjustment, the practice by the Commission and the Council is in conformity with WTO law. However, to refuse adjustments for products that share the same internal codes may be a violation of WTO law if the differences between the products can be identified.

In *Certain side-by-side Refrigerators*,[38] the Council found that the adjustments for physical differences made by the Commission led to distorted normal value. In that particular situation, the adjustments were abandoned, and the normal value was – following a suggestion by the producer – constructed on costs, SAG and profits in accordance with Article 2.3 of the basic Regulation.[39] Since the producer, the Commission, and the Council agreed on the terms, it might not violate WTO law. As described in Chapter 1, the Appellate Body will usually accept an interpretation of a provision if both parties agree to it.

6.1.4.2 Import Charges and Indirect Taxes: Article 2.10(b)

Article 2.10(b) of the basic Regulation is the basis for adjusting for import charges and indirect taxes. In *Polyester Staple Fibres I*, one producer claimed that adjustments should automatically be made for a duty drawback. The Council rejected this claim and stated:

> [A] duty adjustment is only granted provided two conditions are met cumulatively: first, it must be shown that import charges are borne by the like

---

originating in India and collecting definitively the provisional duty imposed, OJ L 183, 26 Jun. 1998, pp. 1-8, recital 13.

37. *Stainless Steel Fasteners and Parts thereof I*, Commission Regulation (EC) No. 1732/97 of 4 Sep. 1997 imposing a provisional anti-dumping duty on imports of stainless steel fasteners and parts originating in the People's Republic of China, India, Malaysia, the Republic of Korea, Taiwan and Thailand, OJ L 243, 5 Sep. 1997, pp. 17-36, recital 44, endorsed in Council Regulation (EC) No. 393/98 of 16 Feb. 1998 imposing a definitive anti-dumping duty on imports of stainless steel fasteners and parts thereof originating in the People's Republic of China, India, the Republic of Korea, Malaysia, Taiwan and Thailand, OJ L 50, 20 Feb. 1998, pp. 1-14, recital 43.
38. *Certain side-by-side Refrigerators*, Commission Regulation (EC) No. 355/2006 of 28 Feb. 2006 imposing a provisional anti-dumping duty on imports of certain side-by-side refrigerators originating in the Republic of Korea, OJ L 59, 1 Mar. 2006, pp. 12-33, endorsed in Council Regulation (EC) No. 1289/2006 of 25 Aug. 2006 imposing a definitive anti-dumping duty and collecting definitively the provisional duty imposed on imports of certain side-by-side refrigerators originating in the Republic of Korea, OJ L 236, 31 Aug. 2006, pp. 11-17.
39. Recital 22 of the Council Regulation.

product and by materials physically incorporated therein when intended for consumption in the exporting country and second, these import charges are refunded or not collected when the product is exported to the Community. If one of the requirements is not fulfilled, the adjustment for duty drawback cannot be granted.[40]

When a duty has been imposed on raw materials that are used in the final product being exported to the EU, the producer must demonstrate that:

- the same material is actually incorporated into both the final product and the like product;
- the import charges must be refunded or not collected when the product is exported.

If both conditions are met, the EU authorities will make adjustments.[41] This line has been upheld in other cases.[42]

The method applied by the Commission and the Council to make adjustments may be changed if the producer can demonstrate a more appropriate method.[43]

---

40. *Polyester Staple Fibres I*, Council Regulation (EC) No. 2852/2000 of 22 Dec. 2000 imposing a definitive anti-dumping duty and definitively collecting the provisional duty imposed on imports of polyester staple fibres originating in India and the Republic of Korea, OJ L 332, 28 Dec. 2000, pp. 17-31, recital 19.
41. See for instance the Commission Regulation in *Polyester Staple Fibres I*, Commission Regulation (EC) No. 1472/2000 of 6 Jul. 2000 imposing a provisional anti-dumping duty on imports of polyester staple fibres originating in India and the Republic of Korea, OJ L 166, 6 Jul. 2000, pp. 1-13, recital 49. See also *Certain Polyethylene Terephthalate II*, Council Regulation (EC) No. 192/2007 of 22 Feb. 2007 imposing a definitive anti-dumping duty on imports of certain polyethylene terephthalate originating in India, Indonesia, Malaysia, the Republic of Korea, Thailand and Taiwan following an expiry review and a partial interim review pursuant to Art. 11(2) and Art. 11(3) of Regulation (EC) No. 384/96, OJ L 59, 27 Feb. 2007, pp. 1-33, recital 57.
42. *Sacks and Bags Made of Polyethylene or Polypropylene*, Commission Regulation (EC) No. 45/97 of 10 Jan. 1997 imposing a provisional anti-dumping duty on imports of sacks and bags made of polyethylene or polypropylene originating in India, Indonesia and Thailand, OJ L 12, 15 Jan. 1997, pp. 8-20, recital 24, endorsed in Council Regulation (EC) No. 1950/97 of 6 Oct. 1997 imposing a definitive anti-dumping duty on imports of sacks and bags made of polyethylene or polypropylene originating in India, Indonesia and Thailand and collecting definitively the provisional duty imposed, OJ L 276, 9 Oct. 1997, pp. 1-8, recitals 19-21; *Stainless Steel Fasteners and Parts thereof I*, Commission Regulation (EC) No. 1732/97 of 4 Sep. 1997 imposing a provisional anti-dumping duty on imports of stainless steel fasteners and parts originating in the People's Republic of China, India, Malaysia, the Republic of Korea, Taiwan and Thailand, OJ L 243, 5 Sep. 1997, pp. 17-36, recital 42, endorsed in Council Regulation (EC) No. 393/98 of 16 Feb. 1998 imposing a definitive anti-dumping duty on imports of stainless steel fasteners and parts thereof originating in the People's Republic of China, India, the Republic of Korea, Malaysia, Taiwan and Thailand, OJ L 50, 20 Feb. 1998, pp. 1-14, recital 36.
43. *Synthetic Fibre Ropes*: Commission Regulation (EC) No. 18/98 of 7 Jan. 1998 imposing a provisional anti-dumping duty on imports of synthetic fibre ropes originating in India, OJ L 4, 8 Jan. 1998, pp. 28-38 endorsed in Council Regulation (EC) No. 1312/98 of 24 Jun. 1998

Although it may be questioned whether the Commission and the Council place an unreasonable burden of proof on the producers, the Commission and the Council are open to suggestions of more appropriate methods to determine whether adjustment should be made. This line by the Commission and the Council seems to be in conformity with the guidelines provided by the Panel in *US – Softwood Lumber V*;[44] see Section 6.1.2.3 above.

6.1.4.3 Discounts, Rebates and Quantities: Article 2.10(c)

Article 2.10(c) of the basic Regulation provides that adjustments must be made for differences in discounts and rebates, including those for differences in quantity, if they are properly quantified and there is a link to the product under consideration. If those conditions are not met, adjustment is refused by the Commission and Council.[45] In *Sulphanilic Acid*, the Commission refused to make adjustments for notional quantity discounts, where the producer claimed that *if* the domestic buyer had bought a similar quantity as the one bought by the EU importer, the domestic buyer would also have qualified to get the discounts. The Commission stated that adjustments will only be made when the discounts are actually given; instead, the Commission tried the claim under 'other factors' in Article 2.10(k); see Section 6.1.4.10 below.[46] The Council endorsed the Commission's finding.[47]

Rules on discounts, rebates and quantities are not provided in Article 2.4 of the ADA, third sentence, and therefore the situation must be dealt with under 'other

imposing a definitive anti-dumping duty on imports of synthetic fibre ropes originating in India and collecting definitively the provisional duty imposed, OJ L 183, 26 Jun. 1998, pp. 1-8, recital 12; *Polyethylene Terephthalate Film*: Commission Regulation (EC) No. 367/2001 of 23 Feb. 2001 imposing a provisional anti-dumping duty on imports of PET film originating in India and the Republic of Korea, OJ L 55, 24 Feb. 2001, pp. 16-39, recitals 61-65, endorsed with some amendments in Council Regulation (EC) No. 1676/2001 of 13 Aug. 2001 imposing a definitive anti-dumping duty and collecting definitively the provisional duty imposed on imports of PET film originating in India and the Republic of Korea, OJ L 227, 23 Aug. 2001, pp. 1-14, recitals 33-34.

44. *US – Softwood Lumber V*, WT/DS264/R, report of the Panel on 13 Apr. 2004.
45. *Polyester Textured Filament Yarn (PTY)*; Commission Regulation (EC) No. 1412/2002 of 29 Jul. 2002 imposing a provisional anti-dumping duty on imports of polyester textured filament yarn (PTY) originating in India, OJ L 205, 2 Aug. 2002, pp. 50-69, recital 37, endorsed in Council Regulation (EC) No. 2093/2002 of 26 Nov. 2002 imposing a definitive anti-dumping duty and collecting definitively the provisional duty imposed on imports of PTY originating in India, OJ L 323, 28 Dec. 2002, pp. 1-20, recital 35.
46. *Sulphanilic Acid*, Commission Regulation (EC) No. 575/2002 of 3 Mar. 2002 imposing a provisional anti-dumping duty on imports of sulphanilic acid originating in the People's Republic of China and in India, OJ L 87, 4 Apr. 2002, pp. 28-44, recital 25.
47. *Sulphanilic Acid*, Council Regulation (EC) No. 1339/2002 of 22 Jul. 2002 imposing a definitive anti-dumping duty and collecting definitively the provisional duty imposed on imports of sulphanilic acid originating in the People's Republic of China and India, OJ L 196, 25 Jul. 2002, pp. 11-18, recital 16.

differences'. In *Korea – Certain Paper*, the Panel stated that the producers must demonstrate that there is a difference in the factors that relate to normal value and export price and that those factors affect the price comparability. If the producer cannot demonstrate that the domestic buyer would have got the same quantity discount, the practice by the Commission and the Council seems to be in conformity with WTO law.[48] It is further to be noted that the Commission and the Council may try a case under Article 2.10(k) if adjustments for discounts are refused under Article 2.10(c). Therefore, a strict burden of proof under Article 2.10(c) does not imply that adjustments cannot be granted, but recourse is taken to Article 2.10(k) instead.

6.1.4.4 Level of Trade: Article 2.10(d)

Pursuant to Article 2.10(d)(i)-(ii) of the basic Regulation, adjustments must be made for differences in the level of trade if such differences affect price comparability. In most cases, a claim for adjustment based on different levels of trade is rejected because the exporter cannot demonstrate the existence of a consistent difference in the functions and prices between the different levels of trade.[49]

If it is demonstrated that a domestic sale is made at a level that does not exist in the EU, then the domestic prices may be disregarded. In *Certain side-by-side Refrigerators*, the Commission and the Council disregarded domestic prices to

---

48. *Korea – Certain Paper*, WT/DS312/R, report of the Panel on 28 Oct. 2005, see Section 6.1.2.5 above.

49. See *Stainless Steel Fasteners and Parts thereof I*, Commission Regulation (EC) No. 1732/97 of 4 Sep. 1997 imposing a provisional anti-dumping duty on imports of stainless steel fasteners and parts originating in the People's Republic of China, India, Malaysia, the Republic of Korea, Taiwan and Thailand, OJ L 243, 5 Sep. 1997, pp. 17-36, recital 44, endorsed in Council Regulation (EC) No. 393/98 of 16 Feb. 1998 imposing a definitive anti-dumping duty on imports of stainless steel fasteners and parts thereof originating in the People's Republic of China, India, the Republic of Korea, Malaysia, Taiwan and Thailand, OJ L 50, 20 Feb. 1998, pp. 1-14, recital 43; *Sacks and Bags Made of Polyethylene or Polypropylene*, Council Regulation (EC) No. 96/1999 of 12 Jan. 1999 amending Regulation (EC) No. 1950/97 imposing a definitive anti-dumping duty on imports of sacks and bags made of polyethylene or polypropylene originating in India, Indonesia and Thailand and collecting definitively the provisional duty imposed, OJ L 11, 16 Jan. 1999, pp. 1-4, recital 12; *Polyethylene Terephthalate Film*, Commission Regulation (EC) No. 367/2001 of 23 Feb. 2001 imposing a provisional anti-dumping duty on imports of PET film originating in India and the Republic of Korea, OJ L 55, 24 Feb. 2001, pp. 16-39, recital 47, endorsed in Council Regulation (EC) No. 1676/2001 of 13 Aug. 2001 imposing a definitive anti-dumping duty and collecting definitively the provisional duty imposed on imports of PET film originating in India and the Republic of Korea, OJ L 227, 23 Aug. 2001, pp. 1-14, recitals 20-22; *Certain Plastic Sacks and Bags*, Council Regulation (EC) No. 1425/2006 of 25 Sep. 2006 imposing a definitive anti-dumping duty on imports of certain plastic sacks and bags originating in the People's Republic of China and Thailand, and terminating the proceeding on imports of certain plastic sacks and bags originating in Malaysia, OJ L 270, 29 Sep. 2006, pp. 4-41, recital 129.

consumers, as that level of trade did not exist in the EU, and because the producer still had a representative domestic sale to establish normal value.[50]

In a situation with *original equipment producers*' sales (OEM sales), i.e., sales where the product carries the buyer's brand name,[51] the Commission and the Council made adjustments for differences in level of trade. See for example *Certain Prepared or Preserved Sweetcorn*, where the Commission accepted a claim by some producers who only exported retailer branded products, but on the domestic market sold the products both under the retailer brand and under the producer's own brand name. There was a difference in the prices between the producer-named products and the retailer-named products.[52]

Again, there is a strong burden of proof put on the producers, and this may be in violation of WTO law. However, the Commission and the Council are open to adjustments if the evidence shows that there is a difference between the levels of trade affecting price comparability. Furthermore, the requirement of a consistent price difference between the different levels is in line with the above-mentioned finding by a Panel in *US – Softwood Lumber V*, where the Panel stated there must be a pattern in the prices between the different levels of trade in order to determine that there is a difference between the prices.[53]

6.1.4.5 Transport, Insurance, Handling, Loading and Ancillary Costs: Article 2.10(e)

Article 2.10(e) of the basic Regulation is not listed on the WTO list in Article 2.4, third sentence, but is apparently another factor that may affect price comparability. In the EU Regulations, this factor seldom gives rise to any controversies.

The Commission and the Council reject adjustments for transport and freight if the transport or freight is invoiced to the producer by a related company. Adjustments are only made for transport costs, etc., in sales between a producer and an

50. *Certain side-by-side Refrigerators*, Commission Regulation (EC) No. 355/2006 of 28 Feb. 2006 imposing a provisional anti-dumping duty on imports of certain side-by-side refrigerators originating in the Republic of Korea, OJ L 59, 1 Mar. 2006, pp. 12-33, recital 28, endorsed in Council Regulation (EC) No. 1289/2006 of 25 Aug. 2006 imposing a definitive anti-dumping duty and collecting definitively the provisional duty imposed on imports of certain side-by-side refrigerators originating in the Republic of Korea, OJ L 236, 31 Aug. 2006, pp. 11-17, recital 26.
51. See I. Van Bael & J. F. Bellis, *Anti-dumping and Other Trade Protection Laws of the EC*, 4th edn (The Hague: Kluwer Law International, 2004), 52-53.
52. *Certain Prepared or Preserved Sweetcorn*; Commission Regulation (EC) No. 1888/2006 of 19 Dec. 2006 imposing a provisional anti-dumping duty on imports of certain prepared or preserved sweetcorn in kernels originating in Thailand, OJ L 364, 20 Dec. 2006, pp. 68-91, recital 36, endorsed in Council Regulation (EC) No. 682/2007 of 18 Jun. 2007 imposing a definitive anti-dumping duty and collecting definitively the provisional duty imposed on imports of certain prepared or preserved sweetcorn in kernels originating in Thailand, OJ L 159, 20 Jun. 2007, pp. 14-25, recital 23.
53. *US – Softwood Lumber V*, WT/DS264/R, report of the Panel on 13 Apr. 2004, para. 7.176.

independent buyer.[54] However, if the producer proves that the price invoiced by the related party is the same as the related party invoices to independent customers, then adjustments may be made.[55]

As seen here, there is not a per se rejection of adjusting freight costs in sales between related parties. However, the Commission and the Council must assure that the related parties are given the opportunity to provide the information necessary to demonstrate that the freight costs from the sales are the same as those from sales to an independent buyer. Under WTO law, if the investigating authorities are not satisfied with the information provided, the investigating authorities are obligated to inform the producers about the information necessary to examine whether adjustments are to be made. See the above-mentioned findings by the Panel in *Argentina – Ceramic Tiles*[56] in Section 6.1.2.3, and the Panel finding in *Argentina – Poultry Anti-dumping Duties*,[57] described in Section 6.3.2.1 below.

6.1.4.6 Packing: Article 2.10(f)

Packing is another factor not listed under the WTO provision in Article 2.4 of the ADA. In EU practice, adjustments for packing have only rarely led to disputes.[58] If there are differences in packing costs, and such differences are demonstrated by the producer or the importer, they must be adjusted for.[59]

In *Recordable Compact Disks*, an anti-dumping duty had been imposed upon some Taiwanese producers, and the dumping margin had been established by the weighted-average-to-transaction method[60] (see more in section 6.2 about this

54. *Potassium Permanganate*, Commission Regulation (EC) No. 178/98 of 23 Jan. 1998 imposing a provisional anti-dumping duty on imports of potassium permanganate originating in India and the Ukraine, OJ L 19, 24 Jan. 1998, pp. 23-34, recital 20, endorsed in Council Regulation (EC) No. 1507/98 of 13 Jul. 1998 imposing a definitive anti-dumping duty on imports of potassium permanganate originating in India and the Ukraine and collecting definitively the provisional duty imposed, OJ L 200, 16 Jul. 1998, pp. 4-8, recital 10.
55. *Certain side-by-side Refrigerators* Council Regulation (EC) No. 1289/2006 of 25 Aug. 2006 imposing a definitive anti-dumping duty and collecting definitively the provisional duty imposed on imports of certain side-by-side refrigerators originating in the Republic of Korea, OJ L 236, 31 Aug. 2006, pp. 11-17, recital 25.
56. *Argentina – Ceramic Tiles*, WT/DS189/R, report of the Panel on 28 Sep. 2001.
57. *Argentina – Poultry Anti-dumping Duties*,WT/DS241/R, report of the Panel on 22 Apr. 2003.
58. See I. Van Bael & J. F. Bellis, *Anti-dumping and Other Trade Protection Laws of the EC*, 4th edn (The Hague: Kluwer Law International, 2004), 111.
59. *Potassium Permanganate*, Commission Regulation (EC) No. 178/98 of 23 Jan. 1998 imposing a provisional anti-dumping duty on imports of potassium permanganate originating in India and the Ukraine, OJ L 19, 24 Jan. 1998, pp. 23-34, recital 19, endorsed in Council Regulation (EC) No. 1507/98 of 13 Jul. 1998 imposing a definitive anti-dumping duty on imports of potassium permanganate originating in India and the Ukraine and collecting definitively the provisional duty imposed, OJ L 200, 16 Jul. 1998, pp. 4-8, recital 10.
60. *Recordable Compact Disks*, Commission Regulation (EC) No. 2479/2001 of 17 Dec. 2001 imposing a provisional anti-dumping duty on imports of recordable compact disks originating in Taiwan, OJ L 334, 18 Dec. 2001, pp. 8-25, recital 29.

method), in which normal value had been constructed based on information about the cost of production of the exported product. The Taiwanese producers claimed that according to the provisional Regulation, the Commission had included *all* packing costs related to exports in the weighted average normal value and then compared the weighted average normal value with the individual export transactions, which also included the same packing costs. Those included packing costs should therefore be adjusted for. The Council accepted the claim by the Taiwanese producers and adjusted the weighted average normal value for the packing costs related to exports.[61]

Again, the Council demonstrates a willingness to take the producers' claim into account. For the reasons stated above, such a flexibility is in conformity with WTO law.

6.1.4.7 Credit: Article 2.10(g)

Pursuant to Article 2.10(g) of the basic Regulation, the Commission and the Council make adjustments for differences in the cost of credit granted for the sales under consideration, provided they are taken into account in the determination of the sale price of the product. It follows from practice that if the producer cannot accurately demonstrate a link between the cost of credit and the sales price, the adjustment is rejected.[62] Even in situations where the producer can refer to contractual obligations of payment charges, it is not sufficient to link the cost of credits with the price charged,[63] nor is a verbal agreement sufficient to demonstrate that credit costs related to the production exist.[64]

---

61. *Recordable Compact Disks*, Council Regulation (EC) No. 1050/2002 of 13 Jun. 2002 imposing a definitive anti-dumping duty and collecting definitively the provisional duty imposed on imports of recordable compact disks originating in Taiwan, OJ L 160, 18 Jun. 2002, pp. 2-13, recitals 22-25.
62. See as examples *Certain side-by-side Refrigerators*, Commission Regulation (EC) No. 355/2006 of 28 Feb. 2006 imposing a provisional anti-dumping duty on imports of certain side-by-side refrigerators originating in the Republic of Korea, OJ L 59, 1 Mar. 2006, pp. 12-33, recital 30, endorsed in Council Regulation (EC) No. 1289/2006 of 25 Aug. 2006 imposing a definitive anti-dumping duty and collecting definitively the provisional duty imposed on imports of certain side-by-side refrigerators originating in the Republic of Korea, OJ L 236, 31 Aug. 2006, pp. 11-17, recital 26; *Certain Polyethylene Terephthalate II*, Council Regulation (EC) No. 192/2007 of 22 Feb. 2007 imposing a definitive anti-dumping duty on imports of certain polyethylene terephthalate originating in India, Indonesia, Malaysia, the Republic of Korea, Thailand and Taiwan following an expiry review and a partial interim review pursuant to Arts 11(2) and 11(3) of Regulation (EC) No. 384/96, OJ L 59, 27 Feb. 2007, pp. 1-33, recital 58.
63. *Polyester Staple Fibres I*, Commission Regulation (EC) No. 1472/2000 of 6 Jul. 2000 imposing a provisional anti-dumping duty on imports of polyester staple fibres originating in India and the Republic of Korea, OJ L 166, 6 Jul. 2000, pp. 1-13, recital 57, endorsed in Council Regulation (EC) No. 2852/2000 of 22 Dec. 2000 imposing a definitive anti-dumping duty and definitively collecting the provisional duty imposed on imports of polyester staple fibres originating in India and the Republic of Korea, OJ L 332, 28 Dec. 2000, pp. 17-31, recital 40.
64. *Sulphanilic Acid*, Commission Regulation (EC) No. 575/2002 of 3 Mar. 2002 imposing a provisional anti-dumping duty on imports of sulphanilic acid originating in the People's

If, however, the Commission and the Council find a link between the cost of credit and the price comparability, adjustments are made. In *Sacks and Bags Made of Polyethylene or Polypropylene*, a number of Indian producers claimed that bank charges for credit, which the Commission had adjusted for in the export price, should not have been taken into account. The producers claimed that those bank charges did not reflect the export prices. The argument by the producers was rejected by the Council, which stated:

> It should be noted that in these cases the bank charges are intrinsically linked to the cost of credit and as such must therefore be taken into consideration when determining the cost of credit. Therefore, the claim could not be accepted.[65]

It is not clear from the text of the Regulation whether an examination of the claim by the Indian producers was made, or whether the Indian producers tried to prove their claim. Under WTO law, adjustments shall only be made for credit costs that in fact affect the price comparison between the export price and normal value. If there is a link between the bank charges and the price comparability, the EU practice is in accordance with WTO law.

6.1.4.8 After-Sales Costs: Article 2.10(h)

The Commission and the Council must make adjustments for direct costs of providing warranties, guaranties, service, etc., as provided by law or by a contractual obligation. If normal value is constructed based on costs and SAG, and the constructed normal value does not include such after-sales costs, a request of deducting after-sales costs from the normal value will be rejected.[66] Under WTO law, after-sales costs may fall under ‘other differences’. Naturally, if the normal value is constructed, and after-sales costs are excluded in the normal value determination, they will not be deducted from the normal value. Otherwise, the normal value would appear to be adjusted for after-sales costs twice, which would violate note 7 re article 2.4 of the ADA. Therefore, the practice by the Commission and the Council is in conformity with WTO law.

Republic of China and in India, OJ L 87, 4 Apr. 2002, pp. 28-44, recital 26, endorsed in Council Regulation (EC) No. 1339/2002 of 22 Jul. 2002 imposing a definitive anti-dumping duty and collecting definitively the provisional duty imposed on imports of sulphanilic acid originating in the People’s Republic of China and India, OJ L 196, 25 Jul. 2002, pp. 11-18, recital 16.

65. *Sacks and Bags Made of Polyethylene or Polypropylene*, Council Regulation (EC) No. 1950/97 of 6 Oct. 1997 imposing a definitive anti-dumping duty on imports of sacks and bags made of polyethylene or polypropylene originating in India, Indonesia and Thailand and collecting definitively the provisional duty imposed, OJ L 276, 9 Oct. 1997, pp. 1-8, recital 18.
66. *Certain Electronic Weighing Scales (REWS)*, Council Regulation (EC) No. 692/2005 of 28 Apr. 2005 amending Regulation (EC) No. 2605/2000 imposing definitive anti-dumping duties on imports of certain electronic weighing scales (REWS) originating, inter alia, in the People’s Republic of China, OJ L 112, 3 May 2005, pp. 1-7, recitals 50-51.

In *Polyester Staple Fibres (PSF) II*, adjustments for after-sales costs are rejected if no condition under law or contractual obligation exists, evidence has not been produced that the cost was an after-sales cost and the technical assistance provided was not demonstrated to affect prices.[67] The rejection seems to be in conformity with WTO law, as the Panel stated in *Korea – Certain Paper* that it must be demonstrated that the price comparability is affected by such differences.[68] If that is not the case, there should be no adjustments. However, it may be questioned whether the requirement of a contractual obligation or a condition under law is in conformity with WTO law. It is not clear what a condition under law in the EU context implies. If, for example, it is customary in the particular field to make after-sales services, in case there is a link to the price comparability and such link is demonstrated by the producer, this is a factor to be considered for adjustment under WTO law.

6.1.4.9 Commissions: Article 2.10(i)

According to Article 2.10(i), adjustments must be made for commissions paid in respect of sales under consideration. Commissions include mark-up received by traders who have a similar function as an agent working on a commission basis. In EU practice, determination of the commission may be based on SAG and profits data from the agent. If profit is influenced by an association, the profit data may be based on data received by an unrelated trader.[69]

In *Kundan and Tata v. Council*, the Court of First Instance was presented with a situation where an Indian producer, Kundan, sold the product, stained steel fasteners, to a domestic buyer, Tata, who resold the product to importers in the EU. The Council had deducted a *notional* commission of approximately 2% from the export price, i.e., from the price between Kundan and Tata. Kundan and Tata claimed the adjustment was inconsistent with Article 2.10 because no commission was paid. The Council claimed that even though no commission was paid, the Council could adjust for it because Kundan made its sales through Tata, which

---

67. *Polyester Staple Fibres (PSF) II*; Commission Regulation (EC) No. 124/2000 of 20 Jan. 2000 imposing a provisional anti-dumping duty on imports of polyester staple fibres (PSF) originating in Australia, Indonesia and Thailand, OJ L 16, 21 Jan. 2000, pp. 30-49, recital 59, apparently endorsed in Council Regulation (EC) No. 1522/2000 of 10 Jul. 2000 imposing a definitive anti-dumping duty on imports of synthetic staple fibres of polyester originating in Australia, Indonesia and Thailand and collecting definitively the provisional duty imposed, OJ L 175, 14 Jul. 2000, pp. 10-28.
68. *Korea – Certain Paper*, WT/DS312/R, report of the Panel on 28 Oct. 2005.
69. *Certain Plastic Sacks and Bags*, Council Regulation (EC) No. 1425/2006 of 25 Sep. 2006 imposing a definitive anti-dumping duty on imports of certain plastic sacks and bags originating in the People's Republic of China and Thailand, and terminating the proceeding on imports of certain plastic sacks and bags originating in Malaysia, OJ L 270, 29 Sep. 2006, pp. 4-41, recital 69.

operated in the same way as an 'agent acting on a commission basis'.[70] The Court of First Instance disagreed with the Council:

> The Council's argument must be rejected. It is apparent from both the wording and the scheme of Article 2(10) of the basic regulation that an adjustment to the export price or the normal value may only be made to take account of differences in factors which affect the prices and therefore their comparability. That is not the case for a commission which has not actually been paid.
>
> To be able to make the adjustment in question, the institutions would have had to base their decision on factors capable of showing, or of giving rise to the inference, that a commission was in fact paid and was such as to have a definite effect on the comparison between the export price and the normal value.
>
> Just as a party who is claiming adjustments under Article 2(10) of the basic regulation in order to make the normal value and the export price comparable for the purpose of determining the dumping margin must prove that his claim is justified (. . .) *it is incumbent upon the institutions, where they consider that they must make an adjustment of the kind made in the present case, to base their decision on direct evidence or at least on circumstantial evidence pointing to the existence of the factors for which the adjustment was made, and to determine its effect on price comparability.*
>
> In the present case, the institutions based their decision solely on the finding that the functions carried out by Tata in the course of its export activity were similar to those of an agent acting on a commission basis. *As they took the view that that finding was sufficient in order to make the adjustment in question, they did not adduce any evidence at all from which it could be inferred that Kundan and Tata had agreed a commission.*[71] (Emphasis added)

In the present case, the Council had not demonstrated that a commission had been paid. Nor was it demonstrated that a commission affected price comparability. The Court of First Instance then concluded that the Council had committed an error of law in applying Article 2.10 of the basic Regulation.[72] The statement by the Court of First Instance is generally made about Article 2.10. The Commission and the Council must be able to demonstrate that

- the factor adjusted for exists; and
- the factor affects price comparability between normal value and export price.

More interestingly, the Court of First Instance states that commission, which is not actually paid, is not a difference in factors affecting prices. The statement seems to

70. *Kundan and Tata v. Council*, Case T-88/98, judgment of the Court of First Instance on 21 Nov. 2001, ECR 2002, p. II-4897, para. 93.
71. Paras 94-97.
72. Para. 98.

be in conflict with the amendment made by the Council to the basic Regulation shortly afterwards,[73] where the Regulation in its present form permits the Commission and the Council to make adjustments for mark-ups received by a trader of the product or the like product if the functions of such a trader are similar to those of an agent working on a commission basis. Therefore, the statement by the Court of First Instance seems to contradict the amendment.[74]

The statement by the Court of First Instance is in line with the findings by the Panel in *Korea – Certain Paper*; see Section 6.2 above, where the Panel also emphasized that a difference must exist and it must affect the price comparability between export price and normal value in order to be adjusted.[75] If the Commission and the Council follow the line in the amended Article 2.10(i), and there is no examination of an actual link between the mark-up and price comparability, it may violate WTO law.

6.1.4.10 Currency Conversions: Article 2.10(j)

When price comparison requires conversion of currencies, the general rule under Article 2.10(j) is to use the currency rate of exchange on the *date of the sale*, which can be the date of invoice, the date of contract or the date of purchase. This requirement is also reflected in practice by the Commission and the Council; therefore, the use of the rate of exchange on the *date of the payment* is rejected.[76]

The Commission and the Council make adjustments for fluctuations between different currencies if they affect price comparability.[77] However, if such fluctuations

73. Council Regulation (EC) No. 1972/2002 of 5 Nov. 2002 amending Regulation (EC) No. 384/96 on the protection against dumped imports from countries not members of the European Community, OJ L 305, 7 Nov. 2002, pp. 1-3, Art. 1.5.
74. See also I. Van Bael & J. F. Bellis, *Anti-dumping and Other Trade Protection Laws of the EC*, 4th edn (The Hague: Kluwer Law International, 2004), 114.
75. *Korea – Certain Paper*, WT/DS312/R, report of the Panel on 28 Oct. 2005, para. 7.138.
76. *Stainless Steel Fasteners and Parts thereof I*, Council Regulation (EC) No. 393/98 of 16 Feb. 1998 imposing a definitive anti-dumping duty on imports of stainless steel fasteners and parts thereof originating in the People's Republic of China, India, the Republic of Korea, Malaysia, Taiwan and Thailand, OJ L 50, 20 Feb. 1998, pp. 1-14, recitals 39 and 41; *Polyethylene Terephthalate Film*, Commission Regulation (EC) No. 367/2001 of 23 Feb. 2001 imposing a provisional anti-dumping duty on imports of PET film originating in India and the Republic of Korea, OJ L 055, 24 Feb. 2001, pp. 16-39, recital 48, apparently endorsed in Council Regulation (EC) No. 1676/2001 of 13 Aug. 2001 imposing a definitive anti-dumping duty and collecting definitively the provisional duty imposed on imports of PET film originating in India and the Republic of Korea, OJ L 227, 23 Aug. 2001, pp. 1-14.
77. *Polyethylene Terephthalate Film*, Commission Regulation (EC) No. 367/2001 of 23 Feb. 2001 imposing a provisional anti-dumping duty on imports of PET film originating in India and the Republic of Korea, OJ L 055, 24 Feb. 2001, pp. 16-39, recital 60, endorsed in Council Regulation (EC) No. 1676/2001 of 13 Aug. 2001 imposing a definitive anti-dumping duty and collecting definitively the provisional duty imposed on imports of PET film originating in India and the Republic of Korea, OJ L 227, 23 Aug. 2001, pp. 1-14, recitals 32 and 34.

are not confirmed during the investigation period, or no fluctuations between the currencies exist, adjustments will be rejected.[78]

By adhering closely to the wordings of Article 2.10(j), which imports the text of Article 2.4.1 of the ADA, the Commission and the Council seem to act in conformity with WTO law.

6.1.4.11 Other Factors: Article 2.10(k)

Pursuant to Article 2.10(k) of the basic Regulation, the Commission and the Council may also make adjustments for *other factors* than those listed in Article 2.10(a)-(j). This provision is rarely applied, probably because differences affecting price comparability usually fall under one of the other factors in Article 2.10(a)-(j).

In *Certain Prepared or Preserved Sweetcorn*,[79] an association of EU importers claimed that adjustment should be made for *other factors* because heavy flooding in Thailand had made the export price relatively low compared to the increased cost of raw material sweetcorn after the flood. The Council refused to make adjustments for several reasons:

(1) the Thai producers themselves had not claimed that adjustment should be made;
(2) since floods are a common occurrence in Thailand, it was possible to take flooding into account when the export price was negotiated; and
(3) the effect on the prices of raw materials after the flooding was limited, and the fact was that most of the raw materials had been bought before the flooding.[80]

---

78. *Malleable Cast Iron Tube or Pipe Fittings*, Commission Regulation (EC) No. 449/2000 of 28 Feb. 2000 imposing a provisional anti-dumping duty on imports of malleable cast iron tube or pipe fittings originating in Brazil, the Czech Republic, Japan, the People's Republic of China, the Republic of Korea and Thailand and accepting an undertaking offered by an exporting producer in the Czech Republic, OJ L 55, 29 Feb. 2000, pp. 3-23, recital 107, apparently endorsed in Council Regulation (EC) No. 1784/2000 of 11 Aug. 2000 imposing a definitive anti-dumping duty and collecting definitively the provisional duty imposed on imports of certain malleable cast iron tube or pipe fittings originating in Brazil, the Czech Republic, Japan, the People's Republic of China, the Republic of Korea and Thailand, OJ L 208, 18 Aug. 2000, pp. 8-23.
79. *Certain Prepared or Preserved Sweetcorn*; Commission Regulation (EC) No. 1888/2006 of 19 Dec. 2006 imposing a provisional anti-dumping duty on imports of certain prepared or preserved sweetcorn in kernels originating in Thailand, OJ L 364, 20 Dec. 2006, pp. 68-91, endorsed in Council Regulation (EC) No. 682/2007 of 18 Jun. 2007 imposing a definitive anti-dumping duty and collecting definitively the provisional duty imposed on imports of certain prepared or preserved sweetcorn in kernels originating in Thailand, OJ L 159, 20 Jun. 2007, pp. 14-25.
80. *Certain Prepared or Preserved Sweetcorn*, Council Regulation (EC) No. 682/2007 of 18 Jun. 2007 imposing a definitive anti-dumping duty and collecting definitively the provisional duty imposed on imports of certain prepared or preserved sweetcorn in kernels originating in Thailand, OJ L 159, 20 Jun. 2007, pp. 14-25, recital 20.

The Council has also refused to make adjustments for increased prices of raw materials during the investigating period, if such an increase is not isolated to the particular geographic market but is worldwide.[81]

In Section 6.1.4.3 above, it was described that the Commission and the Council had refused to make adjustments for notional quantity discounts in *Sulphanilic Acid*. The Commission tried the situation under 'other factors', where the Commission also declined to make adjustments because there was no consistent pattern on the domestic market of the claimed built-in discounts.[82]

Under WTO law, the main determinant is whether a factor affects price comparability between normal value and export price. It must be determined on a case-to-case basis whether the factors adjusted for have such an effect on price comparability. *Other factors* can be anything, and adjustments shall be made if it is demonstrated that the other factors exist and affect the price comparability. Therefore, the rejection by the Commission and the Council to make adjustments if it is not demonstrated that there is a link between a certain factor and a price increase or price reduction seems to be in conformity with WTO law. However, as noted several times, the burden of proof on the producers or exporters must not be too heavy.

6.2 CALCULATING THE DUMPING MARGIN

In this part, it is examined whether the calculation method to compare normal value and export price by the EU authorities is in conformity with WTO law. In Chapter 1, some examples were brought of different calculation methods to determine the dumping margin. The dumping margin could turn out differently depending on how it was calculated, and, for example, the likelihood for finding dumping could be higher in situations where high export prices were *zeroed*.

In this part, the requirement under WTO law will be described through an initial description of WTO legislation, and next a description of practice by Panels and Appellate Body. Subsequently, the methods provided in EU legislation and the methods used by the EU institutions will be compared with the findings under WTO law.

---

81. *Cotton-type Bed linen II*, Council Regulation (EC) No. 695/2006 of 5 May 2006 amending Regulation (EC) No. 397/2004 imposing a definitive anti-dumping duty on imports of cotton-type bed linen originating in Pakistan, OJ L 121, 6 May 2006, pp. 14-26, recital 52.
82. *Sulphanilic Acid*, Commission Regulation (EC) No. 575/2002 of 3 Mar. 2002 imposing a provisional anti-dumping duty on imports of sulphanilic acid originating in the People's Republic of China and in India, OJ L 87, 4 Apr. 2002, pp. 28-44, recital 25, endorsed in Council Regulation (EC) No. 1339/2002 of 22 Jul. 2002 imposing a definitive anti-dumping duty and collecting definitively the provisional duty imposed on imports of sulphanilic acid originating in the People's Republic of China and India, OJ L 196, 25 Jul. 2002, pp. 11-18, recital 16.

6.2.1 WTO Legislation

Under WTO law, the dumping margin is defined in Article VI.2 of GATT 1994, second sentence:

> For the purpose of this Article, the margin of dumping is the price difference determined in accordance with the provisions of paragraph 1.

The dumping margin is the price difference as found under paragraph 1 re Article VI. In the previous chapters, the provision in Article VI.1 basically provided that the price difference is found by comparing normal value with the export price. The methods of calculating the dumping margin are provided in Article 2.4.2 of ADA. It reads:

> Subject to the provisions governing fair comparison in paragraph 4, the existence of margins of dumping during the investigation phase shall normally be established on the basis of a comparison of a weighted average normal value with a weighted average of prices of all comparable export transactions or by a comparison of normal value and export prices on a transaction-to-transaction basis. A normal value established on a weighted average basis may be compared to prices of individual export transactions if the authorities find a pattern of export prices which differ significantly among different purchasers, regions or time periods, and if an explanation is provided as to why such differences cannot be taken into account appropriately by the use of a weighted average-to-weighted average or transaction-to-transaction comparison.

The first noticeable feature is the explicit reference to the fair comparison requirement in Article 2.4. The comparison between normal value and export price made to reach the dumping margins must be fair.

Article 2.4.2 then provides requirements to the methods of calculating the dumping margin. The dumping margin must '*normally*' be based on:

- a *weighted-average-to-weighted-average* method, where the weighted average normal value is compared with the weighted average export price; or
- a *transaction-to-transaction* method, where the calculation of dumping is made by comparison between each normal value transaction with each export transaction.

It is further provided that the *weighted-average-to-weighted-average* method is made between normal value and *all comparable* export transactions. The requirement of including *all comparable* export transactions is not explicitly expressed under the *transaction-to-transaction* method.

A third method may be used: the *weighted-average-to-transaction* method, where the weighted average normal value is compared with selected export transactions. Using the weighted-average-to-transaction method requires that the 'authorities find' that *targeted dumping* takes place, where the authorities find a pattern of export prices that differ significantly among different purchasers, regions or time periods. Furthermore, it is required that the investigating authorities *explain* why the weighted-average-to-weighted-average and the transaction-to-transaction method cannot be used to detect the particular dumping.

6.2.2 PRACTICE BY PANELS AND APPELLATE BODY

In this part, the practice by Panels and Appellate Body in calculating methods to determine the dumping margin is described. The part is divided into three headings: First, the practice concerning the hierarchy of calculating methods in Article 2.4.2 is described. Next, the practice regarding multiple averaging, where investigating authorities have made intermediary calculations of, for example, different types of products and then calculated a final margin, is described. Finally, the practice of zeroing is described.

6.2.2.1 The Hierarchy of the Methods in Article 2.4.2

In the relation between the three methods in Article 2.4.2, it appears from the text in the provision that the weighted-average-to-transaction method is only applicable under exceptional circumstances. The Appellate Body has dealt with whether there is a hierarchy between the two principal methods, the weighted-average-to-weighted-average method and the transaction-to-transaction method. In *US – Softwood Lumber V (Article 21.5 – Canada)*, the Appellate Body stated:

> The first sentence of Article 2.4.2 sets out the two methodologies that 'shall normally' be used by investigating authorities to establish 'margins of dumping'. *Although the transaction-to-transaction and weighted average-to-weighted average comparison methodologies are distinct, they fulfil the same function. They are also equivalent in the sense that Article 2.4.2 does not establish a hierarchy between the two. An investigating authority may choose between the two depending on which is most suitable for the particular investigation.*[83](Emphasis added)

In this passage, the Appellate Body makes it clear that the weighted-average-to-weighted-average method and the transaction-to-transaction method are *equal principal methods* compared to the weighted-average-to-transaction method, as the two methods 'shall normally' be used.[84] In *US – Zeroing (Japan)*, the Appellate Body was more clear about the superiority of the weighted-average-to-weighted-average and the transaction-to-transaction methods compared to the weighted-average-to-transaction method.[85] The Appellate Body stated that the

83. *US – Softwood Lumber V (Art. 21.5 – Canada)*, WT/DS264/AB/RW, report of the Appellate Body on 15 Aug. 2006, para. 93.
84. See also *US – Softwood Lumber V*, WT/DS264/AB/R, report of Appellate Body on 11 Aug. 2004, para. 76.
85. *US – Zeroing (Japan)*, WT/DS322/AB/R, report of the Appellate Body on 9 Jan. 2007, para. 131.

weighted-average-to-transaction method in Article 2.4.2, second sentence, only applies if two conditions are met:

- the investigating authorities find a pattern of export prices that differ significantly among different purchasers, regions or time periods; and,
- an explanation is provided as to why such differences in export prices cannot be taken into account appropriately by the use of either the weighted-average-to-weighted-average method or the transaction-to-transaction method in Article 2.4.2, first sentence. This requirement 'thus contemplates that there may be circumstances in which targeted dumping could be adequately addressed through the normal symmetrical methodologies'.[86]

It is therefore established in WTO practice that the weighted-average-to-weighted-average method and the transaction-to-transaction methods are equal. Furthermore, the weighted-average-to-transaction method is only to be used under exceptional circumstances, in which the two other methods cannot detect the particular dumping.

6.2.2.2 Intermediary Step: Multiple Averaging

Multiple averaging regards those situations where the investigating authorities, before determining the dumping margin, make an intermediate calculation between export price and normal value. This intermediary calculation can, for example, be of different types of products or different periods.

Consider the following situation, in which bed linen is the product under consideration. An Indian exporter sells three types of bed linen, both domestically and abroad. The investigating authorities will then make an intermediary calculation by comparing export price and normal value for each type of bed linen before finding the dumping margin for bed linen; this results in three intermediary calculations. Those calculations will then be aggregated in order to find one dumping margin.

In Chapter 3, it was found that different types of a product under investigation may exist, and in Chapter 4 different type-to-type-based methods to determine normal value were described.

Panels and Appellate Body have dealt with whether the use of intermediary calculations is in conformity with Article 2.4.2 of the ADA. In *US – Stainless Steel*, the issue before the Panel was multiple averaging based on periods. The US had imposed an anti-dumping duty on steel plates and sheets originating from Korea. During the anti-dumping investigation, the US investigating authority, DOC, was faced with a major devaluation of the KRW. Since the comparison between the normal value and export price was made in USD, the DOC had divided the investigating period into two sub-periods – a pre-devaluation period and a post devaluation period – and determined a weighted-average-to-weighted-average

86. Para. 131.

calculation for each period. A final, overall dumping margin was then reached. Korea claimed that a comparison of multiple averages of normal values with multiple averages of export prices was inconsistent with Article 2.4.2 of the ADA.[87] The US, on the other hand, found support in Article 2.4.2 of the ADA for the intermediary step of multiple averaging and claimed that the transactions made before the devaluation were not comparable to the transactions made after the devaluation.[88] The Panel looked into Article 2.4.2 of the ADA and stated:

> In considering this claim, we first make clear that *we do not consider that Article 2.4.2 prohibits the use of multiple averaging* per se, as Korea's first submission could be taken to suggest. To the contrary, Article 2.4.2 provides that the existence of dumping shall normally be established 'on the basis of a comparison of a weighted average normal value with a weighted average of all comparable export transactions' (emphasis added by the Panel). The inclusion of the word 'comparable' is in our view highly significant, as in its ordinary meaning it indicates that a weighted average normal value is not to be compared to a weighted average export price that includes non-comparable export transactions. It flows from this conclusion that *a Member is not required to compare a single weighted average normal value to a single weighted average export price in cases where certain export transactions are not comparable to transactions that represent the basis for the calculation of the normal value*.[89] (Emphasis added)

The Panel found that multiple averaging based on time periods was permissible under Article 2.4.2 in cases where the export prices and normal value were not comparable.

The next question was to determine whether the multiple averaging in the particular situation was permissible. The Panel looked into the term 'comparable' and found that it means 'able to be compared (with)', but that definition did not shed any light on the meaning of the term in Article 2. The Panel then looked at the context in Article 2.4 and found that a comparison must be made for transactions made at *nearly the same time*, and therefore the timing of the sales had implications with respect of the comparability of export and home market transactions. However, the importance of the timing would not preclude comparison of normal value and export price for transactions made at different times. It follows from the nature of the method of weighted-average-to-weighted-average calculations that transactions made in the beginning of a period will be included in a weighted average together with transactions made later in the period. If the 'nearly as same time' text in Article 2.4 means that sales made at different times are not comparable, then WTO Members would be obligated to make as many sub-periods as possible; this would read the weighted-average-to-weighted-average method out

87. *US – Stainless Steel*, WT/DS179/R, report of the Panel on 22 Dec. 2000, para. 6.106.
88. Paras 6.107-6.108.
89. Para. 6.111.

of Article 2.4.2.[90] The Panel then elaborated on the circumstances under which the multiple averaging of periods is permissible:

> *We note that, where changes in normal value, export price or constructed export price during the course of the POI are combined with differences in the relative weights by volume within the POI [period of investigation] of sales in the home market as compared to the export market, the use of weighted averages for the entire POI could indicate the existence of a margin of dumping that did not reflect the situation at any given moment within the POI.* In this situation a Member might in our view be justified in concluding that differences in timing of sales in the home and export markets give rise to a problem of comparability that could be addressed through multiple averaging periods. *We recall however that this situation only arises where two elements – a change in prices and differences in the relative weights by volume within the POI of sales in the home market as compared to the export market – exist.* Thus, while a change in normal value, export price or constructed export price may be a necessary condition for the conclusion that the passage of time affects comparability in the case of an average-to-average comparison, the existence of such a change is not in itself a sufficient condition to conclude that the export transactions are not comparable to the normal value.[91] (Emphasis added)

Since the DOC had not made its sub-division of periods due to the existence of a difference in the relative weights by volume of sales within the period of investigation between the domestic and export markets, the multiple averaging of periods in the specific case was an infringement of Article 2.4.2 of the ADA.[92]

According to the Panel, multiple averaging based on periods is in itself permissible if some transactions from one period cannot be compared with transactions from another period. Two requirements must be met:

(1) there is a change in prices; and
(2) the changes in prices have implied differences in the relative weight of volume of sales on either the domestic or the export market. A change in price is not in itself sufficient to justify the *multiple average method based on periods*.

There have been a few cases about the permissibility of *multiple averaging based on different types* of the product under consideration. In *EC – Bed linen*,which is elaborated on in Section 6.2.2.3.1 below, the Appellate Body stated:

> *We see nothing in Article 2.4.2 or in any other provision of the Anti-dumping Agreement that provides for the establishment of 'the existence of margins of dumping' for types or models of the product under investigation; to the*

90. Paras 6.120-6.122.
91. Para. 6.123.
92. Paras 6.124-6.125.

> *contrary, all references to the establishment of 'the existence of margins of dumping' are references to the product that is subject of the investigation.* Likewise, we see nothing in Article 2.4.2 to support the notion that, in an anti-dumping investigation, two different stages are envisaged or distinguished in any way by this provision of the Anti-dumping Agreement, nor to justify the distinctions the European Communities contends can be made among types or models of the same product on the basis of these 'two stages'.[93] (Emphasis added)

When this statement is taken out of its right context, namely a situation with zeroing, it may appear that multiple averaging based on types is not permitted under Article 2.4.2. Such a reading would be in conflict with the above-mentioned general statement by the Panel in *US – Stainless Steel*, where multiple averaging as such is permissible under Article 2.4.2. The statement by the Appellate Body in *EC – Bed linen* became central to other cases. In *Argentina – Ceramic Tiles*, a Panel discussed the relationship between Article 2.4 and Article 6.10. Article 6.10 provides the general rule that individual dumping margins shall be made for each producer. See more in Section 6.3 about individual dumping margins. The Panel commented on the statements by the Appellate Body from the *EC – Bed linen* case:

> In our view, it is important not to confuse the usefulness of grouping (by size, model, type) for the purpose of making a fair comparison under Article 2.4 and the requirement under Article 6.10 to determine an individual margin of dumping for the product as a whole. *We consider that the use of types or models is a valid method of ensuring a fair comparison between normal value and export price under Article 2.4. We see nothing in the Appellate Body Report in the EC – Bed Linen case that suggests otherwise so long as the investigating authority goes on to determine a margin of dumping for the product as a whole.*[94] (Emphasis added)

This statement clearly supports multiple averaging based on types being permissible under the fairness requirement in Article 2.4. An intermediary calculation can be determined for different types of the product under investigation, as long as the final dumping margin is made for the product under consideration.

In *US – Softwood Lumber V*, the Appellate Body clarified its statements from *EC – Bed linen*. First, the Appellate Body noted that there were no disagreements between the participants to the case, and that multiple averaging based on different types was permissible under Article 2.4.2.[95] The Appellate Body then stated:

> We agree with the participants in this dispute that multiple averaging is permitted under Article 2.4.2 to establish the existence of margins of dumping for

93. *EC – Bed linen*, WT/DS141/AB/R, report of the Appellate Body on 1 Mar. 2001, para. 53.
94. *Argentina – Ceramic Tiles*, WT/DS189/R, report of the Panel on 28 Sep. 2001, para. 6.99.
95. *US – Softwood Lumber V*, WT/DS264/AB/R, report of Appellate Body on 11 Aug. 2004, para. 80.

> the product under investigation. *We disagree with those who suggest that the Appellate Body Report in EC – Bed Linen is premised on an assumption that multiple averaging is prohibited.* The issue of multiple averaging was not before the Appellate Body in EC – Bed Linen and the reasoning of the Appellate Body in that case should therefore not be read as prohibiting that practice. This is not to say that EC – Bed Linen is not relevant in this appeal. Indeed, there are a number of relevant findings to which we refer to below. However, *the Appellate Body did not rule on multiple averaging in that case and therefore it is incorrect to argue, as the United States does, that '[t]he agreement of both parties to this dispute and a unanimous Panel that Article 2.4.2 permits multiple comparisons is a fundamental departure from the premise' of the Appellate Body Report in EC – Bed Linen.*[96] (Emphasis added)

In footnote 142, the Appellate Body referred to the Panel statement:

> [a]lthough multiple averaging based on different types or models may be particularly common, multiple averaging may also be used in other contexts. For example, an investigating authority might perform multiple averaging in respect of sales made at different levels of trade (e.g., retail versus wholesale) or on the basis of sub-periods of the period of investigation (the latter may arise in cases where hyper-inflationary economies are involved). Thus, an investigating authority might well resort to multiple averaging to ensure comparability even in a case of absolute product homogeneity, i.e., where all of the product under investigation is identical and is being compared to transactions involving identical goods in the market of the exporting country.[97]

From this statement, it seems clear that multiple averaging based on different types is permissible under WTO law.[98] There seems to be no conditions about making the type-to-type-based multiple averaging, as is the case with multiple averaging based on time periods. However, the multiple averaging based on the types is not to be confused with finding *different dumping margins* for each type, as there is only to be found one dumping margin; see more just below about such matters and zeroing.

6.2.2.3 Zeroing

One major issue in WTO practice has been whether zeroing is a permissible method under WTO law. On one hand, it can be argued that zeroing will lead

96. Para. 81.
97. *US – Softwood Lumber V*, WT/DS264/R, report of the Panel on 13 Apr. 2004, para. 7.201.
98. See also *US – Zeroing (EC)*, WT/DS294/AB/R, report of the Appellate Body on 18 Apr. 2006, para. 126.

to artificial dumping margins by not considering all export prices. On the other hand, it can be argued that dumping determinations must be based solely on the actual positive values, leaving negative values out of the calculation, as both the ADA and Article VI of GATT 1994 are silent about negative values. It would therefore be left to the investigating authorities to decide whether negative values should be included in the dumping determination.[99]

The starting point in cases about zeroing has been Article 2.4.2 of the ADA, although zeroing has also been tried under Article 2.4. As stated above, Article 2.4.2 provides three methods of calculating the dumping margin: the weighted-average-to-weighted-average method, the transaction-to-transaction method, and the weighted-average-to-transaction method. The last method may justify zeroing. Article 2.4.2 refers to Article 2.4, which requires that a fair comparison be made between the normal value and the export price. In the following part, the WTO practice regarding Article 2.4.2 and Article 2.4 will be examined.

6.2.2.3.1 Zeroing and the Weighted-Average-to-Weighted Average Method: Article 2.4.2

Article 2.4.2 provides the weighted-average-to-weighted-average as one of the two principal methods of calculating the dumping margin. Although the weighted-average-to-weighted-average method was introduced into the ADA as a means to reduce the zeroing methodology under the weighted-average-to-transaction method, investigating authorities have been able to use a zeroing methodology under that method.

In *EC – Bed linen*,[100] the Commission and the Council had zeroed negative intermediary values resulting from the multiple averaging in respect of different types of bed linen produced in India. The zeroing of some types under the weighted-average-to-weighted-average method can be illustrated by the following example:

Consider that the product under consideration – bed linen – is differentiated into three different types; A, B and C. Intermediary calculations are made for each type by using the weighted-average-to-weighted-average method. For type A there are 3 domestic transactions at the price 2, 3, and 4; this will result in a weighted-average normal value of 3, as (2+3+4)/(number of domestic transaction = 3) = 9/3 = 3. For type A, there are three export transactions at the price: 2, 3 and 1. The weighted average export price is 2, as (2+3+1)/(number of export transaction = 3) = 6/3 = 2. The intermediary calculation is here 1, as weighted average domestic price, 3, minus the weighted average export price, 2 = 1.

99. See the different positions taken by the EU, Canada, India and Japan on the one side and the US on the other side in *US – Softwood Lumber V*, WT/DS264/AB/R, report of the Appellate Body on 11 Aug. 2004, paras 88-89.

100. *EC – Bed linen*, WT/DS141/AB/R, report of the Appellate Body on 1 Mar. 2001.

The same methodology is used for types B and C as seen in the table, but with different prices:

Type	*Weighted-Average Domestic Price*	*Weighted-Average Export Price*	*Intermediary Calculation*
A	(2+3+4)/3 = 3	(2+3+1)/3 = 2	3-2 = 1
B	(5+6+7)/3 = 6	(4+5+9)/3 = 6	6-6 = 0
C	(2+3+1)/3 = 2	(2+3+4)/4 = 3	2-3 = −1

As appears from the table, the intermediary calculation for type A is 1, the intermediary calculation for type B is 0, and the intermediary calculation for type C is −1. If those values are aggregated, the dumping margin is 0 as 1+0+−1 is 0. The price of bed linen would therefore not be regarded as dumped.

If, however, the intermediary calculation for type C is instead zeroed, the dumping margin will be different, as the aggregation will show that dumping takes place as 1+0+0 is 1. This sort of zeroing is often referred to as '*model zeroing*'.[101]

In *EC – Bed linen*, the Appellate Body was presented with the question of whether zeroing of the intermediary calculations of some types of bed linen under the weighted-average-to-weighted-average method was consistent with Article 2.4.2 of the ADA. The EU argued that the calculation of margins could be divided into two steps: The first step was a *dumping margin* for each type, and the second step was combining the different margins found during the first step. The EU claimed that Article 2.4.2 did not provide any guidance on how the different margins found at the first stage should be combined. The EU was therefore within its rights to disregard the negative dumping margins found during the first step when the final calculation on the second step was made.[102]

The Appellate Body began its analysis of Article 2.4.2 by stating that the term 'margins of dumping' in Article 2.4.2 refers to margins of dumping for *a product*, as provided in Article 2.1 of the ADA. The Appellate Body found that the EU had defined the product under consideration as cotton-type bed linen. With the definition of the product under consideration, the EU was bound by this definition, as the Appellate Body stated:

> [W]ith respect to Article 2.4.2, the European Communities had to establish' the existence of margins of dumping 'for the product – cotton-type bed linen – and not for the various types or models of that product. *We see nothing in Article 2.4.2 or in any other provision of the Anti-dumping Agreement that provides for the establishment of 'the existence of margins of dumping' for*

101. See *US – Zeroing (Japan)*, WT/DS322/AB/R, report of the Appellate Body on 9 Jan. 2007, para. 3, n. 13, and para. 121 and WT/DS322/R, report of the Panel on 20 Sep. 2006, para. 7.2.
102. *EC – Bed linen*, WT/DS141/AB/R, report of the Appellate Body on 1 Mar. 2001, para. 49.

> *types or models of the product under investigation; to the contrary, all references to the establishment of 'the existence of margins of dumping' are references to the product that is subject of the investigation.* Likewise, we see nothing in Article 2.4.2 to support the notion that, in an anti-dumping investigation, two different stages are envisaged or distinguished in any way by this provision of the Anti-dumping Agreement, nor to justify the distinctions the European Communities contends can be made among types or models of the same product on the basis of these 'two stages'. *Whatever the method used to calculate the margins of dumping, in our view, these margins must be, and can only be, established for the product under investigation as a whole.* We are unable to agree with the European Communities that Article 2.4.2 provides no guidance as to how to calculate an overall margin of dumping for the product under investigation.[103] (Emphasis added)

According to this statement, Article 2.4.2 provides guidance on how to make the dumping margins. The dumping margins must be made for the product under consideration, and not for the different types of products. The Appellate Body then went on to examine whether zeroing was permissible under the weighted-average-to-weighted-average method:

> [W]e recall that Article 2.4.2, first sentence, provides that 'the existence of margins of dumping' for the product under investigation shall normally be established according to one of the two methods. At issue in this case is the first method set out in that provision, under which 'the existence of margins of dumping' must be established:
>
> (. . .) on the basis of a comparison of a weighted average normal value with a weighted average of prices of all comparable export transactions (. . .)
>
> Under this method, the investigating authorities are required to compare the weighted average normal value with the weighted average of all comparable export transactions. Here, we emphasize that Article 2.4.2 speaks of 'all' comparable export transactions (. . .) By 'zeroing' the 'negative dumping margins', the European Communities, therefore, did not take fully into account the entirety of the prices of some export transactions, namely, those export transactions involving models of cotton-type bed linen where 'negative dumping margins' were found. Instead, the European Communities treated those export prices as if they were less than what they were. This, in turn, inflated the result from the calculation of the margin of dumping. Thus, the European Communities did not establish 'the existence of margins of dumping' for cotton-type bed linen on the basis of a comparison of the weighted average normal value with the weighted average of prices of all comparable export transactions – that is, for all transactions involving all models or types of the product under investigation.[104]

---

103. Para. 53.
104. Paras 54-55.

Zeroing of some type-based intermediary calculations is thus a violation of Article 2.4.2, as the weighted-average-to-weighted-average method requires that *all* export transactions of the product concerned must be included in the dumping calculation. When a product under consideration is differentiated into different types, the intermediary calculation for each type has to be included in the aggregation of *all* the different intermediary calculations to determine the dumping margin for the product concerned.

The Appellate Body stated that the term 'comparable' in the wordings of Article 2.4.2, which requires that the investigating authorities make 'a comparison of a weighted average normal value with a weighted average of all *comparable* export transactions', does not diminish the obligation to include *all* export transactions in the determination of the dumping margin. The EU had then violated WTO law by zeroing under the weighted-average-to-weighted-average method.[105]

EU zeroing was also challenged in *EC – Tube or Pipe Fittings*, where the EU had zeroed negative intermediary values of some types of the product under consideration, threaded malleable cast-iron tube or pipe fittings, under the weighted-average-to-weighted-average method. The situation was similar to that in *EC – Bed linen*. The Panel also referred to the finding of the Appellate Body in *EC – Bed linen* and stated that by zeroing the negative intermediary values, the EU had violated Article 2.4.2 of the ADA.[106] The EU did not appeal this finding to the Appellate Body.[107]

The US was challenged by Canada for a similar zeroing methodology in *US – Softwood Lumber V*. The USDOC had differentiated the product under investigation, softwood lumber, into different sub-groups. An intermediary value was calculated for each sub-group by using the weighted-average-to-weighted-average method. Subsequently, the positive intermediary values were aggregated and the negative intermediary values were left out of the aggregation; i.e., the negative intermediary values were zeroed. The US held that non-dumped intermediary values were not *comparable* with dumped intermediary values and thus should be left out from the aggregation of the final dumping margin.[108]

The Appellate Body elaborated on its findings from *EC – Bed linen*. On the inclusion of *all comparable export transactions* in the dumping margin, the Appellate Body stated that Article 2.4.2 does not contain an explicit wording to disregard some export transactions, whereas other provisions in the ADA explicitly make it permissible to disregard certain matters. For example, Article 2.2.1 explicitly provides that sales below costs may be disregarded from the normal value

105. Para. 56.

106. *EC – Tube or Pipe Fittings*, WT/DS219/R, report of the Panel on 7 Mar. 2003, paras 7.214-7.217.

107. *EC – Tube or Pipe Fittings*, WT/DS219/AB/R, report of the Appellate Body on 22 Jul. 2003, para. 83 and n. 79.

108. *US – Softwood Lumber V*, WT/DS264/AB/R, report of the Appellate Body on 11 Aug. 2004, para. 82.

calculation as not being in the ordinary course of trade, and Article 9.4 informs the investigating authority to disregard de minimis margins.[109]

Concerning the term 'margins of dumping' in Article 2.4.2, the Appellate Body referred to the definition of dumping Article 2.1. The Appellate Body found that this definition applied to the entire ADA including, Article 2.4.2. Dumping must be concluded for the entire product, and not only for some types of products.[110] In situations where the investigating authorities determine dumping based on the multiple averaging using a two-step approach, the comparison in the first step – the type or sub-group step – is not to be regarded as anti-dumping margins. Rather, the first step calculation is an intermediary calculation:

> [I]t is *only on the basis of aggregating all these 'intermediary values' that an investigating authority can establish margins of dumping* for the product under investigation as a whole.[111] (Emphasis added)

The Appellate Body found support for its conclusion regarding Article 2.4.2 in Article VI.2 of GATT 1994 and Article 9.3 of the ADA, which both stipulate that dumping is found for the entire product and not only for some types.[112] 'Margins of dumping' refers to the final aggregation of different results from intermediary calculation when authorities apply a multi-step approach.

The Appellate Body could conclude that it was not a permissible act by the USDOC to disregard the negative dumping margins in the final aggregation of the dumping margin for softwood lumber.[113]

Another type of zeroing under the weighted-average-to-weighted-average method arose in *Argentina – Poultry Anti-dumping Duties*. The Dirección de Competencia Desleal (DCD), which is the Argentinean investigating authority, had based the normal value for two Brazilian exporters of poultry on a weighted-average statistical sample instead of on a weighted-average of *all* the domestic sale prices reported by the two Brazilian exporters. The DCD had then compared the weighted average statistical sample normal value with a weighted average export price. Brazil claimed that Argentina had violated Article 2.4.2 by not taking into account *all* domestic sales in the calculation of the dumping margin. Argentina, on the other hand, argued that the sampling was statistically valid and based on information submitted by the producers.[114]

The Panel took its outset in the term 'normal value' in Article 2.1, which defines normal value as 'domestic sales transactions in the exporting country'. The Panel found that Article 2.1 is silent on whether *all* domestic transactions

109. Para. 100.
110. Para. 93.
111. Para. 97. See also *US – Zeroing (Japan)*, WT/DS322/AB/R, Report of the Appellate Body on 9 Jan. 2007, para. 115.
112. Para. 99.
113. Para. 103.
114. *Argentina – Poultry Anti-dumping Duties*, WT/DS241/R, report of the Panel on 22 Apr. 2003, paras 7.268-7.269.

must be included in the normal value.[115] The Panel then referred to Article 2.2.1 and stated:

> Article 2.2.1 states that *domestic sales 'may be disregarded in determining normal value only if' the relevant conditions are met.* We understand these provisions to mean that there are only specific circumstances in which domestic sales transactions may be excluded from normal value.[116] (Emphasis added)

According to the Panel, domestic sales may be disregarded from the normal value determination only when it is explicitly provided in the ADA.

The Panel then looked at Article 2.4.2 and the word 'a weighted average', which indicates that weighted average can be established in more than one way. It does not mean that normal value can be established in various ways.[117] The Panel further stated that this interpretation is not undermined by the fact that Article 2.4.2 does not refer to all domestic transactions in the weighted average normal value, and then concluded its argumentation by saying:

> We believe that the strict rules in Article 2 regarding the determination of normal value require that, in the usual case, *normal value should be established by reference to all domestic sales of the like product in the ordinary course of trade*. There would be no need to stipulate the circumstances in which domestic transactions may be excluded from normal value if there were no general obligation to otherwise include all domestic transactions in normal value.[118] (Emphasis added)

On those grounds, the DCD had violated Article 2.4.2 by excluding some domestic transactions from the weighted average normal value.

Zeroing is not a permissible method when the weighted-average-to-weighted-average method is applied. *All* transactions – both domestic and export – must be taken into account when the dumping margin is determined. Therefore, with multiple averaging, the investigating authorities must not exclude the negative intermediary calculations in the final dumping determination. In subsequent cases, the Appellate Body and Panels have consistently held that zeroing under this method is a violation of Article 2.4.2.[119]

115. Para. 7.272.
116. Ibid.
117. Para. 7.273.
118. Para. 7.274.
119. See *US – Zeroing (EC)*, WT/DS294/AB/R, Report of the Appellate Body on 18 Apr. 2006, para. 126; *US – Softwood Lumber (Art. 21.5 – Canada)*, WT/DS264/AB/RW, Report of the Appellate Body on 15 Aug. 2006, para. 89; *US – Zeroing (Japan)*, WT/DS322/R, Report of Panel on 20 Sep. 2006, para. 7.80; *US – Shrimp (Ecuador)*, WT/DS335/R, Report of the Panel on 30 Jan. 2007, para. 7.40.

6.2.2.3.2 *Zeroing and the Transaction-to-Transaction Method: Article 2.4.2*

In this part, the WTO practice about zeroing under the transaction-to-transaction method is described. As stated above, under the weighted-average-to-weighted-average method, zeroing is a violation of Article 2.4.2 of the ADA, as the Panels and Appellate Body have emphasized the wording *all comparable export transactions* in Article 2.4.2 to conclude that zeroing is an impermissible act. The wording in Article 2.4.2 about the transaction-to-transaction method is different, as it is not provided that the dumping margin must be based on *all comparable export transactions.* Instead, it is provided that the margins of dumping are established '*by a comparison of normal value and export price on a transaction-to-transaction basis*'. The difference in the wordings has led to claims that zeroing is permissible when the transaction-to-transaction method is applied.

US – Softwood Lumber V (Article 21.5 – Canada)[120] is a compliance case to the original *US Softwood Lumber V*,[121] as mentioned above, where the Appellate Body had made it clear that zeroing negative intermediary values for specific types of products in the aggregation of the product as a whole under the weighted-average-to-weighted-average method was an infringement of Article 2.4.2. In the compliance case, Canada asserted that the US investigating authorities continued a zeroing practice, which according to Canada was inconsistent with Article 2.4.2. The zeroing practice was not based on the weighted-average-to-weighted-average method; rather, the US authorities continued a zeroing practice when the transaction-to-transaction method was applied. The differences compared to the original case were that now the authorities made a comparison between individual domestic and export transactions, where the individual export price was deducted from the individual normal price. Some comparisons would end up positive, meaning that the normal price would exceed the export price; others would be negative, with the export price exceeding normal value. In the aggregation of the final dumping margin, all negative amounts would be zeroed.[122] This would as a matter of mathematical fact end up with the normal value exceeding the export price, and thus with higher dumping margins than if the negative amounts had been included.

In the Panel report, the Panel first made a textual approach to Article 2.4.2 and found that zeroing is not prohibited therein, and that there is no guidance on how to use the transaction-to-transaction method.[123] Next, the Panel looked at the scope of the reasoning made by the Appellate Body in the original case regarding the term 'margins of dumping', which had to be found for the product as a whole. The Panel found that the statements by the Appellate Body were limited to situations with the

120. *US – Softwood Lumber V (Art. 21.5 – Canada)*, WT/DS264/AB/RW, report of the Appellate Body on 15 Aug. 2006.
121. See Section 2.1.6.2 above about compliance cases.
122. See para. 2.8. See also Ch. 1 above.
123. *US – Softwood Lumber V (Art. 21.5 – Canada)*, WT/DS264//RW, report of the Panel 3 Apr. 2006, paras 5.17-5.18.

weighted-average-to-weighted-average methods. On that background, the Panel found that this

> suggests strongly that that interpretation was indeed limited to the situation where the term 'margins of dumping' is used in conjunction with the phrase 'all comparable export transactions'.[124]

Therefore, the Panel rejected a deduction from the interpretation by the Appellate Body in the original investigation to the situation with zeroing in a transaction-to-transaction situation.

The Panel then noted that in the absence of the term 'margins of dumping' under Article 2.4.2 and the absence of an obligation to ensure 'all comparable sales' under the transaction-to-transaction method, zeroing was not impermissible under Article 2.4.2. In the transaction-to-transaction method, when aggregating or adding up the results from the comparisons, there is no requirement to include an average of calculations, as is the case in the weighted-average-to-weighted-average method. Thus, according to the Panel, the text of Article 2.4.2 does not provide any requirements to include both positive and negative results from the comparison of the individual domestic and export transactions when the aggregation in the transaction-to-transaction method is performed.[125]

In the Appellate Body report, the Appellate Body reversed the finding by the Panel. First, the Appellate Body looked into the term 'export prices' in the first sentence of Article 2.4.2:

> The reference to 'export prices' in the plural suggests that the comparison will generally involve multiple transactions, as was the case in the anti-dumping investigation before us. At the same time, the reference to 'a comparison' in the singular suggests an overall calculation exercise involving aggregation of these multiple transactions. The transaction-specific results are mere steps in the comparison process. This tallies with the term 'basis' at the end of the sentence, which suggests that these individual transaction comparisons are not the final results of the calculation, but, rather, are inputs for the overall calculation exercise.[126]

The Appellate Body concluded that finding a dumping margin by means of the transaction-to-transaction method is a multi-step approach, where the first step is to make the transaction-to-transaction calculation of normal value and export prices. The result from the first step cannot be regarded as 'dumping margins'. The second step is the aggregation of results found in the first step. The dumping margin is found by this aggregation.[127] The Appellate Body further stated about the export prices:

> [T]he reference to 'export prices' in the plural, without further qualification, suggests that all of the results of the transaction-specific comparisons should

124. Para. 5.20.
125. Paras 5.28-5.29.
126. Para. 87.
127. Ibid.

> be included in the aggregation for purposes of calculating the margins of dumping. In addition, the 'export prices' and 'normal value' to which Article 2.4.2 refers are real values, unless conditions allowing an investigating authority to use other values are met. Thus, in our view, zeroing in the transaction-to-transaction methodology does not conform to the requirement of Article 2.4.2 in that it results in the real values of certain export transactions being altered or disregarded.

The investigating authorities cannot disregard some results from the transaction-to-transaction method in the final aggregation. According to the Appellate Body, Article 2.4.2 does not provide any options where the results – or 'real values' – found in each transaction-to-transaction calculation may be disregarded. The Appellate Body refers in a footnote to Article 2.2 and 2.3 of the ADA as examples where the 'real values' may be disregarded.[128] Such exceptions are not provided in Article 2.4.2.

The Appellate Body then goes on to conclude that the application of the zeroing method on results from transaction-to-transaction calculation of normal value and export prices is inconsistent with Article 2.4.2.

The conclusion contradicted the argumentation by the US and the Panel, as they advocated that the term 'margins of dumping' would have a different meaning when margins of dumping were established under the transaction-to-transaction method rather than under the weighted-average-to-weighted-average method. This was supported by the absence of an obligation to include 'all comparable sales' under the transaction-to-transaction method. The Appellate Body's response to the allegation was that the term 'all comparable export transactions' only applies to the weighted-average-to-weighted-average situations, because investigating authorities may use the multiple averaging approach. Under that approach, the investigating authorities would have to include 'all comparable export transactions' when determining the margins of dumping.[129] The Appellate Body then emphasized the difference compared to the transaction-to-transaction method:

> As transactions are not divided into groups under the transaction-to-transaction comparison methodology, the phrase 'all comparable export transactions' is not pertinent to that methodology and, consequently, no inference may be drawn from the fact that this phrase does not appear in relation to the transaction-to-transaction methodology.[130]

Under the transaction-to-transaction method, the product under consideration is not divided into different types, and thus the term 'all comparable export transactions' is superfluous. The Appellate Body stated in a footnote: '*However, product types could be used as a criterion in selecting which domestic transaction to match with a particular export transaction when carrying out a transaction-to-transaction*

128. Footnote 143 re para. 88.
129. Para 91.
130. Ibid.

comparison.'[131] This means that investigating authorities may use type-based selection of domestic transactions to be compared with specific export transactions under the transaction-to-transaction method.

The Appellate Body continued its rejection of zeroing under the transaction-to-transaction method by looking into the structure in Article 2.4.2, first sentence. As there is no hierarchy between the weighted-average-to-weighted-average method and the transaction-to-transaction method, and both methods serve the same function of establishing the margins of dumping, allowing zeroing under one of the methods would lead to systematically different results.[132] Based on that reasoning, the Appellate Body concluded:

> Given that the two methodologies are alternative means for establishing 'margins of dumping' and that there is no hierarchy between them, it would be illogical to interpret the transaction-to-transaction comparison methodology in a manner that would lead to results that are systematically different from those obtained under the weighted average-to-weighted average methodology.[133]

After interpreting Article 2.4.2 and comparing the transaction-to-transaction method with the weighted-average-to-weighted-average method, the Appellate Body was able to conclude that zeroing is not a permissible act when the transaction-to-transaction method is applied by the investigating authorities.

About a month after the release of the *US – Softwood Lumber V (Article 21.5 – Canada)* Appellate Body report, a Panel released a report regarding the permissibility of zeroing under Article 2.4.2 in *US – Zeroing (Japan)*, where Japan had claimed that the application of US law would lead to zeroing in the dumping calculations. One of the issues that the Panel was faced with concerned the permissibility of zeroing under the transaction-to-transaction methodology. The case was in that respect similar to the case in *US – Softwood Lumber V (Article 21.5 – Canada)*. The Panel emphasized the lack of clear textual guidelines in Article 2.4.2 and then referred to the *Panel* report in *US – Softwood Lumber V (Article 21.5 – Canada)*, stating that zeroing was permissible when authorities applied the transaction-to-transaction methodology.[134] Japan appealed the Panel finding.

In the Appellate Body report, the Appellate Body reversed the Panel's finding. The Appellate Body found that zeroing is not permissible under Article 2.4.2 when the transaction-to-transaction methodology is applied. The Appellate Body referred for most of its argumentation to its findings in *US – Softwood Lumber V (Article 21.5 – Canada)*, but it also added to that argumentation that if each transaction-to-transaction specific calculation could be regarded as margins of dumping, then several margins could be found to exist for an exporter.

131. Footnote 149 re para. 91.
132. Para. 93.
133. Para. 93.
134. *US – Zeroing (Japan)*, WT/DS322/R, report of the Panel on 20 Sep. 2006, para. 7.119 and n. 758.

Several different margins would lead to '*uncertainty and divergences in determinations to be made in original investigations and subsequent stages of anti-dumping proceedings*'.[135]

The Appellate Body also noted that under US law, export transactions that exceeded normal value and thus were disregarded in the calculation of the margins of dumping would be included in the injury determination. The Appellate Body concluded:

> If, as a consequence of zeroing, the results of certain comparisons are disregarded only for purposes of calculating margins of dumping, but taken into consideration for determining injury, this would mean that the same transactions are treated as 'non-dumped' for one purpose, and as 'dumped' for another purpose. This is not in consonance with the need for consistent treatment of a product in an anti-dumping investigation.[136]

The Appellate Body reached the same conclusion as in *US – Softwood Lumber V (Article 21.5 – Canada)*, finding that zeroing under the transaction-to-transaction method is a violation of Article 2.4.2.

In sum, zeroing is not permissible according to Article 2.4.2 of the ADA, when the transaction-to-transaction method is applied.

6.2.2.3.3 Zeroing and the Weighted-Average-to-Transaction Method: Article 2.4.2

Article 2.4.2 of the ADA, second sentence, permits the use of comparison between the weighted-average normal value and individual export transactions. The application of the weighted-average-to-transaction method is limited to exceptional circumstances where the investigating authorities find a pattern of export prices differing significantly among different purchasers, regions or time periods, and where an explanation is provided by the investigating authorities why such differences cannot be taken into account under the weighted-average-to-weighted-average method or the transaction-to-transaction method; see Section 6.2.2.1 above.

In *EC – Bed linen*, the Appellate Body clarified that the weighted-average-to-transaction method only applies to dumped products that are targeted for specific purchasers, regions or time periods. The EU claimed that by prohibiting model zeroing, as described above, the investigating authorities would not be able to counter dumping targeting specific types. The Appellate Body stated:

> [N]either Article 2.4.2, second sentence, nor any other provision of the Anti-dumping Agreement refers to dumping 'targeted' to certain 'models' or 'types' of the same product under investigation. It seems to us that, had

135. *US – Zeroing (Japan)*, WT/DS322/AB/R, report of the Appellate Body on 9 Jan. 2007, para. 126.
136. Para. 128.

> the drafters of the Anti-dumping Agreement intended to authorize Members to respond to such kind of 'targeted' dumping, they would have done so explicitly in Article 2.4.2, second sentence.[137]

It is clear from the statement that the application of the weighted-average-to-transaction method cannot be extended to dumping *targeted specific types* of the product under investigation. However, the Appellate Body does not rule whether zeroing is permissible under the weighted-average-to-transaction method. A few cases have indirectly dealt with that issue. In both *US – Softwood Lumber V (Article 21.5 – Canada)* and *US – Zeroing (Japan)*,the Appellate Body made statements about the second sentence of Article 2.4.2 serving as context for the main issue about zeroing under the transaction-to-transaction method. From those cases, there are indications that zeroing is permissible when Article 2.4.2, second sentence is applied.

In *US – Softwood Lumber V (Article 21.5 – Canada)*, Canada had asserted that the findings by the Appellate Body in *US – Softwood Lumber V*, concerning zeroing and the concepts of 'dumping' and 'margins of dumping', were not only limited to a prohibition of zeroing under the weighted-average-to-weighted-average method. The Panel stated that the argument presented by Canada would imply that zeroing would also be forbidden under the weighted-average-to-transaction method in Article 2.4.2, second sentence, i.e., there would be a general prohibition of zeroing. A prohibition of zeroing under the transaction-to-transaction method in Article 2.4.2, first sentence, would lead to a nullification of the weighted-average-to-transaction method in Article 2.4.2, second sentence.[138]

In the Appellate Body report, the Appellate Body disagreed with the Panel for several reasons: First, the US had never applied the weighted-average-to-transaction methodology.[139] Second, the weighted-average-to-transaction method in Article 2.4.2, second sentence is an exception to the methods provided in Article 2.4.2, first sentence. Therefore, an interpretation of Article 2.4.2, second sentence cannot alone determine the interpretation of the two methods in Article 2.4.2, first sentence.[140] Third, there are uncertainties on how to apply the weighted-average-to-transaction method. The argument by the Panel assumed that zeroing by means of the weighted-average-to-transaction method was prohibited; this assumption had never been tried before the Appellate Body.[141] The Appellate Body was then able to conclude:

> [W]e find the concerns of the Panel and the United States over the third comparison methodology (weighted average-to-transaction) being rendered

137. *EC – Bed linen*, WT/DS141/AB/R, report of the Appellate Body on 1 Mar. 2001, para. 62.
138. *US – Softwood Lumber V (Art. 21.5 – Canada),* WT/DS264/RW, report of the Panel on 3 Apr. 2006, para. 5.33.
139. *US – Softwood Lumber V (Art. 21.5 – Canada)* WT/DS264/AB/RW, report of the Appellate Body on 15 Aug. 2006, para. 97.
140. Ibid.
141. Para. 98.

> inutile by a prohibition of zeroing under the transaction-to-transaction methodology to be overstated. *It could be argued, on the contrary, that the use of zeroing under the two comparison methodologies set out in the first sentence of Article 2.4.2 would enable investigating authorities to capture pricing patterns constituting 'targeted dumping', thus rendering the third methodology inutile.*[142] (Emphasis added)

The Appellate Body does not conclude whether zeroing is permissible under the weighted-average-to-transaction method. However, there are still a few points that should be noted. The Appellate Body distinguishes between the principal methods in Article 2.4.2, first sentence and the exceptional method in Article 2.4.2, second sentence. A statement regarding the impermissibility of zeroing under the principal methods in Article 2.4.2, first sentence cannot be extended to cover the weighted-average-to-transaction method. Furthermore, if zeroing was permitted under the weighted-average-to-weighted-average method and the transaction-to-transaction method, the weighted-average-to-transaction method would be nullified. This statement indicates that zeroing is a permissible act under the weighted-average-to-transaction method.

In *US – Zeroing (Japan)*,[143] the Appellate Body elaborated its findings from *US – Softwood Lumber V (Article 21.5 – Canada)* about the weighted-average-to-transaction method in Article 2.4.2, second sentence as context for the interpretation of Article 2.4.2, first sentence. In the Panel report,[144] the Panel had, in its argumentation for the permissibility of zeroing under the transaction-to-transaction method, found that the comparison under that method is between prices of individual domestic transactions and prices of individual export transactions. According to the Panel, the expression 'prices of individual export transaction' in Article 2.4.2, second sentence does not distinguish the transaction-to-transaction method from the weighted-average-to-transaction method. Therefore, under the transaction-to-transaction method zeroing – or disregarding of some export transactions – was permissible.[145]

The Appellate Body disagreed, as the Panel wrongly seemed to assume that the types of export transaction used under the transaction-to-transaction method would be the same as under the weighted-average-to-transaction method.[146] The Appellate Body then elaborated on the differences between those two methods:

> We disagree with the assumption underlying the Panel's reasoning. The emphasis in the second sentence of Article 2.4.2 is on a 'pattern', namely a 'pattern of export prices which differs significantly among different purchasers, regions or time periods'. The prices of transactions that fall within this pattern must be found to differ significantly from other export prices.

142. Para. 100.
143. *US – Zeroing (Japan)*, WT/DS322/AB/R, report of Appellate Body on 9 Jan. 2007.
144. *US – Zeroing (Japan)*, WT/DS322/R, report of the Panel on 20 Sep. 2006.
145. Para. 7.139.
146. Para. 134.

> We therefore read the phrase 'individual export transactions' in that sentence as referring to the transactions that fall within the relevant pricing pattern. This universe of export transactions would necessarily be more limited than the universe of export transactions to which the symmetrical comparison methodologies in the first sentence of Article 2.4.2 would apply. In order to unmask targeted dumping, an investigating authority may limit the application of the W-T comparison methodology to the prices of export transactions falling within the relevant pattern.[147]

The scope of export transactions that may be used under the weighted-average-to-transaction method is limited to those that have the specific pricing pattern targeted towards purchasers, regions or time periods. The scope of export transactions under the transaction-to-transaction method is different, as export transactions that do not follow the particular pricing pattern cannot be excluded as they can be under the weighted-average-to-transaction method. The statement by the Appellate Body could therefore indicate that zeroing is permissible under the weighted-average-to-transaction method.

6.2.2.3.4 Zeroing under Article 2.4

This section deals with the practice of zeroing and Article 2.4 of the ADA. First, the interaction between Article 2.4 and Article 2.4.2 is described. Next, it is examined whether zeroing is in conformity with the fairness requirement in Article 2.4. The final question is whether zeroing may be an adjustment under Article 2.4, third through fifth sentences.

The first question regarding the interaction between Article 2.4.2 and 2.4 originates from the above-mentioned Panel report in *US – Softwood Lumber V (Article 21.5 – Canada)*[148] and the Panel report in *US – Zeroing (Japan)*,[149] where zeroing according to the Panel was permissible under the transaction-to-transaction method. Even if zeroing would be impermissible under Article 2.4, it could still be permissible under Article 2.4.2, as both Panels regarded Article 2.4.2 as *lex specialis* to Article 2.4.[150] In *US – Softwood Lumber V (Article 21.5 – Canada)*, the Appellate Body rejected this argument and stated:

> This, however, is not a correct representation of the relationship between the two provisions. Rather, the introductionary clause to Article 2.4.2 expressly makes it '[s]ubject to the provisions governing fair comparison' in Article 2.4.[151]

147. Para. 135.
148. *US – Softwood Lumber V (Art. 21.5 – Canada)*, WT/DS264/RW, report of the Panel on 3 Apr. 2006.
149. *US – Zeroing (Japan)*, WT/DS322/R, report of the Panel on 20 Sep. 2006.
150. See para. 5.75 in the Panel report in *US – Softwood Lumber V (Art. 21.5 – Canada)*, and para. 7.158 in the Panel report in *US – Zeroing (Japan)*.
151. *US – Softwood Lumber V (Art. 21.5 – Canada)*, WT/DS264/AB/RW, report of the Appellate Body on 15 Aug. 2006, para. 136.

The Appellate Body repeated this standpoint in *US – Zeroing (Japan).*[152] The findings by the Appellate Body indicate that the methods in Article 2.4.2 are covered by the requirement of fair comparison in Article 2.4. Article 2.4.2 does not supersede Article 2.4.

The second question regards whether zeroing may be a fair comparison under Article 2.4. About the weighted-average-to-weighted-average method, the Appellate Body made two important statements in the above-cited *EC – Bed linen* case:

(1) zeroing 'inflated the results from the calculation of the dumping margin'; and
(2) zeroing is not a 'fair comparison' between export price and normal value, as required by Article 2.4 and Article 2.4.2.[153]

In *US – Corrosion-Resistant Steel Sunset Review*, the Appellate Body elaborated on its argumentation about the unfairness of zeroing. The Appellate Body referred to its findings in *EC – Bed linen* and stated:

> [T]hat methodology will tend to inflate the margins calculated. Apart from inflating the margins, such a methodology could, in some instances, turn a negative margin of dumping into a positive margin of dumping. (. . .) Thus, the inherent bias in a zeroing methodology of this kind may distort not only the magnitude of a dumping margin, but also a finding of the very existence of dumping.[154]

The Appellate Body emphasizes two reasons why zeroing is not fair – and thus inconsistent with Article 2.4:

(1) zeroing may inflate the dumping margin; and
(2) zeroing may find occurrences of dumping which would not have existed without the zeroing.

Under the weighted-average-to-weighted-average methodology, zeroing is thus a violation of Article 2.4 and cannot be included in the determination of the dumping margin.

Concerning zeroing under the transaction-to-transaction method, the Appellate Body reached the same conclusion: zeroing is not a fair comparison methodology and is a violation of Article 2.4. The Appellate Body stated in *US – Softwood Lumber V (Article 21.5 – Canada)* that:

– under the transaction-to-transaction methodology, zeroing 'distorts the prices of certain export transactions because export transactions made at prices above normal value are not considered at their real value. The prices

152. *US – Zeroing (Japan),* WT/DS322/AB/R, report of the Appellate Body on 9 Jan. 2007, para. 143.
153. *EC – Bed linen*, WT/DS141/AB/R, report of the Appellate Body on 1 Mar. 2001, para. 55.
154. *US – Corrosion-Resistant Steel Sunset Review*, WT/DS244/AB/R, report of Appellate Body on 15 Dec. 2003, para. 135.

of these export transactions are artificially reduced when zeroing is applied under the transaction-to-transaction comparison methodology', and;
- the same reasons apply as under the weighted-average-to-weighted-average methodology; the dumping margins are inflated, and negative margins could turn into positive margins.[155]

The first statement applies only to the transaction-to-transaction methodology. As under the weighted-average-to-weighted-average method, *all* prices from the export transactions will be included in the first step under a multiple-comparison calculation. Under the transaction-to-transaction method, zeroing of some export prices will exclude some prices from the calculation; this is an unfair practice. The second statement is the same as the one made by the Appellate Body regarding zeroing under the weighted-average-to-weighted-average methodology.

In *US – Zeroing (Japan)*, the Appellate Body referred to its argumentation in *US – Softwood Lumber V (Article 21.5 – Canada)* and reached the same conclusion: zeroing under the transaction-to-transaction methodology is an infringement of Article 2.4.[156]

Zeroing under weighted-average-to-transaction methodology has not been tried by a WTO body under the fairness requirement in Article 2.4. In light of the conclusions drawn in Section 6.2.2.3.3 above, it must be assumed that the fair comparison is limited to those export prices that have not been disregarded in the first place. If the conditions in Article 2.4.2, second sentence are met, the selection of export prices for comparison may also be seen as fairly selected for the comparison.

Some guidance may be found from GATT practice, where a GATT Panel in *US – Anti-dumping Duties against Imports of Fresh and Chilled Atlantic Salmon* considered whether zeroing under the weighted-average-to-transaction method was a violation of the *fairness* principle in Article 2.6 of the Tokyo ADA, which had some resemblance to the present ADA.[157] The Panel stated:

> While the Panel thus found that Article 2:6 did not explicitly deal with the question of whether normal values and export prices should be compared on an average-to-average basis, it considered that it was possible to interpret the first sentence to reflect a requirement of a 'fair comparison' which applied generally to any aspect of the comparison of normal values and export prices. The Panel considered, however, that this interpretation of Article 2:6 would not permit a conclusion that a method whereby average normal values were compared to individual export prices was *per se* inconsistent with Article 2:6.

155. *US – Softwood Lumber V (Art. 21.5 – Canada)*, WT/DS322/AB/RW, report of Appellate Body on 15 Aug. 2006, paras 139-140.

156. *US – Zeroing (Japan)*, WT/DS264/AB/R, report of the Appellate Body on 9 Jan. 2007, para. 146.

157. See Ch. 2 above.

> Rather, the 'fairness' of such a method would have to be evaluated in the light of the circumstances of each case.[158]

With this statement, the GATT Panel found that it was a case-to-case determination – depending on the circumstances – whether zeroing under the weighted-average-to-transaction method would be permitted under the fairness requirement in the Article 2.6 of the Tokyo ADA. The question under the present ADA is whether a situation could occur in which a WTO Member fulfils the conditions in Article 2.4.2, second sentence, but will still be found to violate the fairness requirement in Article 2.4. This needs still to be resolved in practice.

The final question before the Appellate Body has been whether zeroing is justified as an allowance made under Article 2.4, third to fifth sentences. In *US – Zeroing (EC)*, the EU challenged the US practice of zeroing. The EU referred to Article 2.4, third to fifth sentences and held that zeroing is not a permissible allowance or adjustment according to Article 2.4, third to fifth sentences. Allowances or adjustments can only be made for differences that affect price comparability. The EU argued that adjustments must not be made if there are no such differences.[159] The US opposed the EU arguments, as Article 2.4, third to fifth sentence should be interpreted narrowly to address pre-comparison price adjustments that affect price comparability. This would imply that zeroing is not an adjustment that falls under the wordings of Article 2.4, third to fifth sentences.[160] In the Panel report, the Panel had rejected the argumentation put forward by the EU. The Panel emphasized the structure between Article 2.4, third to fifth sentences and Article 2.4.2, and stated:

> If zeroing is characterized as an impermissible allowance or adjustment, there is no rational basis to explain why an allowance or adjustment that is prohibited because it does not correspond to a difference affecting price comparability is no longer prohibited in the context of the asymmetrical comparison method provided for in the second sentence of Article 2.4.2[161]

According to the Panel, zeroing is not an allowance or adjustment as provided in Article 2.4, third to fifth sentences. Zeroing is the step performed after allowances or adjustments for differences that affect price comparability have been made. It would therefore be illogical to regard zeroing under the allowance or adjustment step.

The Appellate Body reached the same conclusion as the Panel. The Appellate Body began its analysis of Article 2.4 and concluded that allowances should not be made for differences that do not affect price comparability.[162] The Appellate Body

158. *US – Anti-dumping Duties against Imports of Fresh and Chilled Atlantic Salmon*, ADP/87, report of the Panel on 30 Nov. 1992, para. 481.
159. *US – Zeroing (EC)*, WT/DS294/AB/R, report of Appellate Body on 18 Apr. 2006, para. 151.
160. Para. 153.
161. *US – Zeroing (EC)*, WT/DS294/AB/R, report of port of the Panel on 31 Oct. 2005, para. 7.277.
162. *US – Zeroing (EC)*, WT/DS294/AB/R, report of Appellate Body on 18 Apr. 2006, para. 156.

then examined what falls under 'differences affecting price comparability'. The Appellate Body found:

> Article 2.4 specifies that the differences for which due allowance shall be made are those 'which affect price comparability'. In our view, this refers to differences in characteristics of the compared transactions that have an impact, or are likely to have an impact, on the price of the transaction. Likewise, the *a contrario* application of this principle prohibits only those adjustments made in relation to differences in characteristics of the compared transactions that do *not* affect price comparability. These are differences that do not have an impact, or are unlikely to have an impact, on the price of the transaction. Therefore, adjustments or allowances made in relation to *differences in price* between export transactions and domestic transactions—such as zeroing – cannot be adjustments or allowances covered by the third sentence of Article 2.4, including its *a contrario* application. Indeed, whether or not a factor affects the price comparability between export and domestic transactions should be determined before this comparison is made, and not after.[163](Emphasis added)

The Appellate Body is in line with the Panel in paying attention to the *different steps* in the dumping determination where 'allowances or adjustments' take place before the calculation of dumping margins is made. Therefore, zeroing happens *after* the allowances or adjustments for differences affecting price comparability are made. Zeroing is not an allowance or adjustment under Article 2.4. The Appellate Body therefore upheld the Panel findings and rejected the claim by the EU.[164]

The next section concerns the conformity of EU legislation and practice with WTO law.

6.2.3 EU Legislation

Under EU law, the dumping margin is defined in Article 2.12 of the basic Regulation:

> The dumping margin shall be the amount by which the normal value exceeds the export price. Where dumping margins vary, a weighted average dumping margin may be established.

The definition of dumping margin under this provision is the amount by which the normal value exceeds the export price. Under WTO law, the dumping margin was the difference between normal value and export price. Although there may be some difference in the wordings, an anti-dumping duty can nevertheless only be imposed under the circumstances set forth under the EU provision.

163. Para. 157.
164. Para. 159.

The second sentence of Article 2.12 of the basic Regulation provides that the dumping margin may be based on a weighted average if the dumping margins vary. This provision is relevant if only one dumping margin is established for two producers who are associated. See more in part 6.3.

The calculation methods to compare normal value and export price to determine a dumping margin are provided in Article 2.11 of the basic Regulation:

> Subject to the relevant provisions governing fair comparison, the existence of margins of dumping during the investigation period *shall normally* be established on the basis of a *comparison of a weighted average normal value with a weighted average of prices of all export transactions* to the Community, *or* by a *comparison of individual normal values and individual export prices to the Community on a transaction-to-transaction basis*. However, a *normal value established on a weighted average basis may be compared to prices of all individual export transactions to the Community, if there is a pattern of export prices which differs significantly among different purchasers, regions or time periods, and if the methods specified in the first sentence of this paragraph would not reflect the full degree of dumping being practised*. This paragraph shall not preclude the use of sampling in accordance with Article 17. (Emphasis added)

Article 2.11 of the basic Regulation has some resemblance to Article 2.4.2 of the ADA. The first sentence of Article 2.11 of the basic Regulation concerns the establishment of a dumping margin based on either a *weighted-average-to-weighted-average* method or on a *transaction-to-transaction* method, where the method for transaction-to-transaction is found 'by comparison of individual normal values and individual export prices'. The latter term is different from the WTO provision, where 'individual export transactions' are only provided for the weighted-average-to-transaction method. It is not further elaborated on in the EU provision why the transaction-to-transaction method is based on a comparison of individual normal value with individual export transactions. If the term 'individual' gives the Commission and the Council an opportunity to select which transactions will be included in the determination of the dumping margin, this may be a violation of WTO law. The Appellate Body stated in *US – Softwood Lumber V (Article 21.5 – Canada)* that a transaction-to-transaction calculation includes *all real values*, and zeroing under the transaction-to-transaction method is a violation of Article 2.4.2 of the ADA.[165]

The second sentence of Article 2.11 of the basic Regulation regards the weighted-average-to-transaction method, which to some extent resembles the WTO text in Article 2.4.2 of the ADA, second sentence. However, there are a few differences compared to the WTO text:

- Under Article 2.4.2 of the ADA, one of the conditions for applying the weighted-average-to-transaction method is that the investigating authorities

165. See Section 6.2.2.3.2 above.

explain why the differences in pattern of export prices between purchasers, regions or time periods cannot be taken into account under the weighted-average-to-weighted-average method or the transaction-to-transaction method. Under the EU provision, an explanation is not required, provided that the weighted-average-to-weighted-average or the transaction-to-transaction method would not reflect the full degree of dumping being practiced.

- Under the EU provision, it is provided that the weighted average normal value may be compared to 'all' individual export transactions. Under the WTO provision, 'all' is not provided. It is not clear why the word 'all' is included in the EU text, and it would be self-contradictory if *all* export transactions should be included in the determination of the dumping margin; however, at the same time, individual export transactions can be selected for inclusion in the determination of the dumping margin.

The third sentence of Article 2.11 of the basic Regulation is not provided in the WTO legislation. The EU provision ensures that sampling of data under Article 17 of the basic Regulation is not in conflict with Article 2.11.

6.2.4 EU Practice

Turning to the practice used by the EU institutions, it is first examined whether there is a hierarchy between the three methods provided in Article 2.11 of the basic Regulation. Next, the zeroing approaches by the EU institutions are examined.

6.2.4.1 The Preferred Method of Article 2.11

In line with the WTO requirement, there is a hierarchy between the three methods described in Article 2.11. In *Petrotub and Republica v Council*, the EC Court stated:

> [I]t is clear from the actual wording of Article 2(11) of the basic regulation that the existence of a dumping margin is normally to be established using one of the two symmetrical methods and that recourse to the asymmetrical method, by way of an exception to that rule, may be had only on the twofold condition that, on the one hand, the pattern of export prices differs significantly among different purchasers, regions or time periods and, on the other hand, the symmetrical methods do not reflect the full degree of dumping being practised.[166]

The weighted-average-to-transaction method is an exception to the two principal methods, weighted-average-to-weighted-average or transaction-to-transaction

166. *Petrotub and Republica v. Council,* Case C-76/00 P, judgment of the Court on 9 Jan. 2003, ECR 2003, p. I-79, para. 49.

method. The weighted-average-to-transaction method only applies if two conditions are met:

(1) there is a pattern of export prices that differ significantly between different purchasers, regions or time periods; and
(2) dumping is not fully reflected under the weighted-average-to-weighted-average method or the transaction-to-transaction method.

In *Ritek and Prodisc v. Council*, the Court of First Instance came to the same conclusion.[167]

In Commission and Council practice, the preferred method of calculating the dumping margin is the weighted-average-to-weighted-average method.[168]

---

167. *Ritek and Prodisc v. Council*, Case T-274/02, judgment of the Court of First Instance on 24 Oct. 2006, ECR 2006, p. II-4305, para. 49.

168. *Stainless Steel Fasteners and Parts thereof I*, Commission Regulation (EC) No. 1732/97 of 4 Sep. 1997 imposing a provisional anti-dumping duty on imports of stainless steel fasteners and parts originating in the People's Republic of China, India, Malaysia, the Republic of Korea, Taiwan and Thailand, OJ L 243, 5 Sep. 1997, pp. 17-36, recital 45, endorsed in Council Regulation (EC) No. 393/98 of 16 Feb. 1998 imposing a definitive anti-dumping duty on imports of stainless steel fasteners and parts thereof originating in the People's Republic of China, India, the Republic of Korea, Malaysia, Taiwan and Thailand, OJ L 50, 20 Feb. 1998, pp. 1-14, recital 44; *Synthetic Fibre Ropes*, Commission Regulation (EC) No. 18/98 of 7 Jan. 1998 imposing a provisional anti-dumping duty on imports of synthetic fibre ropes originating in India, OJ L 4, 8 Jan. 1998, pp. 28-38, recital 16, endorsed in Council Regulation (EC) No. 1312/98 of 24 Jun. 1998 imposing a definitive anti-dumping duty on imports of synthetic fibre ropes originating in India and collecting definitively the provisional duty imposed, OJ L 183, 26 Jun. 1998, pp. 1-8, recital 15; *Potassium Permanganate*, Commission Regulation (EC) No. 178/98 of 23 Jan. 1998 imposing a provisional anti-dumping duty on imports of potassium permanganate originating in India and the Ukraine, OJ L 19, 24 Jan. 1998, pp. 23-34, recital 24, endorsed in Council Regulation (EC) No. 1507/98 of 13 Jul. 1998 imposing a definitive anti-dumping duty on imports of potassium permanganate originating in India and the Ukraine and collecting definitively the provisional duty imposed, OJ L 200, 16 Jun. 1998, pp. 4-8, recital 11; *Certain Iron or Steel Ropes and Cables,* Commission Regulation (EC) No. 230/2001 of 2 Feb. 2001 imposing a provisional anti-dumping duty on certain iron or steel ropes and cables originating in the Czech Republic, Russia, Thailand and Turkey and accepting undertakings offered by certain exporters in the Czech Republic and Turkey, OJ L 34, 3 Feb. 2001, pp. 4-27, recitals 29, 55, 64 and 74, endorsed in Council Regulation (EC) No. 1601/2001 of 2 Aug. 2001 imposing a definitive anti-dumping duty and definitively collecting the provisional anti-dumping duty imposed on imports of certain iron or steel ropes and cables originating in the Czech Republic, Russia, Thailand and Turkey, OJ L 211, 4 Aug. 2001, pp. 1-19, recitals 26, 45, 53 and 65; *Polyethylene Terephthalate Film*, Commission Regulation (EC) No. 367/2001 of 23 Feb. 2001 imposing a provisional anti-dumping duty on imports of PET film originating in India and the Republic of Korea, OJ L 55, 24 Feb. 2001, pp. 16-39, recital 35, endorsed in Council Regulation (EC) No. 1676/2001 of 13 Aug. 2001 imposing a definitive anti-dumping duty and collecting definitively the provisional duty imposed on imports of PET film originating in India and the Republic of Korea, OJ L 227, 23 Aug. 2001, pp. 1-14, recital 15; *Sulphanilic Acid*, Commission Regulation (EC) No. 575/2002 of 3 Mar. 2002 imposing a provisional anti-dumping duty on imports of sulphanilic acid originating in the People's Republic of China and in India, OJ L 87, 4 Apr. 2002, pp. 28-44, recital 27, endorsed in Council Regulation (EC) No. 1339/2002 of 22 Jul. 2002 imposing a definitive anti-dumping duty and collecting definitively the provisional duty imposed on imports of sulphanilic acid

When the weighted-average-to-weighted-average method is applied, the Commission and the Council – as stated several times already – make type-to-type-based calculations and therefore go into multiple averaging of the different calculations found from each type.[169]

The transaction-to-transaction is rarely used.[170] One reason for not applying the transaction-to-transaction method is that there are often significant differences in the numbers of export transactions and domestic transactions.[171] However, if all export transactions refer to a *different product type*, the transaction-to-transaction method may apply.[172]

---

originating in the People's Republic of China and India, OJ L 196, 25 Jun. 2002, pp. 11-18, recital 17; *Certain Polyethylene Terephthalate II*, Council Regulation (EC) No. 192/2007 of 22 Feb. 2007 imposing a definitive anti-dumping duty on imports of certain polyethylene terephthalate originating in India, Indonesia, Malaysia, the Republic of Korea, Thailand and Taiwan following an expiry review and a partial interim review pursuant to Arts 11(2) and 11(3) of Regulation (EC) No. 384/96, OJ L 59, 27 Feb. 2007, pp. 1-33, recitals 31 and 45; *Certain Plastic Sacks and Bags*, Council Regulation (EC) No. 1425/2006 of 25 Sep. 2006 imposing a definitive anti-dumping duty on imports of certain plastic sacks and bags originating in the People's Republic of China and Thailand, and terminating the proceeding on imports of certain plastic sacks and bags originating in Malaysia, OJ L 270, 29 Sep. 2006, pp. 4-41, recital 56; *Certain Prepared or Preserved Sweetcorn*, Commission Regulation (EC) No. 1888/2006 of 19 Dec. 2006 imposing a provisional anti-dumping duty on imports of certain prepared or preserved sweetcorn in kernels originating in Thailand, OJ L 364, 20 Dec. 2006, pp. 68-91, recital 37, endorsed in Council Regulation (EC) No. 682/2007 of 18 Jun. 2007 imposing a definitive anti-dumping duty and collecting definitively the provisional duty imposed on imports of certain prepared or preserved sweetcorn in kernels originating in Thailand, OJ L 159, 20 Jun. 2007, pp. 14-25, recital 25.

169. *Cotton-type Bed linen I*, Commission Regulation (EC) No. 1069/97 of 12 Jun. 1997 imposing a provisional anti-dumping duty on imports of cotton-type bed linen originating in Egypt, India and Pakistan, OJ L 156, 13 Jun. 1997, pp. 11-33, recital 46, endorsed in Council Regulation (EC) No. 2398/97 of 28 Nov. 1997 imposing a definitive anti-dumping duty on imports of cotton-type bed linen originating in Egypt, India and Pakistan, OJ L 332, 4 Dec. 1997, pp. 1-18, recital 28.
170. Though, it happens in some occasions that the second method is used. See for instance recital 46 in the Commission Regulation in *Cotton-type Bed linen I*, mentioned in the previous footnote, where the second method was used in situations with exporters from Pakistan.
171. *Polyester Staple Fibres I*, Council Regulation (EC) No. 428/2005 of 10 Mar. 2005 imposing a definitive anti-dumping duty on imports of PSF originating in the People's Republic of China and Saudi Arabia, amending Regulation (EC) No. 2852/2000 imposing a definitive anti-dumping duty on imports of PSF originating in the Republic of Korea and terminating the anti-dumping proceeding in respect of such imports originating in Taiwan, OJ L 71, 17 Mar. 2005, pp. 1-33, recital 44; *Recordable Compact Disks*; Council Regulation (EC) No. 1050/2002 of 13 Jun. 2002 imposing a definitive anti-dumping duty and collecting definitively the provisional duty imposed on imports of recordable compact disks originating in Taiwan, OJ L 160, 18 Jun. 2002, pp. 2-13, recital 29.
172. *Cotton-type Bed linen I*, Commission Regulation (EC) No. 1069/97 of 12 Jun. 1997 imposing a provisional anti-dumping duty on imports of cotton-type bed linen originating in Egypt, India and Pakistan, OJ L 156, 13 Jun. 1997, pp. 11-33, recital 46, endorsed in Council Regulation (EC) No. 2398/97 of 28 Nov. 1997 imposing a definitive anti-dumping duty on imports of cotton-type bed linen originating in Egypt, India and Pakistan, OJ L 332, 4 Dec. 1997, pp. 1-18, recital 28.

The preference for the weighted-average-to-weighted-average method over the transaction-to-transaction method is in conformity with WTO law, for which there is no hierarchy between those two methods.[173]

6.2.4.2 Zeroing

In this part, the use of zeroing in EU practice is examined. Above, under WTO practice, it was shown that the EU has violated WTO law by using the zeroing methods. The starting point here is the Regulations, which led to the *EC – Bed linen* case. Subsequently, EU practice after the *EC – Bed linen* case will be described. Finally, the use of the weighted-average-to-transaction method by the EU authorities is examined.

6.2.4.2.1 Zeroing under the Weighted-Average-to-Weighted-Average Method

It was just stated that the Commission and the Council have the weighted-average-to-weighted-average method as their preferred method to determine the dumping margin. As described in 6.2.2.3.1, model zeroing was the exclusion of negative intermediary calculations from the aggregation of the different intermediary calculations from each type under the product definition. However, the regulations released before *EC – Bed linen* offer no clues as to how the actual calculation of intermediary numbers for type-to-type determinations and the final aggregation is made. It is not possible to see whether model zeroing has been the preferred method in other cases. For example, the Commission Regulation in *Cotton-Type Bed Linen I*, which was the challenged EU Regulation in the *EC – Bed linen* case, only reads:

> In general, weighted average constructed normal value by type was compared with weighted average export price by type. However, with regard to five Pakistani exporters/producers, every export transaction referred to a different product type.[174]

On this basis, it cannot be concluded that zeroing of intermediary calculations takes place. However, based on the two WTO reports, *EC – Bed linen* and *EC – Tube or Pipe Fittings*,[175] mentioned above in Section 6.2.2.3.1, it must be assumed that it was a consistent practice by the Commission and the Council to zero the negative intermediary values before the final aggregation, though this was in conflict with WTO law.

---

173. See Section 6.2.2.1 above.
174. *Cotton-type Bed linen I*, Commission Regulation (EC) No. 1069/97 of 12 Jun. 1997 imposing a provisional anti-dumping duty on imports of cotton-type bed linen originating in Egypt, India and Pakistan, OJ L 156, 13 Jun. 1997, pp. 11-33, recital 46, endorsed in Council Regulation (EC) No. 2398/97 of 28 Nov. 1997 imposing a definitive anti-dumping duty on imports of cotton-type bed linen originating in Egypt, India and Pakistan, OJ L 332, 4 Dec. 1997, pp. 1-18, recital 28.
175. *EC – Tube or Pipe Fittings*, WT/DS219/R, report of the Panel on 7 Mar. 2003.

6.2.4.2.2 The Time After EC: Bed Linen

After *EC – Bed linen*, the Commission issued a Notice in the Official Journal, stating that all exporters subject to existing anti-dumping duties could have a review of the anti-dumping measure 'in the light of the legal interpretations regarding the determination of dumping margins contained in the reports, to request a review on the basis of Article 2 of the WTO enabling Regulation'.[176] The Commission and the Council then seemed to be open to reassess *all* other exporters dumping margin if such a margin had been based on the model zeroing under the weighted-average-to-weighted-average method.

In regard to *Cotton-type Bed linen I*,[177] the Council subsequently released Regulation 1644/2001 amending the Regulation that violated WTO law.[178] In Regulation 1644/2001, the Council referred to the report from the Appellate Body and stated that the Commission had reassessed its finding by taking into account the findings in the *EC – Bed linen* report, but that injurious dumping still existed.[179] In the revised finding, the Council emphasized a change in its approach, where zeroing is no longer applied:

> The weighted average constructed normal value by type was compared with weighted average export price by type, (. . .). In compliance with the recommendations of the Report, no 'zeroing' was applied in calculating the overall dumping margin for each company.[180]

In *Polyethylene Terephthalate Film*, the Council also emphasized its non-zeroing line:

> It should be noted that in cases where an exporting producer exported more than one product type to the Community, the weighted average overall dumping margin was determined by computing the dumping found on each type without zeroing 'negative dumping' found on individual types.[181]

---

176. Notice regarding the anti-dumping measures in force following a ruling of the Dispute Settlement Body of the World Trade Organization adopted on 12 Mar. 2001, OJ C 111, 8 May 2002, p. 4.
177. *Cotton-type Bed linen I*, Commission Regulation (EC) No. 1069/97 of 12 Jun. 1997 imposing a provisional anti-dumping duty on imports of cotton-type bed linen originating in Egypt, India and Pakistan, OJ L 156, 13 Jun. 1997, pp. 11-33, endorsed in Council Regulation (EC) No. 2398/97 of 28 Nov. 1997 imposing a definitive anti-dumping duty on imports of cotton-type bed linen originating in Egypt, India and Pakistan, OJ L 332, 4 Dec. 1997, pp. 1-18.
178. *Cotton-type Bed linen I*, Council Regulation (EC) No. 1644/2001 of 7 Aug. 2001 amending Regulation (EC) No. 2398/97 imposing a definitive anti-dumping duty on imports of cotton-type bed linen originating in Egypt, India and Pakistan and suspending its application with regard to imports originating in India, OJ L 219, 14 Aug. 2001, pp. 1-11.
179. Recitals 2 and 4.
180. Recital 11.
181. *Polyethylene Terephthalate Film*, Council Regulation (EC) No. 1676/2001 of 13 Aug. 2001 imposing a definitive anti-dumping duty and collecting definitively the provisional duty imposed on imports of PET film originating in India and the Republic of Korea, OJ L 227, 23 Aug. 2001, pp. 1-14, recital 18.

Apparently, the Commission and the Council have left the model zeroing method and have thus brought the calculation under the weighted-average-to-weighted-average in conformity with WTO law.[182]

It must also be noted that in WTO cases in which EU intervenes as a third party, the EU has after the *EC – Bed linen* case advocated that zeroing methods are in conflict with WTO law. The EU has taken that position in regard to the weighted-average-to-weighted-average method in *US – Softwood lumber V*.[183] The EU has also, in regard to the transaction-to-transaction method, held that zeroing is prohibited under WTO law; see for example EU's position in *US – Softwood Lumber V (Article 21.5 – Canada)*[184] and in *US – Zeroing (Japan)*.[185]

Although there now seems to be a WTO-consistent practice in place, and zeroing under the weighted-average-to-weighted-average method is no longer applied, it has still not been established whether zeroing under that method is a violation of EU law. A case is pending in *Ikea*,[186] concerning the Regulations subject to the *EC – Bed linen* ruling by the Appellate Body. The EC Court has to rule on whether zeroing under the weighted-average-to-weighted-average method is in conformity with Article 2.11 of the basic Regulation. In his opinion, the Advocate General stated that the Commission and the Council violated Article 2.11 by not establishing an anti-dumping margin for the product as a whole and by violating the fairness principle in Article 2.10 of the basic Regulation.[187]

The following sections concern the application of the weighted-average-to-transaction method by the EU authorities. Due to the rarely used transaction-to-transaction method and lack of information from the Regulations, it is not further examined whether EU is zeroing when that method is applied.

6.2.4.2.3 The Weighted-Average-to-Transaction Method: First Condition

The first condition in Article 2.11, second sentence requires that there be a pattern of prices that differs significantly among different purchasers, regions and time periods. In *Ritek and Prodisc v. Council*,[188] the Commission and the Council had applied the weighted-average-to-transaction method because there was a pattern

182. See also the opinion of Advocate General Jacobs in *Petrotub and Republica v. Council*, Case C-76/00 P, opinion delivered on 25 Apr. 2002, ECR 2003, p. I-79, point 17.
183. *US – Softwood Lumber V*, WT/DS264/AB/R, Report of the Appellate Body on 11 Aug. 2004, paras 52-57.
184. *US – Softwood Lumber V (Art. 21.5 – Canada)*, WT/DS264/AB/RW, Report of the Appellate Body on 15 Aug. 2006, paras 45, 46 and 81.
185. *US – Zeroing (Japan)*, WT/DS322/AB/R, Report of the Appellate Body on 9 Jan. 2007, paras 47-49.
186. *Ikea*, Case 351/04, *Ikea v. Commissioners of Customs & Excise*, OJ C 262, 23 Oct. 2004, p. 18.
187. *Ikea*, Case C-351/04, opinion of Advocate General Leger delivered on 6 Apr. 2006, not yet reported in the ECR, point 166-167.
188. *Ritek and Prodisc v. Council*, Case T-274/02, judgment of the Court of First Instance of 24 Oct. 2006, ECR 2006, p. II-4305.

that differed among different time periods.[189] Before the Court of First Instance, the applicants claimed that although such differences did exist, it was not their intentional behaviour to target different time periods but that they had had to do so due to a worldwide decline in prices.[190] It was not contested that there was such a pattern of differences in time periods; rather, the question before the Court of First Instance was whether the Commission and the Council should have taken the intention by the producer into account. The Court of First Instance stated:

> [T]he purpose of the asymmetrical method is to enable the full degree of the dumping practised to be reflected where, in the event that a difference in the export price pattern has been found, irrespective of its cause, this would not be possible using the two other methods. *The question as to whether there is an export price pattern differing according to the purchasers, regions or purchasers is a purely objective one, irrespective, therefore, of the presence or absence of any fraudulent intent underlying that situation.* Requiring proof of intent would prevent use of the asymmetrical method in situations where that method alone would enable the full degree of the dumping practised to be reflected, and thus, by introducing a requirement not provided for under Article 2(11) of the basic regulation, would prevent that provision from operating correctly.[191] (Emphasis added)

The Court Of First Instance finds that the application of weighted-average-to-transaction method rests on an examination of the objective facts on whether a pattern of differences in prices exists. The causes behind such a pattern of differences are irrelevant. Therefore, the producer's intention behind the price setting to particular purchasers, in particular regions or in particular time periods is irrelevant in this respect. The Court of First Instance found support for its finding in the context where the dumping determination is a purely *objective comparison* between the normal value and export prices.[192] For those reasons, the Court of First Instance found that the Commission and the Council had not violated Article 2.11 of the basic Regulation by not taking the producers' intention into account.[193]

Under WTO law, the text of Article 2.4.2 does not include an aspect of intent. Concerning the first condition, it is provided that 'the authorities [shall] find a pattern of export prices which differ significantly among different purchasers, regions or time periods'. What is relevant is the finding of a pattern of export

189. See the disputed Commission and Council Regulations in *Recordable Compact Disks*, Commission Regulation (EC) No. 2479/2001 of 17 Dec. 2001 imposing a provisional anti-dumping duty on imports of recordable compact disks originating in Taiwan, OJ L 334, 18 Dec. 2001, pp. 8-25, recital 29, endorsed in Council Regulation (EC) No. 1050/2002 of 13 Jun. 2002 imposing a definitive anti-dumping duty and collecting definitively the provisional duty imposed on imports of recordable compact disks originating in Taiwan, OJ L 160, 18 Jun. 2002, pp. 2-13, recitals 28-30.
190. Para. 51.
191. Para. 54.
192. Paras 59-60.
193. Para. 64.

prices, which are different in this case between two periods. It cannot be read into Article 2.4.2 of the ADA that the parties' intent is a factor to be taken into account by the Commission and the Council when they decide to apply the weighted-average-to-transaction method.

The finding by the Court of First Instance finds support in an Appellate Body statement in *US – 1916 Act (EC)*:

> We note that, under Article VI:1 of the GATT 1994 and Article 2 of the Anti-dumping Agreement, neither the intent of the persons engaging in 'dumping' nor the injurious effects that 'dumping' may have on a Member's domestic industry are constituent elements of 'dumping'.[194]

Under WTO law, the intention by the producer is not a factor to be taken into account when dumping is determined. The finding by the Court of First Instance seems to be in conformity with WTO law.

6.2.4.2.4 The Weighted-Average-to Transaction-Method: Second Condition

Above, it was stressed that the text of Article 2.11 of the basic Regulation, second sentence, does not provide that reasons shall be stated when the weighted-average-to-transaction method is applied; this is a requirement, however, in WTO law. Even though the weighted-average-to-weighted-average method is the preferred method of the Commission and the Council, the weighted-average-to-transaction method is often applied. In particular, after *EC – Bed linen*, the weighted-average-to-transaction method would be applied.[195] The question is, though, whether the Commission and the Council state reasons when the weighted-average-to-transaction method is used.

The information in the Regulations is limited – and the explanation for applying the weighted-average-to-transaction method is therefore not elaborated on. An example could be: 'there was a pattern of export prices which differed significantly among different time periods and that a calculation based on weighted average would not reflect the full degree of dumping being practised'.[196] Furthermore, the Regulations lack an explanation as to why the differences in the export prices among different purchasers, regions or time periods cannot be taken into account under the weighted-average-to-weighted-average method.

---

194. *US – 1916 ACT (EC)*, WT/DS136/AB/R, report of the Appellate Body on 28 Aug. 2000, para. 107.
195. See I. Van Bael & J. F. Bellis, *Anti-dumping and Other Trade Protection Laws of the EC*, 4th edn (The Hague: Kluwer Law International, 2004), 124.
196. *Stainless Steel Fasteners and Parts thereof I*, Council Regulation (EC) No. 393/98 of 16 Feb. 1998 imposing a definitive anti-dumping duty on imports of stainless steel fasteners and parts thereof originating in the People's Republic of China, India, the Republic of Korea, Malaysia, Taiwan and Thailand, OJ L 50, 20 Feb. 1998, pp. 1-14, recital 45.

Only in rare occasions in the Council Regulations might the reasons for applying the weighted-average-to-transaction be elaborated on.[197]

The lack of reasons has also resulted in a case before the Court of First Instance and the EC Court in *Petrotub and Republica v. Council*.[198] Two Romanian companies, Petrotub and Republica, exported seamless pipes and tubes of iron or non-alloy steel to the EU. The products were subject to an anti-dumping investigation by the Commission and the Council that ended in the imposition of an anti-dumping duty.[199] In the Council Regulation, the dumping margin was based on the weighted-average-to-transaction method. The exporters claimed that the Commission and the Council had not justified the reasons why the weighted-average-to-transaction method was preferred in the particular case over the weighted-average-to-weighted-average or transaction-to-transaction methods, and that the Commission and the Council had thus violated Article 2.4.2 of the ADA. In the Council Regulation, the Council stated:

> This claim was rejected after the methodology used for all Romanian companies was reconsidered and it was found that:
>
> – for one company, there was no difference in dumping margin between both methods as all export transactions were made at dumped prices;
> – for three companies, a pattern of export prices which differed significantly by destination or time period was found.[200]

The result, then, was that the methodology was not changed. The two exporters brought action against the Council before the Court of First Instance, claiming that neither the Commission nor the Council had stated reasons for applying the weighted-average-to-transaction method. They therefore had violated the WTO requirement.

As already stated in Section 2.4.3.1, the Court of First Instance ruled that the provisions in the basic Regulation are the only set of governing EU measures. Therefore, the requirement to state a reason in Article 2.4.2 of the ADA is not an

---

197. *Recordable Compact Disks*, Compare the Commission Regulation (EC) No. 2479/2001 of 17 Dec. 2001 imposing a provisional anti-dumping duty on imports of recordable compact disks originating in Taiwan, OJ L 334, 18 Dec. 2001, pp. 8-25, recitals 28-29, with the Council Regulation (EC) No. 1050/2002 of 13 Jun. 2002 imposing a definitive anti-dumping duty and definitively the provisional duty imposed on imports of recordable compact disks originating in Taiwan, OJ L 160, 18 Jun. 2002, pp. 2-13, recitals 30-31.
198. *Petrotub and Republica v. Council*, Case 76/00 P, judgment of the EC Court on 9 Jan. 2003, ECR 2003, p. I-79, and joined cases T-33/98 and T-34/98, judgment of the Court of First Instance on 15 Dec. 1999, ECR 1999, p. II-3837.
199. See *Certain Seamless Pipes and Tubes of Iron or non-alloy Steel*, Council Regulation (EC) No. 2320/97 of 17 Nov. 1997 imposing definitive anti-dumping duties on imports of certain seamless pipes and tubes of iron or non-alloy steel originating in Hungary, Poland, Russia, the Czech Republic, Romania and the Slovak Republic, repealing Regulation (EEC) No. 1189/93 and terminating the proceeding in respect of such imports originating in the Republic of Croatia, OJ L 322, 25 November 1997, p. 1.
200. Recital 22.

applicable rule, as Article 2.11 of the basic Regulation does not contain a similar rule.[201] The Court of First Instance then referred to Article 253 of the EC Treaty, which requires the Commission and the Council to state their reasons for measures taken. The Court of First Instance concluded that the Commission and the Council had provided sufficient reasons for applying the weighted-average-to-transaction method.[202]

On appeal by Petrotub and Republica, the Council held that due to its wide discretion, the Council was not required to state its reasons for applying the weighted-average-to-transaction method.[203] The EC Court first referred to Article 2.11 of the basic Regulation and stated the above conditions for applying the weighted-average-to-transaction method.[204] The EC Court then contradicted the statement from the Court of First Instance that Article 2.4.2 of the ADA should not be taken into account when it differed from the text of Article 2.11 of the basic Regulation.[205] With reference to Article 2.4.2 of the ADA and Article 253 of the EC treaty, the EC Court stated:

> [I]t must be held that a Council regulation imposing definitive anti-dumping duties and having recourse to the asymmetrical method for the purposes of calculating the dumping margin must in particular contain, as part of the statement of reasons required by Article 190 [now Article 253] of the Treaty, the specific explanation provided for in Article 2.4.2 of the 1994 Anti-dumping Code.
>
> It is evident in this case that the contested regulation does not contain even the merest reference to the second symmetrical method or, a fortiori, the slightest explanation as to why that method would not enable significant differences in the pattern of export prices among different purchasers, regions or time periods to be taken appropriately into account.[206]

The EC Court then stated that the Court of First Instance had erred in law by not taking the requirement to state its reasons in Article 2.4.2 of the ADA into account and by finding that the statement of reasons in the particular Regulation was in accordance with Article 253 of the EC Treaty.

It is clear from the EC Court finding that the lack of reasons behind the selection of the weighted-average-to-transaction method is a violation of both EU and WTO law. The EC Court finding brings EU law in conformity with WTO law. Under EU law, it is required that the Commission and the Council explain why the weighted-average-to-weighted-average or transaction-to-transaction method cannot reflect dumping.

---

201. Para. 105.
202. Paras 106-113.
203. Para. 43.
204. Para. 49.
205. Para. 52.
206. Paras 60-61.

After *Petrotub and Republica v. Council*, it seems that the Commission and the Council state their reasons why the weighted-average-to-weighted-average or transaction-to-transaction methods are disregarded and the weighted-average-to-transaction method applied.[207]

However, in *Ritek and Prodisc v. Council*,[208] where there allegedly was a pattern of prices differing between two time periods, the second condition of applying the weighted-average-to-transaction method was tried again. The Council had explained that under the weighted-average-to-transaction method, the dumping margin was significantly higher than under the weighted-average-to-weighted-average method. The weighted-average-to-weighted-average method would therefore not take into account the effect of the significant decline of export prices to the EU during the second half of the investigation period. Furthermore, export prices during the second half of the investigation period were lower than production costs for the product concerned.[209] The applicants, Ritek and Prodisc, claimed that even though the margins under the weighted-average-to-transaction method had been significantly higher than under the weighted-average-to-weighted-average method, such differences were not sufficient to determine that the weighted-average-to-transaction method would better reflect the full degree of dumping. Therefore, according to Ritek and Prodisc, the Commission and the Council had not stated sufficient reason for applying the weighted-average-to-transaction method.

The Court of First Instance stated that it was a relevant reason by the Commission and the Council to put forward. The exclusion of some export prices would lead to a higher margin than that found under the weighted-average-to-weighted-average method, where all export prices would be included and the

---

207. See for instance *Polyester Staple Fibres I*, Council Regulation (EC) No. 428/2005 of 10 Mar. 2005 imposing a definitive anti-dumping duty on imports of PSF originating in the People's Republic of China and Saudi Arabia, amending Regulation (EC) No. 2852/2000 imposing a definitive anti-dumping duty on imports of PSF originating in the Republic of Korea and terminating the anti-dumping proceeding in respect of such imports originating in Taiwan, OJ L 71, 17 Mar. 2005, pp. 1-33, recitals 44, 134 and 135; *Certain side-by-side Refrigerators*, Commission Regulation (EC) No. 355/2006 of 28 Feb. 2006 imposing a provisional anti-dumping duty on imports of certain side-by-side refrigerators originating in the Republic of Korea, OJ L 59, 1 Mar. 2006, pp. 12-33, recitals 31-34, endorsed in Council Regulation (EC) No. 1289/2006 of 25 Aug. 2006 imposing a definitive anti-dumping duty and collecting definitively the provisional duty imposed on imports of certain side-by-side refrigerators originating in the Republic of Korea, OJ L 236, 31 Aug. 2006, pp. 11-17, recital 27; *Certain Polyethylene Terephthalate II*, Council Regulation (EC) No. 192/2007 of 22 Feb. 2007 imposing a definitive anti-dumping duty on imports of certain polyethylene terephthalate originating in India, Indonesia, Malaysia, the Republic of Korea, Thailand and Taiwan following an expiry review and a partial interim review pursuant to Arts 11(2) and 11(3) of Regulation (EC) No. 384/96, OJ L 59, 27 Feb. 2007, pp. 1-33, recital 67.
208. *Ritek and Prodisc v. Council*, Case T-274/02, judgment of the Court of First Instance of 24 Oct. 2006, ECR 2006, p. II-4305.
209. See the disputed Council Regulation; *Recordable Compact Disks*, Council Regulation (EC) No. 1050/2002 of 13 Jun. 2002 imposing a definitive anti-dumping duty and collecting definitively the provisional duty imposed on imports of recordable compact disks originating in Taiwan, OJ L 160, 18 Jun. 2002, pp. 2-13, recital 31.

weighted-average-to-weighted-average method would not reflect those differences, consequently not fully reflecting dumping. Since the dumping margin for Ritek had been doubled under the weighted-average-to-transaction method compared to the weighted-average-to-weighted-average method, and the dumping margin for Prodisc had been increased by 6% under the weighted-average-to-transaction method compared to the weighted-average-to-weighted-average method, and the export prices during the second half of the investigation period were lower than production costs for the product concerned, the Court of First Instance found that the Council had not violated Article 2.11 of the basic Regulation.[210]

It is further to be noted that in a few cases, the application of the weighted-average-to-transaction method in the Commission regulation would be changed to the weighted-average-to-weighted-average method in the Council Regulation. The Commission and the Council seem to be willing to make such changes if the producer can demonstrate that the pattern in the export prices can be explained by reasons other than price discrimination.[211]

In *Polyethylene Terephthalate Film*, the dumping margin for one exporter was calculated on a weighted-average-to-transaction basis. This was the conclusion reached by the Commission because the export prices differed between different importers.[212] In the Council Regulation, however, it was found that this had no significant effect on the degree of dumping. The methodology was subsequently changed to the weighted-average-to-weighted-average method.[213]

EU practice seems to have been brought more into conformity with WTO law after the judgment of the EC Court in *Petrotub and Republica v. Council*. It appears from recent practice that the Commission and the Council state their reasons to explain why either the weighted-average-to-weighted-average method or the transaction-to-transaction method cannot be applied.

---

210. Paras 83-84.
211. See *Stainless Steel Fasteners and Parts thereof I*, Commission Regulation (EC) No. 1732/97 of 4 Sep. 1997 imposing a provisional anti-dumping duty on imports of stainless steel fasteners and parts originating in the People's Republic of China, India, Malaysia, the Republic of Korea, Taiwan, and Thailand, OJ L 243, 5 Sep. 1997, pp. 17-36, recital 52, amended in Council Regulation (EC) No. 393/98 of 16 Feb. 1998 imposing a definitive anti-dumping duty on imports of stainless steel fasteners and parts thereof originating in the People's Republic of China, India, the Republic of Korea, Malaysia, Taiwan, and Thailand, OJ L 50, 20 Feb. 1998, pp. 1-14, recital 49.
212. *Polyethylene Terephthalate Film*, Commission Regulation (EC) No. 367/2001 of 23 Feb. 2001 imposing a provisional anti-dumping duty on imports of PET film originating in India and the Republic of Korea, OJ L 55, 24 Feb. 2001, pp. 16-39, recital 67.
213. *Polyethylene Terephthalate Film*, Council Regulation (EC) No. 1676/2001 of 13 Aug. 2001 imposing a definitive anti-dumping duty and collecting definitively the provisional duty imposed on imports of PET film originating in India and the Republic of Korea, OJ L 227, 23 Aug. 2001, pp. 1-14, recital 35.

6.2.4.2.5 *Zeroing under the Weighted-Average-to-Transaction Method*

In *Ritek and Prodisc v. Council*, the Court of First Instance was presented with a question of whether the Commission and the Council should take *all* export transactions into account when applying the weighted-average-to-transaction method. The applicants claimed that zeroing was impermissible under the requirement of a fair comparison under Article 2.4.2 of the ADA together with Article 2.4 of the ADA, and they referred to *EC – Bed linen*. The Court of First Instance held that *EC – Bed linen* dealt with the weighted-average-to-weighted-average method and thus was not applicable in the particular case.[214] Furthermore, the Appellate Body had stressed the term 'all' in relation to the weighted-average-to-weighted-average method as provided in the text of Article 2.4.2, first sentence, which indicated that *all* was specifically related to that method.[215] See more in Section 6.2.2.3.1 above. The Court of First Instance then looked into the text of Article 2.11 of the basic Regulation, second sentence, where it is provided that 'a normal value established on a weighted average basis may be compared to prices of *all* individual export transactions' to determine the dumping margin. The Court of First Instance referred to the explanation provided by the Council and stated that there are two ways that the weighted-average-to-transaction method can be applied:

> [E]ither by making a selection of individual export transactions to be compared with the weighted average normal value and, thereby, excluding entirely from that comparison certain exports (those not dumped) or by taking into account all the exports in that comparison, but subject to zeroing of the individual negative dumping margins, precisely in order to prevent those margins from masking the dumping practised elsewhere. The Council states that it is that second approach, which is less severe on the exporters, which was finally adopted by the institutions when Article 2.4.2 of the 1994 Anti-dumping Code was transposed into Community law. It explains that, as an expression of the choice not to exclude certain export transactions, the second sentence of Article 2(11) of the basic regulation provides, in relation to the asymmetrical method, that the weighted average normal value is 'compared to prices of all individual export transactions'.[216]

The explanation is that either the non-dumped export transactions are left out from the comparison with the weighted average normal value, or *all* export transaction are compared with the weighted-average normal value but the negative calculations are zeroed. The text of Article 2.11 reflects the last mentioned method.

The explanation is not convincing. The first method, where non-dumped export transactions are excluded from comparison with the weighted average normal value, is illogical because it cannot be determined that an export price is

214. *Ritek and Prodisc v. Council*, Case T-274/02, judgment of the Court of First Instance on 24 Oct. 2006, ECR 2006, p. II-4305, para. 106.
215. Paras 98-100.
216. Para. 101.

dumped unless it has been compared with the weighted-average normal value. In my view, leaving out non-dumped export transactions, which can logically only be done *after* the comparison with the weighted average normal value, is the same as zeroing.

The Court of First Instance accepted the Council's explanation. The Court of First Instance then stated that neither the wording of Article 2.4.2 of the ADA nor that of Article 2.11 of the basic Regulation prohibits the use of zeroing under the weighted-average-to-transaction method.[217] The Court of First Instance further noted that under the weighted-average-to-transaction, zeroing is not a violation of the fairness requirement under Article 2.10, and thus it concluded that zeroing is not a violation of Article 2.11.[218]

Zeroing under the weighted-average-to-transaction method seems to be in conformity with WTO law. First, Article 2.4.2 of the ADA, second sentence, refers to 'individual export transactions'. The term 'individual' may imply that specific transactions may be selected. Furthermore, it would be illogical if no such selections were made under the weighted-average-to-transaction method, as the purpose is to counter targeted dumping towards purchasers, regions or time periods. Therefore, if a country has two regions, A and B, and dumping takes place in region A but not in region B, the export prices to region B must necessarily be excluded. Although the Appellate Body has not directly dealt with the question, it indirectly appears that zeroing is permissible under the weighted-average-to-transaction method; see Section 6.2.2.3.3. However, under WTO law it can be argued that zeroing may only be permissible when it applies to specific purchasers, regions or time periods. For example, if dumping is targeted in one region, *all* export transactions from that region must be included in the group of selected export transactions, including those with higher value than the weighted-average normal value. Accordingly, all the export transactions from the non-targeted regions are excluded from the comparison with the weighted-average normal value, even those with lower values than the weighted-average normal value.

6.3 INDIVIDUAL OR GENERAL DUMPING MARGINS

This section contains a brief examination of the rules on whether individual or general dumping margins must be calculated for the producers. In this context, it should be borne in mind that the outset for the anti-dumping investigation is dumped products from a specific country and not products from a specific producer. The anti-dumping investigation thus involves *all* producers from the particular country who export the product to the EU – even producers that do not dump the price of the product. Therefore, it is important to describe the rules regarding when the dumping margin is determined for *each* exporting producer, which results in a non-imposition of anti-dumping duties for those producers

217. Para. 103.
218. Para. 107.

who do not dump, and when the dumping margin is determined generally, thereby including those producers who do not dump.

In Chapter 2, it was mentioned that the investigating authorities might apply a sampling method. The sampling method is not further examined here, as the decision to sample lies before the actual dumping investigation is made and is therefore outside the scope of this book.

6.3.1 WTO Legislation

Article 6.10 of the ADA provides:

> The authorities shall, as a rule, determine an individual margin of dumping for each known exporter or producer concerned of the product under investigation. In cases where the number of exporters, producers, importers or types of products involved is so large as to make such a determination impracticable, the authorities may limit their examination either to a reasonable number of interested parties or products by using samples which are statistically valid on the basis of information available to the authorities at the time of the selection, or to the largest percentage of the volume of the exports from the country in question which can reasonably be investigated.

According to the first sentence of Article 6.10, the rule is to establish *individual* dumping margins for *each known* exporter or producer of the product under investigation. Producers that are not known and do not come forth during the investigation may then be under a general dumping margin. Naturally, it is not possible to determine individual dumping margins from producers that are not known.

Furthermore, as noted in Chapter 2, the investigating authorities may decide to determine the dumping margins based on samples from selected producers. The second sentence of Article 6.10 is not further examined here.

6.3.2 Practice by Panels and Appellate Body

In the following part, some of the issues dealt with by the Panel and the Appellate Body concerning general or individual dumping margins will be described.

6.3.2.1 Lack of Information

In *Mexico – Anti-dumping Measures on Rice,* several US producers of long grained rice were all under a general dumping margin, whereas two other producers got individual dumping margins. The US claimed that the Mexican investigating authority, Economía, had been too passive by not investigating whether there would be more than two US producers of long grained rice. Those two producers had been the only producers to come forward at the initial stage of the investigation. According to the US, Mexico had violated Article 6.10 of the

ADA.[219] Mexico claimed that Article 6.10 had not been violated because Economía had made individual dumping margins for the known producers.[220] The Panel found that Mexico had violated Article 6.10 of the ADA:

> Article 6.10 of the AD Agreement is a general requirement that the authority has to comply with, at the latest, at the end of the investigation when making the determinations. This implies that the exporters that are known to the authorities at that point are those that an objective and unbiased investigating authority properly establishing the facts and conducting an active investigation could have and should have reasonably been considered to have knowledge of.[221]

According to the Panel, Economía, had been too passive and should have made an effort to find out whether there would be more than two producers of long grained rice on the US market.

The Appellate Body overruled the finding by the Panel. The Appellate Body referred to the interpretation by the Panel and stated:

> This interpretation is difficult to reconcile with the ordinary meaning of the term: a known exporter or producer is an exporter or producer known to the investigating authority, not an exporter or producer of which it does not know, but should have known. *In our view, the rule set out in the first sentence of Article 6.10 (determining an individual margin of dumping) covers the exporters or foreign producers of which the investigating authority knows at the time the calculation of the margins of dumping is made. Under the first sentence of Article 6.10, the investigating authority is not required to determine an individual margin of dumping for exporters or foreign producers of whose existence it was unaware.*[222] (Emphasis added)

Since Economía had calculated individual margins for the producers who did come forward, the Appellate Body reversed the Panel finding.[223] There is no requirement in the text that the investigating authorities must investigate whether there are more producers than the ones who have made themselves known to the authorities. All other producers will then have a general dumping margin calculated.

In *Argentina – Poultry Anti-dumping Duties*, the Argentinean authorities had made general margins for producers who did not supply the investigating authority with sufficient documentation for its normal value. Brazil claimed that Argentina violated Article 6.10 of the ADA by not determining individual margins for such companies.[224] The Panel noted that Article 6.10 provides a general obligation to

---

219. *Mexico – Anti-dumping Measures on Rice*, WT/DS295//R, report of the Panel on 29 Nov. 2005, para. 7.170.
220. Para. 7.176.
221. Para. 7.187.
222. *Mexico – Anti-dumping Measures on Rice*, WT/DS295/AB/R, report of the Appellate Body on 29 Nov. 2005, para. 255.
223. Para. 257.
224. *Korea – Certain Paper*, WT/DS312/R, report of the Panel on 28 Oct. 2005.

make individual dumping margins. The Panel did not see a requirement in Article 6.10 for producers to submit the documentation needed to determine an individual margin. The Panel then referred to Article 6.8 of the ADA, which allows the investigating authorities to complete the data with regard to a particular exporter in case the information provided is unreliable or necessary information is simply not provided.[225] The Panel then stated:

> The fact that an investigating authority does not receive any information from an exporter, or only receives partial information, or information that is not usable or is unreliable, should not prevent the calculation of an individual margin of dumping for that exporter, since the substantive provisions in [Article 6.8 of the ADA](. . .) expressly allow investigating authorities to complete the data with regard to a particular exporter in order to determine a dumping margin in case the information provided is unreliable or necessary information is simply not provided.[226]

The Panel then concluded that Argentina had violated Article 6.10 of the ADA by not determining individual margins for the producers who did not submit all necessary documentation.[227]

It follows from this decision that the investigating authorities are required to make individual margins for the known producers, even if the data submitted from those producers are not satisfactory. Article 6.8 of the ADA provides a mechanism for the investigating authorities to complete such data.

6.3.2.2 Related Exporters

In *Korea – Certain Paper*, the Panel was faced with a question of whether Article 6.10 of the ADA permits investigating authorities to treat separate legal entities that both export the product under consideration and are somehow related to each other as *one* single exporter. In the specific case, three exporters from Indonesia were organized under a parent company, also from Indonesia, and they shared the same directors. Furthermore, all three exporters conducted their domestic sales through the parent company, but conducted the export of the product individually. The investigating authorities in Korea had made a general dumping margin covering all three exporters.[228]

The Panel noted that Article 6.10 requires that a single margin be calculated for 'exporters' and 'producers', but those two words are not defined in the text.[229] The Panel then turned to the context of Article 6.10 and found guidance in Article 9.5 of the ADA about newcomer reviews. Article 9.5 provides that reviews must be made promptly and individual margins determined for new exporters or producers,

225. Para. 7.215.
226. Para. 7.216.
227. Para. 7.217.
228. *Korea – Certain Paper*, WT/DS312/R, report of the Panel on 28 Oct. 2005.
229. Para. 7.157.

'provided that these exporters or producers can show that they are not related to any of the exporters or producers in the exporting country who are subject to the anti-dumping duties on the product'. The Panel then stated:

> Article 9.5 as context strongly suggests that the term 'exporter' in Article 6.10 should not be read in a way to require an individual margin of dumping for each independent legal entity under all circumstances.[230]

The Panel found further support for its finding in Article 2.3, according to which sales between associated parties are disregarded, and in the Appellate Body interpretation of 'ordinary course of trade' in Article 2.1.[231] Therefore, a general margin may be determined for companies that are related. However, the Panel stated that the discretion to make the general margin determination is not unlimited, and the investigating authorities must determine 'that these companies are in a relationship close enough to support that treatment'.[232] The investigating authorities are thus required to examine the concrete facts on a case-by-case basis in order to determine whether the relationship between two parties is close enough.

The Panel noted that the fact that all three Indonesian exporters had the same parent company, shared the same directors and conducted their domestic sales through the parent company indicated a close legal and commercial relationship between the three exporters. Therefore, the investigating authorities in Korea had been in their right to determine a general dumping margin for the three companies.[233]

6.3.2.3 Margin Based on Product Types

In *Argentina – Ceramic Tiles*, the Argentinean authorities, DCD, had used a sampling technique due to the many exporters. The sample included the EU exporters Bismantova and Caesar. However, the dumping margin was not calculated on an individual basis for the exporters included in the sample but was made for the different sizes of product under investigation, filed tiles. There was a dumping margin for tiles 20 × 20, 30 × 30 and 40 × 40 cm. The EU argued that the margin based on different product types was a violation of Article 6.10 of the ADA.

Argentina, on the other hand, claimed that the dumping margin based on the different sizes was in line with Article 6.10. Argentina asserted that the exporters had not provided the necessary information to calculate individual anti-dumping margins for the exporters included in the sample.

The Panel referred to the Appellate Body in *EC – Bed linen* and stated that the dumping margin must be determined for the product as a whole and not for specific types of the product. The product under investigation was ceramic tiles, and

230. Para. 7.159.
231. Para. 7.160. See Ch. 4 *above*.
232. Para. 7.161.
233. Para. 7.163-7.168.

therefore the DCD was required to determine individual dumping margins for each producer and exporter of ceramic tiles.[234] The Panel then stated:

> Even if Argentina had been entitled to determine margins of dumping with respect to each of three sizes of tile rather than with respect to the product subject to investigation as a whole, we believe the DCD was not justified in not determining an individual margin for each exporter for each of the three sizes of tiles. In our view, even if the DCD were to have doubted the reliability of the information for one or two size categories in the case of Bismantova because of the significant quantity of sales made to a related party, this should not have impeded the DCD from determining an exporter specific margin of dumping for at least the one or two remaining size categories for which the DCD did not identify any problems. Similarly, in the case of Caesar, which only exported one size of tiles, this exporter should have at least received an individual margin for that size based on the information submitted.[235]

Based on this reasoning by the Panel, the investigating authorities are required to determine individual margins for producers. It is not sufficient to determine margins based on different types of product. Furthermore, and in line with the above conclusion in 6.3.2.1, lack of information is not a sufficient factor to preclude determinations of *individual* dumping margins.

The following sections deal with EU legislation, EU practice and the conformity with WTO law.

6.3.3 EU Legislation

As noted in Section 6.2.3, Article 2.12 of the basic Regulation, second sentence, provides that where dumping margins vary, a weighted-average dumping margin may be established. Article 2.12, second sentence, addresses dumping margins for related producers and exporters, and therefore a weighted-average dumping margin may be made for related producers or exporters. As seen above, a Panel has stated that it is in conformity with WTO law to establish a general margin for related exporters if their interrelationship is close enough. There is, however, no direct text in the EU legislation providing that the dumping margin must normally be determined for each known producer or exporter. However, a single margin follows implicitly from other provisions in the basic Regulation. Article 17.1 permits the Commission and the Council to use the sampling techniques as provided under Article 6.10 of the ADA. It is stated in the third paragraph of Article 17 of the basic Regulation:

> In cases where the examination has been limited in accordance with this Article, *an individual margin of dumping shall, nevertheless, be calculated*

234. *Argentina – Ceramic Tiles*, WT/DS189/R, report of the Panel on 28 Sep. 2001, paras 6.98-6.99.
235. Para. 6.100.

> *for any exporter or producer not initially selected* who submits the necessary information within the time limits provided for in this Regulation, except where the number of exporters or producers is so large that individual examinations would be unduly burdensome and would prevent completion of the investigation in good time. (Emphasis added)

The sampling rule is only an option if certain criteria are met. Nevertheless, the Commission and the Council must determine an individual margin for producers that submit the information required. In line with the WTO rules on sampling described in Chapter 2, this rule may be derogated from, but this does not change the fact that the general rule is to calculate individual margins for producers or exporters.

Article 9.5 of the basic Regulation supports this claim. It provides that the general rule is to determine specific *anti-dumping duties* for each *supplier*. The basis for the individual anti-dumping duties is the differences between the normal value and export price from each producer and exporter. Therefore, if the general rule to determine individual anti-dumping duties for each supplier is met, the Commission and the Council have to look at the individual dumping margins. Chinese companies are exempted from this rule, and for Chinese suppliers an anti-dumping duty is based on a countrywide margin, unless certain criteria are met. See more in Section 7.3.

In the following part, the practice by the Commission and the Council concerning the question of general and individual dumping margins is examined.

6.3.4 EU Practice

In Commission and Council practice, the general rule is to determine individual dumping margins for each producer or exporter.[236] The general rule is therefore in conformity with the requirements under Article 6.10 of the ADA to determine individual margins.

The general rule is exempted from in situations of sampling, which is not further examined here, when there is an interrelationship between producers and/or exporters or when producers/exporters are not co-operating. Those situations are described in the following sections.

6.3.4.1 Related Producers

It is settled practice by the Commission and the Council to establish a general dumping margin for related companies. The general dumping margin is based on a weighted average calculation of the price information submitted by the related producers to the Commission.[237]

---

236. See in general the Regulations mentioned *below*.
237. *Stainless Steel Fasteners and Parts thereof I*, Commission Regulation (EC) No. 1732/97 of 4 Sep. 1997 imposing a provisional anti-dumping duty on imports of stainless steel fasteners and parts originating in the People's Republic of China, India, Malaysia, the Republic of Korea,

In *Polyester Staple Fibres I*, the Commission explained that the reason for only calculating one margin for associated exporters is that 'individual dumping margins might encourage circumvention of anti-dumping measures, thus rendering them ineffective, by enabling related companies to channel their exports to the Community through the company with the lowest individual dumping margin'.[238]

In *Sacks and Bags Made of Polyethylene or Polypropylene*, the Council and the Commission stressed that the companies under investigation shared the same directors, the directors owned shares in each company, the companies shared the same production facilities, and one company held shares in the other companies.[239]

Under WTO law, a Panel found in *Korea – Certain Paper*[240]that a general margin for associated producers or exporters is justified under Article 6.10 if the relationship is close enough. The determination must be made on a case-by-case

---

Taiwan and Thailand, OJ L 243, 5 Sep. 1997, pp. 17-36, recital 21, endorsed in Council Regulation (EC) No. 393/98 of 16 Feb. 1998 imposing a definitive anti-dumping duty on imports of stainless steel fasteners and parts thereof originating in the People's Republic of China, India, the Republic of Korea, Malaysia, Taiwan and Thailand, OJ L 50, 20 Feb. 1998, pp. 1-14, recital 28; *Polyester Staple Fibres I*, Commission Regulation (EC) No. 1472/2000 of 6 Jul. 2000 imposing a provisional anti-dumping duty on imports of PSF originating in India and the Republic of Korea, OJ L 166, 6 Jul. 2000, pp. 1-13, recital 58, apparently endorsed in Council Regulation (EC) No. 2852/2000 of 22 Dec. 2000 imposing a definitive anti-dumping duty and definitively collecting the provisional duty imposed on imports of PSF originating in India and the Republic of Korea, OJ L 332, 28 Dec. 2000, pp. 17-31, recitals 41 and 42; *Recordable Compact Disks*, Commission Regulation (EC) No. 2479/2001 of 17 Dec. 2001 imposing a provisional anti-dumping duty on imports of recordable compact disks originating in Taiwan, OJ L 334, 18 Dec. 2001, pp. 8-25, recital 30, endorsed in Council Regulation (EC) No. 1050/2002 of 13 Jun. 2002 imposing a definitive anti-dumping duty and collecting definitively the provisional duty imposed on imports of recordable compact disks originating in Taiwan, OJ L 160, 18 Jun. 2002, pp. 2-13, recital 34; *Certain Plastic Sacks and Bags*, Council Regulation (EC) No. 1425/2006 of 25 Sep. 2006 imposing a definitive anti-dumping duty on imports of certain plastic sacks and bags originating in the People's Republic of China and Thailand, and terminating the proceeding on imports of certain plastic sacks and bags originating in Malaysia, OJ L 270, 29 Sep. 2006, pp. 4-41, recital 58.

238. *Polyester Staple Fibres I*, Commission Regulation (EC) No. 1472/2000 of 6 Jul. 2000 imposing a provisional anti-dumping duty on imports of PSF originating in India and the Republic of Korea, OJ L 166, 6 Jul. 2000, pp. 1-13, recital 58, apparently endorsed in Council Regulation (EC) No. 2852/2000 of 22 Dec. 2000 imposing a definitive anti-dumping duty and definitively collecting the provisional duty imposed on imports of PSF originating in India and the Republic of Korea, OJ L 332, 28 Dec. 2000, pp. 17-31, recital 41.

239. *Sacks and Bags Made of Polyethylene or Polypropylene*, Commission Regulation (EC) No. 45/97 of 10 Jan. 1997 imposing a provisional anti-dumping duty on imports of sacks and bags made of polyethylene or polypropylene originating in India, Indonesia and Thailand OJ L 12, 15 Jan. 1997, pp. 8-20, recital 27, endorsed in Council Regulation (EC) No. 1950/97 of 6 Oct. 1997 imposing a definitive anti-dumping duty on imports of sacks and bags made of polyethylene or polypropylene originating in India, Indonesia and Thailand and collecting definitively the provisional duty imposed, OJ L 276, 9 Oct. 1997, pp. 1-8, recitals 22 and 23. See also Council Regulation (EC) No. 96/1999 of 12 Jan. 1999 amending Regulation (EC) No. 1950/97 imposing a definitive anti-dumping duty on imports of sacks and bags made of polyethylene or polypropylene originating in India, Indonesia and Thailand and collecting definitively the provisional duty imposed, OJ L 11, 16 Jan. 1999, pp. 1-4, recital 13.

240. *Korea – Certain Paper*, WT/DS312/R, report of the Panel on 28 Oct. 2005.

basis, and therefore the use of general margins for associated parties per se may be a violation of WTO law. If the Commission and the Council base their approach on specific factors, as they do in *Sacks and Bags Made of Polyethylene or Polypropylene*,[241] this is consistent with WTO law. However, in several of the cases mentioned in note 237, it is not apparent that a concrete examination of the relationship between the producers or exporters has been carried out. It is thus not clear whether the Commission and the Council in fact carry out concrete examinations of relationships to conclude whether they are so close that only a general dumping margin is required.

6.3.4.2 Non-cooperating Producers

The Commission and the Council determine a general dumping margin for producers and exporters who do not cooperate during the investigation, either by not making themselves known or by not answering the questionnaires. Furthermore, if a producer submits unreliable information, and if no company-specific data can be used, the dumping margin is based on a general margin.[242]

When the general margin is calculated, the consistent EU practice is to use data from other cooperating producers, and the general dumping margin is established on the *highest* dumping margin found from the cooperating companies.[243]

---

241. *Sacks and Bags Made of Polyethylene or Polypropylene*, Commission Regulation (EC) No. 45/97 of 10 Jan. 1997 imposing a provisional anti-dumping duty on imports of sacks and bags made of polyethylene or polypropylene originating in India, Indonesia and Thailand OJ L 12, 15 Jan. 1997, pp. 8-20, endorsed in Council Regulation (EC) No. 1950/97 of 6 Oct. 1997 imposing a definitive anti-dumping duty on imports of sacks and bags made of polyethylene or polypropylene originating in India, Indonesia and Thailand and collecting definitively the provisional duty imposed, OJ L 276, 9 Oct. 1997, pp. 1-8.
242. See *Certain Tube and Pipe Fittings of Iron or Steel II*, Commission Regulation (EC) No. 358/2002 of 26 Feb. 2002 imposing a provisional anti-dumping duty on imports of certain tube and pipe fittings, of iron or steel originating in the Czech Republic, Malaysia, Russia, the Republic of Korea and Slovakia and accepting an undertaking offered by an exporting producer in Slovakia, OJ L 056, 27 Feb. 2002, pp. 4-18, recital 35, endorsed in Council Regulation (EC) No. 1514/2002 of 19 Aug. 2002 imposing a definitive anti-dumping duty and collecting definitively the provisional duty imposed on imports of certain tube and pipe fittings, of iron or steel originating in the Czech Republic, Malaysia, Russia, the Republic of Korea and Slovakia, OJ L 228, 24 Aug. 2002, pp. 1-7, recital 9.
243. *Polyester Staple Fibres I*, Commission Regulation (EC) No. 1472/2000 of 6 Jul. 2000 imposing a provisional anti-dumping duty on imports of PSF originating in India and the Republic of Korea, OJ L 166, 6 Jul. 2000, pp. 1-13, recitals 42-44, endorsed in Council Regulation (EC) No. 2852/2000 of 22 Dec. 2000 imposing a definitive anti-dumping duty and definitively collecting the provisional duty imposed on imports of PSF originating in India and the Republic of Korea, OJ L 332, 28 Dec. 2000, pp. 17-31, recitals 24 and 41; *Certain Prepared or Preserved Sweetcorn*, Commission Regulation (EC) No. 1888/2006 of 19 Dec. 2006 imposing a provisional anti-dumping duty on imports of certain prepared or preserved sweetcorn in kernels originating in Thailand, OJ L 364, 20 Dec. 2006, pp. 68-91, recital 40, endorsed in Council Regulation (EC) No. 682/2007 of 18 Jun. 2007 imposing a definitive anti-dumping duty and collecting definitively the provisional duty imposed on imports of certain prepared or preserved sweetcorn in kernels originating in Thailand, OJ L 159, 20 Jun. 2007, pp. 14-25, recital 26.

However, if the percentage of non-cooperative producers is high, the Commission and the Council find it appropriate to determine a general dumping margin higher than the highest margin found from the cooperating producers. In *Recordable Compact Disks*, the Commission made this argument for the high dumping margin:

> Indeed, there is reason to believe that the high level of non-cooperation results from the non-cooperating producers in Taiwan generally having dumped at a higher level than any cooperating producer. The residual dumping margin for Taiwan was therefore established at a level higher than the highest dumping margin established for a cooperating company. This level corresponds to the weighted average dumping margin of the product types with the highest dumping margin sold in representative quantities.[244]

It is stated that the high percentage of non-cooperative producers indicates dumping *at higher levels* than any of cooperative producers. Therefore, a higher general dumping margin is calculated and, in this case, based on product types with the highest margins instead of being based on the highest margin found for the product under investigation from a cooperative producer.

The Appellate Body stated in *Mexico – Anti-dumping Measures on Rice* that the investigating authorities are not required to seek out the producers and exporters that have not made themselves known.[245] Therefore, the practice by the Commission and Council to determine a general margin for such producers and exporters is in conformity with WTO law.

The question is, however, whether the practice of applying a general dumping margin in situations where the data is unreliable and no company-specific data can be used is in line with the findings by the Panel in *Argentina – Poultry Anti-dumping Duties.* There, it was stated that in case of unreliable information, the investigating authorities shall complete the data.[246] It should be noted here that in Annex II.7 to the ADA about secondary sources to information, it is provided:

> If the authorities have to base their findings, including those with respect to normal value, on information from a secondary source, including the information supplied in the application for the initiation of the investigation, they should do so with special circumspection. In such cases, the authorities should, where practicable, check the information from other independent sources at their disposal, such as published price lists, official import statistics and customs returns, and from the information obtained from other interested parties during the investigation. *It is clear, however, that if an interested party does*

244. *Recordable Compact Disks*, Commission Regulation (EC) No. 2479/2001 of 17 Dec. 2001 imposing a provisional anti-dumping duty on imports of recordable compact disks originating in Taiwan, OJ L 334, 18 Dec. 2001, pp. 8-25, recital 33.
245. *Mexico – Anti-dumping Measures on Rice*, WT/DS295//R, report of the Appellate Body on 29 Nov. 2005.
246. *Argentina – Poultry Anti-dumping Duties*, WT/DS241/R, report of the Panel on 22 Apr. 2003.

> *not cooperate and thus relevant information is being withheld from the authorities, this situation could lead to a result which is less favourable to the party than if the party did cooperate*. (Emphasis added)

The question is, then, whether the Commission and the Council should determine individual dumping margins based on such facts for producers that have made themselves known, instead of the general dumping margins, which apply to the producers that have *not made themselves known*. It must, however, be stressed that non-cooperative producers may be treated less favourably than cooperative producers, and therefore it seems justified if the dumping margins for such producers are higher than the dumping margins for the cooperative producers. Therefore, a dumping margin based on the highest margin for the cooperating producers is reasonable in such circumstances if an individual margin based on other secondary sources would have resulted in a lower margin than the highest margin of the cooperating producers.

6.4 FINAL COMMENTS

This chapter was divided into three parts, all concerning the comparison of the normal value and export price. Part 6.1 dealt with the adjustment of normal value and export price for price comparability, part 6.2 discussed the calculation methods when normal value and export price are compared and, finally, part 6.3 contained a brief examination whether the dumping margin should be individually or generally determined.

Part 6.1 revealed that WTO law offers wide discretion to the investigating authorities when adjustments of normal value and export price are made. The main principle of the investigating authorities is to ensure that the comparison is fair. A non-exhaustive list of factors that may affect price comparability is provided in Article 2.4 of the ADA. The list of factors provided in the EU legislation includes more factors than the WTO list; this is in line with the WTO requirements. In practice, the striking point is whether the EU authorities put too unreasonable a burden on the producers when they suggest adjustments of the prices. In several cases, adjustments have been rejected because the producers have not demonstrated to the satisfaction of the Commission and the Council that the factors had an impact on price comparability. Under WTO law, the burden of proof shall not be unreasonable. However, the Commission and the Council have also showed openness towards changing their initial standpoint about adjustment if suggestions by producers are supported by convincing evidence. This openness by the Commission and the Council is in conformity with a Panel statement in *US – Softwood Lumber V*.

Part 6.2 dealt with the calculation of dumping margins. Under WTO law, the principal methods are the weighted-average-to-weighted-average method or the transaction-to-transaction method. The weighted-average-to-transaction method only applies when the investigating authorities can demonstrate a pattern of different prices targeting different purchasers, regions or time periods, and can explain why the weighted-average-to-weighted-average method or the transaction-to-transaction method cannot be used to catch dumped prices.

The EU legislative approach is the same as outlined under WTO law for most parts, although the requirement to state reasons when the weighted-average-to-transaction is applied is not apparent in the basic Regulation but follows from Article 253 of the EC Treaty. In practice, the Commission and the Council prefer the weighted-average-to-weighted-average method to the transaction-to-transaction method, which, due to the two methods equal status under WTO law, is in conformity with WTO law. However, until recently the Commission and the Council have often applied the weighted-average-to-transaction method without explaining the reasons for derogating from the two principal methods. This practice is found by the EC Court in *Petrotub and Republica v. Council* to be a violation of both EU and WTO law, and it appears that the Commission and the Council have changed their practice and now provides explanations for applying the weighted-average-to-transaction method.

Under WTO law, it was also found that zeroing is an impermissible method under the weighted-average-to-weighted-average method and under the transaction-to-transaction method. Nevertheless, there are strong indications that zeroing is permissible under the weighted-average-to-transaction method.

A few point must, however, be noted about WTO practice. Under the weighted-average-to-weighted-average method, there has been consistency in the approaches by Panels and Appellate Body to the interpretations of Article 2.4.2 of the ADA. Zeroing is here not a permissible method.

This consistency between Panels and Appellate Body is not reflected in the approaches to zeroing under the transaction-to-transaction method. Until recently the Panel line was that zeroing is permissible, but the line by the Appellate Body has been the opposite. By looking into the wordings of Article 2.4.2, both interpretations can be justified. To justify the Panel interpretation, the lack of 'all' export transactions under the transaction-to-transaction method, compared to the wordings about the weighted-average-to-weighted-average, seems to form the basis for concluding that zeroing is permissible under the transaction-to-transaction method. To justify the Appellate Body interpretation, the different nature of the weighted-average-to-weighted-average method and the transaction-to-transaction method and the fairness principle seem to form the basis for such an interpretation. However, although Panels have corrected their approach into conformity with the line of the Appellate Body in subsequent cases, the different lines by the Panel and Appellate Body could have been avoided if the text of Article 2.4.2 of the ADA had been clearer on that point. In Chapter 2, it was stated that the reason why the negotiators made a hierarchy between the two principal methods and the weighted-average-to-transaction method was to reduce the application of zeroing, which was/is a natural element in the weighted-average-to-transaction method. The negotiators should make it clearer now what the line under the transaction-to-transaction method should be. The line by the Appellate Body has led some commentators to argue that the Appellate Body has taken an activist law-creating role, going beyond its powers under the DSU and the WTO Agreement; see Chapter 2, Section 2.2.3.

From the outset, the EU has used model zeroing under the weighted-average-to-weighted-average method. After the Appellate Body in *EC – Bed linen* found that the EU violated its WTO obligations, the Commission and the Council seem to have changed their direction away from zeroing, and they now act in conformity with WTO law.

In part 6.3, there was a brief examination of the application of either individual or general dumping margins. The outset under WTO law is to determine individual margins for each known producer under investigation. The approach by the Commission and the Council is the same. The dumping margins are determined on individual bases.

This general rule is derogated from by the Commission and the Council if some producers are related to one another. Under such circumstances, a general margin is established for the group of related producers. WTO law permits such general margins for related producers if it is examined that they have a close relationship. It is not always clear from Commission and Council practice whether they conduct such an examination, and if they do not, this may violate WTO law.

The general rule is also derogated from by the Commission and the Council if the producer does not cooperate. In situations where the producers do not make themselves known, it is in conformity with WTO law to apply a general dumping margin for those producers. If the producers do not submit reliable information, it may be a violation of WTO law not to determine an individual dumping margin, as the Commission and the Council should determine an individual margin based on available facts.

Chapter 7

Special Anti-dumping Rules Regarding China

This chapter will discuss whether EU dumping determinations towards Chinese producers are in conformity with WTO law. This subject deserves a separate chapter because of the exceptional rules that apply to China, and because China is by far the most targeted country in the EU anti-dumping regime.

The chapter begins with Section 7.1, listing some brief background information about the reason for having special rules towards China. Section 7.2 concerns the normal value determination for Chinese producers, and Section 7.3 deals with the special rules about the general countrywide dumping margin determination for Chinese producers.

7.1 CHINA: THE ACCESSION TO THE WTO

China was one of the original signatories to GATT in 1947, but had not been active in GATT activities since 1949, when Chairman Mao and the Communist Party took over in China. The nationalist government, *Guomindang*, retreated to Taiwan and in 1950 tried to withdraw China from GATT.[1] On 5 May, 1950 the withdrawal took effect, and it was contested by China.[2] In 1986, China applied to re-enter into the GATT.[3] In the years between the withdrawal and the application for re-entry into

1. Wang Gui Guo, *The Law of The WTO – China and the Future of Free Trade* (Hong Kong: Sweet & Maxwell Asia, 2005), 49.
2. R. Bhala, *International Trade Law: Theory and Practice*, 2nd edn (New York/San Fransisco: Lexis Publishing, 2000), 1126-1127.
3. *China's Status as a Contracting Partner*, Communication from the People's Republic of China, GATT doc. L/6017 of 14 Jul. 1986.

GATT, Chairman Mao died and the new leader, Deng Xiaoping, introduced economic reforms, including an open door policy towards the outside world.[4] For example, in 1981 China had become an observer of the Textile Committee under GATT.[5] China had also joined the International Monetary Fund (IMF) and the World Bank.[6]

GATT responded by establishing a GATT Working Party on China's Status. Due to the Uruguay Round and introduction of the WTO, the Working Party changed to the Working Party for China's Accession to the Marrakesh Agreement.[7]

China was, however, far from being accepted under the general terms in GATT 1947 and later under the WTO Agreement, due to the political and economic differences between China and the GATT contracting parties/WTO Members.[8] The negotiations between China and the different WTO Members would last for fifteen years before China was accepted as a WTO Member. In November 2001, China accepted the Protocol on Accession, and since 11 December, 2001 China has been a member of the WTO.[9]

Several members of the Working Party noted in the report on the Accession of China that the Chinese economy was in a transition phase towards a full market economy. There could be difficulties in determining costs and prices in the anti-dumping investigations, and a strict comparison between the domestic Chinese price and export price would not always be appropriate.[10] The result is that WTO law leaves it to the discretion of each WTO Member to decide whether it will regard China as a market economy or not. So far, countries like Australia,[11] Brazil,[12] Argentina[13] and all ASEAN Members[14] treat China as a

4. Kong Qingjiang, *China and the World Trade Organization – A Legal Perspective* (Singapore/New Jersey: World Scientific Publishing, 2002), 3.
5. Ibid., 5.
6. J. Hoogmartens, *EC Trade Law Following China's Accession to the WTO* (The Hague: Kluwer Law International, 2004), 47.
7. *Report of the Working Party on the Accession of China*, WT/ACC/CHN/49, 1 Oct. 2001, para. 1.
8. J. F. Gertler, 'What China's Accession Is All About', in *China and the WTO*, eds. D. Bhattasali, Li Shantong & W. Martin (Washington: The World Bank and Oxford University Press, 2004), 23-24 .
9. Protocol on the Accession of the People's Republic of China, Notification of Acceptance, WLI/100.
10. *Report of the Working Party on the Accession of China*, WT/ACC/CHN/49, 1 Oct. 2001, para. 150.
11. See <www.dfat.gov.au/geo/china/fta/facts/market_economy.html>, which is the homepage for the Australian Department of Foreign Affairs and Trade.
12. See <www.china-embassy.org/eng/xw/t264143.htm>, which is the homepage of the Chinese Embassy in the US.
13. Ibid.
14. Association of South East Asian Nations (ASEAN) consists of ten members; Brunei Darussalam, Cambodia, Indonesia, Laos, Malaysia, Myanmar, Philippines, Singapore, Thailand and Vietnam. It follows from Art. 14 in the Agreement on Trade in Goods of the Framework Agreement on Comprehensive Economic Co-operation between ASEAN and China, from 29 Nov. 2004, that all ASEAN Members must recognize China as a full market economy and shall not apply ss 15 and 16 in the protocol on the WTO accession of China.

market economy – whereas WTO Members like the US and the EU still treat China as a non-market economy.[15]

7.2 NORMAL VALUE FOR CHINESE PRODUCERS

This part deals with the normal value determination in EU of Chinese producers, and its conformity with WTO law. The first step is the WTO legislation. No practice by Panels and Appellate Body exists, so the next step is an examination of EU legislation and EU practice under WTO law.

7.2.1 WTO LEGISLATION

The specific rules on anti-dumping treatment of China are provided in Article 15(a) and Article 15(d) of the Protocol annexed to the Accession Agreement. It follows from Article 15 and Article 15(a) of the Protocol:

> Article VI of the GATT 1994, the Agreement on Implementation of Article VI of the General Agreement on Tariffs and Trade 1994 (Anti-dumping Agreement) and the SCM Agreement shall apply in proceedings involving imports of Chinese origin into a WTO Member consistent with the following:
>
> (a) In determining price comparability under Article VI of the GATT 1994 and the Anti Dumping Agreement, the importing WTO Member shall use either Chinese prices or costs for the industry under investigation or a methodology that is not based on a strict comparison with domestic prices or costs in China based on the following rules:
>   (i) If the producers under investigation can clearly show that market economy conditions prevail in the industry producing the like product with regard to the manufacture, production and sale of that product, the importing WTO Member shall use Chinese prices or costs for the industry under investigation in determining price comparability;
>   (ii) The importing WTO Member may use a methodology that is not based on a strict comparison with domestic prices or costs in China if the producers under investigation cannot clearly show that market economy conditions prevail in the industry producing the like product with regard to manufacture, production and sale of that product.

Article 15(d) of the Protocol reads:

> (d) Once China has established, under the national law of the importing WTO Member, that it is a market economy, the provisions of subparagraph (a) shall be terminated provided that the importing Member's national law contains

15. Changho Sohn, 'Treatment of Non-market Economy Countries under the World Trade Organization Anti-dumping Regime', *Journal of World Trade* 39 (4) (2005): 770 et seq.

> market economy criteria as of the date of accession. In any event, the provisions of subparagraph (a)(ii) shall expire 15 years after the date of accession. In addition, should China establish, pursuant to the national law of the importing WTO Member, that market economy conditions prevail in a particular industry or sector, the non market economy provisions of subparagraph (a) shall no longer apply to that industry or sector.

Before turning to the substantial part of those rules, the legal status of Article 15 of the Protocol must be established.

7.2.1.1 Relation to Article VI of GATT 1994 and ADA

The situation with non-market economies was described in Section 2.1.1.1. It was found that Article VI did not provide sufficient guidelines to deal with non-market economies, but the interpretative note provided that a strict comparison with the actual domestic prices may not always be appropriate when the State has complete monopoly of its trade and where domestic prices are fixed by the State. As seen in Chapter 4, Article 2.2 of the ADA deals with the construction of prices, for example if the sales on domestic markets with a *particular market situation* [. . .] *do not permit a proper comparison*. In that case, the provision suggests the alternative methods mentioned in Chapter 4. In order to avoid conflict between the alternatives in Article 2.2 of the ADA and the interpretative note re Article VI.1 of GATT 1994, Article 2.7 of the ADA reads:

> This article is without prejudice to the second Supplementary Provision to paragraph 1 of Article VI in Annex I to GATT 1994.

The general rule towards non-market economies has thus been written into the interpretative note re Article VI.1, which is not being limited by the rules in Article 2 of the ADA. Nevertheless, the Working Party noted in its report that China is a transition-economy.[16] The anti-dumping rules on China apparently recognize the transition of the economy from non-market towards market, because the WTO Members have the choice to treat China as either a market economy or a non-market economy.

It follows from the Accession Agreement that the WTO Members have decided to grant China a WTO Membership on the terms and conditions set out in the annexed Protocol. Article 1.2 of that Protocol provides that the Protocol is an integral part of the WTO Agreement. Therefore, the rights and obligations in the Protocol are binding on the same terms as those of any other WTO agreement. Article 1.2 of the Protocol furthermore provides that the provisions mentioned in Article 342 of the report by the Working Party are part of the Protocol and also an integral part of the WTO Agreement.

---

16. *Report of the Working Party on the Accession of China*, WT/ACC/CHN/49, report of the Working Party on 1 Oct. 2001, para. 9.

More specifically, it follows from the first sentence in Article 15 of the Protocol that Article VI of GATT 1994 and the ADA must apply consistently with the specific rules provided in the subparagraphs to Article 15. Article 15 of the Protocol seems thus to be an expression of the principle of *lex specialis*.

Article 15(a) provides that the condition on price comparability under Article VI of GATT 1994 and Article 2.1 of the ADA, which was exemplified under Article 2.2 in particular market situations, may be determined on the basis of other prices than prescribed by the general rule. The general rule was described in Chapter 4, where it was found that if domestic prices are comparable with the export prices, they will not be disregarded for the normal value determination. However, concerning China, the prices for normal value may be based on other methods; this is described in the following part.

It must be noted that Article 15(a) of the Protocol only allows the WTO Members to change the Chinese price and cost data with another set of data. Apart from that, the basic requirements in Article VI of GATT 1994 and ADA must be met by the investigating authorities in order to impose Chinese products with an anti-dumping duty.

7.2.1.2 The Special Rules

Article 15(a) of the Protocol leaves the WTO Members with two choices in situations with normal value determinations of products from China:

(1) the normal value must be based on the domestic prices in China in accordance with the general rules on normal value described above in Chapter 4 – i.e., *market economy treatment*; or
(2) the normal value must be determined by other means than the domestic prices.

There are no suggestions provided as to what methodology must be used if the prices are not based on domestic prices. It merely says 'not based on a strict comparison' with domestic prices or costs. Therefore, it may be assumed that there is wide discretion to the WTO Members to determine a price-finding methodology to serve as normal value. Those prices may not be based on the prices in the Chinese domestic market

It is clear from Article 15(a)(ii) that a WTO Member *may* use the general rules on normal value regardless of the market or non-market status of China. It is also clear from Article 15(a)(i) that a WTO Member *must* use the general rules on normal value if Chinese producers under investigation are able to prove that market economy conditions prevail in the industry producing the like product with regard to the manufacture, production and sale of that product. Article 15(a)(i) places the burden of proof on the Chinese producers to demonstrate that market economy conditions prevail. If the producers *clearly* demonstrate that market economy conditions prevail in the industry, normal value shall be based on the prices in the *industry*. However, the term 'market economy' is not defined under Article 15(a).

Pursuant to Article 15(d) of the Protocol, it is left to the individual WTO Members to decide whether China should be granted full market economy status or not. Thus, the decision on granting China full market economy status rests on bilateral or regional agreements. Granting China full market economy status is therefore merely resting on a political decision by the respective WTO Members. Once China has attained a market economy status by the WTO Member, the normal value and dumping margins will be determined in accordance with the general rules described in Chapters 4-6.

However, there are two limitations involved:

(1) Once China has fulfilled the requirements under the specific WTO Member's national law that market economy conditions prevail in China as such, the WTO Member must treat Chinese producers under the general rules on normal value. However, this condition appears only to apply to those WTO Members that had market economy criteria written into national law on the date of China's accession to the WTO.
(2) In 2016, all WTO Members will grant China market economy status.

In the following part, the EU approach towards China as a non-market economy is described. Next, the specific provisions in the basic Regulation are examined, and subsequently the practice by the EU institutions.

7.2.2 EU and the Non-Market Approach towards China

In this part, there is a brief description of the EU position towards China concerning the conditions for granting China a market economy status.

7.2.2.1 No State Specific Market Economy Criteria in EU Law

EU could be obligated to grant China market economy status if EU law contained specific criteria of a market economy on the date of the China's accession to the WTO, and China fulfilled those criteria. No market economy criteria for China are found in the EU Regulations. Nor are there any definitions of a market economy. There are, however, market economy criteria targeting Chinese *producers or exporters* in Article 2.7 of the basic Regulation, but no criteria covering a nation as such. Other countries have statutory criteria of market economies; for example, the US has such criteria in their Tariff Act of 1930.[17]

---

17. Tariff Act of 1930, s. 771 (18), provides:

(A) In general. The term 'nonmarket economy country' means any foreign country that the administering authority determines does not operate on market principles of cost or pricing structures, so that sales of merchandise in such country do not reflect the fair value of the merchandise.
(B) Factors to be considered. In making determinations under subparagraph (A) the administering authority shall take into account

The producer and export-specific criteria in the EU legal framework came into being in 1998 in the 905/98 Regulation,[18] an amendment to the basic Regulation.[19] The specific criteria in Regulation 905/98 will be further elaborated on in Sections 7.2.3 and 7.2.4.

In a few instances, the EC Court has made general comments about non-market economies. In *Technointorg v. Commission and Council*, the EC Court made a teleological interpretation of Article 2.7, stating that '[t]he aim of that provision is to prevent account from being taken of prices and costs in non-market economy countries which are not normally the result of market forces'.[20] The statement, however, is very generally formulated and only indicates that prices and costs in a non-market economy may not be a result of the market forces. The EC Court does not provide any criteria on how to determine whether a country is a non market economy or not.

The lack of nation-based market economy criteria under EU law implies that the EU is not obligated under Article 15(d) to grant China market economy status if certain market economy criteria are met. However, the EU is obligated to grant China market economy status in 2016.

7.2.2.2 Political and Technical Statements

Although EU law does not provide any criteria of a market economy, the Commission issued a document in 2004 containing a preliminary analysis aimed at evaluating the possibility of granting China a market economy status.[21]

(i) the extent to which the currency of the foreign country is convertible into the currency of other countries;
(ii) the extent to which wage rates in the foreign country are determined by free bargaining between labor and management,
(iii) the extent to which joint ventures or other investments by firms of other foreign countries are permitted in the foreign country,
(iv) the extent of government ownership or control of the means of production,
(v) the extent of government control over the allocation of resources and over the price and output decisions of enterprises, and
(vi) such other factors as the administering authority considers appropriate.

18. Council Regulation (EC) No. 905/98 of 27 Apr. 1998 amending Regulation (EC) No. 384/96 on protection against dumped imports from countries not members of the European Community, OJ L 128, 30 Apr. 1998, pp. 18-19.
19. Art. 2.7(a) – Art. 2.7(c) were written into the basic Regulation. The market economy criteria are found in Art. 2.7(c).
20. *Technointorg v. Commission and Council*, Joined cases 294/86 and 77/87, judgment of the Court on 5 Oct. 1988, ECR 1988, p. 6077, para. 29. See also *Neotype Techmashexport v. Commission and Council*, Joined cases C-305/86 and C-160/87, judgment of the Court on 11 Jul. 1990, ECR 1990, p. I-2945, para. 26.
21. *China – Market economy status in trade defence investigations*, Brussels, 28 Jun. 2004. See Commission's homepage; <trade.ec.europa.eu/doclib/html/117795.htm>.

The Commission stated that the analysis was solely technical, not political. The Commission found that China had to improve in four broad areas:

- State influence: ensuring equal treatment of all companies by reducing State interference, which takes place on an *ad hoc* basis or as a result of industrial policies, as well as through export and pricing restrictions on raw materials.
- Corporate governance: increasing the level of compliance with the existing Accounting Law in order to ensure in general the usability of accounting information for the purpose of trade defence investigations.
- Property and bankruptcy law: ensuring equal treatment of all companies in bankruptcy procedures and in respect of property and intellectual property rights.
- Financial sector: bringing the banking sector under market rules, i.e., by removing discriminatory barriers, in order to ensure rational allocation of capital by financial institutions.

In a speech held in February 2005, Trade Commissioner Mandelson mentioned that granting China market economy status was not only a political issue but also a technical matter of China having to fulfil the objective criteria mentioned above.[22]

The above statements have been made after the accession of China, and they are thus not binding on the EU in regard to Article 15(d) of the Protocol, which states that the criteria must be incorporated in national law *on the date of the accession*. Furthermore, the four criteria in the Commission's statement are not part of EU legislation. The document is 'a preliminary analysis'; it is not a regulation in the sense mentioned in Article 300 of the EC Treaty, cf. Article 133.

In any case, the EU is not obligated to grant China market economy status until 2016. In the following sections, the EU legislation and practice about the application of market economy treatment to the producers in concrete cases are examined.

7.2.3 EU Legislation

Article 2.7 of the basic Regulation provides special rules concerning countries with non- or transition economies. Article 2.7 is divided into three parts: Article 2.7(a) is the general rule to non-market economies, which also applies to transition economies like China. The normal value is here based on prices from producers in countries with a market economy, i.e., prices from an analogue country. For transition economies, an exception is written into Article 2.7(b), whereby producers have the possibility to be granted market economy treatment in concrete cases, and the normal value is instead based on the producer's own prices. Article 2.7(c)

22. *The EU and China: Partnership and Responsibility in the Global Economy*, speech by Peter Mandelson at the University of International Business and Economics. Beijing, 24 Feb. 2005. See Commission's homepage on: <ec.europa.eu/comm/commission_barroso/mandelson/speeches_art.s/temp_icentre.cfm?temp=sppm016_en>.

concerns the criteria that the producers from transition economies, including Chinese producers, must meet in order to get market economy treatment. The rules in Article 2.7 are described below:

7.2.3.1 Analogue Country

Article 2.7(a) of the basic Regulation provides:

> In the case of imports from non-market economy countries [*], normal value shall be determined on the basis of the price or constructed value in a market economy third country, or the price from such a third country to other countries, including the Community, or where those are not possible, on any other reasonable basis, including the price actually paid or payable in the Community for the like product, duly adjusted if necessary to include a reasonable profit margin.
>
> An appropriate market economy third country shall be selected in a not unreasonable manner, due account being taken of any reliable information made available at the time of selection. Account shall also be taken of time limits; where appropriate, a market economy third country which is subject to the same investigation shall be used.
>
> The parties to the investigation shall be informed shortly after its initiation of the market economy third country envisaged and shall be given 10 days to comment.
>
> (*) Including Albania, Armenia, Azerbaijan, Belarus, Georgia, North Korea, Kyrgyzstan, Moldova, Mongolia, Tajikistan, Turkmenistan, Uzbekistan

According to the first sentence, normal value for non-market economy countries is based on the price – or constructed on values – from market economy countries, i.e., *analogue countries*. Therefore, when normal value is determined for producers from a non-market economy, reference is made to prices from market economy countries.

There is also an alternative method provided in Article 2.7(a), as the normal value for a non-market economy may be based on the export price from an analogue country to another third country. This includes a price to the EU.

If a normal value cannot be found by either of the two methods described, the EU authorities must determine the normal value for non-market economy producers on any other reasonable basis. This method may be based on prices from sales between EU producers of the like product and EU buyers. Those prices may be adjusted for a reasonable profit margin.

Article 2.7(a), second sentence, provides that the analogue country must be selected in a not unreasonable manner. If a market economy country is also under the same anti-dumping investigation as China, then it may be used if it is considered appropriate. Finally, the third sentence regards the right of the Chinese producers and exporters to comment on the selected analogue country.

Under WTO law, it is provided in Article 15(a) of the Protocol that normal value for China may be based on prices other than the domestic prices. There seems to be wide discretion for the WTO Members to determine the alternatives. Therefore, it seems to be in accordance with WTO law to base the normal value on prices from an analogue country.

7.2.3.2 Opening to Market Economy Treatment

In EU legislation, the WTO requirement of opening up for market economy treatment of China in specific cases is followed. Article 2.7(b) of the basic Regulation reads:

> In anti-dumping investigations concerning imports from the People's Republic of China, Vietnam and Kazakhstan and any non-market-economy country which is a member of the WTO at the date of the initiation of the investigation, normal value will be determined in accordance with paragraphs 1 to 6, if it is shown, on the basis of properly substantiated claims by one or more producers subject to the investigation and in accordance with the criteria and procedures set out in subparagraph (c) that market economy conditions prevail for this producer or producers in respect of the manufacture and sale of the like product concerned. When this is not the case, the rules set out under subparagraph (a) shall apply.

Chinese producers may have normal value based on the general rules described in Chapter 4 if the conditions in Article 2.7(c) are fulfilled. The conditions in Article 2.7(c) are described below. The producer or producers have to demonstrate, *on the basis of a properly substantiated claim*, that market economy conditions prevail *for the producer or producers*, both in regard to the manufacture of the like product and in regard to the sale of the like product.

One difference between the wordings of Article 2.7(b) of the basic Regulation and Article 15(a)(i) of the Protocol lies in the possibility for *one producer or producers* to be granted market economy treatment if the particular producer or producers meet the conditions mentioned in Article 2.7(c). In the Protocol, market economy treatment will be granted if the producers under investigation can clearly show that market economy conditions prevail *for the industry*. The difference in the wordings may question whether the market economy treatment will be granted to the producers in the entire industry if market economy conditions prevail in the industry. Under the EU provisions, it appears to be a market economy examination of single producers, which may imply that only some producers in an industry may be granted market economy treatment, whereas other producers in the same industry are not granted market economy treatment. This issue is more thoroughly examined in Section 7.2.4.1.

It follows that also producers from Vietnam and Kazakhstan may be granted market economy treatment. As Kazakhstan is not a WTO Member, it is left out of the analysis. Vietnam did not become a WTO Member until 2007.[23] The dumping determinations for Vietnam have therefore not been examined here.

23. *Accession of the Socialist Republic of Vietnam*, WT/L662, Decision taken on 15 Nov. 2006, entered into force on 11 Jan. 2007.

7.2.3.3 The Market Economy Criteria

Article 2.7(c) of the basic Regulation provides the criteria that one or more Chinese producers have to fulfil in order to get market economy treatment in accordance with Article 2.7(b):

> A claim under subparagraph (b) must be made in writing and contain sufficient evidence that the producer operates under market economy conditions, that is if:
>
> – decisions of firms regarding prices, costs and inputs, including for example raw materials, cost of technology and labour, output, sales and investment, are made in response to market signals reflecting supply and demand, and without significant State interference in this regard, and costs of major inputs substantially reflect market values,
> – firms have one clear set of basic accounting records which are independently audited in line with international accounting standards and are applied for all purposes,
> – the production costs and financial situation of firms are not subject to significant distortions carried over from the former non-market economy system, in particular in relation to depreciation of assets, other write-offs, barter trade and payment via compensation of debts,
> – the firms concerned are subject to bankruptcy and property laws which guarantee legal certainty and stability for the operation of firms, and
> – exchange rate conversions are carried out at the market rate.

A determination whether the producer meets the abovementioned criteria shall be made within three months of the initiation of the investigation, after specific consultation of the Advisory Committee and after the Community industry has been given an opportunity to comment. This determination shall remain in force throughout the investigation.

The provision lists five criteria that a Chinese producer must meet in order to be granted market economy treatment:

(1) The producer must demonstrate that the market conditions are reflected in prices, costs, input, labour wages, output, sales and investments, and are not a result of State interference.
(2) International accounting principles must be followed.
(3) Production costs and financial situation must not reflect the former non-market economy system.
(4) The producers must be under bankruptcy and property right laws.
(5) Currency exchange rates must be based on market rates.

The determination by the Commission shall be in force throughout the investigation, and the Commission shall come with a determination within three months after the initiation of the investigation. Furthermore, before the determination, the Commission shall consult the Advisory Board and give the EU industry the possibility to comment on the matter.

WTO legislation does not provide any criteria on how to identify a market economy. There seems to be wide discretion for national legislation to provide market economy criteria. The criteria set up in the EU legislation cannot be seen as violating WTO law.

In the following two parts, practice by the EU institutions is examined. There is a change in the order compared to the order in Article 2.7. In part 7.2.4, the practice in relation to the general rule on Chinese producers in Article 2.7(b) and the practice about market economy determination in Article 2.7(c) are examined. In part 7.2.5, the practice of selecting an analogue country is examined. The reason for reversing the order compared to the structure in Article 2.7 is that an analogue country is selected *after* it has been determined whether Chinese producers are granted market economy treatment or not.

7.2.4 EU Practice: The Non-Market Economy Approach for Single Producers

The Commission and the Council follow the setup from Article 2.7(b), according to which the general rule is to meet Chinese producers with a non-market approach. Each Chinese producer is offered the opportunity to demonstrate that market economy conditions prevail for the particular producer in order to get market economy treatment.[24]

In *Shanghai Teraoka Electronic v. Council*, the Court of First Instance stated that the granting of market economy treatment is an exception to the general rule of non-market economy treatment, and therefore it must be interpreted strictly.[25] Furthermore, the Court of First Instance confirmed the general rule that the Commission and the Council have wide discretion. A review by the Court of First Instance is limited to establishing whether the relevant procedural rules have been complied with, whether the facts on which the contested choice is based have been accurately stated and whether there has been a manifest error of assessment of the facts or a misuse of power.[26]

Before turning to the practice on the specific criteria in Article 2.7(c), a few points are made about WTO law and EU practice about individual examination of Chinese producers.

7.2.4.1 Single Producer Examination or Industry Examination?

As mentioned above, Article 15(a)(i) of the Protocol provides that if 'the producers under investigation can clearly show that *market economy conditions prevail in the*

24. See in general the Regulations mentioned in this part.
25. *Shanghai Teraoka Electronic v. Council*, Case T-35/01, judgment of the Court of First Instance on 28 Oct. 2004, ECR 2004, p. II-3663, para. 50. See also *Nanjing Metalink Int. v. Council*, Case T-138/02, judgment of the Court of First Instance of 14 Nov. 2006, ECR 2006, p. II-4347, para. 46.
26. Para. 48-49.

industry', then 'the importing WTO Member *shall use Chinese prices or costs for the industry under investigation* in determining price comparability'. The term 'industry' could imply that the entire group of producers of the like product should be granted market economy treatment if the producers demonstrate that market economy conditions prevail 'for the industry'. Therefore, the EU examination of individual producers – and not an examination of the industry as such – may violate WTO law. This interpretation finds support in the context in Article 4.1 of the ADA, where 'domestic industry' is defined as 'the domestic producers *as a whole* of the like product'. This indicates that 'industry' covers more than just a single producer.

Furthermore, the report by the Working Party provides in paragraph 151(a):

> When determining price comparability in a particular case in a manner not based on a strict comparison with domestic prices or costs in China, the importing WTO Member should ensure that it had established and published in advance (1) the criteria that it used for determining whether *market economy conditions prevailed in the industry or company producing the like product* and (2) the methodology that it used in determining price comparability. (Emphasis added)

This particular text regards the transparency of the criteria used to determine market economy treatment. As emphasized, the Working Party mentions the criteria to determine whether market economy principles prevail in the 'industry or company'. It is here suggested that the examination of market economy conditions can be made for either the industry or individual producers. However, the particular paragraph is not mentioned in paragraph 342 of the Working Party report, and thus it is not an integral part of the WTO Agreements; see Article 1.2 of the Protocol. It could then be argued that if the drafters had wanted the opportunity to make individual producer examinations, they would have written it into the text of Article 15(a)(i).

If the Chinese producers clearly demonstrate that market economy conditions prevail in the industry, the normal value should be based on the regular prices from *all* the Chinese producers in that particular industry. Those producers who are under State influence could have adjustments made under the provision of Article 2.4 of the ADA or have domestic sales disregarded if they are not comparable with the export prices; see Article 2.1 of the ADA, and possibly constructed under Article 2.2 of the ADA. Therefore, the producer-specific examination of market economy conduct instead of an examination of the industry as such by the Commission and the Council may violate WTO law.

7.2.4.2 The Five Criteria in Article 2.7(c)

Article 2.7(c) provides five criteria that a Chinese producer must fulfil in order to be granted market economy treatment. Once they are met, normal value shall be determined on the prices and costs from the Chinese producer. If the conditions are not met, the normal value shall be based on prices and costs from producers in an analogue country. The Court of First Instance stated in *Shanghai Teraoka*

Electronic v. Council that the five criteria are cumulative, and a Chinese producer cannot get market economy treatment unless all five criteria are met.[27]

The burden of proof lies with the Chinese producers; this has also been established in practice.[28] In practice, the claim by Chinese producers to be granted market economy treatment is rejected by the EU authorities if it is not demonstrated to the satisfaction of the EU authorities that market economy conditions prevail for the specific producer.[29]

In situations where one Chinese company is related to another Chinese company and they both manufacture the product under investigation, or the companies have different positions in the product chain, they must both meet the five criteria in order to get market economy treatment. If one of the producers does not fulfil one of the five criteria or does not provide the necessary information, none of the related companies will be granted market economy treatment, even though the other companies meet the five criteria. This is now settled practice by the EU authorities.[30]

Under WTO law, how Chinese associated companies are to be dealt with is not regulated under Article 15 of the Protocol. However, as found in Section 6.3.2.2, it is in conformity with WTO law to determine a *general margin* for producers who are related. It indicates an openness under the WTO system to treat associated companies as a *single company*, which probably also could be advocated in situations with market economy determination for Chinese associated producers. Yet, if the EU made the market economy treatment for the entire industry as such, which would be in conformity with WTO law, this issue would be solved because the associated companies would all be under the market economy treatment.

Practice about the five criteria in Article 2.7(c) of the basic Regulation is described in Sections 7.2.4.2.1 through 7.2.4.2.5. In Section 7.2.4.3, the

---

27. *Shanghai Teraoka Electronic v. Council*, Case T-35/01, judgment of the Court of First Instance on 28 Oct. 2004, ECR 2004, p. II-3663, para. 54.
28. See Art. 2.7 (b) and (c). *Shanghai Teraoka Electronic v. Council*, Case T-35/01, judgment of the Court of First Instance on 28 Oct. 2004, ECR 2004, p. II-3663, para. 59. See also *Granular Polytetrafluoroethylene (PTFE)*; Commission Regulation (EC) No. 862/2005 of 7 Jun. 2005 imposing provisional anti-dumping duties on imports of granular polytetrafluoroethylene (PTFE) originating in Russia and the People's Republic of China, OJ L 144, 8 Jun. 2005, pp. 11-36, recital 32.
29. See in general the Regulations mentioned in this chapter.
30. *Okoumé Plywood*, Commission Regulation (EC) No. 988/2004 of 17 May 2004 imposing provisional anti-dumping duties on imports of okoumé plywood originating in the People's Republic of China, OJ L 181, 18 May 2004, pp. 5-23, recital 34, endorsed in Council Regulation (EC) No. 1942/2004 of 2 Nov. 2004 imposing a definitive anti-dumping duty and collecting definitively the provisional duty imposed on imports of okoumé plywood originating in the People's Republic of China, OJ L 336, 12 Nov. 2004, pp. 4-12, recital 21; *Certain Castings*, Council Regulation (EC) No. 1212/2005 of 25 Jul. 2005 imposing a definitive anti-dumping duty on imports of certain castings originating in the People's Republic of China, OJ L 199, 29 Jul. 2005, pp. 1-27, recital 38; *Sodium Cyclamate*, Council Regulation (EC) No. 435/2004 of 8 Mar. 2004 imposing a definitive anti-dumping duty and collecting definitively the provisional duty imposed on imports of sodium cyclamate originating in the People's Republic of China and Indonesia, OJ L 072, 11 Mar. 2004, pp. 1-4, recital 38. See J. Hoogmartens, *EC Trade Law Following China's Accession to the WTO* (The Hague: Kluwer Law International, 2004), 153, who offers some highly critical remarks to this particular case.

requirement that market economy treatment shall remain in force throughout the investigation in Article 2.7(c) is discussed. In Section 7.2.4.4, EU practice on establishing normal value for Chinese producers granted market economy treatment is described. Finally, Section 7.2.4.5 contains an evaluation of the practice under WTO law. The reason for not making the evaluation of the EU conformity with WTO law in each section is due to the wide discretion left to the WTO Members to determine the market economy treatment. Therefore, Section 7.2.4.5 only describes some overall aspects of WTO law that may be violated in the EU practice.

7.2.4.2.1 State Interference and Market Conditions

The first criterion in Article 2.7(c) regards the way business decisions are carried out. They must be without significant State interference and be on a market that reflects supply and demand. In this section, first, the factors about State influence on the producers' decisions are described. Next, the factors about market conditions are examined.

7.2.4.2.1.1 Determinants Regarding Business Decisions

The Commission and the Council want to ensure that the producer is not under the influence of the State when business decisions are made. Some of the factors used by the Commission and the Council to determine State influence are described here.

The State has a legal right to exercise control: In situations where the State has significant influence on business decisions, market economic treatment cannot be granted.[31] This could, for example, be a situation where the State-owned shareholder in the company under investigation owns the majority of the shares,[32] or when the appointed directors of the board are State officials.[33]

---

31. *Granular Polytetrafluoroethylene (PTFE)*, Commission Regulation (EC) No. 862/2005 of 7 Jun. 2005 imposing provisional anti-dumping duties on imports of granular PTFE originating in Russia and the People's Republic of China, OJ L 144, 8 Jun. 2005, pp. 11-36, recital 35, endorsed in Council Regulation (EC) No. 1987/2005 of 2 Dec. 2005 imposing a definitive anti-dumping duty and collecting definitively the provisional duty imposed on imports of granular PTFE originating in Russia and the People's Republic of China, OJ L 320, 8 Dec. 2005, pp. 1-19, recital 16.
32. *Granular Polytetrafluoroethylene (PTFE)*, Commission Regulation (EC) No. 862/2005 of 7 Jun. 2005 imposing provisional anti-dumping duties on imports of granular PTFE originating in Russia and the People's Republic of China, OJ L 144, 8 Jun. 2005, pp. 11-36, recital 35, endorsed in Council Regulation (EC) No. 1987/2005 of 2 Dec. 2005 imposing a definitive anti-dumping duty and collecting definitively the provisional duty imposed on imports of granular PTFE originating in Russia and the People's Republic of China, OJ L 320, 8 Dec. 2005, pp. 1-19, recital 16; and *Glyphosate*, Council Regulation (EC) No. 1683/2004 of 24 Sep. 2004 imposing a definitive anti-dumping duty on imports of glyphosate originating in the People's Republic of China, OJ L 303, 30 Sep. 2004, pp. 1-18, recital 13.
33. *Glyphosate*, Council Regulation (EC) No. 1683/2004 of 24 Sep. 2004 imposing a definitive anti-dumping duty on imports of glyphosate originating in the People's Republic of China, OJ L 303, 30 Sep. 2004, pp. 1-18, recital 13.

In *Trichloroisocyanuric Acid*, one producer was denied market economy treatment. The producer was owned by three other companies, of which one, ABC, held 48% of the shares in the producer under investigation. The State held 20% of the shares in ABC, while the 1,000 employees of ABC owned 80%. The Commission found that the State had de facto control of ABC, and thus ABC was a State-controlled company.[34] The Commission also found that the producer under investigation had a close relationship to a State-controlled company, DEF, where the link itself was sufficient to reject market economy treatment under the first criterion. The Commission found that the producer:

- shared the same premises as DEF, where the producer subleased the land-rights from DEF;
- purchased some of the most important raw materials from DEF; and
- had lent a significant amount of money to DEF.

The producer argued that those circumstances had commercial explanations. The Commission did not deny that but stated:

> It should first be noted that DEF is indirectly controlled by the State. Secondly, whereas behind each of the observations mentioned in the previous recital, there may be reasons that could be commercially explained, this does not contradict the conclusion that [the company] is closely linked to DEF. Indeed, the main argument against granting MET under this criterion are not the links themselves, but that [the company] has such links with a company which is de facto state-controlled.[35]

This case shows that the first criterion is not fulfilled if there is a close relationship between a Chinese producer under investigation and a State-controlled company. It seems not sufficient to be able to explain such relations on commercial reasons.

Furthermore, in situations with national export quotas, market economy treatment will be denied. In *Bicycles I*, the exporters of bicycles were subject to an export quota system under national regulation approved by the Ministry of Foreign Trade and Economic Cooperation (MOFTEC) and the customs authorities. MOFTEC set up criteria for the allocation of quotas between the exporters, and export prices were controlled by MOFTEC. The exporters had to follow the guidelines in order to get an export license. The exporters would then be restricted from exporting bicycles beyond a maximum allowed quantity. The Council found that 'this restriction indicates clearly that they are not free to determine their export activities

---

34. *Trichloroisocyanuric Acid*, Commission Regulation (EC) No. 538/2005 of 7 Apr. 2005 imposing a provisional anti-dumping duty on imports of trichloroisocyanuric acid originating in the People's Republic of China and the United States of America, OJ L 089, 8 Apr. 2005, pp. 4-31, recitals 51-52.
35. Recital 53, endorsed in Council Regulation (EC) No. 1631/2005 of 3 Oct. 2005 imposing a definitive anti-dumping duty and collecting definitely the provisional duty imposed on imports of trichloroisocyanuric acid originating in the People's Republic of China and the United States of America, OJ L 261, 7 Oct. 2005, pp. 1-12, recital 16.

without significant State interference'.[36] Also, MOFTEC and the customs authorities monitored quantities and prices of bicycles. On those grounds, market economy treatment was denied because of State interference.[37]

Market economy treatment can also be rejected in situations where the producer is subject to a regional or provincial law that lets the local government exercise control over business decisions.[38]

However, a Chinese exporter or producer is not prevented from getting into joint venture agreements with the State or State-controlled companies, as long as the exporter or producer can control business decisions without State interference.[39]

Price control – domestic prices: In practice, if prices are controlled by the State, or there are indications of such a control, market economy treatment is denied. In *Certain Electronic Weighing Scales (REWS)*, the Council rejected market economy treatment because a producer had sold the product at a loss for several years and at uniform prices to all customers. This indicated that the prices were controlled by the State.[40] The Chinese producers challenged the rejection by the Council in *Shanghai Teraoka Electronic v. Council*. The Court of First Instance had to review whether the Council made a manifest error in its assessment of the evidence submitted by the producer, as the producer claimed that prices were determined at different levels to different customers. However, the producer did not demonstrate to the satisfaction of the Court of First Instance that it determined the prices without State interference, as the prices to different customers were not different. Consequently, the Council had not made a manifest error in its assessment of the facts.[41] Nor did the Council make a manifest error of assessment in finding that sales at a loss was a factor from which it could be inferred that the producer did not operate in a market economy. The Court of First Instance stated

36. *Bicycles I*, Council Regulation (EC) No. 1095/2005 of 12 Jul. 2005 imposing a definitive anti-dumping duty on imports of bicycles originating in Vietnam, and amending Regulation (EC) No. 1524/2000 imposing a definitive anti-dumping duty on imports of bicycles originating in the People's Republic of China, OJ L 183, 14 Jul. 2005, pp. 1-36, recital 33.
37. Recitals 31-33.
38. *Certain Magnesia Bricks*, Commission Regulation (EC) No. 552/2005 of 11 Apr. 2005 imposing a provisional anti-dumping duty on imports of certain magnesia bricks originating in the People's Republic of China, OJ L 093, 12 Apr. 2005, pp. 6-30, recital 25, endorsed in Council Regulation (EC) No. 1659/2005 of 6 Oct. 2005 imposing a definitive anti-dumping duty and collecting definitively the provisional duty imposed on imports of certain magnesia bricks originating in the People's Republic of China, OJ L 267, 12 Oct. 2005, pp. 1-14, recital 14.
39. *Certain Electronic Weighing Scales (REWS)*, Council Regulation (EC) No. 692/2005 of 28 Apr. 2005 amending Regulation (EC) No. 2605/2000 imposing definitive anti-dumping duties on imports of certain electronic weighing scales (REWS) originating, inter alia, in the People's Republic of China, OJ L 112, 3 May 2005, pp. 1-7, recital 21.
40. *Certain Electronic Weighing Scales (REWS)*, Council Regulation (EC) No. 2605/2000 of 27 Nov. 2000 imposing definitive anti-dumping duties on imports of certain electronic weighing scales (REWS) originating in the People's Republic of China, the Republic of Korea and Taiwan, OJ L 301, 30 Nov. 2000, pp. 42-60, recital 46.
41. *Shanghai Teraoka Electronic v. Council*, Case T-35/01, judgment of the Court of First Instance on 28 Oct. 2004, ECR 2004, p. II-3663, paras 59-73.

that even though sales at a loss may be made under regular market conditions, it is an indication that the producer does not act in accordance with market economy conditions.[42] The claim by the producer was then rejected.[43]

Price control – export prices: If the State can force the Chinese producer to use a fixed export price set by the State, market economy treatment will not be granted; see for example *Glyphosate*, where the China Chamber of Commerce Metals, Minerals & Chemicals Importers and Exporters could refuse export from producers that were not willing to set their prices based on a pricing system created by the Chamber.[44]

Pricing behaviour: The Commission and the Council have denied market economy treatment if the product concerned is sold domestically at the same price as a lower quality product. This is not, according to the EU authorities, in accordance with market economy principles.[45]

The State influences output: If the Chinese producer has to sell a certain amount of the goods in order to get benefits from the State or to avoid being punished, market economy treatment will not be granted. An example could be a producer who has to pay compensation to the state if the producer does not meet his production, sales and profit targets. In *Certain Electronic Weighing Scales (REWS)*, the Council rejected the claim by the Chinese producer that a compensation paid to the partner – the local authorities, who also owned the land – in a joint venture agreement was under market conditions. When compensation claims were not limited to situations where rent for the land was not paid, such claims would go beyond a market relation between a landlord and a tenant.[46]

Business license with sales restriction: The EU authorities have denied market economy treatment to Chinese producers where the business license or the Articles of Association include sales restrictions on the exporters. Such documents bind the producers, as the producers must act in accordance with the basic documents in order to get the authorization to operate its business.[47]

42. Para. 83.
43. Para. 93.
44. *Glyphosate*, Council Regulation (EC) No. 1683/2004 of 24 Sep. 2004 imposing a definitive anti-dumping duty on imports of glyphosate originating in the People's Republic of China, OJ L 303, 30 Sep. 2004, pp. 1-18, recital 14.
45. *Okoumé Plywood*, Commission Regulation (EC) No. 988/2004 of 17 May 2004 imposing provisional anti-dumping duties on imports of okoumé plywood originating in the People's Republic of China, OJ L 181, 18 May 2004, pp. 5-23, recital 29, endorsed in Council Regulation (EC) No. 1942/2004 of 2 Nov. 2004 imposing a definitive anti-dumping duty and collecting definitively the provisional duty imposed on imports of okoumé plywood originating in the People's Republic of China, OJ L 336, 12 Nov. 2004, pp. 4-12, recital 20.
46. *Certain Electronic Weighing Scales (REWS)*, Council Regulation (EC) No. 692/2005 of 28 Apr. 2005 amending Regulation (EC) No. 2605/2000 imposing definitive anti-dumping duties on imports of certain electronic weighing scales (REWS) originating, inter alia, in the People's Republic of China, OJ L 112, 3 May 2005, pp. 1-7, recitals 16, 20 and 21.
47. *Certain Footwear with Uppers of Leather*, Commission Regulation (EC) No. 553/2006 of 23 Mar. 2006 imposing a provisional anti-dumping duty on imports of certain footwear with uppers of leather originating in the People's Republic of China and Vietnam, OJ L 098,

Unclear ownership: In situations where the shareholders or the owners of the producing company cannot be identified, there is a possibility that the producer may be controlled by the State. In such situations, market economy treatment cannot be granted.[48]

Unclear Articles of Association: If it is not clearly stated in the Articles of Association that a State-owned shareholder cannot exert significant influence on the business decisions, or if the producer can easily change the Articles of Association, market economic treatment will be denied. See as example *Granular Polytetrafluoroethylene (PTFE).*[49]

No respect for Articles of Association: In situations where the producer does not respect the Articles of Associations, market economy treatment cannot be granted. The reason for rejecting market economy treatment is that articles stating that the State has no right to control the decisions in the company under investigation cannot be regarded as reliable if they are not respected.[50]

The right to employ employees: The producer must be the one to decide whom to employ, and the content of the labour contract is a matter between the employer and employee. If the labour contract must be approved by the State, this is regarded as State interference, and market economy treatment will not be granted.[51]

7.2.4.2.1.2 Determinants Regarding Market Conditions

The market must be a reflection of supply and demand. If that is not the case, the Commission and the Council refuse market economy treatment. Some of the

---

6 Apr. 2006, pp. 3-54, recital 73, endorsed in Council Regulation (EC) No. 1472/2006 of 5 Oct. 2006 imposing a definitive anti-dumping duty and collecting definitely the provisional duty imposed on imports of certain footwear with uppers of leather originating in the People's Republic of China and Vietnam, OJ L 275, 6 Oct. 2006, pp. 1-41, recital 78.

48. *Barium Carbonate*, Commission Regulation (EC) No. 145/2005 of 28 Jan. 2005 imposing a provisional anti-dumping duty on imports of barium carbonate originating in the People's Republic of China, OJ L 027, 29 Jan. 2005, pp. 4-23, recital 20, endorsed in Council Regulation (EC) No. 1175/2005 of 18 Jul. 2005 imposing a definitive anti-dumping duty and collecting definitively the provisional duty imposed on imports of barium carbonate originating in the People's Republic of China, OJ L 189, 21 Jul. 2005, pp. 15-23, recital 7.
49. *Granular Polytetrafluoroethylene (PTFE)*, Commission Regulation (EC) No. 862/2005 of 7 Jun. 2005 imposing provisional anti-dumping duties on imports of granular PTFE originating in Russia and the People's Republic of China, OJ L 144, 8 Jun. 2005, pp. 11-36, recital 33, endorsed in Council Regulation (EC) No. 1987/2005 of 2 Dec. 2005 imposing a definitive anti-dumping duty and collecting definitively the provisional duty imposed on imports of granular PTFE originating in Russia and the People's Republic of China, OJ L 320, 8 Dec. 2005, pp. 1-19, recital 16.
50. Ibid.
51. *Lever Arch Mechanisms*, Commission Regulation (EC) No. 134/2006 of 26 Jan. 2006 imposing a provisional anti-dumping duty on imports of lever arch mechanisms originating in the People's Republic of China, OJ L 23, 27 Jan. 2006, pp. 13-33, recital 24, endorsed in Council Regulation (EC) No. 1136/2006 of 24 Jul. 2006 imposing a definitive anti-dumping duty and collecting definitively the provisional duty imposed on imports of lever arch mechanisms originating in the People's Republic of China, OJ L 205, 27 Jul. 2006, pp. 1-12, recital 13.

factors included in the examination of market conditions are described in the following:

Prices of raw materials: The producer must demonstrate that the prices from purchases of raw materials are made under market conditions; otherwise market economy treatment cannot be granted. For example, if the producer cannot satisfactorily explain differences in prices of raw materials, market economy treatment is denied.[52] It should be noted that according to the Commission and the Council, *differences* in prices indicate that the prices are not determined under market economy conditions. Above, it was seen that if the prices from the producer to different domestic buyers *are not different*, this indicates that market economy conditions *do not prevail*. It seems unclear what the line about price differentiation is. On one hand, it indicates State interference; on the other hand, it reflects market behaviour.

Renting land: The price for renting land must reflect market signals. If, for example, a producer does not pay rent to the owner of the land, this does not reflect a market condition, and market economy treatment will not be granted.[53]

Bank loans: In situations where the producer does not pay interest to the bank for its loans, or bank guarantees are free of charge by a third party, this is not regarded as a result of the market conditions, and market economy treatment will not be granted.[54]

State subsidies: When a Chinese exporter is granted some kind of state subsidies, its costs do not reflect market conditions, and market economy treatment is not granted. For example, in *Polyester Staple Fibres I*, a State-owned company had contributed with assets when the producer was established. When the State-owned company subsequently sold its shares, it was not compensated for the increased value of the producer. The Council stated that the producer thereby gained a financial benefit by not paying the market value for the assets necessary to produce the product under investigation. The decisions regarding cost of production would then not reflect market signals.[55]

---

52. *Granular Polytetrafluoroethylene (PTFE)*, Commission Regulation (EC) No. 862/2005 of 7 Jun. 2005 imposing provisional anti-dumping duties on imports of granular PTFE originating in Russia and the People's Republic of China, OJ L 144, 8 Jun. 2005, pp. 11-36, recital 33, endorsed in Council Regulation (EC) No. 1987/2005 of 2 Dec. 2005 imposing a definitive anti-dumping duty and collecting definitively the provisional duty imposed on imports of granular PTFE originating in Russia and the People's Republic of China, OJ L 320, 8 Dec. 2005, pp. 1-19, recital 16.
53. *Certain Electronic Weighing Scales (REWS)*, Council Regulation (EC) No. 692/2005 of 28 Apr. 2005 amending Regulation (EC) No. 2605/2000 imposing definitive anti-dumping duties on imports of certain electronic weighing scales (REWS) originating, inter alia, in the People's Republic of China, OJ L 112, 3 May 2005, pp. 1-7, recital 16.
54. Ibid.
55. *Polyester Staple Fibres I*, Council Regulation (EC) No. 428/2005 of 10 Mar. 2005 imposing a definitive anti-dumping duty on imports of polyester staple fibres originating in the People's Republic of China and Saudi Arabia, amending Regulation (EC) No. 2852/2000 imposing a definitive anti-dumping duty on imports of polyester staple fibres originating in the Republic of Korea and terminating the anti-dumping proceeding in respect of such imports originating in Taiwan, OJ L 071, 17 Mar. 2005, pp. 1-33, recital 56.

Supplier is not private: If the producer in the anti-dumping investigation cannot demonstrate that the suppliers of raw materials and other inputs are not owned by the Chinese State, market economy treatment will not be granted. In *Certain Finished Polyester Filament Fabrics*, the Council stated that this is to ensure that the costs for the company are a response to market signals without State interference.[56]

The administration of the first criterion by the EU authorities has shown that State interference – or possible State interference – on any level of the business chain will lead to market economy treatment being denied. Therefore, the Chinese producer may not be able to control the factors the EU authorities rely on in the determination of market economy treatment.

7.2.4.2.2 *International Accounting Standards*

Pursuant to the second condition in Article 2.7(c) of the basic Regulation, Chinese producers need to fulfil the requirement of reliable accounts based on international accounting principles. In *Polyethylene Terephthalate I*, the Commission, endorsed by the Council, made a general statement that the purpose of the second condition 'is to assess the reliability of the accounts and more particularly of revenues, costs and profit booked by the company since the bulk of the anti-dumping verification visit consists precisely in verifying these three items'.[57]

In *Certain Finished Polyester Filament Fabrics*, the Council made an even clearer statement:

> From a general point of view, it is recalled that the second criterion of Article 2(7)(c) of the basic Regulation requires the companies concerned to demonstrate that they have a basic set of accounts independently audited in line with international accounting standards, in order to assess the reliability of those accounts in view of ensuring a proper assessment of dumping. Indeed, the dumping calculation is mainly based on data included in the accounting records of the companies, such as revenue, costs, profit and inventory,

56. *Certain Finished Polyester Filament Fabrics*, Council Regulation (EC) No. 1487/2005 of 12 Sep. 2005 imposing a definitive anti-dumping duty and collecting definitely the provisional duty imposed on imports of certain finished polyester filament fabrics originating in the People's Republic of China, OJ L 240, 16 Sep. 2005, pp. 1-16, recital 22. in the Council Regulation.
57. *Polyethylene terephthalate I*, Commission Regulation (EC) No. 306/2004 of 19 Feb. 2004 imposing a provisional anti-dumping duty on imports of polyethylene terephthalate originating in Australia, the People's Republic of China and Pakistan, OJ L 052, 21 Feb. 2004, pp. 5-34, recital 68. Without making any comments to the statement of the Commission, the Council confirmed the findings of the Commission in Council Regulation (EC) No. 1467/2004 of 13 Aug. 2004 imposing a definitive anti-dumping duty and collecting definitively the provisional duty imposed on imports of polyethylene terephthalate originating in Australia, the People's Republic of China and terminating the anti-dumping proceeding concerning imports of polyethylene terephthalate originating in Pakistan and releasing the amounts secured by way of the provisional duties imposed, OJ L 271, 19 Aug. 2004, pp. 1-17, recital 38.

which must therefore be reliable. The anti-dumping verification visit precisely consists in verifying those items.[58]

The second criterion has a technical purpose, namely to enable the Commission and the Council to look through the producers' costs and prices of the inputs and outputs of the production. As seen above regarding the first criterion, differences in the prices of the raw materials indicate non-market behaviour, which reliable accounts will reveal. In the following, the factors to determine whether the second condition is met are divided into two parts:

(1) The Accounts must be in Accordance with International Accounting Standards (IAS)

Fair presentation of financial statements: If Assets are booked into the accounts at higher value than actually paid,[59] or if write-offs of loans are not properly booked into the accounts,[60] market economy treatment is rejected.

Changes in accounting policies: If the accounting method concerning bad debt provisions is changed without applying that change retrospectively, market economy treatment is not granted.[61]

Recording at initial recognition of foreign currency transactions: The currency rate for the date of transaction must be used. In *Hand Pallet Trucks and Their Essential Parts*, Chinese companies used one currency rate for the whole year, and market economy treatment was therefore denied.[62]

Depreciation: Depreciation must be done in accordance with accounting standards; otherwise market economy treatment is rejected.[63]

---

58. *Certain Finished Polyester Filament Fabrics*, Council Regulation (EC) No. 1487/2005 of 12 Sep. 2005 imposing a definitive anti-dumping duty and collecting definitely the provisional duty imposed on imports of certain finished polyester filament fabrics originating in the People's Republic of China, OJ L 240, 16 Sep. 2005, pp. 1-16, recital 24.
59. *Hand Pallet Trucks and Their Essential Parts*, Council Regulation (EC) No. 1174/2005 of 18 Jul. 2005 imposing a definitive anti-dumping duty and collecting definitely the provisional duty imposed on imports of hand pallet trucks and their essential parts originating in the People's Republic of China, OJ L 189, 21 Jul. 2005, pp. 1-14, recital 16.
60. Ibid., recital 17.
61. Ibid., recital 17.
62. *Hand Pallet Trucks and Their Essential Parts*, Commission Regulation (EC) No. 128/2005 of 27 Jan. 2005 imposing a provisional anti-dumping duty on imports of hand pallet trucks and their essential parts originating in the People's Republic of China, OJ L 025, 28 Jan. 2005, pp. 16-36, recitals 30-34, endorsed in Council Regulation (EC) No. 1174/2005 of 18 Jul. 2005 imposing a definitive anti-dumping duty and collecting definitely the provisional duty imposed on imports of hand pallet trucks and their essential parts originating in the People's Republic of China, OJ L 189, 21 Jul. 2005, pp. 1-14, recital 16.
63. *Polyester Staple Fibres I*, Council Regulation (EC) No. 428/2005 of 10 Mar. 2005 imposing a definitive anti-dumping duty on imports of polyester staple fibres originating in the People's Republic of China and Saudi Arabia, amending Regulation (EC) No. 2852/2000 imposing a definitive anti-dumping duty on imports of polyester staple fibres originating in the Republic of Korea and terminating the anti-dumping proceeding in respect of such imports originating in Taiwan, OJ L 071, 17 Mar. 2005, pp. 1-33, recital 59.

Borrowing/Lending: If a company under investigation borrows money from a bank or lends money to its shareholders, it must be accounted for in accordance with international accounting standards. If not, market economy treatment cannot be granted.[64]

(2) Relations to the Auditors

In practice, the work or comments by auditors may also lead to rejection of a claim of market economy treatment. For example:

If auditors do not comment on flaws and serious problems in the accounting records, the international accounting principles have not been adhered to by the auditor. This means that the producer will not be granted market economy treatment, as the accounts cannot be seen as reliable. See as examples: *Certain Footwear with Uppers of Leather,*[65] *Certain Electronic Weighing Scales (REWS)*[66] and *Polyester Staple Fibres I.*[67]

If there are discrepancies between the auditors' report and the accounts of the company, market economy treatment will not be granted.[68]

---

64. *Trichloroisocyanuric Acid*, Commission Regulation (EC) No. 538/2005 of 7 Apr. 2005 imposing a provisional anti-dumping duty on imports of trichloroisocyanuric acid originating in the People's Republic of China and the United States of America, OJ L 089, 8 Apr. 2005, pp. 4-31, recital 59, endorsed in Council Regulation (EC) No. 1631/2005 of 3 Oct. 2005 imposing a definitive anti-dumping duty and collecting definitely the provisional duty imposed on imports of trichloroisocyanuric acid originating in the People's Republic of China and the United States of America, OJ L 261, 7 Oct. 2005, pp. 1-12, recital 16.
65. *Certain Footwear with Uppers of Leather*, Commission Regulation (EC) No. 553/2006 of 23 Mar. 2006 imposing a provisional anti-dumping duty on imports of certain footwear with uppers of leather originating in the People's Republic of China and Vietnam, OJ L 098, 6 Apr. 2006, pp. 3-54, recital 74, endorsed in Council Regulation (EC) No. 1472/2006 of 5 Oct. 2006 imposing a definitive anti-dumping duty and collecting definitely the provisional duty imposed on imports of certain footwear with uppers of leather originating in the People's Republic of China and Vietnam, OJ L 275, 6 Oct. 2006, pp. 1-41, recital 78.
66. *Certain Electronic Weighing Scales (REWS)*, Council Regulation (EC) No. 692/2005 of 28 Apr. 2005 amending Regulation (EC) No. 2605/2000 imposing definitive anti-dumping duties on imports of certain electronic weighing scales (REWS) originating, inter alia, in the People's Republic of China, OJ L 112, 3 May 2005, pp. 1-7, recital 17.
67. *Polyester Staple Fibres I*, Council Regulation (EC) No. 428/2005 of 10 Mar. 2005 imposing a definitive anti-dumping duty on imports of polyester staple fibres originating in the People's Republic of China and Saudi Arabia, amending Regulation (EC) No. 2852/2000 imposing a definitive anti-dumping duty on imports of polyester staple fibres originating in the Republic of Korea and terminating the anti-dumping proceeding in respect of such imports originating in Taiwan, OJ L 071, 17 Mar. 2005, pp. 1-33, recital 58.
68. *Granular Polytetrafluoroethylene (PTFE)*, Commission Regulation (EC) No. 862/2005 of 7 Jun. 2005 imposing provisional anti-dumping duties on imports of granular PTFE originating in Russia and the People's Republic of China, OJ L 144, 8 Jun. 2005, pp. 11-36, recital 36, endorsed in Council Regulation (EC) No. 1987/2005 of 2 Dec. 2005 imposing a definitive anti-dumping duty and collecting definitively the provisional duty imposed on imports of granular PTFE originating in Russia and the People's Republic of China, OJ L 320, 8 Dec. 2005, pp. 1-19, recital 16. See also *Certain Finished Polyester Filament Fabrics*, Council Regulation (EC) No. 1487/2005 of 12 Sep. 2005 imposing a definitive anti-dumping duty and collecting definitely the provisional duty imposed on imports of certain finished polyester

In situations where the auditors have made some reservations to the accounts, this can lead to rejection of market economy treatment.[69] In *Certain Finished Polyester Filament Fabrics*, the auditors had commented on:

(1) the company's inability to verify the validity of the year-end balance of stocks and selling costs of the year;
(2) the inability of the second company to check the inventory as of year-end; and
(3) the fact that some company reservations were made in 2002, but no reservations in 2003; with no obvious changes in accounting policies, the 2003 accounts were suspected of not having been independently made. Market economy treatment was therefore rejected.[70]

7.2.4.2.3 Distortions from the Non-market Economy

In a fully non-market economy, the State is the owner of all resources and property, including factories, land, etc., and it can determine their uses. If the State then turns towards a more open economy, and properties change hands from the State to private ownership, it is necessary to determine the value of properties and assets. The third criterion prevents producers from having the possibility of market economy treatment if the transition from State ownership to privatization has not been in line with market economy principles. For example, it prevents the Chinese State from granting a Chinese producer certain competitive advantages by selling the asset at too low a price; this is not a result of the market forces. A market economy treatment will be denied if a Chinese company cannot explain the privatization of a company and re-evaluation of the assets.[71]

---

filament fabrics originating in the People's Republic of China, OJ L 240, 16 Sep. 2005, pp. 1-16, recital 27.

69. *Barium Carbonate*, Commission Regulation (EC) No. 145/2005 of 28 Jan. 2005 imposing a provisional anti-dumping duty on imports of barium carbonate originating in the People's Republic of China, OJ L 027, 29 Jan. 2005, pp. 4-23, recital 21, endorsed in Council Regulation (EC) No. 1175/2005 of 18 Jul. 2005 imposing a definitive anti-dumping duty and collecting definitively the provisional duty imposed on imports of barium carbonate originating in the People's Republic of China, OJ L 189, 21 Jul. 2005, pp. 15-23, recital 7.
70. *Certain Finished Polyester Filament Fabrics*, Council Regulation (EC) No. 1487/2005 of 12 Sep. 2005 imposing a definitive anti-dumping duty and collecting definitely the provisional duty imposed on imports of certain finished polyester filament fabrics originating in the People's Republic of China, OJ L 240, 16 Sep. 2005, pp. 1-16, recital 25.
71. *Lever Arch Mechanisms*, Commission Regulation (EC) No. 134/2006 of 26 Jan. 2006 imposing a provisional anti-dumping duty on imports of lever arch mechanisms originating in the People's Republic of China, OJ L 023, 27 Jan. 2006, pp. 13-33, recital 23, endorsed in Council Regulation (EC) No. 1136/2006 of 24 Jul. 2006 imposing a definitive anti-dumping duty and collecting definitively the provisional duty imposed on imports of lever arch mechanisms originating in the People's Republic of China, OJ L 205, 27 Jul. 2006, pp. 1-12, recital 11.

Some other examples, where distortions from the former non-market system have been – or may have been – carried over to privatization, are described in the following:

Bank loan guarantees: In situations where a producer receives bank loan guarantees and has settlement accounts where invoices and payments cannot be linked, and the bank is a State-owned shareholder of the producer, this will be regarded as a distortion from the non-market system. See for example *Granular Polytetrafluoroethylene (PTFE).*[72]

Land-use rights: If the producer under investigation has not paid land-use rights for several years and the State or local government owns the land, this is an indication of non-market distortions.[73] In *Certain Footwear with Uppers of Leather*, some Chinese producers could not clearly show that their production costs and financial situation were not affected by the former non-market economy system. The producers had land-use rights and machineries, which had been passed to them in a non-market manner. Under those circumstances market economy treatment was rejected.[74] In addition, in situations where the price of land-use rights is remarkably low, this is an indication of distortions carried over from the non-market economy, and market economy treatment will not be granted.[75]

Machineries and production facilities: If the producer cannot satisfactorily prove to the EU authorities that the producer has bought machines from State-owned companies at market economy prices, market economy treatment will be denied. This was for example seen in *Granular Polytetrafluoroethylene (PTFE)*, where the producer had received a substantial discount from the State-owned

72. *Granular Polytetrafluoroethylene (PTFE)*, Commission Regulation (EC) No. 862/2005 of 7 Jun. 2005 imposing provisional anti-dumping duties on imports of granular PTFE originating in Russia and the People's Republic of China, OJ L 144, 8 Jun. 2005, pp. 11-36, recital 37, endorsed in Council Regulation (EC) No. 1987/2005 of 2 Dec. 2005 imposing a definitive anti-dumping duty and collecting definitively the provisional duty imposed on imports of granular PTFE originating in Russia and the People's Republic of China, OJ L 320, 8 Dec. 2005, pp. 1-19, recital 16.
73. *Okoumé Plywood*, Commission Regulation (EC) No. 988/2004 of 17 May 2004 imposing provisional anti-dumping duties on imports of okoumé plywood originating in the People's Republic of China, OJ L 181, 18 May 2004, pp. 5-23, recital 31, endorsed in Council Regulation (EC) No. 1942/2004 of 2 Nov. 2004 imposing a definitive anti-dumping duty and collecting definitively the provisional duty imposed on imports of okoumé plywood originating in the People's Republic of China, OJ L 336, 12 Nov. 2004, pp. 4-12, recital 20.
74. *Certain Footwear with Uppers of Leather*, Commission Regulation (EC) No. 553/2006 of 23 Mar. 2006 imposing a provisional anti-dumping duty on imports of certain footwear with uppers of leather originating in the People's Republic of China and Vietnam, OJ L 098, 6 Apr. 2006, pp. 3-54, recital 75, endorsed in Council Regulation (EC) No. 1472/2006 of 5 Oct. 2006 imposing a definitive anti-dumping duty and collecting definitely the provisional duty imposed on imports of certain footwear with uppers of leather originating in the People's Republic of China and Vietnam, OJ L 275, 6 Oct. 2006, pp. 1-41, recital 78.
75. *Certain Finished Polyester Filament Fabrics*, Council Regulation (EC) No. 1487/2005 of 12 Sep. 2005 imposing a definitive anti-dumping duty and collecting definitely the provisional duty imposed on imports of certain finished polyester filament fabrics originating in the People's Republic of China, OJ L 240, 16 Sep. 2005, pp. 1-16, recital 31.

seller.[76] Another example is found in *Certain Finished Polyester Filament Fabrics*, where the purchases of equipment were made through one of the shareholders in the producing company. The producer could not provide information about the purchases by the shareholder on the open market. For that reason, it could not be ruled out that the purchases by the shareholder were not at market prices, and market economy treatment was denied.[77]

The sale of the company from the State does not follow market conditions: When a company transitions from a State enterprise to a private company, the transition must reflect market conditions. In *Certain Finished Polyester Filament Fabrics*, the Commission denied market economy treatment because the valuation of the company when it went from a State-owned company to a private company was only 25% of its net book value, and the new shareholders paid only a limited proportion of the price. A third company paid the rest. No information about the third company was provided, and the possibility that the third company was owned by the State could not be ruled out.[78]

In addition, if the company cannot explain the transfer of assets from a former State-owned company to a private company, the criterion is not met.[79]

State Subsidies: In general, State subsidies in one form or another that are granted to a producer fall under the third criterion, and market economy treatment is denied. However, the line between the first and the third criterion is not always clear. For example, in *Polyester Staple Fibres I*,[80] the Council had – as seen above

76. *Granular Polytetrafluoroethylene (PTFE)*, Commission Regulation (EC) No. 862/2005 of 7 Jun. 2005 imposing provisional anti-dumping duties on imports of granular PTFE originating in Russia and the People's Republic of China, OJ L 144, 8 Jun. 2005, pp. 11-36, recital 37, endorsed in Council Regulation (EC) No. 1987/2005 of 2 Dec. 2005 imposing a definitive anti-dumping duty and collecting definitively the provisional duty imposed on imports of granular PTFE originating in Russia and the People's Republic of China, OJ L 320, 8 Dec. 2005, pp. 1-19, recital 16.

77. *Certain Finished Polyester Filament Fabrics*, Council Regulation (EC) No. 1487/2005 of 12 Sep. 2005 imposing a definitive anti-dumping duty and collecting definitely the provisional duty imposed on imports of certain finished polyester filament fabrics originating in the People's Republic of China, OJ L 240, 16 Sep. 2005, pp. 1-16, recital 30.

78. *Certain Finished Polyester Filament Fabrics*, Commission Regulation (EC) No. 426/2005 of 15 Mar. 2005 on imposing a provisional anti-dumping duty on imports of certain finished polyester filament apparel fabrics originating in the People's Republic of China, OJ L 069, 16 Mar. 2005, pp. 6-33, endorsed in Council Regulation (EC) No. 1487/2005 of 12 Sep. 2005 imposing a definitive anti-dumping duty and collecting definitely the provisional duty imposed on imports of certain finished polyester filament fabrics originating in the People's Republic of China, OJ L 240, 16 Sep. 2005, pp. 1-16, recital 29.

79. *Barium Carbonate*, Commission Regulation (EC) No. 145/2005 of 28 Jan. 2005 imposing a provisional anti-dumping duty on imports of barium carbonate originating in the People's Republic of China, OJ L 027, 29 Jan. 2005, pp. 4-23, recital 22, endorsed in Council Regulation (EC) No. 1175/2005 of 18 Jul. 2005 imposing a definitive anti-dumping duty and collecting definitively the provisional duty imposed on imports of barium carbonate originating in the People's Republic of China, OJ L 189, 21 Jul. 2005, pp. 15-23, recital 7.

80. *Polyester Staple Fibres I*, Council Regulation (EC) No. 428/2005 of 10 Mar. 2005 imposing a definitive anti-dumping duty on imports of polyester staple fibres originating in the People's Republic of China and Saudi Arabia, amending Regulation (EC) No. 2852/2000 imposing a

in 7.2.4.2.1 – found that decisions regarding cost of production would not reflect market signals because the State was not compensated when the company shares were sold. Also, regarding the third criterion, the Council found that State subsidies would have an impact on the costs of production, meaning that distortions from the former non-market economy were transferred to the present market situation. The line between the two criteria is not clear.

7.2.4.2.4 Property Rights and Bankruptcy Laws

Under the fourth criterion of Article 2.7(c) of the basic Regulation, the Chinese producer must act under laws of bankruptcy and property rights to reflect market conditions and to ensure legal certainty.

In *Granular Polytetrafluoroethylene (PTFE)*, one Chinese producer had been selling at a loss for several years. Its State-owned shareholder rescued the producer. The Commission's statement, which was endorsed by the Council, was:

> Although, as argued by the company, such significant financial difficulties may not necessarily result in bankruptcy, the fact that the State-owned shareholder rescued the company (including through debt write-off), *in a situation where under normal market conditions a shareholder would not have done this, indicates that the application of such law to this particular case is doubtful*. It had therefore to be concluded that there was no evidence that the bankruptcy law applied in practice to the company. In the absence of such evidence this criterion was considered as not being fulfilled.[81] (Emphasis added)

If under usual market economy conditions it is expected that a company would be declared bankrupt rather than be rescued by a shareholder, the company seems not to be under regular bankruptcy conditions if the State as a shareholder rescues the company. In *Okoumé Plywood*, the Commission stated:

> However, it was noted during the verification visit that in a certain financial year the losses were higher than the capital. Therefore, it was found that, whilst the company may in theory be subject to the bankruptcy laws, these de facto did not apply to it, since under those circumstances a proceeding for bankruptcy should have been launched. It is worth noting that the auditors

---

definitive anti-dumping duty on imports of polyester staple fibres originating in the Republic of Korea and terminating the anti-dumping proceeding in respect of such imports originating in Taiwan, OJ L 071, 17 Mar. 2005, pp. 1-33.

81. *Granular Polytetrafluoroethylene (PTFE)*, Commission Regulation (EC) No. 862/2005 of 7 Jun. 2005 imposing provisional anti-dumping duties on imports of granular PTFE originating in Russia and the People's Republic of China, OJ L 144, 8 Jun. 2005, pp. 11-36, recital 39, endorsed in Council Regulation (EC) No. 1987/2005 of 2 Dec. 2005 imposing a definitive anti-dumping duty and collecting definitively the provisional duty imposed on imports of granular PTFE originating in Russia and the People's Republic of China, OJ L 320, 8 Dec. 2005, pp. 1-19, recitals 16 and 39.

> made also no comments in this respect. Hence, the company failed to demonstrate that it operates under a legal framework which guarantees legal certainty. Therefore, this claim was rejected.[82]

Even though the bankruptcy law is applicable on the producer, market economy treatment may be rejected. For instance, if the producer's financial situation would lead to bankruptcy under market economy conditions, but a proceeding on bankruptcy has not been initiated, market economy treatment is rejected.

7.2.4.2.5 Currency Exchanges are Carried Out at Market Rate

The fifth criterion in Article 2.7(c) only rarely leads to rejection of market economy treatment by the Commission and the Council. In *Trichloroisocyanuric Acid*, the Commission had the opportunity to make a statement regarding the situation where the CNY is pegged to the USD.

The Commission stated:

> The fact that the Chinese currency [CNY] is pegged to the USD is *a decision by the Chinese government, against which an applicant for MET cannot be held responsible*. Similar decisions have in the past also been taken by other countries, notably in Latin America. *Again, it is the consistent practice of the Institutions to consider this criterion as fulfilled if the company uses the official exchange rate for all its transactions involving foreign currencies. Thus, it is ensured that no black market practices are applied*. Indeed, all of the co-operating exporters in this investigation were found to be able to purchase and sell foreign currencies obtained in their business operations, despite the fact that the exchange rate RMB/USD is pegged.[83] (Emphasis added)

It is obvious that the Chinese producers are not responsible for State decisions about currency policy. As long as the official exchange rate is followed in transactions between the producers and its different suppliers, employees, customers, etc.,

82. *Okoumé Plywood*, Commission Regulation (EC) No. 988/2004 of 17 May 2004 imposing provisional anti-dumping duties on imports of okoumé plywood originating in the People's Republic of China, OJ L 181, 18 May 2004, pp. 5-23, recital 32, endorsed in Council Regulation (EC) No. 1942/2004 of 2 Nov. 2004 imposing a definitive anti-dumping duty and collecting definitively the provisional duty imposed on imports of okoumé plywood originating in the People's Republic of China, OJ L 336, 12 Nov. 2004, pp. 4-12, recital 20.

83. *Trichloroisocyanuric Acid*, Commission Regulation (EC) No. 538/2005 of 7 Apr. 2005 imposing a provisional anti-dumping duty on imports of trichloroisocyanuric acid originating in the People's Republic of China and the United States of America, OJ L 089, 8 Apr. 2005, pp. 4-31, recital 62, endorsed in Council Regulation (EC) No. 1631/2005 of 3 Oct. 2005 imposing a definitive anti-dumping duty and collecting definitely the provisional duty imposed on imports of trichloroisocyanuric acid originating in the People's Republic of China and the United States of America, OJ L 261, 7 Oct. 2005, pp. 1-12, recital 16.

the fifth criterion will not justify market economy treatment being denied. It seems that the reason for applying the fifth criterion is to avoid black market exchange rates.

7.2.4.3 Market Economy Treatment during the Investigation

Pursuant to Article 2.7(c), last sentence, the determination of whether to grant market economy treatment to Chinese producers must be made within three months after the initiation of the investigation. That determination shall remain in force during the investigation.

In *Nanjing Metalink Int. v. Council*, Nanjing, a Chinese producer of ferro molybdenum, had been granted market economy treatment by the Commission in the provisional regulation. After the imposition of the provisional duty, the China Chamber of Commerce and Minmetals held a meeting. Nanjing was awarded larger exports than other Chinese exporters with a non-market economy status. The Commission withdrew the market economy status for Nanjing without a renewed investigation.[84] The question before the Court of First Instance was whether the Commission had violated Article 2.7(c), last sentence, because the Chinese producer had not been granted a renewed investigation about the market economy treatment. The Court of First Instance stated:

> [T]he last sentence of Article 2(7)(c) of the basic regulation is to be interpreted as meaning that it precludes the institutions from re-evaluating evidence they had at the time of the initial determination as to market economy treatment. That provision does not, however, preclude the grant of market economy treatment from being discontinued if a change in the factual situation on the basis of which such treatment was conferred no longer permits the conclusion that the producer concerned operates under market economy conditions.[85]

The Court of First Instance looked into the facts of the case and concluded that it is not a violation of Article 2.7(c), last sentence to revoke market economy status that a Chinese producer had been granted at the initial stage of the investigation.[86] The Commission and the Council may then withdraw a market economy determination without a renewed investigation. The last sentence in Article 2.7(c) only limits the Commission and the Council from re-examining the evidence from the time of the initial market economy determination.

84. *Nanjing Metalink Int. v. Council*, Case T-138/02, judgment of the Court of First Instance of 14 Nov. 2006, ECR 2006, p. II-4347, paras 7-14.
85. Para. 47.
86. Para. 57.

7.2.4.4 Establishing Normal Value for Chinese Producers Granted Market Economy Treatment

It follows from Article 2.7(b) that if the criteria in Article 2.7(c) are met, the normal value will be established in accordance with the normal procedure in Article 2.1 – 2.6 of the basic Regulation.[87]

It is rare, though, that a Chinese company will be granted market economy treatment. In most cases Chinese producers have failed to demonstrate that *all* five criteria have been fulfilled, and the general methods – analogue country or any other reasonable basis – will be used in establishing normal value.

It is also seen that even in situations where market economy treatment has been granted, normal value is based on prices from an analogue country if the information about the domestic price etc., submitted by the producer is deficient. See *Sodium Cyclamate*, where some of the Chinese producers met the five criteria. However, the information regarding normal value was insufficient, and the normal value was instead based on prices from an analogue country in the Commission Regulation.[88] Afterwards, the necessary information was provided and in the definitive Regulation, normal value could be established pursuant to Article 2.1 – Articles 2-6 of the basic Regulation.[89]

7.2.4.5 The EU Practice and WTO Law

Because of the wide discretion under WTO law to determine the market economy criteria, the few points made concern practice by the Commission and the Council where there might be a violation of WTO law.

In some cases, Chinese producers have claimed that the EU practice regarding the five criteria is in conflict with WTO law. So far, the claims by the Chinese producers have only been adduced for the EU authorities – not for a Panel or Appellate Body. This has left the EU authorities to take a stand regarding the WTO provisions. For example, in *Granular Polytetrafluoroethylene (PTFE)*, the Commission stated:

> In this respect it should be noted that the current investigation, including the assessment of whether an exporting producer operates under market economy

87. *Stainless Steel Fasteners and Parts thereof I*, Council Regulation (EC) No. 2570/2000 of 20 Nov. 2000 amending Regulation (EC) No. 393/98 imposing a definitive anti-dumping duty on imports of stainless steel fasteners and parts thereof originating, inter alia, in the People's Republic of China, OJ L 297, 24 Nov. 2000, pp. 1-3, recitals 12-16.
88. *Sodium Cyclamate*, Commission Regulation (EC) No. 1627/2003 of 17 Sep. 2003 imposing a provisional anti-dumping duty on imports of sodium cyclamate originating in the People's Republic of China and Indonesia, OJ L 232, 18 Sep. 2003, pp. 12-28, recitals 26-29.
89. *Sodium Cyclamate*, Council Regulation (EC) No. 435/2004 of 8 Mar. 2004 imposing a definitive anti-dumping duty and collecting definitively the provisional duty imposed on imports of sodium cyclamate originating in the People's Republic of China and Indonesia, OJ L 072, 11 Mar. 2004, pp. 1-14, recitals 39-42.

> conditions, is made in accordance with the applicable provisions of the basic Regulation, which are fully in line with WTO obligations.[90]

In other instances, the Commission has used similar statements.[91] According to the Commission, the wordings in Article 2.7 of the basic Regulation and its own practice are both in conformity with the WTO obligations. However, the Commission does not provide any thorough examination of the question about the violation of WTO law.

As already mentioned, the WTO rules do not provide any guidelines about market economy conditions, and there is wide discretion to the investigating authorities to set up criteria for market economic treatment. The wide discretion seems to be fully exercised in the EU practice just described. Furthermore, under WTO law, the burden of proof on Chinese producers is heavy, as the producers have to 'clearly' demonstrate that market conditions prevail in the industry in order to get market economy treatment. Therefore, it seems not to be a violation of WTO law for the burden on the producers to be strict in EU practice.

When a Chinese producer fulfils the market economy criteria provided in Article 2.7(c) of the basic Regulation, market economy treatment is granted. This rule is in accordance with Article 15(a)(i) of the Protocol, although there may be a violation by only granting the specific producer market economy treatment instead of the entire industry as discussed in Section 7.2.4.1.

However, it is striking that the Chinese producers are only able to fulfil the five criteria in rare situations. In EU practice, there are however only a few aspects which may violate WTO law.

One aspect is the lack of uniformity in EU practice on price differentiation. If a Chinese producer makes domestic sales to different customers at the same prices, the conduct by the Chinese producer is regarded by the EU authorities as an indication of State interference under the first criterion of Article 2.7(c). However, the producer has to explain different prices of raw materials, as differences on this level are an indication of State interference. It could be in conflict with the fairness principle, since the criteria are not used even-handedly, as the reason for rejecting market economy treatment in one instance is reversed in the other instance. However, in WTO practice, the fairness principle has applied to situations where the *information* is used differently by the authorities. The question is whether the principle also is applicable to the situation described in this part.

---

90. *Granular Polytetrafluoroethylene (PTFE)*, Commission Regulation (EC) No. 862/2005 of 7 Jun. 2005 imposing provisional anti-dumping duties on imports of granular PTFE originating in Russia and the People's Republic of China, OJ L 144, 8 Jun. 2005, pp. 11-36, recital 31.
91. *Certain Magnesia Bricks*, Commission Regulation (EC) No. 552/2005 of 11 Apr. 2005 imposing a provisional anti-dumping duty on imports of certain magnesia bricks originating in the People's Republic of China, OJ L 093, 12 Apr. 2005, pp. 6-30, recitals 24-25, endorsed in Council Regulation (EC) No. 1659/2005 of 6 Oct. 2005 imposing a definitive anti-dumping duty and collecting definitively the provisional duty imposed on imports of certain magnesia bricks originating in the People's Republic of China, OJ L 267, 12 Oct. 2005, pp. 1-14, recital 14.

Another aspect is the situation where the five criteria have been met, but the information is insufficient – and until sufficient information is provided, the Chinese producer will be treated under non-market rules. In the previous chapter, it was seen that the Panel stated in *Argentina – Poultry Anti-dumping Duties*[92] that the investigating authorities have to fill in the missing data in order to determine individual margins. It could then be argued that the EU would have to fill in the missing information instead of revoking the market economy status. Furthermore, it follows from Article 15(a) of the Protocol that if the producers have clearly demonstrated that market economy conditions prevail, then market economy treatment will be granted. It then seems unconvincing to revoke a market economy status if the normal value cannot be determined due to insufficient information because the market economy conduct has already been established – and if there has been no changes in the market economy circumstances, then the market economy status should be kept.

7.2.5 EU Practice: Selection of an Analogue Country

Those Chinese producers who are not fulfilling the five conditions in Article 2.7(c) will have the normal value based on prices and costs from producers in an analogue country in accordance with Article 2.7(a) of the basic Regulation, cf. Article 2.7(b).

Pursuant to Article 2.7(a), the normal value for non-market economies is based on either the domestic price or the constructed value of the like product in an appropriate analogue country with a market economy, or the export price from the analogue country to another third country of the like product. If that is not possible, the Commission and the Council will determine the normal value for a non-market economy on any other reasonable basis.

The text of Article 2.7(a) provides a hierarchy between the principal method on one hand, and prices related to an analogue country and normal value based on any other reasonable method, on the other hand. This line is also adhered to in practice, where the Commission and the Council first establish a normal value based on data from an analogue country.[93] It is only on rare occasions that it has not been possible to find an analogue country, and the Commission and the Council have determined a normal value by any reasonable method.[94]

Pursuant to Article 2.7(a), second sentence, the analogue country selected must be appropriate and not selected in an unreasonable manner. However, the Chinese producers often use their right under the third sentence of Article 2.7(a) to comment on the suggested selection of an appropriate country, and they may suggest other countries. It is – naturally – not an easy task to find a country that

---

92. *Argentina – Poultry Anti-dumping Duties*, WT/DS241/R, report of the Panel on 22 Apr. 2003.
93. See in general the Regulations in this chapter.
94. *Dihydrostreptomycin*, Commission Decision No. 98/90/EC of 21 Jan. 1998 terminating the anti-dumping proceeding concerning imports of dihydrostreptomycin originating in the People's Republic of China, OJ L 017, 22 Jan. 1998, pp. 42-45, recital 14.

resembles China, had China been a market economy. The differences in access to raw materials, labour costs, distribution networks, qualities in both the inputs and outcome of the product concerned, cost structures, economic development, per capita GNP, etc., are all important factors in determining whether a country should be regarded as an appropriate reference for the establishment of the normal value for the Chinese producers.

In the following section, some of the different factors that have an impact in the selection of an appropriate country are described. In Section 7.2.5.2, the normal value determination from such an analogue country is examined, and Section 7.2.5.3 regards the normal value for a Chinese producer based on any other reasonable method. Section 7.2.5.4 concerns EU practice and WTO law, and finally Section 7.2.5.5 discusses some problems arising in case some Chinese producers are granted market economy treatment, while other producers are not.

7.2.5.1 The Factors to Select an Appropriate Third Country

In this section, some of the factors used by the EU authorities in the selection of an appropriate third country are examined. As mentioned above, several factors may have an impact on the comparability between two countries. Such comparison involves complex economic analysis. As stated in Section 7.2.4.1, the Commission and the Council therefore have wide discretion in carrying out such an analysis. However, the discretion is not without limits. In *Paint, Distemper, Varnish and Similar Brushes*, the Commission and the Council found that Sri Lanka was an appropriate analogue country to determine normal value for Chinese producers.[95] Nölle, an EU importer of paintbrushes from China, claimed before the EC Court in *Nölle* that the Chinese products were not like the products in Sri Lanka, because the Chinese paintbrushes were round, flat and radiator paintbrushes, whereas the paintbrushes from Sri Lanka were flat brushes. Furthermore, the Chinese producers had a cost advantage in the direct access to raw materials – pig bristles – in which China also represented 85% of the world market, whereas Sri Lanka had to import pig bristles.[96] Instead, Taiwan was suggested as an appropriate analogue

95. *Paint, Distemper, Varnish and Similar Brushes*, Commission Regulation (EEC) No. 3052/88 of 29 Sep. 1988 imposing a provisional anti-dumping duty on imports of paint, distemper, varnish and similar brushes originating in the People's Republic of China, OJ L 272, 4 Oct. 1988, pp. 16-17, endorsed in Council Regulation (EEC) No. 725/89 of 20 Mar. 1989 imposing a definitive anti-dumping duty on imports of paint, distemper, varnish and similar brushes originating in the people's Republic of China and definitively collecting the provisional anti-dumping duty on such imports, OJ L 79, 22 Mar. 1989, pp. 24-29, recitals 14-18. The Commission Regulation does not mention Sri Lanka, but it follows implicitly from both the Council Regulation and from a Council Decision accepting an undertaking, cf. Council Decision (EEC) 87/104 of 9 Feb. 1987 accepting an undertaking given in connection with the anti-dumping proceeding concerning imports of paint, distemper, varnish and similar brushes originating in the People' s Republic of China, and terminating the investigation, OJ L 46, 14 Jan. 1987, pp. 45-48, recitals 7-9.
96. *Nölle*, Case C-16/90, judgment of the EC Court on 22 Oct. 1991, ECR 1991, p. I-5163, paras 14-24.

country.[97] The Commission stated before the EC Court that the paintbrushes produced in China were like the paint brushes produced in Sri Lanka, that the cost advantage by the direct access to raw materials could not be quantified satisfactorily in a non-market economy, and that adjustments had been made for the imported pig bristles in Sri Lanka.[98] The EC Court stated:

> As regards in particular the choice of reference country it is desirable to verify whether the institutions neglected to take account of essential factors for the purpose of establishing the appropriate nature of the country chosen and whether the information contained in the documents in the case were considered with all the care required for the view to be taken that the normal value was determined in an appropriate and not unreasonable manner.[99]

The Commission and the Council cannot disregard essential factors in the determination of an appropriate analogue country, and the Commission and the Council must consider the information carefully in order to determine an appropriate analogue country. The EC Court found that the Commission and the Council had not demonstrated their claim that low-wage production methods in Sri Lanka were comparable with the production methods in China.[100] However, though the EC Court could not determine whether the products were similar,[101] the EC Court nevertheless stated that the Commission and the Council should have taken the Chinese advantage in easy access to raw materials into account. Furthermore, Nölle had demonstrated that the prices of paintbrushes sold in the EU were lower than the prices of the paintbrushes from Sri Lanka.[102] Nölle had provided sufficient factors to cast doubt on Sri Lanka as an appropriate analogue country. The EC Court further noted that although the Commission and the Council were not supposed to take any suggested analogue country into consideration, they had not made a serious and sufficient attempt to determine whether Taiwan could be considered as an appropriate analogue country. The Regulation was therefore declared invalid.[103]

It is clear from the case that the Commission and the Council must make a thorough examination of the different factors used in the selection of an analogue country. Furthermore, if other third countries are suggested in a convincing manner, the Commission and the Council must make an effort to determine whether the suggested other third country is more appropriate than the one suggested by the Commission and the Council.

---

97. *Paint, Distemper, Varnish and Similar Brushes*, Council Regulation (EEC) No. 725/89 of 20 Mar. 1989 imposing a definitive anti-dumping duty on imports of paint, distemper, varnish and similar brushes originating in the people's Republic of China and definitively collecting the provisional anti-dumping duty on such imports, OJ L 79, 22 Mar. 1989, pp. 24-29, recital 15.
98. Paras 15-25.
99. Para. 13.
100. Para. 24.
101. Para. 17.
102. Para. 29.
103. Paras 32-38.

In the following, some of the factors used in EU practice to select an appropriate country in a reasonable manner are described.

7.2.5.1.1 Same Economic Level

It has been contested whether a selected analogue country has been appropriate because of differences in the level of economic development between China and the selected analogue country. In *Granular Polytetrafluoroethylene (PTFE)*, the Council stated in general terms:

> [I]t must be noted that it is precisely the aim of Article 2(7)(a) of the basic Regulation that an analogue country is selected to determine the normal value on the basis of prices and costs, unbiased by non-market economy conditions. Thus, a simple comparison of prices in the non-market economy country or in the country with an economy in transition with those in the analogue country is as such not meaningful.[104]

In this case, the Chinese producers had compared the overall Chinese production costs with the overall costs in the analogue country. The cost of production and the prices of the product in a non-market economy cannot be directly compared to the costs and prices in a country with a market economy. The Council used similar terms in *Polyester Staple Fibres I*, where the US was chosen as an analogue country, and further stated:

> As far as the different level of economic development of the USA and the PRC is concerned, this in itself is not a relevant factor when selecting an analogue country. Indeed, the selection of a modern and cost efficient market characterised by intensive competition should result in a lower normal value than if the analogue country has a comparable economic development to the non market economy country.[105]

---

104. *Granular Polytetrafluoroethylene (PTFE)*, Council Regulation (EC) No. 1987/2005 of 2 Dec. 2005 imposing a definitive anti-dumping duty and collecting definitively the provisional duty imposed on imports of granular PTFE originating in Russia and the People's Republic of China, OJ L 320, 8 Dec. 2005, pp. 1-19, recital 21.

105. *Polyester Staple Fibres I*, Council Regulation (EC) No. 428/2005 of 10 Mar. 2005 imposing a definitive anti-dumping duty on imports of polyester staple fibres originating in the People's Republic of China and Saudi Arabia, amending Regulation (EC) No. 2852/2000 imposing a definitive anti-dumping duty on imports of polyester staple fibres originating in the Republic of Korea and terminating the anti-dumping proceeding in respect of such imports originating in Taiwan, OJ L 071, 17 Mar. 2005, pp. 1-33, recital 80. See also *Granular Polytetrafluoroethylene (PTFE)*, Commission Regulation (EC) No. 862/2005 of 7 Jun. 2005 imposing provisional anti-dumping duties on imports of granular PTFE originating in Russia and the People's Republic of China, OJ L 144, 8 Jun. 2005, pp. 11-36, where the Commission used similar terms, cf. recital 54, which was endorsed in Council Regulation (EC) No. 1987/2005 of 2 Dec. 2005 imposing a definitive anti-dumping duty and collecting definitively the provisional duty imposed on imports of granular PTFE originating in Russia and the People's Republic of China, OJ L 320, 8 Dec. 2005, pp. 1-19, recital 24.

The statement by the Council is not further elaborated on. The Council seems to be of the point of view that the selection of an analogue country with an efficient market will be an advantage for the Chinese producers because the economy in China – regarding the particular industry – is not as developed as the economy in the analogue country. It is not further elaborated on what 'efficient competition' is.

In *Polyethylene Terephthalate I*, the Council stated that a country at a stage of economic development different from that of China may be selected as an analogue country, and that labour costs that reflect the economic development of the country are not a relevant factor in themselves.[106]

The above statements by the EU authorities may be opposed in other practices by the EU authorities. For example, in *Barium Carbonate*, the differences in economic development between China and the selected analogue country were not a factor rejected by the EU authorities. The Commission stated:

> As far as the level of economic development and the different production processes are concerned it was considered that there might indeed be some differences. USA is a highly industrialised economy and the producer in the USA employed a more advanced and more efficient production method than that used in the PRC. However, it should be noted that even if these differences would affect normal value, they should normally result in a lower normal value in the USA and thus be to the advantage of the Chinese exporting producers.[107]

Another notable point is that in some instances the EU institutions seem to take into account the competitive and market situations in China compared to a situation in the optional analogue countries.[108]

---

106. *Polyethylene Terephthalate I*, Council Regulation (EC) No. 1467/2004 of 13 Aug. 2004 imposing a definitive anti-dumping duty and collecting definitively the provisional duty imposed on imports of polyethylene terephthalate originating in Australia, the People's Republic of China and terminating the anti-dumping proceeding concerning imports of polyethylene terephthalate originating in Pakistan and releasing the amounts secured by way of the provisional duties imposed, OJ L 271, 19 Aug. 2004, pp. 1-17, recital 46.
107. *Barium Carbonate*, Commission Regulation (EC) No. 145/2005 of 28 Jan. 2005 imposing a provisional anti-dumping duty on imports of barium carbonate originating in the People's Republic of China, OJ L 027, 29 Jan. 2005, pp. 4-23, recital 36, endorsed by Council Regulation (EC) No. 1175/2005 of 18 Jul. 2005 imposing a definitive anti-dumping duty and collecting definitively the provisional duty imposed on imports of barium carbonate originating in the People's Republic of China, OJ L 189, 21 Jul. 2005, pp. 15-23, recitals 13-15.
108. See as example *Furfuryl Alcohol*, Commission Regulation (EC) No. 781/2003 of 7 May 2003 imposing a provisional anti-dumping duty on imports of furfuryl alcohol originating in the People's Republic of China, OJ L 114, 8 May 2003, pp. 16-37, recital 33, endorsed in Council Regulation (EC) No. 1905/2003 of 27 Oct. 2003 imposing a definitive anti-dumping duty and collecting definitively the provisional duty imposed on imports of furfuryl alcohol originating in the People's Republic of China, OJ L 283, 31 Oct. 2003, pp. 1-7, recital 16.

7.2.5.1.2 Competition on the Market

There must be some sort of competition on the market in the analogue country used as a reference for the normal value. However, perfect competition is not required on the market of the analogue country:

Several domestic suppliers and lots of imports: A market may be appropriate if there is competition between many domestic suppliers and there is a substantial amount of imports competing with the domestic producers. This was emphasized in *Chamois Leather*, where the US market had many domestic producers of the like product. The US market was also an open market, and there was a considerable level of import.[109]

Only few domestic producers: If there are only a few domestic producers in the national market but those producers are subject to competition from imported goods, such a country can be qualified as an analogue country. See for example *Tartaric Acid.*[110]

Only one domestic producer: In *Rotexchemie*, the EC Court stated that it is not unreasonable to select an analogue country with only *one* producer if there are no barriers to import.[111]

In *Lever Arch Mechanisms*, Iran was selected as an analogue country, even though there was only one supplier. There were several producers in China. However, the EU authorities emphasized the substantial import of the like product from China and thus the competition on the Iranian market between the Iranian supplier and the Chinese exporters.[112]

In *Okoumé Plywood*, the selection of Morocco in the provisional regulation was changed to Turkey in the definitive regulation. In Morocco, there was only one

109. *Chamois Leather*, Commission Regulation (EC) No. 439/2006 of 16 Mar. 2006 imposing a provisional anti-dumping duty on imports of chamois leather originating in the People's Republic of China, OJ L 080, 17 Mar. 2006, pp. 7-22, recital 22, endorsed in Council Regulation (EC) No. 1338/2006 of 8 Sep. 2006 imposing a definitive anti-dumping duty and collecting definitively the provisional duty imposed on imports of chamois leather originating in the People's Republic of China, OJ L 251, 14 Sep. 2006, pp. 1-5, recitals 10-11.

110. *Tartaric Acid*, Commission Regulation (EC) No. 1259/2005 of 27 Jul. 2005 imposing a provisional anti-dumping duty on imports of tartaric acid originating in the People's Republic of China, OJ L 200, 30 Jul. 2005, pp. 73-90, recital 31, endorsed in Council Regulation (EC) No. 130/2006 of 23 Jan. 2006 imposing a definitive anti-dumping duty and collecting definitively the provisional duty imposed on imports of tartaric acid originating in the People's Republic of China, OJ L 023, 27 Jan. 2006, pp. 1-7, recital 13.

111. *Rotexchemie*, Case C-26/96, judgment of the EC Court on 29 May 1997, ECR 1997, p. I-2817, para. 15.

112. *Lever Arch Mechanisms*, Commission Regulation (EC) No. 134/2006 of 26 Jan. 2006 imposing a provisional anti-dumping duty on imports of lever arch mechanisms originating in the People's Republic of China, OJ L 023, 27 Jan. 2006, pp. 13-33, recital 37, endorsed in Council Regulation (EC) No. 1136/2006 of 24 Jul. 2006 imposing a definitive anti-dumping duty and collecting definitively the provisional duty imposed on imports of lever arch mechanisms originating in the People's Republic of China, OJ L 205, 27 Jul. 2006, pp. 1-12, recital 11.

producer, with entry barriers to the market because of high import duties. Turkey was a better choice because there were several domestic competitors.[113]

Barriers to entry: The Commission and the Council consider the market entry possibilities in the proposed analogue country. In practice, it is sometimes seen that a country that has imposed anti-dumping duties on imported products like the one concerned by the EU authorities can be disregarded if there is another country without such anti-dumping duties.[114]

In *Bicycles I*, the Council rejected the claims that the import registration system in Mexico, which was the suggested analogue country by the Council, would have any significant impact on the entry to the Mexican market.[115]

Producers are subject to National Antitrust Charges: If producers in the analogue country act in an anti-competitive way, for example with price agreements, the country will not qualify as appropriate analogue country. In *Polyester Staple Fibres I*, Chinese producers contested the choice of the US as an analogue country because some producers in the US were subject to a national antitrust investigation by the US authorities. The Council stated that the antitrust investigation took place one year before the anti-dumping investigation period and that it had not been proved that the anticompetitive behaviour had had any impact on the prices during the investigation period. In addition, the US authorities had not charged the cooperating producer in the US. The US was therefore suitable as an analogue country. The Council then stated:

> However, it is noted that, in any event, should an investigation find that such anti-competitive practices would have taken place during the investigation

---

113. *Okoumé Plywood*, Commission Regulation (EC) No. 988/2004 of 17 May 2004 imposing provisional anti-dumping duties on imports of okoumé plywood originating in the People's Republic of China, OJ L 181, 18 May 2004, pp. 5-23, recital 56, endorsed in Council Regulation (EC) No. 1942/2004 of 2 Nov. 2004 imposing a definitive anti-dumping duty and collecting definitively the provisional duty imposed on imports of okoumé plywood originating in the People's Republic of China, OJ L 336, 12 Nov. 2004, pp. 4-12, recitals 27-30.

114. See *Trichloroisocyanuric Acid*, Commission Regulation (EC) No. 538/2005 of 7 Apr. 2005 imposing a provisional anti-dumping duty on imports of trichloroisocyanuric acid originating in the People's Republic of China and the United States of America, OJ L 089, 8 Apr. 2005, pp. 4-31, recitals 70-72, endorsed in Council Regulation (EC) No. 1631/2005 of 3 Oct. 2005 imposing a definitive anti-dumping duty and collecting definitely the provisional duty imposed on imports of trichloroisocyanuric acid originating in the People's Republic of China and the United States of America, OJ L 261, 7 Oct. 2005, pp. 1-12, recital 18; *Magnesium Oxide*, Council Regulation (EC) No. 778/2005 of 23 May 2005 imposing a definitive anti-dumping duty on imports of magnesium oxide originating in the People's Republic of China, OJ L 131, 25 May 2005, pp. 1-17, recital 26, where the Council stressed the fact that no anti-dumping duties were applied in the US market for import of magnesium oxide.

115. *Bicycles I*, Council Regulation (EC) No. 1095/2005 of 12 Jul. 2005 imposing a definitive anti-dumping duty on imports of bicycles originating in Vietnam, and amending Regulation (EC) No. 1524/2000 imposing a definitive anti-dumping duty on imports of bicycles originating in the People's Republic of China, OJ L 183, 14 Jul. 2005, pp. 1-36, recital 62.

period or would have distorted the findings of this investigation, the current findings may be subject to a review.[116]

The Council disregards countries where the producers act in an anti-competitive way. Even though it is discovered after the investigation that anti-competitive behaviour has taken place during the investigation, the Council may select another country.

7.2.5.1.3 The Sale must be Representative

The domestic sale in the analogue country must be of some volume to be representative.[117] In *Bicycles I*, the Council was reluctant to use Taiwan as analogue country because the domestic market was small compared to the Mexican market. The one producer in Taiwan that sent reliable information to the EU authorities had such a small domestic sale that Taiwan was rejected. Mexico was then selected as analogue country.[118]

7.2.5.1.4 Similar Production Processes

If the production process in a market economy country is the same as in China, this is a factor that, among others, may justify the selection of a country.[119]

However, the EU authorities may use an analogue country with different production methods if there is competition on the domestic market. In *Tartaric Acid*, Argentina was selected as the analogue country even though the production process was different from the production method in China. The EU authorities

116. *Polyester Staple Fibres I*, Council Regulation (EC) No. 428/2005 of 10 Mar. 2005 imposing a definitive anti-dumping duty on imports of polyester staple fibres originating in the People's Republic of China and Saudi Arabia, amending Regulation (EC) No. 2852/2000 imposing a definitive anti-dumping duty on imports of polyester staple fibres originating in the Republic of Korea and terminating the anti-dumping proceeding in respect of such imports originating in Taiwan, OJ L 071, 17 Mar. 2005, pp. 1-33, recital 84.
117. See *Paracresol*, Commission Regulation (EC) No. 510/2003 of 20 Mar. 2003 imposing provisional anti-dumping duties on imports of paracresol originating in the People's Republic of China, OJ L 075, 21 Mar. 2003, pp. 12-22, recital 22, endorsed in Council Regulation (EC) No. 1656/2003 of 11 Sep. 2003 imposing a definitive anti-dumping duty and collecting definitively the provisional duty imposed on imports of paracresol originating in the People's Republic of China, OJ L 234, 20 Sep. 2003, pp. 1-5, recital 8.
118. *Bicycles I*, Council Regulation (EC) No. 1095/2005 of 12 Jul. 2005 imposing a definitive anti-dumping duty on imports of bicycles originating in Vietnam, and amending Regulation (EC) No. 1524/2000 imposing a definitive anti-dumping duty on imports of bicycles originating in the People's Republic of China, OJ L 183, 14 Jul. 2005, pp. 1-36, recitals 49-67.
119. *Chamois Leather*, Commission Regulation (EC) No. 439/2006 of 16 Mar. 2006 imposing a provisional anti-dumping duty on imports of chamois leather originating in the People's Republic of China, OJ L 080, 17 Mar. 2006, pp. 7-22, recital 22, endorsed in Council Regulation (EC) No. 1338/2006 of 8 Sep. 2006 imposing a definitive anti-dumping duty and collecting definitively the provisional duty imposed on imports of chamois leather originating in the People's Republic of China, OJ L 251, 14 Sep. 2006, pp. 1-5, recital 13.

justified the choice by the fact that there was competition on the Argentinean market.[120] None of the Chinese producers made any comments to the selection of Argentina.

In *Barium Carbonate*, the US was chosen as an analogue country in spite of production methods different than those of the Chinese producers. The Commission stressed that the production methods used in the US were more advanced and efficient than the methods used by the Chinese producers. It would in fact – according to the Commission – be an advantage for the Chinese producers if the US was used as an analogue country.[121]

7.2.5.1.5 Different Types of Quality

In some situations, the producer in the analogue country makes a lower or higher quality product than the Chinese producers. This difference in quality may not disqualify the analogue country from being used as reference to the establishment of the normal value.

In *Granular Polytetrafluoroethylene (PTFE)*, the Commission admitted that there were differences in the quality between the Chinese products and the products from the selected analogue country – the US. The Commission stressed that in spite of such differences, the same industry standards were used, and the products were generally used for the same applications.[122] However, the Commission made an adjustment of 10%. This was upheld in the Council Regulation.[123]

The approach taken in *Granular Polytetrafluoroethylene (PTFE)* is quite different from the one taken in *Okoumé Plywood*. In the Commission regulation imposing provisional anti-dumping duty on okoumé plywood from China, the

---

120. *Tartaric Acid*, Commission Regulation (EC) No. 1259/2005 of 27 Jul. 2005 imposing a provisional anti-dumping duty on imports of tartaric acid originating in the People's Republic of China, OJ L 200, 30 Jul. 2005, pp. 73-90, recital 31, endorsed in Council Regulation (EC) No. 130/2006 of 23 Jan. 2006 imposing a definitive anti-dumping duty and collecting definitively the provisional duty imposed on imports of tartaric acid originating in the People's Republic of China, OJ L 023, 27 Jan. 2006, pp. 1-7, recital 13.
121. *Barium Carbonate*, Commission Regulation (EC) No. 145/2005 of 28 Jan. 2005 imposing a provisional anti-dumping duty on imports of barium carbonate originating in the People's Republic of China, OJ L 027, 29 Jan. 2005, pp. 4-23, recital 36, endorsed by Council Regulation (EC) No. 1175/2005 of 18 Jul. 2005 imposing a definitive anti-dumping duty and collecting definitively the provisional duty imposed on imports of barium carbonate originating in the People's Republic of China, OJ L 189, 21 Jul. 2005, pp. 15-23, recitals 13-15.
122. *Granular Polytetrafluoroethylene (PTFE)*, Commission Regulation (EC) No. 862/2005 of 7 Jun. 2005 imposing provisional anti-dumping duties on imports of granular PTFE originating in Russia and the People's Republic of China, OJ L 144, 8 Jun. 2005, pp. 11-36, recital 53.
123. *Granular Polytetrafluoroethylene (PTFE)*, Council Regulation (EC) No. 1987/2005 of 2 Dec. 2005 imposing a definitive anti-dumping duty and collecting definitively the provisional duty imposed on imports of granular PTFE originating in Russia and the People's Republic of China, OJ L 320, 8 Dec. 2005, pp. 1-19, recital 22.

Commission had selected Morocco as the analogue country.[124] The Chinese producers stressed that there were qualitative differences between their products and the products from Morocco. In the definitive regulation by the Council, Turkey was preferred over Morocco as the analogue country. However, several other factors were included in the choice: in contrast to the Moroccan market, the market in Turkey had several competitors, and contrary to what was the case of the Morocco market, there were no significant import duties.[125]

However, in *Barium Carbonate*, Russia was ruled out as an analogue country because the product quality was much different from that of China and the US, which had been the initial choice as an analogue country by the EU authorities. The EU authorities found that the differences in quality were significant, and thus the products from Russia were not comparable with the Chinese products.[126]

7.2.5.1.6 Access to Raw Materials

In the above-mentioned case, *Nölle*, the EC Court ruled that access to raw materials is a factor to take into account when selecting an appropriate analogue country.[127] However, the line taken in newer practice by the Commission and the Council may differ from the line taken by the EC Court. In *Granular Polytetrafluoroethylene (PTFE)*, the Chinese producers of PTFE contested the choice by the Commission of the US as an analogue country. The Chinese producers claimed that there was a difference in the access to the raw materials of fluorspar. The US producers would have to import the fluorspar from China, which had an export quota on fluorspar.[128] The Commission stated:

> The argument on differences in access to raw materials (fluorspar) was found not to prevent the choice of the USA either. No evidence was provided regarding the effect of the Chinese export quotas on the USA market so as to allow a quantification of such possible effect. It was found however, that fluorspar is the fourth upstream raw material of PTFE and should therefore represent only

---

124. *Okoumé Plywood*, Commission Regulation (EC) No. 988/2004 of 17 May 2004 imposing provisional anti-dumping duties on imports of okoumé plywood originating in the People's Republic of China, OJ L 181, 18 May 2004, pp. 5-23, recital 57.
125. *Okoumé Plywood*, Council Regulation (EC) No. 1942/2004 of 2 Nov. 2004 imposing a definitive anti-dumping duty and collecting definitively the provisional duty imposed on imports of okoumé plywood originating in the People's Republic of China, OJ L 336, 12 Nov. 2004, pp. 4-12, recitals 28-30.
126. *Barium Carbonate*, Commission Regulation (EC) No. 145/2005 of 28 Jan. 2005 imposing a provisional anti-dumping duty on imports of barium carbonate originating in the People's Republic of China, OJ L 027, 29 Jan. 2005, pp. 4-23, recital 34, endorsed by Council Regulation (EC) No. 1175/2005 of 18 Jul. 2005 imposing a definitive anti-dumping duty and collecting definitively the provisional duty imposed on imports of barium carbonate originating in the People's Republic of China, OJ L 189, 21 Jul. 2005, pp. 15-23. The selection of US was not objected to by the Chinese exporters in the Council regulation.
127. *Nölle*, Case C-16/90, judgment of the EC Court on 22 Oct. 1991, ECR 1991, p. I-5163, para 26. See the beginning of Section 7.2.5.1.
128. Apparently, a limited access to raw materials will raise the prices of the raw materials.

> a very small part of its cost of manufacturing (roughly estimated at less than 5 %). In these circumstances, the effect of the Chinese export quotas on the USA market for PTFE would be minimal. Moreover, chloroform is a much more important input of PTFE, in which the PRC has a disadvantage due to its dependence on imports and the high AD duties in force against several exporting countries. It is therefore concluded that any difference in access to raw materials between USA and the PRC is not such as to render the choice of the former as analogue country unreasonable.[129]

Claiming that the parties have different access to raw materials is not sufficient – the Chinese producers must also demonstrate that the different access will have different effects for the Chinese and, in this situation, the US producer. The Commission also seems to disregard the differences in access to the raw materials, because the costs of the raw material only represent a small part of the production costs. Furthermore, this recital shows that in situations with many different inputs (raw materials), the Commission may take into account that limited access to one material may be counterbalanced by an advantage in the access to another raw material.

It follows from that case and in *Certain Magnesia Bricks* that an adjustment will instead be made when the normal value is determined.[130]

However, it is not clear where the line is to be drawn between the practice by the Commission and the Council on one side, and the rule by the EC Court on the other.

7.2.5.1.7 Labour Costs

The costs of labour can have a significant impact on the final price of a product. However, the EU authorities reject direct comparison between the labour cost in the analogue country and the non-market economy country,[131] unless the intensity

---

129. *Granular Polytetrafluoroethylene (PTFE)*, Commission Regulation (EC) No. 862/2005 of 7 Jun. 2005 imposing provisional anti-dumping duties on imports of granular PTFE originating in Russia and the People's Republic of China, OJ L 144, 8 Jun. 2005, pp. 11-36, recital 52, endorsed in Council Regulation (EC) No. 1987/2005 of 2 Dec. 2005 imposing a definitive anti-dumping duty and collecting definitively the provisional duty imposed on imports of granular PTFE originating in Russia and the People's Republic of China, OJ L 320, 8 Dec. 2005, pp. 1-19, recital 53.
130. *Granular Polytetrafluoroethylene (PTFE)*, Council Regulation (EC) No. 1987/2005 of 2 Dec. 2005 imposing a definitive anti-dumping duty and collecting definitively the provisional duty imposed on imports of granular PTFE originating in Russia and the People's Republic of China, OJ L 320, 8 Dec. 2005, pp. 1-19, recital 22; *Certain Magnesia Bricks*, Council Regulation (EC) No. 1659/2005 of 6 Oct. 2005 imposing a definitive anti-dumping duty and collecting definitively the provisional duty imposed on imports of certain magnesia bricks originating in the People's Republic of China, OJ L 267, 12 Oct. 2005, pp. 1-14, recital 24.
131. *Bicycle I*, Council Regulation (EC) No. 1095/2005 of 12 Jul. 2005 imposing a definitive anti-dumping duty on imports of bicycles originating in Vietnam, and amending Regulation (EC) No. 1524/2000 imposing a definitive anti-dumping duty on imports of bicycles originating in the People's Republic of China, OJ L 183, 14 Jul. 2005, pp. 1-36, recital 64.

of labour costs is high. In *Hand Pallet Trucks and Their Essential Parts*, the Council stated:

> [T]he investigation established that the production of hand pallet trucks is not labour intensive (the cost of labour in Canada is not more than 15 % of the total cost of production) and, therefore, any differences in labour cost between Canada and the PRC would not affect significantly the total cost of production. Therefore, the argument that cost differences mainly due to labour render the choice of Canada as an analogue country inappropriate cannot be accepted.[132]

The Council does not focus on the cost of labour, but rather on the percentage of labour costs of the total cost of production. According to the statement, a low percentage with no *significant* affect on the total cost is not a factor that influences the selection of the analogue country.

7.2.5.1.8 Devaluation of Currency

Apparently, the monetary situation in the suggested analogue country can have an impact on the selection. This was the situation in *Silicon*, where EU producers objected to the Chinese proposal of Brazil as an analogue country on account of the devaluation of the local currency and for the non-cooperation by the Brazilian producer. The Council instead selected Norway.[133]

7.2.5.2 Determining Normal Value with an Analogue Country

When the EU authorities have found an appropriate third country as analogue country, the next step is to establish the normal value. This can be done by:

- using the prices from the domestic sales or the constructed value by the cooperating company in the analogue country; or
- by using the company's prices for export to other countries, including export prices to the EU.

The prices from domestic sales must originate from the ordinary course of sale to unrelated customers, and the sale must be representative of the like product.[134] The procedure will then be the same as in situations with market economy countries.

---

132. *Hand Pallet Trucks and Their Essential Parts*, Council Regulation (EC) No. 1174/2005 of 18 Jul. 2005 imposing a definitive anti-dumping duty and collecting definitely the provisional duty imposed on imports of hand pallet trucks and their essential parts originating in the People's Republic of China, OJ L 189, 21 Jul. 2005, pp. 1-14, recital 23.
133. *Silicon*, Council Regulation (EC) No. 398/2004 of 2 Mar. 2004 imposing a definitive anti-dumping duty on imports of silicon originating in the People's Republic of China, OJ L 066, 4 Mar. 2004, pp. 15-30, recitals 21-23.
134. *Chamois Leather*, Council Regulation (EC) No. 1338/2006 of 8 Sep. 2006 imposing a definitive anti-dumping duty and collecting definitively the provisional duty imposed on imports of chamois leather originating in the People's Republic of China, OJ L 251, 14 Sep. 2006, pp. 1-5, recitals 23 and 24; *Bicycles I*, Council Regulation (EC) No. 1095/2005 of

Adjustments will be made for differences between factors in China and the analogue country, such as differences in the quality of the raw materials used, differences in transportation costs and differences in costs for importation for the raw materials, provided such differences exist.[135] However, adjustment will not be made for all types in costs. In *Certain Magnesia Bricks*, the Council stated:

> It must be noted that this claim is irrelevant in the context of the assessment of normal value in the analogue country as any such adjustment on the costs would render the investigation in the analogue country meaningless and it would lead to adjust the normal value to non-market economy levels.[136]

Apparently, the costs in China are regarded as unreliable, and therefore adjustments are not made for costs because the normal value might end up being adjusted to the level of the non-market economy.

Although an analogue country is found to be appropriate for the normal value determination, there may be other difficulties. Far too often, the selected countries cannot be used because the companies in the selected analogue country are not cooperative, i.e., do not want to or cannot provide the necessary information to the EU authorities.[137]

The result is that another country must be selected. However, it cannot be expected that producers in those countries will cooperate either, or there might not

---

12 Jul. 2005 imposing a definitive anti-dumping duty on imports of bicycles originating in Vietnam, and amending Regulation (EC) No. 1524/2000 imposing a definitive anti-dumping duty on imports of bicycles originating in the People's Republic of China, OJ L 183, 14 Jul. 2005, pp. 1-36, recitals 73-74.

135. *Certain Magnesia Bricks*, Council Regulation (EC) No. 1659/2005 of 6 Oct. 2005 imposing a definitive anti-dumping duty and collecting definitively the provisional duty imposed on imports of certain magnesia bricks originating in the People's Republic of China, OJ L 267, 12 Oct. 2005, pp. 1-14, recital 24.

136. Ibid., recital 22.

137. See *Steel Ropes and Cables*, Council Regulation (EC) No. 1796/1999 of 12 Aug. 1999 imposing a definitive anti-dumping duty, and collecting definitively the provisional duty imposed, on imports of steel ropes and cables originating in the People's Republic of China, Hungary, India, Mexico, Poland, South Africa and Ukraine and terminating the anti-dumping proceeding in respect of imports originating in the Republic of Korea, OJ L 217, 17 Aug. 1999, pp. 1-13, recital 22, together with Council Regulation (EC) No. 1858/2005 of 8 Nov. 2005 imposing a definitive anti-dumping duty on imports of steel ropes and cables originating in the People's Republic of China, India, South Africa and Ukraine following an expiry review pursuant to Art. 11(2) of Regulation (EC) No. 384/96, OJ L 299, 16 Nov. 2005, pp. 1-22, recitals 42-48; *Certain Electronic Weighing Scales (REWS)*, Council Regulation (EC) No. 692/2005 of 28 Apr. 2005 amending Regulation (EC) No. 2605/2000 imposing definitive anti-dumping duties on imports of certain electronic weighing scales (REWS) originating, inter alia, in the People's Republic of China, OJ L 112, 3 May 2005, pp. 1-7, recital 32; and; *Furfuryl Alcohol*, Commission Regulation (EC) No. 781/2003 of 7 May 2003 imposing a provisional anti-dumping duty on imports of furfuryl alcohol originating in the People's Republic of China, OJ L 114, 8 May 2003, pp. 16-37, recital 33, endorsed in Council Regulation (EC) No. 1905/2003 of 27 Oct. 2003 imposing a definitive anti-dumping duty and collecting definitively the provisional duty imposed on imports of furfuryl alcohol originating in the People's Republic of China, OJ L 283, 31 Oct. 2003, pp. 1-7, recital 14.

be another appropriate country. If an appropriate country cannot be found, the Commission and the Council have to determine normal value based on any other reasonable method.

7.2.5.3 Determining Normal Value When No Appropriate Analogue Countries Is Found

As stated in the beginning of Section 7.2.5, it happens only rarely that the Commission and the Council have to determine a normal value for Chinese producers based on any other reasonable method. In *Dihydrostreptomycin*, the Commission had considered Brazil, India, Romania and the US as analogue countries to the determination of the normal value for Chinese exporters of dihydrostreptomycin. All the producers in the market economy countries manufactured the product under consideration. However, none of the producers from Brazil, India, Romania, or the US would or could cooperate with the Commission, which stated:

> In the absence of any available third country, *there was no other option than to use the Community* as the analogue market for the establishment of the normal value, in accordance with Article 2(7) of the Basic Regulation.[138]

From this statement, it appears that the absence of an analogue country will lead to a normal value based on domestic prices in the EU. It may be questioned, however, whether there are other alternatives in situations where no appropriate analogue country has been found. The text of Article 2.7(a) does not exhaust the possibilities of finding other methods to determine the normal value, so long as it is reasonable.

7.2.5.4 The EU Practice and WTO law

Under WTO law, there is apparently absolute discretion left to the investigating authorities to determine a normal value based on prices other than Chinese domestic prices. The rule in Article 15(a)(ii) that the export price of Chinese products shall not be strictly compared with the Chinese domestic price has close resemblance to the text in the interpretative note re Article VI.1 of GATT 1994. Since the introduction of that note in 1955 in GATT 1947, it has been a consistent practice by the US – and later the EU – to use the prices from producers in analogue countries towards non-market economy countries. Based on the consistent interpretation of that note, it may be assumed that Article 15(a)(ii) can also be applied in such way.

When the EU selects an analogue country, the Commission and the Council can take any factor into account in determining a reasonable analogue country. However, there is a limitation to the Commission and the Council practice, as the

138. *Dihydrostreptomycin*, Commission Decision No. 98/90/EC of 21 Jan. 1998 terminating the anti-dumping proceeding concerning imports of dihydrostreptomycin originating in the People's Republic of China, OJ L 017, 22 Jan. 1998, pp. 42-45, recital 14.

EC Court stated in *Nölle* that the examination of the third countries shall be thorough, and the Commission and the Council shall take convincing suggestions from other third countries into account. Under WTO law, there are no direct requirements about factors to be used for selecting an appropriate analogue country. However, Article 15 of the Protocol refers to Article VI of GATT 1994. The basic requirements for dumping determinations cannot be ignored. The exceptional rules on China only allow the WTO Members to replace the Chinese data on prices and costs with another set of data. There are then indirect requirements on the selection of the analogue country because the prices from those countries, which are used for comparison with the Chinese export prices, are to be comparable, in the ordinary course of trade, to the like product when destined for consumption in the particular country. It is not written into Article 15 of the Protocol that those basic requirements for normal value can be ignored. If the conditions are not met, recourse must be taken to Article 2.2 of the ADA, and the normal value must be constructed based either on third-country prices for sales of the like product or on costs, SAG and profit information from the producer in the analogue country.

In this respect, the EU authorities must assure that the producer in the analogue country produce the *like product*. It seems that the EU authorities in some cases determine normal value based on products with qualitative differences from the product exported by the Chinese producers. Instead, adjustments are made to ensure price comparability. As noted in Section 3.4.2, it must be assumed that WTO law provides some room for differences between the product under investigation and the like product if these can be adjusted in accordance with Article 2.4 of the ADA.[139] However, if the qualitative differences are of such nature that the products are not identical or do not have physical resemblance to the exported Chinese products, then the products cannot serve as basis for the normal value. If no other like products are found in the selected country, another country must be used.

Under such circumstances, the normal value for Chinese producers would have to be based on another basis. However, it appears that in other cases the Commission and the Council find that the qualitative differences disqualify a country to be appropriate as analogue country and use countries with less difference in product quality.

7.2.5.5 The Problem between Non-Market Treatment and Market Treatment of Chinese Exporters

The Commission and the Council may find that some Chinese producers meet the conditions to be granted market economy treatment, while other Chinese producers

139. See also J. Ulff-Møller Nielsen & A. Rutkowski, 'The EU Anti-dumping Policy Towards Russia and China: Product Quality and the Choice of an Analogue Country, *World Economy* 28 (1) (2005): 131, where no systematic relation between the quality differences and dumping margins is found.

do not meet the requirements. The situation is then that normal value will be based on Chinese prices and costs for those producers being treated under the rules described in Chapter 4, while the other groups of producers have normal value based on prices from an analogue country. The question is, however, whether the normal value determination for the producers not being granted market economy treatment shall be based on the prices from the Chinese producers that get market economy treatment or on prices from an analogue country. This question was raised before the Court of First Instance in *Changzhou/Zheijiang v. Council.* Two Chinese exporters of integrated electronic compact fluorescent lamps had been denied market economy treatment by the Council, while other Chinese exporters had fulfilled the criteria in Article 2.7(c), and their normal value was determined on the basis of their Chinese domestic prices and costs. For the two exporters with no market economy treatment, Mexico had been selected as an analogue country.[140] The two exporters claimed that the normal value should instead be based on the prices from the Chinese producers that had been granted market economy treatment. A normal value based on prices from Mexico resulted in disadvantages, since '*normal value in the analogue country is not adequately adjusted so as to be "as similar as possible" to normal value in market-economy operating conditions in the PRC*', and the '*disadvantage amounts to unequal treatment in that the companies receiving individual treatment and those granted market-economy status compete against each other in the market for other exports to the Community*'.[141] The Court of First Instance stated:

> The competent institutions may choose not to apply the general rule set out in Article 2(7)(a) of the basic regulation for the determination of the normal value of products originating in non-market economy countries, using a different reasonable basis, only where it is impossible to apply that general rule. The Court of First Instance considers that such impossibility arises only where the data required in order to determine normal value are not available or are not reliable. That it happens to be necessary to adjust those data in order to adapt them as closely as possible to the conditions which would obtain for Chinese producers if the PRC were a market-economy country does not demonstrate that it was either impossible or even inappropriate to use the data concerning Philips Mexicana.[142]

---

140. See the Commission Regulation and the Council Regulation, *Integrated Electronic Compact Fluorescent Lamps (CFL-i)*; Commission Regulation (EC) No. 255/2001 of 7 Feb. 2001 imposing a provisional anti-dumping duty on imports of integrated electronic compact fluorescent lamps (CFL-i) originating in the People's Republic of China, OJ L 38, 8 Feb. 2001, pp. 8-21, recitals 27-32, endorsed in Council Regulation (EC) No. 1470/2001 of 16 Jul. 2001 imposing a definitive anti-dumping duty and collecting definitively the provisional duty imposed on imports of integrated electronic compact fluorescent lamps (CFL-i) originating in the People's Republic of China, OJ L 195, 19 Jul. 2001, pp. 8-14, recitals 10-12.
141. *Changzhou/Zheijiang v. Council*, Case T-255/01, judgment of the Court of First Instance on 23 Oct. 2003, ECR 2003, p. II-4741, para. 48.
142. Para. 59.

The Court of First Instance determines that the general rule – use of an analogue country – may only be departed from and normal value based on any other reasonable method if the use of such is impossible. The Court of First Instance thus refers to the hierarchical nature between the methods in Article 2.7(a). The Court of First Instance then rejected the claim by the Chinese producers.[143]

The question is whether the EU position is in conformity with WTO law. Under WTO law, it is clearly provided that the Commission and the Council may use a methodology that is not based on a strict comparison with domestic prices or costs in China if the producers do not clearly demonstrate that market economy conditions prevail in the industry. This could imply that the Commission and the Council may disregard a method according to which prices are based on prices from other Chinese producers, even though those producers have been granted market economy treatment.

However, as stated Section 7.2.4.1, it can be questioned whether the method of making *individual examinations* of Chinese companies is in conformity with WTO law. Instead, it is suggested that the Commission and the Council should determine whether the *industry as such* works under market conditions and whether those companies that might be under State interference should have adjustments made in accordance with Article 2.4 of the ADA. Furthermore, prices could be disregarded if there is a particular market situation, cf. Article 2.1 and Article 2.2 of the ADA, which may include situations with State subsidies or other State interferences. As seen in Section 4.1.4.1, the EU apparently disregards Korean local export sales due to a particular market situation. In those circumstances, the prices for those producers would be based in accordance with Article 2.2 of the ADA. The counter-argument may be that the domestic prices are not reliable for such Chinese producers if the State is able to influence the price setting. This problem could be solved through a general dumping margin for those producers under State influence in accordance with the WTO requirements; see Section 6.3 and next section.

Furthermore, it can be argued that the normal value for Chinese producers that are not granted market economy treatment is supposed to be a price reflecting a situation with market economy situation. The idea behind the EU legislation is to find an appropriate analogue country – and the most appropriate country should be China itself if there are producers working under market conditions. It should here be noted that under WTO law, it is not required that an analogue country is found, but that the EU *may* use a methodology that is not based on a strict comparison with Chinese domestic prices and costs. Therefore, it seems more appropriate to make the normal value determination on the prices by other Chinese producers, as it must be expected that their costs and prices are closer to a market economy situation in China than the costs and prices of a Mexican producer.

Finally, it could be argued that the non-discrimination principle should apply in such cases. Clearly, there is a difference in treatment between the Chinese

143. Para. 62.

market producers and the Chinese non-market producers. However, the situation between the two types of Chinese producers is not similar, as one producer acts under non-market conditions with its possible State interference, whereas the other producer acts under market economy conditions. Therefore, the non-discrimination principle may not apply to such situations.

7.3 DETERMINING THE DUMPING MARGIN

This part concerns the same issue as in Chapter 6, namely whether individual or general margin will be determined. The Chinese companies that are granted market economy treatment will be under the general rules to determine dumping. The normal value, export price and comparison are made as seen in Chapters 4-6. The dumping margin is made in accordance with the rules mentioned in Chapter 6, i.e., a dumping margin is determined individually for each company unless the exceptions mentioned in Chapter 6 apply.

For those Chinese companies that are not granted market economy treatment, the normal value is based on the prices from a company in an analogue country. The dumping margins as a rule will be calculated on a national basis, i.e., a general margin will cover all export transactions from those producers.

The WTO legislation on determining individual or general margins is the same as mentioned in the previous chapter in Section 6.3.

At first glance, the EU legislation is also the same as in the previous chapter. However, when looking further into the basic Regulation, Article 9.5 provides:

> An anti-dumping duty shall be imposed in the appropriate amounts in each case, on a non-discriminatory basis on imports of a product from all sources found to be dumped and causing injury, except as to imports from those sources from which undertakings under the terms of this Regulation have been accepted. The Regulation imposing the duty shall specify the duty for each supplier or, if that is impracticable, and in general where Article 2(7)(a) applies, the supplying country concerned.
>
> Where Article 2(7)(a) applies, an individual duty shall, however, be specified for the exporters, which can demonstrate, on the basis of properly substantiated claims that:
>
> (a) in the case of wholly or partly foreign owned firms or joint ventures, exporters are free to repatriate capital and profits;
> (b) export prices and quantities, and conditions and terms of sale are freely determined;
> (c) the majority of the shares belong to private persons. State officials appearing on the board of Directors or holding key management positions shall either be in minority or it must be demonstrated that the company is nonetheless sufficiently independent from State interference;
> (d) exchange rate conversions are carried out at the market rate; and

(e) State interference is not such as to permit circumvention of measures if individual exporters are given different rates of duty.

Article 9.5 regards the anti-dumping duty – and actually not the dumping margin. It is mentioned here because Article 9.5 has an impact on the dumping margin. For those producers that have not been granted market economy treatment, an individual dumping margin is determined if five conditions are met. The Chinese producer claiming for individual treatment has to demonstrate that if the producer is owned by foreign companies, the capital and profits can be repatriated; the export prices and conditions and terms for the sales are independently determined by the producer; shares are owned by private persons; the market rate governs exchange rates; and State interference does not result in circumvention. The conditions in Article 9.5 were introduced in 2002 in the regulation amending the basic Regulation. Until then, the rules about individual treatment had been based on practice.[144]

The following two sections briefly describe practice by the EU authorities.

7.3.1.1 Individual Treatment

The Chinese producers that have fulfilled the market economy conditions also have individual margins established. Only those producers that did not get market economy treatment are regarded under Article 9.5.

Before the conditions for the *dumping duty* in Article 9.5 were made, the methods by the Commission and the Council to determine individual treatment were unclear, and the practice about individual treatment evolved into a strict set of unclear criteria that could hardly be met by Chinese producers.[145] The strict line by the Commission and the Council led to heavy criticism.[146]

In recent practice – and after the introduction of the conditions in Article 9.5, it seems that more Chinese producers meet the conditions in Article 9.5 of the basic

144. Council Regulation (EC) No. 1972/2002 of 5 Nov. 2002 amending Regulation (EC) No. 384/96 on the protection against dumped imports from countries not members of the European Community, OJ L 305, 7 Nov. 2002, pp. 1-3, Art. 1.6 and recital 7. See also the subsequent section.
145. Compare for instance *Small-screen Colour Television Receivers*, Commission Regulation (EEC) No. 129/91 of 11 Jan. 1991 imposing a provisional anti-dumping duty on imports of small-screen colour television receivers originating in Hong Kong and the people's Republic of China, OJ L 14, 19 Jan. 1991, pp. 31-45, recital 28, amended in Council Regulation (EEC) No. 2093/91 of 15 Jul. 1991 imposing a definitive anti-dumping duty on imports of small-screen colour television receivers originating in Hong Kong and the People's Republic of China and collecting definitively the provisional duty, OJ L 195, 18 Jul. 1991, pp. 1-8, recitals 19-20, with *Bicycles I*, Council Regulation (EEC) No. 2474/93 of 8 Sep. 1993 imposing a definitive anti-dumping duty on imports into the Community of bicycles originating in the People's Republic of China and collecting definitively the provisional anti-dumping duty, OJ L 228, 9 Sep. 1993, pp. 1-9, recitals 15-27.
146. See Donghui Fu, 'EC Anti-dumping Law and Individual Treatment Policy', *Journal of World Trade* 31 (1) (1997): 73 et seq., and I. Van Bael & J. F. Bellis, *Anti-dumping and Other Trade Protection Laws of the EC*, 4th edn (The Hague: Kluwer Law International, 2004), 147-151.

Regulation and, thus, have individual dumping margins. However, it is still the exception rather than the rule that individual treatment is granted.[147]

If a Chinese producer is granted individual treatment, the dumping margin is based on the actual export prices from the particular producer compared with the normal value from the analogue country.[148]

147. See for instance *Integrated Electronic Compact Fluorescent Lamps (CFL-i)*, Commission Regulation (EC) No. 255/2001 of 7 Feb. 2001 imposing a provisional anti-dumping duty on imports of integrated electronic compact fluorescent lamps (CFL-i) originating in the People's Republic of China, OJ L 38, 8 Feb. 2001, pp. 8-21, recitals 35-36, endorsed in Council Regulation (EC) No. 1470/2001 of 16 Jul. 2001 imposing a definitive anti-dumping duty and collecting definitively the provisional duty imposed on imports of integrated electronic compact fluorescent lamps (CFL-i) originating in the People's Republic of China, OJ L 195, 19 Jul. 2001, pp. 8-14, recital 17; *Granular Polytetrafluoroethylene (PTFE)*, Commission Regulation (EC) No. 862/2005 of 7 Jun. 2005 imposing provisional anti-dumping duties on imports of granular PTFE originating in Russia and the People's Republic of China, OJ L 144, 8 Jun. 2005, pp. 11-36, recitals 65-66, apparently endorsed in Council Regulation (EC) No. 1987/2005 of 2 Dec. 2005 imposing a definitive anti-dumping duty and collecting definitively the provisional duty imposed on imports of granular PTFE originating in Russia and the People's Republic of China, OJ L 320, 8 Dec. 2005, pp. 1-19; *Certain Footwear with Uppers of Leather*, Commission Regulation (EC) No. 553/2006 of 23 Mar. 2006 imposing a provisional anti-dumping duty on imports of certain footwear with uppers of leather originating in the People's Republic of China and Vietnam, OJ L 098, 6 Apr. 2006, pp. 3-54, recitals 92-94, endorsed in Council Regulation (EC) No. 1472/2006 of 5 Oct. 2006 imposing a definitive anti-dumping duty and collecting definitely the provisional duty imposed on imports of certain footwear with uppers of leather originating in the People's Republic of China and Vietnam, OJ L 275, 6 Oct. 2006, pp. 1-41, recital 83; *Lever Arch Mechanisms*, Commission Regulation (EC) No. 134/2006 of 26 Jan. 2006 imposing a provisional anti-dumping duty on imports of lever arch mechanisms originating in the People's Republic of China, OJ L 23, 27 Jan. 2006, pp. 13-33, recitals 26-29, endorsed with some amendments in Council Regulation (EC) No. 1136/2006 of 24 Jul. 2006 imposing a definitive anti-dumping duty and collecting definitively the provisional duty imposed on imports of lever arch mechanisms originating in the People's Republic of China, OJ L 205, 27 Jul. 2006, pp. 1-12, recitals 14-15; *Certain Tungsten Electrodes*, Commission Regulation (EC) No. 1350/2006 of 13 Sep. 2006 imposing a provisional anti-dumping duty on imports of certain tungsten electrodes originating in the People's Republic of China, OJ L 250, 14 Sep. 2006, pp. 10-33, recitals 24-25, endorsed with some amendments in Council Regulation (EC) No. 260/2007 of 9 Mar. 2007 imposing a definitive anti-dumping duty and collecting definitively the provisional duty imposed on imports of certain tungsten electrodes originating in the People's Republic of China, OJ L 72, 13 Mar. 2007, pp. 1-9, recital 15; *Certain Frozen Strawberries*, Commission Regulation (EC) No. 1551/2006 of 17 Oct. 2006 imposing a provisional anti-dumping duty on imports of certain frozen strawberries originating in the People's Republic of China, OJ L 287, 18 Oct. 2006, pp. 3-29, recitals 27-28, endorsed in Council Regulation (EC) No. 407/2007 of 16 Apr. 2007 imposing definitive anti-dumping measures and releasing the provisional duty imposed on imports of certain frozen strawberries originating in the People's Republic of China, OJ L 100, 17 Apr. 2007, pp. 1-13, recitals 14-17.

148. *Stainless Steel Fasteners and Parts thereof I*, Commission Regulation (EC) No. 1732/97 of 4 Sep. 1997 imposing a provisional anti-dumping duty on imports of stainless steel fasteners and parts originating in the People's Republic of China, India, Malaysia, the Republic of Korea,

7.3.1.2 The Country-Wide Margin

Chinese producers that do not meet the conditions of getting an individual margin will be covered by the countrywide general margin. In practice, the Commission and the Council will determine the dumping margin by comparing the weighted-average domestic price from the company in the analogue country with the weighted-average export price for *all* the Chinese producers not granted individual treatment; i.e., their respective export data are grouped into one value.[149]

Although it appears that the use of individual dumping margins for Chinese producers is increasing, the practice of determining a general margin for those producers that do not meet either the market economy conditions or the conditions in Article 9.5 may be questioned under WTO law. In *Certain Footwear with Uppers of Leather*, several Chinese producers claimed to the Council that the rejection of individual treatment was a violation of Article 6.10 of the ADA. The Council rejected this claim by stating that the ADA is not directly applicable in the EU and that the general rules for determining dumping margins are derogated from in regard to Chinese exports; see note 2 re Article VI.1 of GATT of 1994.[150]

In this regard it must be noted that in Chapter 2, it was found that the interpretation of the basic Regulation must be interpreted in light of the ADA because there is an explicit reference to both Article VI of GATT 1994 and the ADA in the preamble to the basic Regulation. Therefore, the Council cannot ignore Article 6.10 of the ADA in its application of the basic Regulation.

Taiwan, and Thailand, OJ L 243, 5 Sep. 1997, pp. 17-36, recital 35, endorsed in Council Regulation (EC) No. 393/98 of 16 Feb. 1998 imposing a definitive anti-dumping duty on imports of stainless steel fasteners and parts thereof originating in the People's Republic of China, India, the Republic of Korea, Malaysia, Taiwan, and Thailand, OJ L 50, 20 Feb. 1998, pp. 1-14.

149. See *Integrated Electronic Compact Fluorescent Lamps (CFL-i)*, Commission Regulation (EC) No. 255/2001 of 7 Feb. 2001 imposing a provisional anti-dumping duty on imports of integrated electronic compact fluorescent lamps (CFL-i) originating in the People's Republic of China, OJ L 38, 8 Sep. 2001, pp. 8-21, recitals 35-36, endorsed in Council Regulation (EC) No. 1470/2001 of 16 Jul. 2001 imposing a definitive anti-dumping duty and collecting definitively the provisional duty imposed on imports of integrated electronic compact fluorescent lamps (CFL-i) originating in the People's Republic of China, OJ L 195, 19 Jul. 2001, pp. 8-14, recital 17; *Granular Polytetrafluoroethylene (PTFE)*, Commission Regulation (EC) No. 862/2005 of 7 Jun. 2005 imposing provisional anti-dumping duties on imports of granular PTFE originating in Russia and the People's Republic of China, OJ L 144, 8 Jun. 2005, pp. 11-36, recitals 65-66, apparently endorsed in Council Regulation (EC) No. 1987/2005 of 2 Dec. 2005 imposing a definitive anti-dumping duty and collecting definitively the provisional duty imposed on imports of granular PTFE originating in Russia and the People's Republic of China, OJ L 320, 8 Dec. 2005, pp. 1-19.

150. *Certain Footwear with Uppers of Leather*, Council Regulation (EC) No. 1472/2006 of 5 Oct. 2006 imposing a definitive anti-dumping duty and collecting definitely the provisional duty imposed on imports of certain footwear with uppers of leather originating in the People's Republic of China and Vietnam, OJ L 275, 6 Oct. 2006, pp. 1-41, recitals 84-88.

Before turning to Article 6.10 of the ADA, the Council's reference to note 2 re Article VI.1 of GATT 1994 is not convincing, as it appears that the provision addresses the normal value and not the export price. However, a legal basis for making a countrywide margin may be found elsewhere under WTO law.

The general rule under WTO law is to determine individual margins to the known producers; see Article 6.10 of the ADA. Under WTO law, however, a general margin may be determined for producers that are related. In *Korea – Certain Paper*, the Panel found it a permissible interpretation of Article 6.10 of the ADA to make general margins for related companies; however, the investigating authorities must determine 'that these companies are in a relationship close enough to support that treatment'.[151] The question is here whether the requirements under Article 9.5 of the basic Regulation are sufficient factors to conclude that there is a 'strong enough' connection between the particular Chinese producers under State influence to conclude that an individual margin must be denied. This still needs to be resolved in practice.

7.4 FINAL COMMENTS

WTO law leaves it up to the discretion of the WTO Members to treat China as a market economy or a non-market economy. The EU has so far refused requests from China about market economy status, although in 2016 the EU has to accept China as a market economy; see Article 15(d) of the Protocol.

However, under WTO law market economy treatment will be granted if Chinese producers clearly demonstrate that market economy conditions prevail in the industry. If not, normal value will not be based strictly on Chinese prices and costs. The general rule under EU law is to determine normal value based on prices from producers in an analogue country. This rule seems to be in conformity with WTO law. The rule is exempted from if a Chinese producer demonstrates that he works under market economy conditions. It must be noted that the EU makes an examination of *individual Chinese producers* instead of the *industry*, and this may be in violation of the requirements in Article 15(a) of the Protocol.

The factors used by the Commission and the Council to determine whether market economy treatment should be granted are in conformity with WTO law due to the wide discretion. The very few problems identified regard the inconsistency in practice about price differentiation, which may violate the fairness principle, although the scope of that principle is not clear.

Another problem was the non-market treatment of producers that meet the five criteria, whereby market economy treatment is not granted until the producer has submitted sufficient information. Under WTO law, the investigating authorities are required to fill out data in case of missing information.

In EU practice, several factors are included in the determination of an appropriate analogue country. The Commission and the Council have to take into

151. *Korea – Certain Paper*, WT/DS312/R, report of the Panel on 28 Oct. 2005, para. 7.161.

account convincing suggestions of appropriate countries by the Chinese producers. Again, the WTO legislation is silent, and therefore wide discretion is left to the Commission and the Council in determining an appropriate country. However, the normal value determination must be in accordance with the requirements in Article VI of GATT 1994 and Article 2.1 of the ADA. Therefore, the EU authorities must ensure that the normal value is based on a comparable price in the ordinary course of trade of the like product destined for consumption in the analogue country. The EU may violate WTO law if the products in the analogue country have qualitative differences of such nature that they are not like the products being exported from China.

Another problem occurs when some Chinese producers are granted market economy treatment while others are under the non-market treatment. It seems unreasonable to use prices from an analogue country if those prices are higher than the prices from the Chinese producers with market economy treatment, as the dumping margin then will increase. It is, however, not clear under WTO law whether such situations must be resolved by using the Chinese prices, which are much closer to reflecting the costs and prices in China, than for example a producer in the US. This particular problem would not occur if the *industry as a whole* was subject to market or non-market treatment, which – as just stated – could be the right interpretation of the WTO text.

If this reading of Article 15 is not correct, and the investigating authorities may use the same approach as the EU institutions, making the necessary amendments in the WTO legislation to ensure that the prices come from Chinese producers with a market economy treatment must be strongly advised. Thereby, the normal value for the Chinese producers that do not get a market economy treatment will reflect Chinese prices and costs – instead of prices and costs in, for example, Mexico, the US or Brazil. The purpose must be to find a normal value as close to a market situation in China as possible. Therefore, if some Chinese producers get market economy treatment, their costs and prices must reflect such a Chinese market.

The dumping margin for those producers with market economy treatment is made individually in line with the method described in Chapter 6. See more in Chapter 6 about the conformity with WTO law.

Chinese producers that are under the non-market treatment will as a general rule be under a countrywide dumping duty, but they may apply for individual treatment using their own export prices compared with the normal value from the analogue country. The EU authorities grant individual treatment if several conditions are fulfilled. It often occurs that such a request is rejected, and the dumping margin for the particular producer is the countrywide margin. Under WTO law, general dumping margins are only calculated if there is a close association between producers. In the situation with China, the question is instead whether the relationship between the producers under State influence is close enough to regard the producers as related. If the Commission and the Council can demonstrate such a connection, for example if the Chinese State is able to determine the price setting or the supply volume for the group of producers, the EU practice may not be a violation of WTO law.

Chapter 8
Final Thoughts

In the preceding chapters, the aim has been to examine whether EU legislation on dumping and EU practice on dumping towards mainly Asian countries are in conformity with WTO law. The overall picture from those chapters is that the EU violates WTO law in several areas: the EU has both a global and a type-to-type based 5% test concerning low volume sales; the EU rejects *all* domestic sales when only 10% of the sales are equal to or above costs; the EU uses *other producers*' price and cost data for the construction of the normal value; the EU makes individual market economy examinations of Chinese producers, etc.

Thus, the findings in this book to some extent support the claims made in the literature that the EU is violating WTO law. However, there are also several areas where the EU acts in conformity with WTO law. Furthermore, it must be noted that the EU seems to bring its illegal practice into conformity with WTO law when a ruling by a Panel or Appellate Body is against EU practice. For example, the illegal zeroing practice has now been changed to conform with WTO law. That goes both for the zeroing practice and for making statements when the weighted-average-to-transaction method is applied.

The reason for looking into the question of EU conformity with WTO law is the frequent use of the anti-dumping instrument by the EU authorities, in particular targeted at Asian countries. The imposition of anti-dumping duties is a trade barrier to the import of foreign products, and the WTO framework dealing with anti-dumping is an exception to the general aim of the WTO to remove trade barriers. However, such trade barriers might be justified when the exporting producer eliminates the competitors in the importing country and thereafter raises the price. Predatory pricing leads to welfare losses. In addition, from a political perspective there might be an interest in avoiding unemployment if inefficient industries are ousted. On the other hand, the protection of inefficient industries might harm consumers, importers and the producers in the exporting countries.

The EU violations of WTO law lead to *legal uncertainty*. The exporting producer cannot rely solely on WTO law, as the exporting producer cannot challenge the EU measures in the WTO system, but needs the exporting State to bring the EU before the DSB. Nor can the exporting producer expect the application of WTO law in the EU system – or at least only to some extent – as there are several unclear aspects of the application of WTO anti-dumping law in the EU system. The EU violations may then not be challenged under WTO law. The exporting producers cannot be certain of the exact price paid by the importer in advance, as the importer might – besides the actual price demanded by the exporting producer – consider an anti-dumping duty that is based on an arbitrary dumping determination. That might affect both the price setting and the products demanded by the importer. The legal uncertainty then creates a trade barrier.

Legal uncertainty for the exporting producers/importers is a result of the violation of WTO law by the EU authorities. However, merely looking at the EU approach to anti-dumping seems insufficient. Legal uncertainty is also a result of the WTO anti-dumping framework itself. WTO anti-dumping law can be criticized for lack of predictability and for not being able to work sufficiently for developing and least developed countries. The WTO anti-dumping framework is an obstacle to trade in itself, and it leads to legal uncertainty for the exporting producers/importers.

By looking at the legal definition of dumping under WTO law, it is not sufficient to define dumping just as an export price lower than the domestic price in the exporting country. The legal definition of dumping is the setting of an export price lower than the normal value. The normal value consists of 4 elements:

(1) comparable price;
(2) ordinary course of trade;
(3) like product; and
(4) being destined for consumption in the exporting country.

If one looks at the *normal value*, the concept is based on several unclear elements that affect the dumping determination. Domestic sales which are not *comparable* with the export sales, and which cannot be adjusted to reach comparability with the export sales, must be disregarded. The problem here lies in the degree of comparability. What are the conditions to have two sales – export and domestic – comparable? It follows indirectly from the WTO provisions that domestic unrepresentative sales and domestic sales on a market with a particular situation are not comparable with the export sale. Looking at the condition about the representative sale, the WTO rules seem clear enough. That condition under WTO law should not lead to any uncertainty for the user of anti-dumping law, although the EU performs the two-test determination, which clearly violates WTO law. The second condition about particular market is not clear. What is a market with a particular situation? The term 'market' is not defined anywhere under WTO law. Using the 'particular market situation' as basis for disregarding the domestic sales must imply a difference between a 'market' and a 'market with the particular situation'. That difference is not easily predictable for the exporting producer/importer, as 'market' is not defined. The exporting producer/importer can only rely on a statement from GATT Panel practice, as there must be a difference in comparability between the domestic sales and export sales in order to use the 'particular market situation' as basis for disregarding the domestic sales. The term 'market' is also a major concept concerning anti-dumping investigations towards China and Vietnam, since both countries are regarded as transition economies and left with the bilateral or regional agreements whether being granted market economy status or not. Now, the EU anti-dumping treatment of Vietnam is not examined in this book due to Vietnam's late entry to the WTO, but the problem is the same for Vietnam as for China. What is a market economy?

The *ordinary course of trade* condition also lacks a clear definition. What are the elements used to determine that a sale is ordinary? A few examples are found in WTO law. In the ADA, below-cost sales may be seen as outside the ordinary course of trade. Furthermore, the Appellate Body has come up with some guidelines. A sale is ordinary if it is a 'normal' transaction. Sales between associated parties are less likely to be in the ordinary course of trade than sales between non-associated parties. Nevertheless, the investigating authorities are left with wide discretion to determine whether a transaction is an ordinary sale or not. The exporting producer is left with little chance to predict whether sales to domestic purchasers are ordinary, in particular sales to an associated party. The EU appears to leave sales between associated parties out from the investigation *per se*, although reservations must be made to this statement due to the lack of information in the EU Regulations. Furthermore, the ordinary course of trade condition has been used by the EU authorities to disregard subsidized sales that would have been more appropriate to categorize and discuss under the particular market situation condition. WTO law should have a clear definition of ordinary course of trade by writing ordinary course of trade criteria into the ADA. *Destined for consumption in the exporting country* is also a concept without clear guidelines. As seen in this book, the condition has not led to many difficulties in EU practice, although in *Polyester Stable Fibres I*, local export sales were regarded as export in violation of WTO law. However, the term 'consumption' is still an unclear concept under WTO law, which leads to some uncertainty. The concept of *like product* is the only normal value factor defined under WTO law.

The construction of the normal value – third country prices or costs, SAG and profits – is also a source of some uncertainty. The construction of domestic prices is, *ceteris paribus*, only an estimated value of how the domestic price would be or is in reality. In addition, the normal value determination for most Chinese exporting producers is based on prices from analogue countries, the dumping margin being impossible to predict for the Chinese exporting producers and the EU importers. Attempts should be made to set up criteria for the selection of analogue countries.

In addition to the uncertainty about the concept of normal value, the concept of *export price* is not defined under WTO law. Furthermore, the reasons for departing from the actual export price due to association or compensatory agreements are to a large extent left to the discretion of the investigating authorities. It must be stressed here, in line with the argument made by Wenxi Li, that the normal value and the export price are not symmetrically determined. This leaves the dumping determinations biased. For instance, the export price determination does not have a 5% low volume test like the normal value determination. Furthermore, the alternatives to normal value are different than those to the export price. Such asymmetrical approaches will reduce the objectivity in the dumping determination and provide the investigating authorities with wider flexibility to determine dumping.[1]

Finally, the *comparison* between the normal value and export price revealed the two different approaches by Panels and Appellate Body concerning 'zeroing'. Such different interpretations of the WTO text indicate that the text is simply not clear enough; this is just another element of uncertainty in WTO law on dumping determination. Apparently, the zeroing issues are debated at the Doha-negotiations in order to clarify the WTO rules.[2]

It is important to note that the uncertainties described here are not only affecting the Asian exporting producers of products into the EU and the EU importers of Asian products. The EU is far from the only WTO Member using the anti-dumping instrument, and the EU is not the only WTO Member extending the application of the anti-dumping instrument beyond the limits of WTO law. The use of the anti-dumping instrument is a worldwide phenomenon. Some Asian countries are heavy users of anti-dumping. In June 2007, China had 103 measures in force compared to only 88 in 2006. Yet, there has been a decline in anti-dumping cases initiated by the Chinese authorities, from 16 in 2006 to 11 in 2007. India, on the other hand, initiated 27 cases in 2007, but only 11 in 2006. However, the last number does not convey the full picture of the Indian application of anti-dumping, as the Indian authorities did not report its anti-dumping activities in the period from 1 January, 2006 to 20 June, 2006. By June 2007, 179 anti-dumping measures were in force in India, but in 2006 the numbers of measures in force were not reported. The EU initiated 18 anti-dumping investigations in 2007, which is less than the 25 initiated in 2006, and 149 measures were in force on June 2007, which is also less than the 154 in force on June 2006.[3] The numbers show that India is a more frequent user of anti-dumping than the EU.

It is not the aim here to come up with a determination of whether the use of the anti-dumping instrument is decreasing or increasing worldwide. What is clear from those numbers is that the anti-dumping instrument is being heavily used, also by Asian countries. The book does not examine whether other countries are violating WTO law, but, as seen from several of the reports by Panels and Appellate Body, anti-dumping law is often being violated by other countries as well, the US in particular. In addition, Asian countries have been violating WTO law, as for instance seen in *Thailand – H-Beams* and *Korea – Certain Paper*.[4] Besides

1. See Wenxi Li, *Anti-dumping Law of the WTO/GATT and EC – Gradual Evolution of Anti-dumping Law in Global Economic Integration* (Lund: Lund University, 2001), 150 et seq.
2. See Art. 2.4.3 of the Draft Consolidated Chair Texts of the AD and SCM Agreements, TN/RL/W/213 of 30 Nov. 2007.
3. Compare the Report of the Committee of Anti-dumping Practices, G/L/830, of 26 Oct. 2007 with the Report of the Committee of Anti-dumping Practices, G/L/791, of 27 Oct. 2006.
4. *Thailand – H-Beams*, WT/DS122, and *Korea – Certain Paper*, WT/DS312.

those cases, India and the Philippines have been brought before the DSB. In *India – Anti-dumping Measure on Batteries from Bangladesh*, India and Bangladesh reached a satisfactory solution between them.[5] In *India – Anti-dumping Measures on Imports of Certain Products from the European Communities*, *India – Anti-dumping Measures on Certain Products from the Separate Customs Territory of Taiwan, Penghu, Kinmen and Matsu*, and *Philippines – Anti-dumping Measures Regarding Polypropylene Resins from Korea*, no Panels were established and no solutions were reported to the DSB. It is not clear whether the request for consultation is just a strategic means in trade negotiations.[6]

The uncertainties described here are worldwide, and they may affect *all* exporting producers and importers on a worldwide basis. It is here important to bear in mind that unlike competition law, which addresses specific uncompetitive behaviour by specific companies that end up being fined, anti-dumping is directed at a specifically defined product from a specific country. That means *all* producers of that product from the particular country are under investigation, and *all* may be imposed with an anti-dumping duty. Even though the duty is concretely determined for each producer, and some producers may not even be imposed such duties if their products are not found to be dumped, the discretionary room for the investigating authorities and political considerations for the importing country make it uncertain beforehand for the producer to predict whether his product will be imposed a duty or not.

The consequences of the legal uncertainty may be particularly heavy on those exporting producers who base their income on the export, for instance those with only a limited domestic sale. Such producers may end up bankrupt because the dumping determination has not been predictable. The producers have not been able to set an export price in advance that would not be considered as dumped, or the anti-dumping duty might reduce the export to a degree where the exporting producer is losing money by the production. Workers from such companies might lose their jobs. In developing and least developed countries, where the social security is not well developed, the result might be disastrous, as such workers might end up with no income at all and no other options of finding another job. In the worst cases, the only alternative is prostitution or the sale of children for child labour or human trafficking.[7] Article 15 of the ADA, which deals with anti-dumping measures towards developing countries, states that special regard must be given to developing countries when a developed country is considering the use of anti-dumping duty towards the developing country. Yet the WTO does not provide for any

5. See *India – Anti-dumping Measure on Batteries from Bangladesh*, WT/DS306.
6. See *India – Anti-dumping Measures on Imports of Certain Products from the European Communities*, WT/DS304 and *India – Anti-dumping Measures on Certain Products from the Separate Customs Territory of Taiwan, Penghu, Kinmen and Matsu*, WT/DS318, and *Philippines – Anti-dumping Measures Regarding Polypropylene Resins from Korea*, WT/DS215.
7. See C. Barton, M. Khor, S. Narain & V. Tauli-Corpuz, *Civil Society Perspectives on the Millennium Development Goals* (New York: United Nations Development Programme, Bureau for Resources and Strategic Partnerships, 2005), 6.

guidelines about those special considerations. Furthermore, WTO does not provide a definition of a developing country – only least developed countries are defined with regard to the definition provided by the UN.[8]

Besides affecting the exporting producer and the importers, the legal uncertainty has an impact on the State level. Legal uncertainty makes room for political manoeuvres to impose anti-dumping duties in cases where the actual dumping is hard to find. However, the legal uncertainties and the wide discretionary power to the investigating authorities provide the different WTO Members with an instrument that can serve as a political strategic tool towards other WTO Members. The threat of imposing anti-dumping duties on products from another WTO Member in situations where the actual dumping is hard to see might be used towards the other WTO Member in international negotiations, or as an instrument to counter issues over trade, threats of disputes by the other WTO Member or other related situations. For example, the threat of anti-dumping duties can be used to put pressure on other WTO Members, encouraging them to improve in the field of human rights, environmental issues, etc. An example already mentioned in this book is the EU position towards China concerning the Chinese request for market economy status. One condition for granting China market economy status is that the enforcement of intellectual property rights is being strengthened in China, and this will apparently reduce the import of pirated products entering at the EU border. Pirated products are a major problem for the EU. The WTO anti-dumping rules concerning China provide the other WTO Members, who have not granted China market economy status, with a tool to put pressure on China in other fields.

Naturally, it is important to strike a balance between a free trade market and the protection of the importing markets. Within the EU there is a political interest in keeping EU producers able to manufacture and sell their products on both the EU market and the global market, thereby keeping the wheels running and EU citizens employed. Being ousted by cheaper Asian products could lead to unemployment and economic instability in the EU region. From that perspective, the use of anti-dumping measures seems an important instrument to protect such industries. However, the losers are instead the EU importers and the EU consumers, and it is important to weigh those interests against one another, also taking into account the economic and social situation in the exporting countries. The world is becoming smaller with the tide of globalization, and the EU is depending on the foreign markets as well.

With present-day eyes focused on globalization and the global exchange of products, the WTO anti-dumping framework seems to have another problem concerning legal uncertainty. It seems that the WTO anti-dumping instrument is not working sufficiently well for developing and least developed countries. The anti-dumping instrument lays down the rules allowing the use of anti-dumping duties. At the same time, the rules are meant to protect exporting countries from illegal anti-dumping duties. Developing and least developed countries are

---

8. <www.wto.org/english/thewto_e/whatis_e/tif_e/org7_e.htm>.

particularly reluctant to use the DSB in situations where a developed country is using illegal anti-dumping duties, with some exceptions, for instance, India and Brazil. The book has pointed out areas where the EU is violating WTO law; the EU is still not being brought before the DSB. Naturally, the political considerations may have an impact in such situations. Using the DSB before important political negotiations with the EU might not be a good signal to convey. There may be higher economic considerations at stake.

The anti-dumping instrument does not seem sufficient in dealing with the opposite situations, either – situations where the EU producers are dumping the prices in developing and least developed countries. The EU subsidies on export agricultural products to developing and least developed countries pose an example hereof; the export prices are being dumped. Apparently, the export subsidies on agricultural products are being dealt with in the present Doha negotiations. Under the present rules, export subsidies on agricultural products are not prohibited. However, the dumped prices can be targeted by the importing countries. The question is, then, why the EU agricultural products are not being imposed with anti-dumping duties. Again, there may be higher considerations at stake. The aid provided by the EU countries to some importing countries could come at the risk of the imposition of anti-dumping duties towards the dumped agricultural products. You do not bite the hand that feeds you. Furthermore, the lack of legal education and capacity in some countries makes it problematic to deal with such cases. The result, however, is that the farmers in the importing countries are left bankrupt, and the production in those countries may be injured badly.[9]

The haziness surrounding the present legal framework on dumping determinations leads to the question of amending the existing WTO rules. Legal certainty could be improved for the exporting producers and importers in the global market. In the anti-dumping field, this author would welcome a more appropriate dumping standard based on objective and predictable factors with less national discretion, or perhaps an international standard of competition rules only targeting those exporting producers with predatory behaviour. Thereby, the WTO's aim of reducing trade barriers seems more likely be achieved.

Another way to overcome the legal uncertainty might be the use of bilateral or regional agreements on anti-dumping. The EU itself can serve as an example, as the EU Members may not impose anti-dumping duties on goods coming from another EU country. Other regional agreements like *North American Free Trade Agreement* (NAFTA), *Common Market for Eastern and Southern Africa* (COMESA), *Andean Community* and *Economic Community of West African States* (ECOWAS) are dealing with anti-dumping – although not prohibiting the use of

9. See S. Dehlsten, 'Key Policy Coherence Issues in Agriculture and Migration' Room Document 4 given at The Institutional Approaches to Policy Coherence for Development OECD Policy Workshop (OECD, 2004); C. Godfrey, 'Stop the Dumping! – How EU Agricultural Subsidies are Damaging Livelihoods in the Developing World', *Oxfam Briefing Paper No. 31* (Washington: Oxfam International, 2002); P. Goodison, 'EU trade Policy & the Future of Africa's Trade Relationship with the EU', *Review of African Political Economy* 34 (112) (2007): 248.

anti-dumping between the Members as seen in the EU. Here it is interesting to note that the Andean Community has a neutral Board to investigate dumping and injury.[10] In the case with ECOWAS, dumping is prohibited, and if dumping allegedly occurs, the importing Member State may appeal to the ECOWAS Council to resolve the matter.[11] By using neutral organs to determine dumping, the arbitrary dumping determinations might be reduced.

The changes in the anti-dumping field must come from the WTO Members themselves in the WTO negotiations, like Doha, and from the anti-dumping approach taken by the WTO Members in their legislation and practice. If the EU is interested in taking part in increasing legal certainty in the anti-dumping field, a change in EU legislation on dumping and a change in practice by the Commission, the Council and the EC courts on the WTO-violating points could, as suggested in this book, be a place to start.

10. ANDEAN Community comprises Bolivia, Columbia, Ecuador and Peru. See *Rules for preventing or correcting distortions in competition caused by dumping or subsidy practices*, Decision 283.
11. ECOWAS is the Economic Community of West African States comprising of Benin, Burkina Faso, Cape Verde, Côte d'Ivoire, Gambia, Ghana, Guinea, Guinea-Bissau, Liberia, Mali, Niger, Nigeria, Senegal, Sierra Leone and Togo. *See* Economic Community of West African States, Revised Treaty, Art. 42.

Abbreviations

ADA	WTO Anti-dumping Agreement
AJIL	*American Journal of International Law*
ASEAN	Association of South East Asian Nations
CNY	Chinese Yuan Renmibi
DCD	Dirección de Competencia Desleal (Argentinean investigating authority)
DOC	See USDOC
DSB	Dispute Settlement Body
DSU	Dispute Settlement Understanding
EC	European Community
ECR	European Court Report
EIOP	European Integration Online Papers
ELJ	*European Law Journal*
EU	European Union
EUR	Euro
GATT	General Agreement on Tariffs and Trade
IA	Investigating Authority
IMF	International Monetary Fond
INR	Indian Rupee
ITO	International Trade Organization
JFC	*Journal of Financial Crime*
JITL	*Journal of International Trade Law*
JWT	*Journal of World Trade*
KRW	South Korean Won
MET	Market Economy Treatment
MOFTEC	Ministry of Foreign Trade and Economic Cooperation
OEM	Original Equipment Producers

OJ	Official Journal of the European Union
POI	Period of Investigation
POSAM	Pohang Steel America Corporation
POSCO	Pohang Iron and Steel Company
PRC	People's Republic of China
SAG	Sales, administrative and general costs
SAJE	*South African Journal of Economy*
SEJ	*Southern Economic Journal*
USDOC	United States Department of Commerce
WE	World Economy
WTO	World Trade Organization
WTR	World Trade Review

Appendix I
Article VI of GATT 1994

Article VI

Anti-dumping and Countervailing Duties

(1) The contracting parties recognize that dumping, by which products of one country are introduced into the commerce of another country at less than the normal value of the products, is to be condemned if it causes or threatens material injury to an established industry in the territory of a contracting party or materially retards the establishment of a domestic industry. For the purposes of this Article, a product is to be considered as being introduced into the commerce of an importing country at less than its normal value, if the price of the product exported from one country to another (*a*) is less than the comparable price, in the ordinary course of trade, for the like product when destined for consumption in the exporting country, or, (*b*) in the absence of such domestic price, is less than either:

(i) the highest comparable price for the like product for export to any third country in the ordinary course of trade; or
(ii) the cost of production of the product in the country of origin plus a reasonable addition for selling cost and profit.

Due allowance shall be made in each case for differences in conditions and terms of sale, for differences in taxation, and for other differences affecting price comparability.*

(2) In order to offset or prevent dumping, a contracting party may levy on any dumped product an anti-dumping duty not greater in amount than the margin of dumping in respect of such product. For the purposes of this Article, the margin of dumping is the price difference determined in accordance with the provisions of paragraph 1.*

(3) No countervailing duty shall be levied on any product of the territory of any contracting party imported into the territory of another contracting party in excess of an amount equal to the estimated bounty or subsidy determined to have been granted, directly or indirectly, on the manufacture, production or export of such product in the country of origin or exportation, including any special subsidy to the transportation of a particular product. The term 'countervailing duty' shall be understood to mean a special duty levied for the purpose of offsetting any bounty or subsidy bestowed, directly, or indirectly, upon the manufacture, production or export of any merchandise.*

(4) No product of the territory of any contracting party imported into the territory of any other contracting party shall be subject to anti-dumping or countervailing duty by reason of the exemption of such product from duties or taxes borne by the like product when destined for consumption in the country of origin or exportation, or by reason of the refund of such duties or taxes.

(5) No product of the territory of any contracting party imported into the territory of any other contracting party shall be subject to both anti-dumping and countervailing duties to compensate for the same situation of dumping or export subsidization.

(6) (*a*) No contracting party shall levy any anti-dumping or countervailing duty on the importation of any product of the territory of another contracting party unless it determines that the effect of the dumping or subsidization, as the case may be, is such as to cause or threaten material injury to an established domestic industry, or is such as to retard materially the establishment of a domestic industry.

(*b*) The CONTRACTING PARTIES may waive the requirement of subparagraph (*a*) of this paragraph so as to permit a contracting party to levy an anti-dumping or countervailing duty on the importation of any product for the purpose of offsetting dumping or subsidization which causes or threatens material injury to an industry in the territory of another contracting party exporting the product concerned to the territory of the importing contracting party. The CONTRACTING PARTIES shall waive the requirements of subparagraph (*a*) of this paragraph, so as to permit the levying of a countervailing duty, in cases in which they find that a subsidy is causing or threatening material injury to an industry in the territory of another contracting party exporting the product concerned to the territory of the importing contracting party.*

(*c*) In exceptional circumstances, however, where delay might cause damage which would be difficult to repair, a contracting party may levy a countervailing duty for the purpose referred to in subparagraph (*b*) of this paragraph without the prior approval of the CONTRACTING PARTIES; *Provided* that such action shall be reported immediately to the CONTRACTING PARTIES and that the countervailing duty shall be withdrawn promptly if the CONTRACTING PARTIES disapprove.

(7) A system for the stabilization of the domestic price or of the return to domestic producers of a primary commodity, independently of the movements of export prices, which results at times in the sale of the commodity for export at a price lower than the comparable price charged for the like commodity to buyers in

the domestic market, shall be presumed not to result in material injury within the meaning of paragraph 6 if it is determined by consultation among the contracting parties substantially interested in the commodity concerned that: (*a*) the system has also resulted in the sale of the commodity for export at a price higher than the comparable price charged for the like commodity to buyers in the domestic market, and (*b*) the system is so operated, either because of the effective regulation of production, or otherwise, as not to stimulate exports unduly or otherwise seriously prejudice the interests of other contracting parties.

*** Note Ad Article VI**

Paragraph 1

(1) Hidden dumping by associated houses (that is, the sale by an importer at a price below that corresponding to the price invoiced by an exporter with whom the importer is associated, and also below the price in the exporting country) constitutes a form of price dumping with respect to which the margin of dumping may be calculated on the basis of the price at which the goods are resold by the importer.

(2) It is recognized that, in the case of imports from a country which has a complete or substantially complete monopoly of its trade and where all domestic prices are fixed by the State, special difficulties may exist in determining price comparability for the purposes of paragraph 1, and in such cases importing contracting parties may find it necessary to take into account the possibility that a strict comparison with domestic prices in such a country may not always be appropriate.

Paragraphs 2 and 3

As in many other cases in customs administration, a contracting party may require reasonable security (bond or cash deposit) for the payment of anti-dumping or countervailing duty pending final determination of the facts in any case of suspected dumping or subsidization.

Appendix II

Agreement on Implementation of Article VI of GATT 1994 (ADA)

Members hereby *agree* as follows:

PART I

Article 1

Principles

An anti-dumping measure shall be applied only under the circumstances provided for in Article VI of GATT 1994 and pursuant to investigations initiated[1] and conducted in accordance with the provisions of this Agreement. The following provisions govern the application of Article VI of GATT 1994 in so far as action is taken under anti-dumping legislation or regulations.

Article 2

Determination of Dumping

2.1 For the purpose of this Agreement, a product is to be considered as being dumped, i.e., introduced into the commerce of another country at less than its normal value, if the export price of the product exported from one country to

1. The term 'initiated' as used in this Agreement means the procedural action by which a Member formally commences an investigation as provided in Art. 5.

another is less than the comparable price, in the ordinary course of trade, for the like product when destined for consumption in the exporting country.

2.2 When there are no sales of the like product in the ordinary course of trade in the domestic market of the exporting country or when, because of the particular market situation or the low volume of the sales in the domestic market of the exporting country,[2] such sales do not permit a proper comparison, the margin of dumping shall be determined by comparison with a comparable price of the like product when exported to an appropriate third country, provided that this price is representative, or with the cost of production in the country of origin plus a reasonable amount for administrative, selling and general costs and for profits.

2.2.1 Sales of the like product in the domestic market of the exporting country or sales to a third country at prices below per unit (fixed and variable) costs of production plus administrative, selling and general costs may be treated as not being in the ordinary course of trade by reason of price and may be disregarded in determining normal value only if the authorities[3] determine that such sales are made within an extended period of time[4] in substantial quantities[5] and are at prices which do not provide for the recovery of all costs within a reasonable period of time. If prices which are below per unit costs at the time of sale are above weighted average per unit costs for the period of investigation, such prices shall be considered to provide for recovery of costs within a reasonable period of time.

2.2.1.1 For the purpose of paragraph 2, costs shall normally be calculated on the basis of records kept by the exporter or producer under investigation, provided that such records are in accordance with the generally accepted accounting principles of the exporting country and reasonably reflect the costs associated with the production and sale of the product under consideration. Authorities shall consider all available evidence on the proper allocation of costs, including that which is made available by the exporter or producer in the course of the investigation provided that such allocations have been historically utilized by the exporter or producer, in particular in relation to establishing appropriate amortization and

2. Sales of the like product destined for consumption in the domestic market of the exporting country shall normally be considered a sufficient quantity for the determination of the normal value if such sales constitute 5% or more of the sales of the product under consideration to the importing Member, provided that a lower ratio should be acceptable where the evidence demonstrates that domestic sales at such lower ratio are nonetheless of sufficient magnitude to provide for a proper comparison.
3. When in this Agreement the term 'authorities' is used, it shall be interpreted as meaning authorities at an appropriate senior level.
4. The extended period of time should normally be one year but shall in no case be less than six months.
5. Sales below per unit costs are made in substantial quantities when the authorities establish that the weighted average selling price of the transactions under consideration for the determination of the normal value is below the weighted average per unit costs, or that the volume of sales below per unit costs represents not less than 20% of the volume sold in transactions under consideration for the determination of the normal value.

depreciation periods and allowances for capital expenditures and other development costs. Unless already reflected in the cost allocations under this subparagraph, costs shall be adjusted appropriately for those non-recurring items of cost which benefit future and/or current production, or for circumstances in which costs during the period of investigation are affected by start-up operations.[6]

2.2.2 For the purpose of paragraph 2, the amounts for administrative, selling and general costs and for profits shall be based on actual data pertaining to production and sales in the ordinary course of trade of the like product by the exporter or producer under investigation. When such amounts cannot be determined on this basis, the amounts may be determined on the basis of:

(i) the actual amounts incurred and realized by the exporter or producer in question in respect of production and sales in the domestic market of the country of origin of the same general category of products;
(ii) the weighted average of the actual amounts incurred and realized by other exporters or producers subject to investigation in respect of production and sales of the like product in the domestic market of the country of origin;
(iii) any other reasonable method, provided that the amount for profit so established shall not exceed the profit normally realized by other exporters or producers on sales of products of the same general category in the domestic market of the country of origin.

2.3 In cases where there is no export price or where it appears to the authorities concerned that the export price is unreliable because of association or a compensatory arrangement between the exporter and the importer or a third party, the export price may be constructed on the basis of the price at which the imported products are first resold to an independent buyer, or if the products are not resold to an independent buyer, or not resold in the condition as imported, on such reasonable basis as the authorities may determine.

2.4 A fair comparison shall be made between the export price and the normal value. This comparison shall be made at the same level of trade, normally at the ex-factory level, and in respect of sales made at as nearly as possible the same time. Due allowance shall be made in each case, on its merits, for differences which affect price comparability, including differences in conditions and terms of sale, taxation, levels of trade, quantities, physical characteristics, and any other differences which are also demonstrated to affect price comparability.[7] In the cases referred to in paragraph 3, allowances for costs, including duties and taxes, incurred between importation and resale, and for profits accruing, should also

6. The adjustment made for start-up operations shall reflect the costs at the end of the start-up period or, if that period extends beyond the period of investigation, the most recent costs which can reasonably be taken into account by the authorities during the investigation.
7. It is understood that some of the above factors may overlap, and authorities shall ensure that they do not duplicate adjustments that have been already made under this provision.

be made. If in these cases price comparability has been affected, the authorities shall establish the normal value at a level of trade equivalent to the level of trade of the constructed export price, or shall make due allowance as warranted under this paragraph. The authorities shall indicate to the parties in question what information is necessary to ensure a fair comparison and shall not impose an unreasonable burden of proof on those parties.

2.4.1 When the comparison under paragraph 4 requires a conversion of currencies, such conversion should be made using the rate of exchange on the date of sale,[8] provided that when a sale of foreign currency on forward markets is directly linked to the export sale involved, the rate of exchange in the forward sale shall be used. Fluctuations in exchange rates shall be ignored and in an investigation the authorities shall allow exporters at least sixty days to have adjusted their export prices to reflect sustained movements in exchange rates during the period of investigation.

2.4.2 Subject to the provisions governing fair comparison in paragraph 4, the existence of margins of dumping during the investigation phase shall normally be established on the basis of a comparison of a weighted average normal value with a weighted average of prices of all comparable export transactions or by a comparison of normal value and export prices on a transaction-to-transaction basis. A normal value established on a weighted average basis may be compared to prices of individual export transactions if the authorities find a pattern of export prices which differ significantly among different purchasers, regions or time periods, and if an explanation is provided as to why such differences cannot be taken into account appropriately by the use of a weighted average-to-weighted average or transaction-to-transaction comparison.

2.5 In the case where products are not imported directly from the country of origin but are exported to the importing Member from an intermediate country, the price at which the products are sold from the country of export to the importing Member shall normally be compared with the comparable price in the country of export. However, comparison may be made with the price in the country of origin, if, for example, the products are merely transshipped through the country of export, or such products are not produced in the country of export, or there is no comparable price for them in the country of export.

2.6 Throughout this Agreement the term 'like product' ('produit similaire') shall be interpreted to mean a product which is identical, i.e., alike in all respects to the product under consideration, or in the absence of such a product, another product which, although not alike in all respects, has characteristics closely resembling those of the product under consideration.

2.7 This Article is without prejudice to the second Supplementary Provision to paragraph 1 of Article VI in Annex I to GATT 1994.

---

8. Normally, the date of sale would be the date of contract, purchase order, order confirmation, or invoice, whichever establishes the material terms of sale.

Article 3

Determination of Injury[9]

3.1 A determination of injury for purposes of Article VI of GATT 1994 shall be based on positive evidence and involve an objective examination of both *(a)* the volume of the dumped imports and the effect of the dumped imports on prices in the domestic market for like products, and *(b)* the consequent impact of these imports on domestic producers of such products.

3.2 With regard to the volume of the dumped imports, the investigating authorities shall consider whether there has been a significant increase in dumped imports, either in absolute terms or relative to production or consumption in the importing Member. With regard to the effect of the dumped imports on prices, the investigating authorities shall consider whether there has been a significant price undercutting by the dumped imports as compared with the price of a like product of the importing Member, or whether the effect of such imports is otherwise to depress prices to a significant degree or prevent price increases, which otherwise would have occurred, to a significant degree. No one or several of these factors can necessarily give decisive guidance.

3.3 Where imports of a product from more than one country are simultaneously subject to anti-dumping investigations, the investigating authorities may cumulatively assess the effects of such imports only if they determine that *(a)* the margin of dumping established in relation to the imports from each country is more than *de minimis* as defined in paragraph 8 of Article 5 and the volume of imports from each country is not negligible and *(b)* a cumulative assessment of the effects of the imports is appropriate in light of the conditions of competition between the imported products and the conditions of competition between the imported products and the like domestic product.

3.4 The examination of the impact of the dumped imports on the domestic industry concerned shall include an evaluation of all relevant economic factors and indices having a bearing on the state of the industry, including actual and potential decline in sales, profits, output, market share, productivity, return on investments, or utilization of capacity; factors affecting domestic prices; the magnitude of the margin of dumping; actual and potential negative effects on cash flow, inventories, employment, wages, growth, ability to raise capital or investments. This list is not exhaustive, nor can one or several of these factors necessarily give decisive guidance.

---

9. Under this Agreement the term 'injury' shall, unless otherwise specified, be taken to mean material injury to a domestic industry, threat of material injury to a domestic industry or material retardation of the establishment of such an industry and shall be interpreted in accordance with the provisions of this Article.

3.5 It must be demonstrated that the dumped imports are, through the effects of dumping, as set forth in paragraphs 2 and 4, causing injury within the meaning of this Agreement. The demonstration of a causal relationship between the dumped imports and the injury to the domestic industry shall be based on an examination of all relevant evidence before the authorities. The authorities shall also examine any known factors other than the dumped imports which at the same time are injuring the domestic industry, and the injuries caused by these other factors must not be attributed to the dumped imports. Factors which may be relevant in this respect include, inter alia, the volume and prices of imports not sold at dumping prices, contraction in demand or changes in the patterns of consumption, trade restrictive practices of and competition between the foreign and domestic producers, developments in technology and the export performance and productivity of the domestic industry.

3.6 The effect of the dumped imports shall be assessed in relation to the domestic production of the like product when available data permit the separate identification of that production on the basis of such criteria as the production process, producers' sales and profits. If such separate identification of that production is not possible, the effects of the dumped imports shall be assessed by the examination of the production of the narrowest group or range of products, which includes the like product, for which the necessary information can be provided.

3.7 A determination of a threat of material injury shall be based on facts and not merely on allegation, conjecture or remote possibility. The change in circumstances which would create a situation in which the dumping would cause injury must be clearly foreseen and imminent.[10] In making a determination regarding the existence of a threat of material injury, the authorities should consider, inter alia, such factors as:

(i) a significant rate of increase of dumped imports into the domestic market indicating the likelihood of substantially increased importation;
(ii) sufficient freely disposable, or an imminent, substantial increase in, capacity of the exporter indicating the likelihood of substantially increased dumped exports to the importing Member's market, taking into account the availability of other export markets to absorb any additional exports;
(iii) whether imports are entering at prices that will have a significant depressing or suppressing effect on domestic prices, and would likely increase demand for further imports; and
(iv) inventories of the product being investigated.

No one of these factors by itself can necessarily give decisive guidance but the totality of the factors considered must lead to the conclusion that further dumped

10. One example, though not an exclusive one, is that there is convincing reason to believe that there will be, in the near future, substantially increased importation of the product at dumped prices.

exports are imminent and that, unless protective action is taken, material injury would occur.

3.8 With respect to cases where injury is threatened by dumped imports, the application of anti-dumping measures shall be considered and decided with special care.

Article 4

Definition of Domestic Industry

4.1 For the purposes of this Agreement, the term 'domestic industry' shall be interpreted as referring to the domestic producers as a whole of the like products or to those of them whose collective output of the products constitutes a major proportion of the total domestic production of those products, except that:

(i) when producers are related[11] to the exporters or importers or are themselves importers of the allegedly dumped product, the term 'domestic industry' may be interpreted as referring to the rest of the producers;

(ii) in exceptional circumstances the territory of a Member may, for the production in question, be divided into two or more competitive markets and the producers within each market may be regarded as a separate industry if *(a)* the producers within such market sell all or almost all of their production of the product in question in that market, and *(b)* the demand in that market is not to any substantial degree supplied by producers of the product in question located elsewhere in the territory. In such circumstances, injury may be found to exist even where a major portion of the total domestic industry is not injured, provided there is a concentration of dumped imports into such an isolated market and provided further that the dumped imports are causing injury to the producers of all or almost all of the production within such market.

4.2 When the domestic industry has been interpreted as referring to the producers in a certain area, i.e., a market as defined in paragraph 1(ii), anti-dumping duties shall be levied[12] only on the products in question consigned for final consumption

---

11. For the purpose of this paragraph, producers shall be deemed to be related to exporters or importers only if *(a)* one of them directly or indirectly controls the other; or *(b)* both of them are directly or indirectly controlled by a third person; or *(c)* together they directly or indirectly control a third person, provided that there are grounds for believing or suspecting that the effect of the relationship is such as to cause the producer concerned to behave differently from non-related producers. For the purpose of this paragraph, one shall be deemed to control another when the former is legally or operationally in a position to exercise restraint or direction over the latter.
12. As used in this Agreement 'levy' shall mean the definitive or final legal assessment or collection of a duty or tax.

to that area. When the constitutional law of the importing Member does not permit the levying of anti-dumping duties on such a basis, the importing Member may levy the anti-dumping duties without limitation only if *(a)* the exporters shall have been given an opportunity to cease exporting at dumped prices to the area concerned or otherwise give assurances pursuant to Article 8 and adequate assurances in this regard have not been promptly given, and *(b)* such duties cannot be levied only on products of specific producers which supply the area in question.

4.3 Where two or more countries have reached under the provisions of paragraph 8(a) of Article XXIV of GATT 1994 such a level of integration that they have the characteristics of a single, unified market, the industry in the entire area of integration shall be taken to be the domestic industry referred to in paragraph 1.

4.4 The provisions of paragraph 6 of Article 3 shall be applicable to this Article.

Article 5

Initiation and Subsequent Investigation

5.1 Except as provided for in paragraph 6, an investigation to determine the existence, degree and effect of any alleged dumping shall be initiated upon a written application by or on behalf of the domestic industry.

5.2 An application under paragraph 1 shall include evidence of *(a)* dumping, *(b)* injury within the meaning of Article VI of GATT 1994 as interpreted by this Agreement and *(c)* a causal link between the dumped imports and the alleged injury. Simple assertion, unsubstantiated by relevant evidence, cannot be considered sufficient to meet the requirements of this paragraph. The application shall contain such information as is reasonably available to the applicant on the following:

(i) the identity of the applicant and a description of the volume and value of the domestic production of the like product by the applicant. Where a written application is made on behalf of the domestic industry, the application shall identify the industry on behalf of which the application is made by a list of all known domestic producers of the like product (or associations of domestic producers of the like product) and, to the extent possible, a description of the volume and value of domestic production of the like product accounted for by such producers;

(ii) a complete description of the allegedly dumped product, the names of the country or countries of origin or export in question, the identity of each known exporter or foreign producer and a list of known persons importing the product in question;

(iii) information on prices at which the product in question is sold when destined for consumption in the domestic markets of the country or countries of origin or export (or, where appropriate, information on the prices at which the product is sold from the country or countries of origin or export to a third country or countries, or on the constructed value of the product) and information on export prices or, where appropriate, on the prices at which the product is first resold to an independent buyer in the territory of the importing Member;

(iv) information on the evolution of the volume of the allegedly dumped imports, the effect of these imports on prices of the like product in the domestic market and the consequent impact of the imports on the domestic industry, as demonstrated by relevant factors and indices having a bearing on the state of the domestic industry, such as those listed in paragraphs 2 and 4 of Article 3.

5.3 The authorities shall examine the accuracy and adequacy of the evidence provided in the application to determine whether there is sufficient evidence to justify the initiation of an investigation.

5.4 An investigation shall not be initiated pursuant to paragraph 1 unless the authorities have determined, on the basis of an examination of the degree of support for, or opposition to, the application expressed[13] by domestic producers of the like product, that the application has been made by or on behalf of the domestic industry.[14] The application shall be considered to have been made 'by or on behalf of the domestic industry' if it is supported by those domestic producers whose collective output constitutes more than 50% of the total production of the like product produced by that portion of the domestic industry expressing either support for or opposition to the application. However, no investigation shall be initiated when domestic producers expressly supporting the application account for less than 25% of total production of the like product produced by the domestic industry.

5.5 The authorities shall avoid, unless a decision has been made to initiate an investigation, any publicizing of the application for the initiation of an investigation. However, after receipt of a properly documented application and before proceeding to initiate an investigation, the authorities shall notify the government of the exporting Member concerned.

5.6 If, in special circumstances, the authorities concerned decide to initiate an investigation without having received a written application by or on behalf of a domestic industry for the initiation of such investigation, they shall proceed only if they have sufficient evidence of dumping, injury and a causal link, as described in paragraph 2, to justify the initiation of an investigation.

---

13. In the case of fragmented industries involving an exceptionally large number of producers, authorities may determine support and opposition by using statistically valid sampling techniques.
14. Members are aware that in the territory of certain Members employees of domestic producers of the like product or representatives of those employees may make or support an application for an investigation under para. 1.

5.7 The evidence of both dumping and injury shall be considered simultaneously *(a)* in the decision whether or not to initiate an investigation, and *(b)* thereafter, during the course of the investigation, starting on a date not later than the earliest date on which in accordance with the provisions of this Agreement provisional measures may be applied.

5.8 An application under paragraph 1 shall be rejected and an investigation shall be terminated promptly as soon as the authorities concerned are satisfied that there is not sufficient evidence of either dumping or of injury to justify proceeding with the case. There shall be immediate termination in cases where the authorities determine that the margin of dumping is *de minimis*, or that the volume of dumped imports, actual or potential, or the injury, is negligible. The margin of dumping shall be considered to be *de minimis* if this margin is less than 2%, expressed as a percentage of the export price. The volume of dumped imports shall normally be regarded as negligible if the volume of dumped imports from a particular country is found to account for less than 3% of imports of the like product in the importing Member, unless countries which individually account for less than 3% of the imports of the like product in the importing Member collectively account for more than 7% of imports of the like product in the importing Member.

5.9 An anti-dumping proceeding shall not hinder the procedures of customs clearance.

5.10 Investigations shall, except in special circumstances, be concluded within one year, and in no case more than eighteen months, after their initiation.

Article 6

6.1 All interested parties in an anti-dumping investigation shall be given notice of the information which the authorities require and ample opportunity to present in writing all evidence which they consider relevant in respect of the investigation in question.

6.1.1 Exporters or foreign producers receiving questionnaires used in an anti-dumping investigation shall be given at least thirty days for reply.[15] Due consideration should be given to any request for an extension of the thirty-day period and, upon cause shown, such an extension should be granted whenever practicable.

6.1.2 Subject to the requirement to protect confidential information, evidence presented in writing by one interested party shall be made available promptly to other interested parties participating in the investigation.

15. As a general rule, the time-limit for exporters shall be counted from the date of receipt of the questionnaire, which for this purpose shall be deemed to have been received one week from the date on which it was sent to the respondent or transmitted to the appropriate diplomatic representative of the exporting Member or, in the case of a separate customs territory Member of the WTO, an official representative of the exporting territory.

6.1.3 As soon as an investigation has been initiated, the authorities shall provide the full text of the written application received under paragraph 1 of Article 5 to the known exporters[16] and to the authorities of the exporting Member and shall make it available, upon request, to other interested parties involved. Due regard shall be paid to the requirement for the protection of confidential information, as provided for in paragraph 5.

6.2 Throughout the anti-dumping investigation all interested parties shall have a full opportunity for the defence of their interests. To this end, the authorities shall, on request, provide opportunities for all interested parties to meet those parties with adverse interests, so that opposing views may be presented and rebuttal arguments offered. Provision of such opportunities must take account of the need to preserve confidentiality and of the convenience to the parties. There shall be no obligation on any party to attend a meeting, and failure to do so shall not be prejudicial to that party's case. Interested parties shall also have the right, on justification, to present other information orally.

6.3 Oral information provided under paragraph 2 shall be taken into account by the authorities only in so far as it is subsequently reproduced in writing and made available to other interested parties, as provided for in subparagraph 1.2.

6.4 The authorities shall whenever practicable provide timely opportunities for all interested parties to see all information that is relevant to the presentation of their cases, that is not confidential as defined in paragraph 5, and that is used by the authorities in an anti-dumping investigation, and to prepare presentations on the basis of this information.

6.5 Any information which is by nature confidential (for example, because its disclosure would be of significant competitive advantage to a competitor or because its disclosure would have a significantly adverse effect upon a person supplying the information or upon a person from whom that person acquired the information), or which is provided on a confidential basis by parties to an investigation shall, upon good cause shown, be treated as such by the authorities. Such information shall not be disclosed without specific permission of the party submitting it.[17]

6.5.1 The authorities shall require interested parties providing confidential information to furnish non-confidential summaries thereof. These summaries shall be in sufficient detail to permit a reasonable understanding of the substance of the information submitted in confidence. In exceptional circumstances, such parties may indicate that such information is not susceptible of summary. In such exceptional circumstances, a statement of the reasons why summarization is not possible must be provided.

---

16. It being understood that, where the number of exporters involved is particularly high, the full text of the written application should instead be provided only to the authorities of the exporting Member or to the relevant trade association.
17. Members are aware that in the territory of certain Members disclosure pursuant to a narrowly-drawn protective order may be required.

6.5.2 If the authorities find that a request for confidentiality is not warranted and if the supplier of the information is either unwilling to make the information public or to authorize its disclosure in generalized or summary form, the authorities may disregard such information unless it can be demonstrated to their satisfaction from appropriate sources that the information is correct.[18]

6.6 Except in circumstances provided for in paragraph 8, the authorities shall during the course of an investigation satisfy themselves as to the accuracy of the information supplied by interested parties upon which their findings are based.

6.7 In order to verify information provided or to obtain further details, the authorities may carry out investigations in the territory of other Members as required, provided they obtain the agreement of the firms concerned and notify the representatives of the government of the Member in question, and unless that Member objects to the investigation. The procedures described in Annex I shall apply to investigations carried out in the territory of other Members. Subject to the requirement to protect confidential information, the authorities shall make the results of any such investigations available, or shall provide disclosure thereof pursuant to paragraph 9, to the firms to which they pertain and may make such results available to the applicants.

6.8 In cases in which any interested party refuses access to, or otherwise does not provide, necessary information within a reasonable period or significantly impedes the investigation, preliminary and final determinations, affirmative or negative, may be made on the basis of the facts available. The provisions of Annex II shall be observed in the application of this paragraph.

6.9 The authorities shall, before a final determination is made, inform all interested parties of the essential facts under consideration which form the basis for the decision whether to apply definitive measures. Such disclosure should take place in sufficient time for the parties to defend their interests.

6.10 The authorities shall, as a rule, determine an individual margin of dumping for each known exporter or producer concerned of the product under investigation. In cases where the number of exporters, producers, importers or types of products involved is so large as to make such a determination impracticable, the authorities may limit their examination either to a reasonable number of interested parties or products by using samples which are statistically valid on the basis of information available to the authorities at the time of the selection, or to the largest percentage of the volume of the exports from the country in question which can reasonably be investigated.

6.10.1 Any selection of exporters, producers, importers or types of products made under this paragraph shall preferably be chosen in consultation with and with the consent of the exporters, producers or importers concerned.

18. Members agree that requests for confidentiality should not be arbitrarily rejected.

6.10.2 In cases where the authorities have limited their examination, as provided for in this paragraph, they shall nevertheless determine an individual margin of dumping for any exporter or producer not initially selected who submits the necessary information in time for that information to be considered during the course of the investigation, except where the number of exporters or producers is so large that individual examinations would be unduly burdensome to the authorities and prevent the timely completion of the investigation. Voluntary responses shall not be discouraged.

6.11 For the purposes of this Agreement, 'interested parties' shall include:

(i) an exporter or foreign producer or the importer of a product subject to investigation, or a trade or business association a majority of the members of which are producers, exporters or importers of such product;
(ii) the government of the exporting Member; and
(iii) a producer of the like product in the importing Member or a trade and business association a majority of the members of which produce the like product in the territory of the importing Member.

This list shall not preclude Members from allowing domestic or foreign parties other than those mentioned above to be included as interested parties.

6.12 The authorities shall provide opportunities for industrial users of the product under investigation, and for representative consumer organizations in cases where the product is commonly sold at the retail level, to provide information which is relevant to the investigation regarding dumping, injury and causality.

6.13 The authorities shall take due account of any difficulties experienced by interested parties, in particular small companies, in supplying information requested, and shall provide any assistance practicable.

6.14 The procedures set out above are not intended to prevent the authorities of a Member from proceeding expeditiously with regard to initiating an investigation, reaching preliminary or final determinations, whether affirmative or negative, or from applying provisional or final measures, in accordance with relevant provisions of this Agreement.

Article 7

Provisional Measures

7.1 Provisional measures may be applied only if:

(i) an investigation has been initiated in accordance with the provisions of Article 5, a public notice has been given to that effect and interested parties have been given adequate opportunities to submit information and make comments;

(ii) a preliminary affirmative determination has been made of dumping and consequent injury to a domestic industry; and

(iii) the authorities concerned judge such measures necessary to prevent injury being caused during the investigation.

7.2 Provisional measures may take the form of a provisional duty or, preferably, a security – by cash deposit or bond – equal to the amount of the anti-dumping duty provisionally estimated, being not greater than the provisionally estimated margin of dumping. Withholding of appraisement is an appropriate provisional measure, provided that the normal duty and the estimated amount of the anti-dumping duty be indicated and as long as the withholding of appraisement is subject to the same conditions as other provisional measures.

7.3 Provisional measures shall not be applied sooner than thirty days from the date of initiation of the investigation.

7.4 The application of provisional measures shall be limited to as short a period as possible, not exceeding four months or, on decision of the authorities concerned, upon request by exporters representing a significant percentage of the trade involved, to a period not exceeding six months. When authorities, in the course of an investigation, examine whether a duty lower than the margin of dumping would be sufficient to remove injury, these periods may be six and nine months, respectively.

7.5 The relevant provisions of Article 9 shall be followed in the application of provisional measures.

Article 8

Price Undertakings

8.1 Proceedings may[19] be suspended or terminated without the imposition of provisional measures or anti-dumping duties upon receipt of satisfactory voluntary undertakings from any exporter to revise its prices or to cease exports to the area in question at dumped prices so that the authorities are satisfied that the injurious effect of the dumping is eliminated. Price increases under such undertakings shall not be higher than necessary to eliminate the margin of dumping. It is desirable that the price increases be less than the margin of dumping if such increases would be adequate to remove the injury to the domestic industry.

8.2 Price undertakings shall not be sought or accepted from exporters unless the authorities of the importing Member have made a preliminary affirmative determination of dumping and injury caused by such dumping.

19. The word ‘may’ shall not be interpreted to allow the simultaneous continuation of proceedings with the implementation of price undertakings except as provided in para. 4.

8.3 Undertakings offered need not be accepted if the authorities consider their acceptance impractical, for example, if the number of actual or potential exporters is too great, or for other reasons, including reasons of general policy. Should the case arise and where practicable, the authorities shall provide to the exporter the reasons which have led them to consider acceptance of an undertaking as inappropriate, and shall, to the extent possible, give the exporter an opportunity to make comments thereon.

8.4 If an undertaking is accepted, the investigation of dumping and injury shall nevertheless be completed if the exporter so desires or the authorities so decide. In such a case, if a negative determination of dumping or injury is made, the undertaking shall automatically lapse, except in cases where such a determination is due in large part to the existence of a price undertaking. In such cases, the authorities may require that an undertaking be maintained for a reasonable period consistent with the provisions of this Agreement. In the event that an affirmative determination of dumping and injury is made, the undertaking shall continue consistent with its terms and the provisions of this Agreement.

8.5 Price undertakings may be suggested by the authorities of the importing Member, but no exporter shall be forced to enter into such undertakings. The fact that exporters do not offer such undertakings, or do not accept an invitation to do so, shall in no way prejudice the consideration of the case. However, the authorities are free to determine that a threat of injury is more likely to be realized if the dumped imports continue.

8.6 Authorities of an importing Member may require any exporter from whom an undertaking has been accepted to provide periodically information relevant to the fulfilment of such an undertaking and to permit verification of pertinent data. In case of violation of an undertaking, the authorities of the importing Member may take, under this Agreement in conformity with its provisions, expeditious actions which may constitute immediate application of provisional measures using the best information available. In such cases, definitive duties may be levied in accordance with this Agreement on products entered for consumption not more than ninety days before the application of such provisional measures, except that any such retroactive assessment shall not apply to imports entered before the violation of the undertaking.

Article 9

Imposition and Collection of Anti-dumping Duties

9.1 The decision whether or not to impose an anti-dumping duty in cases where all requirements for the imposition have been fulfilled, and the decision whether the amount of the anti-dumping duty to be imposed shall be the full margin of dumping or less, are decisions to be made by the authorities of the importing Member. It is desirable that the imposition be permissive in the territory of all Members, and that the duty be less than the margin if such lesser duty would be adequate to remove the injury to the domestic industry.

9.2 When an anti-dumping duty is imposed in respect of any product, such anti-dumping duty shall be collected in the appropriate amounts in each case, on a non-discriminatory basis on imports of such product from all sources found to be dumped and causing injury, except as to imports from those sources from which price undertakings under the terms of this Agreement have been accepted. The authorities shall name the supplier or suppliers of the product concerned. If, however, several suppliers from the same country are involved, and it is impracticable to name all these suppliers, the authorities may name the supplying country concerned. If several suppliers from more than one country are involved, the authorities may name either all the suppliers involved, or, if this is impracticable, all the supplying countries involved.

9.3 The amount of the anti-dumping duty shall not exceed the margin of dumping as established under Article 2.

9.3.1 When the amount of the anti-dumping duty is assessed on a retrospective basis, the determination of the final liability for payment of anti-dumping duties shall take place as soon as possible, normally within twelve months, and in no case more than eighteen months, after the date on which a request for a final assessment of the amount of the anti-dumping duty has been made.[20] Any refund shall be made promptly and normally in not more than ninety days following the determination of final liability made pursuant to this sub-paragraph. In any case, where a refund is not made within ninety days, the authorities shall provide an explanation if so requested.

9.3.2 When the amount of the anti-dumping duty is assessed on a prospective basis, provision shall be made for a prompt refund, upon request, of any duty paid in excess of the margin of dumping. A refund of any such duty paid in excess of the actual margin of dumping shall normally take place within twelve months, and in no case more than eighteen months, after the date on which a request for a refund, duly supported by evidence, has been made by an importer of the product subject to the anti-dumping duty. The refund authorized should normally be made within ninety days of the above- noted decision.

9.3.3 In determining whether and to what extent a reimbursement should be made when the export price is constructed in accordance with paragraph 3 of Article 2, authorities should take account of any change in normal value, any change in costs incurred between importation and resale, and any movement in the resale price which is duly reflected in subsequent selling prices, and should calculate the export

20. It is understood that the observance of the time-limits mentioned in this subparagraph and in subpara. 3.2 may not be possible where the product in question is subject to judicial review proceedings.

price with no deduction for the amount of anti-dumping duties paid when conclusive evidence of the above is provided.

9.4 When the authorities have limited their examination in accordance with the second sentence of paragraph 10 of Article 6, any anti-dumping duty applied to imports from exporters or producers not included in the examination shall not exceed:

(i) the weighted average margin of dumping established with respect to the selected exporters or producers or,

(ii) where the liability for payment of anti-dumping duties is calculated on the basis of a prospective normal value, the difference between the weighted average normal value of the selected exporters or producers and the export prices of exporters or producers not individually examined, provided that the authorities shall disregard for the purpose of this paragraph any zero and de minimis margins and margins established under the circumstances referred to in paragraph 8 of Article 6. The authorities shall apply individual duties or normal values to imports from any exporter or producer not included in the examination who has provided the necessary information during the course of the investigation, as provided for in subparagraph 10.2 of Article 6.

9.5 If a product is subject to anti-dumping duties in an importing Member, the authorities shall promptly carry out a review for the purpose of determining individual margins of dumping for any exporters or producers in the exporting country in question who have not exported the product to the importing Member during the period of investigation, provided that these exporters or producers can show that they are not related to any of the exporters or producers in the exporting country who are subject to the anti-dumping duties on the product. Such a review shall be initiated and carried out on an accelerated basis, compared to normal duty assessment and review proceedings in the importing Member. No anti-dumping duties shall be levied on imports from such exporters or producers while the review is being carried out. The authorities may, however, withhold appraisement and/or request guarantees to ensure that, should such a review result in a determination of dumping in respect of such producers or exporters, anti-dumping duties can be levied retroactively to the date of the initiation of the review.

Article 10

Retroactivity

10.1 Provisional measures and anti-dumping duties shall only be applied to products which enter for consumption after the time when the decision taken under paragraph 1 of Article 7 and paragraph 1 of Article 9, respectively, enters into force, subject to the exceptions set out in this Article.

10.2 Where a final determination of injury (but not of a threat thereof or of a material retardation of the establishment of an industry) is made or, in the case of a final determination of a threat of injury, where the effect of the dumped imports would, in the absence of the provisional measures, have led to a determination of injury, anti-dumping duties may be levied retroactively for the period for which provisional measures, if any, have been applied.

10.3 If the definitive anti-dumping duty is higher than the provisional duty paid or payable, or the amount estimated for the purpose of the security, the difference shall not be collected. If the definitive duty is lower than the provisional duty paid or payable, or the amount estimated for the purpose of the security, the difference shall be reimbursed or the duty recalculated, as the case may be.

10.4 Except as provided in paragraph 2, where a determination of threat of injury or material retardation is made (but no injury has yet occurred) a definitive anti-dumping duty may be imposed only from the date of the determination of threat of injury or material retardation, and any cash deposit made during the period of the application of provisional measures shall be refunded and any bonds released in an expeditious manner.

10.5 Where a final determination is negative, any cash deposit made during the period of the application of provisional measures shall be refunded and any bonds released in an expeditious manner.

10.6 A definitive anti-dumping duty may be levied on products which were entered for consumption not more than ninety days prior to the date of application of provisional measures, when the authorities determine for the dumped product in question that:

- (i) there is a history of dumping which caused injury or that the importer was, or should have been, aware that the exporter practises dumping and that such dumping would cause injury, and
- (ii) the injury is caused by massive dumped imports of a product in a relatively short time which in light of the timing and the volume of the dumped imports and other circumstances (such as a rapid build-up of inventories of the imported product) is likely to seriously undermine the remedial effect of the definitive anti-dumping duty to be applied, provided that the importers concerned have been given an opportunity to comment.

10.7 The authorities may, after initiating an investigation, take such measures as the withholding of appraisement or assessment as may be necessary to collect anti-dumping duties retroactively, as provided for in paragraph 6, once they have sufficient evidence that the conditions set forth in that paragraph are satisfied.

10.8 No duties shall be levied retroactively pursuant to paragraph 6 on products entered for consumption prior to the date of initiation of the investigation.

Article 11

Duration and Review of Anti-dumping Duties and Price Undertakings

11.1 An anti-dumping duty shall remain in force only as long as and to the extent necessary to counteract dumping which is causing injury.

11.2 The authorities shall review the need for the continued imposition of the duty, where warranted, on their own initiative or, provided that a reasonable period of time has elapsed since the imposition of the definitive anti-dumping duty, upon request by any interested party which submits positive information substantiating the need for a review.[21] Interested parties shall have the right to request the authorities to examine whether the continued imposition of the duty is necessary to offset dumping, whether the injury would be likely to continue or recur if the duty were removed or varied, or both. If, as a result of the review under this paragraph, the authorities determine that the anti-dumping duty is no longer warranted, it shall be terminated immediately.

11.3 Notwithstanding the provisions of paragraphs 1 and 2, any definitive anti-dumping duty shall be terminated on a date not later than five years from its imposition (or from the date of the most recent review under paragraph 2 if that review has covered both dumping and injury, or under this paragraph), unless the authorities determine, in a review initiated before that date on their own initiative or upon a duly substantiated request made by or on behalf of the domestic industry within a reasonable period of time prior to that date, that the expiry of the duty would be likely to lead to continuation or recurrence of dumping and injury.[22] The duty may remain in force pending the outcome of such a review.

11.4 The provisions of Article 6 regarding evidence and procedure shall apply to any review carried out under this Article. Any such review shall be carried out expeditiously and shall normally be concluded within twelve months of the date of initiation of the review.

11.5 The provisions of this Article shall apply mutatis mutandis to price undertakings accepted under Article 8.

---

21. A determination of final liability for payment of anti-dumping duties, as provided for in para. 3 of Art. 9, does not by itself constitute a review within the meaning of this Article.
22. When the amount of the anti-dumping duty is assessed on a retrospective basis, a finding in the most recent assessment proceeding under subpara. 3.1 of Art. 9 that no duty is to be levied shall not by itself require the authorities to terminate the definitive duty.

Article 12

Public Notice and Explanation of Determinations

12.1 When the authorities are satisfied that there is sufficient evidence to justify the initiation of an anti-dumping investigation pursuant to Article 5, the Member or Members the products of which are subject to such investigation and other interested parties known to the investigating authorities to have an interest therein shall be notified and a public notice shall be given.

12.1.1 A public notice of the initiation of an investigation shall contain, or otherwise make available through a separate report,[23] adequate information on the following:

(i) the name of the exporting country or countries and the product involved;
(ii) the date of initiation of the investigation;
(iii) the basis on which dumping is alleged in the application;
(iv) a summary of the factors on which the allegation of injury is based;
(v) the address to which representations by interested parties should be directed;
(vi) the time-limits allowed to interested parties for making their views known.

12.2 Public notice shall be given of any preliminary or final determination, whether affirmative or negative, of any decision to accept an undertaking pursuant to Article 8, of the termination of such an undertaking, and of the termination of a definitive anti-dumping duty. Each such notice shall set forth, or otherwise make available through a separate report, in sufficient detail the findings and conclusions reached on all issues of fact and law considered material by the investigating authorities. All such notices and reports shall be forwarded to the Member or Members the products of which are subject to such determination or undertaking and to other interested parties known to have an interest therein.

12.2.1 A public notice of the imposition of provisional measures shall set forth, or otherwise make available through a separate report, sufficiently detailed explanations for the preliminary determinations on dumping and injury and shall refer to the matters of fact and law which have led to arguments being accepted or rejected. Such a notice or report shall, due regard being paid to the requirement for the protection of confidential information, contain in particular:

(i) the names of the suppliers, or when this is impracticable, the supplying countries involved;
(ii) a description of the product which is sufficient for customs purposes;

23. Where authorities provide information and explanations under the provisions of this Article in a separate report, they shall ensure that such report is readily available to the public.

(iii) the margins of dumping established and a full explanation of the reasons for the methodology used in the establishment and comparison of the export price and the normal value under Article 2;
(iv) considerations relevant to the injury determination as set out in Article 3;
(v) the main reasons leading to the determination.

12.2.2 A public notice of conclusion or suspension of an investigation in the case of an affirmative determination providing for the imposition of a definitive duty or the acceptance of a price undertaking shall contain, or otherwise make available through a separate report, all relevant information on the matters of fact and law and reasons which have led to the imposition of final measures or the acceptance of a price undertaking, due regard being paid to the requirement for the protection of confidential information. In particular, the notice or report shall contain the information described in subparagraph 2.1, as well as the reasons for the acceptance or rejection of relevant arguments or claims made by the exporters and importers, and the basis for any decision made under subparagraph 10.2 of Article 6.

12.2.3 A public notice of the termination or suspension of an investigation following the acceptance of an undertaking pursuant to Article 8 shall include, or otherwise make available through a separate report, the non-confidential part of this undertaking.

12.3 The provisions of this Article shall apply mutatis mutandis to the initiation and completion of reviews pursuant to Article 11 and to decisions under Article 10 to apply duties retroactively.

Article 13

Judicial Review

Each Member whose national legislation contains provisions on anti-dumping measures shall maintain judicial, arbitral or administrative tribunals or procedures for the purpose, inter alia, of the prompt review of administrative actions relating to final determinations and reviews of determinations within the meaning of Article 11. Such tribunals or procedures shall be independent of the authorities responsible for the determination or review in question.

Article 14

Anti-dumping Action on Behalf of a Third Country

14.1 An application for anti-dumping action on behalf of a third country shall be made by the authorities of the third country requesting action.

14.2 Such an application shall be supported by price information to show that the imports are being dumped and by detailed information to show that the alleged dumping is causing injury to the domestic industry concerned in the third country. The government of the third country shall afford all assistance to the authorities of the importing country to obtain any further information which the latter may require.

14.3 In considering such an application, the authorities of the importing country shall consider the effects of the alleged dumping on the industry concerned as a whole in the third country; that is to say, the injury shall not be assessed in relation only to the effect of the alleged dumping on the industry's exports to the importing country or even on the industry's total exports.

14.4 The decision whether or not to proceed with a case shall rest with the importing country. If the importing country decides that it is prepared to take action, the initiation of the approach to the Council for Trade in Goods seeking its approval for such action shall rest with the importing country.

Article 15

Developing Country Members

It is recognized that special regard must be given by developed country Members to the special situation of developing country Members when considering the application of anti-dumping measures under this Agreement. Possibilities of constructive remedies provided for by this Agreement shall be explored before applying anti-dumping duties where they would affect the essential interests of developing country Members.

PART II

Article 16

Committee on Anti-dumping Practices

16.1 There is hereby established a Committee on Anti-dumping Practices (referred to in this Agreement as the 'Committee') composed of representatives from each of the Members. The Committee shall elect its own Chairman and shall meet not less than twice a year and otherwise as envisaged by relevant provisions of this Agreement at the request of any Member. The Committee shall carry out responsibilities as assigned to it under this Agreement or by the Members and it shall afford Members the opportunity of consulting on any matters relating to the operation of the Agreement or the furtherance of its objectives. The WTO Secretariat shall act as the secretariat to the Committee.

16.2 The Committee may set up subsidiary bodies as appropriate.

16.3 In carrying out their functions, the Committee and any subsidiary bodies may consult with and seek information from any source they deem appropriate. However, before the Committee or a subsidiary body seeks such information from a source within the jurisdiction of a Member, it shall inform the Member involved. It shall obtain the consent of the Member and any firm to be consulted.

16.4 Members shall report without delay to the Committee all preliminary or final anti-dumping actions taken. Such reports shall be available in the Secretariat for inspection by other Members. Members shall also submit, on a semi-annual basis, reports of any anti-dumping actions taken within the preceding six months. The semi-annual reports shall be submitted on an agreed standard form.

16.5 Each Member shall notify the Committee *(a)* which of its authorities are competent to initiate and conduct investigations referred to in Article 5 and *(b)* its domestic procedures governing the initiation and conduct of such investigations.

Article 17

Consultation and Dispute Settlement

17.1 Except as otherwise provided herein, the Dispute Settlement Understanding is applicable to consultations and the settlement of disputes under this Agreement.

17.2 Each Member shall afford sympathetic consideration to, and shall afford adequate opportunity for consultation regarding, representations made by another Member with respect to any matter affecting the operation of this Agreement.

17.3 If any Member considers that any benefit accruing to it, directly or indirectly, under this Agreement is being nullified or impaired, or that the achievement of any objective is being impeded, by another Member or Members, it may, with a view to reaching a mutually satisfactory resolution of the matter, request in writing consultations with the Member or Members in question. Each Member shall afford sympathetic consideration to any request from another Member for consultation.

17.4 If the Member that requested consultations considers that the consultations pursuant to paragraph 3 have failed to achieve a mutually agreed solution, and if final action has been taken by the administering authorities of the importing Member to levy definitive anti-dumping duties or to accept price undertakings, it may refer the matter to the Dispute Settlement Body ('DSB'). When a provisional measure has a significant impact and the Member that requested consultations considers that the measure was taken contrary to the provisions of paragraph 1 of Article 7, that Member may also refer such matter to the DSB.

17.5 The DSB shall, at the request of the complaining party, establish a panel to examine the matter based upon:

(i) a written statement of the Member making the request indicating how a benefit accruing to it, directly or indirectly, under this Agreement has been nullified or impaired, or that the achieving of the objectives of the Agreement is being impeded, and

(ii) the facts made available in conformity with appropriate domestic procedures to the authorities of the importing Member.

17.6 In examining the matter referred to in paragraph 5:

(i) in its assessment of the facts of the matter, the panel shall determine whether the authorities' establishment of the facts was proper and whether their evaluation of those facts was unbiased and objective. If the establishment of the facts was proper and the evaluation was unbiased and objective, even though the panel might have reached a different conclusion, the evaluation shall not be overturned;

(ii) the panel shall interpret the relevant provisions of the Agreement in accordance with customary rules of interpretation of public international law. Where the panel finds that a relevant provision of the Agreement admits of more than one permissible interpretation, the panel shall find the authorities' measure to be in conformity with the Agreement if it rests upon one of those permissible interpretations.

17.7 Confidential information provided to the panel shall not be disclosed without formal authorization from the person, body or authority providing such information. Where such information is requested from the panel but release of such information by the panel is not authorized, a non-confidential summary of the information, authorized by the person, body or authority providing the information, shall be provided.

PART III

Article 18

Final Provisions

18.1 No specific action against dumping of exports from another Member can be taken except in accordance with the provisions of GATT 1994, as interpreted by this Agreement.[24]

---

24. This is not intended to preclude action under other relevant provisions of GATT 1994, as appropriate.

18.2 Reservations may not be entered in respect of any of the provisions of this Agreement without the consent of the other Members.

18.3 Subject to subparagraphs 3.1 and 3.2, the provisions of this Agreement shall apply to investigations, and reviews of existing measures, initiated pursuant to applications which have been made on or after the date of entry into force for a Member of the WTO Agreement.

18.3.1 With respect to the calculation of margins of dumping in refund procedures under paragraph 3 of Article 9, the rules used in the most recent determination or review of dumping shall apply.

18.3.2 For the purposes of paragraph 3 of Article 11, existing anti-dumping measures shall be deemed to be imposed on a date not later than the date of entry into force for a Member of the WTO Agreement, except in cases in which the domestic legislation of a Member in force on that date already included a clause of the type provided for in that paragraph.

18.4 Each Member shall take all necessary steps, of a general or particular character, to ensure, not later than the date of entry into force of the WTO Agreement for it, the conformity of its laws, regulations and administrative procedures with the provisions of this Agreement as they may apply for the Member in question.

18.5 Each Member shall inform the Committee of any changes in its laws and regulations relevant to this Agreement and in the administration of such laws and regulations.

18.6 The Committee shall review annually the implementation and operation of this Agreement taking into account the objectives thereof. The Committee shall inform annually the Council for Trade in Goods of developments during the period covered by such reviews.

18.7 The Annexes to this Agreement constitute an integral part thereof.

Annex I

Procedures for On-the-Spot Investigations Pursuant To Paragraph 7 of Article 6

(1) Upon initiation of an investigation, the authorities of the exporting Member and the firms known to be concerned should be informed of the intention to carry out on-the-spot investigations.

(2) If in exceptional circumstances it is intended to include non-governmental experts in the investigating team, the firms and the authorities of the exporting Member should be so informed. Such non-governmental experts should be subject to effective sanctions for breach of confidentiality requirements.

(3) It should be standard practice to obtain explicit agreement of the firms concerned in the exporting Member before the visit is finally scheduled.

(4) As soon as the agreement of the firms concerned has been obtained, the investigating authorities should notify the authorities of the exporting Member of the names and addresses of the firms to be visited and the dates agreed.

(5) Sufficient advance notice should be given to the firms in question before the visit is made.

(6) Visits to explain the questionnaire should only be made at the request of an exporting firm. Such a visit may only be made if *(a)* the authorities of the importing Member notify the representatives of the Member in question and *(b)* the latter do not object to the visit.

(7) As the main purpose of the on-the-spot investigation is to verify information provided or to obtain further details, it should be carried out after the response to the questionnaire has been received unless the firm agrees to the contrary and the government of the exporting Member is informed by the investigating authorities of the anticipated visit and does not object to it; further, it should be standard practice prior to the visit to advise the firms concerned of the general nature of the information to be verified and of any further information which needs to be provided, though this should not preclude requests to be made on the spot for further details to be provided in the light of information obtained.

(8) Enquiries or questions put by the authorities or firms of the exporting Members and essential to a successful on-the-spot investigation should, whenever possible, be answered before the visit is made.

Annex II

Best Information Available in Terms of Paragraph 8 of Article 6

(1) As soon as possible after the initiation of the investigation, the investigating authorities should specify in detail the information required from any interested party, and the manner in which that information should be structured by the interested party in its response. The authorities should also ensure that the party is aware that if information is not supplied within a reasonable time, the authorities will be free to make determinations on the basis of the facts available, including those contained in the application for the initiation of the investigation by the domestic industry.

(2) The authorities may also request that an interested party provide its response in a particular medium (e.g., computer tape) or computer language. Where such a request is made, the authorities should consider the reasonable ability of the interested party to respond in the preferred medium or computer language, and should not request the party to use for its response a computer system other than that used by the party. The authority should not maintain a request for a computerized

response if the interested party does not maintain computerized accounts and if presenting the response as requested would result in an unreasonable extra burden on the interested party, e.g., it would entail unreasonable additional cost and trouble. The authorities should not maintain a request for a response in a particular medium or computer language if the interested party does not maintain its computerized accounts in such medium or computer language and if presenting the response as requested would result in an unreasonable extra burden on the interested party, e.g., it would entail unreasonable additional cost and trouble.

(3) All information which is verifiable, which is appropriately submitted so that it can be used in the investigation without undue difficulties, which is supplied in a timely fashion, and, where applicable, which is supplied in a medium or computer language requested by the authorities, should be taken into account when determinations are made. If a party does not respond in the preferred medium or computer language but the authorities find that the circumstances set out in paragraph 2 have been satisfied, the failure to respond in the preferred medium or computer language should not be considered to significantly impede the investigation.

(4) Where the authorities do not have the ability to process information if provided in a particular medium (e.g., computer tape), the information should be supplied in the form of written material or any other form acceptable to the authorities.

(5) Even though the information provided may not be ideal in all respects, this should not justify the authorities from disregarding it, provided the interested party has acted to the best of its ability.

(6) If evidence or information is not accepted, the supplying party should be informed forthwith of the reasons therefor, and should have an opportunity to provide further explanations within a reasonable period, due account being taken of the time-limits of the investigation. If the explanations are considered by the authorities as not being satisfactory, the reasons for the rejection of such evidence or information should be given in any published determinations.

(7) If the authorities have to base their findings, including those with respect to normal value, on information from a secondary source, including the information supplied in the application for the initiation of the investigation, they should do so with special circumspection. In such cases, the authorities should, where practicable, check the information from other independent sources at their disposal, such as published price lists, official import statistics and customs returns, and from the information obtained from other interested parties during the investigation. It is clear, however, that if an interested party does not cooperate and thus relevant information is being withheld from the authorities, this situation could lead to a result which is less favourable to the party than if the party did cooperate.

Appendix III

Article 15 of the Protocol on Accession of China to the WTO Price Comparability in Determining Subsidies and Dumping

Article VI of the GATT 1994, the Agreement on Implementation of Article VI of the General Agreement on Tariffs and Trade 1994 ('Anti-dumping Agreement') and the SCM Agreement shall apply in proceedings involving imports of Chinese origin into a WTO Member consistent with the following:

(a) In determining price comparability under Article VI of the GATT 1994 and the Anti-dumping Agreement, the importing WTO Member shall use either Chinese prices or costs for the industry under investigation or a methodology that is not based on a strict comparison with domestic prices or costs in China based on the following rules:

   (i) If the producers under investigation can clearly show that market economy conditions prevail in the industry producing the like product with regard to the manufacture, production and sale of that product, the importing WTO Member shall use Chinese prices or costs for the industry under investigation in determining price comparability;

   (ii) The importing WTO Member may use a methodology that is not based on a strict comparison with domestic prices or costs in China if the producers under investigation cannot clearly show that market economy conditions prevail in the industry producing the like product with regard to manufacture, production and sale of that product.

(b) In proceedings under Parts II, III and V of the SCM Agreement, when addressing subsidies described in Articles 14(a), 14(b), 14(c) and 14(d), relevant provisions of the SCM Agreement shall apply; however, if there are special difficulties in that application, the importing WTO Member may then use methodologies for identifying and measuring the subsidy benefit which take into account the possibility that prevailing terms and conditions in China may not always be available as appropriate benchmarks. In applying such methodologies, where practicable, the importing WTO Member should adjust such prevailing terms and conditions before considering the use of terms and conditions prevailing outside China.

(c) The importing WTO Member shall notify methodologies used in accordance with subparagraph (a) to the Committee on Anti-dumping Practices and shall notify methodologies used in accordance with subparagraph (b) to the Committee on Subsidies and Countervailing Measures.

(d) Once China has established, under the national law of the importing WTO Member, that it is a market economy, the provisions of subparagraph (a) shall be terminated provided that the importing Member's national law contains market economy criteria as of the date of accession. In any event, the provisions of subparagraph (a)(ii) shall expire fifteen years after the date of accession. In addition, should China establish, pursuant to the national law of the importing WTO Member, that market economy conditions prevail in a particular industry or sector, the non-market economy provisions of subparagraph (a) shall no longer apply to that industry or sector.

Appendix IV
Basic Regulation

COUNCIL REGULATION (EC) No. 384/96 of 22 December 1995 on protection against dumped imports from countries not members of the European Community with amendments.[1]

THE COUNCIL OF THE EUROPEAN UNION; Having regard to the Treaty establishing the European Community, and in particular Article 113 thereof; Having regard to the Regulations establishing the common organization of agricultural markets and the Regulations adopted pursuant to Article 235 of the Treaty applicable to goods manufactured from agricultural products, and in particular the provisions of those Regulations which allow for derogation from the general principle that protective measures at frontiers may be replaced solely by the measures provided for in those Regulations; Having regard to the proposal from the Commission (1); Having regard to the opinion of the European Parliament (2):

(1) whereas, by Regulation (EC) No. 2423/88 (3), the Council adopted common rules for protection against dumped or subsidized imports from countries which are not members of the European Community;
(2) whereas those rules were adopted in accordance with existing international obligations, in particular those arising from Article VI of the General Agreement on Tariffs and Trade (hereinafter referred to as 'GATT'), from the Agreement on Implementation of Article VI of the

1. Council Regulation (EC) No. 384/96 of 22 Dec. 1995 on protection against dumped imports from countries not members of the European Community, OJ L 56, 6 Mar. 1996, pp. 1-20, amended by Council Regulation (EC) No. 2331/96 of 2 Dec. 1996, OJ L 317, 6 Dec. 1996, pp. 1-2; Council Regulation (EC) No. 905/98 of 27 Apr. 1998, OJ L 128, 30 Apr. 1998, pp. 18-19; Council Regulation (EC) No. 2238/2000 of 9 Oct. 2000, OJ L 257, 11 Oct. 2000, pp. 2-3; Council Regulation (EC) No. 1972/2002 of 5 Nov. 2002, OJ L 305, 7 Nov. 2002, pp. 1-3; Council Regulation (EC) No. 461/2004 of 8 March 2004, OJ L 77, 13 Mar. 2004, pp. 12-20; and Council Regulation (EC) No. 2117/2005 of 21 December 2005, OJ L 340, 23 Dec. 2005, p. 17.

GATT (1979 Anti-dumping Code) and from the Agreement on Interpretation and Application of Articles VI, XVI and XXIII of the GATT (Code on Subsidies and Countervailing Duties);

(3) whereas the multilateral trade negotiations concluded in 1994 have led to new Agreements on the implementation of Article VI of GATT and it is therefore appropriate to amend the Community rules in the light of these new Agreements; whereas is it also desirable, in the light of the different nature of the new rules for dumping and subsidies respectively, to have a separate body of Community rules in each of those two areas; whereas, consequently, the new rules on protection against subsidies and countervailing duties are contained in a separate Regulation;

(4) whereas, in applying the rules it is essential, in order to maintain the balance of rights and obligations which the GATT Agreement establishes, that the Community take account of how they are interpreted by the Community's major trading partners;

(5) whereas the new agreement on dumping, namely, the Agreement on Implementation of Article VI of the General Agreement on Tariffs and Trade 1994 (hereinafter referred to as 'the 1994 Anti-dumping Agreement'), contains new and detailed rules, relating in particular to the calculation of dumping, procedures for initiating and pursuing an investigation, including the establishment and treatment of the facts, the imposition of provisional measures, the imposition and collection of anti-dumping duties, the duration and review of anti-dumping measures and the public disclosure of information relating to anti-dumping investigations; whereas, in view of the extent of the changes and to ensure a proper and transparent application of the new rules, the language of the new agreements should be brought into Community legislation as far as possible;

(6) whereas it is desirable to lay down clear and detailed rules on the calculation of normal value; whereas in particular such value should in all cases be based on representative sales in the ordinary course of trade in the exporting country; whereas, it is expedient to define the circumstances in which domestic sales may be considered to be made at a loss and may be disregarded, and in which recourse may be had to remaining sales, or to constructed normal value, or to sales to a third country; whereas it is also desirable to provide for a proper allocation of costs, even in start-up situations; whereas it is also appropriate to lay down guidance as to definition of start-up and the extent and method of allocation; whereas it is also necessary, when constructing normal value, to indicate the methodology that is to be applied in determining the amounts for selling, general and administrative costs and the profit margin that should be included in such value;

(7) whereas when determining normal value for non-market economy countries, it appears prudent to set out rules for choosing the appropriate market-economy third country that is to be used for such purpose and,

where it is not possible to find a suitable third country, to provide that normal value may be established on any other reasonable basis;

(8) whereas it is expedient to define the export price and to enumerate the adjustments which are to be made in those cases where a reconstruction of this price from the first open-market price is deemed necessary;

(9) whereas, for the purpose of ensuring a fair comparison between export price and normal value, it is advisable to list the factors which may affect prices and price comparability and to lay down specific rules as to when and how the adjustments should be made, including the fact that any duplication of adjustments should be avoided; whereas it is also necessary to provide that comparison may be made using average prices although individual export prices may be compared to an average normal value where the former vary by customer, region or time period;

(10) whereas it is desirable to lay down clear and detailed guidance as to the factors which may be relevant for the determination of whether the dumped imports have caused material injury or are threatening to cause injury; whereas, in demonstrating that the volume and price levels of the imports concerned are responsible for injury sustained by a Community industry, attention should be given to the effect of other factors and in particular prevailing market conditions in the Community;

(11) whereas it is advisable to define the term 'Community industry' and to provide that parties related to exporters may be excluded from such industry and to define the term 'related'; whereas, it is also necessary to provide for anti-dumping action to be taken on behalf of producers in a region of the Community and to lay down guidelines on the definition of such region;

(12) whereas it is necessary to lay down who may lodge an anti-dumping complaint, including the extent to which it should be supported by the Community industry, and the information on dumping, injury and causation which such complaint should contain; whereas it is also expedient to specify the procedures for the rejection of complaints or the initiation of proceedings;

(13) whereas it is necessary to lay down the manner in which interested parties should be given notice of the information which the authorities require, and should have ample opportunity to present all relevant evidence and to defend their interests; whereas it is also desirable to set out clearly the rules and procedures to be followed during the investigation, in particular the rules whereby interested parties are to make themselves known, present their views and submit information within specified time limits, if such views and information are to be taken into account; whereas it is also appropriate to set out the conditions under which an interested party may have access to, and comment on, information presented by other interested parties; whereas there should also be cooperation between the Member States and the Commission in the collection of information;

(14) whereas it is necessary to lay down the conditions under which provisional duties may be imposed, including the condition that they may be imposed no earlier than sixty days from initiation and not later than nine months thereafter; whereas, for administrative reasons, it is also necessary to provide that such duties may in all cases be imposed by the Commission, either directly for a nine-month period or in two stages of six and three months;

(15) whereas it is necessary to specify procedures for accepting undertakings which eliminate dumping and injury instead of imposing provisional or definitive duties; whereas it is also appropriate to lay down the consequences of breach or withdrawal of undertakings and that provisional duties may be imposed in cases of suspected violation or where further investigation is necessary to supplement the findings; whereas, in accepting undertakings, care should be taken that the proposed undertakings, and their enforcement, do not lead to anti-competitive behaviour;

(16) whereas it is necessary to provide that the termination of cases should, irrespective of whether definitive measures are adopted or not, normally take place within twelve months, and in no case later than fifteen months, from the initiation of the investigation; whereas investigations or proceedings should be terminated where the dumping is de minimis or the injury is negligible, and it is appropriate to define those terms; whereas, where measures are to be imposed, it is necessary to provide for the termination of investigations and to lay down that measures should be less than the margin of dumping if such lesser amount would remove the injury, as well as to specify the method of calculating the level of measures in cases of sampling;

(17) whereas it is necessary to provide for retroactive collection of provisional duties if that is deemed appropriate and to define the circumstances which may trigger the retroactive application of duties to avoid the undermining of the definitive measures to be applied; whereas it is also necessary to provide that duties may be applied retroactively in cases of breach or withdrawal of undertakings;

(18) whereas it is necessary to provide that measures are to lapse after five years unless a review indicates that they should be maintained; whereas it is also necessary to provide, in cases where sufficient evidence is submitted of changed circumstances, for interim reviews or for investigations to determine whether refunds of anti-dumping duties are warranted; whereas it is also appropriate to lay down that in any recalculation of dumping which necessitates a reconstruction of export prices, duties are not to be treated as a cost incurred between importation and resale where the said duty is being reflected in the prices of the products subject to measures in the Community;

(19) whereas it is necessary to provide specifically for the reassessment of export prices and dumping margins where the duty is being absorbed by the exporter through a form of compensatory arrangement and the

measures are not being reflected in the prices of the products subject to measures in the Community;

(20) whereas the 1994 Anti-dumping Agreement does not contain provisions regarding the circumvention of anti-dumping measures, though a separate GATT Ministerial Decision recognizes circumvention as a problem and has referred it to the GATT Anti-dumping Committee for resolution; whereas given the failure of the multilateral negotiations so far and pending the outcome of the referral to the GATT Anti-dumping Committee, it is necessary to introduce new provisions into Community legislation to deal with practices, including mere assembly of goods in the Community or a third country, which have as their main aim the circumvention of anti-dumping measures;

(21) whereas it is expedient to permit suspension of anti-dumping measures where there is a temporary change in market conditions which makes the continued imposition of such measures temporarily inappropriate;

(22) whereas it is necessary to provide that imports under investigation may be made subject to registration upon importation in order to enable measures to be applied subsequently against such imports;

(23) whereas in order to ensure proper enforcement of measures, it is necessary that Member States monitor, and report to the Commission, the import trade of products subject to investigation or subject to measures, and also the amount of duties collected under this Regulation;

(24) whereas it is necessary to provide for consultation of an Advisory Committee at regular and specified stages of the investigation; whereas, the Committee should consist of representatives of Member States with a representative of the Commission as chairman;

(25) whereas it is expedient to provide for verification visits to check information submitted on dumping and injury, such visits being, however, conditional on proper replies to questionnaires being received;

(26) whereas it is essential to provide for sampling in cases where the number of parties or transactions is large in order to permit completion of investigations within the appointed time limits;

(27) whereas it is necessary to provide that where parties do not cooperate satisfactorily other information may be used to establish findings and that such information may be less favourable to the parties than if they had cooperated;

(28) whereas provision should be made for the treatment of confidential information so that business secrets are not divulged;

(29) whereas it is essential that provision be made for proper disclosure of essential facts and considerations to parties which qualify for such treatment and that such disclosure be made, with due regard to the decision-making process in the Community, within a time period which permits parties to defend their interests;

(30) whereas it is prudent to provide for an administrative system under which arguments can be presented as to whether measures are in the Community interest, including the consumers' interest, and to lay down the time

periods within which such information has to be presented as well as the disclosure rights of the parties concerned;

(31) whereas, by Regulation (EC) No. 3283/94 of 22 December 1994 on protection against dumped imports from countries not members of the European Community (4), the Council repealed Regulation (EEC) No. 2423/88 and instituted a new common system of defence against dumped imports from countries not members of the European Community;

(32) whereas significant errors in the text of Regulation (EC) No. 3283/94 became apparent on publication;

(33) whereas, moreover, that Regulation has already been twice amended;

(34) whereas, in the interests of clarity, transparency and legal certainty, that Regulation should therefore be repealed and replaced, without prejudice to the anti-dumping proceedings already initiated under it or under Regulation (EEC) No. 2423/88.

HAS ADOPTED THIS REGULATION:

Article 1

Principles

(1) An anti-dumping duty may be applied to any dumped product whose release for free circulation in the Community causes injury.

(2) A product is to be considered as being dumped if its export price to the Community is less than a comparable price for the like product, in the ordinary course of trade, as established for the exporting country.

(3) The exporting country shall normally be the country of origin. However, it may be an intermediate country, except where, for example, the products are merely transhipped through that country, or the products concerned are not produced in that country, or there is no comparable price for them in that country.

(4) For the purpose of this Regulation, the term 'like product' shall be interpreted to mean a product which is identical, that is to say, alike in all respects, to the product under consideration, or in the absence of such a product, another product which although not alike in all respects, has characteristics closely resembling those of the product under consideration.

Article 2

Determination of Dumping

A Normal Value

(1) The normal value shall normally be based on the prices paid or payable, in the ordinary course of trade, by independent customers in the exporting country.

However, where the exporter in the exporting country does not produce or does not sell the like product, the normal value may be established on the basis of prices of other sellers or producers.

Prices between parties which appear to be associated or to have a compensatory arrangement with each other may not be considered to be in the ordinary course of trade and may not be used to establish normal value unless it is determined that they are unaffected by the relationship.

In order to determine whether two parties are associated account may be taken of the definition of related parties set out in Article 143 of Commission Regulation (EEC) 2454/93 of 2 July 1993 laying down provisions for the implementation of Council Regulation (EEC) No. 2913/92 establishing the Community Customs Code(*).

(*)OJ L 253, 11 October 1993, p. 1. Regulation as last amended by Commission Regulation (EC) No. 444/2002 (OJ L 68, 12 March 2002, p. 11).

(2) Sales of the like product intended for domestic consumption shall normally be used to determine normal value if such sales volume constitutes 5% or more of the sales volume of the product under consideration to the Community. However, a lower volume of sales may be used when, for example, the prices charged are considered representative for the market concerned.

(3) When there are no or insufficient sales of the like product in the ordinary course of trade, or where because of the particular market situation such sales do not permit a proper comparison, the normal value of the like product shall be calculated on the basis of the cost of production in the country of origin plus a reasonable amount for selling, general and administrative costs and for profits, or on the basis of the export prices, in the ordinary course of trade, to an appropriate third country, provided that those prices are representative. A particular market situation for the product concerned within the meaning of the preceding sentence may be deemed to exist, inter alia, when prices are artificially low, when there is significant barter trade, or when there are non-commercial processing arrangements.

(4) Sales of the like product in the domestic market of the exporting country, or export sales to a third country, at prices below unit production costs (fixed and variable) plus selling, general and administrative costs may be treated as not being in the ordinary course of trade by reason of price, and may be disregarded in determining normal value, only if it is determined that such sales are made within an extended period in substantial quantities, and are at prices which do not provide for the recovery of all costs within a reasonable period of time.

If prices which are below costs at the time of sale are above weighted average costs for the period of investigation, such prices shall be considered to provide for recovery of costs within a reasonable period of time.

The extended period of time shall normally be one year but shall in no case be less than six months, and sales below unit cost shall be considered to be made in substantial quantities within such a period when it is established that the weighted average selling price is below the weighted average unit cost, or that the volume of sales below unit cost is not less than 20% of sales being used to determine normal value.

(5) Costs shall normally be calculated on the basis of records kept by the party under investigation, provided that such records are in accordance with the generally accepted accounting principles of the country concerned and that it is shown that the records reasonably reflect the costs associated with the production and sale of the product under consideration. If costs associated with the production and sale of the product under investigation are not reasonably reflected in the records of the party concerned, they shall be adjusted or established on the basis of the costs of other producers or exporters in the same country or, where such information is not available or cannot be used, on any other reasonable basis, including information from other representative markets.

Consideration shall be given to evidence submitted on the proper allocation of costs, provided that it is shown that such allocations have been historically utilized. In the absence of a more appropriate method, preference shall be given to the allocation of costs on the basis of turnover. Unless already reflected in the cost allocations under this subparagraph, costs shall be adjusted appropriately for those non-recurring items of cost which benefit future and/or current production.

Where the costs for part of the period for cost recovery are affected by the use of new production facilities requiring substantial additional investment and by low capacity utilization rates, which are the result of start-up operations which take place within or during part of the investigation period, the average costs for the start-up phase shall be those applicable, under the abovementioned allocation rules, at the end of such a phase, and shall be included at that level, for the period concerned, in the weighted average costs referred to in the second sub-paragraph of paragraph 4. The length of a start-up phase shall be determined in relation to the circumstances of the producer or exporter concerned, but shall not exceed an appropriate initial portion of the period for cost recovery. For this adjustment to costs applicable during the investigation period, information relating to a start-up phase which extends beyond that period shall be taken into account where it is submitted prior to verification visits and within three months of the initiation of the investigation.

(6) The amounts for selling, for general and administrative costs and for profits shall be based on actual data pertaining to production and sales, in the ordinary course of trade, of the like product, by the exporter or producer under investigation. When such amounts cannot be determined on this basis, the amounts may be determined on the basis of:

(a) the weighted average of the actual amounts determined for other exporters or producers subject to investigation in respect of production and sales of the like product in the domestic market of the country of origin;
(b) the actual amounts applicable to production and sales, in the ordinary course of trade, of the same general category of products for the exporter or producer in question in the domestic market of the country of origin;

(c) any other reasonable method, provided that the amount for profit so established shall not exceed the profit normally realized by other exporters or producers on sales of products of the same general category in the domestic market of the country of origin.

(7) (a) In the case of imports from non-market economy countries (*), normal value shall be determined on the basis of the price or constructed value in a market economy third country, or the price from such a third country to other countries, including the Community, or where those are not possible, on any other reasonable basis, including the price actually paid or payable in the Community for the like product, duly adjusted if necessary to include a reasonable profit margin.

An appropriate market economy third country shall be selected in a not unreasonable manner, due account being taken of any reliable information made available at the time of selection. Account shall also be taken of time limits; where appropriate, a market economy third country which is subject to the same investigation shall be used.

The parties to the investigation shall be informed shortly after its initiation of the market economy third country envisaged and shall be given ten days to comment.

(b) In anti-dumping investigations concerning imports from the People's Republic of China, Vietnam and Kazakhstan and any non-market-economy country which is a member of the WTO at the date of the initiation of the investigation, normal value will be determined in accordance with paragraphs 1 to 6, if it is shown, on the basis of properly substantiated claims by one or more producers subject to the investigation and in accordance with the criteria and procedures set out in subparagraph (c) that market economy conditions prevail for this producer or producers in respect of the manufacture and sale of the like product concerned. When this is not the case, the rules set out under subparagraph (a) shall apply,

(c) A claim under subparagraph (b) must be made in writing and contain sufficient evidence that the producer operates under market economy conditions, that is if:

- decisions of firms regarding prices, costs and inputs, including for instance raw materials, cost of technology and labour, output, sales and investment, are made in response to market signals reflecting supply and demand, and without significant State interference in this regard, and costs of major inputs substantially reflect market values,
- firms have one clear set of basic accounting records which are independently audited in line with international accounting standards and are applied for all purposes,
- the production costs and financial situation of firms are not subject to significant distortions carried over from the former non-market economy system, in particular in relation to depreciation of assets, other write-offs, barter trade and payment via compensation of debts,
- the firms concerned are subject to bankruptcy and property laws which guarantee legal certainty and stability for the operation of firms, and
- exchange rate conversions are carried out at the market rate.

A determination whether the producer meets the abovementioned criteria shall be made within three months of the initiation of the investigation, after specific consultation of the Advisory Committee and after the Community industry has been given an opportunity to comment. This determination shall remain in force throughout the investigation.

(*) Including Albania, Armenia, Azerbaijan, Belarus, Georgia, North Korea, Kyrgyzstan, Moldova, Mongolia, Tajikistan, Turkmenistan, Uzbekistan.

B Export Price

(8) The export price shall be the price actually paid or payable for the product when sold for export from the exporting country to the Community.

(9) In cases where there is no export price or where it appears that the export price is unreliable because of an association or a compensatory arrangement between the exporter and the importer or a third party, the export price may be constructed on the basis of the price at which the imported products are first resold to an independent buyer, or, if the products are not resold to an independent buyer, or are not resold in the condition in which they were imported, on any reasonable basis.

In these cases, adjustment for all costs, including duties and taxes, incurred between importation and resale, and for profits accruing, shall be made so as to establish a reliable export price, at the Community frontier level.

The items for which adjustment shall be made shall include those normally borne by an importer but paid by any party, either inside or outside the Community, which appears to be associated or to have a compensatory arrangement with the importer or exporter, including usual transport, insurance, handling, loading and ancillary costs; customs duties, any anti-dumping duties, and other taxes payable in the importing country by reason of the importation or sale of the goods; and a reasonable margin for selling, general and administrative costs and profit.

C Comparison

(10) A fair comparison shall be made between the export price and the normal value. This comparison shall be made at the same level of trade and in respect of sales made at as nearly as possible the same time and with due account taken of other differences which affect price comparability. Where the normal value and the export price as established are not on such a comparable basis due allowance, in the form of adjustments, shall be made in each case, on its merits, for differences in factors which are claimed, and demonstrated, to affect prices and price comparability. Any duplication when making adjustments shall be avoided, in particular in relation to discounts, rebates, quantities and level of trade. When the specified conditions are met, the factors for which adjustment can be made are listed as follows:

(a) Physical characteristics: An adjustment shall be made for differences in the physical characteristics of the product concerned. The amount of the adjustment shall correspond to a reasonable estimate of the market value of the difference.

(b) Import charges and indirect taxes: An adjustment shall be made to normal value for an amount corresponding to any import charges or indirect taxes borne by the like product and by materials physically incorporated therein, when intended for consumption in the exporting country and not collected or refunded in respect of the product exported to the Community.

(c) Discounts, rebates and quantities: An adjustment shall be made for differences in discounts and rebates, including those given for differences in quantities, if these are properly quantified and are directly linked to the sales under consideration. An adjustment may also be made for deferred discounts and rebates if the claim is based on consistent practice in prior periods, including compliance with the conditions required to qualify for the discount or rebates.

(d) Level of trade: (i) An adjustment for differences in levels of trade, including any differences which may arise in OEM (Original Equipment Manufacturer) sales, shall be made where, in relation to the distribution chain in both markets, it is shown that the export price, including a constructed export price, is at a different level of trade from the normal value and the difference has affected price comparability which is demonstrated by consistent and distinct differences in functions and prices of the seller for the different levels of trade in the domestic market of the exporting country. The amount of the adjustment shall be based on the market value of the difference. (ii) However, in circumstances not envisaged under (i), when an existing difference in level of trade cannot be quantified because of the absence of the relevant levels on the domestic market of the exporting countries, or where certain functions are shown clearly to relate to levels of trade other than the one which is to be used in the comparison, a special adjustment may be granted.'

(e) Transport, insurance, handling, loading and ancillary costs: An adjustment shall be made for differences in the directly related costs incurred for conveying the product concerned from the premises of the exporter to an independent buyer, where such costs are included in the prices charged. Those costs shall include transport, insurance, handling, loading and ancillary costs.

(f) Packing: An adjustment shall be made for differences in the directly related packing costs for the product concerned.

(g) Credit: An adjustment shall be made for differences in the cost of any credit granted for the sales under consideration, provided that it is a factor taken into account in the determination of the prices charged.

(h) After-sales costs: An adjustment shall be made for differences in the direct costs of providing warranties, guarantees, technical assistance and services, as provided for by law and/or in the sales contract.

(i) Commissions: An adjustment shall be made for differences in commissions paid in respect of the sales under consideration. The term 'commissions' shall be understood to include the mark-up received by a trader of the product or the like product if the functions of such a trader are similar to those of an agent working on a commission basis.

(j) Currency conversions: When the price comparison requires a conversion of currencies, such conversion shall be made using the rate of exchange on the date of sale, except that when a sale of foreign currency on forward markets is directly linked to the export sale involved, the rate of exchange in the forward sale shall be used. Normally, the date of sale shall be the date of invoice but the date of contract, purchase order or order confirmation may be used if these more appropriately establish the material terms of sale. Fluctuations in exchange rates shall be ignored and exporters shall be granted sixty days to reflect a sustained movement in exchange rates during the investigation period.

(k) Other factors: An adjustment may also be made for differences in other factors not provided for under subparagraphs (a) to (j) if it is demonstrated that they affect price comparability as required under this paragraph, in particular that customers consistently pay different prices on the domestic market because of the difference in such factors.

D Dumping Margin

(11) Subject to the relevant provisions governing fair comparison, the existence of margins of dumping during the investigation period shall normally be established on the basis of a comparison of a weighted average normal value with a weighted average of prices of all export transactions to the Community, or by a comparison of individual normal values and individual export prices to the Community on a transaction-to-transaction basis. However, a normal value established on a weighted average basis may be compared to prices of all individual export transactions to the Community, if there is a pattern of export prices which differs significantly among different purchasers, regions or time periods, and if the methods specified in the first sentence of this paragraph would not reflect the full degree of dumping being practised. This paragraph shall not preclude the use of sampling in accordance with Article 17.

(12) The dumping margin shall be the amount by which the normal value exceeds the export price. Where dumping margins vary, a weighted average dumping margin may be established.

Article 3

Determination of Injury

(1) Pursuant to this Regulation, the term 'injury' shall, unless otherwise specified, be taken to mean material injury to the Community industry, threat of material injury to the Community industry or material retardation of the establishment

of such an industry and shall be interpreted in accordance with the provisions of this Article.

(2) A determination of injury shall be based on positive evidence and shall involve an objective examination of both (a) the volume of the dumped imports and the effect of the dumped imports on prices in the Community market for like products; and (b) the consequent impact of those imports on the Community industry.

(3) With regard to the volume of the dumped imports, consideration shall be given to whether there has been a significant increase in dumped imports, either in absolute terms or relative to production or consumption in the Community. With regard to the effect of the dumped imports on prices, consideration shall be given to whether there has been significant price undercutting by the dumped imports as compared with the price of a like product of the Community industry, or whether the effect of such imports is otherwise to depress prices to a significant degree or prevent price increases, which would otherwise have occurred, to a significant degree. No one or more of these factors can necessarily give decisive guidance.

(4) Where imports of a product from more than one country are simultaneously subject to anti-dumping investigations, the effects of such imports shall be cumulatively assessed only if it is determined that (a) the margin of dumping established in relation to the imports from each country is more than de minimis as defined in Article 9 (3) and that the volume of imports from each country is not negligible; and (b) a cumulative assessment of the effects of the imports is appropriate in light of the conditions of competition between imported products and the conditions of competition between the imported products and the like Community product.

(5) The examination of the impact of the dumped imports on the Community industry concerned shall include an evaluation of all relevant economic factors and indices having a bearing on the state of the industry, including the fact that an industry is still in the process of recovering from the effects of past dumping or subsidization, the magnitude of the actual margin of dumping, actual and potential decline in sales, profits, output, market share, productivity, return on investments, utilization of capacity; factors affecting Community prices; actual and potential negative effects on cash flow, inventories, employment, wages, growth, ability to raise capital or investments. This list is not exhaustive, nor can any one or more of these factors necessarily give decisive guidance.

(6) It must be demonstrated, from all the relevant evidence presented in relation to paragraph 2, that the dumped imports are causing injury within the meaning of this Regulation. Specifically, this shall entail a demonstration that the volume and/or price levels identified pursuant to paragraph 3 are responsible for an impact on the Community industry as provided for in paragraph 5, and that this impact exists to a degree which enables it to be classified as material.

(7) Known factors other than the dumped imports which at the same time are injuring the Community industry shall also be examined to ensure that injury

caused by these other factors is not attributed to the dumped imports under paragraph 6. Factors which may be considered in this respect include the volume and prices of imports not sold at dumping prices, contraction in demand or changes in the patterns of consumption, restrictive trade practices of, and competition between, third country and Community producers, developments in technology and the export performance and productivity of the Community industry.

(8) The effect of the dumped imports shall be assessed in relation to the production of the Community industry of the like product when available data permit the separate identification of that production on the basis of such criteria as the production process, producers' sales and profits. If such separate identification of that production is not possible, the effects of the dumped imports shall be assessed by examination of the production of the narrowest group or range of products, which includes the like product, for which the necessary information can be provided.

(9) A determination of a threat of material injury shall be based on facts and not merely on allegation, conjecture or remote possibility. The change in circumstances which would create a situation in which the dumping would cause injury must be clearly foreseen and imminent.

In making a determination regarding the existence of a threat of material injury, consideration should be given to such factors as:

(a) a significant rate of increase of dumped imports into the Community market indicating the likelihood of substantially increased imports;
(b) sufficient freely disposable capacity of the exporter or an imminent and substantial increase in such capacity indicating the likelihood of substantially increased dumped exports to the Community, account being taken of the availability of other export markets to absorb any additional exports;
(c) whether imports are entering at prices that would, to a significant degree, depress prices or prevent price increases which otherwise would have occurred, and would probably increase demand for further imports; and
(d) inventories of the product being investigated.

No one of the factors listed above by itself can necessarily give decisive guidance but the totality of the factors considered must lead to the conclusion that further dumped exports are imminent and that, unless protective action is taken, material injury will occur.

Article 4

Definition of Community Industry

(1) For the purposes of this Regulation, the term 'Community industry' shall be interpreted as referring to the Community producers as a whole of the like products or to those of them whose collective output of the products constitutes a major

proportion, as defined in Article 5 (4), of the total Community production of those products, except that:

(a) when producers are related to the exporters or importers or are themselves importers of the allegedly dumped product, the term 'Community industry' may be interpreted as referring to the rest of the producers;
(b) in exceptional circumstances the territory of the Community may, for the production in question, be divided into two or more competitive markets and the producers within each market may be regarded as a separate industry if (i) the producers within such a market sell all or almost all of their production of the product in question in that market; and (ii) the demand in that market is not to any substantial degree supplied by producers of the product in question located elsewhere in the Community. In such circumstances, injury may be found to exist even where a major portion of the total Community industry is not injured, provided there is a concentration of dumped imports into such an isolated market and provided further that the dumped imports are causing injury to the producers of all or almost all of the production within such a market.

(2) For the purpose of paragraph 1, producers shall be considered to be related to exporters or importers only if (a) one of them directly or indirectly controls the other; or (b) both of them are directly or indirectly controlled by a third person; or (c) together they directly or indirectly control a third person provided that there are grounds for believing or suspecting that the effect of the relationship is such as to cause the producer concerned to behave differently from non-related producers. For the purpose of this paragraph, one shall be deemed to control another when the former is legally or operationally in a position to exercise restraint or direction over the latter.

(3) Where the Community industry has been interpreted as referring to the producers in a certain region, the exporters shall be given an opportunity to offer undertakings pursuant to Article 8 in respect of the region concerned. In such cases, when evaluating the Community interest of the measures, special account shall be taken of the interest of the region. If an adequate undertaking is not offered promptly or the situations set out in Article 8 (9) and (10) apply, a provisional or definitive duty may be imposed in respect of the Community as a whole. In such cases, the duties may, if practicable, be limited to specific producers or exporters.

(4) The provisions of Article 3 (8) shall be applicable to this Article.

Article 5

Initiation of Proceedings

(1) Except as provided for in paragraph 6, an investigation to determine the existence, degree and effect of any alleged dumping shall be initiated upon a written

complaint by any natural or legal person, or any association not having legal personality, acting on behalf of the Community industry.

The complaint may be submitted to the Commission, or to a Member State, which shall forward it to the Commission. The Commission shall send Member States a copy of any complaint it receives. The complaint shall be deemed to have been lodged on the first working day following its delivery to the Commission by registered mail or the issuing of an acknowledgement of receipt by the Commission.

Where, in the absence of any complaint, a Member State is in possession of sufficient evidence of dumping and of resultant injury to the Community industry, it shall immediately communicate such evidence to the Commission.

(2) A complaint under paragraph 1 shall include evidence of dumping, injury and a causal link between the allegedly dumped imports and the alleged injury. The complaint shall contain such information as is reasonably available to the complainant on the following:

(a) identity of the complainant and a description of the volume and value of the Community production of the like product by the complainant. Where a written complaint is made on behalf of the Community industry, the complaint shall identify the industry on behalf of which the complaint is made by a list of all known Community producers of the like product (or associations of Community producers of the like product) and, to the extent possible, a description of the volume and value of Community production of the like product accounted for by such producers;

(b) a complete description of the allegedly dumped product, the names of the country or countries of origin or export in question, the identity of each known exporter or foreign producer and a list of known persons importing the product in question;

(c) information on prices at which the product in question is sold when destined for consumption in the domestic markets of the country or countries of origin or export (or, where appropriate, information on the prices at which the product is sold from the country or countries of origin or export to a third country or countries or on the constructed value of the product) and information on export prices or, where appropriate, on the prices at which the product is first resold to an independent buyer in the Community;

(d) information on changes in the volume of the allegedly dumped imports, the effect of those imports on prices of the like product on the Community market and the consequent impact of the imports on the Community industry, as demonstrated by relevant factors and indices having a bearing on the state of the Community industry, such as those listed in Article 3 (3) and (5).

(3) The Commission shall, as far as possible, examine the accuracy and adequacy of the evidence provided in the complaint to determine whether there is sufficient evidence to justify the initiation of an investigation.

(4) An investigation shall not be initiated pursuant to paragraph 1 unless it has been determined, on the basis of an examination as to the degree of support for, or opposition to, the complaint expressed by Community producers of the like product, that the complaint has been made by or on behalf of the Community industry. The complaint shall be considered to have been made by or on behalf of the Community industry if it is supported by those Community producers whose collective output constitutes more than 50% of the total production of the like product produced by that portion of the Community industry expressing either support for or opposition to the complaint. However, no investigation shall be initiated when Community producers expressly supporting the complaint account for less than 25% of total production of the like product produced by the Community industry.

(5) The authorities shall avoid, unless a decision has been made to initiate an investigation, any publicising of the complaint seeking the initiation of an investigation. However, after receipt of a properly documented complaint and before proceeding to initiate an investigation, the government of the exporting country concerned shall be notified.

(6) If in special circumstances, it is decided to initiate an investigation without having received a written complaint by or on behalf of the Community industry for the initiation of such investigation, this shall be done on the basis of sufficient evidence of dumping, injury and a causal link, as described in paragraph 2, to justify such initiation.

(7) The evidence of both dumping and injury shall be considered simultaneously in the decision on whether or not to initiate an investigation. A complaint shall be rejected where there is insufficient evidence of either dumping or of injury to justify proceeding with the case. Proceedings shall not be initiated against countries whose imports represent a market share of below 1%, unless such countries collectively account for 3% or more of Community consumption.

(8) The complaint may be withdrawn prior to initiation, in which case it shall be considered not to have been lodged.

(9) Where, after consultation, it is apparent that there is sufficient evidence to justify initiating a proceeding, the Commission shall do so within forty five days of the lodging of the complaint and shall publish a notice in the Official Journal of the European Communities. Where insufficient evidence has been presented, the complainant shall, after consultation, be so informed within forty five days of the date on which the complaint is lodged with the Commission.

(10) The notice of initiation of the proceedings shall announce the initiation of an investigation, indicate the product and countries concerned, give a summary of the information received, and provide that all relevant information is to be communicated to the Commission; it shall state the periods within which interested parties may make themselves known, present their views in writing and submit information if such views and information are to be taken into account during the

investigation; it shall also state the period within which interested parties may apply to be heard by the Commission in accordance with Article 6 (5).

(11) The Commission shall advise the exporters, importers and representative associations of importers or exporters known to it to be concerned, as well as representatives of the exporting country and the complainants, of the initiation of the proceedings and, with due regard to the protection of confidential information, provide the full text of the written complaint received pursuant to paragraph 1 to the known exporters and to the authorities of the exporting country, and make it available upon request to other interested parties involved. Where the number of exporters involved is particularly high, the full text of the written complaint may instead be provided only to the authorities of the exporting country or to the relevant trade association.

(12) An anti-dumping investigation shall not hinder the procedures of customs clearance.

Article 6

The Investigation

(1) Following the initiation of the proceeding, the Commission, acting in cooperation with the Member States, shall commence an investigation at Community level. Such investigation shall cover both dumping and injury and these shall be investigated simultaneously. For the purpose of a representative finding, an investigation period shall be selected which, in the case of dumping shall, normally, cover a period of not less than six months immediately prior to the initiation of the proceeding. Information relating to a period subsequent to the investigation period shall, normally, not be taken into account.

(2) Parties receiving questionnaires used in an anti-dumping investigation shall be given at least thirty days to reply. The time limit for exporters shall be counted from the date of receipt of the questionnaire, which for this purpose shall be deemed to have been received one week from the day on which it was sent to the exporter or transmitted to the appropriate diplomatic representative of the exporting country. An extension to the thirty day period may be granted, due account being taken of the time limits of the investigation, provided that the party shows due cause for such extension, in terms of its particular circumstances.

(3) The Commission may request Member States to supply information, and Member States shall take whatever steps are necessary in order to give effect to such requests. They shall send to the Commission the information requested together within the results of all inspections, checks or investigations carried out. Where this information is of general interest or where its transmission has been requested by a Member State, the Commission shall forward it to the Member States, provided it is not confidential, in which case a non-confidential summary shall be forwarded.

(4) The Commission may request Member States to carry out all necessary checks and inspections, particularly amongst importers, traders and Community producers, and to carry out investigations in third countries, provided that the firms concerned give their consent and that the government of the country in question has been officially notified and raises no objection. Member States shall take whatever steps are necessary in order to give effect to such requests from the Commission. Officials of the Commission shall be authorized, if the Commission or a Member State so requests, to assist the officials of Member States in carrying out their duties.

(5) The interested parties which have made themselves known in accordance with Article 5 (10) shall be heard if they have, within the period prescribed in the notice published in the Official Journal of the European Communities, made a written request for a hearing showing that they are an interested party likely to be affected by the result of the proceeding and that there are particular reasons why they should be heard.

(6) Opportunities shall, on request, be provided for the importers, exporters, representatives of the government of the exporting country and the complainants, which have made themselves known in accordance with Article 5 (10), to meet those parties with adverse interests, so that opposing views may be presented and rebuttal arguments offered. Provision of such opportunities must take account of the need to preserve confidentiality and of the convenience to the parties. There shall be no obligation on any party to attend a meeting, and failure to do so shall not be prejudicial to that party's case. Oral information provided under this paragraph shall be taken into account in so far as it is subsequently confirmed in writing.

(7) The complainants, importers and exporters and their representative associations, users and consumer organizations, which have made themselves known in accordance with Article 5 (10), as well as the representatives of the exporting country may, upon written request, inspect all information made available by any party to an investigation, as distinct from internal documents prepared by the authorities of the Community or its Member States, which is relevant to the presentation of their cases and not confidential within the meaning of Article 19, and that it is used in the investigation. Such parties may respond to such information and their comments shall be taken into consideration, wherever they are sufficiently substantiated in the response.

(8) Except in the circumstances provided for in Article 18, the information which is supplied by interested parties and upon which findings are based shall be examined for accuracy as far as possible.

(9) For proceedings initiated pursuant to Article 5 (9), an investigation shall, whenever possible, be concluded within one year. In any event, such investigations shall in all cases be concluded within fifteen months of initiation, in accordance with the findings made pursuant to Article 8 for undertakings or the findings made pursuant to Article 9 for definitive action.

Article 7

Provisional Measures

(1) Provisional duties may be imposed if proceedings have been initiated in accordance with Article 5, if a notice has been given to that effect and interested parties have been given adequate opportunities to submit information and make comments in accordance with Article 5 (10), if a provisional affirmative determination has been made of dumping and consequent injury to the Community industry, and if the Community interest calls for intervention to prevent such injury. The provisional duties shall be imposed no earlier than sixty days from the initiation of the proceedings but not later than nine months from the initiation of the proceedings.

(2) The amount of the provisional anti-dumping duty shall not exceed the margin of dumping as provisionally established, but it should be less than the margin if such lesser duty would be adequate to remove the injury to the Community industry.

(3) Provisional duties shall be secured by a guarantee, and the release of the products concerned for free circulation in the Community shall be conditional upon the provision of such guarantee.

(4) The Commission shall take provisional action after consultation or, in cases of extreme urgency, after informing the Member States. In this latter case, consultations shall take place ten days, at the latest, after notification to the Member States of the action taken by the Commission.

(5) Where a Member State requests immediate intervention by the Commission and where the conditions in paragraph 1 are met, the Commission shall within a maximum of five working days of receipt of the request, decide whether a provisional anti-dumping duty shall be imposed.

(6) The Commission shall forthwith inform the Council and the Member States of any decision taken under paragraphs 1 to 5. The Council, acting by a qualified majority, may decide differently.

(7) Provisional duties may be imposed for six months and extended for a further three months or they may be imposed for nine months. However, they may only be extended, or imposed for a nine-month period, where exporters representing a significant percentage of the trade involved so request or do not object upon notification by the Commission.

Article 8

Undertakings

(1) Upon condition that a provisional affirmative determination of dumping and injury has been made, the Commission may accept satisfactory voluntary

undertaking offers submitted by any exporter to revise its prices or to cease exports at dumped prices, if, after specific consultation of the Advisory Committee, it is satisfied that the injurious effect of the dumping is thereby eliminated. In such a case and as long as such undertakings are in force, the provisional duties imposed by the Commission in accordance with Article 7(1) or the definitive duties imposed by the Council in accordance with Article 9(4) as the case may be shall not apply to the relevant imports of the product concerned manufactured by the companies referred to in the Commission decision accepting undertakings, as subsequently amended. Price increases under such undertakings shall not be higher than necessary to eliminate the margin of dumping and they should be less than the margin of dumping if such increases would be adequate to remove the injury to the Community industry.

(2) Undertakings may be suggested by the Commission, but no exporter shall be obliged to enter into such an undertaking. The fact that exporters do not offer such undertakings, or do not accept an invitation to do so, shall in no way prejudice consideration of the case. However, it may be determined that a threat of injury is more likely to be realized if the dumped imports continue. Undertakings shall not be sought or accepted from exporters unless a provisional affirmative determination of dumping and injury caused by such dumping has been made. Save in exceptional circumstances, undertakings may not be offered later than the end of the period during which representations may be made pursuant to Article 20 (5).

(3) Undertakings offered need not be accepted if their acceptance is considered impractical, if such as where the number of actual or potential exporters is too great, or for other reasons, including reasons of general policy. The exporter concerned may be provided with the reasons for which it is proposed to reject the offer of an undertaking and may be given an opportunity to make comments thereon. The reasons for rejection shall be set out in the definitive decision.

(4) Parties which offer an undertaking shall be required to provide a non-confidential version of such undertaking, so that it may be made available to interested parties to the investigation.

(5) Where undertakings are, after consultation, accepted and where there is no objection raised within the Advisory Committee, the investigation shall be terminated. In all other cases, the Commission shall submit to the Council forthwith a report on the results of the consultation, together with a proposal that the investigation be terminated. The investigation shall be deemed terminated if, within one month, the Council, acting by a qualified majority, has not decided otherwise.

(6) If the undertakings are accepted, the investigation of dumping and injury shall normally be completed. In such a case, if a negative determination of dumping or injury is made, the undertaking shall automatically lapse, except in cases where such a determination is due in large part to the existence of an undertaking. In such cases it may be required that an undertaking be maintained for a reasonable period. In the event that an affirmative determination of dumping and injury is made, the undertaking shall continue consistent with its terms and the provisions of this Regulation.

(7) The Commission shall require any exporter from which an undertaking has been accepted to provide, periodically, information relevant to the fulfilment of such undertaking, and to permit verification of pertinent data. Non-compliance with such requirements shall be construed as a breach of the undertaking.

(8) Where undertakings are accepted from certain exporters during the course of an investigation, they shall, for the purpose of Article 11, be deemed to take effect from the date on which the investigation is concluded for the exporting country.

(9) In case of breach or withdrawal of undertakings by any party to the undertaking, or in case of withdrawal of acceptance of the undertaking by the Commission, the acceptance of the undertaking shall, after consultation, be withdrawn by Commission Decision or Commission Regulation, as appropriate, and the provisional duty which has been imposed by the Commission in accordance with Article 7 or the definitive duty which has been imposed by the Council in accordance with Article 9(4) shall automatically apply, provided that the exporter concerned has, except where he himself has withdrawn the undertaking, been given an opportunity to comment.

Any interested party or Member State may submit information showing *prima facie* evidence of a breach of an undertaking. The subsequent assessment of whether or not a breach of an undertaking has occurred shall normally be concluded within six months, but in no case later than nine months following a duly substantiated request. The Commission may request the assistance of the competent authorities of the Member States in the monitoring of undertakings.

(10) A provisional duty may, after consultation, be imposed in accordance with Article 7 on the basis of the best information available, where there is reason to believe that an undertaking is being breached, or in case of breach or withdrawal of an undertaking where the investigation which led to the undertaking has not been concluded.

Article 9

Termination without Measures; Imposition of Definitive Duties

(1) Where the complaint is withdrawn, the proceeding may be terminated unless such termination would not be in the Community interest.

(2) Where, after consultation, protective measures are unnecessary and there is no objection raised within the Advisory Committee, the investigation or proceeding shall be terminated. In all other cases, the Commission shall submit to the Council forthwith a report on the results of the consultation, together with a proposal that the proceeding be terminated. The proceeding shall be deemed terminated if, within one month, the Council, acting by a qualified majority, has not decided otherwise.

(3) For a proceeding initiated pursuant to Article 5 (9), injury shall normally be regarded as negligible where the imports concerned represent less than the volumes set out in Article 5 (7). For the same proceeding, there shall be immediate termination where it is determined that the margin of dumping is less than 2%, expressed as a percentage of the export price, provided that it is only the investigation that shall be terminated where the margin is below 2% for individual exporters and they shall remain subject to the proceeding and may be reinvestigated in any subsequent review carried out for the country concerned pursuant to Article 11.

(4) Where the facts as finally established show that there is dumping and injury caused thereby, and the Community interest calls for intervention in accordance with Article 21, a definitive anti-dumping duty shall be imposed by the Council, acting on a proposal submitted by the Commission after consultation of the Advisory Committee. The proposal shall be adopted by the Council unless it decides by a simple majority to reject the proposal, within a period of one month after its submission by the Commission. Where provisional duties are in force, a proposal for definitive action shall be submitted not later than one month before the expiry of such duties. The amount of the anti-dumping duty shall not exceed the margin of dumping established but it should be less than the margin if such lesser duty would be adequate to remove the injury to the Community industry.

(5) An anti-dumping duty shall be imposed in the appropriate amounts in each case, on a non-discriminatory basis on imports of a product from all sources found to be dumped and causing injury, except as to imports from those sources from which undertakings under the terms of this Regulation have been accepted. The Regulation imposing the duty shall specify the duty for each supplier or, if that is impracticable, and in general where Article 2(7)(a) applies, the supplying country concerned.

Where Article 2(7)(a) applies, an individual duty shall, however, be specified for the exporters which can demonstrate, on the basis of properly substantiated claims that:

(a) in the case of wholly or partly foreign owned firms or joint ventures, exporters are free to repatriate capital and profits;
(b) export prices and quantities, and conditions and terms of sale are freely determined;
(c) the majority of the shares belong to private persons. State officials appearing on the board of Directors or holding key management positions shall either be in minority or it must be demonstrated that the company is nonetheless sufficiently independent from State interference;
(d) exchange rate conversions are carried out at the market rate; and
(e) State interference is not such as to permit circumvention of measures if individual exporters are given different rates of duty.

(6) When the Commission has limited its examination in accordance with Article 17, any anti-dumping duty applied to imports from exporters or producers which

have made themselves known in accordance with Article 17 but were not included in the examination shall not exceed the weighted average margin of dumping established for the parties in the sample. For the purpose of this paragraph, the Commission shall disregard any zero and de minimis margins, and margins established in the circumstances referred to in Article 18. Individual duties shall be applied to imports from any exporter or producer which is granted individual treatment, as provided for in Article 17.

Article 10

Retroactivity

(1) Provisional measures and definitive anti-dumping duties shall only be applied to products which enter free circulation after the time when the decision taken pursuant to Articles 7 (1) or 9 (4), as the case may be, enters into force, subject to the exceptions set out in this Regulation.

(2) Where a provisional duty has been applied and the facts as finally established show that there is dumping and injury, the Council shall decide, irrespective of whether a definitive anti-dumping duty is to be imposed, what proportion of the provisional duty is to be definitively collected. For this purpose, 'injury' shall not include material retardation of the establishment of a Community industry, nor threat of material injury, except where it is found that this would, in the absence of provisional measures, have developed into material injury. In all other cases involving such threat or retardation, any provisional amounts shall be released and definitive duties can only be imposed from the date that a final determination of threat or material retardation is made.

(3) If the definitive anti-dumping duty is higher than the provisional duty, the difference shall not be collected. If the definitive duty is lower than the provisional duty, the duty shall be recalculated. Where a final determination is negative, the provisional duty shall not be confirmed.

(4) A definitive anti-dumping duty may be levied on products which were entered for consumption not more than ninety days prior to the date of application of provisional measures but not prior to the initiation of the investigation, provided that imports have been registered in accordance with Article 14 (5), the Commission has allowed the importers concerned an opportunity to comment, and:

(a) there is, for the product in question, a history of dumping over an extended period, or the importer was aware of, or should have been aware of, the dumping as regards the extent of the dumping and the injury alleged or found; and

(b) in addition to the level of imports which caused injury during the investigation period, there is a further substantial rise in imports which, in the light of its timing and volume and other circumstances, is likely to seriously undermine the remedial effect of the definitive anti-dumping duty to be applied.

(5) In cases of breach or withdrawal of undertakings, definitive duties may be levied on goods entered for free circulation not more than ninety days before the application of provisional measures, provided that imports have been registered in accordance with Article 14 (5), and that any such retroactive assessment shall not apply to imports entered before the breach or withdrawal of the undertaking.

Article 11

Duration, Reviews and Refunds

(1) An anti-dumping measure shall remain in force only as long as, and to the extent that, it is necessary to counteract the dumping which is causing injury.

(2) A definitive anti-dumping measure shall expire five years from its imposition or five years from the date of the conclusion of the most recent review which has covered both dumping and injury, unless it is determined in a review that the expiry would be likely to lead to a continuation or recurrence of dumping and injury. Such an expiry review shall be initiated on the initiative of the Commission, or upon request made by or on behalf of Community producers, and the measure shall remain in force pending the outcome of such review.

An expiry review shall be initiated where the request contains sufficient evidence that the expiry of the measures would be likely to result in a continuation or recurrence of dumping and injury. Such a likelihood may, for example, be indicated by evidence of continued dumping and injury or evidence that the removal of injury is partly or solely due to the existence of measures or evidence that the circumstances of the exporters, or market conditions, are such that they would indicate the likelihood of further injurious dumping.

In carrying out investigations under this paragraph, the exporters, importers, the representatives of the exporting country and the Community producers shall be provided with the opportunity to amplify, rebut or comment on the matters set out in the review request, and conclusions shall be reached with due account taken of all relevant and duly documented evidence presented in relation to the question as to whether the expiry of measures would be likely, or unlikely, to lead to the continuation or recurrence of dumping and injury.

A notice of impending expiry shall be published in the Official Journal of the European Communities at an appropriate time in the final year of the period of application of the measures as defined in this paragraph. Thereafter, the Community producers shall, no later than three months before the end of the five-year period, be entitled to lodge a review request in accordance with the second subparagraph. A notice announcing the actual expiry of measures pursuant to this paragraph shall also be published.

(3) The need for the continued imposition of measures may also be reviewed, where warranted, on the initiative of the Commission or at the request of a Member State or, provided that a reasonable period of time of at least one year has elapsed since the imposition of the definitive measure, upon a request by any

exporter or importer or by the Community producers which contains sufficient evidence substantiating the need for such an interim review.

An interim review shall be initiated where the request contains sufficient evidence that the continued imposition of the measure is no longer necessary to offset dumping and/or that the injury would be unlikely to continue or recur if the measure were removed or varied, or that the existing measure is not, or is no longer, sufficient to counteract the dumping which is causing injury.

In carrying out investigations pursuant to this paragraph, the Commission may, inter alia, consider whether the circumstances with regard to dumping and injury have changed significantly, or whether existing measures are achieving the intended results in removing the injury previously established under Article 3. In these respects, account shall be taken in the final determination of all relevant and duly documented evidence.

(4) A review shall also be carried out for the purpose of determining individual margins of dumping for new exporters in the exporting country in question which have not exported the product during the period of investigation on which the measures were based.

The review shall be initiated where a new exporter or producer can show that it is not related to any of the exporters or producers in the exporting country which are subject to the anti-dumping measures on the product, and that it has actually exported to the Community following the abovementioned investigation period, or where it can demonstrate that it has entered into an irrevocable contractual obligation to export a significant quantity to the Community.

A review for a new exporter shall be initiated, and carried out on an accelerated basis, after consultation of the Advisory Committee and after Community producers have been given an opportunity to comment. The Commission Regulation initiating a review shall repeal the duty in force with regard to the new exporter concerned by amending the Regulation which has imposed such duty, and by making imports subject to registration in accordance with Article 14 (5) in order to ensure that, should the review result in a determination of dumping in respect of such an exporter, anti-dumping duties can be levied retroactively to the date of the initiation of the review.

The provisions of this paragraph shall not apply where duties have been imposed under Article 9 (6).

(5) The relevant provisions of this Regulation with regard to procedures and the conduct of investigations, excluding those relating to time limits, shall apply to any review carried out pursuant to paragraphs 2, 3 and 4 of this Article. Reviews carried out pursuant to paragraphs 2 and 3 shall be carried out expeditiously and shall normally be concluded within twelve months of the date of initiation of the review. In any event, reviews pursuant to paragraphs 2 and 3 shall in all cases be concluded within fifteen months of initiation. Reviews pursuant to paragraph 4 shall in all cases be concluded within nine months of the date of initiation. If a review carried out pursuant to paragraph 2 is initiated while a review under paragraph 3 is ongoing in the same proceeding, the review pursuant to paragraph 3 shall be concluded at the same time as foreseen above for the review pursuant to paragraph 2.

The Commission shall submit a proposal for action to the Council not later than one month before the expiry of the above deadlines.

If the investigation is not completed within the above deadlines, the measures shall:

- expire in investigations pursuant to paragraph 2 of this Article,
- expire in the case of investigations carried out pursuant to paragraphs 2 and 3 of this Article in parallel, where either the investigation pursuant to paragraph 2 was initiated while a review under paragraph 3 was ongoing in the same proceeding or where such reviews were initiated at the same time, or
- remain unchanged in investigations pursuant to paragraphs 3 and 4 of this Article.

A notice announcing the actual expiry or maintenance of the measures pursuant to this paragraph shall then be published in the Official Journal of the European Union.

(6) Reviews pursuant to this Article shall be initiated by the Commission after consultation of the Advisory Committee. Where warranted by reviews, measures shall be repealed or maintained pursuant to paragraph 2, or repealed, maintained or amended pursuant to paragraphs 3 and 4, by the Community institution responsible for their introduction. Where measures are repealed for individual exporters, but not for the country as a whole, such exporters shall remain subject to the proceeding and may, automatically, be reinvestigated in any subsequent review carried out for that country pursuant to this Article.

(7) Where a review of measures pursuant to paragraph 3 is in progress at the end of the period of application of measures as defined in paragraph 2, such review shall also cover the circumstances set out in paragraph 2.

(8) Notwithstanding paragraph 2, an importer may request reimbursement of duties collected where it is shown that the dumping margin, on the basis of which duties were paid, has been eliminated, or reduced to a level which is below the level of the duty in force.

In requesting a refund of anti-dumping duties, the importer shall submit an application to the Commission. The application shall be submitted via the Member State of the territory in which the products were released for free circulation, within six months of the date on which the amount of the definitive duties to be levied was duly determined by the competent authorities or of the date on which a decision was made definitively to collect the amounts secured by way of provisional duty. Member States shall forward the request to the Commission forthwith.

An application for refund shall only be considered to be duly supported by evidence where it contains precise information on the amount of refund of anti-dumping duties claimed and all customs documentation relating to the calculation and payment of such amount. It shall also include evidence, for a representative period, of normal values and export prices to the Community for the exporter or producer to which the duty applies. In cases where the importer is not associate with the exporter or producer concerned and such information is not immediately available, or where the exporter or producer is unwilling to release it to the importer, the application shall contain a statement from the exporter or producer that the dumping margin has been reduced or eliminated, as specified in this Article, and that the relevant supporting evidence will be provided to the Commission. Where such evidence is not forthcoming from the exporter or producer within a reasonable period of time the application shall be rejected.

The Commission shall, after consultation of the Advisory Committee, decide whether and to what extent the application should be granted, or it may decide at any time to initiate an interim review, whereupon the information and findings from such review carried out in accordance with the provisions applicable for such reviews, shall be used to determine whether and to what extent a refund is justified. Refunds of duties shall normally take place within twelve months, and in no circumstances more than eighteen months after the date on which a request for a refund, duly supported by evidence, has been made by an importer of the product subject to the anti-dumping duty. The payment of any refund authorized should normally be made by Member States within ninety day of the abovementioned decision.

(9) In all review or refund investigations carried out pursuant to this Article, the Commission shall, provided that circumstances have not changed, apply the same methodology as in the investigation which led to the duty, with due account being taken of Article 2, and in particular paragraphs 11 and 12 thereof, and of Article 17.

(10) In any investigation carried our pursuant to this Article, the Commission shall examine the reliability of export prices in accordance with Article 2. However, where it is decided to construct the export price in accordance with Article 2 (9), it shall calculate it with no deduction for the amount of anti-dumping duties paid when conclusive evidence is provided that the duty is duly reflected in resale prices and the subsequent selling prices in the Community.

Article 12

(1) Where the Community industry or any other interested party submit, normally within two years from the entry into force of the measures, sufficient information showing that, after the original investigation period and prior to or following the imposition of measures, export prices have decreased or that there has been no movement, or insufficient movement in the resale prices or subsequent selling prices of the imported product in the Community, the investigation may, after consultation, be reopened to examine whether the measure has had effects on the abovementioned prices.

The investigation may also be reopened, under the conditions set out above, at the initiative of the Commission or at the request of a Member State.

(2) During a reinvestigation pursuant to this Article, exporters, importers and Community producers shall be provided with an opportunity to clarify the situation

with regard to resale prices and subsequent selling prices: if it is concluded that the measure should have led to movements in such prices, then, in order to remove the injury previously established in accordance with Article 3, export prices shall be reassessed in accordance with Article 2 and dumping margins shall be recalculated to take account of the reassessed export prices. Where it is considered that the conditions of Article 12(1) are met due to a fall in export prices which has occurred after the original investigation period and prior to or following the imposition of measures, dumping margins may be recalculated to take account of such lower export prices.

(3) Where a reinvestigation pursuant to this Article shows increased dumping, the measures in force may, after consultation, be amended by the Council, acting on a proposal from the Commission in accordance with the new findings on export prices. The proposal shall be adopted by the Council unless it decides by a simple majority to reject the proposal, within a period of one month after its submission by the Commission. The amount of the anti-dumping duty imposed pursuant to this Article shall not exceed twice the amount of the duty imposed initially by the Council.

(4) The relevant provisions of Article 5 and 6 shall apply to any reinvestigation carried out pursuant to this Article, except that such reinvestigation shall be carried out expeditiously and shall normally be concluded within six months of the date of initiation of the reinvestigation. In any event, such reinvestigations shall in all cases be concluded within nine months of initiation of the reinvestigation.

The Commission shall submit a proposal for action to the Council not later than one month before the expiry of the above deadline.

If the reinvestigation is not completed within the above deadlines, measures shall remain unchanged. A notice announcing the maintenance of the measures pursuant to this paragraph shall be published in the Official Journal of the European Union.

(5) Alleged changes in normal value shall only be taken into account under this Article where complete information on revised normal values, duly substantiated by evidence, is made available to the Commission within the time limits set out in the notice of initiation of an investigation. Where an investigation involves a re-examination of normal values, imports may be made subject to registration in accordance with Article 14 (5) pending the outcome of the reinvestigation.

Article 13

Circumvention

(1) Anti-dumping duties imposed pursuant to this Regulation may be extended to imports from third countries, of the like product, whether slightly modified or not; or to imports of the slightly modified like product from the country subject to

measures; or parts thereof, when circumvention of the measures in force is taking place. Anti-dumping duties not exceeding the residual anti-dumping duty imposed in accordance with Article 9(5) of this Regulation may be extended to imports from companies benefiting from individual duties in the countries subject to measures when circumvention of the measures in force is taking place. Circumvention shall be defined as a change in the pattern of trade between third countries and the Community or between individual companies in the country subject to measures and the Community, which stems from a practice, process or work for which there is insufficient due cause or economic justification other than the imposition of the duty, and where there is evidence of injury or that the remedial effects of the duty are being undermined in terms of the prices and/or quantities of the like product, and where there is evidence of dumping in relation to the normal values previously established for the like product, if necessary in accordance with the provisions of Article 2.

The practice, process or work referred to in paragraph 1 includes, inter alia, the slight modification of the product concerned to make it fall under customs codes which are normally not subject to the measures, provided that the modification does not alter its essential characteristics; the consignment of the product subject to measures via third countries; the reorganization by exporters or producers of their patterns and channels of sales in the country subject to measures in order to eventually have their products exported to the Community through producers benefiting from an individual duty rate lower than that applicable to the products of the manufacturers; and, in the circumstances indicated below under Article 13(2), the assembly of parts by an assembly operation in the Community or a third country.

(2) An assembly operation in the Community or a third country shall be considered to circumvent the measures in force where:

(a) the operation started or substantially increased since, or just prior to, the initiation of the anti-dumping investigation and the parts concerned are from the country subject to measures; and
(b) the parts constitute 60% or more of the total value of the parts of the assembled product, except that in no case shall circumvention be considered to be taking place where the value added to the parts brought in, during the assembly or completion operation, is greater than 25% of the manufacturing cost, and
(c) the remedial effects of the duty are being undermined in terms of the prices and/or quantities of the assembled like product and there is evidence of dumping in relation to the normal values previously established for the like or similar products.

(3) Investigations shall be initiated pursuant to this Article on the initiative of the Commission or at the request of a Member State or any interested party on the basis of sufficient evidence regarding the factors set out in paragraph 1. Initiations shall be made, after consultation of the Advisory Committee, by Commission Regulation which may also instruct the customs authorities to make imports

subject to registration in accordance with Article 14(5) or to request guarantees. Investigations shall be carried out by the Commission, which may be assisted by customs authorities and shall be concluded within nine months. When the facts as finally ascertained justify the extension of measures, this shall be done by the Council, acting on a proposal submitted by the Commission, after consultation of the Advisory Committee. The proposal shall be adopted by the Council unless it decides by a simple majority to reject the proposal, within a period of one month after its submission by the Commission. The extension shall take effect from the date on which registration was imposed pursuant to Article 14(5) or on which guarantees were requested. The relevant procedural provisions of this Regulation with regard to initiations and the conduct of investigations shall apply pursuant to this Article.

(4) Imports shall not be subject to registration pursuant to Article 14(5) or measures where they are traded by companies which benefit from exemptions. Requests for exemptions duly supported by evidence shall be submitted within the time limits established in the Commission Regulation initiating the investigation. Where the circumventing practice, process or work takes place outside the Community, exemptions may be granted to producers of the product concerned that can show that they are not related to any producer subject to the measures and that are found not to be engaged in circumvention practices as defined in Article 13(1) and 13(2). Where the circumventing practice, process or work takes place inside the Community, exemptions may be granted to importers that can show that they are not related to producers subject to the measures.

These exemptions are granted by decision of the Commission after consultation of the Advisory Committee or decision of the Council imposing measures and shall remain valid for the period and under the conditions set down therein.

Provided that the conditions set in Article 11(4) are met, exemptions may also be granted after the conclusion of the investigation leading to the extension of the measures.

Provided that at least one year has lapsed from the extension of the measures, and in case the number of parties requesting or potentially requesting an exemption is significant, the Commission may decide to initiate a review of the extension of the measures. Any such review shall be conducted in accordance with the provisions of Article 11(5) as applicable to reviews pursuant to Article 11(3).

(5) Nothing in this Article shall preclude the normal application of the provisions in force concerning customs duties.

Article 14

General Provisions

(1) Provisional or definitive anti-dumping duties shall be imposed by Regulation, and collected by Member States in the form, at the rate specified and according to

the other criteria laid down in the Regulation imposing such duties. Such duties shall also be collected independently of the customs duties, taxes and other charges normally imposed on imports. No product shall be subject to both anti-dumping and countervailing duties for the purpose of dealing with one and the same situation arising from dumping or from export subsidization.

(2) Regulations imposing provisional or definitive anti-dumping duties, and Regulations or Decisions accepting undertakings or terminating investigations or proceedings, shall be published in the Official Journal of the European Communities. Such Regulations or Decisions shall contain in particular and with due regard to the protection of confidential information, the names of the exporters, if possible, or of the countries involved, a description of the product and a summary of the material facts and considerations relevant to the dumping and injury determinations. In each case, a copy of the Regulation or Decision shall be sent to known interested parties. The provisions of this paragraph shall apply mutatis mutandis to reviews.

(3) Special provisions, in particular with regard to the common definition of the concept of origin, as contained in Council Regulation (EEC) No. 2913/92 (6), may be adopted pursuant to this Regulation.

(4) In the Community interest, measures imposed pursuant to this Regulation may, after consultation of the Advisory Committee, be suspended by a decision of the Commission for a period of nine months. The suspension may be extended for a further period, not exceeding one year, if the Council so decides, acting on a proposal from the Commission. The proposal shall be adopted by the Council unless it decides by a simple majority to reject the proposal, within a period of one month after its submission by the Commission. Measures may only be suspended where market conditions have temporarily changed to an extent that injury would be unlikely to resume as a result of the suspension, and provided that the Community industry has been given an opportunity to comment and these comments have been taken into account. Measures may, at any time and after consultation, be reinstated if the reason for suspension is no longer applicable.

(5) The Commission may, after consultation of the Advisory Committee, direct the customs authorities to take the appropriate steps to register imports, so that measures may subsequently be applied against those imports from the date of such registration. Imports may be made subject to registration following a request from the Community industry which contains sufficient evidence to justify such action. Registration shall be introduced by Regulation which shall specify the purpose of the action and, if appropriate, the estimated amount of possible future liability. Imports shall not be made subject to registration for a period longer than nine months.

(6) Member States shall report to the Commission every month, on the import trade in products subject to investigation and to measures, and on the amount of duties collected pursuant to this Regulation.

(7) Without prejudice to paragraph 6, the Commission may request Member States, on a case by case basis, to supply information necessary to monitor efficiently the application of measures. In this respect, the provisions of Articles 6(3) and 6(4) shall apply. Any data submitted by Member States pursuant to this Article shall be covered by the provisions of Article 19(6).

Article 15

Consultations

(1) Any consultations provided for in this Regulation shall take place within an Advisory Committee, which shall consist of representatives of each Member State, with a representative of the Commission as chairman. Consultations shall be held immediately at the request of a Member State or on the initiative of the Commission and in any event within a period of time which allows the time limits set by this Regulation to be adhered to.

(2) The Committee shall meet when convened by its chairman. He shall provide the Member States, as promptly as possible, but no later than ten working days before the meeting, with all relevant information.

(3) Where necessary, consultation may be in writing only; in that event, the Commission shall notify the Member States and shall specify a period within which they shall be entitled to express their opinions or to request an oral consultation which the chairman shall arrange, provided that such oral consultation can be held within a period of time which allows the time limits set by this Regulation to be adhered to.

(4) Consultation shall cover, in particular:

- (a) the existence of dumping and the methods of establishing the dumping margin;
- (b) the existence and extent of injury;
- (c) the causal link between the dumped imports and injury;
- (d) the measures which, in the circumstances, are appropriate to prevent or remedy the injury caused by dumping and the ways and means of putting such measures into effect.

Article 16

Verification Visits

(1) The Commission shall, where it considers it appropriate, carry out visits to examine the records of importers, exporters, traders, agents, producers, trade associations and organizations and to verify information provided on dumping and

injury. In the absence of a proper and timely reply, a verification visit may not be carried out.

(2) The Commission may carry out investigations in third countries as required, provided that it obtains the agreement of the firms concerned, that it notifies the representatives of the government of the country in question and that the latter does not object to the investigation. As soon as the agreement of the firms concerned has been obtained the Commission should notify the authorities of the exporting country of the names and addresses of the firms to be visited and the dates agreed.

(3) The firms concerned shall be advised of the nature of the information to be verified during verification visits and of any further information which needs to be provided during such visits, though this should not preclude requests made during the verification for further details to be provided in the light of information obtained.

(4) In investigations carried out pursuant to paragraphs 1, 2 and 3, the Commission shall be assisted by officials of those Member States who so request.

Article 17

Sampling

(1) In cases where the number of complainants, exporters or importers, types of product or transactions is large, the investigation may be limited to a reasonable number of parties, products or transactions by using samples which are statistically valid on the basis of information available at the time of the selection, or to the largest representative volume of production, sales or exports which can reasonably be investigated within the time available.

(2) The final selection of parties, types of products or transactions made under these sampling provisions shall rest with the Commission, though preference shall be given to choosing a sample in consultation with, and with the consent of, the parties concerned, provided such parties make themselves known and make sufficient information available, within three weeks of initiation of the investigation, to enable a representative sample to be chosen.

(3) In cases where the examination has been limited in accordance with this Article, an individual margin of dumping shall, nevertheless, be calculated for any exporter or producer not initially selected who submits the necessary information within the time limits provided for in this Regulation, except where the number of exporters or producers is so large that individual examinations would be unduly burdensome and would prevent completion of the investigation in good time.

(4) Where it is decided to sample and there is a degree of non-cooperation by some or all of the parties selected which is likely to materially affect the outcome of the investigation, a new sample may be selected. However, if a material degree of non-cooperation persists or there is insufficient time to select a new sample, the relevant provisions of Article 18 shall apply.

Article 18

Non-cooperation

(1) In cases in which any interested party refuses access to, or otherwise does not provide, necessary information within the time limits provided in this Regulation, or significantly impedes the investigation, provisional or final findings, affirmative or negative, may be made on the basis of the facts available. Where it is found that any interested party has supplied false or misleading information, the information shall be disregarded and use may be made of facts available. Interested parties should be made aware of the consequences of non-cooperation.

(2) Failure to give a computerized response shall not be deemed to constitute non-cooperation, provided that the interested party shows that presenting the response as requested would result in an unreasonable extra burden or unreasonable additional cost.

(3) Where the information submitted by an interested party is not ideal in all respects it should nevertheless not be disregarded, provided that any deficiencies are not such as to cause undue difficulty in arriving at a reasonably accurate finding and that the information is appropriately submitted in good time and is verifiable, and that the party has acted to the best of its ability.

(4) If evidence or information is not accepted, the supplying party shall be informed forthwith of the reasons therefor and shall be granted an opportunity to provide further explanations within the time limit specified. If the explanations are considered unsatisfactory, the reasons for rejection of such evidence or information shall be disclosed and given in published findings.

(5) If determinations, including those regarding normal value, are based on the provisions of paragraph 1, including the information supplied in the complaint, it shall, where practicable and with due regard to the time limits of the investigation, be checked by reference to information from other independent sources which may be available, such as published price lists, official import statistics and customs returns, or information obtained from other interested parties during the investigation. Such information may include relevant data pertaining to the world market or other representative markets, where appropriate.

(6) If an interested party does not cooperate, or cooperates only partially, so that relevant information is thereby withheld, the result may be less favourable to the party than if it had cooperated.

Article 19

Confidentiality

(1) Any information which is by nature confidential (e.g., because its disclosure would be of significant competitive advantage to a competitor or would have a

significantly adverse effect upon a person supplying the information or upon a person from whom he has acquired the information) or which is provided on a confidential basis by parties to an investigation shall, if good cause is shown, be treated as such by the authorities.

(2) Interested parties providing confidential information shall be required to furnish non-confidential summaries thereof. Those summaries shall be in sufficient detail to permit a reasonable understanding of the substance of the information submitted in confidence. In exceptional circumstances, such parties may indicate that such information is not susceptible of summary. In such exceptional circumstances, a statement of the reasons why summarization is not possible must be provided.

(3) If it is considered that a request for confidentiality is not warranted and if the supplier of the information is either unwilling to make the information available or to authorize its disclosure in generalized or summary form, such information may be disregarded unless it can be satisfactorily demonstrated from appropriate sources that the information is correct. Requests for confidentiality shall not be arbitrarily rejected.

(4) This Article shall not preclude the disclosure of general information by the Community authorities and in particular of the reasons on which decisions taken pursuant to this Regulation are based, or disclosure of the evidence relied on by the Community authorities in so far as is necessary to explain those reasons in court proceedings. Such disclosure must take into account the legitimate interests of the parties concerned that their business secrets should not be divulged.

(5) The Council, the Commission and Member States, or the officials of any of these, shall not reveal any information received pursuant to this Regulation for which confidential treatment has been requested by its supplier, without specific permission from the supplier. Exchanges of information between the Commission and Member States, or any information relating to consultations made pursuant to Article 15, or any internal documents prepared by the authorities of the Community or its Member States, shall not be divulged except as specifically provided for in this Regulation.

(6) Information received pursuant to this Regulation shall be used only for the purpose for which it was requested. This provision shall not preclude the use of information received in the context of one investigation for the purpose of initiating other investigations within the same proceeding in relation to the product concerned.

Article 20

Disclosure

(1) The complainants, importers and exporters and their representative associations, and representatives of the exporting country, may request disclosure of the details underlying the essential facts and considerations on the basis of which

provisional measures have been imposed. Requests for such disclosure shall be made in writing immediately following the imposition of provisional measures, and the disclosure shall be made in writing as soon as possible thereafter.

(2) The parties mentioned in paragraph 1 may request final disclosure of the essential facts and considerations on the basis of which it is intended to recommend the imposition of definitive measures, or the termination of an investigation or proceedings without the imposition of measures, particular attention being paid to the disclosure of any facts or considerations which are different from those used for any provisional measures.

(3) Requests for final disclosure, as defined in paragraph 2, shall be addressed to the Commission in writing and be received, in cases where a provisional duty has been applied, not later than one month after publication of the imposition of that duty. Where a provisional duty has not been applied, parties shall be provided with an opportunity to request final disclosure within time limits set by the Commission.

(4) Final disclosure shall be given in writing. It shall be made, due regard being had to the protection of confidential information, as soon as possible and, normally, not later than one month prior to a definitive decision or the submission by the Commission of any proposal for final action pursuant to Article 9. Where the Commission is not in a position to disclose certain facts or considerations at that time, these shall be disclosed as soon as possible thereafter. Disclosure shall not prejudice any subsequent decision which may be taken by the Commission or the Council but where such decision is based on any different facts and considerations, these shall be disclosed as soon as possible.

(5) Representations made after final disclosure is given shall be taken into consideration only if received within a period to be set by the Commission in each case, which shall be at least ten days, due consideration being given to the urgency of the matter.

Article 21

Community Interest

(1) A determination as to whether the Community interest calls for intervention shall be based on an appreciation of all the various interests taken as a whole, including the interests of the domestic industry and users and consumers; and a determination pursuant to this Article shall only be made where all parties have been given the opportunity to make their views known pursuant to paragraph 2. In such an examination, the need to eliminate the trade distorting effects of injurious dumping and to restore effective competition shall be given special consideration. Measures, as determined on the basis of the dumping and injury found, may not be applied where the authorities, on the basis of all the information submitted, can clearly conclude that it is not in the Community interest to apply such measures.

(2) In order to provide a sound basis on which the authorities can take account of all views and information in the decision as to whether or not the imposition of measures is in the Community interest, the complainants, importers and their representative associations, representative users and representative consumer organizations may, within the time limits specified in the notice of initiation of the anti-dumping investigation, make themselves known and provide information to the Commission. Such information, or appropriate summaries thereof, shall be made available to the other parties specified in this Article, and they shall be entitled to respond to such information.

(3) The parties which have acted in conformity with paragraph 2 may request a hearing. Such requests shall be granted when they are submitted within the time limits set in paragraph 2, and when they set out the reasons, in terms of the Community interest, why the parties should be heard.

(4) The parties which have acted in conformity with paragraph 2 may provide comments on the application of any provisional duties imposed. Such comments shall be received within one month of the application of such measures if they are to be taken into account and they, or appropriate summaries thereof, shall be made available to other parties who shall be entitled to respond to such comments.

(5) The Commission shall examine the information which is properly submitted and the extent to which it is representative and the results of such analysis, together with an opinion on its merits, shall be transmitted to the Advisory Committee. The balance of views expressed in the Committee shall be taken into account by the Commission in any proposal made pursuant to Article 9.

(6) The parties which have acted in conformity with paragraph 2 may request the facts and considerations on which final decisions are likely to be taken to be made available to them. Such information shall be made available to the extent possible and without prejudice to any subsequent decision taken by the Commission or the Council.

(7) Information shall only be taken into account where it is supported by actual evidence which substantiates its validity.

Article 22

Final Provisions

This Regulation shall not preclude the application of:

(a) any special rules laid down in agreements concluded between the Community and third countries;
(b) the Community Regulations in the agricultural sector and Council Regulations (EC) No. 3448/93 (7), (EEC) No. 2730/75 (8) and (EEC) No. 2783/75 (9); this Regulation shall operate by way of complement to those

Regulations and in derogation from any provisions thereof which preclude the application of anti-dumping duties;

(c) special measures, provided that such action does not run counter to obligations pursuant to the GATT.

Article 23

Repeal of existing legislation and transitional measures

Regulation (EC) No. 3283/94 is hereby repealed, with the exception of the first paragraph of Article 23 thereof.

However, the repeal of Regulation (EC) No. 3283/94 shall not prejudice the validity of proceedings initiated thereunder.

References to Regulation (EEC) No. 2423/88 and to Regulation (EC) No. 3283/94 shall be construed as references to this Regulation, where appropriate.

Article 24

Entry into force

This Regulation shall enter into force on the day of its publication in the Official Journal of the European Communities.

However, the time limits provided for in Articles 5 (9), 6 (9) and 7 (1) shall apply to complaints lodged under Article 5 (9) as from 1 September 1995 and investigations initiated pursuant to such complaints.

This Regulation shall be binding in its entirety and directly applicable in all Member States.

Done at Brussels, 22 December 1995.
For the Council
L. ATIENZA SERNA
The President

(1) OJ No. C 319, 30. 11. 1995.
(2) OJ No. C 17, 22. 1. 1996.
(3) OJ No. L 209, 2. 8. 1988, p. 1, as last amended by Regulation (EC) No. 522/94 (OJ No. L 66, 10. 3. 1994, p. 10).
(4) OJ No. L 349, 31. 12. 1994, p. 1. Regulation as last amended by Regulation (EC) No. 1251/95 (OJ No. L 122, 2. 6. 1995, p. 1).
(5) OJ No. L 67, 10. 3. 1994, p. 89.
(6) OJ No. L 302, 19. 10. 1992, p. 1.
(7) OJ No. L 318, 20. 12. 1993, p. 18.
(8) OJ No. L 281, 1. 11. 1975, p. 20. Regulation as amended by Commission Regulation (EEC) No. 222/88 (OJ No. L 28, 1. 2. 1988, p. 1).
(9) OJ No. L 282, 1. 11. 1975, p. 104. Regulation as last amended by Regulation (EEC) No. 3290/94 (OJ No. L 349, 31. 12. 1994, p. 105).

Reports from Panels and Appellate Body (by Name)

Appellate Body Reports

Panel Reports

GATT Panel Reports

Council and Commission Regulations and Decisions

Council Regulations

Commission Regulations

Commission and Council Decisions

Regulations and Decisions (by Name)

Barium Carbonate, Commission Regulation (EC) No. 145/2005 of 28 January 2005 imposing a provisional anti-dumping duty on imports of barium carbonate originating in the People's Republic of China, OJ L 027, 29 January 2005, pp. 4-23, endorsed by Council Regulation (EC) No. 1175/2005 of 18 July 2005 imposing a definitive anti-dumping duty and collecting definitively the provisional duty imposed on imports of barium carbonate originating in the People's Republic of China, OJ L 189, 21 July 2005, pp. 15-23.

Basic Regulation, Council Regulation (EC) No. 384/96 of 22 December 1995 on protection against dumped imports from countries not members of the European Community, OJ L 56, 6 March 1996, pp. 1-20, amended by Council Regulation (EC) No. 2331/96 of 2 December 1996, OJ L 317, 6 December 1996, pp. 1-2; Council Regulation (EC) No. 905/98 of 27 April 1998, OJ L 128, 30 April 1998, pp. 18-19; Council Regulation (EC) No. 2238/2000 of 9 October 2000, OJ L 257, 11 October 2000, pp. 2-3; Council Regulation (EC) No. 1972/2002 of 5 November 2002, OJ L 305, 7 November 2002, pp. 1-3; Council Regulation (EC) No. 461/2004 of 8 March 2004, OJ L 77, 13 March 2004, pp. 12-20; and Council Regulation (EC) No. 2117/2005 of 21 December 2005, OJ L 340, 23 December 2005, p. 17.

Bicycles I, Council Regulation (EEC) No. 2474/93 of 8 September 1993 imposing a definitive anti-dumping duty on imports into the Community of bicycles originating in the People's Republic of China and collecting definitively the provisional anti-dumping duty, OJ L 228, 9 September 1993, pp. 1-9, and Council Regulation (EC) No. 1095/2005 of 12 July 2005 imposing a definitive anti-dumping duty on imports of bicycles originating in Vietnam, and amending Regulation (EC) No. 1524/2000 imposing a definitive anti-dumping duty on imports of bicycles originating in the People's Republic of China, OJ L 183, 14 July 2005, pp. 1-36.

Bicycles II, Council Regulation (EC) No. 397/1999 of 22 February 1999 imposing a definitive anti-dumping duty on imports of bicycles originating in Taiwan and collecting definitively the provisional duty imposed, OJ L 049, 25 February 1999, pp. 1-14.

Certain Ball Bearings and Tapered Roller Bearings, Council Regulation (EEC) No. 1739/85 of 24 June 1985 imposing a definitive anti-dumping duty on imports of certain ball bearings and tapered roller bearings originating in Japan, OJ L 167, 27 June 1985, pp. 3-9.

Certain Castings, in Council Regulation (EC) No. 1212/2005 of 25 July 2005 imposing a definitive anti-dumping duty on imports of certain castings originating in the People's Republic of China, OJ L 199, 29 July 2005, pp. 1-27.

Certain Electronic Weighing Scales (REWS), Council Regulation (EC) No. 2605/2000 of 27 November 2000 imposing definitive anti-dumping duties on imports of certain electronic weighing scales (REWS) originating in the People's Republic of China, the Republic of Korea and Taiwan, OJ L 301, 30 November 2000, pp. 42-60, amended in Council Regulation (EC) No. 692/2005 of 28 April 2005 amending Regulation (EC) No. 2605/2000 imposing definitive anti-dumping duties on imports of certain electronic weighing scales (REWS) originating, inter alia, in the People's Republic of China, OJ L 112, 3 May 2005, pp. 1-7.

Certain Finished Polyester Filament Fabrics, Commission Regulation (EC) No. 426/2005 of 15 March 2005 on imposing a provisional anti-dumping duty on imports of certain finished polyester filament apparel fabrics originating in the People's Republic of China, OJ L 069, 16 March 2005, pp. 6-33, endorsed in Council Regulation (EC) No. 1487/2005 of 12 September 2005 imposing a definitive anti-dumping duty and collecting definitely the provisional duty imposed on imports of certain finished polyester filament fabrics originating in the People's Republic of China, OJ L 240, 16 September 2005, pp. 1-16.

Certain Footwear with Textile Uppers, Commission Regulation (EC) No. 165/97 of 28 January 1997 imposing a provisional anti-dumping duty on imports of certain footwear with textile uppers originating in the People's Republic of China and Indonesia, OJ L 029, 31 January 1997, pp. 3-18 endorsed in Council Regulation (EC) No. 2155/97 of 29 October 1997 imposing a definitive anti-dumping duty on imports of certain footwear with textile uppers originating in the People's Republic of China and Indonesia and collecting definitively the provisional duty imposed, OJ L 298, 1 November 1997, pp. 1-18.

Certain Footwear with Uppers of Leather, Commission Regulation (EC) No. 553/2006 of 23 March 2006 imposing a provisional anti-dumping duty on imports of certain footwear with uppers of leather originating in the People's Republic of China and Vietnam, OJ L 098, 6 April 2006, pp. 3-54 endorsed in Council Regulation (EC) No. 1472/2006 of 5 October 2006 imposing a definitive anti-dumping duty and collecting definitely the provisional duty imposed on imports of certain footwear with uppers of leather originating in the People's Republic of China and Vietnam, OJ L 275, 6 October 2006, pp. 1-41.

Certain Footwear with Uppers of Leather or Plastics, Council Regulation (EC) No. 467/98 of 23 February 1998 imposing a definitive anti-dumping duty on imports of certain footwear with uppers of leather or plastics originating in the People's Republic of China, Indonesia and Thailand, OJ L 60, 28 February 1998, pp. 1-29.

Certain Frozen Strawberries, Commission Regulation (EC) No. 1551/2006 of 17 October 2006 imposing a provisional anti-dumping duty on imports of certain frozen strawberries originating in the People's Republic of China, OJ L 287, 18 October 2006, pp. 3-29, endorsed in Council Regulation (EC) No. 407/2007 of 16 April 2007 imposing definitive anti-dumping measures and releasing the provisional duty imposed on imports of certain frozen strawberries originating in the People's Republic of China, OJ L 100, 17 April 2007, pp. 1-13.

Certain Graphite Electrode Systems, Commission Regulation (EC) No. 1009/2004 of 19 May 2004 imposing a provisional anti-dumping duty on imports of certain graphite electrode systems originating in India, OJ L 183, 20 May 2004, pp. 61-82, endorsed in Council Regulation (EC) No. 1629/2004 of 13 September 2004 imposing a definitive anti-dumping duty and collecting definitively the provisional duty imposed on imports of certain graphite electrode systems originating in India, OJ L 295, 18 September 2004, pp. 10-14.

Certain Iron or Steel Ropes and Cables, Commission Regulation (EC) No. 230/2001 of 2 February 2001 imposing a provisional anti-dumping duty on certain iron or steel ropes and cables originating in the Czech Republic, Russia, Thailand and Turkey and accepting undertakings offered by certain exporters in the Czech Republic and Turkey, OJ L 34, 3 February 2001, pp. 4-27, endorsed in Council Regulation (EC) No. 1601/2001 of 2 August 2001 imposing a definitive anti-dumping duty and definitively collecting the provisional anti-dumping duty imposed on imports of certain iron or steel ropes and cables originating in the Czech Republic, Russia, Thailand and Turkey, OJ L 211, 4 August 2001, pp. 1-19.

Certain Magnesia Bricks, Commission Regulation (EC) No. 552/2005 of 11 April 2005 imposing a provisional anti-dumping duty on imports of certain magnesia bricks originating in the People's Republic of China, OJ L 093, 12 April 2005, pp. 6-30, endorsed in the Council in Council Regulation (EC) No. 1659/2005 of 6 October 2005 imposing a definitive anti-dumping duty and collecting definitively the provisional duty imposed on imports of certain magnesia bricks originating in the People's Republic of China, OJ L 267, 12 October 2005, pp. 1-14.

Certain Polyester Yarn, Council Regulation (EEC) No. 407/83 of 21 February 1983 amending Regulation (EEC) No. 3439/80 imposing a definitive anti-dumping duty on imports of certain polyester yarn originating in the United States of America, OJ L 050, 23 February 1983, p. 1.

Certain Polyethylene Terephthalate I, Commission Regulation (EC) No. 1742/2000 of 4 August 2000 imposing a provisional anti-dumping duty on imports of certain polyethylene terephthalate (PET) originating in India, Indonesia, Malaysia, the Republic of Korea, Taiwan and Thailand, OJ L 199, 5 August 2000, pp. 48-77, endorsed in Council Regulation (EC) No. 496/2002 of 18 March 2002 amending Regulation (EC) No. 2604/2000 imposing a definitive anti-dumping duty on imports of certain polyethylene terephthalate originating, amongst other countries, in India, OJ L 78, 21 March 2002, pp. 4-6.

Certain Polyethylene Terephthalate II, Council Regulation (EC) No. 192/2007 of 22 February 2007 imposing a definitive anti-dumping duty on imports of certain polyethylene terephthalate originating in India, Indonesia, Malaysia, the Republic of Korea, Thailand and Taiwan following an expiry review and a partial interim review pursuant to Article 11(2) and Article 11(3) of Regulation (EC) No. 384/96, OJ L 59, 27 February 2007, pp. 1-33.

Certain Plastic Sacks and Bags, Council Regulation (EC) No. 1425/2006 of 25 September 2006 imposing a definitive anti-dumping duty on imports of certain plastic sacks and bags originating in the People's Republic of China and Thailand, and terminating the proceeding on imports of certain plastic sacks and bags originating in Malaysia, OJ L 270, 29 September 2006, pp. 4-41.

Certain Prepared or Preserved Sweetcorn, Commission Regulation (EC) No. 1888/2006 of 19 December 2006 imposing a provisional anti-dumping duty on imports of certain prepared or preserved sweetcorn in kernels originating in Thailand, OJ L 364, 20 December 2006, pp. 68-91, endorsed in Council Regulation (EC) No. 682/2007 of 18 June 2007 imposing a definitive anti-dumping duty and collecting definitively the provisional duty imposed on imports of certain prepared or preserved sweetcorn in kernels originating in Thailand, OJ L 159, 20 June 2007, pp. 14-25.

Certain Ringbinder Mechanisms I, Council Regulation (EC) No. 1208/2004 of 28 June 2004 extending the definitive anti-dumping measures imposed by Regulation (EC) No. 119/97 on imports of certain ring-binder mechanisms originating in the People's Republic of China to imports of the same product consigned from the Socialist Republic of Vietnam, OJ L 232, 1 July 2004, pp. 1-8.

Certain Ringbinder Mechanisms (RBM) II, Council Regulation (EC) No. 976/2002 of 4 June 2002 imposing a definitive anti-dumping duty on imports of certain ring binder mechanisms (RBM) originating in Indonesia and terminating the anti-dumping proceeding in respect of imports of certain RBM originating in India, OJ L 150, 8 June 2002, pp. 1-16.

Certain Seamless Pipes and Tubes of Iron or non-alloy Steel, Council Regulation (EC) No. 2320/97 of 17 November 1997 imposing definitive anti-dumping duties on imports of certain seamless pipes and tubes of iron or non-alloy steel originating in Hungary, Poland, Russia, the Czech Republic, Romania and the Slovak Republic, repealing Regulation (EEC) No. 1189/93 and terminating the proceeding in respect of such imports originating in the Republic of Croatia, OJ 25 November 1997 L 322, p. 1.

Certain side-by-side Refrigerators, Commission Regulation (EC) No. 355/2006 of 28 February 2006 imposing a provisional anti-dumping duty on imports of certain side-by-side refrigerators originating in the Republic of Korea, OJ L 59, 1 March 2006, pp. 12-33, endorsed in Council Regulation (EC) No. 1289/2006 of 25 August 2006 imposing a definitive anti-dumping duty and collecting definitively the provisional duty imposed on imports of certain side-by-side refrigerators originating in the Republic of Korea, OJ L 236, 31 August 2006, pp. 11-17.

Certain Tube or Pipe Fittings of Iron or Steel I, Commission Regulation (EC) No. 2318/95 of 27 September 1995 imposing a provisional anti-dumping duty on imports of certain tube or pipe fittings, of iron or steel, originating in the People' s Republic of China, Croatia and Thailand and terminating the anti-dumping proceeding in respect of imports of these fittings, originating in the Slovak Republic and Taiwan, OJ L 234, 3 October 1995, pp. 4-15, endorsed in Council Regulation (EC) No. 584/96 of 11 March 1996 imposing a definitive anti-dumping duty on imports of certain tube or pipe fittings, of iron or steel, originating in the People's Republic of China, Croatia and Thailand, and collecting definitively the provisional duty imposed, OJ L 84, 3 April 1996, pp. 1-7.

Certain Tube and Pipe Fittings of Iron or Steel II, Commission Regulation (EC) No. 358/2002 of 26 February 2002 imposing a provisional anti-dumping duty on imports of certain tube and pipe fittings, of iron or steel originating in the Czech Republic, Malaysia, Russia, the Republic of Korea and Slovakia and accepting an undertaking offered by an exporting producer in Slovakia, OJ L 056, 27 February 2002, p. 4-18 endorsed in Council Regulation (EC) No. 1514/2002 of 19 August 2002 imposing a definitive anti-dumping duty and collecting definitively the provisional duty imposed on imports of certain tube and pipe fittings, of iron or steel originating in the Czech Republic, Malaysia, Russia, the Republic of Korea and Slovakia, OJ L 228, 24 August 2002, pp. 1-7.

Certain Tungsten Electrodes, Commission Regulation (EC) No. 1350/2006 of 13 September 2006 imposing a provisional anti-dumping duty on imports of certain tungsten electrodes originating in the People's Republic of China, OJ L 250, 14 September 2006, pp. 10-33, endorsed in Council Regulation (EC) No. 260/2007 of 9 March 2007 imposing a definitive anti-dumping duty and collecting definitively the provisional duty imposed on imports of certain tungsten electrodes originating in the People's Republic of China, OJ L 72, 13 March 2007, pp. 1-9.

Certain Unbleached Cotton Fabrics, Commission Regulation (EC) No. 773/98 of 7 April 1998 imposing a provisional anti-dumping duty on imports of certain unbleached cotton fabrics originating in the People's Republic of China, Egypt, India, Indonesia, Pakistan and Turkey, OJ L 111, 9 April 1998, pp. 19-64. Not endorsed by the Council.

Chamois Leather, Commission Regulation (EC) No. 439/2006 of 16 March 2006 imposing a provisional anti-dumping duty on imports of chamois leather originating in the People's Republic of China, OJ L 080, 17 March 2006, pp. 7-22, endorsed in Council Regulation (EC) No. 1338/2006 of 8 September 2006 imposing a definitive anti-dumping duty and collecting definitively the provisional duty imposed on imports of chamois leather originating in the People's Republic of China, OJ L 251, 14 September 2006, pp. 1-5.

Colour Television Receivers, Commission Regulation (EC) No. 2376/94 of 27 September 1994 imposing a provisional anti-dumping duty on imports of colour television receivers originating in Malaysia, the people's Republic of China, the Republic of Korea, Singapore and Thailand, OJ L 255, 1 October 1994, pp. 50-69, endorsed in Council Regulation (EC) No. 710/95 of 27 March 1995 imposing a definitive anti-dumping duty on imports of colour television receivers originating in Malaysia, the People's Republic of China, the Republic of Korea, Singapore and Thailand and collecting definitively the provisional duty imposed, OJ L 73, 1 April 1995, pp. 3-12.

Cotton-type Bed linen I, Commission Regulation (EC) No. 1069/97 of 12 June 1997 imposing a provisional anti-dumping duty on imports of cotton-type bed linen originating in Egypt, India and Pakistan, OJ L 156, 13 June 1997, pp. 11-33, endorsed in Council Regulation (EC) No. 2398/97 of 28 November 1997 imposing a definitive anti-dumping duty on imports of cotton-type bed linen originating in Egypt, India and Pakistan, OJ L 332, 4 December 1997, pp. 1-18. Council Regulation (EC) No. 1644/2001 of 7 August 2001 amending Regulation (EC) No. 2398/97 imposing a definitive anti-dumping duty on imports of cotton-type bed linen originating in Egypt, India and Pakistan and suspending its application with regard to imports originating in India, OJ L 219, 14 August 2001, pp. 1-11 and Council Regulation (EC) No. 160/2002 of 28 January 2002 amending Council Regulation (EC) No. 2398/97 imposing a definitive anti-dumping duty on imports of cotton-type bed linen originating in Egypt, India and Pakistan, and terminating the proceeding with regard to imports originating in Pakistan, OJ L 26, 30 January 2002, pp. 1-4; Council Regulation (EC) No. 1644/2001 of 7 August 2001 amending Regulation (EC) No. 2398/97 imposing a definitive anti-dumping duty on imports of cotton-type bed linen originating in Egypt, India and Pakistan and suspending its application with regard to imports originating in India, OJ L 219, 14 August 2001, pp. 1-11 and Council Regulation (EC) No. 2239/2003 of 17 December 2003 terminating the partial interim review and the expiry review concerning the anti-dumping measures imposed by Regulation (EC) No. 2398/97 on imports of cotton-type bed linen originating, inter alia, in India, OJ L 333, 20 December 2003, pp. 3-8.

Cotton-type Bedlinen II, Council Regulation (EC) No. 695/2006 of 5 May 2006 amending Regulation (EC) No. 397/2004 imposing a definitive anti-dumping duty on imports of cotton-type bed linen originating in Pakistan, OJ L 121, 6 May 2006, pp. 14-26.

Coumarin, Council Regulation (EC) No. 2272/2004 of 22 December 2004 extending the definitive anti-dumping duty imposed by Regulation (EC) No. 769/2002 on imports of coumarin originating in the People's Republic of China to imports of coumarin consigned from India or Thailand, whether declared as originating in India or Thailand or not, OJ L 396, 31 December 2004, pp. 18-27.

Electronic Typewriters, Commission Regulation (EEC) No. 3643/84 of 20 December 1984 imposing a provisional anti-dumping duty on imports of electronic typewriters originating in Japan and terminating the anti-dumping proceeding with regard to Nakajima All Co. Ltd, OJ L 335, 22 December 1984, pp. 43-48, endorsed in Council Regulation (EEC) No. 1698/85 of 19 June 1985 imposing a definitive anti-dumping duty on imports of electronic typewriters originating in Japan, OJ L 163, 22 June 1985, pp. 1-11.

Farmed Atlantic Salmon, Council Regulation (EC) No. 1890/97 of 26 September 1997 imposing a definitive anti-dumping duty on imports of farmed Atlantic salmon originating in Norway – Council Declaration, OJ L 267, 30 September 1997, pp. 1-18.

Ferro-silicon, Council Regulation (EEC) No. 341/90 of 5 February 1990 accepting undertakings and imposing a definitive anti-dumping duty on imports of ferro-silicon originating in Iceland, Norway, Sweden, Venezuela or Yugoslavia, except those sold for export to the Community by companies whose undertakings have been accepted, OJ L 38, 10 February 1990, pp. 1-8.

Furfuryl Alcohol, Commission Regulation (EC) No. 781/2003 of 7 May 2003 imposing a provisional anti-dumping duty on imports of furfuryl alcohol originating in the People's Republic of China, OJ L 114, 8 May 2003, pp. 16-37, endorsed in Council Regulation (EC) No. 1905/2003 of 27 October 2003 imposing a definitive anti-dumping duty and collecting definitively the provisional duty imposed on imports of furfuryl alcohol originating in the People's Republic of China, OJ L 283, 31 October 2003, pp. 1-7.

Gas-fuelled, non-refillable Pocket Flint Lighters, Council Regulation (EC) No. 192/1999 of 25 January 1999 extending the definitive anti-dumping duty, imposed by Regulation (EEC) No. 3433/91 on imports of gas-fuelled, non-refillable pocket flint lighters originating in the People's Republic of China to imports of certain disposable refillable pocket flint lighters originating in the People's Republic of China or consigned from or originating in Taiwan and to imports of non-refillable lighters consigned from or originating in Taiwan, and terminating the proceeding in respect of imports of non-refillable lighters consigned from Hong Kong and Macao OJ L 22, 29 January 1999, pp. 1-9.

Glyphosate, Council Regulation (EC) No. 1683/2004 of 24 September 2004 imposing a definitive anti-dumping duty on imports of glyphosate originating in the People's Republic of China, OJ L 303, 30 September 2004, pp. 1-18.

Granular Polytetrafluoroethylene (PTFE), Commission Regulation (EC) No. 862/2005 of 7 June 2005 imposing provisional anti-dumping duties on imports of PTFE originating in Russia and the People's Republic of China, OJ L 144, 8 June 2005, pp. 11-36, endorsed in Council Regulation (EC) No. 1987/2005 of 2 December 2005 imposing a definitive anti-dumping duty and collecting definitively the provisional duty imposed on imports of PTFE originating in Russia and the People's Republic of China, OJ L 320, 8 December 2005, pp. 1-19.

Hand Pallet Trucks and Their essential Parts, Commission Regulation (EC) No. 128/2005 of 27 January 2005 imposing a provisional anti-dumping duty on imports of hand pallet trucks and their essential parts originating in the People's Republic of China, OJ L 025, 28 January 2005, pp. 16-36, endorsed in Council Regulation (EC) No. 1174/2005 of 18 July 2005 imposing a definitive anti-dumping duty and collecting definitely the provisional duty imposed on imports of hand pallet trucks and their essential parts originating in the People's Republic of China, OJ L 189, 21 July 2005, pp. 1-14.

Integrated Electronic Compact Fluorescent Lamps (CFL-I), Commission Regulation (EC) No. 255/2001 of 7 February 2001 imposing a provisional anti-dumping duty on imports of integrated electronic compact fluorescent lamps (CFL-i) originating in the People's Republic of China, OJ L 38, 8 February 2001, pp. 8-21, endorsed in Council Regulation (EC) No. 1470/2001 of 16 July 2001 imposing a definitive anti-dumping duty and collecting definitively the provisional duty imposed on imports of integrated electronic compact fluorescent lamps (CFL-i) originating in the People's Republic of China, OJ L 195, 19 July 2001, pp. 8-14, extended in Council Regulation (EC) No. 866/2005 of 6 June 2005 extending the definitive anti-dumping measures imposed by Regulation (EC) No. 1470/2001 on imports of integrated electronic compact fluorescent lamps (CFL-i) originating in the People's Republic of China to imports of the same product consigned from the Socialist Republic of Vietnam, the Islamic Republic of Pakistan and the Republic of the Philippines, OJ L 145, 9 June 2005, pp. 1-15.

Lever Arch Mechanisms, Commission Regulation (EC) No. 134/2006 of 26 January 2006 imposing a provisional anti-dumping duty on imports of lever arch mechanisms originating in the People's Republic of China, OJ L 23, 27 January 2006, pp. 13-33, endorsed in Council Regulation (EC) No. 1136/2006 of 24 July 2006 imposing a definitive anti-dumping duty and collecting definitively the provisional duty imposed on imports of lever arch mechanisms originating in the People's Republic of China, OJ L 205, 27 July 2006, pp. 1-12.

Magnesium Oxide, Council Regulation (EC) No. 778/2005 of 23 May 2005 imposing a definitive anti-dumping duty on imports of magnesium oxide originating in the People's Republic of China, OJ L 131, 25 May 2005, pp. 1-17.

Malleable Cast Iron Tube or Pipe Fittings, Commission Regulation (EC) No. 449/2000 of 28 February 2000 imposing a provisional anti-dumping duty on imports of malleable cast iron tube or pipe fittings originating in Brazil, the Czech Republic, Japan, the People's Republic of China, the Republic of Korea and Thailand and accepting an undertaking offered by an exporting producer in the Czech Republic,

OJ L 55, 29 February 2000, pp. 3-23, endorsed in Council Regulation (EC) No. 1784/2000 of 11 August 2000 imposing a definitive anti-dumping duty and collecting definitively the provisional duty imposed on imports of certain malleable cast iron tube or pipe fittings originating in Brazil, the Czech Republic, Japan, the People's Republic of China, the Republic of Korea and Thailand, OJ L 208, 18 August 2000, pp. 8-23.

MSG, Council Regulation (EEC) No. 1798/90 of 27 June 1990 imposing a definitive anti-dumping duty on imports of MSG originating in Indonesia, the Republic of Korea, Taiwan and Thailand and definitively collecting the provisional anti-dumping duty imposed on such imports, OJ 1990 L 167 30 June 1990, p. 1, amended by Council Regulation (EEC) No. 2966/92 of 12 October 1992, OJ 1992 L 299, p. 1, and by Council Regulation (EEC) No. 2455/93 of 2 September 1993, OJ 1993 L 225, p. 1.

Okoumé Plywood, Commission Regulation (EC) No. 988/2004 of 17 May 2004 imposing provisional anti-dumping duties on imports of okoumé plywood originating in the People's Republic of China, OJ L 181, 18 May 2004, pp. 5-23, endorsed in Council Regulation (EC) No. 1942/2004 of 2 November 2004 imposing a definitive anti-dumping duty and collecting definitively the provisional duty imposed on imports of okoumé plywood originating in the People's Republic of China, OJ L 336, 12 November 2004, pp. 4-12.

Paint, Distemper, Varnish and similar Brushes, Commission Regulation (EEC) No. 3052/88 of 29 September 1988 imposing a provisional anti-dumping duty on imports of paint, distemper, varnish and similar brushes originating in the people's Republic of China, OJ L 272, 4 October 1988, pp. 16-17, endorsed in Council Regulation (EEC) No. 725/89 of 20 March 1989 imposing a definitive anti-dumping duty on imports of paint, distemper, varnish and similar brushes originating in the people's Republic of China and definitively collecting the provisional anti-dumping duty on such imports, OJ L 79, 22 March 1989, pp. 24-29; and Council Decision (EEC) 87/104 of 9 February 1987 accepting an undertaking given in connection with the anti-dumping proceeding concerning imports of paint, distemper, varnish and similar brushes originating in the People's Republic of China, and terminating the investigation, OJ L 46, 14 February 1987, pp. 45-48.

Paracresol, Commission Regulation (EC) No. 510/2003 of 20 March 2003 imposing provisional anti-dumping duties on imports of paracresol originating in the People's Republic of China, OJ L 075, 21 March 2003, pp. 12-22, endorsed in Council Regulation (EC) No. 1656/2003 of 11 September 2003 imposing a definitive anti-dumping duty and collecting definitively the provisional duty imposed on imports of para-cresol originating in the People's Republic of China, OJ L 234, 20 September 2003, pp. 1-5.

Polyester Staple Fibres I, Commission Regulation (EC) No. 1472/2000 of 6 July 2000 imposing a provisional anti-dumping duty on imports of polyester staple fibres originating in India and the Republic of Korea, OJ L 166, 6 July 2000, pp. 1-13, endorsed in Council Regulation (EC) No. 2852/2000 of 22 December

2000 imposing a definitive anti-dumping duty and definitively collecting the provisional duty imposed on imports of polyester staple fibres originating in India and the Republic of Korea, OJ L 332, 28 December 2000, pp. 17-31; Council Regulation (EC) No. 428/2005 of 10 March 2005 imposing a definitive anti-dumping duty on imports of polyester staple fibres originating in the People's Republic of China and Saudi Arabia, amending Regulation (EC) No. 2852/2000 imposing a definitive anti-dumping duty on imports of polyester staple fibres originating in the Republic of Korea and terminating the anti-dumping proceeding in respect of such imports originating in Taiwan, OJ L 71, 17 March 2005, pp. 1-33.

Polyester Staple Fibres (PSF) II, Commission Regulation (EC) No. 124/2000 of 20 January 2000 imposing a provisional anti-dumping duty on imports of polyester staple fibres (PSF) originating in Australia, Indonesia and Thailand, OJ L 16, 21 January 2000, pp. 30-49, endorsed in Council Regulation (EC) No. 1522/2000 of 10 July 2000 imposing a definitive anti-dumping duty on imports of synthetic staple fibres of polyester originating in Australia, Indonesia and Thailand and collecting definitively the provisional duty imposed, OJ L 175, 14 July 2000, pp. 10-28.

Polyethylene Terephthalate I, Commission Regulation (EC) No. 306/2004 of 19 February 2004 imposing a provisional anti-dumping duty on imports of polyethylene terephthalate originating in Australia, the People's Republic of China and Pakistan, OJ L 052, 21 February 2004, pp. 5-34, endorsed in Council Regulation (EC) No. 1467/2004 of 13 August 2004 imposing a definitive anti-dumping duty and collecting definitively the provisional duty imposed on imports of polyethylene terephthalate originating in Australia, the People's Republic of China and terminating the anti-dumping proceeding concerning imports of polyethylene terephthalate originating in Pakistan and releasing the amounts secured by way of the provisional duties imposed, OJ L 271, 19 August 2004, pp. 1-17.

Polyethylene Terephthalate II, Council Regulation (EC) No. 192/2007 of 22 February 2007 imposing a definitive anti-dumping duty on imports of certain polyethylene terephthalate originating in India, Indonesia, Malaysia, the Republic of Korea, Thailand and Taiwan following an expiry review and a partial interim review pursuant to Article 11(2) and Article 11(3) of Regulation (EC) No. 384/96, OJ L 59, 27 February 2007, pp. 1-33.

Polyethylene Terephthalate Film, Commission Regulation (EC) No. 367/2001 of 23 February 2001 imposing a provisional anti-dumping duty on imports of polyethylene terephthalate film originating in India and the Republic of Korea, OJ L 055, 24 February 2001, pp. 16-39, endorsed in Council Regulation (EC) No. 1676/2001 of 13 August 2001 imposing a definitive anti-dumping duty and collecting definitively the provisional duty imposed on imports of polyethylene terephthalate film originating in India and the Republic of Korea, OJ L 227, 23 August 2001, pp. 1-14, extended in Council Regulation (EC) No. 1975/2004 of 15 November 2004 extending the definitive anti-dumping duty imposed by Regulation (EC) No. 1676/2001 on imports of polyethylene terephthalate (PET) film originating, inter alia, in India to imports of polyethylene terephthalate (PET) film consigned from Brazil and from Israel, whether declared as originating in Brazil or Israel or not, OJ L 342, 18 November 2004, pp. 1-7, amended in Council Regulation (EC) No. 366/2006 of 27 February 2006 amending Regulation (EC) No. 1676/2001 imposing a definitive anti-dumping duty on imports of polyethylene terephthalate (PET) film originating, inter alia, in India, OJ L 068, 8 March 2006, pp. 6-14.

Council Regulation (EC) No. 390/2005 of 7 March 2005 terminating the partial interim review of the anti-dumping measures applicable to imports of polyethylene terephthalate (PET) film originating, inter alia, in India, OJ L 63, 10 March 2005, pp. 1-3.

Polyester Textured Filament Yarn (PTY), Commission Regulation (EC) No. 1412/2002 of 29 July 2002 imposing a provisional anti-dumping duty on imports of polyester textured filament yarn (PTY) originating in India, OJ L 205, 2 August 2002, pp. 50-69, endorsed in Council Regulation (EC) No. 2093/2002 of 26 November 2002 imposing a definitive anti-dumping duty and collecting definitively the provisional duty imposed on imports of polyester textured filament yarn (PTY) originating in India, OJ L 323, 28 November 2002, pp. 1-20.

Potassium Permanganate, Commission Regulation (EC) No. 178/98 of 23 January 1998 imposing a provisional anti-dumping duty on imports of potassium permanganate originating in India and the Ukraine, OJ L 19, 24 January 1998, pp. 23-34, endorsed in Council Regulation (EC) No. 1507/98 of 13 July 1998 imposing a definitive anti-dumping duty on imports of potassium permanganate originating in India and the Ukraine and collecting definitively the provisional duty imposed, OJ L 200, 16 July 1998, pp. 4-8.

Recordable Compact Disks, Commission Regulation (EC) No. 2479/2001 of 17 December 2001 imposing a provisional anti-dumping duty on imports of recordable compact disks originating in Taiwan, OJ L 334, 18 December 2001, pp. 8-25, endorsed in Council Regulation (EC) No. 1050/2002 of 13 June 2002 imposing a definitive anti-dumping duty and collecting definitively the provisional duty imposed on imports of recordable compact disks originating in Taiwan, OJ L 160, 18 June 2002, pp. 2-13.

Sacks and Bags Made of Polyethylene or Polypropylene, Commission Regulation (EC) No. 45/97 of 10 January 1997 imposing a provisional anti-dumping duty on imports of sacks and bags made of polyethylene or polypropylene originating in India, Indonesia and Thailand, OJ L 12, 15 January 1997, pp. 8-20, endorsed in Council Regulation (EC) No. 1950/97 of 6 October 1997 imposing a definitive anti-dumping duty on imports of sacks and bags made of polyethylene or polypropylene originating in India, Indonesia and Thailand and collecting definitively the provisional duty imposed, OJ L 276, 9 October 1997, pp. 1-8 and Council Regulation (EC) No. 1763/2002 of 30 September 2002 amending Regulation (EC) No. 1950/97 imposing definitive anti-dumping measures on imports of sacks and bags made of polyethylene or polypropylene originating, inter alia, in India, OJ L 267, 4 October 2002, pp. 1-7.

Silicon, Council Regulation (EC) No. 398/2004 of 2 March 2004 imposing a definitive anti-dumping duty on imports of silicon originating in the People's Republic of China, OJ L 066, 4 March 2004, pp. 15-30.

Small-screen Colour Television Receivers, Commission Regulation (EEC) No. 129/91 of 11 January 1991 imposing a provisional anti-dumping duty on imports of small-screen colour television receivers originating in Hong Kong and the people's Republic of China, OJ L 14, 19 January 1991, pp. 31-45, endorsed in Council Regulation (EEC) No. 2093/91 of 15 July 1991 imposing a definitive anti-dumping duty on imports of small-screen colour television receivers originating in Hong Kong and the People's Republic of China and collecting definitively the provisional duty, OJ L 195, 18 July 1991, pp. 1-8.

Sodium Cyclamate, Commission Regulation (EC) No. 1627/2003 of 17 September 2003 imposing a provisional anti-dumping duty on imports of sodium cyclamate originating in the People's Republic of China and Indonesia, OJ L 232, 18 September 2003, pp. 12-28, endorsed in Council Regulation (EC) No. 435/2004 of 8 March 2004 imposing a definitive anti-dumping duty and collecting definitively the provisional duty imposed on imports of sodium cyclamate originating in the People's Republic of China and Indonesia, OJ L 072, 11 March 2004, pp. 1-14.

Stainless Steel Bars, Commission Regulation (EC) No. 1084/98 of 28 May 1998 imposing a provisional anti-dumping duty on imports of stainless steel bars originating in India, OJ L 155, 29 May 1998, pp. 3-13, endorsed in Council Regulation (EC) No. 2450/98 of 13 November 1998 imposing a definitive countervailing duty on imports of stainless steel bars originating in India and collecting definitively the provisional duty imposed, OJ L 304, 14 November 1998, pp. 1-12.

Stainless Steel Fasteners and Parts thereof I, Commission Regulation (EC) No. 1732/97 of 4 September 1997 imposing a provisional anti-dumping duty on imports of stainless steel fasteners and parts originating in the People's Republic of China, India, Malaysia, the Republic of Korea, Taiwan and Thailand, OJ L 243, 5 September 1997, pp. 17-36, endorsed in Council Regulation (EC) No. 393/98 of 16 February 1998 imposing a definitive anti-dumping duty on imports of stainless steel fasteners and parts thereof originating in the People's Republic of China, India, the Republic of Korea, Malaysia, Taiwan and Thailand, OJ L 50, 20 February 1998, pp. 1-14; Council Regulation (EC) No. 2570/2000 of 20 November 2000 amending Regulation (EC) No. 393/98 imposing a definitive anti-dumping duty on imports of stainless steel fasteners and parts thereof originating, inter alia, in the People's Republic of China, OJ L 297, 24 November 2000, pp. 1-3 and Council Regulation (EC) No. 695/2003 of 14 April 2003 amending Regulation (EC) No. 393/98 imposing a definitive anti-dumping duty on imports of stainless steel fasteners and parts thereof originating in the People's Republic of China, India, the Republic of Korea, Malaysia, Taiwan and Thailand, OJ L 99, 17 April 2003, pp. 22-23.

Stainless Steel Fasteners and Parts thereof II, Council Regulation (EC) No. 1890/2005 of 14 November 2005 imposing a definitive anti-dumping duty and collecting definitively the provisional duty imposed on imports of certain stainless steel fasteners and parts thereof originating in the People's Republic of China, Indonesia, Taiwan, Thailand and Vietnam and terminating the proceeding on imports of certain stainless steel fasteners and parts thereof originating in Malaysia and the Philippines, OJ L 302, 19 November 2005, pp. 1-13.

Steel Ropes and Cables, Council Regulation (EC) No. 1796/1999 of 12 August 1999 imposing a definitive anti-dumping duty, and collecting definitively the provisional duty imposed, on imports of steel ropes and cables originating in the People's Republic of China, Hungary, India, Mexico, Poland, South Africa and Ukraine and terminating the anti-dumping proceeding in respect of imports originating in the Republic of Korea, OJ L 217, 17 August 1999, pp. 1-13 and Council Regulation (EC) No. 1886/2004 of 25 October 2004 extending the definitive anti-dumping duty imposed by Council Regulation (EC) No. 1796/1999 on imports of steel ropes and cables originating, inter alia, in the People's Republic of China to imports of steel ropes and cables consigned from Morocco, whether declared as originating in Morocco or not, and terminating the investigation in respect of imports from one Moroccan exporter, OJ L 328, 30 October 2004, pp. 1-6, and Council Regulation (EC) No. 1858/2005 of 8 November 2005 imposing a definitive anti-dumping duty on imports of steel ropes and cables originating in the People's Republic of China, India, South Africa and Ukraine following an expiry review pursuant to Article 11(2) of Regulation (EC) No. 384/96, OJ L 299, 16 November 2005, pp. 1-22.

Sulphanilic Acid, Commission Regulation (EC) No. 575/2002 of 3 March 2002 imposing a provisional anti-dumping duty on imports of sulphanilic acid originating in the People's Republic of China and in India, OJ L 87, 4 April 2002, pp. 28-44, endorsed in Council Regulation (EC) No. 1339/2002 of 22 July 2002 imposing a definitive anti-dumping duty and collecting definitively the provisional duty imposed on imports of sulphanilic acid originating in the People's Republic of China and India, OJ L 196, 25 July 2002, pp. 11-18.

Synthetic Fibres of Polyesters I, Council Regulation (EC) No. 1489/96 of 23 July 1996 amending Regulation (EEC) No. 54/93 imposing a definitive anti-dumping duty on imports of synthetic fibres of polyesters originating in India and the Republic of Korea, OJ L 189, 30 July 1996, pp. 10-12 and Council Regulation (EC) No. 907/97 of 20 May 1997 amending Regulation (EEC) No. 54/93 imposing a definitive anti-dumping duty on imports of synthetic fibres of polyesters originating in India and the Republic of Korea, OJ L 131, 23 May 1997, pp. 1-3.

Synthetic Fibres of Polyester II, Council Regulation (EC) No. 1728/1999 of 29 July 1999 imposing a definitive anti-dumping duty on imports of synthetic fibres of polyesters originating in Taiwan and terminating the proceeding in respect of imports of synthetic fibres of polyesters originating in the Republic of Korea, OJ L 204, 4 August 1999, pp. 3-12, and Council Regulation (EC) No. 976/2002 of 4 June 2002 imposing a definitive anti-dumping duty on imports of certain ring binder mechanisms (RBM) originating in Indonesia and terminating the anti-dumping proceeding in respect of imports of certain RBM originating in India, OJ L 150, 8 June 2002, pp. 1-16.

Synthetic Fibre Ropes, Commission Regulation (EC) No. 18/98 of 7 January 1998 imposing a provisional anti-dumping duty on imports of synthetic fibre ropes originating in India, OJ L 4, 8 January 1998, pp. 28-38 endorsed in Council Regulation (EC) No. 1312/98 of 24 June 1998 imposing a definitive anti-dumping duty on imports of synthetic fibre ropes originating in India and collecting definitively the provisional duty imposed, OJ L 183, 26 June 1998, pp. 1-8.

Tartaric Acid, Commission Regulation (EC) No. 1259/2005 of 27 July 2005 imposing a provisional anti-dumping duty on imports of tartaric acid originating in the People's Republic of China, OJ L 200, 30 July 2005, pp. 73-90, endorsed in Council Regulation (EC) No. 130/2006 of 23 January 2006 imposing a definitive anti-dumping duty and collecting definitively the provisional duty imposed on imports of tartaric acid originating in the People's Republic of China, OJ L 23, 27 January 2006, pp. 1-7.

Trichloroisocyanuric Acid, Commission Regulation (EC) No. 538/2005 of 7 April 2005 imposing a provisional anti-dumping duty on imports of trichloroisocyanuric acid originating in the People's Republic of China and the United States of America, OJ L 089, 8 April 2005, pp. 4-31, endorsed in Council Regulation (EC) No. 1631/2005 of 3 October 2005 imposing a definitive anti-dumping duty and collecting definitely the provisional duty imposed on imports of trichloroisocyanuric acid originating in the People's Republic of China and the United States of America, OJ L 261, 7 October 2005, pp. 1-12.

Tungsten Carbide and Fused Tungsten Carbide, Commission Regulation (EEC) No. 763/90 of 26 March 1990 imposing a provisional anti-dumping duty on imports of tungsten carbide and fused tungsten carbide originating in the people's Republic of China and terminating the anti-dumping proceeding concerning imports of those products from the Republic of Korea, OJ L 83, 30 March 1990, pp. 36-44, endorsed in Council Regulation (EEC) No. 2737/90 of 24 September 1990 imposing a definitive anti-dumping duty on imports of tungsten carbide and fused tungsten carbide originating in the People's Republic of China and definitively collecting the provisional duty, OJ L 264, 27 September 1990, pp. 7-11, reviewed in Council Regulation (EC) No. 2268/2004 of 22 December 2004 imposing a definitive anti-dumping duty on imports of tungsten carbide and fused tungsten carbide originating in the People's Republic of China, OJ L 395, 31 December 2004, pp. 56-67.

Decisions

Certain Flat-rolled Products of Iron or Non-alloy Steel, of a Width of 600 mm or more, Commission Decision No. 1357/2001/ECSC of 4 July 2001 amending Decision No. 283/2000/ECSC imposing a definitive anti-dumping duty on imports of certain flat-rolled products of iron or non-alloy steel, of a width of 600 mm or more, not clad, plated or coated, in coils, not further worked than hot-rolled, originating, inter alia, in India, OJ L 182, 5 July 2001, pp. 27-33.

Dihydrostreptomycin, Commission Decision No. 98/90/EC of 21 January 1998 terminating the anti-dumping proceeding concerning imports of dihydrostreptomycin originating in the People's Republic of China, OJ L 017, 22 January 1998, pp. 42-45.

Hematite Pigs Iron, Commission Decision No. 962/98/ECSC of 7 May 1998 repealing Decisions No. 1751/94/ECSC and No. 55/96/ECSC with respect to the imposition of definitive anti-dumping duties on imports of hematite pig iron originating in Brazil, the Czech Republic, Poland, Russia and the Ukraine, OJ L 135, 8 May 1998, pp. 7-17.

MSG, Commission Decision 92/493/EEC of 12 October 1992 accepting undertakings offered in connection with the review of anti-dumping measures applicable to certain imports of monosodium glutamate originating in Indonesia and terminating the investigation, OJ L 299, 15 October 1992, pp. 40-42 and Commission Decision 93/479/EEC of 30 July 1993 accepting undertakings offered in connection with the review of anti-dumping measures applicable to certain imports of monosodium glutamate originating in Indonesia, the Republic of Korea, Taiwan and Thailand, OJ L 225, 4 September 1993, pp. 35-39.

Judgments of the EC Court and Court of First Instance and Opinions of Advocate Generals

Judgments of the EC Court

Judgments of Court of First Instance

Opinions from Advocate Generals

Bibliography

Ahlborn, C. & B. Allen, 'The Napp Case: A Study of Predation?', *World Competition* 26 (3) (2003): 233-262.

Andersen, H., 'EU's anti-dumpingpraksis mod varer med oprindelse i Kina', in *Julebog 2005*, edited by S. Treumer. Copenhagen: Jurist- og Økonomforbundets Forlag, 2005, 119-143.

Anderson, S. P., N. Schmidt & J.F. Thisse, 'Who Benefits from Anti-dumping Legislation?', in *The WTO and Anti-dumping – Volume I*, edited by D. R. Nelson & H. Vandenbussche. Cheltenham Glos: Edward Elgar Publishing Ltd, 2005, 411-427.

Aust, A., *Handbook of International Law*. Cambridge: Cambridge University Press, 2005.

Barton, C., M. Khor, S. Narain & V. Tauli-Corpuz, *Civil Society Perspectives on the Millennium Development Goals*. New York United Nations Development Programme, Bureau for Resources and Strategic Partnerships, 2005.

Bekker, D., 'The Strategic Use of Anti-dumping in International Trade', *South African Journal of Economics* 74 (3) (2006): 501-521.

Bernt, J. F. & D. R. Doublet, *Vitenskapsfilosofi for jurister*. Bergen: Fagboksforlaget, 1998.

Bhala, R., *International Trade Law: Theory and Practice*, 2nd edn. New York/San Fransisco, Lexis Publishing, 2000.

Bhala, R., *Modern GATT Law – A Treatise on the General Agreement on Tariffs and Trade*. London: Sweet & Maxwell, 2005.

Blume, P., 'Kritisk retsteori. Et blik tilbage og et blik frem', *Retfærd* 29 (2) (2006): 58-71.

Bronckers, M. C. E. J. & N. McNellis, *A Cross-Section of WTO Law*. London: Cameron May, 2000.

Brownlie, I., *Principles of Public International Law*, 5th edn. Oxford: Oxford University Press, 1998.

Chakravarthy, S., 'India', in *Competition Policy and Development in Asia*, edited by D. H. Brooks & S. J. Evenett. Hampshire: Palgrave Macmillan, 2005, 107-160.

Changho Sohn, 'Treatment of Non-market Economy Countries under the World Trade Organization Anti-dumping Regime', *Journal of World Trade* 39 (4) (2005): 763-786.

Cheng Bin, *General Principles of Law as Applied by International Courts and Tribunals*, reprint (Cambridge: Cambridge Grotius Publications Ltd, 1987).

Confucius, *Confucius – The Analects (Lun yü)*, translated by D.C. Lau, first edition, Penguin Books, 1979.

Craig, P. & G. De Búrca, *EU Law – Text, Cases, and Materials*, 3rd edn. Oxford: Oxford University Press, 2003.

Craig, P., *EU Administrative Law*. Oxford: Oxford University Press, 2006.

Czako, J., J. Human & J. Miranda, *A Handbook on Anti-dumping Investigations*. Cambridge: Cambridge University Press, 2003.

Daniel, B. T., 'Interpretation, Sources of Law and Precedents', in *WTO Law – from an European perspective*, edited by B. Egelund Olsen, M. Steinicke & K. Engsig Sørensen. Copenhagen: Forlaget Thomson, 2006, 75-90.

Das, S. S., 'Evolution and Political Economy of Trade Protectionism: Anti-dumping and Safeguard Measures', *IIMB Management Review* 17 (4) (2005): 51-65.

Degan, V. D., *Sources of International Law* (The Hague: Kluwer Law International, 1997).

Dehlsten, S., 'Key Policy Coherence Issues in Agriculture and Migration' Room Document 4 given at The Institutional Approaches to Policy Coherence for Development OECD Policy Workshop (OECD, 2004).

Didier, P., 'The WTO Anti-dumping Code and EC Practice – Issues for Review in Trade Negotiations', *Journal of World Trade* 35 (1) (2001): 33-54.

Donghui Fu, 'EC Anti-dumping Law and Individual Treatment Policy', *Journal of World Trade* 31 (1) (1997): 73-105.

Durling, J. P. & M. R. Nicely, *Understanding the WTO Anti-dumping Agreement, Negotiation History and Subsequent Interpretation*. London: Cameron May, 2002.

Durling, J. P., 'Deference, But Only When Due: WTO Review of Anti-dumping Measures', *Journal of International Economic Law* 6 (1) (2003): 125-153.

Egelund Olsen, B., M. Steinicke & K. Engsig Sørensen (eds.). with contributions by B. T. Daniel, H. Kirk Deichmann & P. Wegener Jessen, *WTO Law – From an European perspective*. Copenhagen: Forlaget Thomson, 2006.

Ehlermann, C. D. & L. Ehring, 'The Authoritative Interpretation under Article IX:2 of the Agreement of Establishing the World Trade Organization: Current Law, Practice and Possible Improvements', *Journal of International Economic Law* 8 (4) (2005): 803-824.

Evenett, S. J. & E. Vermulst, 'The Politicisation of EC Anti-dumping Policy: Member States, Their Votes and the European Commission', *The World Economy* 28 (2005): 701-717.

Farrar, J. H. & A. M. Dougdale, *Introduction to Legal Method*, 2nd edn. London: Sweet & Maxwell, 1984.

Finger, M. (ed.), *Anti-dumping – How It Works and Who Gets Hurt*. Michigan: The University of Michigan Press, 1993.

Franck, T. M., *Fairness in International Law and Institutions*. Oxford: Clarendon Press, 1995.

Gertler, J. F., 'What China's Accession is all About', in *China and the WTO*, edited by D. Bhattasali, Li Shantong & W. Martin. Washington: The World Bank and Oxford University Press 2004, 21-28.

Godfrey, C., 'Stop the Dumping! – How EU Agricultural Subsidies Are Damaging Livelihoods in the Developing World', *Oxfam Briefing Paper No. 31*. Washington: Oxfam International, 2002.

Goodison, P., 'EU Trade Policy & the Future of Africa's Trade Relationship with the EU. *Review of African Political Economy* 34 (112) (2007): 247-266.

Greenwald, J., 'WTO Dispute Settlement: An Exercise in Trade Law Legislation?', *Journal of International Trade Law* 6 (1) (2003): 113-124.

Hindley, B. & P. A. Messerlin, *Anti-dumping Industrial Policy – Legalized Protectionism in the WTO and What To Do About It*. Washington, DC: The AEI Press, 1996.

Hoekman, B. M. & M. M. Kostecki, *The Political Economy of the World Trading System – From GATT to the WTO*. Oxford: Oxford University Press, 1995.

Hoekman B. M. & P. C. Mavroidis, 'Dumping, Anti-dumping and Antitrust', *Journal of World Trade* 30 (1) (2006): 27-52.

Hoogmartens, J., *EC Trade Law Following China's Accession to the WTO*. The Hague: Kluwer Law International, 2004.

Horlick, G. N., 'How the GATT Became Protectionist – An Analysis of the Uruguay Round Draft Final Anti-dumping Code', *Journal of World Trade* 27 (5) (2003): 5-17.

Horlick G. N. & E. C. Shea, 'The World Trade Organization Anti-dumping Agreement', *Journal of World Trade* 29 (1) (1995): 5-31.

Hudec, R. E., *The GATT Legal System and World Trade Diplomacy*, 2nd edn. Salem: Butterworth Legal Publishers, 1990.

Jackson, J. H., *The World Trading System*. London: The MIT Press, 1989.

Jackson, J. H., 'Global Economics and International Economic Law', *Journal of International Economic Law* 1 (1) (1998): 1-23.

Kelsen, H., *General Theory of Law and State*, translated by Anders Wedberg. Cambridge: Harvard University Press, 1945.

Kong Qingjiang, *China and the World Trade Organization – A Legal Perspective*. Singapore/New Jersey: World Scientific Publishing, 2002.

Krarup, O., 'Arbejdsret og korporativ retfærdighed' (U1983B) *Ugeskrift for retsvæsen*, p. 303.

Krauss, M., *How Nations Grow Rich*. Oxford: Oxford University Press, 1997.

Kuijper, P. J. & M. Bronckers, 'WTO Law in the European Court of Justice', *Common Market Law Review* 42 (5) (2005): 1313-1355.

Lando, O., *Kort indføring i komparativ ret*, 2nd edn. København: Jurist- og Økonomforbundets Forlag, 2004.

Lao Tzu, *Tao Te Ching*, translated by D. C. Lau. Hong Kong: The Chinese University Press, 2001.

Lauridsen, S., 'Deliberativt demokrati eller intern retslig legitimitet – En retsfilosofisk discussion af Kaarlo Tuoris teori om kritisk retspositivisme', *Retfærd* 28 (1) (2005): 26-41.

Lenaerts, K. & P. Van Nuffel, *Constitutional Law of the European Union*. London: Thomson/Sweet & Maxwell, 2005.

Lennard, M., 'Interpreting China's Accession Protocol: A Case Study in Anti-dumping', in *China and the World Trading System – Entering the New Millennium*, edited by D. Z. Cass, B. G. Williams & G. Barker. Cambridge: Cambridge University Press, 2003, 387-412.

Livdahl, D. A., Huawei Lin & Yukiko Masudo, 'China's Antimonopoly Control Strengthens', *Licensing Journal* May (2005): 31-36.

Matsushita, M., T. H. Schoenbaum & P. C. Mavroidis, *The World Trade Organization – Law, Practice, and Policy*, 2nd edn. Oxford: Oxford University Press, 2006.

Marceau, G., *Anti-dumping and Anti-Trust Issues in Free-Trade Areas*. Oxford: Oxford University Press, 1994.

Marceau, G., 'Conflicts of Norms and Conflicts of Jurisdiction – The Relationship between the WTO Agreement and MEAs and other Treaties', *Journal of World Trade* 35 (6) (2001): 1081-1131.

Neergaard, U. and R. Nielsen, *EU Ret*, 4th edn. Copenhagen: Forlaget Thomsen/ GADJura, 2005.

Nielsen, R. & C. D. Tvarnø, *Retskilder & Retsteorier*. Copenhagen: Jurist- og Økonomforbundets Forlag, 2005.

O'Brien, J., *International Law*. London: Cavendish Publishing Limited, 2001.

Palmeter, D. & P. Mavroidis, 'The WTO Legal System: Sources of Law', *American Journal of International Law* 92 (1) (1998): 398-413.

Palmeter, D. & P. Mavroidis, *Dispute Settlement in the World Trade Organization – Practice and Procedure*, 2nd edn. Cambridge: Cambridge University Press, 2004.

Pauwelin, J., *Conflict of Norms in Public International Law*. Cambridge: Cambridge University Press, 2003.

Peerenboom, R., *China's Long March Toward Rule of Law*. Cambridge: Cambridge University Press, 2002.

Petersmann, E. U., *The GATT Dispute Settlement System – International Law, International Organizations and Dispute Settlement*. The Hague: Kluwer Law International, 1997.

Prusa, T. J., 'East Asia's Anti-dumping Problem', *World Economy* 29 (6) (2006): 743-761.

Qureshi, A. H., *Interpreting WTO Agreements – Problems and Perspectives*. Cambridge: Cambridge University Press, 2006.

Reitzes, J. D., 'Anti-dumping Policy', in *The WTO and Anti-dumping*, edited by D. R. Nelson & H. Vandenbussche. Cheltenham Glos: Edward Elgar Publishing Ltd, 2005, 392-410.

Ross, A., *On Law and Justice*. Los Angeles: University of California Press, 1958.

Ross, A., *Lærebog i Folkeret*, revised by O. S. Andersen, T. Lehmann & P. Magid, 6th edn. Copenhagen: Nyt Nordisk Forlag Arnold Busck, 1984.

Rothbard, M. N., *Protectionism and the Destruction of Prosperity*, monograph. Ludwig: Von Mises Institute, 1986.

Schaumburg-Müller, S., *Internationale handelsrelationer i retsteoretisk belysning*. Copenhagen: Jurist- og Økonomforbundets Forlag, 1997.

Snyder, F., 'The Origins of the "Nonmarket Economy": Ideas, Pluralism and Power in EC Anti-dumping Law about China', *European Law Journal* 7 (4) (2001): 369-434.

Spiermann, O., *Moderne Folkeret*, 3rd edn. Copenhagen: Jurist- og Økonomforbundets Forlag, 2006.

Staiger, R. W., 'Some Remarks on Reforming WTO AD/CDV Rules', *World Economy* 28 (5) (2005): 739-743.

Steel, K. (ed.), *Anti-dumping under the WTO: A comparative Review* (London: Kluwer Law International and International Bar Association, 1996).

Steinberg, R. H., 'Judicial Lawmaking at the WTO: Discursive, Constitutional, and Political Constraints', *American Journal of International Law* 98 (2) (2004): 247-275.

Stewart, T. P. (ed.), *The GATT Uruguay Round – A Negotiating History (1986-1992) – Volume II: Commentary* (Deventer: Kluwer Law and Taxation Publishers, 1993).

Stewart, T. P. & A. S. Dwyer, *WTO Anti-dumping and Subsidy Agreements – A Practioner's Guide to 'Sunset' Reviews in Australia, Canada, the European Union, and the United States*. The Hague: Kluwer Law International, 1998.

Stieglitz, J. E., 'Dumping on Free Trade: The U.S. Import Trade Laws', *Southern Economic Journal* 64 (2) (1997): 402-424.

Swinbank, A., 'Like Products, Animal Welfare and the World Trade Organization', *Journal of World Trade* 40 (4) (2006): 687-711.

Syrstad, H., 'Rettens tre realitetskretser og nivåer', *Retfærd* 28 (2) (2005): 4-15.

Tarullo, D. K., 'Paved with Good Intentions: The Dynamic Effects of WTO Review of Anti-dumping Action', 2 (3) (2003): 373-393.

Tuori, K., *Critical Legal Positivism*. Burlington: Ashgate, 2002.

Ulff-Møller Nielsen, J. & A. Rutkowski, 'The EU Anti-dumping Policy Towards Russia and China: Product Quality and the Choice of an Analogue Country, *World Economy* 28 (1) (2005): 103-136.

Van Bael, I. & J. F. Bellis, *Anti-dumping and Other Trade Protection Laws of the EC*, 4th edn. The Hague: Kluwer Law International, 2004.

Van den Bossche, P., *The Law and Policy of the World Trade Organization*. Cambridge: Cambridge University Press, 2005.

Vermulst, E. & F. Graafsma, *WTO Disputes – Anti-dumping, Subsidies and Safeguards.* London: Cameron May, 2002.

Vermulst, 'The 10 Major Problems With the Anti-dumping Instrument in the European Community', *Journal of World Trade* 39 (1) (2005a): 105-113.

Vermulst, E., *The WTO Anti-dumping Agreement.* Oxford: Oxford University Press, 2005b.

Viner, J., *Dumping – A Problem in International Trade*, Reprint of Economic Classics. New York: Augstus M. Kelley Publishers, 1966.

Wang G. G., *The Law of The WTO – China and the Future of Free Trade.* Hong Kong: Sweet & Maxwell Asia, 2005.

Wegener Jessen, P., 'Anti-dumping', in *WTO Law – From an European perspective*, edited by B. Egelund Olsen, M. Steinicke & K. Engsig Sørensen. Copenhagen: Forlaget Thomson, 2006, 379-418.

Weinberger, O., *Law, Institution and Legal Politics – Fundamental Problems of Legal Theory and Social Philosofy.* London: Kluwer Academics Publishers, 1991.

Wenig, H., 'The European Community's Anti-dumping System: Salient Features', *Journal of World Trade* 39 (4) (2005): 787-794.

Wenxi Li, *Anti-dumping Law of WTO/GATT and EC – Gradual Evolution of Anti-dumping Law in Global Economic Integration.* Lund: Lund University, 2001.

Williams, M., *Competition Policy and Law in China, Hong Kong and Taiwan* Cambridge: Cambridge University Press, 2005.

Willig, R. D., 'Economic Effects of Anti-dumping Policy', in *The WTO and Anti-dumping*, edited by D. R. Nelson & H. Vandenbussche. Cheltenham Glos: Edward Elgar Publishing Ltd, 2005, 286-308.

Wilson, J. & Lan Tao, 'China's New Company Law – Recent Changes in PRC Corporate Law Are Welcome News to Foreign Investors', *China Business Review* March-April (2006): 30-32.

World Trade Organization; Appellate Body Secretariat, *WTO Appellate Body Repertory of Reports and Awards 1995 – 2004.* Cambridge: Cambridge University Press, 2005.

World Trade Organization, *Guide to GATT Law and Practice – Volume I.* Geneva: WTO, 1995.

Xiang Liu & H. Vandenbussche, *EU Anti-dumping Cases against China: An Overview and Future Prospects with Respect to China's WTO Membership.* LICOS Discussion Paper, LICOS Centre for Transition Economies, Katholieke Universiteit Leuven, 2002.

Yuhan Liu, 'Anti-dumping Measures and China', *Journal of Financial Crime* 12 (3) (2005): 272-289.

Index

GLOBAL TRADE LAW SERIES

1. Emmanuel T. Laryea, Paperless Trade: Opportunities, Challenges and Solutions. 2002. ISBN 90-411-9897-0
2. Xiang Gao. The Fraud Rule in the Law of Letters of Credit: A Comparative Study. 2002. ISBN 90-411-9898-9
3. Yuwa Wei, Comparative Corporate Governance: A Chinese Perspective. 2003. ISBN 90-411-9908-X
4. Ross P. Buckley (ed.), The WTO and the Doha Round: The changing Face of World Trade. 2003. ISBN 90-411-9947-0
5. Bradley J. Condon, Joyce C. Sadka, Tapen Sinha (eds), Insurance Regulationin North America: Integrating American, Canadian and Mexican Markets. 2003. ISBN 90-411-2301-6
6. Jan Hoogmartens, EC Trade Law Following China's Accession to the WTO. 2004. ISBN 90-411-2301-6
7. Yang Guohua, Bryan Mercurio, Li Yongjie, WTO Dispute Settlement Understanding: A Detailed Interpretation. 2005. ISBN 90-411-2361-X
8. Jan Job de Vries Robbé, Paul U. Ali, Securitisation of Derivatives and Alternative Asset Classes, Yearbook. 2005. ISBN 90-411-2375-X
9. Markus W. Gehring, Marie-Claire Cordonier Segger, Sustainable Development in World Trade Law. 2005. ISBN 90-411-2366-0
10. Yann Aubin, Arnaud Idiart. Export Control Law and Regulations Handbook: A Practical Guide to Military and Dual-Use Goods Trade Restrictions and Compliance. 2007. ISBN 90-411-2601-5
11. Henry Kibet Mutai, Compliance with International Trade Obligations. The Common Market for Eastern and Southern Africa. 2007. ISBN 978-90-411-2664-1
12. Yong-Shik Lee, Economic Development through World Trade: A DevelopingWorld Perspective. 2007. ISBN 978-90-411-2681-8
13. Yanning Yu, Circumvention and Anti-Circumvention Measures. The Impact on Anti-Dumping Practice in International Trade. 2007. ISBN 978-90-411-2686-3
14. Ross Buckley, Vai Io Lo, Laurence Boulle, Challenges to Multilateral Trade: The Impact of Bilateral, Preferential and Regional Agreements. 2008. ISBN 978-90-411-2711-2
15. K.D. Raju, World Trade Organization Agreement on Anti-dumping: A GATT/ WTO and Indian Jurisprudence. 2008. ISBN 978-90-411-2780-8
16. Xiaochen Wu, Anti-dumping Law and Practice in China. 2008. ISBN 978-90-411-2790-7
17. Amin Alavi, Legalization of Development in the WTO: Between Law and Politics. 2008. ISBN 978-90-411-2795-2
18. Henrik Andersen, EU Dumping Determinations and WTO Law. 2009. ISBN 978-90-411-2827-0